AMERICAN BODY POLITICS

American Body Politics

RACE, GENDER, AND BLACK

LITERARY RENAISSANCE

Felipe Smith

The University of Georgia Press

Athens and London

© 1998 by the University of Georgia Press
Athens, Georgia 30602
All rights reserved
Designed by Erin Kirk New
Set in 10 on 14 Electra by G & S Typesetters, Inc.
Printed and bound by Braun-Brumfield, Inc.
The paper in this book meets the guidelines for permanence and
durability of the Committee on Production Guidelines for Book
Longevity of the Council on Library Resources.
Printed in the United States of America

02 01 00 99 98 C 5 4 3 2 1

Library of Congress Cataloging in Publication Data

Smith, Felipe.
American body politics : race, gender, and Black literary renaissance / Felipe Smith.
p.   cm.
Includes bibliographical references and index.
ISBN 0-8203-1933-3 (alk. paper)
1. United States—Race relations.   2. Body language—United States—History
—20th century.   3. Racism—United States—History—20th century.   4. Sex customs—
United States—History—20th century.   5. Sexism—United States—History
—20th century.   6. Afro-Americans—Intellectual life.   7. American literature—
Afro-American authors—History and criticism.   I. Title.
E185.61.S628   1998
305.896'073—dc21   97-30335

British Library Cataloging in Publication Data available

Contents

Preface   vii

PART ONE: AMERICAN BODIES

Chapter One: American Body Politics   3

Chapter Two: Meanwhile, in Black America   52

Chapter Three: The S/ness of the Mother   84

Chapter Four: The "White Delilah"   122

PART TWO: AMERICAN SOULS

Chapter Five: W. E. B. Du Bois and the Progress of the Black Soul   199

Chapter Six: The Quest of the Black Soul   248

Chapter Seven: The Darkness of the Mother   276

Chapter Eight: The Whiteness of the Witch   307

Chapter Nine: Conclusion   339

Notes   353

Works Cited   399

Index   415

Preface

We are a numerous family by the Great Law of Natural Selection; we hold our
patent directly from Nature herself, our *Alma Mater,* . . . who has from time
immemorial, away back to the geological ages, cared for, improved, favored and
developed, out of all mankind, the great "Smith family."
  —James McCune Smith, "A Word for the 'Smith Family'" (1860)

When I began this project, I had no idea that my path would cross that of another Tulane University professor named Smith. In 1904, William Benjamin
Smith, then a professor of mathematics, took time off from "studies far more
congenial and fascinating" to write a book in support of the South's policies of
racial separation. Published in 1905 as *The Color Line: A Brief in Behalf of the
Unborn,* the book offered a "scientific" defense of state-sanctioned racism to argue that the inevitable extinction of blacks in America required special precau-
tions by whites to protect their "unborn."[1] Why he would even bother to interrupt his "congenial and fascinating" work in mathematics, history, linguistics,
economics, philosophy, and other fields to add yet one more diatribe against a
people he thought were well on their way to extinction might seem, at first
glance, unclear.[2] But to understand Smith's concern, one has to understand the
mythic world of race at the turn of the century, especially the emotional appeal
generated by the idea of America as a "white man's country" for both popular
and professional audiences.

Smith was afraid that the intellectual debate over the meaning of race was beginning to tilt in the favor of advocates of racial equality. Smith felt that despite

the recent *Plessy v. Ferguson* decision and other signs that the federal government was willing to allow the states to handle the "Negro problem" with little interference, a concerted campaign by academics to undermine the scientific basis of state-sanctioned racism, in concert with modest efforts supporting Booker T. Washington's recently brokered compromise of black political equality in return for philanthropic assistance, might affect public policy in the long run. Because he saw such philanthropy as a dangerous circumvention of a "natural" competition that would ensure the survival of the "favored" race—that is, whites—he argued against the industrial education championed by Booker T. Washington as strenuously as he opposed the higher education of blacks advocated by W. E. B. Du Bois.[3] He singled out for criticism Columbia University's Franz Boas, then becoming the most influential voice in American anthropology because of his rigorous critique of the comparative methodology that grounded much of the racist content of the field.[4] Atlanta University's W. E. B. Du Bois was an explicit target of Smith's ire as well, for having demanded in *The Souls of Black Folk* (1903) that citizens of African descent be guaranteed unqualified inclusion in all facets of American life.[5]

Smith's writing betrays that note of hysteria so characteristic of the prophets of racial holocaust, as when he explained that "compared with the vital matter of pure Blood, all other matters, as of tariff, of currency, of subsidies, of civil service, of labour and capital, of education, of forestry, of science and art, and even of religion, sink into insignificance" (ix). Smith thought that no "kind or degree of institutional excellence could permanently stay the race decadence that would follow surely in the wake of any considerable contamination of [the pure strain of Caucasian blood] by the blood of Africa." He believed that if nothing was done to prevent it, he and his colleagues in academia would someday face the consequences of racial intermingling in the form of a physically and mentally debased population incapable of receiving the knowledge a university like Tulane offered. His belief that fears of "blood" pollution took precedence over religious principles reflects both his own prickly skepticism and his justified assumption that even the strongly Calvinist South would view race purity as the higher priority.

Despite Smith's reliance upon Cornell University's Walter Willcox for data predicting black decrepitude and eventual extinction, he strongly disagreed with the northerner on one aspect of America's racial future. Then serving as chief statistician of the U.S. Census Bureau, Willcox, like Smith, had embraced Frederick L. Hoffman's prediction in 1896 that blacks in America would gradually become extinct owing to "race traits and tendencies."[6] Willcox told a conference on race in Montgomery, Alabama, that "Negroes [would] continue to become, as they [were then] becoming, a steadily smaller portion of the population" as a result of "disease, vice and profound discouragement"—the "race traits and tendencies" that would ultimately make their race an evolutionary dead end. Willcox's model for the disappearance of blacks from America—the mythical "vanishing Indian"—was a familiar theme to an audience steeped in the lore of the "manifest destiny" of the white race to rule the world: "The [black] race will follow the fate of the Indians. . . . The great majority will disappear before the whites, and . . . the remnant found capable of elevation to the level of the white man's civilization will ultimately be merged and lost in the lower classes of the whites, leaving almost no trace to mark their former existence."[7] It was apparently this casual attitude toward the likelihood of intermarriage by academics like Willcox that made Smith drop everything to write *The Color Line*.

Smith's extensive reading in the classics had taught him a great truth he wanted to share with those who might have felt secure in Willcox's prediction of black extinction: "inferior blood" always leaves a trace. The difference between their positions can be summed up in their disagreement about the South's emerging redefinition of race through the "one-drop rule," which asserted that any traceable African ancestry, even so little as one drop of "black blood," made the bearer genetically black and therefore a threat to pollute the gene pool of white America if not screened out.[8] Body politics, in the form of constraints on the reproductive options of *white women and black men only*, were necessary, Smith felt, to save the "unborn" whites, whose genetic security depended on the measures taken to exclude black "blood."[9] In calling attention to Willcox's casual attitude toward the inevitability of racial intermixture, Smith adopted and embellished Willcox's spatial/hierarchical model of society in which blacks migrated from the upper echelons of their social classification into the lower echelon of white America, in violation of the southern racist doctrine that "the lowest white man [should always] count for more than the highest negro":[10] "But even suppose that only the lower strata of Whites mingle with the upper strata of Negroes, the result would be . . . fatal. . . . Let the mongrel poison assail the humbler walks of life, and it will spread like a bubonic plague. . . . Up from the Gulf regions the foul contagion would let fly its germs beyond the lakes and mountains. . . . Generations might pass before the darkening tinge could be seen distinctly above the Ohio, but it would be only a question of time. The South alone would suffer total eclipse, but the dread penumbra would deepen insensibly over all the continent" (18–19). In Smith's imagination, race difference created contiguous, hierarchical, sociogeographical worlds of black and white America divided by the mythic "color line" that he hoped to preserve. For Smith, if the social "map" of the Jim Crow South could be superimposed over the geographical map of the nation, readers would have a visual analogue—an increasingly blacker "America"—that would graphically convey the danger of "black blood" seeping into the white gene pool.

It did not matter that W. E. B. Du Bois, whom Smith derisively referred to as "the Boston Negroid," had insisted that blacks did not wish to "Africanize America, for America has too much to teach the world and Africa" (*Souls*, 3). To Smith, nothing threatened the white race more than Du Bois's demand that the "doors of Opportunity" not be "closed roughly in his face" and that he be welcomed as "a co-worker in the kingdom of culture, to escape both death and isolation." It is no exaggeration to say that Smith considered the presence of blacks in America as contaminating the nation—a "one-drop"-ism of the American body politic. In Smith's estimation, only the literal death of Du Bois and his kind would save the "kingdom of culture" from "mongrelism." I am convinced that what Smith hoped to accomplish by announcing that the gradual extinction of blacks would only increase the threat of "mongrelism" in the short term was to make his intended audience comfortable with the idea that any measures taken to expedite black extinction, however dubious on moral grounds, would pay off eventually in continued American economic prosperity and social harmony. Like other so-called social Darwinists, Smith insisted that altruism or charity in any form was contrary to the long-term survival interests of whites: "We must dismiss, then, this vision of a higher race stooping down with arms of love and lifting up the lower to its altitude, as merely a pious imagination. The higher race may indeed stoop down; it has often done so; but never to rise again" (189).

William B. Smith's rhetoric was characteristic of discursive inventions of "white space"—the theorizing of a social classification called "the white race" that occupies an exclusive phylogenetic space and therefore requires, analogously, a bounded, exclusive geographical and/or social space for the undisturbed preservation of its unique attributes. Smith's appeal for a white America telescopes narratives of geographical, social, political, domestic, and corporeal boundaries in a clear instance of what "interaction" theorists of metaphor have described as the creation of new knowledge through the literalization of analogy.[11] The "interactive" principle of metaphor allows each individual body to be seen as a microcosm of its nation, race, or household, making the reproductive behavior of each individual a security issue in the race-identified state. Each body is crucial to the creation and maintenance of racialized space, or "ethnic" space, for that matter, as indicated by the use of rape as a central element in the "ethnic cleansing" and polluting campaigns in Bosnia-Herzegovina in the 1990s.[12] My study focuses on the durability of this discourse of raced and gendered bodies as microcosms of "nation" through every phase of the American experience, but especially the utility of such politicized language of American bodies in revitalizing fantasies of separate white and black Americas during the decades straddling the turn of the twentieth century.

Forty-four years before William B. Smith wrote *The Color Line*, another Smith, Dr. James McCune Smith, had already prepared a rebuttal to all denials of a common past and of a common future among the races based on the idea that the races stemmed from different origins. Nancy Leys Stepan and Sander L. Gilman have summarized J. M. Smith's tongue-in-cheek review of Darwin's *On the Origin of Species*, titled "A Word for the Smith Family": "The very commonness of the name Smith was . . . proof of the evolutionary success of black people, . . . [and] also implicitly used to poke fun at the pretensions of all the white Smiths who thought they were distinct and superior to black Smiths. All Smiths, the author suggested, were linked together in an evolutionary kinship" (Stepan and Gilman, 83). "The Smiths are older than the Anglo-Saxons," observed J. M. Smith (77), a black physician, making the kinship of Smiths older than the idea of Anglo-Saxon race purity as well.

The different interpretations given to Darwin by the black and white Smiths highlight an interesting struggle over the *nature* of "Nature" in the nineteenth century. J. M. Smith employed the more traditional rhetoric of embodied abstraction in his reference to "Nature herself," as "our *Alma Mater*" in the passage used as the epigraph to this preface. William B. Smith likewise constructed a feminized embodiment of "Nature" that reflects his racial ideology. His is a remorseless, "leaden-footed" "Nature" that has "demanded" the extinction of the inferior black race "in sacrifice on the altar of the evolution of Humanity," though, he says with obvious regret, "it is extremely difficult to quicken her pace" (x, xiv–xv). It was within the power of whites to speed up this "natural" process of black extinction, he argued, and more important, it was their *duty* to the unborn whites.

Behind this struggle over the nature of "Nature" lies a strategic appropriation of gender attributes made possible by the personification of abstractions. J. M. Smith's "Nature" is an open-hearted mother who, like the "Alma Mater" illustrated in the frontispiece of Jean de Crèvecoeur's 1787 French edition of *Letters from an American Farmer*, welcomes all varieties of Americans into her "broad

lap."[13] William B. Smith's "Nature," on the other hand, registers a cold, unfeeling, pseudo-Darwinian bias against the racially "unfit." His imperial Nature
separates the winners from the losers in the survival sweepstakes, supervising the
"*Selection . . .* of favoured individuals and of favoured races" (13). Each feminized abstraction implicitly argues a national policy toward the nonwhite population that mirrors its author's idealized image of the state, appropriating the female body for the ideological work of two often competing strands of American
nationalism: America as "melting pot" and America as the fulfillment of white
Western culture. Both narratives about nature establish as their intended objects
those other important dramatis personae of Europe's Enlightenment—"Race"
and "Nation"—which, imagined in female form, enact the politics of American
bodies as well.

Forty-four years after William B. Smith's *The Color Line*, another member of
the extended "Smith Family," Lillian Smith, explained the totalizing potential of
spatial discourses of race difference implicit in anatomical models of society in
Killers of the Dream (1949). Her retrospective on growing up as a white woman
in the Jim Crow South revealed that the laws creating racialized space by drawing the "color line" through every conceivable aspect of American life established a social space for blacks that was at once terrifying and seductive: the restricted erogenous and excretory zones of the "body politic." She recounts, "The
lesson on segregation was only a logical extension of the lessons on sex and white
superiority and God. Not only Negroes but everything dark, dangerous, evil
must be pushed to the rim of one's life. Signs put over doors in the world outside
and over minds seemed natural enough to children like us, for signs had already
been put over forbidden areas of our bodies. The banning of people and books
and ideas did not appear more shocking than the banning of our wishes which
we learned early enough to send to the Dark-town of our unconscious" (90).
Lillian Smith's observations about the boundaries of the body politic, reflected
in the Jim Crow South's hypersensitivity to the positioning and properties of individual raced and gendered bodies, show how homologies of the social and the
biological were inevitably exploited to create new forms of knowledge. Social
and political institutions *imagined* in the form of human bodies enabled the political manipulation of actual bodies into divisions of American social space.

My study examines this analogical discourse of the "body politic" and the attendant *body politics*. I trace the instrumentality of human bodies in the invention of white and black genetic, geographical, social, and cultural space. I am
particularly concerned with how interrelated discourses on race, gender, and
nation shaped the development of black American literature from the turn of the

century to the modern period. I show that the pronouncement of a death sentence upon black America by William B. Smith, Hoffman, Willcox, and their contemporaries gave special urgency to the conscious collective "renaissance" of black American artistic production beginning at the turn of the century.

The term *renaissance* in African American culture is usually associated with the Harlem period of the twenties and thirties. But Houston A. Baker Jr.'s term *renaissancism* suggestively looks further back, toward "a *spirit* of nationalistic engagement that begins with intellectuals, artists, and spokespersons at the turn of the century," signaling "a resonantly and continuously productive set of tactics, strategies, and syllables."[14] I examine the importance of body politics to the development of that turn-of-the-century nationalistic spirit in the work of Charles Waddell Chesnutt, Pauline E. Hopkins, Sutton E. Griggs, James Weldon Johnson, and W. E. B. Du Bois. Much of this early writing holds interest for current audiences primarily as artifacts of a critical moment in the shaping of modern America. But these writers' grappling with theories of race, body ideas, and concepts of nationness inaugurated a series of archetypal and thematic innovations that would influence the literature that followed in important ways. Struggles with myths of the black body's incompetence for full participation in the life of the nation gave impetus to what Baker has called "the canonical appearance—as consecration and promise—of an African body carrying an alternative story of founding."[15] By focusing on the politics of American bodies, I investigate the canonical status of black bodies as the antithesis of a presumed "black body of death" retarding the growth and the wholeness of the nation. In the process, I pay special attention to the way that myths of race difference spawned mythic representations of the body in the cultural imaginary, particularly showing how the rhetoric of white nationalism constructed the figure of the fatal white woman who blocks black (typically, male) aspiration in American society and how the language of black nationalism ultimately gave expression to the nurturing black mother figure whose enshrinement as the guiding spiritual force in the black bourgeois household announced the cultural renaissance as an alternative path toward national inclusion. These figures are mythic both in fulfilling specific ritualistic social functions and also in Barthes's sense of language that has been "stolen" and reinvested with significance.[16]

Prior to W. E. B. Du Bois's important 1897 essays, "The Conservation of Races" and "Strivings of the Negro People" (the latter essay reprinted as the opening chapter of *The Souls of Black Folk*, retitled "Of Our Spiritual Strivings"), the white press had saturated discussions of African American national belonging with tropes of a diseased and dysfunctional blackness, figurations that became more and more sharply etched in the national consciousness through the campaigns for Jim Crow legislation, the lynching epidemic, debt peonage, chain gangs, and the widely circulated predictions of black extinction. After Du Bois's redefining of the terms of national belonging as "spiritual," rather than "embodied," African American literature almost immediately began to adopt his strategy of promoting the excellence of the black American "soul" as a basis of national inclusion. In part 1 of this work, "American Bodies," I examine the way that anthropological, historical, sociological, medical, and literary representations of black bodies in American culture produced what Du Bois called the false consciousness of "a world that looks on with amused contempt and pity" (*Souls*, 3). These images of black corporeal inadequacy migrated into the consciousness of all who participated in American life, including, disastrously, black Americans themselves, requiring a separate sphere of black self-imagining, the founding moment of "renaissancism." In part 2, "American Souls," I describe how the trope of the racial soul shaped the development of black literature, reinventing images of embodied nationness in the process.

In chapter 1, I discuss the importance of body ideas for the definition of citizenship and the access to rights and privileges in American public life. I single out moments in the historical evolution of American racial difference to show how specific language about and interpretations of bodies became naturalized through colonial statutes that inscribed race difference into governance; formulations of the "body politic" in the discourse of American independence; the politicized aesthetics attendant to renderings of artistic allegories of "America"; pollution fears of the postemancipation era; and especially the way that concerted efforts to distribute racial bodies in time and space through *Plessy v. Ferguson* and other Jim Crow enactments instituted the mythic world of race difference to which black writers responded. The problems of kinship ties created by "miscegenation" found expression in the "body of death" imagery that governed American social policy, lent urgency to the "one-drop rule" of racial classification, and shaped the literary emergence of the figure I call the "revenant," which I introduce in chapter 2.

In chapter 3, I discuss the essentializing rhetoric of black motherhood that authorized social and economic assaults on black home life and subsequently gave rise to a counterimage of black domestic integrity, the black madonna. In chapter 4, I discuss the emergence of the fatal white woman, a figure who threatens the incipient black patriarchy by offering would-be black nation builders fatal dreams of inclusion into American blood kinship.

In part 2, I consider Du Bois's career as the chief "mythologist" of race for early African American literature.[17] In chapter 5, I trace Du Bois's sources in Goethe and discuss how the trope of "double-consciousness" as a psychic dualism arising from black body ideas in the cultural imaginary gives way in Du Bois's work to the new body image of the two-souled black protagonist, Du Bois's alternative to Booker T. Washington's body politics. In chapter 6, I describe Sutton E. Griggs's and Pauline Hopkins's elaborations on the discourse of racial soul development. In chapter 7, I examine Du Bois's poetry, prose essays, short fiction, and his novel *The Quest of the Silver Fleece* for their constructions of black and white women's bodies as sites of black nationalist desire.

In chapter 8, I look at the appropriation of this mythic construct by James Weldon Johnson. Johnson's 1915 poem, "The White Witch," enables a discussion of the black urban migration—the movement into white American social space by large numbers of blacks from the South. I conclude with a discussion of Du Bois's *Dark Princess* as a contrast to the body politics of Harlem's New Negro artists in the twenties and thirties, indicating the divergence of Harlem's modernist sensibility from this important strain of Du Boisian race development.

In spite of William B. Smith, there has never been a "color line" of the intellect. One of his deepest fears was that higher education would produce individuals of color whose personal excellence would push them socially and occupationally into spaces reserved for whites, causing Smith to argue that color, not qualifications, should remain the sole criterion of social status: "If the race barrier be removed, and the individual standard of personal excellence be established, the twilight of this century will gather upon a nation hopelessly sinking in the mire of Mongrelism" (xiv). Du Bois, in defiance of all like Smith who wanted to ensure black exclusion no matter how they had to violate American ideals to do so, visualized himself *reborn* above the "Veil" of race as the embodiment of his own text, *The Souls of Black Folk*, sitting with Shakespeare (who does not wince) and moving "arm in arm" with Balzac and Dumas (*Souls*, 76). My own fortuitous arrival upon the contested terrain of "the color line" with the other members of the "Smith Family" was made possible, then, by the visionary intervention in American body politics by Du Bois and his generation of writers about a century ago.

I wish to thank the following people who generously gave of their time and helpful ideas during the writing of this book. Among the earliest believers and supporters of this project, none was more important than Janice Carlisle, whose careful reading and helpful suggestions at the outset steered me toward a much needed focus and whose strong support for the project freed me to work with a minimum of distraction at a difficult time. Raymond T. Diamond was always ready to lend an ear when I needed a considered opinion. Molly Rothenberg was thoughtful in giving her time to help me clarify the early drafts organizationally, and from my first days as a faculty member at Tulane, she was willing to share her knowledge of literary theory. Thanks also to Michael Kuczynski, Cynthia Lowenthal, Rebecca Mark, Joseph Roach, Teresa Toulouse, Peter Cooley, Gerald Snare, Supriya Nair, Donald Pizer, Catherine Den Tandt, Felicia McCarren, and all those who took an interest in the project. I particularly wish to acknowledge Pat Boyer, whose work provided me with insights that were crucial to the evolution of the book in its present form.

I also owe a debt to Susan Bergman, whose research and helpful observations at crucial stages of the project were of inestimable assistance. Hannah and Pamela Bassett were there when it occurred to me that my random thoughts on these matters might actually become a book. Production assistance was generously provided by Sandra Haro and Janice Mulvihill, no small task, as I well know. Thanks, too, to Annie L. Bullock, whose assistance in securing library materials and general morale boosting made my job easier. I wish to acknowledge the staffs of the Howard-Tilton Library, especially the librarians of the Louisiana Collection, the Rare Books Collection, the Interlibrary Loan Department, and Bruce Raeburn of the Hogan Jazz Archive. Thanks as well to the directors and staff at the Amistad Research Center and to the staff of the Schomburg Research Center of the New York Public Library.

I could not have gotten this project into print without the support and generous help of John Roberts, Craig Werner, and especially Aldon Lynn Nielsen. All gave timely and thoughtful advice, and Aldon particularly gave generously of his time to promote the project. Thanks as well to Houston A. Baker Jr. for all of his past support, and to the other members of the "History, Content, and Method in Afro-American Studies" Summer Seminar at the University of Pennsylvania, which John Roberts directed in 1991. Sander L. Gilman took time to give me advice about the direction of the project that I wish I had done a better job of following. I wish to thank also the directors and participants of the Tulane University Literary Theory Seminar, Geoffrey Harpham and John Rouse, and the organizers and participants of the Cultural Studies Seminar on Performance, especially Amy Koritz. The Newcomb College Center for Research on Women provided, very early in my career at Tulane, a series of seminars on feminist theory that were immeasurably important to the conception and completion of the work. I also appreciate the opportunities to talk about my work provided to me by Francis Dodoo, Judy Zwolak, and Jean Rahier.

I also wish to thank the editorial and production staffs of the University of Georgia Press. I could not have done this without the support and inexhaustible patience of Karen Orchard, who believed in the project in its infancy, the editorial assistance of Kristine Blakeslee, or the judicious copyediting of Grace Buonocore. No one has been more supportive than those of my immediate family—my parents, Felipe and Bernice S. Lazo; my brothers and sisters, Raquel, Leonardo, Ceola, Sidney, Frances, and Andrea, and their families; and the members of the Johnson family. I am deeply grateful to my children, Gian and Saia, who were remarkably patient throughout the writing of this work. Finally, my love and gratitude go to my wife, Roslyn, who has been my constant source of inspiration.

PART ONE

American Bodies

CHAPTER ONE

American Body Politics

At the close of the Reconstruction period in United States history, the question of national reconciliation was crucial to the reinvention of an American nation capable of achieving its world-historical potential. This was a period in which Americans debated the future of the largely former-slave black population within the Republic, including the possibility of separate white and black Americas, the wholesale expulsion of black Americans from the country, or the acceleration of a process of extinction that would solve the "Negro problem" once and for all. In "What America Would Be Like without Blacks," Ralph Ellison mused that "despite its absurdity, the fantasy of a blackless America continues to turn up," at least in part because it seems the easiest solution to the problem of creating a cohesive "national" identity out of a heterogeneous citizenry: "Since the beginning of the nation, white Americans have suffered from a deep inner uncertainty as to who they really are. One of the ways that have been used to simplify the answer has been to seize upon the presence of black Americans and use them as a marker, a symbol of limits, a metaphor for the 'outsider.'" This solution, in Ellison's words, "envisaged an attempt to relieve an inevitable suffering that marked the growing pains of the youthful body politic by an operation which would have amounted to the severing of a healthy and indispensable member."[1]

The dream of ridding the American body politic of its citizens of African descent is merely one phase of the complex political history of American bodies. My study focuses on the broad utility of body images in the discourse of black national belonging, which includes the relation of black and white bodies in American physical and social space; the notion of the black body as a contaminant in the national body politic; the importance of gender and gender roles; controls on sexuality and reproduction; black family stability; and discourses of racial "soul." Body politics have played a decisive role in American literature, especially in the works of black Americans, whose sensitivity to the tradition of misrepresenting black bodies in American culture has left indelible traces. I use these issues to outline the cultural bases of a theme in black literature that attempted the "conservation" of the black American from schemes of expulsion or extinction on the one hand and from assimilation into the body and soul of white America on the other. This tradition imagines national belonging in terms of two opposed forms of kinship: relation by shared ancestry and relation by social contract. Thus the literary debate over the ambiguous national status of black Americans often pits one type of kinship claim, "race," against another, democratic citizenship.

Benedict Anderson suggests that modern nations come into being through the collective imagining of their constituents. Nations are "imagined" communities because "the members of even the smallest nation will never know most of their fellow-members, meet them, or even hear of them, yet in the minds of each lives the image of their communion" (6). To Anderson, this "image of their communion" gives nationness more in common with "kinship" and "religion" than with ideologies like "racism" because "regardless of the actual inequality and exploitation that may prevail in each, the nation is always conceived as a deep, horizontal comradeship" (5, 7). By shifting to a passive construction, however, Anderson dodges the critical issue of subjectivity—the fact that those legally entitled to call themselves members of the nation, the "dreamers," determine the image of the community "dreamed."

Anderson tries to anticipate objections to his claim that nationness depends on a disinterestedness about such accidents of birth as "skin-colour, gender, parentage and birth-era" (143): "The fact of the matter is that nationalism thinks in terms of historical destinies, while racism dreams of eternal contaminations, transmitted from the origins of time through an endless sequence of loathsome copulations: outside history. Niggers are, thanks to the invisible tar-brush, forever niggers; Jews, the seed of Abraham, forever Jews, no matter what passports they carry or what language they speak or read" (149). But what, then, of societies that emerged in the New World and elsewhere, whose leading philosophers, scientists, and statesmen assumed that fulfilling "historical destiny" depended entirely on restricting national kinship and subjectivity to only those individuals believed to be "racially" capable of producing or recognizing history? Who believed that their "national destiny" lay in the subjugation or extermination of "lower races"?

The problem with Anderson's opposition of "kinship" to "ideology" is that it does not address the crucial third term—let's call it the "ideology of kinship"— that functions in societies in which "racism" or other "isms" emerge as a culmination of long-standing practices and habits of thought. If there is nothing in nationness that encourages racist imaginings, there is nothing in nationness that prevents national representation from finding expression almost entirely through external markings of gender and race. Racist rhetoric that places blacks and Jews, to use Anderson's examples, "outside history" removes them from the conceptual field of national belonging: citizens of preferred ancestry can effectively "imagine" them *out* of the nation by creating educational, economic, social, and political barriers to official and unofficial avenues of national belonging. Once official policy denies their national "kinship," the state assumes the power to act in the national interest by quarantining ethnic undesirables to spaces where they will not disturb the dream of a racially homogeneous nation, or, if they insist on being seen and heard in national life, by endorsing "final solutions."

Anderson's "imagined community" serves as an intriguing paradigm for my discussion of the social circumstances of America at the turn of the last century, in spite of his largely utopian formulation. Because Anderson locates national imagining in periodical and contemporary literature, a simple test of his "deep, horizontal comradeship" requires a glance at the literature of a historical period. In fact, the literature of the era served as a key mechanism for the imposition of what Orlando Patterson has called "natal alienation," a defining aspect of the "social death" of slavery. Patterson asserts that *slavery is the permanent, violent domination of natally alienated and generally dishonoured persons,"* a condition that specifically denied all kinship claims between slave and slaveholder.[2] In the "Progressive Era," America's newspapers and novels, with a few notable exceptions, overwhelmingly reflected the opinion that Americans of African descent were unfit for full citizenship and participation in modern America, so much so that the discussion of black American "kinship" in the print medium might be termed a literature of estrangement, alienation, and disaffiliation. Thus, through the corporeal violence of lynchings, work farms, and chain gangs, the psychological violence of Jim Crow quarantine, and the rhetorical violence of literary and popular cultural caricature, Americans of European descent reinvented the "social death" of slavery to contain black American aspirations for inclusion into full citizenship. The fashion of emphasizing racial dissimilarity in "national" literature (not only the race romanticists but also the naturalists and realists were instrumental in this trend, as Ralph Ellison has pointed out)[3] helped to undermine black national subjectivity, drawing on a vast body of purportedly scientific writings on the irremediable differences between blacks and whites.[4]

Theorists of race difference disproportionately influenced both literary representation and American public policy toward African Americans. Joseph A. Tillinghast begins *The Negro in Africa and America* (1902) by lamenting, "No African exclusion act [like those targeting Asians] was passed in the days when such action might have delivered us from the black peril, consequently the homogeneity of our national society . . . is dangerously broken."[5] In "Science and the African Problem" (1890), published one month after the cum laude graduation of his student W. E. B. Du Bois, Harvard geologist and amateur anthropologist Nathaniel Southgate Shaler declared that the "African and European races must remain distinct in blood" for the good of the nation (37). In terms that seem to echo Anderson's opposition of the "imagined community" of nationness to the tribal idea of kinship in blood, Shaler asserted that "there must be a perfect civil union without a perfect social accord, . . . without the bond of kinship in blood to unite [Negroes to whites] in the work of life."

Despite his overt appeal for cordial relations among America's many ethnic populations (with the exception of non-Teutonic immigrants, whom he opposed),[6] Shaler's ideology of American kinship rejected a "deep, horizontal comradeship" in favor of the separation of blacks and whites into hierarchically arranged social spheres that prevented any practical comradeship between the groups, let alone any horizontal relations. Shaler could support only the provisional social equality of "parallel lives" of the races, despite the implicit assumption that whites were always to be "on top." "To make this divided life comfortable to both and safe for the state is our immediate object" (44), Shaler concluded. To him, the "African problem" was the *only* potentially insoluble problem of American life (37), reiterating his earlier assertion that the problems of all other nations, past and present, were "light burdens when compared with this load of African negro blood that an evil past has imposed upon us."[7]

The consensus of social scientists was that the impossibility of sharing national kinship with black Americans had to do with innate and ineradicable deficiencies in black bodies. Tillinghast could offer black Americans no greater hope than to remain collectively "the nation's 'ward,'" since in his view they were "psychically" indistinguishable from native Africans, whose lack of a strong sense of family, he claimed, led to parental neglect, adultery, infanticide, and canni-balizing of dead relatives (60–67). The virulent negrophobe Robert W. Shufeldt likewise argued that African Americans had no functional concept of kinship that might link them to other Americans. "So far as I am aware, no single negro in this country has ever made any attempt to hunt up, so to speak, his or her rela-tives left behind in Africa," Shufeldt jokes, accounting for "the extremely low po-sition" of blacks in the evolutionary scale by their alleged indifference to family ties (*Negro*, 66). This would not be possible for whites, he says, who would have "returned en masse to their own country" in an attempt to regain their relatives. Further evidence of black disqualification for any form of kinship was that, ac-cording to Thomas Nelson Page, not only did blacks abandon their spouses with regularity, but black children grew up and abandoned their aging parents "with scarcely less unconcern than do any order of the lower animals" (175). Shufeldt explained that black national kinship was impossible because "the negroes who still practise[d] [cannibalism] in Africa [were] . . . close blood relations of the race in the United States."

The popularity of the works of antiblack southern apologists such as Thomas Dixon Jr. and of the antebellum nostalgia of Thomas Nelson Page shows that the cumulative effect of scientific preachments on black "racial inferiority," an up-surge of racial violence in the form of lynchings, the fictitious epidemic of black rapists, political campaigns for Jim Crow laws, and other public sector eruptions of America's "race problem" had primed audiences for fictional "final solutions" to the endless debate over race.[8] In a sense, the power of antebellum myth and Ku Klux Klan romances was in creating a space of national imagining based largely on the exclusion or suppression of the black masses. Dixon expressly cele-brated the Spanish-American War, in which white northerners and southerners fought side by side against a common external enemy, as a turning point in do-mestic race relations: "From the first, it was seen by thoughtful men that the Ne-gro was an impossibility in the newborn unity of national life. When the Anglo-Saxon race was united into one homogeneous mass in the fire of this crisis, the Negro ceased that moment to be a ward of the nation" (*Leopard's Spots*, 409). Note here Dixon's interest in marking the exact historical moment of white America's national founding based on the exclusion of blacks from a spurious kinship as national wards. The simultaneous, collective effort of northerners and southerners in a conflict defined by the American press as part of a global test of American racial "fitness" allowed them to reimagine a basis for unity that the memories of Civil War antagonism had obscured, as if they suddenly recognized that their fundamental similarity in contrast to the blacks' profound difference was the only legitimate form of national kinship.

Yet despite long-standing custom, outright violence, and official governmental policies of exclusion, black Americans never ceased imagining themselves as part of the nation, even if only to argue that they should leave it as a group to form their own. As Ellison points out, blacks themselves were not "immune to the fantasy" of a white America ("What America Would Be," 105). The dream of a self-sufficient black nation within or outside America itself was contemporary with, and not entirely contradictory to, claims to fuller citizenship rights in America.[9] Wilson J. Moses notes

> There is a difference between citizenship and nationality, and although Afro-Americans are, for the most part, loyal citizens of the United States of America, they tend to perceive themselves, and to be perceived by others, as a "nation within a nation." The "Negro People of the United States," as they were once called, have a sense of identity as Americans, which coexists, somewhat uneasily, with feelings of identity with other black peoples throughout the world. While black Americans think of themselves as part of the "American People," they nonetheless feel somewhat disassociated from them. (Moses, *Wings*, 35)

Although many black Americans modeled their nationalist idealism on the possibility of founding a homogeneous race state, many more responded to the pervasive fantasies of a white America with their own imagined community of black America. For these, black nationalism was more than an expression of race pride; it was the only available psychological defense in the face of whites determined to act out dreams of black extermination.

One prominent millenarian strain of black nationalism called Ethiopianism imagined a black nation as antitype to the prophecy in Ps. 68:31: "Princes shall come out of Egypt; Ethiopia shall soon stretch out her hands unto God." "Ethiopianism," Moses explains, "was concerned with the destiny of black people to create an exemplary civilization, usually in Africa, but not only there" (Moses, *Wings*, 102). Ethiopianism served the purposes of those who envisioned a literal African return on the one hand (colonizers like Alexander Crummel and Edward Blyden and later organizers like Marcus Garvey) and on the other hand those who, like W. E. B. Du Bois, felt that a figurative African kinship (Pan-Africanism) could result from a collective global struggle against white oppression. The common thread in the various Ethiopianist expressions was the call for a social rehabilitation of the image of the black body as the agent of a progressive, world-historical mission, emblematized in the appropriated biblical image of Ethiopia as an *embodied* nation "stretch[ing] out her hands." But the disparagement of African descent in American literature of racial estrangement made Ethiopia's outstretched arms an ambiguous sign of Africa's perpetual alienation from the West.

The Condition of the Mother

Houston Baker has declared that "the space of the African body" is the "creative dreamwork of American democracy" ("Promised Body," 343). But as Hortense Spillers points out, the bodies of African slaves interested slavery's efficiency experts even earlier than the era of national founding, initially through attempts at maximizing the limited space in the transoceanic vessels used to transport the slaves: "Let it now be supposed," writes one slave ship captain, "that every man slave is to be allowed six feet by one foot four inches for room, every woman five feet ten by one foot four, every boy five feet by one foot two, and every girl four feet six by one foot." [10] Spillers cites the owner of a ship called "The Brookes" as recommending that "five females be reckoned as four males, and three boys or girls as equal to two grown persons." Against this historical background, the Constitution's "three-fifths compromise" merely continued the quantification of black bodies in spaces of American confinement.

If the confinement of blacks in American space historically grounded the issue of race, the use of the black body itself to *define* nationality and social "place" had a long tradition before the movement of national independence as well. The cooperation of law, custom, and science in the maintenance of racial divisions also placed great importance on the coincidence of somatic differences of color and gender markings, and because white and black women occupied bodies doubly objectified by mythic language centered in biological difference, their representations in the literature of the period superimposed myths of gender onto myths of race. The history of the founding of two American racial castes in the bodies of women was therefore overdetermined by the convergence of these mythic discourses.

Differential access to the entitlements and privileges of citizenship became crucial to the definition of social position in the developing caste system in the American colonies, as anxieties about the future racial composition of the American nation influenced more drastic and permanent mechanisms of social control over the Africans being imported as laborers. The historical record shows that in the first one hundred years of American slavery, various localities struggled over the implications of race and American nationality and that in the transition from a system of indentured servitude to a chattel slavery based on "race difference," fluid, nonuniform definitions of race allowed for a number of socially disturbing occurrences. The disruption of black "property" rights in America—real, chattel, or corporeal—was the historical foundation of American slavery itself, and discourses of race difference became useful tools to the promoters of the idea that privileged access to American social space should be the exclusive "property" of whites. The earliest statutes and customs sited female bodies as the theoretical and functional dividing points of slave and free status, and, by extension, effected the division of the races based on "the condition of the mother."

In 1620, the first African servants arrived in the English colonies in America, at Jamestown. In 1630 in the Virginia colony, a white man, Hugh Davis, was sentenced to a public whipping for "dishonoring" God "by defiling his body in lying with a Negro."[11] To put this sequence into perspective, it means that within a decade of the first Africans arriving in the Anglo-American colonies in a condition of servitude, official discourse began to single out black women as special cases in the process of colonial self-definition, attracting a mythology pointedly at variance with, for example, the Pocahontas legend.[12] This early episode points as well to the "dishonor" attending the "social death" of the slave, such that prior to the full evolution of permanent enslavement, the African body served as a point of reference for communal behavior, social status, and traditions of honor and shame (Patterson, 10–13).

In dubious interracial sexual attachments, the whites were the ones "defiled" by the contact. The Maryland "Act Concerning Negroes & other Slaves" (1664), which officially differentiated African slaves from indentured servants by pronouncing their term of servitude as "Durante Vita," for example, defined interracial sexual contact as a "disgrace of our Nation" and the white participants as "shamefull" (Cassity, 20). Two important transformations in this act mark the evolution of official language on interracial sexual activity as a form of violence against national imagining. First, those whom the law cites as transgressors are not mere fornicators—they are English citizens who have voluntarily "intermarr[ied] with Negro Slaves" (Cassity, 20). Thus, unlike the Hugh Davis case, we can be certain that the interracial nature of the sexual conduct, and not the marital status of the participants, is what drew the condemnation.[13] Second, the nature of the sexual activity addressed by the law shows the movement toward a gendering of unlawful interracial sexual conduct: "all Negroes and other slaves

already within the Province," or "imported," or "Children born of any Negro
or other slave shall be Slaves as their ffathers were for the terme of their lives"
(Cassity, 20). The violator targeted by the second clause of the law is necessarily
a white female, then, whose punishment would specifically apply to her legal offspring by a black male but not to illegitimate offspring by a white male. As I will
show, this act achieves the same effect as the "condition of the mother" statute of
Virginia by an act of erasure.

Since the Marylanders, like their Virginia neighbors, were concerned with
clarifying the status of slave offspring, to follow Virginia's "condition of the mother"
rule would mean that Maryland slave men could ensure the freedom of their offspring by mating with white females. The Maryland 1664 law thus took pains to
differentiate the "condition" of white women (most likely indentured servants)
as one that required a special type of social responsibility:

> And forasmuch as divers freeborne English women forgettfull of their free Condi-
> cion and to the disgrace of our Nation doe intermarry with Negro Slaves by which
> alsoe divers suites may arise touching the Issue of such woemen [sic] and a great
> damage doth befall the Masters of such Negros for preuention whereof for deterring
> such freeborne women from such shamefull Matches, . . . whatsoever free borne
> woman shall inter marry with any slave . . . shall Serve the master of such slave dure-
> ing the life of her husband And that all the issue of such freeborne woemen so mar-
> ryed shall be Slaves as their fathers were. (Cassity, 20–21)

The act goes on to specify any currently living offspring of a white mother and a
black slave father to be the slave of its parents' master for thirty years. The importance of the language here cannot be overstated. While Hugh Davis's interracial contact shamed himself and dishonored God, the English women cited in
the 1664 Maryland act disgrace the "Nation." Clearly, Benedict Anderson's exception of racism from national imagining has no application to the American
context, for by the 1660s, the colonies had already embarked upon a tradition of
civil distinctions founded on the imagination of "loathsome copulations," identifying white females as the only potential avenue of corruption of the dream of a
white America. The distinction here is twofold. On the one hand, the actions of
Hugh Davis as a male had no impact on the integrity of the "Nation," nor would
the numberless fornications of white males with nonwhite women, so long as
they maintained a semblance of "mastery." On the other hand, the distinction
between dishonoring God and disgracing the nation reflects, in part, the increased secularization of the colonies. White women who voluntarily cohabited

with slave men were disciplined by law as a key definitional moment in the construction of a national ideal, threatened with the replacement of their "free Condicion" by the "condition of the [slave] mother." This state coercion, it bears repeating, represented an intervention into a "natural" interinvolvement of those in servant capacities in the colonies forming matrimonial unions.

The 1662 Virginia statute that preceded this one by two years superficially was more concerned with crossings of the race line by white males. The statute tellingly begins, "Whereas some doubts have arrisen whether children got by any Englishman upon a negro should be slave or ffree," but when it continues, it is to announce that "all children borne in this country shalbe held bond or free only according to the condition of the mother" (Cassity, 22). It doubled the fines for interracial fornication but barred the interracial offspring born of slave women and white men (apparently including freeholders and indentured servants) from legal claims to their father's status, protecting white male property interests. By legally designating their mixed-race offspring "property" too, the colonials sought to preempt the ability of these potential claimants to "own" anything, themselves included.[14] The Virginia and Maryland statutes used gender to define who was a slave and for how long. The importance of the language and the logic of these statutes lies in the fact that the seventeenth-century *partus sequitur ventrem* statutes of the Virginia colony became the model for other colonial regulations of slave identity.[15]

Because the Maryland 1664 law does not mention white male interracial sexual behavior, the law, in effect, assumes a preexisting "condition of the mother." If "divers suites" in regard to the legal status of the offspring of white women with slave husbands might result in "a great damage" to "the Masters of such Negros," why, unless a prior law or custom existed relative to the status of children born of the mother, would not the numerically greater mixed-race offspring of slave mothers become the basis of similar loss to the master? The answer must be that Maryland had already arrived, as did the Virginians in 1662, at a "condition of the mother" that was customary but not yet legally articulated. The masters, worried that their slave men would be able to deliver their mixed offspring from slavery by marrying white women, must have had no comparable fears of slave women's claims to free status for their own mixed-race children. Thus, the attempt by black males to form unions with white women in order to emancipate their offspring suggests a standing convention for determining status through the mother. By legislating a reduced social "condition" for a white mother of mixed offspring in the 1664 "condition of the father" statute, Marylanders were presumably plugging a loophole that decreased the value of male slaves relative to females, who could breed "interest" on the original investment. In practical terms, the Virginia and Maryland laws of the 1660s simplified caste status and social identity assignment by assuming that a person of African ancestry must have had an African mother and was therefore a slave, or if the mother was white, by assigning her a social status equivalent to the African mother's. The constant in slave identity in both colonies, then, was a socially debased "condition of the mother," regardless of the father's status.

Virginia's interest in establishing the duration of black servitude as the lifetime of the slave simply grandfathered the already widespread practice of differentiating between white "Christian" servants indentured for specific terms and black slaves, whom the colonial leaders did not envision as potential full participants in the community. According to Winthrop Jordan, "After 1640, when surviving Virginia county court records began to mention Negroes, sales for life, *often including any future progeny*, were recorded in unmistakable language. In 1646 Francis Pott sold a Negro woman and a boy to Stephen Charlton 'to the use of him . . . forever.' Similarly, six years later William Whittington sold to John Pott 'one Negro girle named Jowan; aged about Ten yeares *and with her Issue and produce duringe her (or either of them) for their Life tyme. And their Successors forever*'" (Jordan, 75).[16] The chilling last line with ominous finality stipulates female reproductivity as both a contractual commodity and a legal basis for future proprietary claims to the entire reproductive capacity of all offspring of the slave child until the exhaustion of the maternal line. Ownership of the black womb enabled the Virginia worthies to freeze the "condition of the mother," in this scheme, into a permanent race space: all black wombs were collapsed into one primordial mother, sharing her original enslavement in perpetuity.

According to Joel Williamson, the Virginia assembly in 1662 decided to contravene the standing principle governing inherited status in order to institute the "condition of the mother" rules: it "wrenched itself away from the English rule that the child followed the status of its father" in an attempt to clarify the social place of the growing number of mixed-race children in the colony (Williamson, *New People*, 8). Thus the Maryland statute that specified that blacks must be slaves "as their fathers were" merely reiterated existing English custom in order to perform a similar but differently targeted colonization of the female womb. The "condition" of white womanhood had to be plainly articulated, apparently, to make it clear that one could not be both a white woman and the mother and wife of slaves. So long as a black man had privileged access to any white womb (implicit in the phrase "dureing the life of her husband") or, as was later specified, unauthorized access to one, that womb was disqualified as a point of entry into the white body politic. Any "Issue" had to spend thirty years in the wilderness of slavery.

Enslaved African colonials and their progeny fit into the social niche described by Orlando Patterson as "intrusive . . . social death" (39). "Ritually incorporated as the permanent enemy on the inside, . . . intruder[s] in the sacred space" of the community, they technically lived at the sufferance of their owners. They existed in social limbo with a perpetual capital sentence looming over them. Only the word of powerful whites stayed the execution of the sentence, a stay that could be revoked for any act transgressing the strictures of their nonpersonhood.[17] White women, on the other hand, by marrying or otherwise cohabiting with slaves, would suffer the "extrusive" social death of nonentity, the fate of the "insider who had fallen, . . . who ceased to belong and had been expelled from normal participation in the community because of the failure to meet certain minimal . . . norms of behavior" (Patterson, 41). The different treatment of white women and white men discovered in interracial relationships speaks to inequalities of power, to patriarchal property interests in white female bodies, and to a cultural predisposition to interpret unsanctioned female behavior as a sign of depravity.

For example, when Maryland's lawmakers had to adjust the 1664 law because of the unforeseen cunning of the English slaveholders, they inscribed suspicion of a white female predilection for interracial sex into the new statute. The 1681 "Act concerning Negroes & Slaves" sought to remedy the fact that "diverse ffreeborne Englishe or White-woman sometimes by the Instigacon Procurem or Conievance of theire Masters Mistres or dames" would be forced to marry a black slave man as a means of making the white woman herself a slave for life (Cassity, 32). The practice of masters and mistresses forcing white indentured servants into slavery through the 1664 act—in effect, the owner purchased a slave for life at the lower price of an indentured servant—was apparently a lucrative scheme for unscrupulous parties until the enactment of the 1681 law created fines for such activity, in addition to loss of the white woman slave and her children to manumission as a further penalty (Cassity, 33). But significantly, the wording of the act did not completely absolve the white women forced into such unions of all responsibility. It pointedly did not extend manumission to the black slave husband, almost as if testing the truth of the claim of forced marriage, so that a white woman could not win the freedom of a slave husband in the process of making such an accusation. The assumption, in other words, was that the accusation of slave owner connivance would require the accusing woman to abandon the slave husband and rejoin the white community from which she was separated by slave status.

Presumption of female depravity, then, drove the statement that such inter-racial marriages were *sometimes* due to the instigation and connivance of the slave master, but they were due *"always to the Satisfaccon of theire* [that is, the white women's] *Lascivious & Lustful desires, & to the disgrace not only of the English butt allso of many other Christian Nations"* (Cassity, 32; my emphasis). Amazingly, the writers of the act, while acknowledging and redressing the forced enslavement of white women by powerful white males through such arranged marriages, felt compelled to register their suspicion that there must be a consensual aspect to such relations that would explain a white woman's acquiescence to the slave master's schemes. Thus the myth of black male sexual prowess intruded in the form of an implied conjugal benefit mitigating the white servant women's communal ostracism. The Maryland fathers, perhaps to assuage their own guilt about the lighter penalties on white male interracial peccadilloes, inscribed white and black female sexual desire into such laws as pretexts for their gender-specific system of "race chastity." [18] But once again, it was the English "nation" that white female lust injured, the religious qualms about dalliances with heathens coming in only as an afterthought.

A Virginia law of 1691 addressed the still disruptive question of intermarriage through a combination of banishment and temporary enslavement. Augmenting the 1662 law that imposed double fines on men and women for interracial forni-cation, the 1691 law condemned both white men and women who participated in the procreation of "abominable mixture and spurious issue." Those who mar-ried blacks would pay the ultimate secular penalty—banishment from the colony forever. But significantly, the law reserved punitive enslavement for white women only. White women who, in an attempt to avoid banishment, did not marry black men yet produced bastard children by slave fathers were subject to tempo-rary enslavement in a legal maneuver that regulated the behavior of specifically lower-class women, current or former indentured servants. "Any English woman being free" who had an illegitimate child by a black man would be forced to pay a fine of fifteen pounds sterling within a month, or be sold into servitude by the fathers of the church. The money from the fine or sale would then be split three ways, with the government, the church, and the informant each getting equal shares (Cassity, 35). Clearly, women of modest financial means would be the most affected by the stiff fine imposed for the violation, and the specific intent of the statute seems to have been the creation of a mechanism by which lower-class white women, long exempt through custom from slavery per se, could be forced at least temporarily into slavery to give the Virginians an enforcement mechanism similar to the 1664 Maryland law.

In stating the principle that race mixture was a route to social anarchy, the colonial fathers chose enforcement policies that were more symbolic than effective in reducing the growing mulatto population but were very effective in deterring interracial relations involving white women. The circumscription of white female behavior must be seen, then, as the primary, not the secondary, intent of the laws. If interracial sexual relations increased, and the "abominable" and "spurious" offspring multiplied with the tacit approval of colonial governments, it could only be because the forms of interracial unions that predominated—white men in both casual and enduring relationships with black women—not only did not disrupt the operation of the colonies but in fact became crucial to the economics of slavery.[19] The greater difficulty of assigning paternity in cases involving powerless slave women, along with the value of fertile slave women to the wealth of the colonies, allowed the authorities to wink at white male fornication with women slaves. But for white women, bearing a child by a black father was a hazardous undertaking whether in or out of wedlock. The stakes were purposely made high for white women because only a self-replenishing stock of women certified to be "white" could ensure the social and cultural legitimacy of the white male descent line in a patriarchal, caste-partitioned economic system. The law's specification of punishments solely aimed at white women's infractions suggests that if the reproductive race line was to be policed at all, it would be on the white female's body, not on the black female's. Despite the racial differential in enforcement, both groups of women became the earliest and most consistent foci of race definition and the formation of a dual American identity: American nationality was founded upon the white female body; slavery, perpetual estrangement from the surrounding nation—social death—was founded on the black female body.

Thus the suspicion of white female consent to "forced" intermarriage set in motion the principle that the state was empowered to act in behalf of the race interest, even where that meant infringement upon the freedom of the individual right to association. The use of private persons to police the race line, as well as the very specific interest of the state in controlling the behavior of white women, reflects what Thomas Heilke has said of the encroachment of the race idea into the definition of the body politic: "For each individual race, the state is the political vessel of the race, and the race is the state's content" (149). Quoting Hitler's *Mein Kampf*, Heilke notes that in the race-identified state, "the state's highest task [becomes] the preservation and intensification of the race" (149). An individual white woman could not, according to colonial statutes, provide a black man with national affiliation without herself surrendering kinship. The *partus sequitur ventrem* laws already enjoined the white father of a mixed-race child from giving access to the white world, and since the child remained with the mother, the white father did not need to have any personal or legal connection with it at all. But white women could not be expected to keep a child of mixed descent and remain a part of the white world.[20] So long as white women remained "mindfull" of their special condition as the privileged space of race origin and destiny, they retained a relatively protected status within the body social. Two hundred years before the lynching craze of the late nineteenth century, the mechanism by which *any* interracial activity involving white women, even if "consensual," could be described as rape—as violent intrusion into spaces exclusive to whites—was set in motion.

Hugh Davis's 1630 punishment for "defiling" himself with a black female was both exceptional and definitive, in the sense that white male crossings of the race line would rarely ever again be available for such public condemnation, but the lore of the sexually active black female as a threat to white communal purity and intactness would become a commonplace. Through slavery and beyond, report the scholars of black women's history, the moral status of black womanhood has been the focal point of attempts to hold blacks entirely responsible for their social condition, even during the period when race agency became overidentified with the image of the black brute rapist. A 1668 Virginia law sought to extend the principle of the "condition of the mother" as a means of defining the social status of the blacks as a race, above and beyond the condition of servitude, proclaiming that "Negro women, though permitted to enjoy their freedom yet ought not in all respects to be admitted to a full fruition of the exemptions and impunities of the English" (Chambers, 37). By strictly controlling access to white wombs and legally inscribing black wombs as the source of perpetual slavery, colonial authorities systematized the social status of black and white women into a reflection of "natural" race and gender distinctions. Under the "condition of the mother," black race pollution and white race purity acquired female bodies.

The ways that the open black and restricted white spaces of female reproductivity served white patriarchal interests were manifold, but opportunities for sexual and economic exploitation were definitive. Consider, for example, the impressive detachment with which Sir Sydney Olivier assessed material and labor resources in the empire's African colonies in *White Capital and Coloured Labor* (1907). Olivier frankly encouraged the maintenance of British imperialism by a systematic colonization of the racial wombs. On the benefits of intermarriage as a means of producing a loyal workforce suited to the tropics, Olivier had this to say:

> Whatever the potentialities of the African stocks as a vehicle for human manifestation, and I myself believe them to be exceedingly important and valuable, . . . the white races are now, in fact, by far the farther advanced in effectual human development, and it would be expedient on this account alone that their maternity should be economized to the utmost. A woman may be the mother of a limited number of children, and our notion of the number advisable is contracting: *it is bad natural economy . . . to breed backwards from her* [that is, the white female]. There is no such reason against the begetting of children by white men . . . with women of coloured or mixed races. The offspring of such breeding, whether legitimate or illegitimate, is, from the point of view of efficiency, an acquisition to the community, and under favourable conditions, an advance on the pure-bred African. (Archer, 228; my emphasis)

Unfettered by the all-encompassing theology of the earlier wave of American colonists and buttressed by Darwinian evolutionary principles the Virginians and Marylanders did not have at their disposal, Olivier advocated "economizing" white wombs for the advance of civilization. Efficiently "breeding upward," in effect, from African wombs, would create offspring emotionally allied to the Crown that their English fathers served, but lacking any legal claim to the nation for which they toiled.

As governor of Jamaica, Olivier's theory of social and economic development by colonizing black wombs and nationalizing white wombs accounts in part for the phenomenon noted by Zora Neale Hurston: "When a Jamaican is born of a black woman and some English or Scotsman, the black mother is literally and figuratively kept out of sight as far as possible, but no one is allowed to forget that white father, however questionable the circumstances of birth. You hear about

'My father this and my father that, and my father who was English, you know,' until you get the impression that he or she *had* no mother" (8–9). In describing the social erasure of the black mother, Hurston foregrounds the analogy between the black mother and the sentient landscape of Jamaica itself, a natural resource awaiting European "development": "Black skin is so utterly condemned that the black mother is not going to be mentioned nor exhibited. You get the impression that these virile Englishmen do not require women to reproduce. They just come out to Jamaica, scratch out a nest and lay eggs that hatch into 'pink' Jamaicans" (8–9). But the process by which "pink" Americans were to be reproduced was left much less to chance. The economic motivation behind slavery's institution in the body of the black mother coexisted with a persistent aesthetic ideal of America as a "white man's country" that required the body of the white mother as a point of origin.

Real Distinctions

Some of the most serious challenges to the official American creed of freedom and opportunity as fundamental rights of citizenship have come from chattel slavery based on race difference, from racially motivated violence, from the racial limits on rights and entitlements collectively known as Jim Crow, and from the vast literature of racial disaffiliation that culturally grounded these efforts at circumventing cherished national ideals. How the Founding Fathers and signers of the Declaration of Independence themselves explained the persistence of racial discrimination as a basis of national self-definition is a case in point. Within a century after the *partus sequitur ventrem* legislation in the colonies, most American colonials looked upon corporeal distinctions in the population as fixed and immutable markers of separate social destinies. With slavery strongly entrenched in somatic differentiation, they were then free to pretend that they were only allowing the "natural" separation of races to run its course.

Thomas Jefferson's *Notes on the State of Virginia* (1785) expressed strong reservations about the possibility of racial coexistence within a democratic society without the ultimate "extermination of one or the other race" (132). Jefferson's assessment of the future of race relations was to become orthodoxy, recycled by racial moderates like Abraham Lincoln and extremists like Hilton Rowan Helper as justification for a variety of solutions to the race problem.[21] At the time Jefferson's words were written, the Sally Hemings scandal was more than fifteen years in the future,[22] but even in the mid-1780s, a decade before the birth of Sally's first child by a white male of the Jefferson household, Jefferson ought to have had enough practical experience as a planter not to make physiognomic difference the basis of his prediction of interracial warfare.

Answering his own rhetorical question, "Why not retain and incorporate the blacks into the State?" Jefferson listed several general problems with black integration into the nation before predicting that the net result of these various frictions would be a race war to the death. But without in-depth discussion of his preliminary list, Jefferson immediately introduced a second general area of conflict: "To these objections, which are political, may be added others, which are physical and moral" (133). Jefferson, however, was being redundant, having *already* included the category of "physical and moral" differences in his list of "political" objections, under the phrasing "the real distinctions which nature has made." "I advance it, therefore," he sums up, "as a suspicion only, that the blacks, whether originally a distinct race, or made distinct by time and circumstances, are inferior to the whites in the endowments both of body and mind" (138). In short, though Jefferson lists a number of contributing factors to his prediction of a race war and extermination, his *Notes* examines at length only one root cause, the physical, aesthetic, and moral "inferiority" of African bodies.[23] Despite his hedging about a possible common origin and his seeming to leave open the question for further investigation, Jefferson, author of the Declaration of Independence, argued that Americans ought not to establish institutions that might counteract the "natural" hierarchy of races. His argument is patently circular: if Africans were not inferior, they would long since have "melted" into the general population. But since they have retained their physical distinction, the persistence of African bodies in America was irrefutable proof of their repugnance and their "natural" inferiority.[24]

Still, *someone* was sleeping with the Hemings women. A white man had fathered Sally, and another white man would father her children—in all likelihood, a man of the gentleman class, if not Jefferson himself.[25] For Jefferson to argue against the successful integration of the races in America based on the supposed white abhorrence of black flesh flies in the face of what was happening in the bed chambers of Jefferson's Monticello and on most of the plantations in the South. As the foremost scholar of his state, furthermore, Jefferson should have known of the frequent interventions by Virginia authorities into the interpersonal affairs of the colony through laws prohibiting marriage and sexual relations between blacks and whites, interventions necessitated by the lack of an instinctive white abhorrence of African bodies. But if Jefferson had acknowledged that white "repugnance" had to be invented in law because the "real distinctions which nature has made" proved no obstacle to physical intimacy between black and white populations, then his apocalyptic vision of an American racial Armageddon would have collapsed, and with it, the basis of all those declarations of irreconcilable differences.

Jefferson's *Notes* represents an all too familiar pattern in the history of race in America, in which the predilections of a powerful individual or group become projected onto an entire population, declared "natural," and thereafter serve to buttress the similar prejudices of other powerful persons or to authorize acts of mass inhumanity. I am not suggesting that race prejudice was imposed upon the masses of whites from above, as it were; but the undeniable fact is that powerful voices constructed the narratives of disaffiliation that were circulated in moments of economic, political, and social tension among the races as "proof" of the justness of denying kinship to nonwhites. Whenever such narratives conflicted with observed or direct experience (as, witness, Jefferson's amnesia about the illicit sexual congress within his own household), the deciding factor became a *national* will to exclusivity that overrode individual exceptions, with an "imagined" America superimposed over the actual one. When such leaders insisted that racial solidarity and superiority were necessary to preserve their ideal of the nation, citizens typically responded as if the personal "disinterestedness" of appeals to exclusivity ennobled them. Benedict Anderson has described the basis of the nation's ability to ask its citizens to die for it as a "disinterestedness" that lends all sacrifice purity of motive (144). What I am suggesting here is that appeals to biblical curses, "distinctions in nature," and evolutionary progress are all terms for "disinterestedness" by which the nation's narrators ask its citizens to hate for it. It is what William B. Smith had in mind when he claimed that what is personally immoral may be racially moral (190).

This appeal to "disinterestedness" explains the conjectural, offhanded tone of the scholar-racists who adopted a pose of objectivity behind which to mask personal antipathies. (Evangelical racists like Helper and Dixon, because they appealed to scriptural authority, did not cloak themselves in "objectivity," relying instead on the "disinterestedness" of divine ordinance.) Jefferson achieves this effect by the use of rhetorical questions to which he supplies the self-evident "facts" of white superiority in body, mind, and morals as answers.[26]

Embodied America: "The Lovely White and Red"

Jefferson's moral and aesthetic reading of African bodies reflects his conventional understanding of somatic features as indexes to character. This aesthetic vocabulary also prevails in allegorical representations of "America" in bodily form. Corporeal models of society are meaningful only to the extent that society can be imagined in bodily terms. In classical and medieval thought, "the true polis" was, "as it were, *the body writ large*," according to John O'Neill in *Five Bodies: The Human Shape of Modern Society* (68–69). As Eric Voegelin explains, the body is an important source of political ideas because "body experiences are basic human experiences and every symbol which can use them as a material starting point can be sure of a strong emotional hold over its believers." [27]

In *The Selling of Joseph* (1700), Samuel Sewall summed up his rationale for advocating the abolition of African slavery and its replacement by white indentured servitude entirely as a necessary step in constructing an aesthetically pleasing body politic: "There is such a disparity in [the Negroes'] Conditions, Colour & Hair, that they can never embody with us, and grow up into orderly Families, to the Peopling of the Land: but still remain in our Body Politick as a kind of extravasat Blood. As many Negro men as there are among us, so many empty places there are in our Train Bands, and the places taken up of Men that might make Husbands for our Daughters. And the Sons and Daughters of *New England* would become more like *Jacob* and *Rachel*, if this Slavery were thrust quite out of doors." [28] To the extent that Sewall and other colonials imagined the nation as a "body," they often held that the racial markings of that body politic should accord with the prevailing concepts of physical perfection. A dark America would necessarily, then, be estranged from Europe as a bastard offspring of European misadventure. [29] Sewall urged a scheme of emancipation and expulsion similar to Jefferson's advice a century later that the black slave be freed and "removed beyond the reach of mixture" so as to avoid "staining the blood of his master" (139). According to Winthrop Jordan, "if any white Americans conceived of their nation or community, at whatever level of conception, as a body of white men, *as a white body*, then the simultaneous expulsion of black men and noxious slavery could scarcely help but afford a measure of cathartic relief" (567; my emphasis). Like the framers of the colonial "condition of the mother" statutes, Sewall promoted the economic utilization of white wombs for race-identified somatic continuity in the "Peopling of the Land," convinced that the preferred European aesthetic was crucial to American identity.

Patrick Henry's blunt statement of the choices—"Our country will be peopled. The question is, shall it be with Europeans or with Africans?" (in Jordan, 544)—resonates through the ages, as each crisis of changed relation between whites and blacks raised the specter of legal, wholesale racial intermarriage. Benjamin Franklin expressed his preference for whites in his *Observations Concerning the Increase of Mankind* (1751), wishing their "Numbers were increased" in relation to the number of Africans and others of "swarthy Complexion": "And while we are, as I may call it, *Scouring* our Planet, by clearing America of Woods, and so making this side of our Globe reflect a brighter Light to the Eyes of Inhabitants in Mars or Venus, why should we in the Sight of Superior Beings, darken its people? Why increase the Sons of Africa, by Planting them in America, where we have so fair an Opportunity, by excluding all Blacks and Tawneys, of increasing the lovely White and Red?" (in Jordan, 143). Franklin's "Partiality" to the "lovely White and Red" complexion of a specifically European imagined body politic illustrates the Enlightenment's complicity with racism in its equation of "white" skin with wisdom and beauty.

In his *Notes*, Jefferson elaborated on his own preference for the "lovely White and Red" in his speculations about black inferiority:

> Whether the black of the negro resides in the reticular membrane, . . . proceeds from the color of the blood, the color of the bile, or from that of some other secretion, the difference is fixed in nature, and is as real as if its seat and cause were better known to us. And is this difference of no importance? Is it not the foundation of a greater or less share of beauty in the two races? Are not the fine mixtures of red and white, the expressions of every passion by greater or less suffusions of color in the one preferable to that eternal monotony, which reigns in the countenances, that immovable veil of black which covers the emotions of the other race? Add to these, flowing hair, a more elegant symmetry of form, their own judgment in favor of the whites, declared by their preference of them, as uniformly as is the preference of the Oranootan for the black woman over those of his own species.

Aware that he was straddling a line between rationality and emotion, Jefferson concluded with an apology for this attention to the clearly superficial, adding, "The circumstance of superior beauty, is thought worthy attention in the propagation of our horses, dogs and other domestic animals; why not in that of man?" (133).

To his earlier arguments Jefferson added two others that attested to the physical and moral repugnance of African bodies—the fact that blacks themselves clearly preferred white somatic features, and the "ape" libel. The myth of black female copulation with large primates was a staple of the black Venus lore, as we shall see, and it is not unconnected to the question of black desires to "embody" with whites, for as Jefferson's analogy suggests, there is an "upward" aspiration in the sexual attraction of blacks for whites that is exactly analogous to the interest of the apes toward the next "highest" rung in the chain of being, the black female. Just as Franklin's Enlightenment preference for the "lovely White and Red" European complexion spawned a fantasy of the "whitening" of America, Jefferson's analogy reveals his rationalist bias against whites mating *downward* in the chain of being.

Feminized, embodied images of America in the visual arts reflect this American politicizing of aesthetics and the evolution of nation body ideas. In the earliest visualizations of the allegorical America, the feminized land mass appeared as an Amazonian Indian Queen.[30] The Indian Queen emblem of the sixteenth century was a sometimes ruthless embodiment of the savage New World landscape who, with human head in hand, gave fierce representation to the challenges and perils of the age of European exploration.[31] But according to Joshua Taylor, the Indianized female as national symbol did not reflect at all on American race identity, in fact, since "until well into the eighteenth century, America was for many only a place, and the dusky brown maiden served as well as any symbol might to indicate the *location* without giving any particular thought to the inhabitants" (5–6; my emphasis). To Taylor, the colonists were not trying to "depict themselves as belonging to the rich coloration of the new environment. They were simply Europeans away from home."[32] Taylor did not raise the question of why the Anglo-American colonists seemed content to adopt traditions of representing America that originated among Italian, French, Flemish, and Dutch artists, artists who were capturing the spirit of a continent as seen through the eyes of mostly Spanish explorers.[33]

His interpretation of the racial features of embodied America comes through more clearly when he explains the transformation that occurred later, the evolution of the national (as opposed to geographical) figure called the "Indian Princess," which succeeded the Indian Queen, into the America/Columbia/Liberty figures: "When a shift in image came, the 'Indian Princess,' as the early image has been called, gave way not to a new symbol for *place* but to *personified virtues*: Independence, Freedom, Wisdom. When the figure of America, or Columbia as she was often called, eventually developed, she belonged not to geography or to a particular race, but to the family of personified virtues. With the

Revolution, America in symbol stood for a social ideal or a cluster of ideals, and the symbol was recognized as such both at home and abroad" (6–7; my emphases). Taylor's opposition of race and geography to "personified virtues" shows that he understands the eighteenth-century artists' use of race to localize nationness in space. But by describing the colonists' values as "universal," Taylor reveals a blindness to the way that their formal innovations do not so much transcend race as accent it.

First, Taylor mistakenly calls the Indian Princess the early "geographical" symbol. As E. McClung Fleming points out in "The American Image as Indian Princess, 1765–1783," the "Indian Queen" was the geographical embodiment of the continent that emerged in response to the European contact with the tropical Caribbean landscape, as her association with armadillos, alligators, monkeys, and parrots and her characteristic tropical vegetation attest (67–68). Not just the figure's Indianness but the tropical context localizes her allegorical representation. Second, Taylor is not quite accurate in suggesting that Europeans in America were not concerned with the figure's racial markings. As Fleming says, "Universal acceptance by the Atlantic Community of the Indian as a symbol of the Spanish America of the Caribbean did not necessarily guarantee that the native would be considered an equally appropriate symbol of the English America that lay between the Alleghenies and the Atlantic seaboard" ("American Image as Indian Princess," 69). For Fleming, Anglo-American acceptance of the Indian symbol was "evidence of the force this strange, distinctive, new race exerted on the imagination of the Englishmen." His discussion of the Indian as *national* symbol of "English America" takes into consideration the protracted evolution away from this localized embodiment of America toward a classicized European ideal that gradually erased the dark, Indian body of "America."

It is in his discussion of this transformation from Indian female to abstract "personified virtue" as national symbol that Taylor most unconsciously reflects Anglo-American body politics. His ascription of virtual racelessness to what are clearly European female images in the representations of Liberty and Columbia underwrites his opposition of Indianness to "universality" and abstraction. From Taylor's perspective, nonwhiteness is always "local," geographical, and historicized by the moment of European "discovery," while only classicized European forms can embody "transcendent," "universal" attributes. Taylor's use of "classical" as a transcendent category of representation mirrors the appeal to order, measured form, discipline, and nobility of style implicit in the neoclassicism of American governmental architecture and national monuments, a fashion begun during the defining early republican period.[34] The point, says Taylor, was to make the appeal to balance, rationality, and dignity through neoclassical design—concepts offering America as the successor to democratic Athens and republican Rome—the basis of a transformation of America's image from frontier society to ideal polis (16, 20). To Taylor, this association with eternal verities translates as racelessness, but as Fleming's discussion of the evolution of the Indian Princess into Columbia shows, the universalizing impulse was, on a practical level, an attempt to figure America's new post-Revolution self-image as clearly analogous to the idealized self-images of the European nations. In other words, the emergence of Liberty as America mimics the apotheosis of newly independent America into white nationhood.

Fleming explains the evolution of the Indian Queen into the Indian Princess by noting that "the Indian Princess is not the creature of an alien race but is the daughter of Britannia; her major concern is not the domination of savage enemies but the attainment of liberty" ("American Image as Indian Princess," 71). She is "less barbarous" and "less Caribbean" than her predecessor but still "has a swarthy complexion and long dark hair, wears a feathered headdress," carries a bow and arrows, and so on (70, 73).[35] The fluctuating complexion of the Princess is one sign of the eventual transformation into what Fleming calls the "Plumed Greek Goddess," the neoclassical transformation of the Indian Princess who shed Indian somatic markings while maintaining much of the identifying context of America, including her plumed headdress.[36]

The less "native" the Plumed Goddess figure became, the more important her iconic context became in identifying her Americanness, though, and the depictions of this figure around the beginning of the nineteenth century begin to use racial others as foils for the Plumed Goddess: "These prints also illustrate the popularity of a curious, new American figure—the young African Negro Boy dressed in American Indian feathers. It is as though the elimination of the Indian element from the dress of the Plumed Goddess required restoring it to the concept in the form of the Indian Boy. Perhaps because the Negro was a more familiar American figure than the Indian at this time, artists emphasized the African Negro Boy, but dressed him in Indian feathers" (Fleming, "From Indian Princess," 52). A more decisive interpretation of the use of the African-Indian Boy is available, though, especially since his emphatic *difference* from the Plumed Goddess moves him in a direction precisely opposite to her increasing Europeanization. The pronounced alterity of the marginal ethnic figure (his complexion and dress make him *doubly* "other") contrasts with the classicism of the central figure in a way that allows her prior ethnic identifying traits to become abstracted, drained off, and resituated at the margins of this allegory of American identity.

The African-Indian Boy's dwarf stature enhances the Goddess's comparative maturity into "personified virtue," the next stage in the apotheosis of embodied America, without compromising her youthfulness. He does not merely play around and about the Goddess in perpetual childlikeness; in picture after picture, he appears in poses adoring her or studying the virtuous life of other exemplary historico-mythic figures of American life, such as George Washington.[37] The appropriation by the abolitionists of the successors to the Plumed Goddess— America, Columbia, and Liberty—in their propaganda battles against slavery would again use the extreme somatic contrast of black and white bodies simultaneously to elevate the Goddess's aesthetic appeal while magnifying the abjectness of the kneeling, supplicating black slave. Though the abolitionists may have had the noble intent of reinstating a long-denied kinship ("Am I Not a Man/ Woman and a Brother/Sister?" they ask), their manipulation of the existing symbolic economy of asymmetrical power representation helped them to fashion a marketable image of the relation between American egalitarian idealism and the enslaved populations in the South.[38] This iconic tradition mirrors the aesthetic politics of the national founders in their scripting of the "lovely White and Red" of European complexions as analogies of national moral and intellectual "enlightenment," encoding an official preferment of European bodies into the written and iconic documentation of the era of national founding.

The evolution of the African-Indian Boy into the supplicating slave of the antislavery movement provides an important perspective on a seeming anomaly of American "embodiment." As the nominal citizen in the Constitution of the young Republic became officially identified as "white" and "male," the presence of African bodies in the nation began to be rationalized and allegorized by physical contrast to a classicized white female figure. The Indian as somatic middle term gradually disappeared, producing a starker, more enduring, more irreconcilable somatic opposition. America was intended forever after to be a land of distinct bodies, if need be—bodies that could share the cultural space of America but only in arrangements that encoded "race" and gender as dividing lines in the formation of social identities.

The Sable Venus

Far from reducing interracial intercourse, the "condition of the mother" laws increased and systematized sexual contact into an overwhelmingly white-male/

black-female pattern that facilitated a racial caste system. In effect, the laws attempted to define different social destinies for black and white mothers and their
families by creating different sexual identities for them. In a social economy that
considered women of all colors to be the "property" of males, white and black
women's roles were functionally differentiated by the race of the males who
could *not* legally have access to their wombs. The laws decreed one class of
racially unrestricted (black) wombs and one of racially exclusive (white) wombs.
In response to this system that legitimized white male access to all women grew
a tradition that questioned the social consequences of establishing black females
as objects of economic and sexual desire.

According to the narrative of the 1676 Virginia rebellion of indentured servants and slaves also known as "Bacon's Rebellion," which hastened the elimination of the indentured servant system in favor of a strictly racial form of chattel
slavery, one burgess of the Virginia assembly named Richard Lawrence assisted
in the rebellion.[39] Lawrence was made the specific object of ridicule and an object lesson in the surrender of reason to passion because his lapses of judgment
included revolt not only against the colony but against all the principles and beliefs that he as an educated man and a cleric should have supported. Cited as evidence of his errant behavior was his choice of a black female slave as his lover:
"He was a Parson not meanly acquainted with such learning . . . that inables
Man for the management of more then ordnary imployments, Which he subjected to an eclips, as well in the transactings of the present affaires, as in the darke
imbraces of a Blackamoore, his slave: And that in so fond a Maner, as though
Venus was cheifely to be worshiped in the Image of a Negro, or that Buty con-
sisted all together in the Antipethy of Complections: to the noe meane Scandle
and affrunt of all the Vottrisses in or about towne" (Cassity, 28). The levity with
which the account records Lawrence's transgressive choice of a "Negro" Venus
suggests a connection between his aesthetic anarchy and his instigation of communal discord. Yet far more than just the "Antipethy of Complections" is in evidence here: the "Sable Venus" is the very antithesis of European order, beauty,
and decorum. She embodies the chaos threatening to engulf the European expansion into the formless wilderness.[40] Lawrence's crime was not, as with Hugh
Davis, treated as a momentary lapse of moral probity but as evidence of a radical
and systemic erosion of colonial values.

The lore of the black Venus underscored specifically the threat to the white
population when the black female became more than just an object of momentary lust or economic investment. Long-standing liaisons and the availability of

"sooty dames, well vers'd in Venus' school" (Jordan, 150) made white males like
Lawrence less inclined to marry white women, causing friction between white
men and their potential white mates. On another level, the lore of the black
Venus protested through ridicule the importation of an aberrant, destabilizing,
maternal line of descent and desire into the American experience.

Allegorical treatments such as Thomas Stothard's *The Voyage of the Sable Venus*
(1781) commemorated the division in American law and custom between the
official preferment of white European somatic standards and the simultaneous,
cynical facilitation of black female sexual exploitation as the cultural divide that
imposed separate destinies on black and white women. Stothard's illustration
fancifully depicts the arrival in America of the black Venus, accompanied by
white cherubs (several of whom appear to be smirking) and a wayward white Cu-
pid.[41] The poem in honor of the painting suggests that this black Venus and her
white sister were "Both just alike, except the white, / No difference, no — none at
night" (Honour, *Image of the Black*, 34). The snide suggestion that a subordinate
aesthetic system must be imported to govern the growing African population —
except at night — reflects the moral temporizing of Jefferson's contemporaries.
The poem pokes fun at official pronouncements about the ugliness of Africans
in the face of ample evidence that black women had become the staple commodity of the erotic economy functioning in the slave states. But because the
parodic black Venus, whom only the cover of night made agreeable, subverted
the Enlightenment preference for the visual above the other senses, her power
lay entirely in her ability to seduce whites into surrendering to their "lower,"
"animal" nature.

The historical development of images of embodied America from the Indian
Queen to Columbia illustrates the distinction drawn by Mikhail Bakhtin between the classical and the grotesque, in that, like Galle's recumbent Indian
Queen, the grotesque emphasizes the bodily parts "that are open to the outside
world," in opposition to the classical body's finished, enclosed features, which
"acquire an essential meaning as the border of a closed individuality that does
not merge with other bodies and with the world" (quoted in Stallybrass, 124).
The racially "open" black womb and the "closed" white womb found iconic representation through the black Venus and Columbia, respectively. As the image
of embodied America came more and more to feature the race-chaste white female as the apotheosis of transcendent virtues, the logic of the American separation of race through the "condition of the mother" acquired another level of
cultural reinforcement. The legitimation of only the white female's offspring

emphasized the modal distinctions between the white female body's official function and the black female body's illicit utility, distinctions between white "propriety" and black "property" that governed the division of American cultural space through the bodies of black and white women.

The Invention of White Space

The nineteenth century was dominated by the terms of an America with separate racial populations defined through the bodies of women. Echoing Jefferson and anticipating Lincoln, Alexis de Tocqueville, in his 1835 study *Democracy in America*, pointed to the inevitability of a racial contest over space if the restrictions of slavery were removed. One American informant had told Tocqueville in very clear terms the precise cause of the American race problem: "The black and white population are in a state of war. Never will they mingle. One of them will have to yield to the other" (Fredrickson, 21).

Based on this type of testimony and his own observations, Tocqueville concluded that so long as blacks and whites coexisted in the same geographical space, there would never be racial harmony in America and that the only possible outcome of the contest over space was some system of racial dominance. From this principle, we can extract a "Tocqueville Corollary": racial equality in a harmonious multiracial society means intermarriage. Having denied legal intermarriage between Africans and Europeans as a way of defining national kinship, whites had in effect made intermarriage the ultimate entitlement of the imagined community. This equivalence, magnified into a natural law in the American South, took concrete form in the elaborate system of social protections around white women, as attempts to preserve white race identity involved contests over geography, social space, and the race-exclusive space of individual female bodies. Driving nineteenth-century race theory and race-based social exclusion policies were the twin threats of racial extermination, resulting from a race war over control of American territory, and the quieter holocaust of amalgamation—the protracted, systematic absorption of whites into the black race. But the sequestration of white women emphasized the danger of intermarriage—a formal relationship—so as to call attention away from the illicit, informal sexual commerce engaged in by white men with black women.

Thus Tocqueville's prediction was perhaps more influential in articulating a white nationalist agenda of social engineering than it was accurate in assessing the nation's ability to accommodate racial heterogeneity. The populations did mingle extensively, though usually not legally or with public approval. Thus the presence of blacks in America continued to influence white national imaginings.[42] Abraham Lincoln told a group of free black men in 1862, "But for your race among us there could not be war. . . . It is better for us both, therefore, to be separated" (Osofsky, 124). His debates with Stephen Douglas had already established his belief that black bodies were unsuitable for American "embodiment,"[43] but when pressed for a model of society inclusive of blacks, Lincoln could only respond, "Inasmuch as [the two races] cannot [live together on terms of social and political equality], while they do remain together there must be the position of superior and inferior." Lincoln, of course, counted himself in the number who were "in favor of having the superior position assigned to the white race" (quoted in Gossett, 254). Later racists would exploit Lincoln's unconsciously sexual metaphor of racial bodies in positions of dominance and subordination, as with the popular analogy of "Negro dominance" during Reconstruction to the "rape" of the South.[44]

Lillian Smith's segregated body model of society nearly a century later conveyed the social reality of Jim Crow in the South, in that the economic and psychological benefits provided by a docile black population enabled southerners to cede space to black Americans, using the formula that difference requires distance.[45] In the post–Civil War era, the dream of a monoracial America kept in circulation the idea that political separation of the races, in the form of movements to disfranchise blacks all across the South, coupled with social separation, in the recurrent themes of extermination, expulsion, and racial quarantine, would "remove" blacks from the American body politic.

To many race spokespersons in the postwar Progressive Era, the establishment of parallel race worlds was an invitation to disaster. W. E. B. Du Bois lamented the attempt to purge blacks from civic life, describing a town divided by the "Veil" of race in Virginia: "You who live in single towns will hardly comprehend the double life of this Virginia hamlet. . . . It is two worlds separate yet bound together like those double stars that, bound for all time, whirl around each other separate yet one" (Du Bois, *Against Racism*, 49). On the other hand, white supremacists like Philip Alexander Bruce were alarmed at the prospect of large numbers of unsupervised blacks given unprecedented freedom of movement by means of a "social separation . . . so wide in the future that every community inhabited by . . . both [races] [would] be as distinctively divided into two social bodies as if they had no local connection" (Bruce, 242). However fundamental to the economic life of the state as cheap laborers, in the "white man's country" of the South, black Americans were systematically to be severed from the body politic and the body social.[46] In the words of John Temple Graves, radical means of racial separation would provide the "knife that severs the limb, but saves the life" of the nation.[47]

The intensity and duration of this reproduction of the body in discourses of American kinship make all corporeal language of national imagining mythical, even (and perhaps, especially) the "scientific" language of race difference. Roland Barthes's definition of mythic language holds that although a mythical form may enjoy a transhistorical existence, it gains significance only when motivated by a specific historical circumstance. Neither the form nor the underlying concept undergoes reality testing: they do not appeal to reason but to predispositions. They persuade by invoking culturally conditioned emotional responses, reactions so overdetermined that the mythic utterance may even be exposed as self-contradictory or factually baseless and yet will still elicit the desired response. Thus mythic discourse presents truth claims that rely solely on the self-evidentiary persistence and "naturalness" of its motivating concepts.[48] According to Barthes, the "repetition of the concept through different forms is precious to the mythologist, it allows him to decipher the myth; it is the insistence of a type of behaviour which reveals its intention" (120). The deciphering of mythic discourse involves tracking the repetition of its motivating concepts invested in various forms through different historical eras, as they become appropriated and recycled by each generation to serve its particular interests.[49]

David Theo Goldberg's analysis of discourse about race shares a common assumption with Barthes's "mythology": "In a field of discourse like racism, what is generally circulated and exchanged is not simply truth but truth claims or representations" (Goldberg, "Social Formation," 298). "If discursive unity is to be achieved" in this system, "it can only be a product of those underlying factors that directly generate the discursive field. Foucault calls this set of factors the *preconceptual* level" (300). The Foucaultian preconceptual level functions in Goldberg's reading of racist discourse much as the conceptual level of the myth functions for Barthes.[50] Goldberg provides a detailed description of the "underlying factors" of race mythology: "The coherence of the racist project . . . is a function of the preconceptual elements that have structured racist dispositions. These include classification and order, value and hierarchy, differentiation and identity; discrimination and identification; exclusion and domination, subjection and subjugation; entitlement and restriction, and in a general way, violence and violation" (301). A survey of racist literature shows that since race concepts attribute significance to "observable differences," racist discourse becomes coherent as narrative only when the intent to distinguish, to differentiate, to *distance*, is understood as the driving mechanism within its often self-contradictory utterances.

One way of simplifying a discussion of Goldberg's "preconceptual primitive terms" is to understand racist discourse as an attempt to organize racially distinct bodies spatially into clusters on horizontal and vertical planes. As we have seen, limiting access to social, political, and economic entitlements through law, custom, or physical violence gives a sense of permanence, "naturalness," and divine sanction to social formations based in observable differences. Whether hierarchical or center/periphery descriptors frame group relations, racist beliefs appeal to an idealized superindividual entity that must preserve its pristine bodily form, and which particularly must protect itself from inferior, devalued bodies that seek to invade its privileged spaces. The "color line" may, according to need, serve as threshold, floor, and ceiling.

At base, then, the governing processes of racist discourse enable narratives of inclusion within and exclusion from, of supremacy over or subordination to—narratives that proliferate, expand, adopt local features, insinuate themselves into folkways, serve as the analogical postulates for scientific inquiry and scientific explanations, and especially make themselves available to bureaucracies and demagogues. Racism must become constructed in language before it can be institutionalized, and those institutions must, to survive, manifest the intent to exclude and to subordinate.[51] I. A. Newby maintained that racist discourse in defense of Jim Crow contained "two themes [that] were constantly repeated: socially, the races must be segregated, and politically, the whites must be supreme" (114). This process of differential exclusion and hierarchy systematically racialized space—into "white space" and, necessarily, "black space."[52] Race-differentiated distribution, discipline, or access to entitlements and privileges characteristically argues a "need" for racially homogeneous territorial and governmental structures—for example, the South as "white man's country." White space fantasies provided rationalizing narratives of differential treatment, making myths of radical race difference more coherent without necessarily serving as the sole or primary cause of individual acts of race discrimination.

Although spatial solutions are the typical results of such fears of intrusion or contamination, in the language of racial science "inferior races" also threaten backward movement in the progress narrative of the "superior race." The key defenses of slavery in pre-Darwinian discourses of race had cited curses on biblical figures such as Ham and Cain as the origins of a new category of people specially marked out for divine punishment by their dark skin. Modern scientific racism, by contrast, maintained the mythicized forms—that is, "chosen people," "cursed races"—but updated the Bible's anthropology (Fredrickson, 60–61, 87–89). This transition from sacred to secular (that is, "evolutionary") time was a slow (and perhaps not entirely complete) one. The metamorphosis of terms for spiritual status into terms for racial division sustained the original categorical intent: separating the saved from the unsaved. This transition featured such discursive innovations as the use of the term *white* to replace the term *Christian* and the replacement of terms like *ethnic, heathen,* and *savage* with *Africans* or *blacks* (Jordan, 94, 95). The vogue of the "noble savage" romanticized otherness for a time, before comparative anthropology exploded the myth of the "happy primitive" (Stocking, 35–41), but the circle was completed when nineteenth-century science revived the terms *savage* and *primitive* in evolutionary and moral taxonomies to distinguish the chosen from the unchosen.

These discursive developments illustrate what Johannes Fabian has called the "politics of time." According to Fabian, evolutionist theories of human difference insisted on "*spatializing* Time" through a "taxonomic approach to sociocultural reality. . . . Efforts to construct relations with [the] Other by means of temporal devices implied affirmation of difference as *distance*" (15, 16). The use of a term such as *primitive* masquerades in scientific objectivity its effect of describing evolutionary and, necessarily, *metaphysical* distance from normative white Western civilization. According to nineteenth-century French anthropologist Joseph Marie Degerando, every anthropological encounter with the non-Western racial other was like a mythic journey through time and space.[53] For Fabian, anthropological study made itself available to conservative politics by denying its object an equivalence in time—"coevalness." This denial leads to judgments about the relative worth of "people outside of history," in Anderson's phrase, and thereafter potentially to denials of kinship.

Anderson's concept of nation is pertinent to this discussion because it relies heavily on the concept of time as a means of imagining community. Anderson explains that novels and newspapers helped the evolution of the modern concept of nation by forcing readers to envision multiple characters simultaneously experiencing the "novelties" of contemporary existence. Anderson borrows a term from Walter Benjamin to describe this temporal basis of community: "homogeneous, empty time."[54] According to Anderson, routine behavior (like reading the morning newspaper as a cultural ritual) helps national constituents to imagine their "kinship" through visualizing other citizens performing the same actions simultaneously in calendrical, clocked time. Such imaginings are necessitated by the need to envision the nation as an extended family, despite the impossibility of knowing all other national constituents. The critical term in this process is, surprisingly, "meanwhile,"[55] because it enables the citizen reading about his or her contemporaries to see numerous destinies as connected not so much by personal contact as by simultaneity. This connection in time provides a glimpse of the "many as one": "The idea of a sociological organism moving calendrically through homogeneous, empty time is a precise analogue of the idea of the nation, which also is conceived as a solid community moving steadily down (or up) history" (26).

But no nation can imagine itself except through the specific kinship practices of its constituent cultures, and Fabian reminds us that "*kinship*, on the surface one of the most innocent descriptive terms one could imagine, is fraught with temporal connotations" (75). In a nation divided into social castes based on ideas of ancestral origins and maintained by the closing off of opportunities for citizens to cross temporal boundaries of "primitive" and "modern," citizens cannot be expected to invent a category of nonhierarchical kinship entirely at odds with their routine social practice. If national history builds on the dynamics of ethnic communities thrust into conflicts over space, the prevailing modes of distinguishing "us" from "them" will necessarily shape the imagined nation. As Fabian explains,

> It is not difficult to transpose from physics to politics one of the most ancient rules which states that it is impossible for two bodies to occupy the same space at the same time. When in the course of colonial expansion a Western body politic came to occupy, literally, the space of an autochthonous body, several alternatives were conceived to deal with that violation of the rule. The simplest one, if we think of North America and Australia, was of course to move or remove the other body. Another one is to pretend that space is being divided and allocated to separate bodies. . . . Most often the preferred strategy has been simply to manipulate the other variable— Time. With the help of various devices of sequencing and distancing one assigns to the conquered populations a *different* Time. (29–30)

Fabian calls this systemic denial of "coevalness" *allochronism* (32). By denying simultaneity to nonwhite others, the politics of time, in effect, creates not Anderson's homogeneous but Fabian's allochronic (or *heterogeneous*) time. Implicit in Anderson's own formulation, too, is the temporal marking of his "imagined community" as a *modern innovation*. Self-consciously modern citizens are entirely free to imagine a kinship with other self-conscious moderns, and free, too, to imagine their fundamental *unlikeness* to the unlettered who do not read the newspaper, the unfranchised who do not participate in democratic institutions, the unemployed who do not share workday routines, and those otherwise genetically unfitted for the "progress" narrative that drives calendrical, clocked time. Privileged racial ancestry therein still determines access to the homogeneous time of the nation. Devalued descent taxonomizes all "others" into a descending evolutionary scale, with the "unevolved" and "unevolving" African at the extreme opposite from the white European.[56] Comparable to the way that Christian adventurers imagined themselves as the rightful supplanters of pagan empires, a dominant ethnicity may imagine itself as the temporal successor of a "primitive" native population ticketed for erasure, justifying its paternalistic attitude toward what it considers the "older" but still "childlike" people through its politics of "progress." It was precisely such politics of time that came forcefully into play in post-Reconstruction America to reinforce the racial hierarchies called into question by postwar egalitarianism.

White Americans constructed temporal boundaries between populations that freed them to imagine an America without blacks. One important factor in this process was the stereotyped representation of black Americans as irremediably trapped in the allochronic time of the primitive. Atlanta newspaperman John Temple Graves justified black suppression on the grounds that "the negro is an accident, . . . an unwholesome, unwelcome, helpless, unassimilable element in our civilization. *He is not made for our times.* He is not framed to share in the duty and the destiny which he perplexes and beclouds" (in Shufeldt, *Negro*, 252; my emphasis). The prolonged attack on the wisdom of educating blacks like other citizens in social policy discussions laid stress on Africans' "unequal aptitude for development and progress" and asserted that tax money was better spent on whites, who were educable and who at the very least could more fully apply an education, given the severe occupational restrictions on blacks.[57] Advances in black literacy were derided as false and misleading because blacks had not "evolved" into a race capable of creating or sustaining a high culture on its own. Black education was only "imitation" and thus would not "take hold" among the masses.[58] Ultimately, the widespread calls to limit black Americans to industrial education at most (that is, education of the "hand and heart," in Nathaniel Shaler's phrase, but not of the "head") was the final step in defining an intellectual sphere available only to whites through both genetic legacy and state fiat.

If whites were free from imagining black Americans as linked to them in a ritual of simultaneous literate self-imagining, then they could, by Anderson's definition, expel blacks from the community of dreamers. If they did not have to grapple with recognition of black citizens as "co-workers in the kingdom of culture," in Du Bois's words, then they were free to imagine that every meaningful achievement of American society was biologically determined. Du Bois recalled that "science" had pegged the evolutionary gap between the races at one thousand years during his university days,[59] but primitive black and the modern white could comfortably share the same geographical boundaries so long as they did not share the same national time. Wherever they physically resided, they would exist, for all practical purposes, in different "imagined" communities. The imagining of America as parallel racial time-spaces, one progressive, the other static to regressive, sought to exclude black Americans from the intellectual and creative production of modernity, the time-space of the nation. William B. Smith, though, argued for protecting the hermetic realm of white "history" through both the politics of time and more drastic measures. Even though Smith's "'true saviour is Time'" (xv), he seemed unconvinced that the politics of time alone could contain "the man of yesterday." Nothing less than expulsion of all black citizens—the ethnic cleansing of American space—would suffice.

Time, Space, and American Bodies

In the aftermath of Darwinian evolution, social Darwinists attributed teleological import to somatic traits, arguing that separate social and political statuses for the races were necessary to protect the white somatic distinctions that had "produced" civilization. Arguments for preserving the "evolutionary space" of the white body inviolate from nonwhite genes through territorialization of the female womb revived the spatial logic of polygenism as polyspecification.[60] This and other variations on the concept of "separate origins, separate destinies" formed the key topoi that enabled a wide variety of mythic expressions on race difference grounded in spatiotemporal exclusion. The idea that individual bodies were microcosms of their space of origin buttressed the vogue of somatic quantification (anthropometry) and the temporal discourses of evolutionary regression, recapitulation, neoteny, race gendering, and atavism. Belief that all blacks were regressing into a essential "type" spurred the redefinition of race in America and helped to restore practices of abjection and physical distance dating from slavery to assert the unquestioned supremacy of whiteness.

Proponents of polygenism, including Josiah C. Nott, Louis Aggasiz, and George R. Gliddon, argued that the Genesis tale of human creation was accurate but incomplete because the extremes of race difference could not have developed within the time frame of biblical events (Fredrickson, 73–90). Other races must therefore represent "separate creations" not specified in Genesis, undoubtedly because these peoples were not meant to share the Judeo-Christian salvation history (Horsman, 118–19; 29–138). According to George Fredrickson, the Swiss-American naturalist Louis Aggassiz "immediately won wide support for the general concept [of "zoological provinces," that is, race-specific natural environments], even among those who were unwilling to accept the idea that separate human creations had literally occurred in each zone" (137). Later, the postslavery consensus that the races should not mix often took the form of assertions that the races should stay within their "God-given" (that is, "natural") places.

But the concept of race-specific zones did nothing to prevent white Western migration. The nineteenth-century vogue of the manifest destiny of Anglo-Saxonism to conquer the temperate zone of the Northern Hemisphere, "the truly historic zone" of world civilization, according to Hegel,[61] was an important component of the American "progress" narrative of the nineteenth century. Rather than condemning apparent contradictions in the principle that each race should stay within a fixed racial zone, many white racialists welcomed the possibility of white global dominance as proof of their racial chosenness.[62] The fusion of narratives of chosenness with the scientific racism of social Darwinist thought resulted in the discourse of "racial fitness" that William B. Smith espoused, allowing "the essence of polygenist thinking about race [to be] preserved in a Darwinian framework" (Fredrickson, 232).[63]

Although Darwin did not describe evolution as progress toward a transcendent state, his popularizers in the late nineteenth century found this misreading useful in weaning public attitudes away from the sacred calendar's anticipation of divine apocalyptic intervention in human history. As Henry Adams noted, natural selection became for scientists the prime mover of all human experience: "It seemed a form of religious hope; a promise of ultimate perfection."[64] This modification of the earlier biblical paradigm of racial chosenness allowed social evolutionists to invest the updated Darwinian narrative with a telos that included a radically secularized apocalypse, wherein deviation from the "true" evolutionary path (that is, "racial purity") became synonymous with damnation and the slippery slope to race extinction (Heilke, 145–46). No longer was Judeo-Christian morality sufficient grounds for salvation; "proper" evolutionary trajectory described a morality as crucial to God's will as any biblical injunction.[65] William B. Smith best articulates this secular racial salvation, pointing out the error of

Christian charity: "There is a personal and even a social morality that may easily become racially immoral. There are diseases whose evolutionary function is to weed out the weak, and so to preserve the future for the strong. . . . The hope of humanity lies not in strengthening the weak, but in perfecting the strong" (190–91).

A second key area of racialist discourse followed through on the logic that biological difference based in adaptation to a particular environment makes each body a reflection—a microcosm, in fact—of its point of origin. The proponents of comparative anthropology were heavily invested in quantifying the spatial dimensions of race-identified bodies—their dimensions, "properties," and "capacities"—in the search for an infallible predictor of differential racial "achievement" (Gould, 73–82). If they could link biological differences to intellectual differences based in race particularly, and, by extension, to a race's potential for full participation in a modern industrialized society, scientists could conclusively settle the question of equal participation of the races in the political and social life of the nation. The belief in radical incompatibility between the bodies of blacks and whites beyond even the evidence of the senses led to the institutionalization of the sciences of craniology, physiognomy, and phrenology in the determination of quantifiable race difference, whose key theorists asserted that nonwhite bodies were stuck in the "primitive" time-space of their place of origins and consequently were limited by insufficient or maladaptive anatomical *space* for the acquisition of white race traits and potentials.[66] Joseph Tillinghast thought Africans were hopelessly trapped in a "state of transition" that showed no evidence of "perceptible progress" within known history, a psychic state that simply mirrored the arrested transitional state of the African body from a lower evolutionary form.[67] Such readings of the physical form are based on an untenable assumption identified by Eric Voegelin. As Thomas Heilke explains, "The error of race theorists is to suppose that vaguely defined mental and physical elements are all determined by the same biological and/or geographical factors, so that a study of the body will yield insights into the nature of the mind."[68]

Preordained findings of a hierarchy of racial types based on physical and intellectual capacities, with whites on top and blacks on the bottom, helped to confirm the idea that the races occupied distinct and distant evolutionary spaces. Charles A. Lofgren's study of the social climate during the time of the *Plessy v. Ferguson* decision includes a chart drawn from a statistical analysis of social science discussions of race done by George Stocking. Among the essays that represented social science research considered to be reputable, by authors whose journal publications began to appear in 1896 or earlier, Stocking's data show that 94 percent explicitly or implicitly agreed with the idea of a racial hierarchy; 100 percent agreed with the idea of a cultural hierarchy; 94 percent agreed that races had different mental capacities; and 83 percent agreed that hereditary race differences caused cultural differences (Lofgren, 104).

Racial taxonomy operated on a principle of analogy that further distinguished races in time and space. Where enlightened white Western man represented the furthest point of evolution of the human species in this scheme (that is, species maturity), other races could be phylogenetically classified along an ontogenetic developmental chart through a principle of racial *neoteny*.[69] In 1875, social Darwinist Herbert Spencer proposed that "how races differ in respect of the more or less involved structures of their minds will best be understood on recalling that unlikeness between the juvenile mind and the adult mind among ourselves" (quoted in Gossett, 149). According to Thomas Gossett, Spencer was applying the principle that ontogeny recapitulates phylogeny, and therefore, by analogy, "the mind of a child recapitulates the history of human races in a development from savagery to civilization" (149). This specialized category of allochronism encompasses pronouncements such as Hegel's designation of Africa as "the land of childhood" (Hegel 91).[70]

Other corporeal analogies led similarly to the invention of "new knowledge" about race, such as descriptions of races having more or less "energy" or "vitality." Analogies of energetic, conquering races to "masculine" organisms and sentient, localized ones to "feminine" creatures led to the popularization of race gendering (Horsman 74).[71] In contrast to the white masculine ideal of dominance, there arose, according to Fredrickson, a "romantic racialism" among defenders of black civil rights that played up the positive attributes of black docility as a type of "feminine" refinement, even as detractors of the race contemptuously rebuked the same qualities as "feminine" weakness (108–9). Darwin's *The Descent of Man* approved of the notion that because males experienced a longer and more differentiated process of maturity, females were closer physically to both lower animals and "lower races."[72] The race/gender analogy itself became frozen into a seemingly immutable, natural law, as Nancy Stepan has argued: "The analogies concerning racial and gender and class differences in the human species developed in the biosocial sciences in the nineteenth century . . . had the social consequences of helping perpetuate the racial and gender status quo. The analogies were used by scientists to justify resistance to efforts at social change on the part of women and 'lower races,' on the grounds that inequality was a 'fact' of nature and not a function of power relations in a society" ("Race and Gender," 40–41, 43, 52).

In configuring the social space that black people should occupy, then, the governing assumption was that their relation to whites be as female to male — that is, inherently unfit for any but a subordinate role. Similarly, the operative Victorian constructions of gender, which assume a white masculine norm, base the assignment of gender roles on "physical differences" analogous to the relation between "higher" and "lower" races.[73] The allochronic circularity of this associative chain becomes even more pronounced when we consider that both constructions of subordinate status are overdetermined by analogy to "child-likeness."[74] As we have seen, Spencer's belief in black neoteny as a form of black incapacity for Caucasian mental and moral functioning was an important way of framing black ineligibility for the rights and responsibilities of modern civilization.[75]

The most sensational and politically resonant feature of the science of black race incapacity was the pervasive belief in black somatic regression. If blacks were evolutionarily and physiognomically "closer" in time to the higher primates, the question went, might not they also be more likely to fall all the way back into brute behavior? Paul A. Barringer's *The American Negro: His Past and Future* (1900) provides a typical detailing of the theoretical underpinnings of the belief in black regression. Barringer says that if "the ontogeny is the repetition of the phylogeny," then "the life history is the repetition of the race history." Since the "degradation" of Africa formed the basis of black race history, no more could be expected of the southern black removed from the disciplined participation in civilization that slavery afforded than a total reversion "through hereditary forces to savagery" (Gossett, 253). The "brute Negro" type so prominent in the literature of the era is preeminently a postemancipation Negro who has been allowed to slide back to the evolutionary level from which he had been raised by white intervention in his phylogenetic trajectory. Tillinghast's study *The Negro in Africa and America*, published, like Hoffman's earlier work, by the American Economic Association, assumed that blacks in America had had insufficient time to change the physical and psychic orientation of their bodies from African time-space, and thus they were virtually indistinguishable from those who had never left Africa. For Tillinghast, environment and heredity were separate causal factors in human behavior, but since in evolutionary terms the human variety evolves through selection within a specific physical and cultural environment, a "race" could not change its makeup except after millennia of further evolution in a changed environment. Since the equatorial climate of Africa did not reward a work ethic, and since the moral and cultural climate did not encourage high standards, according to Tillinghast, Africans had been *selected* for indolence and criminality. There was no hope that education or other forms of intervention in African racial destiny would improve black American capacity for civilized existence.[76] Tillinghast's work is a more sophisticated version of Thomas Dixon's racial romance *The Leopard's Spots*, published the same year and hammering at the same theme, that black Americans cannot shed the shaping influence of their African origins.

Spatial restrictions on black mobility were intricately related to the fear of black regression as well as to a third category of race mythology—the fear of contagious ethnicity: the "Africanization of America." Though its earliest expressions targeted disease, the epidemiological trope covered any form of contact with blacks that could possibly be injurious to whites. Philip A. Bruce noted in an 1899 article that the campaigns to disfranchise black voters were successful in ensuring that blacks were "no longer a menace to organized government," that is, no longer a threat to the body politic. But the "filth" and "debauchery" of black lifestyle imperiled the body social, "menac[ing] the moral well-being of the communities" in which they lived (Fredrickson, 268). William Lee Howard was even more explicit about the epidemiological implications of unstructured race contact: "There is every prospect of checking and reducing . . . diseases in the white race, if the race is socially—in every aspect of the term—quarantined from the African" (424). While they professed that race competition would eventually favor the "fittest," social scientists also feared that short-term contact with the "unfit" was eroding white Anglo-Saxon moral fiber and even, in some cases, its genetic stock.

The more radical of the two common spatial solutions to this race-conflict model was complete expulsion of nonwhite populations outside the continental United States, or restriction of nonwhites to areas of the South or Southwest that would be off-limits to whites (Helper, 14–15). Plans for expulsion rarely got as far as official policy, and large-scale voluntary migrations of blacks from the Northern Hemisphere did not occur either, but both assumed that blacks would actually survive their "racial unfitness," at least in the short term. Quarantine emerged gradually as public policy in the South and the North, acquiring its own mythology as its popularity spread. Residential segregation in the North and public access laws in the South temporarily resolved the issue of black inclusion in American life by creating race worlds with limited points of mutual access.

The concept of parallel race worlds invested even the most casual interpersonal contacts with the significance of cosmic evolutionary processes, romanticizing white repugnance to racial difference and frequently justifying violent suppression of racial others as a "natural" and necessary instinct for self-preservation.[77]

While quarantine appears on the surface to be a less radical solution than expulsion, its adoption and standardization often received impetus from the belief that black Americans would eventually die out as a group and therefore like other sick populations should be prevented from infecting whites. Many social scientists (and William B. Smith) were convinced that such isolation would allow the "natural" competition between races to result, within several generations, in the gradual extinction of nonwhites. According to the standard narrative, blacks had thrived in America because slavery had permitted them to avoid any actual struggle for survival as individuals. With the protecting arm of the kindly slave owners removed after emancipation, blacks were not prepared to survive on their own. Those who did not rush back to the safe haven of the plantation but crowded instead in the large cities would be the first to die out from disease and criminality induced by their inability to adapt to new surroundings.[78]

The increasingly frequent sight of blacks in large cities with no hopes of employment and with no direct supervision as in antebellum days fueled the legislation by "Redeemer" governments enacting Jim Crow segregation and various strategies for keeping blacks out of electoral politics in the 1890s. But according to John S. Haller, "segregation and disfranchisement . . . were not means of achieving eventual equality, or for that matter, even complete separation; rather they were first steps toward preparing the Negro race for its extinction" (210). If we include the upsurge in lynching and rioting in the last decade of the nineteenth century among what Haller calls "policies of anticipation for a singular white society in America," it becomes clear that the cumulative effect of the philosophical alliance of social Darwinism and comparative anthropology was to validate a growing tendency among whites to see themselves as the agents of an evolutionary process of racial extinction, what Paul Barringer ominously called the "sacrifice of a race" (*Race Problems of the South*, 194).

It was but a small step from the imagining of blacks dying to urging governmental facilitation of the foreordained event so as to cause the least disruption in the lives of white Americans.[79] Robert W. Shufeldt, in a plea to create an environment safe for white evolution, advocated the ethnic cleansing of America: "Nature has no pity, or so far as we know, no designs in such matters. . . . In other words, it remains entirely with ourselves to control our environment in such matters, and were there a consensus of opinion upon the point, followed by a consensus of action, we have it in our power to render the negro race extinct in the United States in very short order."[80] Hilton R. Helper had argued even before the great vogue of social Darwinism that like vermin, blacks should be "permitted to decay and die, and then to disappear, at once and forever" in nature's "wonderful fossilizing processes, which are now rapidly removing from the fair face of the earth all ugly and useless organisms" (105). William B. Smith himself looked eagerly forward to the day when the extinction of Africans, "which the unfeeling process of Nature demands in sacrifice on the altar of the evolution of Humanity" (x), would finally make the world safe for whites. The consensus of white social scientists at the turn of the century was that whether or not black Americans acquiesced in the new social death of Jim Crow quarantine, there was every possibility that they faced utter extinction.

William B. Smith's pollution fears centered more on "amalgamation" than infection by disease from dying blacks. In the popular mind of Progressive Era America, black sexuality was doubly diseased by venereal infection and the ultimate pollution of genetic inferiority. The widespread conviction that all blacks were preternaturally sexually promiscuous reinforced the popular link between blacks and venereal disease specifically.[81] This epidemiological model of race interaction extended into theories of hematic contamination as well. "Blood" was widely believed to be a magical determinant of character even in the absence of racial considerations. The taboos against sexual contact with blacks thus had two powerful emotional appeals among whites: the need to avoid contaminating the individual body's reproductive organs through interracial sexual contact and to avoid contaminating the communal bloodstream with black "blood."

In the Jim Crow statutes of the post-Reconstruction era, the state stepped in to facilitate the "natural" division of humans through rules of race classification that made possession of any amount of African genes the basis of social quarantine. But the promulgation of the "one-drop rule" increased rather than decreased the need for vigilance along the color line, because it now meant that the old system, public acceptance of a person as white, was a potential hazard to an entire community. Over but a few generations, a whole community could be "polluted" by the original "one drop" replicating and proliferating, spreading from parent to child in a chain of inevitability. The war against race contamination had to be fought on the level of the individual white body if it was to be won. Once again, because white male adventurism might help spread disease but could not introduce black genes into the "white" world, the prohibitions on personal conduct focused on white women (Smith, *Color Line*, 9–10).

"One drop" mythology also included a further appeal to Jim Crow quarantine. If "one drop" meant that every person of traceable black blood was more related to a single black ancestor than to any white ancestor, it also meant that any so-defined black person was also more related to *all* black people as a class than to *any* consanguineous person defined as white. To put this another way, it means that the differences between the black and white races are always more profound than differences *within* either race. According to Robert W. Shufeldt, "true negroes anywhere are remarkably uniform with respect to their moral and physical characters, — more so, in fact, than any other people of whatever nationality they may be" (*Problem*, 27). The reason for this, according to Philip A. Bruce, was that black allochronism had deprived the race of evolutionary progress to the level of meaningful individuation: "The most remarkable feature of the general moral disposition of the blacks is the almost phenomenal development of the characteristics of the type as compared with the development of the characteristics of the mere individual; in other words, as members of one of the great families of mankind, they have the most pronounced traits as a race to distinguish them from all other races, but few peculiarities of their own as men to distinguish them sharply from each other" (126). According to Tillinghast, this original lack of differentiation among blacks allowed for the complete homogenization of an African type in America, with an attendant uniformity of psychic characteristics (26, 113, 117–18). Bruce claimed that this undifferentiated difference became more pronounced the more blacks congregated in groups, being more influenced by internal than external pressures (167). Bruce concluded that the further removed blacks became from the ameliorative contact with whites of the slave era, the less individuated they would become (244). Thus the atavistic return of the original black African body was emblematic of the group reversion to a near-animal state of indistinguishableness commensurate with the undifferentiated, unevolved landscape and culture of Africa itself.[82]

The most famous literary application of this principle is in Joseph Conrad's *Heart of Darkness*. The Africans' indistinguishableness from the flora and fauna of the primeval landscape anchors Charles Marlow's allochronistic assertion that "Going up the [Congo] was like travelling back to the earliest beginnings of the world." The farther up the Congo Marlow traveled, the more pronounced the confusion of humanity and landscape became: "suddenly, as though a veil had been removed from my eyes, I made out, deep in the tangled gloom, naked breasts, arms, legs, glaring eyes—the bush was swarming with human limbs in movement" (61). Such representations of African humanity as an undifferentiated mass personality strongly reinforced dystopian imagery of the black American citizenry as a mob—what *Atlanta Constitution* editor Henry W. Grady referred to as a "vast *swarm*, ignorant, purchasable" and available to be "impacted and controlled by desperate and unscrupulous white men and made to hold the balance of [electoral] power when white men are divided."[83]

Tropes of diseased African alterity easily translated into fears of cultural pollution on the order of Kurtz's, as the concepts of contagious, migratory, and involuntary ethnicities proliferated in discourses of race difference. The metaphysical realm of whiteness was not merely a biological but an intellectual, aesthetic, and moral plane as well. Even though the primary line of racial defense was erected around the white body, an assault on any aspect of white culture could lead to somatic corruption. Simply put, difference was dangerous to the white body social and to the white body proper, so if the biological and cultural heritage of Europe was to proceed undisturbed into posterity, strict measures would be necessary to prevent pollution. Any deed that had the intent or the effect of reversing white superiority and exclusivity was a source of pollution, and all legal and extralegal measures to preserve white superiority were justified.

The net result in the postemancipation "Progressive Era" was the intensification of public policy initiatives to quarantine nonwhite bodies physically, genetically, and epistemologically. To Orlando Patterson, one useful distinction between slavery and social caste statuses is that slavery's social death allows slaves to coexist in the personal space of the master class without polluting it, a necessary requirement for those who must be available as body servants and other household help (49–50). At the same time, nonslave pariah castes create pollution anxieties. Because somatic markings in American slavery came to stand for social nonentity, manumitted slaves, whose technical freedom threatened the integrity of definitional social boundaries, were the subject of frequent *antebellum* legislation. "Bills to expel all free blacks were repeatedly introduced all over the South, although not all states enacted them. Seven states required freedmen to leave the state, and thirteen made their immigration illegal" (Patterson, 259). The enactment of postwar Jim Crow legislation, "black codes" restricting the freedom of movement and association for former slaves, and campaigns of violence against emancipated blacks signaled the expansion of these pollution fears when the former slaves were set loose, en masse, in the South. Periodic fears of unstructured contact between racially differentiated bodies found expression in tropes of somatic purity and pollution, fostering the residential restriction of black Americans to contagious ethnic zones called "little Africas." Whites in the South (and those in the North as well) found interracial coexistence tolerable only insofar as blacks were locked into the ultimate allochronisms: the social death of slavery or the literal death of extinction. Jim Crow–era hybridophobia was as symptomatic of anxieties about blacks pushing for inclusion in all the rights and privileges of native-born citizens as it was of fears of genetic pollution and infectious diseases.

The core narrative that rationalized American racial separation thus emphasized the folly of allowing unstructured, unsupervised contact between the "races" at even the individual level. Separate origins, planned by God or executed by natural forces, argue for governmental policies and social customs that perpetuate division, except when personal interaction benefits the dominant race. Since individual actions have far-reaching consequences, the experiential "wisdom" of the group on matters of interracial contact should overrule personal choice or freedom of association. The strict rules of individual conduct both reinforced and derived from the idea that each individual body was a microcosm of the body politic.

Undifferentiated Difference

The mythic world of race difference appeared to black and white alike as a vast network of visible and invisible boundaries, originating in law and custom, that designated the ephemeral imagined landscape of white America. The 1896 *Plessy v. Ferguson* decision was the federal government's most influential and enduring postslavery sanction of white space quarantine, lasting until two other public-access confrontations, the *Brown* school desegregation decision in 1954 and the Montgomery bus boycott in 1955, signaled the turning of the tide against Jim Crow restrictions. For all the myth it occasioned, *Plessy* as a document reveals the powerful grip of race mythology on the country in the Progressive Era. Albion Tourgée's brief in defense of Homer Plessy's right to ride in the "whites only" car argued that separation based on theories of race difference ensures inequality, a logic that the Supreme Court officially disagreed with but tacitly acknowledged. The Court ruled that Homer Plessy was violating a "law" higher than even the Court itself—a law of nature: "Legislation is powerless to eradicate racial instincts or to abolish distinctions based upon physical differences," observed Justice Henry Billings Brown in the majority opinion. "If one race be inferior to the other socially, the Constitution of the United States cannot put them upon the same plane" (Olsen, 112). While the Court argued that it could not force the races onto the same social plane, it apparently had no problem forcing them onto separate ones.

The question of an instinctive avoidance of racial others was a thorny one that achieved, through *Plessy*, official standing as a basis for governmental policy. But the theory of instinctive antipathy turned upon recognition of supposedly telltale external markings of race difference such as skin color, hair texture, odor, and the like. For Nathaniel S. Shaler, racial hostility toward black Americans stemmed from the appearance of blacks, perceived by whites as a shocking "antithesis of ourselves" (*Neighbor*, 290). "The disgust," said Shaler, "is not due to the fact that the Negro has this or that peculiarity of body, but that he, like the maimed or deformed person, violates our ideal of the human form."[84] Shaler speculated that since such people "often complain that the negroes all look alike," their response is a form of "herd instinct" that prevents their perception of individuality in the other.[85] Though Shaler felt that culture in the form of training citizens to be sympathetic to racial others could eventually overcome "natural" antipathy, the Court clearly felt no obligation existed for government to promote feelings of kinship among its heterogeneous population. The Court sanctioned racial prejudice against blacks as a constitutional right of white citizenship that the government was required to uphold.

In his brief on behalf of Homer Plessy, Tourgée highlighted the constitutional problems in any practice making whiteness the requirement for entry into American public space by raising the issue of Plessy's mixed ancestry. In choosing Plessy, a man with no visible trace of African ancestry, the challengers of the Jim Crow laws in Louisiana hoped to exploit the sheer arbitrariness of laws quarantining those presumed to offend whites' "ideal of the human form" by possession of black "blood." The case against instinctive antipathy was tacitly made by Plessy's petitioners' raising the arbitrariness of racial distinctions, as well as the state's authorization of a railroad conductor to make such discriminations spontaneously.[86] But the Court, implicitly agreeing that race designation conferred certain social privileges, used Plessy's admission of African ancestry to deny his claim to white race entitlements, since his lack of external markings peculiar to the inferior caste did not justify his assumption of rights not "proper" to his "race" (Olsen, 110–11). In practical terms, race classification as a basis of political entitlement meant that public knowledge of African ancestry (knowledge that Plessy himself had provided) automatically invalidated access to designated white public spaces and all other "racial properties."[87] Only Justice Harlan in dissent noted that arbitrary restriction of the freedom to associate on rail cars meant that the government could carve up all public and private spaces into racially exclusive zones.[88]

The decision, in effect, gave legal standing to the idea that American public space should be differentially accessible based on skin color, even though skin color was not Plessy's problem. As Tourgée made clear in his brief, the laws separating railroad passengers by race legitimized social caste differences forced on a minority by a majority: "A law assorting the citizens of a State in the enjoyment of a public franchise on the basis of race, is obnoxious to the spirit of republican institutions, because it is a legalization of *caste*, . . . *reducing* [black people] *to the condition of a subject race*" (Olsen, 87, 89). As the superior caste, whites were given their preference of space to occupy, and because it was not their freedom of "locomotion" that was in question, they were not the objects of spatial restriction by such statutes as blacks were. They were simply being guaranteed that a "white" environment would always be available to them, should their "instinct" for racial exclusivity require one.

The tag line that haunts American democracy in the wake of *Plessy*—"separate but equal"—thus has a corollary that typically goes undiscussed: what racially segregated facilities must be equal to is not each other, for that would support indirectly a claim to the planar equivalence that *Plessy* dismisses out of hand; rather, the equivalence should be with their respective ontological positions in the hierarchy of races.[89] As Joel Williamson explains, black riders challenged the railroads' assertion that Jim Crow coaches were not inherently inferior given the fact that many of the same coaches were also used for whites on other rail lines. These riders understood the message that Jim Crow was psychologically designed to deliver and therefore knew that an inferior physical space for black patrons was required: "[Whites] wanted black people to have clearly inferior accommodations and to know that they were inferior" because "arbitrary relegation to always inferior facilities was a sign of where the power actually lay, and where it was likely to lie in the future" (Williamson, *Crucible*, 254). The Jim Crow coach, which Robert Stepto has described as a "nefarious design" for inflicting the "stasis of social structure upon blacks in motion,"[90] was the very emblem of black powerlessness—a facsimile of black social space.

Underlying the logic of Jim Crow was a key supposition of racial classification, the notion of blackness as an undifferentiated difference. Appeals to this belief that the ratio of African somatic difference from the Anglo-Saxon norm was inversely proportional to the somatic difference *among* Africans allowed for such popular adages as "all blacks look alike" and thus "all could be treated essentially alike" (Williamson, *Crucible*, 464). Jim Crow necessarily mimics a presumed evolutionary distinction between the races, then, in refusing to allow blacks to disperse themselves into "classes" of patrons as whites did. As such, Jim Crow served as much to create and enforce the illusory nonindividuation of black Americans as it did to ensure the social privilege of whites.

White race nationalists could articulate a desire that every white person be "higher"—socially, economically, intellectually, and every other way—than every black person only because the aggregate life and death power of economics, political authority, and legal and extralegal violence over black citizens allowed them to do so. Racists like Robert Shufeldt would unhesitatingly ascribe any individual accomplishment by black Americans that contradicted an absolute racial hierarchy to infusions of white blood into the black elite.[91] Others, like William B. Smith, could admit to individual exceptions to the "rule" of white superiority, but only in order to argue that such exceptions were a social danger for violations of a principle necessary for the preservation of American civilization: "If the best Negro in the land is the social equal of the best Caucasian, then it will be hard to prove that the lowest White is higher than the lowest Black; the principle of division is lost, and complete social equality is established" (17).

The concept of undifferentiated difference underlies one of the strongest and yet most untenable of nineteenth-century race myths—the idea that race is always a better predictor of ability than individual achievement. Therefore, despite his acceptance of the existence of variations among blacks, as outlined by Shaler in "The Future of the Negro in the South," William B. Smith asserted the justness and the necessity of the policy that the "lowest" variety of African was "typical" of the race (52–53) and therefore this type should determine the way all blacks would be treated.[92] It would take decades before Franz Boas's assaults on the "pure type" mythology through data revealing overlapping frequency-distribution curves in somatic measurements would begin to gain acceptance among social scientists,[93] but Smith's insistence on a "racial" rather than an individual standard of social status amounts to an admission that nonindividuation had to be forced on black Americans by whites through law, custom, and violent intimidation because it did not exist in "nature."

Despite signal achievements throughout the history of the nation, black Americans have been enormously easy to stereotype as being essentially alike. As a mass personality in the national imaginary, blacks simultaneously embodied

American fears of the internalized "outsider" and of the specter of "mobocracy" that shadowed democratic governance—the perpetual self-doubts about government "by the people." In a nation officially committed to heterogeneity and unity (*e pluribus unum*), blackness has served as a cultural sign of democracy's potential for subverting the "national character" through an uncritical absorption of unassimilable others into the body politic. The "welfare mother" who haunts contemporary debates about race and national character is merely the latest in the series of America's shadow personalities, the eternal return of unassimilable blackness.

The myth of black nonindividuation always signifies the eternal return of race as the single determining factor in human destiny. It therefore serves as one of the strategic tropes of race mythology arguing for racial hierarchy, explaining the social quarantine of black citizens via the "one-drop rule" and recurrent fears that contagious blackness would doom America to the scrap heap of history. It influenced American literature, graphic art, cinema, and performance art immeasurably through essentialized portrayals of Africanness as an unassimilable biological and cultural difference—at best, comically misplaced within American modernity; at worst, a corrosive threat to the moral, intellectual, and hygienic progress of the nation. And it influenced black American literature profoundly, surfacing in Du Bois's figure "the Veil of color," in Richard Wright's "etiquette of living Jim Crow," and in Ellison's trope of invisibility as one of the most distinctive and defining violations of American national idealism.

Although deconstructing the mythic world of race difference was not difficult for writers of the late nineteenth century, their general lack of a sophisticated language of race often ended in the perpetuation of many of the very mythic forms they set out to refute. Black writers were themselves products of American education; thus, even in their attempts to contest the discourse of white nationalism, they often unconsciously circulated much mythic language about race as well. This study describes those moments of resistance and complicity by black writers in the body politics of American racial mapping. I offer no global theory of the production of black literature. Instead, I am interested in seeing how what has been largely dismissed as a "literature of protest" without great artistic merit functions within the literary tradition as a site of black national imagining.

CHAPTER TWO

Meanwhile, in Black America

It was as much within as against the mythic discourse of race difference and national belonging that authors such as Pauline Hopkins and Charles W. Chesnutt began their writing careers. Hopkins's preface to her 1900 novel *Contending Forces* leaves no doubt that her objective is inclusion in the national dialogue on race as a speaking subject: "Fiction is of great value to any people as a preserver of manners and customs—religious, political and social. It is a record of growth and development from generation to generation. *No one will do this for us; we must ourselves develop the men and women who will faithfully portray the inmost thoughts and feelings of the Negro with all the fire and romance which lie dormant in our history*, and, as yet, unrecognized by writers of the Anglo-Saxon race" (13–14). Hopkins's interest in "manners and customs" as a generational "record of growth and development" portrays her writing as an irruption into the time-space of national imagining through narratives of black American simultaneity. Black America's "manners and customs" stand in implicit correspondence to white America's, demonstrating both continuity with a heroic past and "development" toward a future steeped in national values and progressive idealism. Novels by authors of African descent were a way of saying, in effect, "Meanwhile, in black America."

Hopkins's literature of black national affiliation is partial to stories in which tangled racial genealogies and hidden or unknown kinships frame social relations in a modern America. Hazel Carby suggests that Hopkins manipulates popular narrative conventions like "passing," disguises, and double identities to produce an "alternative history of close blood ties through miscegenation":[1] "Popular fiction formulas allowed a white character to darken his skin and move into and out of black communities. . . . But American popular culture offered no equivalent convention that would allow black characters access to a fictional or theatrical white society. At the height of the era of Jim Crow, narratives of 'passing' appeared to offer the only fictional mechanism that could enable representation of the relation between the races" (xxxviii–xxxix). Carby notes that "in *Contending Forces*, Hopkins's black characters are revealed to be related to the British aristocracy. In *Hagar's Daughter*, the threads of black inheritance and heritage extend to the Washington elite" (xliii). Hopkins was not interested in plots that resolved personal conflicts through "passing," since at the end of her works the characters acknowledge all aspects of their ancestry. Rather, Hopkins wanted her characters to have access to a fictional white world in which, by their indisputable social success, they would undermine charges of the atavistic properties of black genes.

Hopkins, though, was not entirely satisfied with the constructive potential of conventional miscegenation plots. Her 1902 novel *Of One Blood*, published serially, like *Hagar's Daughter*, in the *Colored American Magazine*, imagines a glorious African past to which her characters are also linked by "blood." The character Reuel Briggs is a black American who returns to Africa to search for a lost African civilization and finds, in the process, "his previously unknown family heritage . . . [and] the heritage of black people throughout the diaspora." According to Carby, "the narrative asserts that contemporary black Americans are Ethiopians, and the fiction was externally authenticated by a series of documentary articles written by A. Kirkland Soga and entitled 'Ethiopians of the Twentieth Century,' which ran concurrently with the novel" (xiv). The complementarity of the fictional and documentary modes facilitated the imagining of black modernity, allowing black American readers to envision their contemporaneity to both mainland Africans and white Americans.

Hopkins drew the title of *Of One Blood* from Acts 17:26, where the apostle Paul, faced with a skeptical group of Jews, Epicureans, and Stoics in Athens, proclaims that God "hath made of one blood all nations" to assert the unifying power of Christianity. As such, the novel preemptively engages strategies of disaffiliation by race nationalists like Thomas Dixon Jr., who perhaps in direct response to Hopkins's novel, but certainly in reaction to a very established tradition of citing this biblical sanction of universal human kinship,[2] stages the following exchange in *The Clansman* (1905):

"We can never attain the ideal Union our fathers dreamed, with millions of an alien, inferior race among us, whose assimilation is neither possible nor desirable. The

Nation cannot now exist half white and half black, any more than it could exist half slave and half free."

"Yet 'God hath made of one blood all races,'" quoted the cynic with a sneer.

"Yes—but finish the sentence—'and fixed the bounds of habitation.' God never meant the Negro should leave his habitat or the white man invade his home. Our violation of this law is written in two centuries of shame and blood. And the tragedy will not be closed until the black man is restored to his home."

The first (and last) to speak is Abraham Lincoln, the martyr-hero of *The Clansman*, whose intention to expel the emancipated slaves as a means of effecting national reconciliation was left unfulfilled by his untimely murder. The second speaker is Radical Republican senator Austin Stoneman, maliciously modeled after Massachusetts's Thaddeus Stevens, who wants to use ignorant, pliable former slaves to punish southerners for secession. Stoneman's substitution of "races" for "nations" in the biblical misquotation of Paul drives home a point that is put into play by Lincoln's (read Dixon's) reference to America as "The Nation." To use the wording of the King James Bible would make America but one of many "nations" united by blood. But Dixon's consciousness of defending a theory of nationness that restores the divine separation of races points America's evolution toward the Founding Fathers' dream of ideal "Union" as progress toward expulsion of difference. Behind this lies Dixon's conviction that all races are not equally capable of forming "nations," so that even in the process of iterating a fiendish scheme for a racial dictatorship of blacks over whites in the South, Stoneman still shrinks from conferring national status upon the former slaves.[3]

Hopkins's insistence on a unifying "one blood" of national belonging over an alienating "one drop" reveals her indebtedness to the color line stories of Charles Waddell Chesnutt, who himself was related, through his white grandfather, to the North Carolina propertied elite. In 1880, as a twenty-two-year-old with a family to support and a social conscience to accommodate, Chesnutt set down certain terms for his writing career:

> The subtle, almost indefinable feeling of repulsion toward the negro, which is common to most Americans . . . cannot be stormed and taken by assault; the garrison will not capitulate: so their position must be mined, and we will find ourselves in their midst before they think it. . . . The Negro's part is to prepare himself for recognition and equality, and it is the province of literature to open the way for him to get it—*to accustom the public mind to the idea; to lead people out, imperceptibly, unconsciously, step by step, to the desired state of feeling.* If I can do anything to further this work, and can see any likelihood of success in it, I would gladly devote my life to the work.[4]

Chesnutt's aim was to write fiction that took black enterprise and accomplishment for granted. In his intimations of the need for a black national literature, Chesnutt looked at fiction as a means of systematically defamiliarizing notions of black incapacity for national kinship, for it was his belief, as he wrote in an unsent letter addressed to the Congregationalist newspaper the *Christian Union*, that "the American People [would] recognize worth[,] ability or talent, wherever it show[ed] itself, . . . and the *Colored Man* in America [would] be considered, not as a separate race, not as a stranger and a pariah, but as a friend and brother; that he [might] become a strong pillar in the Temple of American Liberty, and be 'bone of one bone, flesh of one flesh' with the New American Nation!" (Brodhead, 108). If Chesnutt became less certain by the century's turn that Americans were willing to acknowledge black Americans' kinship, his later pessimism was clearly in response to the growing popularity in the eighties and nineties of Jim Crow, disfranchisement, and lynch law.

In 1890 Chesnutt wrote to George Washington Cable that literary racism in the United States distinguished America from other Western nations: "I have read a number of English and French novels recently, in which Negroes, and 'Coloured people' play either principal or subordinate parts. They figure as lawyers, as doctors, as musicians, as authors, as judges, as people of wealth and station. They love and they marry without reference to their race, or with only such reference to it as to *other personal disabilities*. They seem to find nothing extraordinary in a talented well-bred colored man, nothing amorphous in a pretty gentle-spirited colored girl. But our American writers are different."[5] Though Chesnutt had not rid himself of his own association of race difference with disability, he went on to note that an English writer would treat race difference as one more *fact* of character development, not *the* fact of characterization. "He would not be obliged to kill off his characters or immerse them in convents as [Albion] Tourgée does his latest heroine, to save them from a fate worse than death, i.e., the confession of inferiority by reason of color" (xv). Death or the convent, or some other form of social invisibility, but by no means an uncomplicated routine existence in national life were the choices available in literature by even the most sympathetic white writers such as Tourgée.[6] Chesnutt notes that "Judge Tourgée's cultivated Negroes are always bewailing their fate and cursing the drop of black blood which 'taints'—I hate the word, it implies corruption— their otherwise pure race." As Pauline Hopkins suggested, this inability among white writers to imagine an unconflicted multiracial national community made it imperative that blacks themselves become participants in the literary construction of America. To do so, they decided to work from within the "tragic mulatto" literary theme to establish the fact that hybridity was a normative condition arising out of a long tradition of consensual relations across the color line, including marriage.

The Marrying of Black Folk

As Joel Williamson has shown, the marriage theme had already reached formulaic status in race nationalist literature. By 1905, it was somewhat cliché for Thomas Dixon to close *The Clansman* with a southern brother/sister pair marrying a northern brother/sister pair, symbolizing white national reunification. According to Williamson, "[Thomas] Page, probably the most often read and best-selling Southern author in the last quarter of the nineteenth century, candidly confessed that his literary formula was to take one Southern belle and add a handsome Yankee, let love blossom, introduce an obstacle between them, and overcome the difficulty to effect in the end the promise of everlasting bliss" (*Crucible*, 336). For Page and for Dixon, the "obstacle" was typically the unsettled "Negro problem" in some immediate form. The fact that the white press regularly proclaimed the dangerous consequences of black demands for social and political equality provided this New South literary revival with the perfect expression of the nonrelation between the races as the "problem" to be overcome: the "bad marriage." The "bad marriage" in racial terms was, of course, intermarriage—"miscegenation." Terms such as *deception, rape,* and *coercion* often applied to such unions were superfluous, since laws against intermarriage denied whites the right to consent.

The belief that whites could never knowingly or willingly love or marry a person with African ancestry grew out of the myth of instinctive racial repugnance that blinded Jefferson, and attends, in part, to the allegorical function of the marriage theme in national literature.[7] The dream of America as a nation built by immigrants has always sustained the possibility of aspiring individuals trading outsider status for insider status through personal initiative. Whereas for ethnic immigrants the sacrament of national belonging found ritual expression in the multiethnic marriage, the rationale most often given for resisting black political and economic equality was that of keeping black bodies out of "American" families. As one wit observed, the real threat to America was not "black warriors, but colored brothers-in-law" (Newby, 131).

In his discussion of American culture and literature, Werner Sollors uses the terms *descent* and *consent* to identify two opposing patterns of national identifi-

cation: "the conflict between contractual and hereditary, self-made and ancestral, definitions of American identity—between *consent* and *descent*—[is] the
central drama in American culture. . . . Descent relations are those defined by
anthropologists as relations of 'substance' (by blood or nature); consent relations
describe those of 'law' or 'marriage.' Descent language emphasizes our position
as heirs, our hereditary qualities, liabilities, and entitlements; consent language
stresses our abilities as mature free agents and 'architects of our fates' to choose
our spouses, our destinies, our political systems" (5–6). Sollors explains that
"since the eighteenth century American culture has in an exceptionally intense
way emphasized [a] naturalized construct of romantic love as the basis for marriage" (166). This tradition refuses to see "blood" claims as more powerful than
the "natural" power of love to overcome mere social conventions like ethnic and
political boundaries. As such, the love/marriage theme serves as a valuable expression of the "volitional political allegiance" (167) that buttresses a modern
democracy.

If, as Sollors claims, the tension between consent and descent relations explains American culture generally, it has overwhelmingly been the descent variables that have represented the most persistent obstacles to blacks being welcomed as full partners in American "ethnogenesis."[8] Racist imaginings insisted
that African *descent* made black Americans incapable of informed *consent* in the
rights and responsibilities of the modern nation-state. Love can therefore overcome differences of descent in literature by ethnic European outsiders, reflecting the first blush of egalitarianism among those plunging headlong into the
"melting pot." But as the objective correlative of patriotism in white nationalist
romance, love cannot be engendered by a white American for someone unqualified for full citizenship.

Doris Sommer shows in *Foundational Fictions* that novels of heterosexual love
in Latin America promoted nationalism in a special way: "eroticism and nationalism became figures for each other in modernizing fictions," producing "mutual allegories, as if each discourse were grounded in the allegedly stable other"
(31). Similarly, a staple white nationalist allegorization of Reconstruction in the
United States as a coup d'état forced on a war-torn white citizenry sensational-
ized the equation of perverted Eros with corrupt Polis by placing the threat of
black rapists at the center of the plot, and by extension, of national division.

Black writers charged with establishing that which was *novel* in the post-
Reconstruction world felt compelled to raise the question of assimilation
through marriage that ethnic immigrants handled with less self-consciousness.

The assimilationist drama in African American fiction is structural in the sense that social norms militating against interracial sexual relations by black males represented a prohibition so insistent in American life as to become almost a dare, while the sexual exploitation of black women by white males remained a fact of interracial relations well after the end of the slavery period. If marriage choices in ethnic dramas may be simplistically rendered as choices between endogamic traditionalism ("blood," "Mother country," "descent") and exogamic assimilation ("America the bride," "consent"), then decisions about whom to marry in black American fiction also represent choices for and against the preservation of the black body and "soul," the physical and cultural reminders of the African descent into, through, and from American slavery.

Racist imaginings of a specific difference between the races implied that intermarriage would forever be haunted by the specter of extinction in the form of infertility, unviable offspring, and the potential for monstrous birth.[9] Thus intermarriage fell into the same category as incest as an occasion for state intervention in a potentially catastrophic alliance, explaining in part the hysteria of white nationalists over preserving laws against "miscegenation." As I will show, the successful evasion of divine, governmental, and scientific sanctions against race mixing still left a couple vulnerable to the fantasy of racial regression and extinction, which in black literature of the Progressive Era adopted a distinctive and influential form.

The Body of Death

The key political struggle of Progressive Era black America concerned how to respond to attempts across the nation to reinstitute the social death of slavery through Jim Crow legislation, disfranchisement, and lynching. No more graphic depiction of black allochronism emerged from the Progressive Era than the fantastic image of black America as an already dead appendage to the white body politic. The irony is that Booker T. Washington, in an effort to gain support for his program of racial uplift through industrial education, would be the crucial figure in popularizing this typological discourse. One of the interesting aspects of Washington's "Atlanta Exposition Address" (1895), unflatteringly dubbed the "Atlanta Compromise" by W. E. B. Du Bois, is his rhetoric of the body politic signaling to the nation his willingness to compromise on the issue of full citizenship: "In all things that are purely social we can be as separate as the fingers, yet one as the hand in all things essential to mutual progress."[10]

Two paragraphs further into Washington's speech, another, more striking corporeal metaphor occurs: "Nearly sixteen millions of *hands* will aid you in pulling the load upwards, or they will pull against you the load downwards. We shall constitute one-third and more of the ignorance and crime of the South, or one-third of its intelligence and progress; we shall contribute one-third to the business and industrial prosperity of the South, or we shall prove *a veritable body of death*, stagnating, depressing, retarding every effort to advance the *body politic*." The potential for a strong adverse reaction to this "body of death" rhetoric explains Washington's abrupt tonal shift into his "scandalous" blackface minstrel routine—the infamous "chicken-thief" joke—at this precise moment in the speech, to allay any apprehensions about the conciliatory nature of his address.[11] By reassuring whites of their superiority to the ragtag host of chicken-thieving blacks, Washington rendered absurd the idea that the nation had any cause to fear black competition for social space or economic preeminence.[12]

It is possible that Washington's source for the "body of death" rhetoric was scriptural, an adaptation of Paul's epistle to the Romans stressing the dangers of fleshly indulgence: "O wretched man that I am! who shall deliver me from the body of this death?" (Rom. 7:24). Paul's text is replete with images of sinful "members" at war with the mind, enslaving the mind to the "law of sin." But Washington is specific in his reference to *two* bodies—the black "body of death" and the white body politic. Whether by way of some intermediate source or his own ingenuity, Washington provided the South with an enduring image of racially distinct bodies politic in language that would take on a specific social meaning after Frederick Hoffman's prediction, one year later, that "racial traits and tendencies" doomed blacks to extinction.[13]

Part of the intrigue of the "body of death" figure is the way it haunted Washington's career. Thomas Dixon Jr. certainly had Washington in mind in his appropriation of the figure. In his novel *The Leopard's Spots* (1902), Dixon asks, "*Can you build, in a Democracy, a nation inside a nation of two hostile races?*" (242). Dixon's surrogate (all of his novels used surrogates, who gave identical speeches on the need for race purity) later answers this rhetorical question with another: "What is our condition to-day in the dawn of the twentieth century? If we attempt to move forward we are literally chained to the body of a festering Black Death! . . . We lag behind the age dragging the decaying corpse to which we are chained. 'Who shall deliver us from the body of this death?'" (436). More damaging was the appropriation of the "body of death" rhetoric by Washington's white benefactors. After former president Grover Cleveland opened a Tuskegee fund-raiser at Madison Square Garden in 1903 by lamenting the "grievous amount of ignorance, a sad amount of laziness and thriftlessness" afflicting southern blacks, white southern moderate Edgar Gardner Murphy urged support for Washington on the grounds of enlightened self-interest. If black America was doomed to extinction, then Murphy warned that the "rotting body of its dissolution is polluting the atmosphere we breathe."[14]

In an obvious attempt to recast and reclaim the metaphor, Washington had already begun after his Atlanta speech to use the phrase "body of death" in expanded contexts. In one speech in Topeka, Kansas, he used it to indict the South's one-crop agricultural policy.[15] And at the unveiling ceremony for the monument dedicated to Robert Gould Shaw, Washington equated the "body of death" with slavery, not with black America.[16] But even this attempt at salvaging the phrase was unsuccessful. In 1907, "Pitchfork" Ben Tillman of South Carolina would make this "body of death" image the emotional climax of one of his U.S. Senate speeches on behalf of white supremacy: "'O who will deliver me from the body of this death?' What does it mean? It was the law of the Jews that for certain forms of homicide, certain black and bloody murders, the murderer should be stripped naked and his victim stripped naked and the dead man's body chained to the body of the living man, back to back, limb to limb, and the two left alone. The flies and the vermin which are produced and attracted by putrefication brought about the inevitable result. The decaying carcass fastened to the living in the end produced death in the most horrible form." Tillman, to whom Washington had written a groveling "open letter" in 1895 in which he portrayed himself and 650,000 black South Carolinians as "suppliants at [Tillman's] feet," indicates here an alternative but probably apocryphal source for Washington's phrase.[17] Describing the postwar South, "prostrate, bleeding and helpless," as having had the "dead carcass of slavery chained to it by the fourteenth and fifteenth amendments," Tillman makes the South the victim of both the crime and the punishment: "There the carcass hangs, riveted to our civilization. The putrefication is going on."[18]

A final irony of this typological discourse surfaced in the publicity surrounding Booker T. Washington's death. In the absence of his personal physician, Washington was treated in his final illness by a Dr. Walter A. Bastedo of St. Luke's Hospital in New York, who made a startling announcement to the press in November 1915: "I made an examination of Dr. Washington a few days ago and found him completely worn out. . . . We have thoroughly overhauled him and find that he is ageing rapidly. . . . Racial characteristics are, I think, in part responsible for Dr. Washington's breakdown" (Harlan, *Booker T. Washington*, 2:451–52). In the discourse of race difference, "racial characteristics" had a specific meaning that Dr. Bastedo may not have quite understood. George C. Hall, Washington's regular physician, was quick to notify Julius Rosenwald, an important Washington supporter, that this statement was an incredible blunder, since "racial characteristics" was a code for "a 'syphilitic history' when referring to Colored people."[19] Syphilis, of course, was one of the "racial traits and tendencies" that Frederick Hoffman had cited as a cause for the eventual extinction of blacks.[20] Whether Bastedo was only being indiscreet in violating doctor-patient confidentiality or in fact indicating that he considered Washington's nervous collapse to be symptomatic of black incapacity to handle the demands of political leadership in modern America, as Louis Harlan surmises,[21] he made it impossible for Washington to end his controversial career uncontroversially. Washington in the end had become the black body of death he had himself prophesied.

As Sander Gilman observes, "the blackness of the African, like the blackness of the Jew, was credited to the effect of certain diseases, specifically syphilis, on the skin of the African" (*Body*, 99–100). Gilman goes on to show how Hitler's campaign against the Jews manipulated an analogical series connecting dark skin, the "Black Death" of the Middle Ages, and, inevitably, intermarriage as synonymous threats to the German body politic (100–101). Clearly the same series operates in the "body of death" typology, even to the extent of Tillman's ascription of the antitype to the ancient Jews.

Nor should it go unnoticed that Tillman strategically gendered the "body politic." Evoking the iconography of the feminized "Prostrate South," the image made famous by James S. Pike's 1871 book *The Prostrate State*, an account of South Carolina's Reconstruction sufferings "under Negro government," and magnified into an image of the Reconstruction South as a whole in Henry W. Grady's famous "New South" address in 1886,[22] Tillman luridly suggested that the white body politic chained to the black "body of death" had become the unconsenting victim of diseased black sexuality. Tillman played on representations of Reconstruction such as Pike's that characterized any black participation in government, through a perverse Tocquevillean logic, as "Negro dominance."[23] Black presumption of mastery equated with masculine sexual dominance, by analogy to the sexual mastery of white males during slavery. Thus the inevitable outcome of any claim to social equality immediately evoked images of brute black masculinity run amuck. The hysteria over violent seizure of the body politic by black hands during Reconstruction quickly evolved into the black brute rapist motif, becoming the characteristic expression of white fears of black political and social aspirations. By linking the "body of death" figure to the lore of Reconstruction and the more immediate rhetoric of the "one crime" of inter-racial rape, Tillman depicted racial coexistence in America as a perverse, cor-rupting miscegenation.

In his retelling of the "Wilmington Massacre" of 1898, during which rioting whites expelled an elected, biracial city government,[24] Charles W. Chesnutt credited characterizations of black civic participation as a form of "Negro domi-nation"—a black "body of death" metaphorically raping the helpless South—with instigating the violence. Chesnutt made white resistance to black normativ-ity the centerpiece of his 1901 novel *The Marrow of Tradition*. Early in the novel, the Bourbon white supremacist General Belmont, a lawyer by profession, pro-vides an image of racial heterogeneity as the ultimate subversion of the social or-der: "Things are in an awful condition! A negro justice of the peace has opened an office on Market Street, and only yesterday summoned a white man to appear before him. Negro lawyers get most of the business in the criminal court. Last evening a group of young white ladies, going quietly along the street arm-in-arm, were forced off the sidewalk by a crowd of negro girls. Coming down the street just now I saw a spectacle of social equality and negro domination that made my blood boil with indignation,—a white and a black convict, chained together, crossing the city in charge of a negro officer! We cannot stand that sort of thing" (238–39). The image of the two felons chained together as the "spectacle" of "so-cial equality" itself is an arresting echo of the way that the "body of death" rhetoric criminalized all levels of racial interaction.

Equally intriguing is the way that black entrepreneurial success and assump-tions of equality before the law become conceptually linked to antagonistic and criminal behavior. Black "criminality" was used to justify, both in the novel and in the historical Wilmington, the actions of the heavily armed white insurrec-tionists, whose real objective was the suppression of legitimate black economic enterprise and nominal black governmental participation in a majority black city.[25] The explanation that would later prove satisfactory to northern onlookers of the Wilmington Massacre, both as individual citizens and collectively through the federal government's refusal to intervene, similarly derived from the local white newspapers' description of the coup d'état as an understandable re-sponse to provocative and criminal behavior by blacks (Prather, 54, 174). The de-scription of Wilmington given by Alfred M. Waddell, coup leader and later the elected mayor of Wilmington, portrayed the premassacre city as a "Negro Paradise" where blacks openly committed crimes upon law-abiding whites.[26] At the same time, Waddell, who might have served as a model for Belmont in Chesnutt's novel, asserted that political equality would lead to black extinction (Southern Society, 46). Thus black criminality, one of Frederick Hoffman's "racial traits and tendencies" supposedly ushering blacks toward extinction, could be inferred from any black refusal to confer a privileged status upon whites.

Acts of black assertiveness and upward mobility were considered crimes against the white race—attacks aimed at undermining its superior fitness for civilization—and would typically spark a demonstration of white supremacy that would be explained away as an instinct for racial preservation. When wealthy northern whites journey to Wellington (Chesnutt's fictional Wilmington), for example, the Bourbon social elite reassure them that violent repression of blacks is unavoidable: "It was sad, they said, to witness this spectacle of a dying race, unable to withstand the competition with the superior type" (303). The "severe reprisals taken by white people for certain crimes committed by negroes" were a justifiable form of self-preservation, by this logic, against the wild death throes of a dying race.

If, as Benedict Anderson asserts, the newspaper is "merely an 'extreme form' of the book" that improves on the novel's promotion of homogeneous, empty time by fostering an "extraordinary mass ceremony: the almost precisely simultaneous consumption ('imagining') of the newspaper-as-fiction" (35), then Chesnutt was correct in making the fictional Wellington's newspaper publisher, Major Carteret, another of the novel's villains. Carteret uses his *Morning Chronicle* to promote white nationalism, after the victory of a Fusionist ticket in the local election aligns whites and blacks of the proletarian class against the local Bourbons. Carteret is chiefly responsible for fomenting the riot through the steady drumbeat of antiblack rhetoric in the *Chronicle*, forging white solidarity based on suppression of black political rights. At one point, a powerful Bourbon backer of the paper, General Belmont, explains to Carteret, "You, Carteret, represent the Associated Press. Through your hands passes all of the news of the state. What more powerful medium for the propagation of an idea? The man who would govern a nation by writing its songs was a blethering idiot beside the fellow who can edit its news dispatches" (278).[27] Though Chesnutt focuses on the power of the press to provoke the disaffiliation of large segments of the public, his fictional version of the events leading to the riot actually downplays the newspapers' prominent role in instigating the Wilmington Massacre.[28] Because the city of Wilmington was a majority black city by 56 to 44 percent (Prather, 31), the white press decided that it had to deny the humanity of most of the city's occupants in its drive to rid the city of the handful of black elected officials and public servants whose visibility disturbed the dream of a "white man's country."

Chesnutt's attention to the importance of narratives of racial alienation creates specific parallels between the instigation and the cover-up of the massacre in the public sphere and the troubled kinship between the Carteret and the Miller families. Striking in Chesnutt's portrayal of Janet and Dr. Miller is the unexceptionalness of their lifestyle. They, not the whites who riot and clamor for blood, lead the "normal" lives with which Americans would be expected to identify. Despite social ostracism and the active ill will of her white half sister, Olivia Carteret, Janet Miller and her husband do not bewail their fate. The Millers are content to make their own way in the world so long as they are not unduly penalized by their racial classification, and ultimately, their white relations have more to gain from acknowledging kinship than they. But their disturbing presence in Wellington represents the personal dimension of the public sector crusade against black national belonging.

The story of the buffoon Jerry, a black factotum of the white conspirators at the *Morning Chronicle*, serves as a pointed burlesque of the Millers' ill-fated quest for social normality. When Jerry, attracted by ads in a local black daily newspaper, uses a hair straightener and a skin lightener to erase traces of his African ancestry, Carteret again reads the incident as a sign of the environmental unfitness of blacks, seeing the attempts by blacks to blend into America artificially as a foreshadowing of the eventual extinction of the whole race: "These grotesque advertisements had their tragic side. They were proof that the negroes had read the handwriting on the wall. These pitiful attempts to change their physical characteristics were an acknowledgment, on their own part, that the negro was doomed, and that the white man was to inherit the earth and hold all other races under his heel. For as the months had passed, Carteret's thoughts, centering more and more upon the negro, had led him farther and farther, until now he was firmly convinced that there was no permanent place for the negro in the United States, if indeed anywhere in the world, except under the ground" (402). Since the specific occasion that Jerry interrupts with his grotesque appearance is one of the final gatherings of the conspirators before the coup, Chesnutt shows in some detail here how Carteret moves step by step from belief in the inevitable extinction of blacks to participation in a specific plan for eliminating blacks from the time-space of white civilization.

It is the collective assessment of the coup plotters in the office of the *Morning Chronicle* that blacks must be eliminated as a social and political consideration: "It remained for Carteret and his friends to discover, with inspiration from whatever supernatural source the discriminating reader may elect, that the darker race, docile by instinct, humble by training, patiently waiting upon its as yet uncertain destiny, was *an incubus, a corpse chained to the body politic,* and that the negro vote was a source of danger to the state" (276; my emphasis). The undeniable echoes of Washington's "Atlanta Compromise" and Pike's *The Prostrate State* subtly critique the collusion of Washington in the "body of death" mythology, making clear that Washington's stress on black docility, suitability for industrial training, and abdication of political rights was tacitly complicit in the white-on-black violence of Wilmington and elsewhere in the South.

Hybridophobia

Ultimately, the "body of death" was only a small part of an increasingly paranoid discourse of race, combining the wish for black race extinction with the fear of white race extinction—the zero-sum game that drove (and perhaps still drives) American body politics. Even after disfranchisement, Jim Crow, and lynch law had reduced southern blacks to a condition analogous to the social death of slavery, whites were increasingly fearful. Anxieties about black assertiveness and northern criticism over lynching and violations of black voting rights merged with fears of surreptitious black intrusion into the body politic via "passing." These fears found expression in the southern obsession with "blood pollution," as traditions of defining whiteness by percentages of white ancestry gave way in this era to the "one-drop rule" of race classification. As Joel Williamson explains in *The Crucible of Race,* "Southerners came to fear hidden blackness, the blackness within seeming whiteness. They began to look with great suspicion upon mulattoes who looked white, white people who behaved as black, and a whole congeries of aliens insidious in their midst who would destroy their whole moral universe. The continuous search for invisible blackness, the steady distrust of the alien, and the ready belief in the existence of the enemy hidden within gave rise to a distinctly paranoid style in Southern white culture in the twentieth century" (464–65). What drove their obsession with the unseen "one drop" of black blood was fear of the *revenant,* of a reversion to the original African body by which that one drop of black blood would manifest its presence. Fear of black atavism grew out of claims of postwar blacks reverting to savagery without the uplifting experience of slavery to restrain them, along with the belief that blacks were in-distinguishable from each other, allowing any individual traits to be swallowed up by a mass racial identity trapped in an evolutionary backwash. This fantasy of regression undoubtedly created anxiety for those who actually passed from the official category of black to social acceptance as white, but it seems to have fasci-nated whites even more. Dixon gave his audience an indelible image of the figure Robert W. Shufeldt was to call "the hybrid" as a vision of the embodied na-tion nightmarishly transformed by the African presence: "One drop of Negro blood makes a negro. It kinks the hair, flattens the nose, thickens the lip, puts out the light of intellect, and lights the fires of brutal passions. The beginning of Ne-gro equality as a vital fact is the beginning of the end of this nation's life. There is enough negro blood here to make mulatto the whole Republic" (*Spots*, 242). For Dixon, the equivalence between somatic features and fitness for civilization was so exact that his virulent opposition to any black presence in America amounted to a "one-drop rule" of national identity.

Chesnutt used this fear of the eternal return of the black body to good effect. In *The Marrow of Tradition*, Major Carteret translates Jerry's misery after unsuc-cessfully using "whitening products" as an example of the folly of social integra-tion, since he believed that the black body's inherent unfitness could at best be partially disguised but never escaped. He reflects that "more pathetic even than Jerry's efforts to escape from the universal doom of his race was his ignorance that even if he could, by some strange alchemy, bleach his skin and straighten his hair, there would still remain, underneath it all, only the unbleached darky,— the ass in the lion's skin" (402). Carteret, undoubtedly, has in mind more than Jerry's antics with the whitening products, for his subsequent lecture to Jerry stresses themes that touch on his anxieties over the presence of the Millers in Wellington: "'white people do not like negroes who want to be white. A man should be content to remain as God made him and where God placed him'" (403). Carteret later "washes his hands" of the affair and holds himself blameless when the rioting whites go far beyond his expectations: "'I meant to keep them in their places,—I did not intend wholesale murder and arson'" (449). Naturally, both the Millers, the hybrid couple who so disturb the sense of "place" in Wellington, and the self-despising stooge Jerry become victims of this white ram-page dedicated to the "restoration" of social order.

In the climax of *The Marrow of Tradition*, which takes place after the riot, Olivia Carteret must break with social custom to save the life of her only child. She openly acknowledges that she has known for some time that her relation to

Janet Miller is not, as everyone had suspected, the result of an illicit interracial affair but in fact a "legal" kinship. Janet is the daughter of Samuel Merkell's former household servant, whom he secretly married after the death of Olivia's mother. But the discovery of Janet's "legitimacy" unnerves Olivia, largely because public knowledge of her legal kinship with a person of traceable African descent would cast suspicion upon her own "legitimacy" and, as a mother, on the legitimacy of her son. Olivia and her aunt had both worked secretly, and independently, to suppress or destroy all records of a legal claim by Janet to the Merkell legacy.

But Janet's very coexistence in Wellington, where so many know of her blood relation to Olivia, evokes paranoid fear in Olivia. On one occasion, Olivia is prostrated for several days when her child almost falls from a window. Olivia blames Janet for what her faithful servant, the race traitor Mammy Jane, calls putting the "evil eye" on the child. The "evil eye," however, turns out to have been merely Janet's wistful glance toward her half sister as she passed the Carteret house in a buggy. The look strikes Olivia as impertinent and intrusive—a plea for recognition and belonging that could not be tolerated. The moment is richly suggestive of Nathaniel S. Shaler's description of instinctive "racial antipathy" as recognizing "enough of likeness in the alien . . . to indicate kinship, and at the same time so much that denies the kinship as to arouse . . . race hatred" (*Neighbor*, 291).

Hybridophobia was fertile ground for racial folklore. As Joel Williamson explains, the persistent myth of mulatto infertility "functioned to relieve the Southern white mind of a great irritation. . . . If one could believe . . . that mulattoes were a dying people, in fact *a people already dead by dint of their certain dying*, then everyone was saved, both black and white" from the threat mulattoes presented to the southern image of an ordered society (*New People*, 95; my emphasis). Robert W. Shufeldt's *The Negro: A Menace to American Civilization* (1907) uses as its frontispiece a photograph of a grinning skull propped up by two volumes of antiblack pseudoscientific tracts, with the caption "Skull of Hybrid" below, a signifier of the inevitable extinction of nonwhites and of the dangers of intermarriage, but even more tellingly, of anthropology's massive investment, as far back as the grave-robbing anatomist George Cuvier, in the procurement and display of black corpses.[29]

A Philadelphia physician with an intellectual bloodline that ran through the neo-Lamarckian zoologist Edward Drinker Cope back to the polygenist Louis Aggasiz, Shufeldt tells an incredible tale of "atavism" about a young Virginia couple's experience: "At the end of a year a boy child is born to them, but, horror of horrors, it is found to be as black as coal, and with hair as kinky as the veriest young Congo that a negress of that race ever gave birth to in Africa. . . . Her first child was simply a reversion to the black ancestry on her maternal side, and had inherited the Ethiopian characters, and among them the black skin and kinky hair" (*Negro*, 95–96).[30] Shufeldt goes on to dramatize the consequence of inter-marriage as the demise of America in international stature as a nation descended from "a mixed race, a large part of which were formerly eaters of human flesh."[31]

In the Virginia case cited by Shufeldt, and in fact all cases, the atavism is ulti-mately a product of matrilineal descent from an original African body. Thus fas-cination with the "racial throwback" always unmasks those who attempt to escape descent from the original black mother. If, according to this belief, one drop of black blood could spawn the birth of a nightmare figure that Paul Barringer would call "our prognathic, dolichocephalic cannibal,"[32] then the source of that one drop, the womb of the original black slave mother, could never be escaped. Marital unions involving racial hybrids, thus, were haunted both by the "condi-tion of the mother" that survived in the mythical "one drop" and fear of the atavistic birth that would reveal the African mother's inopportune return. Be-cause mulattoes were so often the vehicles of narratives of affiliation in Progres-sive Era black literature, their accommodation of the imminent return of the black mother's body forms one of the earliest plot conventions of the tradition. Philip A. Bruce was an influential historian of southern race relations who used his family's huge Virginia plantation as a laboratory for observing what he de-scribed as the "evolutionary regression" of the "new issue" blacks of the postwar era (that is, those who had grown up without the "civilizing" influence of slavery) in *The Plantation Negro as a Freeman* (1889). Central to this process of "regres-sion" was the alleged atavism of the black female, who according to Bruce was dramatically regressing in physical character, owing to the lessening of sexual contact with whites since the end of slavery. "Into this class, all the females of the race are slowly merging, which fact, when fully accomplished, will produce an unpleasing appearance and temper that will be universal," according to Bruce (54).

This process of morphological regression into the undifferentiated difference of originary black atavism would eventually transform black womanhood collec-tively into the revenant black body of the white imaginary. Individuals carrying that "one drop" were never out of the allochronistic time of African ahistoricity. The atavistic child was thus the essence of that slave mother herself, subject to innumerable returns to reclaim her descendants for Africa. The "one drop" re-creates the African mother as withered hag, born already dying—the cannibal foremother reclaiming her progeny.

The Mother's Return

If, as Henry Louis Gates Jr. has asserted, "Anglo-African writing arose as a re-sponse to allegations of its absence" ("*Race*," 11), then certainly Progressive Era black writers saw increased literary production as a necessary response to the widespread anticipation of their *erasure*. In keeping with their intervention into the discourse of race, black writers sought to recast the hybrid from the image of diseased body politic to one of the embodied America of the utopian future. In the process, these writers had to come to grips with the "condition of the mother" as a point of origin of the historical imagining of race in America. In confronting the inescapable original slave mother, though, these writers would explore the paranoia of atavistic return as an affliction of the unenlightened, paving the way for a return of race as a liberating rather than enslaving moment of the hybrid experience. In Pauline Hopkins's novel *Hagar's Daughter*, the key scenes of discovery hinge on confrontation with the debased "condition of the mother" of the slavery experience. Hopkins draws on the biblical figure Hagar as archetypal slave mother, the concubine through whom the legitimate nation cannot be fulfilled. Setting much of the story in Washington, D.C., accents the national import of the discovery of hidden blackness in three prominent so-cialites of the capital.

In the novel's first section, which takes place on the eve of the Civil War, the ne'er-do-well St. Clair Enson returns to the home of his older brother, Ellis En-son, accompanied by a slave trader named Walker, who knows that Ellis's young wife has black ancestry. Because he has papers proving his legal ownership of Hagar, who learns through Walker the terrible import of her name, Walker forces Ellis to pay his price in return for Hagar's freedom. Yet it is not until Walker raises the subject of Ellis and Hagar's daughter that Ellis comes to a con-sciousness of the meaning of slavery defined through the mother.

"As for the pickaninny—"
"What!" thundered Ellis, "the child, too?"
"In course," replied Walker, . . . "the child follows the condition of the mother, so I scoop the pile." (55–56)

Ellis's introduction to slavery, despite his ownership of a large plantation with many slaves, arises out of this occasion to consider the meaning of phrases like "condition of the mother" in reference to two people whom he has grown accustomed to thinking of as near kin. Walker can "scoop the pile" because he owns Hagar *and* "her issue forever." Ellis's paternity is irrelevant to questions of legal ownership to mother and child because Walker's titular claim to Hagar's womb supersedes Ellis's rights as her husband.

After a long night of anguish, Ellis decides that he will give up everything for Hagar, including remarrying her and resettling with her in Europe. For her sake, he is willing to "plunge outside of history," to use Ralph Ellison's phrase, but not before Hagar has had an opportunity to contemplate the meaning of the "condition of the mother" as an involuntary return to the body of the original African mother: "Could it be true, or was it but a hideous nightmare from which she would soon awake? Her mother a slave! She wondered that the very thought did not strike her dead. With shrinking horror she contemplated the black abyss into which the day's events had hurled her. . . . Her name gone, her pride of birth shattered at one blow! Was she, indeed, a descendant of naked black savages of the horrible African jungles? . . . Her education, beauty, refinement, what did they profit her now?" (57). When Hagar sees her maid Marthy, her response is to scrutinize the girl's "black skin, crinkled hair, flat nose and protruding lips," as if searching for the face of the foremother who has determined her fate. Hagar's response to the sight of her own face in the mirror is to smash the glass, now that behind the image of the white woman she thought herself to be lurks the visage of the naked savage of the jungle. Hagar, to whom slavery had always seemed so right, takes immediate recourse in manic self-repudiation.

Ironically, Ellis, stalking his library at night, manages himself to conquer the image of the revenant, in large part, I believe, because a visit to the nursery has reassured him that his daughter is not atavistic: "The clock ticked slowly on the mantel, but the beating of his heart outstripped it. He could not follow the plans he had laid out as the path of duty. His visit to the nursery had upset them; parental love, love for his innocent wife, was too strong to be easily cast aside. The ticking of the clock maddened him. It seemed the voice of doom pursuing him—condemning him as a coward—coward—coward" (60). Hopkins places heavy symbolic weight on the clock here, for what Ellis Enson must surrender if he is to keep Hagar is time itself—history, legacy of the past, family name. He decides to follow his heart away from the patriarchal path blazed by Abraham before him, choosing to reaffirm his sense of kinship with his outcast wife and daughter through a second marriage to Hagar.

Ellis's dilemma is akin to what Werner Sollors describes as the ethnic purist's fear of losing offspring through intermarriage. "The products of consent relations across dramatic boundaries were, well into the twentieth century, considered to be exclusively and negatively shaped by one aspect of their descent. In the United States, the country of consent, mulattoes were not to be viewed as architects of their own fates. In the American imagination, mixed bloods were the culmination of the fear of losing generations" (226). Ellis is not concerned about the myth of mulatto sterility. His daughter is living proof that no specific difference between the races exists, negating any analogy to the mule, the animal who gave the mulattoes their generic name. But the fear of generational loss for Ellis is related to his own determination to plunge outside of history. If there were to be more Ensons lording it over Enson Hall, it would not be through him. By choosing to link his reproductive future to Hagar, he forfeits his past. He becomes chained to the black mother haunting Hagar's body.

Later in the novel, after a lapse of twenty years, Hagar's true identity is revealed to the Washington social world she has been a part of under a different identity. Cuthbert Sumner, the wealthy aristocratic husband of Hagar's stepdaughter Jewel, feels sympathy for Hagar, but Sumner is determined to separate Jewel from her stepmother before public suspicion can fix upon his wife's ancestry as well. Cuthbert confronts Ellis Enson, newly unmasked and back from the "dead," over his decision to remarry Hagar twenty years later, to return with her to Enson Hall, and to acknowledge her publicly as his wife. In the conversation between this offspring of the New England abolitionist Sumners and the reformed southern aristocrat, Hopkins locates the source of white paranoia over intermarriage, as Cuthbert protests, "'But my dear Enson, you do not countenance such a—such a—well—terrible action as a wholesale union between whites and blacks? Think of it, my dear man! Think of our refinement and intelligence linked to such black bestiality!'" (270). When Ellis reminds Cuthbert of his prior infatuation with Aurelia Walker, quadroon daughter of the slave trader Walker, Cuthbert reacts predictably, unaware of the discovery in store for him about Jewel: "'I think that the knowledge of her origin would kill all desire in me,' replied Sumner. 'The mere thought of the grinning, toothless black hag that was her foreparent would forever rise between us'" (271). Jewel's discovery that she is Hagar's daughter, not her stepdaughter, links her, by the condition of *her* mother, to the original black hag of Cuthbert's imagination. She must replay the earlier scene in the novel between her parents in which she must come to terms with the shifting grounds of her former social prominence as the daughter of a western state U.S. senator. Cuthbert, for his part, hesitates too long in deciding that he would prefer to lose caste than to lose his wife. Unlike the scene between Ellis and Hagar, though, there is no tangible reassurance for Cuthbert that his offspring will not be lost in atavistic regression. The twenty-four hours that it takes him to stare down the "grinning, toothless black hag" of Jewel's ancestry causes him to miss her departure with Ellis and Hagar for Europe. A year later, after extensively traveling on the Continent himself, Cuthbert returns to find Jewel dead and buried, a victim of "Roman fever." Cuthbert's final insight is that his crime is *national* as much as it is personal: "the sin is the nation's. It must be washed out" (283).

Jewel's death is purposely conventional. Contracting "Roman fever" on a trip to the Continent is a modern, romantic death, quite in contrast to a lingering death from "racial traits and tendencies." If Jewel's death is fashionably circumspect, her life in Washington high society is incomparable. The daughter of a millionaire statesman, the wife of an aristocratic heir to a fortune, Jewel is caught up in the pulse of the national tempo. Hopkins no doubt intends that Cuthbert's obsession with the revenant be an ironic reflection on the transformative power of racism to distort perception of reality. Cuthbert, twice given the opportunity to allow experience to master his prejudices, fails on both occasions to extend an unconventional acceptance of kinship, first with Aurelia, the woman he almost married before he met Jewel, and then with Hagar, his mother-in-law. These two prior denials and his hesitation to accept Jewel at the critical moment link him firmly to the national guilt of disaffiliation.

Yet in order to make such a point, Hopkins must make Cuthbert's fear seem unreasonable. In doing so, she patently adopts the prevailing standard of physical beauty that by definition excludes women of visible African descent from acceptance as equals. Not a "hag," but *Hagar*, herself a conventionally beautiful woman of Anglo-Saxon appearance, stands behind Jewel. On the periphery of the narrative are the Sargeant women—Aunt Henny, Marthy, and Venus. Largely played for comedy, their scenes reveal black postslavery normativity as a gradual uplift through education, confirmed by a perceptible lightening of skin color in successive generations through selective marriage.[33] Aunt Henny and Marthy, though, continue to live an existence defined by slavery standards in a largely matriarchal household with an improvident, absent male father figure, surviving on the women's domestic labor. In Marthy's son Oliver, a brilliant college student, Hopkins demonstrates the hope for a progressive, responsible black patriarchy. But because Venus has had to sacrifice her own education to help to pay for Oliver's, he seems almost like a fourth generation by comparison to the women of the house. The two maternal lines that define black America in the novel move slightly toward convergence in the contemporaries Venus and Jewel, although clearly the older Sargeants are still trapped largely in the heterogeneous time of the primitive. Through dialect spelling, conjure, "superstitions," and other local color markings of the primitive, Hopkins develops an environmentalist discourse of race difference that equates temporal and somatic distance from the slave past with capacity to function in the time of the nation.

Thus, while Hopkins does not connect virtue to skin color, she does equate upward mobility with gradual erasure of the mythical "pure African type." Her body politics reflect what Houston Baker has called the "daughter's departure" from the body, "spirit," and vernacular culture of black motherhood. Baker connects the "mulatto aesthetics" of Hopkins and other women authors of the period to an unconscionable "black northern fondness, awe, approbation, and approval" of "the sign of white, patriarchal hegemony, . . . recuperated by the departed daughters as a 'pleasing' set of features" (*Spirit*, 25). Because these features derive from the systematic rape and concubinage of black women during and after the slavery period, Baker sees this aesthetic preference for Anglo-Saxon somatic features as a "transmutation" of that brutal history into a "black code of beauty, grace, intelligence, and historically embodied presence" (24). Citing an underlying impulse to please white audiences, Baker indicts the whole generation of women writers for their headlong flight from the body of the black mother:

> "Are black women who are not northern, in whiteface, and bearing Greek attributes capable of moral virtue?" Summoning to view black southern mothers—even in their gardens or at the frames of their patchwork quilts—was for the daughters at the turn of the century taboo. For such a summons could only evoke a place of inescapable erring and difficulty whose representation might well bring *contempt* and not the fiercely sought sympathetic white public opinion. Hence, rather than return to a southern place, the daughters chose to dream dreams and project visions of a universal white-faced American *no-place*—a mulatto utopia. (30)

The designation of mulatto features as a social space of placelessness here recalls a turn-of-the-century vogue of referring to mulattoes as "no-nations" (Lewis, *Biography*, 214).

Baker is clearly correct with regard to the aesthetic economy that prevails in *Hagar's Daughter*, although he verges on essentializing black womanhood as a specific physical and cultural type. It is important to distinguish between a

preference for Caucasian somatic traits and a preference for white American culture, just as it is important to assert that the cultural phenomenon of "lightening
up the race" responded to a white America that, in the words of Du Bois, "yields
[the Negro] no true self-consciousness, but only lets him see himself . . . through
the eyes of . . . a world that looks on in amused contempt and pity" (*Souls*, 3).
Hopkins is careful to denounce any absolute moral relevance to skin color. Jewel
vouches for the moral stature of Hagar, Aunt Jenny, and Venus when Cuthbert
tries to question the moral character of the race (269). And Hopkins depicts
Aurelia as morally inferior to the Sargeant women even though Aurelia passes
for white.

To Hopkins, "Aurelia . . . deserves our pity" (159) because women like her
lacked "honorable" means of "gratify[ing] their luxurious tastes." Hopkins invokes the "condition of the mother" in a fashion both conventional and striking.
Her Lamarckian explanation is that through mothers "like themselves," women
such as Aurelia were "helpless" victims of circumstance: "The education of generations of her foreparents has entered into her blood," Elsie Bradford says to
Sumner. Hopkins's discourse of blood pollution thus does not trace Aurelia's
moral corruption to an original African body but to the intervening slave experience. But because it is in this context that the literal "hag" of the novel appears,
Hopkins's ambivalent aesthetics suggest that, on the one hand, slavery is the ultimate corrupting agent in American life, but, on the other hand, the only salvation available is through escape from the revenant image of blackness spawned
in the white imaginary.

Although Hagar looks into Marthy's face and her own for signs of the revenant,
the novel's true ghost inhabits Enson Hall only *after* the disappearance of Hagar
and her daughter, summoned to assist in St. Clair Enson's (Colonel Benson's)
aborted attempt to secure the Bowen fortune:

> The Hall was in charge of an old Negress, known all over the country as "Auntie
> Griffin." She was regarded with awe by both whites and blacks, being a reputed
> "witch woman" used to dealing and trafficking with evil spirits.
>
> Tall and raw-boned, she was a nightmare of horror. Her body was bent and twisted
> by disease from its original height. Her protruding chin was sharp like a razor, and
> the sunken jaws told of toothless gums within.
>
> Her ebony skin was seamed by wrinkles; her eyes, yellow with age. . . . The de-
> formed hands were horny and toilworn. (228)

This detailed description of Auntie Griffin as the revenant places the black hag
in the genealogy of Venus, ironically, but not Marthy. Auntie Griffin, whose

name suggests her monstrosity, is Venus's paternal aunt, and like Venus's father, Ike, she remains enslaved to St. Clair Enson long after the official demise of slavery. Because she represents a return to the corrupted black body of slavery, not the original African body, Auntie Griffin has more in common, ironically, with the fair-skinned seductress Aurelia than with Venus's matrilinear cluster. The revenant that haunts Enson Hall is slavery itself—the debased black body enslaved to a monstrous white tradition.

Yet the greater narrative attention afforded to Aurelia than to Auntie Griffin reveals Hopkins's disturbing assumption that reader interest is color-coded. Dark-skinned women such as Auntie Griffin, Aunt Henny, and Marthy primarily provide comic relief or Gothic effect, while Venus, Aurelia, Hagar, and Jewel command increasingly greater narrative attention in direct proportion to their whiteness of appearance. The expectation that the reading public could not identify with dark-skinned characters in central dramatic roles leaves undisturbed the association of skin color and social value. Only Chesnutt's premonition that white America would not respond well to a literary "frontal assault" on the fortress of race privilege explains in any way the reluctance of writers like Hopkins and himself to dispense with conventional racial characterizations.

Chesnutt's stories and novels of the "color line" reveal his own interest in white hybridophobia. The death of the Miller child in *The Marrow of Tradition* suggests fear of the hybrid, rather than hybridity itself, as the agent of fatality. In other works, Chesnutt also stresses that the social consequences of acknowledging kinship across racial lines pale before the human cost of maintaining caste barriers. In "The Sheriff's Children," the sheriff's mulatto son Tom decides that he must kill his father as an act of self-preservation. To save himself, the sheriff appeals to their kinship, but Tom reminds him that their blood relation has never previously interested the sheriff. Only the timely appearance of the sheriff's other child, his white daughter, saves his life, as she shoots her half brother before he can shoot their father. After this incident, the sheriff decides to make good on his kinship responsibilities, but in a final gesture of alienation, Tom removes his bandage and allows the blood that unites them to seep from his uncovered wound.

Chesnutt again develops dramatic closure around acknowledgment of kinship in *The Marrow of Tradition*. When Olivia Carteret's son lies dying of an illness, Janet Miller's husband is the only doctor who can save him. But Janet's own son has fallen victim to the rioting whites, and when Major Carteret goes to the Miller household to get the doctor, he is shown the boy's body and he realizes the blunt justice of the fact that his own son's life will be forfeited in reparation for his unleashing of the forces of vigilantism. Olivia Carteret, though, swallows her pride and goes to the Miller house to plead with Janet: "'You are my sister;—the child is your own near kin!'" (466).

As Hopkins's *Hagar's Daughter* shows, the potential of marriage as a disruptive as well as a unifying force was important to this period of national imagining because of the intense pressure created by the "one-drop rule" to keep blacks out of the body politic. At the same time, marriages haunted by questions of race placed characters in the position of either reaffirming or disrupting social distinctions of race and color. Werner Sollors has pointed out the centrality of the marriage plot to the issue of racial allegiance in Chesnutt's "The Wife of His Youth,"[34] but the observation might as easily be made with regard to a number of his other works. In "The Wife of His Youth," Chesnutt tells of a "Blue Vein" society in Groveland (Cleveland) whose "custodian of standards" and "preserver of . . . traditions," Mr. Ryder, comes face to face with a ghost of the past on the night he plans to announce his engagement to a young widow. Ryder has changed his name from Sam Taylor and has shed his southern rural past for a new life in the northern city, where he becomes the spokesman for the near-white social group determined to preserve its store of Caucasian genetic traits against the day when whites will intermarry with them freely. His summation of the choices of affiliation facing the Blue Veins certifies that they have not missed the point that the newly promulgated "one-drop rule" is aimed at them, not at their dark-skinned relations: "'Our fate lies between absorption by the white race and extinction in the black. The one does n't want us yet, but may take us in time. The other would welcome us, but it would be for us a backward step. . . . We must do the best we can for ourselves and those who are to follow us. Self-preservation is the first law of nature" (*Stories*, 105). In order to preserve their advantage of white race features in a land that openly reviled black bodies, the Blue Veins have tacitly agreed to exclude any blacks who would make more likely the "backward step" of regression to the original African body. Thus, Ryder's betrothal to the fair Molly Dixon solemnizes Blue Vein endogamy as exorcism of the revenant.

The ghost from the past is Sam Taylor's common-law slave wife, though Sam was never a slave himself. When 'Liza Jane appears on the very day of Ryder's betrothal party in search of her long-departed Sam, she does not recognize Ryder as the man in the picture she has carried with her for twenty-five years, and even Ryder must search his face in a mirror to determine if any trace of Sam Taylor remains. Ryder must decide whether to reveal himself to this "wife of his youth" or to ward her off as the toothless black hag she clearly is: "she seemed quite old; for her face was crossed and re-crossed with a hundred wrinkles, and around the edges of her bonnet could be seen protruding a tuft of short gray wool. . . . And she was very black, — so black that her toothless gums, revealed when she opened her mouth to speak, were not red, but blue. She looked like a bit of the old plantation life, summoned up from the past by the wave of a magician's wand" (106–7). To emphasize the spectral quality of 'Liza, Chesnutt makes her a "blue gum," a "regressive type" credited with the power to poison anyone she bites.[35] As Sollors points out, 'Liza seems more a "mother (or even grandmother) figure" (159) than a spouse for the more youthful Ryder. This motherliness reflects more than just her embodiment of the past; it signals as well the "condition of the mother," repackaged via the "one-drop rule," that threatens all of the Blue Veins with being swallowed by the undifferentiated difference of the mythicized African body.

Ryder's public acknowledgment of 'Liza as the wife of his youth is a choice for moral obligation to the past over future social "mobility and upward drift" (Sollors, 160), a choice that will become central to the marriage plot in black national literature. Ryder does the "right thing" in renouncing his youthful fiancée for the old bride, who, despite her faithful devotion, has no *legal* claim to Ryder. Ryder's voluntary embrace of the revenant seems on the surface to be a blow to the self-preservation of the Blue Veins against the ancient claims of the "blue gums." But Ryder's act also owes something to the fact that 'Liza was the one who saved him from being unlawfully sold into slavery. Ryder's self-unmasking ironically does not produce the expected revelation of a slave past. But the enslavement that he averted in the past through an act of disaffiliation returns in the form of 'Liza to shackle him to the black body of death. 'Liza epitomizes the perdurance of the black body throughout American history as the cultural sign of deficiency, ensuring the inescapableness of descent claims inhibiting Blue Vein progress into the American body politic.

There is something funereal in Ryder's manner as he introduces 'Liza as his wife, as though he has resigned himself to the extinction of his lineage in her withered womb. But closer examination reveals that the whiff of mortality looms as well about the young widow, Molly Dixon, whom he might have chosen instead. There is death lurking in either direction for Ryder, suggesting that his former abstention from matrimony had given way to a pro forma obligation to "preserve" his Caucasian features by mating with a woman "whiter than he, and better educated" (104), not from any personal affection for Molly.

Financially secure as a result of her deceased husband's insurance money, Molly is as conventionally a good match for Ryder as 'Liza is a poor one, and though Sollors uses the story as an allegory of the competition between consent claims (Molly) and descent claims ('Liza), the neat formulation bears closer scrutiny. Consent and descent claims become intelligible if we see the choice Ryder makes as between mother figure and wife. But Molly's childless widowhood casts her into an ambiguous category between wife and mother, as though the death of her husband and her failure to reproduce are intricately connected. Childless widowhood, as it happens, also characterizes 'Liza, such that her embodiment of the "condition of the mother" disguises the truth of her barrenness. In this the women are near equivalents, perhaps even threateningly so, given the fates of their past spouses.

Ryder's choice is further complicated, "one drop" notwithstanding, by the whole meaning of the Blue Vein Society's fight for "self-preservation": that he is *more related*, genetically, to other hybrids like Molly than to the unmixed "blue gums" like 'Liza. His choice is between the hag-that-is and the hag-that-will-be, each bearing descent claims hierarchalized according to the social value placed upon her physical appearance, each choice entailing an element of self-negation. If descent claims were Ryder's overriding concern, he may well have chosen Molly on such grounds. More likely, his choice is between two attitudes about descent, as if the women actually embodied the two forms of annihilation that Ryder has earlier described: eventual "absorption" in whiteness and immediate "extinction" in blackness. "It is a pity . . . that men cannot select their mothers," says Judge Straight in Chesnutt's *The House behind the Cedars* (41). Chesnutt, though, gives Ryder such a choice to construct himself retroactively as white or black through selective affiliation, and from one perspective, it is not entirely surprising that the onetime orphan should choose the mother-bride of his youth over the child-bride of his maturity.

Ryder's choice provides an object lesson for whites as well as fair-skinned blacks because his acknowledgment of kinship with 'Liza brings him no social benefit. If the return of the repressed African body idea was to be used as evidence of black Americans' undifferentiated difference from white Americans, Chesnutt's Ryder ironically can only *disprove* the pernicious stereotype by embracing 'Liza. No one else would have known of his deception had he turned 'Liza away—not even 'Liza. Thus the only way that he can attain moral stature consonant with "civilized" behavior is to make a principled stand at odds with his own interests. His situation purposely parallels that of many whites who stood

to lose more than to gain from acknowledging kinship to blacks, the overwhelming majority of whom could not summon the social courage to do the "white"
thing. In this regard, we might consider Ryder as the prototype of the Du Boisian
quest hero, a fictional response by the volunteer Negro Chesnutt to Du Bois's
question in "The Conservation of Races" (1897), "is self-obliteration the highest
end to which Negro blood dare aspire?"[36]

In his story "Her Virginia Mammy," Chesnutt again uses a black mother
figure as revenant to illustrate the centrality of attitudes toward descent in color-
line politics. Faced with a decision about whether or not to marry the suggestively named John Winthrop (who can, of course, trace his ancestry back to the
Mayflower) Clara Hohlfelder holds back her consent until she can ascertain that
her status as "Miss Nobody, from Nowhere" will do no harm to John's social
standing. "What are a lot of musty, mouldy old grandfathers, compared with life
and love and happiness," asks John (*Stories*, 117), blithely articulating a most
American belief in the power of love to transcend social obstacles.[37] Yet Clara deliberately summons the ghost from the past who comes to bring her the facts of
her ancestry.

The "Virginia mammy" who provides the links to Clara's past is, of course, her
real mother, though Clara's adoption by a German immigrant couple has secured
for Clara a place in the white world. The mammy, who calls herself Mrs. Harper,
gambles that by speaking up, she can settle Clara's nagging doubts without revealing her destabilizing kinship. She assures Clara of the social acceptability of
her white relations (they turn out to be a "first family Virginia" clan known as the
Staffords) while withholding information about the slave condition of her
mother, Mary Fairfax, saying only that Mary "*belonged* to one of the first families
of Virginia, and in her veins flowed some of the best blood of the Old Domin-
ion" (127–28; my emphasis). When Clara attempts to tell John that her fears of
social "disability" have proved unfounded, he sees what she cannot—that the
woman she calls her "Virginia mammy" is biologically related to her. What
Clara takes as a sign of her elevation to John's social plane—her "first family Virginia" mammy against his *Mayflower*—John sees more clearly as her ultimate social invalidity. Amazingly, Mrs. Harper wordlessly appeals to John not to reveal
the secret to Clara, as though *Clara* were the one who had to be protected from
the taint of blackness.

John, then, must make a decision about his own consent/descent dilemma.
Having previously declared rather whimsically that he would marry Clara even if
she were colored like her dance students, John makes good on his word, agreeing

to bestow the Winthrop name upon Clara as a protection against her and society's paranoid obsession with ancestry. John's indifference to the return of the black mother as a potential complication of his children's ancestry reveals, ironically, the "true" aristocrat's self-assurance, a gesture mirroring Clara's father, who stood firm against the Staffords out of love for Clara's mother. As a tangible link to the slave past, Mrs. Harper disguises the "condition of the mother" behind the ambiguous signifier "mammy," implicitly reminding white southerners that even their claims to the social elite derive from their relation to a black mother figure. But John extends kinship to Clara only as a way of negating the social liability of her kinship to Mrs. Harper. The story finally turns on the poignant *necessity* of the daughter's departure, but it is not a conscious departure, and we are given every assurance that Clara would never have consciously chosen to mask her racial antecedents.

In his novel *The House behind the Cedars* (1900), Chesnutt places the "condition of the mother" again at the center of a family melodrama, the complication arising from Rena's need to decide whether to ignore her mother's illness and continue to pass for white in Clarence, or to return to her mother in Patesville and risk exposure by temporarily resuming life as a Negro. Her decision to return casts her back across the color line permanently, as her romance with George Tryon crumbles upon his discovery of her black ancestry. Unlike John Winthrop, Tryon fails the test of his own unreflective boast that he would love Rena even if she were like the mulatto servant girl Mimy. The misunderstanding stems from Tryon's seeing only Mimy's class where Rena sees only Mimy's race.

When Tryon learns of Rena's ancestry, "love . . . [gave] place to astonishment and horror" (127). Chesnutt clearly associates the transformation of Rena from the woman Tryon crowned as "Queen of Love and Beauty" to a "horror" in his eyes with Tryon's absorption of the culture's pervasive hybridophobia. The discourse of atavism first enters the narrative rather innocuously, when John Warwick, Rena's older brother, returns to the house behind the cedars to see the mother and sister he has abandoned to cross the color line. His announcement that he has had a child whose white mother has died is a prelude to explaining his selfish errand of taking Rena with him to Clarence to become the woman of his household, in effect forcing her to cross the color line and abandon their mother as he has. The news of the child sparks a conventional response from his mother and sister, as they "made minute inquiries about the age and weight and eyes and nose and other important details of this precious infant" (20). In the larger context of the novel's somatic politics, this questioning is more than the curiosity of the near kin for the new family addition. Behind their questions is an anxiety about racial "regression to type" that will reduce the offspring's chances for social success.

The justification for this anxiety becomes evident when Rena leaves her mother to live with Warwick, falls in love with Tryon, and then must face the prospect of his discovery of their ancestry. "'George Tryon loves you for yourself alone; it is not your ancestors that he seeks to marry,'" Warwick counsels Rena (73). He could not be more wrong. Tryon succumbs to the paranoia about invisible race that he passively consumes in casual conversations, in ritual social affirmations of race difference, and in news articles framing the latest "scientific evidence" within the immediate objectives of race politics: "The [news article] writer maintained that owing to a special tendency of the Negro blood, however diluted, to revert to the African type, any future amalgamation of the white and black races, which foolish and wicked Northern negrophiles predicated as the ultimate result of the new conditions confronting the South, would therefore be an ethnological impossibility; for the smallest trace of Negro blood would inevitably drag down the superior race to the level of the inferior, and reduce the fair Southland . . . to the frightful level of Hayti, the awful example of Negro incapacity" (96–97). Having the paranoid image of the inevitable return of the African body thus implanted in his imagination, Tryon reacts predictably in renouncing Rena, despite his heartfelt belief in his saner moments that she could not be the hybrid of the white cultural imaginary.

Tryon's mind becomes the battleground between race theory on the one hand and personal experience with Rena on the other. Whenever he seems on the verge of breaking with tradition and accepting Rena at face value, he becomes haunted by her cultural significance. Tryon decides that he cannot blame Rena for her deception because "nature's great law of self-preservation" had forced her to seek escape from her doomed race (133). Still, "she was worse than dead to him; for if he had seen her lying in her shroud before him, he could at least have cherished her memory" (131). This "consolation" is denied to him because every recollection of her beauty reverts to the life-in-death image of her gross racial essence: "In all her fair young beauty she stood before him [in his dream], and then by some hellish magic she was slowly transformed into a hideous black hag. With agonized eyes he watched her beautiful tresses become mere wisps of coarse wool, wrapped round with dingy cotton strings; he saw her clear eyes grow bloodshot, her ivory teeth turn to unwholesome fangs" (133). Tryon, though, tries to find a way around his persistent desire for Rena and his haunted imaginings. In a reflex that echoes both Frank Fowler and Mary Walden's inventions of a fairy tale past for Rena as changeling, Tryon decides to confront Rena in Patesville to determine if there could be any chance of her being an illegitimate white child passed on to a black household to disguise her white mother's sin.

Tryon convinces himself that even if Rena was not a changeling white girl, he would be willing to run away with her where they could start off with new identities. But when he at last sights Rena again, the spectacle of her enjoying herself at a frolic in her home, apparently undeterred by any emotional reaction to the failure of their romance, causes Tryon to feel at last he has glimpse the "real" Rena, her racial essence on full display: "Tonight his eyes had been opened—he had seen her with the mask thrown off, a true daughter of a race in which the sensuous enjoyment of the moment took precedence. . . . With the monkey-like imitativeness of the Negro she had copied the manners of white people while she lived among them, and had dropped them with equal facility when they ceased to serve a purpose. . . . If he had yielded to the momentary weakness of the past night . . . he would have regretted it soon enough. The black streak would have been sure to come out in some form, sooner or later, if not in the wife, then in her children" (199–201). To console himself, Tryon reverts to the scripted iteration of despair that would scapegoat an entire race because of the moral dilemmas its existence creates: "As slaves, Negroes were tolerable. As freemen, they were an excrescence, an alien element incapable of absorption into the body politic of white men. He would like to send them all back to . . . Africa" (227).

Rena is neither the hag of Tryon's imaginings nor the changeling princess "Rowena Warwick" of the elaborate Anglo-Saxon fantasy that John Warwick has thrust her into. Her hybridity creates problems for others to resolve through fantastic myths of racial essence. Tryon thinks of his near escape from marrying Rena as avoiding "the unpardonable sin against his race" (130), and the narrator, having firmly established the humanity and simultaneity of Rena's family, explains why southerners did not permit themselves to think in such terms: "The Southern mind, in discussing abstract questions relative to humanity, makes always, consciously or unconsciously, the mental reservation that the conclusions reached do not apply to the Negro, unless they can be made to harmonize with the customs of the country" (131). The "customs of the country" include the concubinage of black and mulatto women but not lawful marriage with them, a "custom" that accounts for the "low standards" of Mary Walden, who sees her abandonment by her children as a just punishment for her sins. Chesnutt, though, sees the "customs of the country" themselves as the unpardonable sin. Mary Walden is, as even her selfish son realizes, "more sinned against than sinning" (26) in the matter of her acceptance of concubinage in a society that would not let her be a white man's wife. The outcome of this legacy of exploitation by white men is both the unacknowledgeability of cross-racial kinship and the fear of invisible blackness.

Where Hopkins formulaically resorts to aristocratic origins to provide closure for her works, Chesnutt's realism interrogates the obligations and failures of those who adopt the aristocratic pose. The mother's return becomes an important trope for both because of their felt obligation to the past and because of the persistence of social structures defined through the mother's body. They did not acquiesce in the characterization of their ancestry as a "body of death" but sought, as the next chapter explains, to redefine the meaning of blackness in America by reimagining black womanhood.

CHAPTER THREE

The S/ness of the Mother

The uterine family is far from being rare in negro Africa.
—Charles Letourneau, *The Evolution of Marriage, and of the Family* (1900)

The black "body of death" rhetoric derived in part from centuries of myth mak-ing about black bodies, including relentless Victorian-era assaults on specifi-cally black women's moral and physical character. Laura Doyle, in *Bordering on the Body: The Racial Matrix of Modern Fiction and Culture* (1994), summarizes the importance of discourse about women's bodies in turn-of-the-century body politics:

> The dominant kin group's presumption of access to women of the subordinate group . . . disrupts the formation of identity and the accumulation of resources by the subjugated group, . . . not only practically—whether through rape or harassment or restriction of job opportunities—but also symbolically, in cultural discourse and aesthetics. As has been amply documented by feminist critics, dominant-group women serve the aesthetic and myth-making practices of dominant-group men, as muses, virgins, whores, or metaphors for nature, . . . images of women that mirror and reinforce the actual circulation of women. . . . In a stratified kinship culture men of the dominant kin group control the mainstream images of subordinate-group women as well. Thus they deprive subordinate-group men not only of the power to circulate women freely and gain material resources but also of the power to disseminate images of "their" women so as to develop their own cultural traditions and resources. (26)

Through economic practices that deprived many black men of gainful employ-ment while coercing black women into domestic service in white households, whites maintained a practical mastery of black females that authorized ante-bellum representations of black women as mammies or bed wenches (the black Venus) and reinforced suspicions of black females as racially disloyal, domestically incompetent in their own homes, and sexually aggressive in relations with white and black men. Progress toward a racial renaissance, as Doyle suggests, would necessarily involve a struggle over the cultural definition and social mastery of black female bodies.

The early and continuously prurient interest in black women's bodies during the period of European exploration and colonization in Africa and the Americas spawned insidious myths of black female sexuality that coalesced into the image of the black Venus as the essential black female. Jefferson's charge that black females had routinely mated with orangutans in Africa was a far-reaching indictment in Enlightenment terms, influencing the downward classification of blacks in hierarchies of race developed during the era of expanding contact with dark-skinned people (Jordan, 229). In contrast to the white lady ideal of asexuality, the myth of black female bestiality marked black womanhood as a site of spiritual violation for the entire Chain of Being. Her supposedly insatiable sexuality compromised all humanity, in that her womb was accessible to both the white male, creation's pinnacle, and the ape.[1]

The ape libel reflects the polygenetic underpinnings of race/space assumptions: the idea that the racial body is metaphysically continuous with its original environment, a mapping of deterministic geography in the human body itself. By this reasoning, Africans could aspire to no higher "development" than that which a savage, feminized, exploitable Africa itself could claim. This feminization of Africa was made possible by some of the earliest European accounts of the continent during the age of discovery, as when Jean Bodin's 1566 work, *Method for Easy Comprehension of History*, cites Ptolemy's report "that on account of southern sensuality Venus chiefly is worshiped in Africa and that the constellation of Scorpion, which pertains to the pudenda, dominates the continent" (Jordan, 34). Many early accounts focused erotic interest in Africa on accounts of the abnormal size of African male genitalia (Jordan, 34–35), but by the nineteenth century, the idea of Africa as the world's erogenous zone became associated as well with aberrant female sexual anatomy through Europe's fascination with the lineal descendant of the parodic black Venus, the "Hottentot Venus."

What made the Hottentot Venus such a sensation was her possession of primary and secondary sexual features that seemed gross, exaggerated, and savage emblems of feminine essence: steatopygia, or protruding buttocks, and the so-called Hottentot apron, a "hypertrophy of the labia and nymphae caused by manipulation of the genitalia and serving as a sign of beauty among certain tribes" (Gilman, "Black Bodies," 232). That this cultural enhancement of human anatomy would become, for Europeans, an emblem of "natural" race differences was inevitable, since the enlarged vagina—open, from all appearances, to animal entry (Gilman, "Black Bodies," 236)—gave visual representation to the putative elasticity and incontinence of the black womb, securing the myth of a debased, feminized black female essence against which the sanctity and exclusivity of the white womb could be defined.[2]

In her bodily contravention of European idealism, this icon of the essential black female provoked an unmistakable ambivalence on the part of those who set out to define her. On the one hand, Africa feminized was not only deformed but the mother of deformity as well, "bringing dailie foorth newe monsters." Jean Bodin imagined Africa as the place where "promiscuous coition of men and animals took place, wherefore the regions of Africa produce for us so many monsters" (Jordan, 31). As the travel notes of Sir John Barrow reflect, African female sexuality was not merely seductive but often repellent by European standards. After observing that the Bushmen of southern Africa were "among the ugliest of all human beings," Barrow went on to focus attention to the "Hottentot apron," the "peculiar corporeal appearance which [he could not] help terming beast-like" (Helper, 56). Barrow mentions prominently, as expected, the "deformity" of the genitalia as the signature of black female sexual aberration: "The well-known story of the Hottentot women possessing an unusual appendage to those parts that are seldom exposed to view, *which belongs not to the sex in general, ridiculous as it may appear*, is perfectly true with regard to the [Bushmen]" (Helper, 54; my emphasis). Barrow goes on to emphasize the way that the "Hottentot apron" remains available to observation "without the least offence to modesty." All ages of females have the feature, says Barrow, leaping to the conclusion that it indicates a racial "predisposition": "The longest that was measured somewhat exceeded five inches. . . . Many were said to have them much longer. These protruded nymphae, collapsed and pendent, *leave the spectator in doubt as to what sex they belong*. Their color is that of livid blue, inclining to a reddish tint, *not unlike the excrescence on the beak of a turkey*, which indeed may serve to convey a tolerably good idea of the whole appearance, both as to color, shape and size" (Helper, 55; my emphasis). Barrow avails himself of two analogies that certify the women as grotesque: the Bushman female genitalia appear identical to male genitalia and to a turkey wattle. As with other descriptions of black somatic deviance, the principle of an undifferentiated difference—so profound that it confuses bestial with human qualities, so irreducible that it collapses all gender distinctions—frames all discourse about the "Hottentot Venus." Because the passage is quoted in Hinton Helper's unapologetically racist appeal for genocide, *Nojoque*, it is worth noting that Helper borrows from Barrow in his own description of white feminists as gynanders.[3]

Barrow was likewise bemused by the way that the Bushman women's bodies seemed to approximate the letter S, with their "pendulous" bellies and pronounced posteriors: "If the letter S be considered as one expression of the line of beauty, . . . some of the women of this nation are entitled to the first rank in point of form" (Helper, 57). This wink at the parodic discourse of the black Venus, the celebration of the "grotesque" African body as object of irrational desire, stands Hogarth's "serpentine line" of the body, the "S/ness" of beauty in European aesthetics, on its head.[4]

On the other hand, the lore of the black Venus also betrayed as pronounced an element of desire as of abhorrence. While the concept of an embodied black beauty maintained much of its early satiric edge, the high incidence of mixed-race individuals with black mothers required an explanation that did not exclude the possibility that white men could prefer African women as sexual partners. Thus, out of the image of an absurd black female competitor to the idealized white lady gradually emerged a more seductive and an aesthetically more Europeanized black Venus, as embodied by the mixed-race fancy girls and the *placées* of the famous New Orleans quadroon balls, those whose function as concubines for white males *placed* them and their offspring athwart the cultural divide called race (Blassingame, 17–19, 202–3). Often "white" in body but always "morally" African, the quadroon courtesan was a third-generation product of white male sexual adventurism who mediated European aesthetics and the "African" pleasure principle. Thus while Josephine Baker's twentieth-century "Svarta Venus" made iconic gestures toward the Hottentot Venus of nineteenth-century European invention,[5] the "S/ness" of her embodied art derived more immediately from the quadroon seductresses who danced along the color line of American body politics.

The medical folklore of black female sexuality at the turn of the nineteenth century continued the themes of genital gigantism, inordinate sexual appetite, gynandromorphism, and gross immodesty from the lore of the Hottentot Venus. William Lee Howard, a Baltimore physician, implicitly linked black racial inferiority to black female anatomy in a series of fantastic non sequiturs. To Howard, "the African is . . . unlike the Caucasian in secondary sexual characters, and . . .

so he can never be absolutely alike in the highest psychical processes" (423). Later, Howard explained that the gigantism of their penises made black males susceptible to "sexual madness," creating a danger for white women. But Howard interestingly accounted for black male sexual gigantism by referring "to the general law . . . [that] the genital organs of the male are in *proper proportion*, as regards size, to the dimensions of the female organs" (425; my emphasis). If I read Howard correctly, he was suggesting that black *female* genital abnormality is the starting point in a causal chain culminating in the mental and consequently the social inferiority of blacks as a race.

Philip A. Bruce's theme throughout *The Plantation Negro as a Freeman* was that the postwar decrease of direct supervision of blacks meant less infusion of white blood through female concubinage (hence *somatic* regression) and less infusion of white civilization (hence *moral* regression). But clearly, for Bruce, physical regression was the source of moral regression too, since in his experience "pure" Africans did not demonstrate any capacity for moral behavior. Because black women were incapable of refusing sexual advances, according to Bruce, "new issue" black men, having seen nothing but black women all their lives, did not understand that there were women who were capable of sexual restraint, causing an epidemic of rapes of white women (84–85). Bruce argued further that because of an ancestry acquired through its black mother "as nearly allied to the beasts of the field as to any human type, and to a certain extent sunk even below the animals, by their superstitious and cannibalistic customs," the black child grew up in a home "calculated to implant the spirit of evil in his nature, whether it was there before or not by inheritance" (170). The modest benefits of marriage that slavery "enforced" on the blacks were, he claimed, doomed to extinction by black female unchastity, which allowed "promiscuous intercourse" to become "more open and unreserved" (246). This fantasy of public licentiousness coupled with somatic reversion to "type" kept alive the image of the African Venus, her sexuality accessible without limit, as the essential black female, from whom no descendant could escape.

Bruce and his admirers, in effect, updated the phrase "condition of the mother" by reaching back to the earliest myths of black female essence to recast the image of Progressive Era African American womanhood in a new Darwinian language of regression and undifferentiated difference. In 1900, Charles Letourneau reiterated Bruce's conclusions: "in humanity, as well as in animality, the uterine family establishes itself spontaneously, whenever the male abandons the female and her progeny. . . . In every ethnic group living in promiscuity, for example, *uterine filiation* shows itself" (Shufeldt, *Problem*, 355). The problem with the African mother's condition, by this reasoning, was that an aberrant, pathological kinship pattern established through the mother dominated African cultures, trapping African communal life in a "pre-clanship" stage of development. To Joseph Tillinghast, the African inheritance of property through uterine kinship created the only locus of actual family feeling among them, the mother-son bond (66). Tillinghast, like his contemporaries, brought the discussion back to black female promiscuity as the root of all racial evil, calling the custom of property succession through the female "a survival of the time when paternity was too uncertain to be relied upon to trace blood kinship, and it still is for no small portion of the population" (87). Tillinghast thus cast African ahistoricity further back than "pre-clanship" to a "pre-paternal" stage of social evolution, dangerously close to the demarcation line between human and ape drawn by Shaler.[6] In this fashion, the assault on black family life in the Progressive Era would largely focus on the way that a matriarchal, "uterine affiliated" culture deprived black Americans of the wherewithal for national belonging.

Homes and Wildernesses

The question of black familial stability—that is, the precariousness of black patriarchy and the uncertainty of female sexual restraint—became the fixation of social science examinations of black life, during and after the Jim Crow era. Insistence on the patriarchal model within a discourse of gender roles that America did not willingly grant black men and women additionally set the stage for a protracted period of self-scrutiny and self-loathing by "upwardly mobile" black Americans. Both white and black social scientists propounded theories invoking genetic, historical, and environmental influences on black familial dysfunction. While midcentury discourse on the black family gradually replaced references to savage regression with discussions of the impact of slavery conditions on black family cohesion, recent sociohistorical assessments have placed more emphasis on the postslavery period of Jim Crow as the origin of distinctive black familial patterns. The debate over the "matriarchal" structure of black households, for example, draws most attention.

According to Joel Williamson, economic conditions in the South drove large numbers of blacks off the land in the decades when the removal of federal pressure allowed the South to institute Jim Crow statutes and simultaneously disenfranchise black voters. The result was a black urban underclass in the South removed from access to (and thus hostile to the values of) middle-class life: "Loosened males tended to congregate in the cities, and Negro families in the urban situation tended to lose the forms of family that farm life had supported. . . . Trapped in the city, young black men might sometimes take to a street-corner, pool-hall hustling, and petty criminal way of life. Of necessity, they generated a set of values to justify their lives, values that directly countered those of the Victorians. If the black male could find no decent job, it was because he was too smart to work. If he seemed to travel from one woman to another, . . . and if his children did not all live under the same roof, it was simply because he was too much man for one woman to handle." To Williamson, the "black matriarchy" was a complement to this "street-corner, counter-value, male-worshiping society": despite the slavery experience, "both were new, and they were the unfortunate children of the marriage of the industrial revolution to white racism" (*Crucible*, 59).

Herbert Gutman's findings on postslavery attempts by African Americans to form stable family units make it difficult to accept broad generalizations about a "black matriarchy" or to give credence to claims of pandemic black female sexual license. Gutman cites data showing that the newly emancipated slaves went to great lengths to establish familial relationships removed from the external controls and whims of the master class and that black families during the time period his study considers were highly two-parented in constitution (443–44). Immediately after emancipation, there was an overwhelming rush to legalize slave marriages and to untangle multiple marriages created by slave owners selling off slaves to distant plantations.[7] Gutman agrees that impoverished urban ghetto existence took a toll on black family cohesion, as his data from the 1880 and 1900 censuses show: "The simple nuclear household greatly declined in importance [in the urban area, but] . . . the nuclear household retained its commanding importance among rural blacks." Thus, "the typical southern black household in 1900 still had at its head a lower-class husband or father" (448–49). Citing Hylan Lewis's critique of the "Moynihan Report" to the effect that "inculcating marriage and family values" was not the solution to black familial problems but rather "find[ing] ways and means for the young adult male to meet the economic maintenance demands of marriage and family life" (463), Gutman suggests that the decline in family cohesion after emancipation had less to do with mores, values, or regression to savagery than with economics (448).

However, descriptions of black home life by social scientists and cultural observers at the century's turn portrayed black familial instability as normative.

Bruce defined the postwar black community as "an aggregation of ignorant homes, and each home is but a circle of thoughtless individuals" (9). Ray Stannard Baker's 1908 study of black life in America concluded that "the home life of the great mass of Negroes" was "still primitive": "They are crowded together in one or two rooms, they get no ideas of privacy or of decency" (169). Sociologist Howard Odum, who, like Baker, considered himself a racial progressive and a friend of the Negro people, also took a dim view of black home life, arguing that sexual unrestraint lay at the center of black familial dysfunction.[8]

Even evidence of upward mobility was held against black families. William Archer, in his travels along the "color line" in the first decade of this century, found the black homes he visited, to his evident disappointment, to be "very nice little houses, scrupulously neat and well kept, . . . being intended rather for show than use" (160). Clearly, Archer was primed for a firsthand glimpse of the black belt squalor Baker had described, and so he disparaged the functioning black households in the same terms that others criticized dysfunctional black homes — that they were not really "homes" at all: "What troubled me throughout my domiciliary visits was the sense that (with one or two exceptions) these homes were not homes at all. . . . They were no more homelike than the shopwindow rooms of the up-to-date upholsterer. If they were lived in at all, it was from a sense of duty, a self-conscious effort after a life of 'refinement.' They were, in short, entirely imitative and mechanical tributes to the American ideal of the prosperous, cultivated home" (162–63). Inevitably, the myth of black household dysfunction placed emphasis on the failings of black women. Patricia Morton devotes two entire chapters to the "disfiguration" of black women in the historical and sociological discourse of the black family of the late nineteenth and early twentieth centuries, showing how this expectation of black female depravity grounded representations of black home life.[9] Black social historians tended to agree with their white counterparts that unrestrained female sexuality was the cause of the race's poor public image and thus the cause of its social inferiority.[10]

William Hannibal Thomas, a case in point, went furthest in his denunciation of black home life toward shifting the primary onus of immorality from predatory males to libidinous females: "In negro homes, . . . their intimates, devoid of either modesty or discretion, indulge in the utmost freedom of speech and action, and the female members, regardless of the presence of their male relatives and friends, go about in scanty clothing which invites a familiar caress that is rarely forbidden or resented as an insult. Not only does the semi-nude attire of the adult negresses invite lascivious carousal at home, but their young daughters are permitted to parade the streets and visit their associates clad in a scantiness of attire that ought never to be seen outside a bedroom." Black men, according to Thomas, were not only willing to sell their womenfolk to white men, but they also took "strange women into their homes and cohabit[ed] with them with the knowledge, but without protest, from their wives," and they fathered children by their step-daughters "with the consent of the wife and mother of the girl" (177, 179).

Clearly, the acquiescence of women in these outrages by men was the crucial factor in establishing the moral atmosphere of black homes, according to Thomas, who returned again and again to this theme: "there is a fundamental difference in the racial character, habits, integrity, courage, and strength of negro and white Americans. What makes it? The answer lies in one word—their women" (200). "Women unresistingly betray their wifely honor to satisfy a bestial instinct, [and] . . . every notion of marital duty and fidelity is cast to the winds when the next moment of passion arrives" (198). "Most Negro women marry young," Thomas reports; "when they do not, their spinsterhood is due either to physical disease or sexual morbidity [lesbianism], or to a desire for unrestrained sexual freedom" (184).

His concluding endorsement of formal matrimony invokes a familiar, if not overworked, comparison between blacks and Jews: "Is it not obvious that the negro people will never become great, wise, or true, until its women . . . institute such safeguards and assurances of chaste maidenhood as characterize Hebrew social life?" (200–201). This appeal for blacks to become an endogamous community modeled on Jewish tradition boils down, as Thomas makes abundantly clear, to female "race chastity." As William Archer reports, Booker T. Washington held out the ideal of Jewish insularity as a model for black American nationalism in a conversation with H. G. Wells: "'May we not become a peculiar people—like the Jews? Isn't that possible?'" (Archer, 215 n. *). Archer's sarcastic response to Washington's rhetorical question echoes Thomas: "What so long kept the Jews a peculiar people was the constancy with which Jewish women declined to intermingle with the Gentiles around them. If negro women showed such a spirit of racial chastity, the problem would be very different."

In this fashion, the whole question of black national inclusion became a matter of black males' success in reining in the mythic black Venus's voluptuousness, of taming her into the household nun and familial soul keeper. That such constraint on black female sexual expression had both advantages and disadvantages for black males is evident, since black male sexual prowess, as a symbolic expression of manhood denied by law and custom, depended in large part on the absence of a functioning black patriarchy for the large numbers of "unprotected" women from whom to select partners.[11] Without women under constraint, there could be no black patriarchy, but conversely, without a black patriarchy willing and able to police female sexuality, there could be no race-chaste black women.[12]

As Patricia Morton has demonstrated, the degrading images of the black female propounded a "bad mother" image that seemed to clash in every particular with the mammy legend. The rise in popularity of the mammy icon in the late nineteenth and early twentieth centuries coincided with the increase of attacks on black female morality, a sharp demarcation of mythic constructs that illustrates again the inseparability of the mythic form from cultural politics. The fact that a sizable number of black households with no male breadwinner (or, perhaps, no male willing to commit to a serious relationship owing, in part, to the mythology of black female promiscuity) enabled the oversupply of black female domestics willing to work at low wages suggests a connection between these mythic forms.[13] If the myth of the bad black mother forced women into domestic service, the mammy mythology, in return, helped to exacerbate the destabilization of black households by making sexual harassment from white employers a condition of life for tens of thousands of underpaid, undereducated black women with no practical means of avoiding poverty (Dollard, 152), and especially by keeping these women away from their own households for extended periods of time. As with the "lady" image, the mammy icon requires an antithetical formulation to perform its cultural work of subduing black females into domestic service. Asserting that the only virtuous black woman is the black woman under external constraint, the mammy icon does more than merely allow space for the bad mother; it is the bad mother in disguise. The bad black woman, in turn, is the mammy unbound, the black Venus rampant.[14] The lore of the bad black mother argues that only a white household can give black women familial stability and moral constancy.

The propaganda proclaiming black female unchastity also facilitated the myth of impending black extinction. The diseases attributed to blacks, often described as outgrowths of social formations but as often translated as the effects of "natural," evolutionary processes on "inferior organisms" and, predictably, the wrath of God, ranged from blackness itself as a skin disorder often seen as a form of leprosy, to scrofula, tuberculosis, smallpox, and other diseases of "filth" and "uncleanness."[15] Because among the chief threats to black survival were those illnesses thought to arise from their morally "contaminated" lifestyle—diseases acquired through unrestrained worship at the shrine of the black Venus—post-slavery domestic employment practices revitalized the fear that black females might undermine the white household too, by bringing immorality and disease with them. According to Lawrence J. Friedman, the underlying message to whites was that intimacy with blacks was threatening to the body social: "sexual inter-course between white and black was particularly dangerous, serving notice on white men to abandon their long-standing associations with black women. And now more than ever before, black men had to be kept away from white women. The venereal disease that might result could literally destroy the white race, body and soul." The alarm over unstructured interracial contact thus became another argument reinforcing Jim Crow legislation and custom: only "rigid across-the-board segregation of white from black" would assure "the health and safety of white civilization" (124).[16]

Such schemes of radical separation would be possible only if black female promiscuity, acting as a magnet for white male sexual curiosity, did not under-mine whites' better judgment, according to the apologists of white misbehavior. For his part, William B. Smith declared a universal depravity among black fe-male household servants: "Ask [a respectable Negro] to recommend some 'nice colored girl' as a domestic, and she will probably reply frankly that she knows of none, that they are altogether become unprofitable, that they are scandalously unchaste, that there is none that doeth good—no, not one. At this point we speak from personal knowledge" (243). An outpouring of sympathy for the white males who had to run this gauntlet of temptation arose from observers like William Archer: "The youth and manhood of the white South is subjected to an alto-gether unfair and unwholesome ordeal by the constant presence of a multitude of physically well-developed women, among whom, in the lower levels, there is no strong tradition of chastity, and to whom the penalties of incontinence are very slight. . . . Temptation may in myriads of cases be resisted; but this order of temptation ought not to be in the air." "It cannot be good for any race of men," Archer remarks, "to be surrounded by strongly-accentuated Sex, which, for ulte-rior reasons, whereof the mere animal nature takes little account, is placed un-der tabu."[17] For Archer, the "S/ness" of black womanhood was a disorienting sexuality that undermined rationality, order, and progress. In America, black women served a dual mythic function as the upholders and destroyers of white families.[18]

Reading backward to Barrow's description of his encounter with the black Venus in Africa, we can make the connection between Archer's vision of destructive black female sexuality and the mystique of the black Venus more precise. Barrow finds significance in the Bushman women's bodies' seeming to form a capital S. Archer, too, sees "S/ness" in the alluring "well-developed" black women of the American South, whom he collectively denominates "Sex." He might have, following the theme through to a conclusion, otherwise used "Seduction" and, of course, "Sin" as signs of the black female body in the semiotic of American race relations. The outlines of a morality play of race purity are visible here, revealing the lingering traces of the "blessed race" narrative in whose terms black Venus and her diseased attendants are all the devil's minions, cast into the American landscape to test the mettle of the chosen people. Because the availability to white males of black female sexual partners *on premises* represented a threat to the sanctity and stability of the white household, some fanciful histories of the Civil War featured the black Venus as an erotic warrior who defeated the South through passive aggression: "Some of the most thoughtful [white southerners] ascribed the fall of the South to the surrender of white men to the sex of black women. Flesh had smothered soul" (Williamson, *Crucible*, 448).

In his novel *The Clansman*, Thomas Dixon Jr. makes the hidden demonic power behind Austin Stoneman a mulatto housekeeper who sexually enthralls the senator, explaining the true origin of his hatred and humiliation of white southerners as the black Venus's revenge. Dixon depicts Lydia Brown as "a woman of extraordinary animal beauty and the fiery temper of a leopardess" (57), whose imitativeness and social aspirations were strongly marked by her "animal" reservoir of race instincts: "No more curious or sinister figure ever cast a shadow across the history of a great nation than did this mulatto woman in the most corrupt hour of American life. The grim old man who looked into her tawny face and followed her catlike eyes was steadily gripping the Nation by the throat. Did he aim to make this woman the arbiter of its social life, and her ethics the limits of its moral laws?" (94). In answer to this rhetorical question, Dixon reveals the personal pagan shrine Lydia Brown has set up in Stoneman's home, where beneath the "huge painting of a leopard . . . stood the magic green [gambling] table on which men staked their gold and lost their souls."

Dixon personifies Reconstruction's victimization of the South as the sexual sway of the leopard woman over the Nation's rational faculties. Having corrupted Stoneman, Lydia Brown tries to accomplish the corruption of his daughter by encouraging Stoneman's mulatto protégé Silas Lynch to court Elsie. The plan results in the near rape of Elsie; thus Dixon's portrayal of Reconstruction as the symbolic rape of the South focuses on white male seduction by black women as the point of origin for the "rape epidemic" of the Progressive Era. Stoneman's outrage at Lynch's attempt to marry his daughter finally awakens him from the sexual spell of Lydia Brown, as he confesses: "My will alone forged the chains of Negro rule. . . . When I first fell victim to the wiles of the yellow vampire who kept my house, I dreamed of lifting her to my level. [But instead] . . . I felt myself sinking into the black abyss of animalism, I, whose soul had learned the pathway of the stars" (371). Both a "human leopard" and a vampire, Lydia Brown simultaneously corrupts the white domestic sanctuary and the nation at large.[19]

What some have referred to as the cult of the "black lady" responds to this mythology by accepting the "condition of the black mother" as debased and in need of radical overhaul. Michelle Wallace's negative assessment of the campaign for black female uplift sponsored by the women's club movement stresses, like contemporary white critics of the "black lady" phenomenon, its "imitativeness": "One of the fundamental goals of these organizations was to uplift the black woman to the white woman's level. To achieve this, it seemed necessary to make her more of a lady, more clean, more proper than any white woman could hope to be. . . . Black women enacted a charade of teas, cotillions, and all the assorted paraphernalia and pretensions of society life. It was a desperate masquerade which seemed to increase in frenzy as time went on" (156). In contrast, Hazel Carby points to the club movement as an effort "to confront the various modes of [black women's] oppression," by agitating against imperialism, "Jim Crow segregation and the terrorizing practices of lynching and rape" and by pressing for women's rights, including suffrage (Carby, "'Threshold,'" 303–4).

The spirit that typifies the uplift movement for Carby was its "desire for the possibilities of the uncolonized black female body": "Black feminists understood that the struggle would have to take place on the terrain of the previously colonized: the struggle was to be characterized by redemption, retrieval and reclamation—not, ultimately, by an unrestrained utopian vision" (Carby, "'Threshold,'" 315). Yet Carby's focus on political agency does not entirely answer the critiques offered by Houston Baker and by Wallace, for even in their social agitation, black women uplifters typically idealized domesticity as a privileged realm from which black women were unjustly excluded. Literature's function of imagining black America would directly address the difficulties faced by this redemptive project and would similarly hold up the image of domesticated black womanhood as the measure of world-historical emergence. Thus Claudia Tate argues that black Victorian "domestic" texts emphasized upward mobility as a strategy for asserting social and political equality, such that even novels by black women writers featuring "raceless" characters foregrounded the bourgeois ideals of individuation and self-actualization as liberational discourses sure to resonate with black readers (59, 87).

Social Intercourse

The coincidence of the lynching craze of the late nineteenth century and the public agitation for segregation laws leaves little doubt that preventing inter-racial intimacy was a central concern of post-Reconstruction white "Redeemer" governments (Lofgren, 23). In 1890, during the campaign for legislation that ultimately led to the *Plessy v. Ferguson* decision, the editors of the *New Orleans Times Democrat* argued that Jim Crow should be extended to public transportation as well as hotels, restaurants, and schools: "The law—private, not public—which prohibits the negroes from occupying the same place in a hotel, restaurant or theater as the whites, should prevail as to cars also. . . . Whites and blacks may there be crowded together, squeezed close to each other in the same seats, using the same conveniences, and to all intents and purposes in social intercourse" (Olsen, 53). This lurid image of "social intercourse" between the races pictures white commuters squeezed into the same seats with blacks, forced to use the same rest rooms, and thus involuntarily exposed, it implies, to diseased black sexuality.[20] In describing equal public access ambiguously as "intercourse," the essay effectively genders the races by imputing a "masculine" aggression to the intrusive black passengers, while "feminizing" the passive, put-upon white populace attempting to defend its racial exclusivity.

These gender markings become explicit in the editorial's subsequent observation that "a man that would be horrified at the idea of his wife or daughter seated by the side of a burly negro in the parlor of a hotel or at a restaurant cannot see her occupying a crowded seat in a car next to a negro without the same feeling of disgust." For the scenario to generate the maximum emotional impact, the white female passenger embodies the white populace's reluctant coexistence with blacks. To further leverage public indignation, the editorial visualizes the black populace in the person of "a burly negro," imputing not only physical power but a transgressive bulk to the black body. Without specifying "Negro man," the wording requires such a reading, considering that this intrusive black body has forced itself into "social intercourse" with a physically defenseless white female body.

This use of the "white lady" class to justify Jim Crow separation reveals yet another instance of the interdependent analogies of bodies in space and bodies *as* social spaces. Customs regarding the access of black citizens to private white spaces had long since established this equivalence. Because of the strategic attachment of "race" to the body, nearly all physiological operations in the Jim Crow South, from dining to excretory functions, were politicized and mythicized (Myrdal, 610). One aspect of race discourse that nearly every postwar observer noted was the "post-prandial non-sequitur"—the idea that "if a Negro eats with a white man he is assumed to have the right to marry his daughter" (Myrdal, 603). White nationalists often cited interracial dining as a false first step of unconscious kindness into which the unwary white might blunder, an admission of blacks to the same social plane as defined by the common table, which "opened the door" to further demands for equality. Dixon's novel *The Leopard's Spots* offers this defense of the etiquette: "If you ask [the Negro] to your house, he will break bread with you at last. And if he eats at your table, he has the right to ask your daughter's hand in marriage" (242).[21] Dining in a white household was a boundary that could not be crossed in the South without incredible repercussions, as President Teddy Roosevelt discovered from the overwhelmingly negative public response after he asked Booker T. Washington to dine at the White House (Harlan, *Booker T. Washington*, 2:3–5).

But we can only dismiss the practice as a "non-sequitur" if we focus solely on its logical assumptions. Consider, for example, Nathaniel Shaler's explanation of the "post-prandial" prohibition as a measure enjoined primarily against white adolescents, a coming-of-age ritual signifying the need to shed their childhood black dialects as a precondition for entrance into proper white society.[22] Looking at its ritual function as a purgation of a contaminating African trace not permitted to survive in whites past the nondifferentiation of childhood makes the practice coherent as sympathetic magic.[23] Arnold van Gennep's *The Rites of Passage* compares ritual transitions between social states to a three-stage progression across territorial boundaries: separation, transition, and incorporation.[24] Van Gennep explains that threshold (that is, portal) rites form the most evocative class of separation practices, while banqueting and feasting usually mark the final rite of "incorporation," a rite structurally analogous to coitus in some magico-religious contexts (131, 169–70). Thus, "the commonest . . . taboos [in the Jim Crow South were] those against eating at a table with Negroes, having them in the parlor of one's house as guests, sitting with them on the front porch of one's home, and the like" (Dollard, 350), while blacks were forced to "come in at the back doors of houses and [were] quite strictly forbidden entering and even knocking on the front door, . . . carr[ying] the automatic implication that they [were] servants" (Dollard, 352). As John Dollard speculates, "our traditional techniques of court-ship center around the dining table, the parlor, and the front porch, as well as freedom of access by the front sidewalk and the front door. One who cannot share these privileges can hardly be expected to court the daughter of the family" (351).

For Dixon, the issue at hand was preventing the gradual erosion of a privileged domestic space by the systematic exclusion of the black citizen from the intimate operations of the white world. Prohibited from the front door, front porch, and parlor, blacks were effectively denied any foothold in American "kinship." For blacks in the Jim Crow South, the stage of separation from the social death of the enslaved black body was never supposed to occur. Nor were they ever to aspire to "incorporation." If indulgence of any bodily function as an expression of social parity symbolically binds those bodies, "marriage" merely giving a patina of re-spectability to the magical significance of the communal meal, then blacks were especially denied incorporation—intimacy, embodiment—with whites.

Such rhetoric of intrusive black presence builds on concepts of an ideal white "woman's sphere" that must be accorded protected status. According to Eliza-beth Fox-Genovese, the gender role assigned southern white women during the antebellum period emphasized their place in the home but not their preroga-tive to control domestic space: "Southerners, unlike northerners, did not view either families or households as primarily female preserves, but as terrain that contained woman's sphere. According to this view, women did not belong abroad alone; a woman alone on public thoroughfares was a woman at risk. . . . They were not fit to meet men on equal terms in the combat of public life and, should they attempt to, they would open themselves to being bested by superior physical strength" (195). "Women, like children, have only one right—the right to pro-tection. The right to protection involves the obligation to obey" (199). To obey means to stay in one's assigned place, to forgo competition with the household patriarch. Therefore, the discourse that invokes the image of a defenseless white female aboard public transportation cuts in two directions, emphasizing both the need for protection of women who travel alone and the need for women to remain in their secure domestic space away from the putative hazards of the modern world.

Hotel parlors and restaurants had come under Jim Crow restraints earlier than public transportation because as private establishments they clearly suggested extensions of white domestic space. The addition of public transportation to the category of racially restricted spaces goes one step further, then, in defining the boundaries of the sacred white hearth and home as coextensive with the white female body. "Whites should understand how it 'feels to get up from a first-class berth in one of the sleepers, to find that a Negro man has occupied the next berth during the night,'" complained a North Carolina woman in a letter to a southern newspaper (Lofgren, 14). Rhetoric invoking the sacredness of the southern woman's integrity would extend the required white male protection into public spaces without granting any authority to women over their own persons, since their need for protection merely certified their unfitness to be men's equals. Thus the gender mythology of the antebellum South was adapted to fit the greater social mobility of the Jim Crow era. If white women would not stay home, the concept of "home" would travel with them.

No such assumption applied to black women and black households. Albion Tourgée's legal brief in the *Plessy* case used similar rhetoric about the vulnerability of the female away from home and of public space as an extension of domestic space: "A man may be white and his wife colored; a wife may be white and her children colored. Has the State the right to compel the husband to ride in one car and the wife in another? Or to assign the mother to one car and the children to another?" (Olsen, 84). Tourgée then described the only circumstance in which the state did permit interracial cohabitation of space, under the doctrine of "preserving" domestic relations—the provision "applying to nurses attending children of the other race." As Tourgée pointed out, there were probably no cases of white nurses attending black children that would require such an exemption, so the statute must be designed to benefit the white race solely: "[The provision] simply secures to the white parent traveling on the railroads of the state, the right to take a colored person in the coach set apart for whites *in a menial relation.* . . . In other words, the act is simply intended to promote the comfort and sense of exclusiveness and superiority of the white race. They do not object to the colored person in an inferior or menial capacity . . . *but only when as a man and a citizen he seeks to claim equal right and privilege* on a public high-

way" (Olsen, 99; my emphasis).[25] Claiming that whites could actually enhance a
sense of spatial exclusivity by the selective *inclusion* of black people as menials,
Tourgée showed how whites manipulated gender beliefs to reinforce the concept
of blacks as a servile, *female* race. The black nurse therefore created rather than
destroyed white space, by ensuring that the social role of the "lady" would not be
disrupted by maternal obligations. The privilege of the white household to reconstitute itself in transit was absolute, while the law entirely disregarded the existence of the black household.

The convention of the "Ladies Car" on railroads (that is, for white women
only) illustrates the way that the state militarized the white populace against all
forms of black self-actualization, seizing upon the perceived discrepancy between white "ladyhood" and the "S/ness" of black womanhood into a division of
public space. "Usually," explains Charles Lofgren, "one first-class car would be
set aside for 'ladies and gentlemen accompanying them'" (11). This "Ladies Car"
would have strict codes of behavior, forbidding smoking and profanity alto-
gether: "These ladies cars were modern, with separate toilets for each sex, adequate heating and lighting, carpets, and upholstered seats," according to Lofgren.
The other cars, by contrast, "were combination affairs, the rear half for smoking
by both sexes and races, the front part for Negroes of both sexes, with a divider
and door between the halves" (144). In some instances, the Jim Crow car *was* the
smoking car, a situation that subjected black women and men to coarse behavior
by white males. Such cars often carried baggage, animals, and convicts being
transported by law enforcement officials (Lofgren, 22). Booker T. Washington,
arguing that "separate but equal" accommodations were not really "separate"
(let alone "equal"), complained about the lack of spatial exclusivity and "integrity" for blacks: "White men are permitted in the car for colored people.
Whenever a poorly dressed, slovenly white man boards the train he is shown into
the colored half coach. When a white man gets drunk or wants to lounge around
in an indecent position he finds his way into the colored department" (Lofgren,
16). Even Washington could see that Jim Crow separation had the important
function of reminding blacks and whites of the *dishonor* of caste inferiority by
the types of behavior the state considered permissible in the presence of black
women.

Two literary examples indicate the psychology of mastery implicit in white
male access to the Jim Crow car. In Chesnutt's *The Marrow of Tradition*, the
mulatto doctor Miller feels slighted by being locked in the Jim Crow car with

lower-class blacks.[26] Miller observes that the enforcement of Jim Crow laws actually mandated a condition of undifferentiated difference for black citizens: "It was a veritable bed of Procrustes, this standard which the whites had set for the negroes. Those who grew above it must have their heads cut off, figuratively speaking, — must be forced back to the level assigned to their race; those who fell beneath the standard set had their necks stretched, literally" (260). At the same time, Miller protests the right of white males to use the Jim Crow car for smoking over the objections of black occupants. Even when told by the conductor that he must leave, the racist Captain George McBane refuses to move, invoking the unwritten Jim Crow law that no white conductor can take the cause of a black rider in a dispute with a white customer. When he does decide to leave the car, McBane throws the cigar stump on the already unclean floor and adds "a finishing touch by way of expectoration" (258).

In Nella Larsen's 1928 novel *Quicksand*, a similar scene in a Jim Crow car occurs during Helga Crane's departure from the South, where she has been teaching. "A man, a white man, strode through the packed car and spat twice, once in the exact centre of the dingy door panel, and once into the receptacle which held the drinking water. Instantly, Helga became aware of a stinging thirst" (25). Mulatto Helga's toleration of the sights, smells, and sounds of American black public space dissolves once "that disgusting door panel to which her purposely averted eyes were constantly, involuntarily straying" reminded her of white America's contempt and unchallengeable right to defile black space. Helga understands that gesture as a territorial intrusion that emphasizes the powerlessness of those who have no alternative to the state-mandated black space of the Jim Crow car, so she pays a price twice the legal rate for a temporary domestic haven in a sleeper car. It is a minor incident but an important factor in Helga's determination to use her part-white ancestry to flee the dishonor attached to black social space.

Such unsupervised, unlimited white male access to the Jim Crow car was made possible by the existence of a "white lady" class that had to be "protected" from impropriety in as controlled and homelike an environment as could be managed. Since black women could not be ladies in the eyes of the state by definition, they were not entitled to similar deference, and sexual harassment by white males publicly reinforced their unprotected, dishonored status. The case of Mrs. Vera Miles in Pennsylvania in 1867, a black woman evicted from a rail car for refusing to move to a racially restricted zone, established a precedent, further, that allowed carriers to discriminate by race because the practice of gender separation—that is, the very existence of a "ladies car"—was so widely accepted that it argued the "reasonableness" of separation based on physical distinctions.[27] The very concept of gender, thus, was integral to the maintenance of Jim Crow: a racial dichotomy grounded in the differential social value of black and white female bodies governed Jim Crow distribution of the races into white and black public spaces. In the imagination of the black traveler, closed white space and unbounded black space were feminized terrains permeable in one direction only.

Jim Crow, Brownlow

According to Ray Stannard Baker, racial tensions on the streetcar and railroad lines were symptomatic of fluid definitions of race/gender boundaries. Where to place and how strictly to police the race line in the South was a problem each locality solved individually, the most economical system being not to designate specific seats by race but to allow the race line to move back and forth so as to accommodate the maximum number of passengers. Black passengers had to be prepared for rules that changed abruptly from one locality to another, and they had to be adept at reading shifting boundaries so as to avoid confrontations that could become violent. To Baker, the "absence of a clear demarcation is significant of many relationships in the South. The color line is drawn, but neither race knows just where it is. Indeed, it can hardly be definitely drawn in many relationships, because it is constantly changing" (31).

Baker's sense of a fluid, relational color line as a general condition of southern life identifies the way that the South accommodated economic reality in the enforcement of white space privilege. Because of the expense to the white community of complete separation from blacks, and because of the immense psychological gain afforded whites by allowing blacks conditionally into white space (as with the nurse exemptions),[28] the discourse of white nationalism in the South often depended on ritual performance of social space rather than territorial exclusivity. White space and black space emerged as functions of the mythicized relation of black and white bodies in motion. The psychic territory of race provisionally existed in the physical landscape for the convenience of whites, who required both exclusivity and freedom of movement. The notion of "the South as white man's country" tactically did not rule out the presence of blacks in that white nation, making for fluid, interpersonal demarcations of national identity.

The black traveler, moving through the racial map of the South, had to be able to read and script the body itself at a moment's notice to negotiate proliferating, shifting white space boundary rituals.

In his 1937 study *The Etiquette of Race Relations in the South: A Study in Social Control*, Bertram Doyle observed that race conflict in the postwar South occurred only when blacks refused to give appropriate signs of deference to the superiority of whites, explaining, "The free Negro was the source and origin of whatever race problems there were" (xxi). A proponent of Robert E. Park's sociological focus on stages of race conflict and accommodation, Doyle seems, in places, as much a catechist of Jim Crow behavior as an observer of race decorum in the South.[29] As Barbara Babcock has noted, "What is socially peripheral is often symbolically central." [30] If we accept Doyle's logic as representative, it is clear that the failure of blacks to maintain voluntarily the outward forms of social death, all the old obsequiousness and self-effacement of slavery that so reassured whites of their superiority, induced a crisis in white identity.

The compromise that allowed limited black interaction in the "white man's country" of the South was the one that directly addressed the hierarchical relation of legally free black and white bodies in space—what Lawrence J. Friedman has referred to as the "Brownlow tradition." Much like Doyle's description of race etiquette, the "Brownlow tradition" prescribed, in effect, the restoration of the outward forms of slavery's social death that emancipation had technically discarded. By returning to the social formalities of slavery, blacks would sufficiently reassure whites of their mastery to circumvent violent confrontation, as Doyle prescribed. This reconstruction of the black body took place quietly, involving only the psychic violence of enforced self-humiliation, while the violence of lynch law and rioting kept before the public eye the consequences of failure to conform. What the "Brownlow tradition" demanded of blacks was the performance of social abjection by a slavery-molded black body perpetually enacting its phylogenetic confinement to the "evolutionary backwash" of African time-space, an unthreatening allochronism of competent nonentity. The Brownlowed black body that Joel Williamson called "neo-Sambo" (*Crucible*, 479–80) stooped toward the ground, hung its head, made no sudden moves, removed its hat and always stood in the presence of whites, waited for whites to initiate social contact, averted its eyes to avoid seeming insolent, and tried, above all, to convince whites of its ineffectualness with an ingratiating smile.[31] In performing this social death, blacks placed themselves out of direct competition with whites by acting out their unequivocal unfitness for national affiliation.

According to Friedman, the Brownlow tradition combined the seeming contradictions of race expulsion and neoslavery by making white-approved enactment of blackness the basis of limited access to white space: "Brownlow would
permit *docile Negroes* to remain near whites, . . . [but] demanded the exclusion
of all *insolent, disrespectful blacks.*"[32] To Friedman, the essence of the Brownlow
tradition was a concept that could only be expressed as a contradiction: "The essential demand, it seemed, was for Negroes *to be in two places at once*—distant
from, yet near to whites" (31; my emphasis). This performed allochronism allowed blacks to be physically near, in order to better serve southern white aristocratic aspirations, while being metaphysically distant, in order to reinforce white
claims to superiority. If whites were seated, blacks had to stand at attention; if
whites stood, blacks had to crouch, emphatically avoiding the possibility of being
at the eye level of whites: in short, blacks constantly had to adjust their bodies so
as never to reside within the same social plane as whites, whether they met in a
public place, a white household, or even a black one. This performative race difference made it necessary for blacks to theorize the body, to become self-critical
of their bodies, and to develop arts of formal improvisation to meet changing circumstances. Despite evidence of numerous personal relationships that violated
this etiquette, what made it so psychologically destabilizing was that any white at
any time could suddenly demand performance and could enforce the demand
through violence, as Richard Wright made abundantly clear in his works.[33]

Conceptually, the Brownlow tradition created a new paradigm for the national body idea by reenvisioning the permanent presence of nonslave aliens
within the sphere of privilege. Even so, the idea of permanence was held in abey-
ance by fluid demarcations of black time-space. Gunnar Myrdal, writing during
the fourth decade of the twentieth century, was able to see in the South innumerable performances conforming to the ideology that the "lowest white man"
should count for more than the "highest Negro":[34] "[Southern white opinion] is
not satisfied with the natural rules of polite conduct that no individual, of whatever race, shall push his presence on a society where he is not wanted. It asks for
a general order according to which *all* Negroes are placed under *all* white
people and excluded from not only the white man's society but also from the ordinary symbols of respect. No Negro shall ever aspire to" such "symbols," explains Myrdal, "and no white shall be able to offer them" (Myrdal, 65).

To Joel Williamson, like Ray Stannard Baker, there was no "color line" in the
South, only this self-regulating system of ritualized interpersonal contacts wherever white bodies encountered black bodies (*Crucible*, 257–58). Gunnar Myrdal

saw this process as well, pointing out that such contacts at the boundaries of the parallel race worlds were the essence of Jim Crow, because the excessive formality of the ritual behavior made it almost impossible for any real communication to occur. Rather than actively avoid blacks, whites would often seek out opportunities for interaction with them because of the psychic benefits of such contacts with designated inferiors. A society that denied poor whites economic sufficiency compensated them primarily by technical inclusion into the time-space of the white nation. Poor whites' abusive enjoyment of status elevation by waylaying unwary blacks and making them perform rituals of self-abasement was legendary. In conversations that required whites to be condescending and even contemptuous, while blacks could not express any hostility, contradiction, or aggression, what got communicated was the asymmetry of power: "The racial etiquette is a most potent device for bringing persons together physically and have them cooperate for economic ends, while at the same time separating them completely on a social and personal level" (Myrdal, 612).

Myrdal refers to this social form as "'ceremonial' distance rather than spatial distance" (621). In fact, though, the concept of space is, as I have insisted, implicit in discourses invoking the "civilized" or the "primitive." To know the Jim Crow neo-Sambo was to know its discipline, the kinetic limitations of the docile black body enacting its incapacity for evolutionary progress.[35] Ironically, this black body imagined as black time-space itself, as the veil of mythicized flesh manipulable to white desire, invited speculation by white observers about the "plasticity" of black life—its limitless somatic freedom for childlike and regressive behavior. Blacks exploited knowledge of this paradoxical freedom-through-conformity by plying whites' psychic need for acquiescent, docile black bodies into the granting of material boons (Myrdal, 594). Whites and blacks who did this dance on the color line of American life invented, deconstructed, contested, and negotiated the social space that was called "race."

As Bertram Doyle suggested, black improvisation at the shifting boundaries of white space adopted a spirit of gamesmanship that disguised the black body's complicity in its own delegitimation (168). The "true emancipation of the Negro," for Doyle, was a pretended *preference* for Brownlow black space, a compensatory masking against self-recognition that discovered enormous freedom in the performance of white space threshold rituals. White nationalist anxieties over social hierarchy demanded abjection of blacks and invented the term "nigger lover" to discipline independent-minded whites who did not observe ceremonial distance

(Dollard, 353–54). For Gunnar Myrdal, the most striking aspect of American race ritual was its utter refusal to allow forms of interracial intimacy that challenged the formal requirements of Brownlow black docility. Whites were often scrupulous in their observance of race etiquette so as not to alarm their neighbors, and blacks even more so because of the potential dangers that could befall anyone with a reputation as a "sassy" Negro. Each white person encountered presented the possibility for violent verbal or physical confrontation, and to ward off such potential evil, blacks resorted to ritualized, magical behavior.

Dancing on the Color Line

In his short story collection *The Wife of His Youth and Other Stories of the Color Line* (1899), Charles W. Chesnutt included a story of an interracial encounter on an integrated street car. In "Uncle Wellington's Wives," Chesnutt captured the absurdity of Jim Crow through satire. When Wellington Braboy becomes terrified, in a predictable Brownlow tradition reflex, at the prospect of having to take a street car's only vacant seat between two white women during his first trip to the North, his fear of bodily contact with white women precipitates a chain of events that leads to the greatest of all southern horrors—racial intermarriage. Entering the car, Braboy will not even take the word of his northern host that it is permissible for him to run a gauntlet of white flesh, at the end of which the two women sit: "Wellington shrank from walking between those two rows of white people, to say nothing of sitting between the two women, so he remained standing in the rear part of the car. A moment later, as the car rounded a short curve, he was pitched sidewise into the lap of a stout woman magnificently attired in a ruffled blue calico gown" (*Collected Stories*, 219). Later, when Wellington applies for a job as a household handyman in the Ohio city of Groveland, the housekeeper who greets him turns out to be the very woman into whose lap he had fallen in the car—the widow Mrs. Katie Flannigan—announcing her lap's function as an ironic site of the American melting pot.[36]

A romance and then marriage ensue when the Irish Katie, "with a little of the native coquetry of her race," encourages Wellington's attention. "The prospect of securing a white wife had been one of the principal inducements offered by a life at the North" for Wellington (224), and Chesnutt takes the opportunity to poke fun at both Wellington's idle fantasy and the fears of the proponents of Jim Crow. By the story's end, Katie has abandoned Wellington for her first husband, who has returned after being presumed dead, and Wellington likewise returns to the South to the "wife of his youth."

The seduction and abandonment of the black male aspirant to American embodiment is the narrative core of Chesnutt's fable, a plot destined to become more familiar to black audiences in the years before the mass migrations to urban centers in the North.[37] Chesnutt's use of an Irish immigrant as a figure for the fickle North is intriguing cultural politics. First, Chesnutt knew the northern black men with white wives typically found them among immigrants unschooled in American racism (Ray Stannard Baker, 172). Second, in choosing an Irish woman, he focused on an immigrant group that was held in such low esteem in America as to make them the butt of ethnic jokes by blacks.[38] Broadly using Katie Flannigan to symbolize white America's immigrant past, Chesnutt also joins the question implicit in the color line regulations: how far were whites willing to go in propounding the myth of white female race chastity?

While the gross, opportunistic Katie embodies the brusqueness of northern interpersonal relations, the "wife of his youth" who patiently awaits his return to the South, Aunt Milly, is a black woman who gives a new twist to the mammy tradition, a southern Earth Mother with a progressive middle-class uplift agenda: "Externally she would have impressed the casual observer as a neat, well-preserved, and good-looking black woman, of middle age, every curve of whose ample figure—and her figure was all curves—was suggestive of repose. So far from being indolent, or even deliberate in her movements, she was the most active and energetic woman in the town" (209). Like 'Liza Jane in the title story of the collection, Aunt Milly seems more a mother figure to Wellington than a spouse. Her combination of girth and energy contrasts markedly with Wellington's childlikeness and lack of initiative. Wellington is a dreamer, and his departure from the South is hastened by the economic leverage that the industrious Aunt Milly holds over him. When the story opens, Aunt Milly's mild scolding of Wellington's improvidence drives him to seek an environment in which he can assert himself as the patriarch.

Wellington's departure for the North is akin to "the daughter's departure" that Houston Baker analyzes, similarly framed as a quest for the white world mapped in the patriarchal imprint upon his facial features: "Uncle Wellington was a mulatto, and his features were those of his white father, though tinged with the hue of his mother's race; and as he lifted the kerosene lamp at evening, and took a long look at his image in the little mirror over the mantelpiece, he said to himself that he was a very good-looking man, and could have adorned a much higher sphere in life" (207).[39] His quest is to embody the white father through that perquisite of power most jealously denied him by the South—the possession of the white woman's body. Learning from a lawyer that their slave marriage was not considered legal gave him a pretext for leaving Aunt Milly. Wellington's stereotypical lack of industry provides a "racial" context for his departure from this feminized figure of the South that tolerates Braboy but does not value him. Nominally both *"uncle"* and *"boy,"* he is never securely "husband," "father," or "man" in the Jim Crow South.

Chesnutt uses each of Wellington's wives as a pole of social experience in the belated coming-of-age of Uncle Wellington Braboy. In staking her own romantic claim, Katie Flannigan invokes the myth of black female depravity: "'Colored lady, indade! Why, Misther Braboy, ye don't nade ter demane yerself by marryin' a colored lady—not but they're as good as anybody else, so long as they behave themselves. There's many a white woman 'u'd be glad ter git as fine a lookin' man as ye are'" (225). But Aunt Milly's irreproachable domesticity undercuts Katie's devaluation of black womanhood, as one look at her house reveals: "Her savings were carefully put by, and with them she had bought and paid for the modest cottage which she and her husband occupied. Under her careful hand it was always neat and clean; in summer, the little yard was gay with bright-colored flowers, and woe to the heedless pickaninny who should stray into her yard to pluck a rose or a verbena" (210). Edward Mapp's observation that "the thin line between black mammy and black matriarch may be distinguished largely by whether the old girl is presiding over a white or black household" (quoted in Morton, 7) seems appropriate here. The childless Aunt Milly's hostility toward the ubiquitous "pickaninny" who threatens the orderliness of the domestic regime from without, as Wellington undermines it from within, is in the tradition of the mammy who, in the words of Patricia Morton, "regarded her own family with indifference at best," in contrast to "her tenderness to . . . white children" (34). In his paean to the mammy, Thomas Nelson Page charged that she was hostile to her own but devoted to her white "children," a cue taken by Shaler in *The Neighbor* and by Tillinghast in *The Negro in Africa and America,* in which he traces the black mother's indifference to her children to African origins.[40] Thus Aunt Milly's progressive uplift agenda betrays a scarcely concealed hostility toward black male and infantile delinquency, characteristics combined in Wellington Braboy.

In contrast to this emasculating South is the North of Wellington's fantasies. Chesnutt gives him an "imaginative faculty . . . freely bestowed upon him by [his] race" (206)—a gift that allows him to dream himself into the homogeneous, empty time of the nation. Conditioned by constant indulgence in a daydream of "an ideal state of social equality, . . . he saw in the North a land flowing with milk and honey," among whose "noble men and beautiful women, . . . colored men and women moved with the ease and grace of acknowledged right" (207). The most "pleasant of his dreams" is that of a having a white spouse who signifies his eligibility for national affiliation, and again Chesnutt uses domestic spaces to define character. In Wellington's fantasy, "the gracious white lady he might have called wife" had he been born in the North lives in a well-accommodated white household, "a two-story brick house, with a spacious flower garden in front, the whole inclosed by a high iron fence, [where] he kept a carriage and servants, and never did a stroke of work" (207). In the North, he will find such a house, but not as its genteel owner. Instead, he will be the servant who has charge of the carriage, while his stout immigrant wife runs the kitchen, as he squanders his comfortable stake in the black world for a tenuous foothold in white America.

Despite Aunt Milly's brusque treatment of Wellington, she proves to be a true woman in the end. Wellington returns home after his northern adventure to watch, through a "crack in the wall" of the little cottage, the courtship of Aunt Milly by that legendary racial miscreant, the rural black preacher.[41] Aunt Milly's profession of loyalty toward the husband who has abandoned her allows Chesnutt to make a case for the steadfastness of maligned black womanhood. Aunt Milly's neat, clean, bounded cottage is a product of her *restraint*; in direct contrast stands Katie Flannigan's abrupt departure one day when Wellington goes out to find work, taking with her all the household furnishings she can carry. Chesnutt's fanciful morality tale contrasts white female seduction and treachery with black female virtue and patience to describe a black male crisis of identity that strands him between gendered spaces of race affiliation. It helps the telling that Wellington is a mulatto, indulging a psychic duality that makes him restless for the horizon. But Wellington Braboy is clearly too a black Everyman who must choose between the seductive freedom of opportunity offered by the North and the circumscribed but physically undemanding life of the South.[42] Chesnutt's allegory simultaneously uses women to demystify white womanhood and to prescribe black female subservience as foundational gestures in black patriarchal development.

Imperium in Imperio

A different sort of color-line encounter occurs in a novel published the same year as "Uncle Wellington's Wives." In the fantastic events of Sutton E. Griggs's racial romance, *Imperium in Imperio* (1899), several key terms of the debate over public space also come into play. Where Griggs's hero, Belton Piedmont, differs from Wellington Braboy most strongly is that he has not been trained in Jim Crow race etiquette, and he comes close to losing his life through insensitivity toward the social boundaries surrounding the white female body.

Belton travels from the relative social freedom of Washington, D.C., on his way through the Deep South to take a position in Louisiana as a schoolmaster. The irregularity of the restrictions from one state to another are confusing to him, because "at that time, the law providing separate coaches for colored and white people had not been enacted by any of the Southern States. But in some of them the whites had an unwritten but inexorable law, to the effect that no Negro should be allowed to ride in a first-class coach. Louisiana was one of these states, but Belton did not know this. So, being in a first-class coach when he entered Louisiana, he did not get up and go into a second-class coach" (140). Whites of the South in Griggs's story, unlike their northern counterparts in Chesnutt's, do not hesitate to take offense at Belton's unwitting intrusion, particularly when a white woman enters the first-class car and has difficulty finding a vacant seat. Immediately, the white male passengers single out Belton as the cause of the white woman's momentary distress, and they seize him. After a brief, principled stand by Belton, the white passengers throw him bodily from the moving train.

Stranded at the next station, Belton compounds the error by taking a seat in a segregated restaurant. When the owner castigates him for trying to eat on the premises, Belton refuses to purchase the food that has been prepared, whereupon the owner summons policemen, who jail Belton and fine him for vagrancy. Arriving at his destination, Belton attracts the attention of a ghoulish doctor, who covets a black body with Belton's physique for his dissecting experiments. An equally sadistic postmaster, secret leader of the local "Nigger Rulers," agrees to kill the schoolmaster and deliver his body to the doctor, as soon as he steps out of line.

That moment comes years later when Belton, returning a courtesy call from a white minister, goes to a white church and takes a seat: "During the opening exercises a young white lady who sat by his side experienced some trouble in finding the hymn. Belton had remembered the number given out and kindly took the book to find it. In an instant the whole church was in an uproar. A crowd of men gathered around Belton and led him out of doors. . . . They decided that as it was Sunday, they would not lynch him" (151). The minister slams the door in Belton's face when he tries to explain himself, and it clearly is only a matter of time before Belton's inability to conform to Jim Crow performance expectations leads to calamity.

Lynched by the mob—they hang him and shoot him once in the head—Belton miraculously survives owing to the doctor's lust for his body.[43] At the doctor's insistence, Belton has not been burned or riddled with bullets, as was customary in lynchings, and upon being taken to the doctor's dissecting room, he recovers in time to kill the doctor and escape. In the even more fantastic conclusion to the episode, Belton goes on trial for murder before a jury composed of the postmaster and other "Nigger Rulers," but he ultimately gains acquittal when the Supreme Court overturns his conviction. While not deliberately verging into satire, Griggs counteracts the mythic dimensions of Jim Crow with surrealism and melodrama, illustrating in the process the reliance of the amateur anthropologist, criminally in league with the forces of social and political suppression of black citizens, on a steady supply of black corpses.

Framing the story of Belton's adventure in Louisiana is the issue of the shattered home life that causes his departure. His wife, Antoinette Nermal, "famed throughout the city for her beauty, intelligence and virtue" (113), bears a child in a scene that would seem a parody of white fears of atavistic birth were the social context not so obviously critical to black familial stability. "Belton bent forward to look at his infant son. A terrible shriek broke from his lips. . . . The color of Antoinette was brown. The color of Belton was dark. But the child was white!" (186). Prior to the appearance of this specter of slavery's despoliation of black family relations, Belton's own penchant for the bizarre had already poisoned his mind on the subject of black female virtue. Forced by poverty to take various odd jobs, he had resorted to transvestism, disguising himself as a woman on occasion in order to secure work as a household domestic. Part of his education had been the discovery, while disguised as a maid, that white men saw any economically dependent black female as fair sexual game, and when, after rebuffing his seducers, he became known as a "virtuous prude," Belton found that his reputation for modesty only strengthened the resolve of white men "to corrupt him at all hazards," including kidnap and attempted rape (134).

As a "defender" of black women's character ever since his college days, Belton does not entirely disown Antoinette after the scandalous birth; instead, he "buries" her image in his heart and strikes out to Louisiana to devote his life to racial uplift. "Woman . . . occupied the same position in Belton's eye as she did in the eye of the Anglo-Saxon," the narrator assures us. "There is hope for that race or nation that respects its women" (82). Griggs's sentimentality shows no trace of irony, in spite of Belton's contradictory experience as a "woman" among the Anglo-Saxons. Eventually, when he has given up all hope of a normal home life with Antoinette and has become active in a radical organization called the "Imperium," Belton returns home to discover that his child has turned dark! The lightness of skin had been a temporary state, preventing everyone from seeing that his features are identical to Belton's. In a nod to recapitulationist ideas of unitary racial origins accounting for infantile nondifferentiation, Griggs has called into question the very concept of atavism. Antoinette's vindication in the end comes too late to save Belton, but he dies a martyr to his ideals, happily assured that his wife's virtue is intact and therefore that he is a martyr to the founding of a black patriarchal order.

Griggs's incredible tale, like Chesnutt's of the same year, identifies black female restraint as the critical factor in the black male quester's successful return to the domestic circle. While Chesnutt's black mother figure Aunt Milly (whose daughter has died in infancy) must prove herself in the face of the preacher's amorous assault, Antoinette has had to bear her husband's alienation of affections and communal ostracism, owing, in both cases, to the low esteem in which black womanhood was held. Seeing Aunt Milly as a mammylike surrogate of the system that has emasculated him, Wellington abandons her for the woman whose embrace means freedom from corporeal and psychic restraint. Leaving Antoinette under a cloud of suspicion, Belton too has struck out on the road, only to encounter white female images of danger and freedom that all but doom him. Scarcely concealed behind this pattern is the suggestion that black men who are secure in their domestic integrity have no need to venture abroad.

Both Griggs and Chesnutt chose to emphasize counterimages to the dominant culture's representation of black women. Their combined message that black female virtue would be proved over time, after much persecution and condemnation, strikes a mystical note—an anticipation of black female (and through her, black race) redemption in the discourse of the domestic black madonna. Griggs was explicit in the terms of this redemption—as explicit as the detractors of black women were in the source of their condemnation: blacks would have to become, like Anglo-Saxons, a race that practiced female virtue and race chastity to develop race integrity. The black patriarchy must be secure in the legitimacy of its offspring and the exclusivity of its women's affections. In this regard, Belton's situation is only slightly less incredible than the marital history of his friend (and alter ego) Bernard Belgrave. Bernard's fiancée commits suicide after reading too much "scientific" race mythology. Convinced by a book that increased hybridity would lead to racial extinction, she kills herself rather than marry mulatto Bernard (173–75). Ultimately, Griggs's story is more fascinating as an allegorical staging of concepts influencing the future of the black body in America than as a work of realism.

The approved solution to a destabilizing hybridity was race chastity, a systematic filtering of the racial stock to achieve a lost "purity" and, by extension, an elusive wholeness. But the first step to "race chastity" was the institution of codes of female sexual conduct. The legacy of slavery's delegitimization of black female chastity would have to be overcome before black women could be elevated into vessels of racial purity. The true "empire within the empire" is the black family circle, which partially explains why the Imperium failed. Unstable familial relations make Bernard Belgrave dogmatic and inflexible as a leader and make the martyr Belton Piedmont practically suicidal in his persistent testing of the color line.

Thus Chesnutt's and Griggs's stories collectively appraise the circumstances under which black patriarchy could reasonably take hold. In each instance, female submission to male dominance is part of the equation. Wellington returns to North Carolina intending to throw himself at Aunt Milly's mercy, going back to a condition wherein she is the "undisputed head of the establishment" (209). But when he hears Aunt Milly explain to the preacher that in spite of Wellington's exposing her to abuse and ridicule, she would take him back if he were to return, he walks in confidently, acting as if he had never really left. Belton's wife submits to his withdrawal of affection and eventual departure without complaint and greets his return without bitterness or criticism. In an extreme of self-abnegation, Bernard Belgrave's fiancée kills herself rather than precipitate the extinction of the race. Such gestures of feminine submission interpellate, or call into subjectivity, a responsible black patriarchy;[44] Wellington signals his return by performing the final chore Aunt Milly had set him to before his escape, and Belton and Bernard go on to their individual martyrdoms secure in the knowledge that their women have not mocked their heroics by giving aid and comfort to their enemies. But each inaugural step toward black patriarchy is voluntary. The lack of communal pressure enforcing masculine responsibility toward women reveals how each generation of black families symptomatically has had to face a potential vacuum of masculine authority and the consequences thereof.

The Test of Manhood

The discourse of utopian black ladyhood emerged as forcefully from the struggles of black men over territorial rights to "the previously colonized" bodies of black women as from the women's club movement, whose agitation for feminist causes put them at odds with the proprietary claims of the emergent black patriarchy. This explains why Aunt Milly's program of social uplift in "Uncle Wellington's Wives" features a domestic antisepsis that denies Wellington's manhood rights as well as emancipates Aunt Milly from the troublesome presence of "pickaninnies." By the end of the narrative, Aunt Milly's signal of willingness to submit herself to the wayward Wellington, as well as her display of exemplary sexual fidelity, allow Wellington to return to the household with his manhood intact, rather than as a supplicant.

Even more idealized images of black women as essentially beautiful and chaste arose in a countermythology of black womanhood that openly challenged the myth of the wanton black female. William Pickens of the NAACP wrote that "the most virtuous creature in the United States of America is the Negro woman. Her resisting and enduring powers are of the highest order" (quoted in Friedman, 141). In the rhetoric of black female reconstruction, the black Venus metamorphosed into a deified image of chaste, sapient womanhood: "Free from white violation, she was the Athena of the race" (Friedman, 141). But the rhetoric of redeemed black womanhood was saturated with masculine desire. According to Friedman, "though the black men who exalted her obviously wanted to protect her from the white male, they may also have wanted exclusive rights to her body. . . . Efforts to protect black women were elements in a broader campaign . . . for blacks to fornicate exclusively with other blacks." As one postemancipation spokesman observed, *"All we ask of the white man is to let our ladies alone,* and they need not fear us. The difficulty has heretofore been our *ladies were not always at our disposal"* (Gutman, 388). The black madonna was therefore born out of the utopian desire for both a sexually innocent black womanhood and a sexually responsive but race-exclusive black womanhood.

The myth of black female depravity, so important in imagining the difference between the white and black communities, became a crucial question in the development of black national literature. Black writers vehemently attacked the casual assumption that an animal nature lay at the root of black female sexual history in America. Instead, they insisted that the experience of slavery, "two centuries of systematic legal defilement of Negro women, . . . had meant not only the loss of ancient African chastity, but also the hereditary weight of a mass of corruption from white adulterers, threatening almost the obliteration of the Negro home" (Du Bois, *Souls*, 6).[45] In disputing the assumed benevolence of slavery, writers such as Frederick Douglass and Harriet Jacobs established slavery's dual violation of women's domestic sanctity: its sexual exploitation of black women and its transformation of the white household into a hell through the demonization of white women.[46]

The history of the black home during and after slavery contrasts sharply with the discourse of domestic sanctity that permeated white nationalism. Race demagogue James K. Vardaman campaigned for governor of Mississippi in 1900 exclaiming, "We would be justified in slaughtering every Ethiop on the earth to preserve unsullied the honor of one Caucasian home" (quoted in Gossett, 271), effectively illustrating W. J. Cash's assertion that the white woman was "the standard for [southern chivalry's] rallying, the mystic symbol of its nationality in face of the foe" (Cash, 86). White nationalism locates its origin in the "unsullied . . . Caucasian home," and more specifically, in unsullied Caucasian womanhood, according to Cash, to divert attention from the rampant tales of southern white male lechery. "The only really satisfactory escape [from distant northern criticism of white male sexual promiscuity] . . . would be fiction"—the myth of the white lady.

If the white female was the spiritual essence of the white household—the woman as domestic space—then the black woman, except where attached to the white household, served as an image of the allochronistic wilderness of black life, the embodiment of the essentialized African continent. This concept of the black race as a wilderness, upon whose docile, feminized body whites expanded their drive for mastery, anchored the movement toward the "benevolent internal colonialism" of Jim Crow (Fredrickson, 325). So pervasive was the association of the black home with wilderness that Bertram Doyle recounts an anecdote of a respectable black woman arrested for "vagrancy" while she sat on her own front porch (155). One of the achievements of African American writers at the turn of the century was in showing that lynch law and black female concubinage continued the tradition of imagining the black household as an open, un-bounded, primeval space—as wilderness.

In Pauline Hopkins's novel *Contending Forces* (1900), the home-as-wilderness motif dramatically underscores the tragic histories of Grace Montfort and Sappho Clark. Grace Montfort's African ancestry is the pretext for the murder of her hus-band, English-born West Indian planter Charles Montfort, by the Carolina whites among whom he has moved. Headed by Anson Pollock, a citizens' "committee on public safety" attacked the members of the Montfort family and, "to legalize the looting of the house, took possession of the mansion," stripping it "of its fur-niture and all the articles of value. The house itself was fired, and . . . the dead body of [Montfort] flung amid the burning rafters of his dwelling" (70). Tradi-tional associations of women with domestic space allow Hopkins to dramatize the dismantling of the house as correlative to the state-sanctioned rape of Grace Montfort, an event that occurs therefore figuratively, if not actually, prevented in all likelihood by Grace's suicide after she and her children become the personal property of Anson Pollock. Pollock takes Grace's foster sister and personal ser-vant Lucy to be his concubine in her place, and the Montfort sons are separated, never to see each other again.

The story of Sappho Clark likewise centers on the violation of the sanctity of the household. Her story is told at a mass rally in Boston of the American Col-ored League, a meeting called to protest a brutal lynching in the South. White Republican congressman Herbert Clapp addresses the assembly in Tocquevil-lean terms, explaining that "miscegenation [by law in the South] . . . being out of the question, nothing remains for the Negro but to be dominated by the white man there" (246). He declares that the "Negro in American civilization" repre-sents a "national" problem that can only be solved by the voluntary withdrawal of blacks from politics. In response, Luke Sawyer rises to tell the story of his own family's destruction by whites jealous of his father's prosperity. His father was lynched, his mother and sister raped and killed, his baby twin brothers killed by having their brains dashed out against the side of the house, and finally, the house itself burned. Luke escaped to the temporary haven of a planter named Beaubean, who had married a quadroon woman. But later, the daughter of this household, Mabelle, was kidnaped by her white uncle from a school outing at the age of fourteen, raped, and discarded in a house of prostitution. When Beaubean threatened legal retaliation against his brother, he too fell victim to mob violence, and his house burned to the ground.

The synonymous violation of households and women continues into the novel's present in the Progressive Era, when Sappho Clark, the erstwhile Mabelle Beaubean, is confronted about her history by a mulatto descendant of Anson Pollock. John Pollock Langley barges uninvited into Sappho's room in the Smiths' boardinghouse, reenacting all of the past spatial violations of black women's domestic sphere, and threatens to use Sappho's past sexual history to destroy her impending marriage to Will Smith unless she becomes his mistress. Sappho flees Boston for the South, leaving Will Smith to decide how his patriarchal aspirations might be affected by his newfound knowledge of her sexual past. Hopkins stresses that violation of domestic sanctity is structural to black life. "'Your child is no better than her mother or her grandmother,'" Mabelle's uncle explains to his brother, offering a thousand dollars to pay for any "damage" he has done. "'What does a woman of mixed blood, or any Negress, for that matter, know of virtue?" (260–61). Guided by the sentiments of the imperious club woman, Mrs. Willis, to the effect that black women should not be judged for actions committed "under compulsion," the discussion of black female virtue as a consequence of American slavery makes possible the imagining of a utopian past ("Travelers tell us that the native African woman is impregnable in her virtue") that disrupts assumptions of an essential black female depravity (149). Still, a prevailing "condition of the mother" marks women like Grace Montfort and Sappho Clark as perpetually vulnerable to violation in the absence of a patriarchy capable of defending their domestic integrity.

In a short story that looks back toward Chesnutt's "Uncle Wellington's Wives" and "The Wife of His Youth," Hopkins makes the mulatto male's choice to return to the black mother figure "The Test of Manhood" (1902). Mark Myers deserts his mother, "who could not be mistaken for a white woman" (115), leaving the South to pass as white in the North. He becomes the fabled poor boy who makes good, though he is periodically troubled by thoughts of his mother, who, meanwhile, has ventured to the North in search of him. The red-turbaned Aunt Cloty becomes the pet social rehabilitation project of Katherine Brown, the daughter of Mark's employer, and on Christmas Eve, Katherine inadvertently effects a reunion of mother and son when Mark goes to visit her at home with the intent of proposing marriage. In the act of announcing his engagement to Katherine, Mark encounters Aunt Cloty, who unmasks him by claiming him to be her son: "Mark stood as if carved in stone, in an instant he saw his life in ruins, Katherine lost to him, chaos about the social fabric of his life" (119). Defiantly, he embraces his mother, formally renouncing any claims to marriage with Katherine and the life of material ease that was to be his future for the chaos and ruin of black life to which he must return.

Hopkins's Christmas story, with its ghost of the past who reclaims Mark for the descent line that begins in Africa, locates in an ironic epiphany of madonna and child the topos of the son's departure and return. Mark's physical features bespeak Aunt Cloty's dalliance with a white man, so to embrace Aunt Cloty means for Mark to embrace the sexual history that produced him. His dilemma is parallel to Will Smith's before him in the sense that his dream of social ascendancy must come to terms with the revenant horror of black female concubinage. Mark must bridge the "gulf he saw yawning between them" (115) in their social stations by voluntary return to the mother. Unlike Wellington Braboy or Mr. Ryder, Mark's return to the black mother here is not a matrimonial one but one that redeems the mother's sexual past through her idealized maternal role. Mark's challenge, further, is not in being accepted as a man at home but in surrendering his privilege as a white man in the world at large to become a black man able and willing to support and protect his womenfolk.

Will Smith has also assumed a figurative paternity after the disappearance of Sappho, by making plans to develop a school of higher learning for gifted black students: "No wife or child would ever be his, he told himself; but he would be a father to the youth of his race" (386). An appeal on behalf of his ailing mother, now living in the South with his sister, brings him to New Orleans. On the way he dreams of being in a cathedral, when, standing before the altar, he sees a vision of the "Virgin and Child, but the face of the mother was Sappho's" (386–87). This dream vision confirms the transformation that has occurred with Sappho, who, returning to the Holy Family Convent where she attended school as a girl, devotes herself to being a mother to the child she bore after her violation by her uncle. Will finally meets Sappho at the convent quite by accident, and the reunion ends happily with the sanctification of their marriage.

Sappho achieves in full acceptance of her motherhood a redemption she could not accomplish by trying to escape her past. In Louisiana, she not only has been dutiful toward her son but has been gainfully employed as a governess in a mulatto family. Not quite a "mammy," she conducts herself with such dignity that her employer offers her an honorable marriage prior to Will's reappearance. Hopkins's granting to Will a vision of the Virgin signifies his acknowledgment of Sappho's essential blamelessness as a woman "more sinned against than sinning."

His return to Sappho occurs primarily because she returns to her motherly duty, and Hopkins draws her tragic history to a happy conclusion by the constitution of a family unit both conscious of and adjusted to the past, as well as dedicated to uplift in the future.

The emergence of a black domestic madonna as a literary type and a cultural icon negotiates a range of definitions of black female essence. The madonna redeems the black Venus by respecifying her origin as slavery, not Africa, and by finding a male protector who can counteract the corruptive force of white male sexual predation, removing the stigma of centuries of "uterine filiation" legislated by slave statutes. She redeems the mammy, too, by redirecting the mammy's energies toward the stabilization of the black household, again through the presence of a black male breadwinner who can afford to have his wife remain at home. And she revises the black lady's aspiration to social equality with men by concluding that what the race needs at this historical moment is "manhood." Thus, while she may work for uplift in church or school, she refrains from active competition with men for social recognition.

For its advocates, the social emergence of this deified black lady would rouse latent black manhood, just as the rhetoric of Jim Crow called upon white men to prove their manhood by protecting white women's virtue. But it was a curious manhood, in terms of the way that white southerners understood the term, that could serve as protector of womanhood yet forswear all aggressive behavior, for the Brownlow tradition of the South would accept no action that even hinted that blacks thought themselves men. One can imagine Dr. Lewis, Will's brother-in-law and a Booker T. Washington–style head of an industrial education program, prospering in the South, what with his denunciation of politics for blacks and his other accommodationist postures. But Will would not thrive in such an environment, given his ambitions for black youth. What whites taught through the various reigns of terror during the unsettled days after emancipation and Reconstruction was that the sustenance of a class of unapproachable ladyhood required a willingness to kill anyone who intentionally or accidentally challenged the concept of female purity. Blacks in the South were certainly in no position to do anything of the sort to protect the reputation of black women, and so the cult of the black lady found more success in the North and in the large southern cities, where interracial contact and conflict could be minimized.

The myth of undefiled white womanhood that became so politically useful to the South that it even influenced national politics and legislation was burned into the brains of blacks in the South—a nightmare image, not of the black collective imagination, but a psychosis implanted deliberately by whites through acts of incredible cruelty. In opposition to woman as embodied black wilderness stood woman, the image of white nationalism. The usefulness of black and white female bodies in establishing the boundaries of social space became a central feature of ritual behavior in the South that spawned a second revenant, the fatal white woman, as the eternal return of white American will to exclusivity.

CHAPTER FOUR

The "White Delilah"

The negro, now, by eternal grace,
  Must learn to stay in the negro's place.
In the Sunny South, the Land of the Free,
  Let the WHITE SUPREME forever be.
Let this a warning to all negroes be,
  Or they'll suffer the fate of the DOGWOOD TREE.
    — "The Dogwood Tree," the caption to a picture of five lynched black men in
      Sabine County, Texas, in 1908

In W. E. B. Du Bois's 1928 novel *Dark Princess: A Romance*, a scene aboard a train in the South conveys a hint of the precariousness of color-line etiquette in the era of Jim Crow. Matthew Towns is a college-educated medical school dropout whose career crisis comes when he fails to get permission to study in the obstetrics hospital because as a black man he cannot be given access to white women's bodies, especially not to their reproductive organs. Working as a Pullman porter after leaving medical school, Matthew inadvertently precipitates a tragedy aboard a train carrying whites to a Klan convention when he substitutes in his co-worker Jimmie's car while Jimmie finishes a hand of poker. In Compartment D, a white woman passenger commands Matthew to open her window, a task requiring him to transgress the social space around her body: "There came over him at the moment a subtle flash of fear. She was a large woman — opulent and highly colored, and she lay there on her back looking straight up into his eyes. Her breasts were half covered — one scarcely at all. . . . The window flew up, but his hand came down lightly on the woman's bosom. Again came that gust of fear. He glanced down. She did not stir, but looked up at him with slightly closed eyes" (76). The collision of these two bodies in the social stasis of the Jim Crow car is fraught with tension, mythicized by the white female's interposition of her body between Matthew's safety and the fulfillment of his menial role. The commonplace act of raising a window becomes a test of southern black male socialization because if he fails to perform the task, the woman can charge Matthew with disobedience to a caste superior; on the other hand, by performing the act, he makes forbidden contact, which even more puts him at the woman's mercy. Whether as doctor or as manual laborer, as upwardly mobile member of the bourgeoisie or as lowly guarantor of whites' status elevation, Matthew has been moving irrevocably toward such a test of his ability to negotiate the crosscutting boundaries of "white space," the shifting, contingent prerogatives of American color caste preference. Matthew's double jeopardy leaves no room for manly assertion or manly retreat; each docile act requires a potentially fatal transgression of race decorum.

A sharp transformation occurs when the woman's male companion walks in on the encounter precipitating the very crisis Matthew had feared: "The woman's face changed in a flash. She screamed shrilly as Matthew started back and drew the sheet about her: 'Get out of here, you black nigger! How dare you touch me! I asked you to raise the window!'" Matthew's willingness to approach the woman despite the obvious danger suggests a pattern earlier hinted at in his application for the obstetrics hospital—underestimation of the potency of the custom that used white women's bodies to delimit the range of black physical and social mobility. Later, after Matthew has gone into hiding, the Klansmen on the train discover that the car had been assigned to Jimmie and they lynch him. The summary execution of Jimmie is a refusal to grant black men any individuality. By the lore of the undifferentiated difference of blackness, they are irrevocably linked in their biological predisposition to commit sexual assault, in any case, so "guilt" is not so much a matter of whether a black male has committed a crime as it is a matter of whether a black male has had an *opportunity* to commit a crime. As a Georgia penitentiary official summed it up, "The only difference between colored convicts and the colored people at large consists in the fact that the former have been caught in the commission of a crime . . . and the latter have not. The entire race is destitute of character" (Tolnay and Beck, 18). For Jimmie, blackness itself was the crime.

The significance of Jimmie's lynching goes beyond the whites' refusal to grant individuality to black men, for Jimmie's death represents yet another lost opportunity for the development of black patriarchy. Prior to the train trip, Jimmie had taken Matthew to his Atlanta home, "a pretty little cream and green cottage. It was tiny, but neat, and there was a yard in front with roses still blooming. Before Matthew could ask what it all meant, out of the house came a girl and the tiniest of babies" (74). Du Bois describes the wife as demure, race chaste, and African featured. "Never thought of marrying a black girl," Jimmie confessed of the woman who redeemed his faith in black womanhood after he had been betrayed by a "high yaller" in Harlem.[1] Jimmie's wife is more than simply the clean, neat emblem of black ladyhood; she is the symbol of black domestic integrity—the madonna with child. A foreshadowing of his own future, this image touches Matthew in a way that activates an instinctive urge to protect them: "Suppose something happened in Chicago or to this train; to this boy with his soul full of joy, and to this sweet-faced little black wife?" (75) he had asked himself, before Jimmie's death by lynching.

Racial divisions marked by, on, and reproduced through the bodies of women in African American literature gave them a major role in shaping the critical moral choices posed by those works. The South's elevation of white Christian womanhood as the thing it dedicated itself to preserving necessitated the utter separation of white women from black males to maintain "her enormous remoteness to the males of the inferior group" (Cash, 116). Its designers intended this remoteness to exist both as a social space, in the form of specific taboos concerning black male interaction with white female bodies, and as a phylogenetic space, symbolizing the "evolutionary gap" between the races as represented by the physical differences between their respective bodies. As a rhetorical gambit, the mythic confrontation of the white woman and the black male in white nationalist literature served both to silence distant critics of southern violence and to suppress internal agitation for equality by black males and white females alike. Inscribing all white female bodies with a text of white nationalist desire, such discourse defined the black egalitarian as, by definition, an intruder, a rapist, a violent claimant to the feminized, nonconsenting white body politic. If the race line existed anywhere, it existed on the body of the white female, the always/ already victim of violent black intrusion.

But if southerners were, in their own words, fighting race mixture to preserve their style of life, it was not a fight directed against a system of sexual interaction that, in symbolism and material advantages, sustained the concept of white male

mastery—black female concubinage. Rather, "race mixture" almost always translated into images of a black male penetration of privileged white space implied
by black male/white female relations. The explicit threat presented by emancipation was its undoing of the statutes that had created slavery and race in America through fixed lines of descent, opening the way for individual desire to find
expression in the absence of state suppression. Even outside the South, whites
associated black American political and social equality with black male desire
for the bodies of white women as a confirmation of national belonging. Ronald
Takaki's summary of antiblack sentiment in the North prior to the Civil War reveals that the South's postwar paranoia about black "brothers-in-law" had already
cropped up in other parts of the country wherever blacks gained any degree of
personal freedom.[2] Thomas Dixon's "test" of white egalitarianism—"giving"
one's daughter in marriage to a black—challenged white men naive enough to
believe in a color-blind nation to stake their family honor and the fate of their
lineage on the consequences of their misguided idealism: "When she sinks with
her mulatto children into the black abyss of a Negroid life, then ask him!" (Clansman, 460). Dixon supported the South's disproportionate attention to white female "race chastity," asserting that "the South must guard with flaming sword
every avenue of approach to this holy of holies" because the survival of a "white
man's government, conceived by white men, and maintained by white men
through every year of its history . . . [until] the end of time" (Clansman, 333, 442)
rested upon the determination of white men to protect the "holy of holies," the
white womb, from even the covetous gaze of the defiling black male.[3]

The political analogue to this "test" of white egalitarianism was the attempt to
smear Abraham Lincoln as the "father" of a racially hybrid America during his
presidential reelection campaign in 1864. The "misalliance" of American idealism and black social ambition to rise above "nature" was the theme of David
Croly and George Wakeman's subversive pamphlet Miscegenation: The Theory of
the Blending of the Races, Applied to the American White Man and Negro. In a
Democratic Party attempt to smear Republican politics as race mixing, Croly
and Wakeman published the pamphlet anonymously, posing as Republican supporters of Lincoln's Emancipation Proclamation who exulted in the fact that the
Civil War would not stop with securing the freedom of blacks but was merely the
first step toward ensuring "the blending of the white and the black."[4] L. Seaman's later pamphlet, published after the election, What Miscegenation Is!: What
We Are to Expect, Now That Mr. Lincoln Is Re-elected, raised the rhetorical stakes.
Its cover showed a white female and a grotesque black male in profile, kissing.

Seaman exaggerated the sharp physical contrast between their "racial" features: the woman's straight, flowing hair, her extreme paleness, her high brow, thin nose, and thin lips are deliberate contrasts to the tightly curled hair, fleshy nose, thick, brutish hands, and extreme darkness of complexion of the black man.[5] While the woman's facial features are rather conventional, the black man is clearly a figure out of the minstrel iconography of African morphological difference. As Robert Toll has noted, "Minstrel blacks did not have hair, they had 'wool.' . . . They had bulging eyeballs, flat, wide noses, gaping mouths with long, dangling lower lips, and gigantic feet with elongated, even flapping heels. At times, minstrels even claimed that Negroes had to have their hair filed, not cut; that when blacks got sick and pale, they drank ink to restore their color. . . . Male minstrel characters described ideal women with feet so big they 'covered up de whole sidewalk' or lips 'as large as all out doors,' or so large a lover could not kiss them all at once" (67). Seaman's black man, too, has lips "so large a lover could not kiss them all at once," threatening to engulf his mate's.

The same "racial" disparity emphasizing faces in profile would later be used in Nazi propaganda against Jews. George Mosse's *Toward the Final Solution: A History of European Racism* (1978) reprints a Nazi propaganda drawing from *Antisemitismus der Welt in Wort und Bild* (1935) that shows an Aryan maiden in profile superimposed over an older, Jewish male, also in profile, who faces in the same direction.[6] In both the American and Nazi propaganda drawings, sensual, thick lips, the "Jewish" nose with its phallic suggestiveness,[7] and the animalistic and carnivorous "snout" of the black help to metaphorize social "deviance" into a specific threat to white women. In the Nazi art, the Jew has a distinct leer on his face, while the dazed Negro of Seaman's cover art tilts the woman's face up- ward to receive his kiss, circling her shoulder with his pawlike hand. The exag- geration of the facial features contrasts the white females' greater elevation of forehead to the more "prognathous" facial features of the ethnic males. Their broad coarseness seems poised to overwhelm the delicate women, because, and I will return to this point later, the facial disparity encodes the threatening geni- tal disparity of the lower-body stratum. The strongly accented sexual threat in both drawings invokes white male intervention that leads, in one direction, to lynch- ing and, in the other, to a "final solution."

These uses of profile in graphic body politics stem from the ideological propo- sition that spatial dimensions of bodies reflect their relative capacities for intel- lectual and moral achievement. What faces in profile show most clearly is the "race" trait that seemed so critical to craniometrists since the early nineteenth century, the facial angle. According to John S. Haller,

> the facial angle was the most extensively elaborated and artlessly abused criterion for racial somatology. To compare the races, Petrus Camper (1722–1789) had suggested the facial angle. Basically it was a "horizontal line . . . drawn through the lower part of the nose . . . and the orifice of the ear." The angle formed by this horizontal line and the characteristic line of the face made up the facial angle. Using this index, Camper arranged the forms of crania. "The two extremities . . . of the facial line are from 70 to 100 degrees," he wrote, *from the negro to the Crecian antique*; make it under 70, and you describe an orang or an ape; lessen it still more, and you have the head of a dog." (9; my emphasis)

This politicizing of aesthetics into a spatial gradation of intellectual gifts arranges the human varieties into a veritable "Chinese box" of cranial capacities, with the greater facial angles of white Europeans encompassing and surpassing the phylogenetic potentials of all others.[8]

As with the body politics of visual allegories of America, black somatic atavism would be juxtaposed to classicized white faces to argue graphically the disparity not only of race difference but of evolutionary predisposition. An illustration in *Indigenous Races of the Earth* (1868) by Josiah C. Nott (who described his field of study as "niggerology")[9] and George Gliddon clearly shows the order of "descent," using the profiles and crania of "Apollo Belvedere," a Negro, and a young chimpanzee in sequence to illustrate the contrast between the African and the classical Greek.[10] As Haller points out, the facial angle was not only classicized but classical in origin, having been "used as early as Aristotle as an indication of intelligence. . . . The Greek sculptors, in representing superhuman attributes of their gods, gave the deities a facial angle of 100 degrees, exceeding that of the highest human" (9). Classical Greek aesthetics established the ideal of the superhuman with respect to the way that certain somatic features of nose, jawline, and brow reflected an expansive cranial capacity, spawning, among other race myths, the teachings of the pre-Adamites, who argued that Africans departed so demonstrably from traditional concepts of deity that they could not possibly have been created, as Adam was, in God's image.[11]

The use of the classicized white female form by Seaman to personify the sublime exaggerated the somatic difference of black male bodies not simply as a fact of science but as a specific threat to the socius. The very act of placing the classicized white female in physical contact with the grotesque ethnomorph was provocative, a "violation" of the peculiar spatial demands of the classical. As Peter Stallybrass and Allon White explain, "The classical body . . . keeps its distance. In a sense, it is disembodied" (22). According to Hugh Honour, the influence of the anatomical theories of men like Camper and Lavater on aesthetics became so pronounced by the early nineteenth century that Western art in general came under revisionist scrutiny. Staging a white Desdemona across from a black Othello, according to Honour, came to be seen as a perversion of Shakespeare: "Even the gentle and usually humane Charles Lamb asked if anyone who had seen a black-face actor in the part [of Othello] 'did not find something completely revolting in the courtship and wedding caresses of Othello and Desdemona.' The conjunction had come to seem almost a form of bestiality." According to Honour, two dramatic interpretive innovations developed as a result: an 1803 editor of Shakespeare wondered whether the deaths of the lovers should not, in light of Othello's blackness, be considered "fit" rather than tragic; and later artistic representations of the Moor rendered him "tawny" rather than black, Europeanized his profile, and reconstructed his nose, brow, and jawline to give him a classicized "nobility." [12]

Provocative juxtapositioning of black male bodies and white female bodies similarly lent a coherence to the rhetoric of lynching in the post-Reconstruction era. The South after white political "Redemption" set about the task of stripping black men of the citizenship rights they had gained through the Fourteenth and Fifteenth Amendments to reduce the black population to an antebellum state of political and economic powerlessness, and one of its chief propaganda weapons was broad circulation of a narrative of white women and children besieged by an "epidemic" of sexual assaults by black men. "When a knock is heard at the door, [the southern woman] shudders with nameless horror. The black brute is lurking in the dark, a monstrous beast, crazed with lust. . . . A whole community is frenzied with horror" (Fredrickson, 278). In the Jim Crow South, this indelible image of postslavery black regression came to stand for the whole principle of race separation, as the logic of keeping the black brute away from the vulnerable white female through legislation, forced conscription of blacks into chain gangs and work farms, and extralegal violence became conventional wisdom in southern life. To fashion this narrative into an all-purpose political instrument required two acts of erasure: interracial rape had to be reinvented as the "new crime" of postwar conditions, and the long-standing fear of white female depravity had to yield, at least publicly, to a new presumption of race chastity.

"It is a fact that no one will deny," said Thomas Nelson Page, "that the crime of rape was substantially unknown during the period of slavery, and was hardly known during the first years of freedom: it is the fatal product of new conditions" (84). The image of the noble male slave faithfully manning the domestic fortress while the master went off to war found adherents among African Americans also, who seized upon this grudging concession to counter charges of a biological predisposition by blacks toward sexual assault.[13] But for Page and other racists, the praise was an insignificant part of an argument that only the close supervision, strict discipline, and limited mobility allowed by slavery could hold in check the African's biological imperative. Despite southern nostalgia for the trustworthy slave of old, however, according to Martha Hodes, "convictions for the rape of white women were not, in fact, unknown to black men before and during the Civil War" (73). Hodes cites records indicating an unexpected leniency to black males accused of rape before the Civil War, suggesting that the antebellum understanding of forced or consensual interracial sex involving white women was contingent upon specific social circumstances, a radical difference from postwar narratives of race. "Black men could be acquitted or pardoned on charges of raping white women; white husbands could be denied divorces even if their wives had committed adultery with black men; and the black men in such adultery cases could go without retribution" (Hodes, 59).[14] The key to this pronounced discrepancy in antebellum and postwar treatment of interracial sexual activity was twofold. First, the monetary investment in black male slaves made capital punishment a costly remedy, and so slaveholders' property interests sometimes could and did take precedence over claims by lower-status whites.

And second, the tradition of white female purity was largely a class-based phenomenon: "Those who held authority in antebellum Southern communities were likely to consider poorer white women to be the depraved agents of illicit liaisons, including liaisons with black men. Thus could white ideology about lower-class female sexuality overshadow ideas about the dangers of black male sexuality" (Hodes, 60). This tradition of white female depravity, as we have seen, was very pronounced in the colonial period and continued as a way of framing class distinctions. Thus in order to produce the hysteria about the "new crime" of rape from Reconstruction on, apologists of lynching simultaneously had to ennoble the long-lost, lamented black of slavery times and to invent the new tradition of universal white female race chastity. The second objective required violent male intervention and an intensification of social pressure to ensure universal conformity, in spite of which white females continued to test the boundaries of permissible behavior. The result was a discourse about the way that political and economic opportunity had bestialized black males into a threat to white women, whom, prior to the decimation of white males during the Civil War, the blacks had feared to approach. To get to the fatal white female depicted in Du Bois's *Dark Princess* required the invention of a "crime" and a punishment—lynching—with unprecedented social implications.

Recent historians of lynching have raised important cautions about psycho-historical approaches.[15] Lynching did not, despite its advocates' claims, restore white supremacy or squelch all black enterprise. Its contingent, arbitrary application as punishment at best served to shore up the ideological fiction of white solidarity, but the symbolism of a united white populace did nothing to change the material relations between the planter elite and the landless sharecroppers and yeoman farmers. According to Stewart Tolnay and E. M. Beck, white yeoman farmers were dramatically pushed toward landlessness and sharecropping during the height of the lynching craze, and their economic marginality resulting from fluctuations in the price of the staple cotton crop increased their competition with blacks for scarcer and scarcer resources. Prevented by the retaliatory capability of the planter elite from taking out their frustration on grasping white landowners, the lower-status whites turned to the virtually risk-free substitute of violence against blacks as a way of reaffirming their social status and in many cases violently wrested property from black competitors (Tolnay and Beck, 157–60). Instances of terrorism against the planter class likewise typically took the form of "whitecapping" the cheaper black labor and sharecroppers the landowners relied on to increase their profit margin, in order to force whites to employ whites only (Brundage, 23–25). Because black scapegoating did not address the causes of severe divisions among whites, lynching could not be counted on to produce any lasting white solidarity or to effect any lasting structural changes. Yet it did have as important outcomes the maintenance of a docile black population and a visual representation of white nationalist desire, either in accordance with the planter ideal of racial hierarchical feudalism or the white yeoman ideal of race-exclusive geopolitics.

Despite the difficulty of "typifying" lynchings as ritually identical events with predictable social outcomes, I will nonetheless offer a psychohistorical reading of lynch law. W. Fitzhugh Brundage's *Lynching in the New South* aims at showing the hazards of uncritically classifying lynchings as communal exercises (17–19), but he discounts the importance of two aspects of lynch law that did provide coherence over an incredible three-fourths of a century. One was the rhetoric condoning lynch law that Ida B. Wells-Barnett identified as the myth of the "one crime" of rape (*Lynchings: Southern Horrors*, 4). This rhetoric did not make distinctions between lynchings but sought, rather, to justify lynching in general as the only effective means of controlling sexual assaults by black males against white females. According to Tolnay and Beck, lynchings on the grounds of sexual assault decreased markedly after the height of the lynching craze in the 1890s, yet the rhetoric of the "one crime" did not change (49–50). The "one crime," therefore, was for most of the period of lynching inarguably a subterfuge behind which whites concealed a wide range of political, economic, and status-related violence. What was strikingly consistent about the phenomenon was not its causation but its justification, the persistence of the "one crime" rhetoric over time and against the widely disseminated statistical evidence to the contrary.[16] For decades, federal antilynching legislation failed because powerful southern legislative lobbies argued that black "barbarism" required equally "barbaric" retribution, reminiscent of contemporary arguments that private citizens should have access to assault weapons, despite the potential for their tragic misuse, because criminals have such weapons. Lynching's apologists insisted that the social cost of lynchings used to remedy trifling affronts to white status claims or for the prosecution of personal vendettas against blacks was a small enough price to pay in terms of social disruption in order to sustain the availability of the only reliable expedient against black sexual assaults. Lynching's coherence as a social phenomenon of the late nineteenth and twentieth centuries was not based on any singleness of cause or on the regularity of its ritual performance, then, but on the way that the myth of the "one crime" was endlessly enlisted in the suppression of internal communal dissent, in the exoneration of the lynchers, and in the organized opposition of southern politicians to federal intervention.

The second factor was the rhetoric of the violence itself. Brundage has asked, fairly, how diverse events with different motives, audiences, and levels of attention to ritual practice could deliver a coherent "message" about such vague concepts as "white solidarity" or "white supremacy" (12–13, 18–19). But the "message," I will argue, was the event itself: the murder of black citizens by whites who with reason felt little fear of retribution. The message was that whites could plot and execute the murder of blacks, whether singly, in small groups, or in mobs brought in by special excursion trains, on a bewildering variety of petty and nonsensical pretexts, and with almost absolute impunity. The relationship between the "one crime" rhetoric and the lack of consequences for white lynchers was what sustained lynch law for more than three-quarters of a century in "modern" America, and to do so, it must have had compelling conscious and un-conscious significances for its practitioners and apologists. Understanding lynch-ing's rhetoric as a restaging of the old problematic of black and white bodies in American space helps to situate lynching's cultural meanings as a folk institution and mechanism of social repression.

I intend, therefore, to discuss lynch law to illustrate how its narrative of "one crime" authorized and graphically set about accomplishing the era's black body of death through two types of violence, rhetorical and corporeal. Lynch law vio-lence shaped body ideas in American culture during the era of black renaissance by expelling African Americans from the human community and by arguing that black deaths were the necessary precondition for white race survival in America. As a result, the black body of death gained a recurring visual representation through lynching and its justification, repeated with gruesome regularity and of-fered as a morality tale crucial to national imagining through circulation in print and visual media. The longevity of lynching as rhetoric and ritual asserted the appropriateness of black national disaffiliation by expulsion, Jim Crow quaran-tine, and, especially, the reimposition of the performative social death of the Brownlow black body—social death as the only alternative to literal death. Be-cause lynch law rhetoric was as important an influence on black literature of the period as the lynching ritual itself, I will first explore the ways that lynching encoded its social significance into the body politics of its core narrative.

Race, Incorporated

The aftermath of the *Miscegenation* controversy, the enfranchisement of black males and the extension of black citizenship rights through the Fourteenth and Fifteenth Amendments produced a new set of social relations in the defeated South that spawned both legislative and vigilante suppression of former slaves as well as the political allegory of the "besieged South." This allegory drew emo-tional power from graphic representations of the South as an imperiled white female, picking up where the symbolism of Seaman's *What Miscegenation Is!* drawing left off. James S. Pike offered an indelible portrait of Reconstruction as an overtly sexual death struggle between the black male, newly endowed with political power, and the besieged southern body politic in his 1873 book *The Prostrate State: South Carolina under Negro Government*. Pike lamented, "The negro . . . rests like an incubus upon [the southern states]. Their vital forces pul-sate under ribs of iron which will not give them play. It is the man from Africa who today bestrides them like a colossus. He came in helpless, he has risen in strength. He was the servant of South Carolina; he has become her master" (68). Pike hinted that white male mobilization was the subtext of this narrative, observing, "[It cannot] be expected that the white man will long stand passively by" (68–69).

The appeal to white male intervention likewise infused the incendiary 1871 leaflet by A. Zenneck on the plight of another "prostrate state." Zenneck's drawing depicts the metaphorical rape of the state of Louisiana, over the legend "Murder of Louisiana/Sacrificed on the Altar of Radicalism." [17] Zenneck personified Louisiana as a half-naked, supinated white female body with her arms and legs stretched over an "altar" by brutish blacks under the control of an imperious "Ulysses I," who, with a sword dangling suggestively over the figure's pelvis, has cut out her heart under the guidance of Attorney General George H. Williams, depicted as a winged demon. A second white male figure (apparently William Pitt Kellogg, later Reconstruction governor of the state) [18] holds the still bleeding heart aloft in one hand, resting his other hand inside the exposed, bleeding chest cavity, a slightly displaced but barely disguised genital wounding that symbolizes the unlawful intrusion of the federal government into the "internal affairs" of the states. To the right, the other states embodied as classically garbed "virtues" await their turn on the altar behind "South Carolina," who kneels, chained at the neck, hands, and feet. It would take the evolution of the myth of the "one crime" to turn this political allegory into a social threat believable enough to complete the mythicizing of Reconstruction as rape in the public mind. Once in circulation, the political allegory of rape—the unlawful seizure of and intrusion into the body politic—gave an entirely new resonance to any actual sexual assaults that occurred. Rather than a powerful white slavemaster to defend him against bodily harm, a black male accused of assault had only the hated (and by 1880, long departed) federal troops to save him from the mob. The myth of the "one crime" would thereafter equate black political, social, or economic assertiveness with fiendish erotic desire, such that any physical contact with actual white female bodies would be scripted as the inevitable outcome of a new postwar black male assertiveness.

"The [black] rapist is a product of the reconstruction period," Myrta Avary proclaimed bluntly in her 1906 "history" of Reconstruction, *Dixie after the War*. William S. Morrison's 1909 history of South Carolina also depicted Reconstruction as a time when blacks were "taught by designing leaders that they were as good as white men, entitled to sit in the white man's parlor, to take to wife the white man's daughter": "The negro rapist, the black brute, fear of whom hangs like a dark cloud all over the south land—who is in latter days found and lynched—is a direct product of the teachings and practices of the days of reconstruction" (102–3). To Thomas Nelson Page, white "Redemption" produced a "temporary and partial ending" of both rape and lynching. But the taste of freedom experienced by "new issue" blacks had whetted the black male appetite for white women: "The intelligent Negro may understand what social equality truly means, but to the ignorant and brutal young Negro, it signifies but one thing: the opportunity to enjoy, equally with white men, the privilege of cohabiting with white women" (112–13).

Discounting such late revivals of the romance of the "prostrate South" as Claude Bowers's *Tragic Era* (1929), which proclaimed that "rape is the foul daughter of Reconstruction" (308), W. J. Cash theorized the existence of a "Southern rape complex" in the "mind of the South," a form of mass hysteria that interpreted "any assertion of any kind on the part of the Negro . . . [as] an attack on the Southern woman. What they saw more or less consciously in the conditions of Reconstruction was a passage toward a condition for her as degrading in their view as rape itself" (119). To Cash, because the status "degradation" of the white woman that resulted from black males suddenly appearing in positions of equality or even superiority was "thought of as being absolutely forced upon her as rape, . . . the term 'rape' stood as truly as for the *de facto* deed."

Interracial sex involving white women struck at the core of white identity, capturing the anxiety of a white population deprived of its signature social institution, slavery, and forced for a period of years by federal troops to submit to equal treatment with its former bondsmen. According to anthropologist Mary Douglas, "no other social pressures are potentially so explosive as those which constrain sexual relations," because to a beleaguered minority, "these social conditions lend themselves to beliefs which symbolize the body as an imperfect container which will only be perfect if it can be made impermeable" (157–58). South Carolina—which Pike called *A Prostrate State*, where Thomas Dixon set *The Clansman* and Myrta Avary set much of her sentimental history *Dixie after the War*, and where Ben Tillman came to power after employing fraud and intimidation to thwart majority rule—became a special case in the southern lore of Reconstruction precisely because whites there *were* a minority. But even in other parts of the South where whites were numerically superior, the cherished postwar illusion of being a besieged stronghold of natural aristocracy helped to define its "paranoid style" and activate pollution rituals as expressions of patriotism. Lynch law's seemingly spurious insistence on the "one crime" of sexual assault may have been less a stubborn refusal by whites to acknowledge the statistical data to the contrary than a revelation of lynching's social function of making the "imperfect container" of white space "impermeable" to black intrusion.[19]

The symbolic interrelationship between the corporeal, domestic, political, and geographical domains in the discourse of race nationalism insisted that hierarchical transgression in any of these realms signaled a society in crisis. Lynching and other vigilante violence during Reconstruction attempted symbolically to reverse the supplanting of loyalist white male rule, while post-Reconstruction lynch law attempted, conversely, to counteract the symbolic erosion of white male authority exacted by the remaining vestiges of black political, social, and economic assertiveness. The very act of expelling transgressive black bodies from society through lynching, regardless of the nature of the offense punished, restored the white body politic to its idealized image as a classical, exclusive, virginal, intact, pedestalized emblem of social order. Thus Thomas Nelson Page envisioned the "destruction of Negro domination at the South" as a resuscitation of the injured body politic: "burdened as she was by debt; staggering under disasters that had well-nigh destroyed her; scarred by the struggle through which she had gone, and scorched by the passions of that fearful time, [the South] set herself with all her energies to recovering through the arts of peace her old place in the path of progress" (52). On the other extreme, the dystopian picture of an egalitarian South presented by William B. Smith played on the theme of the social equality of races as "pollution": "The standing of the South would be lost irretrievably. . . . The world would turn away from her, and point back the finger of suspicion, and whisper "Unclean!" (18).

D. W. Griffith's 1915 film *Birth of a Nation*, based on Thomas Dixon's *The Clansman*, tapped into this symbolic language equating bodies, domestic spaces, and the body politic, depicting in its grand finale of the Ku Klux Klan's rescue of white women from the clutches of uniformed black rapists an allegory of southern "Redemption." Besieged white women and besieged white houses throughout the film effectively characterize political equality as a pretext for black intrusion into every cherished social institution. Early scenes dramatize the security of the southern home as a refuge from the public space of the streets, where upstart black Union soldiers brusquely shove the former Confederates off the sidewalks and openly ogle their women. Midway, the film's sacrificial white virgin,

Flora Cameron, kills herself to escape being waylaid and raped after she strays from the protective environs of the home where her father and brother wait help-less to assist her.[20]

Ultimately, the white home as an institution is nearly reduced to a wasteland beneath the force of relentless black male assaults. In the movie's climax, Griffith repeatedly cuts back and forth from claustrophobic close-ups of black federal soldiers breaking down doors and windows of two white households (in one in-stance, they reach their hands through windows and doors to pull swooning white women out) to panoramic outdoor shots of the gathering Klan riding to the rescue. At one point Griffith frames a white father preparing to use his sym-bolically empty pistol to club his daughter to death to protect her from a fate worse than death. But he narrowly avoids catastrophe when the timely sounding of the Klan horn alerts him that salvation is imminent. The sometime scholar Woodrow Wilson assisted this mythicizing of Reconstruction with his remark af-ter a private screening that Griffith's film "history" written in "lightning" was "all so terribly true" (Cripps, 52). To the extent that Dixon and Griffith were able translators of the dream of a white nation, their depiction of "social equality" as permission to rape white women was less a case of "writing history with light-ning" than capturing mythopoeia in celluloid.

Such suggestive transformations of Dixon's verbal harangues in *The Clansman* into Griffith's indelible images of "social equality" run amok apparently called forth from Dixon a title more expressive of his white nationalist sentiments: *Birth of a Nation* (Williamson, *Crucible*, 175). Not only were blacks intruders poised to invade white houses and white female bodies, but their very presence in a "mod-ern" civilization was a form of intrusion. The content of the film seems at first glance inhospitable to any sentiment favoring innovation, given its overt ante-bellum nostalgia. But the film's promotional campaign featuring its technologi-cal novelties established its status in cinema history from the outset, subtly con-flating the mythic time-space of race nationalist romance with the unfolding drama of technological progress framing the event. The film's publicity pitches made sure that the audience would make this connection by giving the technical merits of the production equal billing with the movie's "historical" content. The advertising stressed the *national* import of the film, proclaiming it "A Red Blooded Tale of True American Spirit" and "A Composition of National Figures with the Universe as Its Background." Making much of the novelty of the event, the promotional ad boasted that this "Mightiest Spectacle Ever Produced" provided "The Most Realistic and Stupendous View of Stirring Events in the

Development of Our Country," using technology so new that the Liberty Theatre had to have the "House Remodeled According to Scientific Adjustment of
Focal Requirements."[21] This emphasis on the ambient modernity of the theatrical experience made the presence of politically and sexually assertive black characters doubly transgressive. In contrast to conventions of race difference that made
spatial coexistence possible by means of temporal distancing, Dixon's rhetoric of
black regression, filmed with only a few revisions by Griffith, was a compelling
argument for the wholesale expulsion of blacks.[22]

   Griffith's script turns Austin Stoneman's constant commands to his mulatto
protégé to stand up "like a man" into a visual pun on black regression, having the
white actors in black roles make exaggerated simian gestures, especially an "anthropoidal slouch" that has them practically dragging their knuckles across the
floor.[23] Such clever stagings of the old ape libel, along with the grotesque blackface makeup on the "Negro" characters in a drama trumpeting its documentary
fidelity, emphasize the otherworldliness of blacks and make it irrelevant that the
whites are in period dress themselves. Thus in spite of the film's celebration of
white men putting on sheets, pretending to be knights of old and pledging a
return to rites of the ancient Scottish clans as a kinship pattern somehow crucial
to the future of America, Griffith's cinematography, through improved technological "authentication" of the past, and his staging of blackness as evolutionary
regression simultaneously reinforced the belief that whites possessed a "racial"
monopoly on modernity. Looking back at Reconstruction "outrages" from the
privileged time-space of national progress assured white audiences of the allochronistic rightness of Jim Crow, lynch law, disfranchisement, peonage, chain
gangs, and all other practices promoting racial disaffiliation. Lawrence J. Friedman
has noted the contemporary audiences' consumption of Griffith's images as a
fantasy solution of the "Negro problem," and Dixon's national promotional campaign made sure that the "Presidentially endorsed" epic would indelibly link the
efflorescence of the modern cinema with the dream of a white America (171–72).

   Dixon's novel staged its appeal to modernity and evolutionary progress in a
more explicit fashion than the Griffith film, using popular science theatrics to
expose regressive black criminality. In The Clansman, the renegade Gus, along
with "four black brutes," succeeds in raping young Marion and the widow Lenoir
in their home, in contrast to the film's botched rape attempt on Flora. Flora (imported into the film script from Dixon's The Leopard's Spots) jumps to her death
before Gus can ravage her; the Lenoir women in The Clansman jumped after
the fact. After the suicides of the two Lenoir women, and after the discovery of a

footprint bearing "the deep wide mark of the African's foot" near the house, Doctor Cameron conducts a pseudoscientific experiment to discover the identity of their attacker. Believing that "nothing is lost from the memory of man," Cameron uses a microscope to find the photographic, "fire-etched record of this crime" (313) on the retina of the dead women's eyes.

Dixon's flair for popular science here mimics Twain's use of fingerprints to distinguish between the black and white principals in *Pudd'nhead Wilson*. Dixon's constant reminders that vestigial animal features distinguished black bodies gave ample occasion for the whites to establish their Darwinian superiority. "The white man was never born who could make that track," Dixon says of Gus's footprint. His science taught that the African body always betrayed itself, always left traces.[24] Whether the picture on the retina was truly Gus or just Dr. Cameron's imagination, its significance lies in the fact that the African particularly always leaves a trace when it comes into contact with the white female body, even if only in the prophetic imagination of the white scientist. Yet the scientific tracing of the African "footprint" at the scene of the crime merely substitutes the locus and method of discovery of the physical examination previously made by Dr. Cameron offstage. The other, unannounced examination for sexual assault was one that sought a more telling "footprint" of black male intrusion, a trace that was, in the discourse of the "one crime," "unspeakable."

Robert Shufeldt insisted that the mere presence of blacks in American social space was "extremely bad and the knowledge of [black sexual interest in white females] react[ed] disastrously upon the minds of [white men's] daughters and wives throughout the country" (*Problem*, 112–13). Shufeldt's insistence that the very sight of blacks permanently scarred the white female psyche explains why blacks caught in the field of vision of white women were sometimes lynched. Dixon's interest in anatomy, biochemistry, mesmerism, and human psychology suggests that for him the purpose of science was primarily the revelation of innate black criminality as the single threat to American modernity and progress.

The appeal to progress is part of a larger rhetorical strategy that surfaced in this era, ironically arguing the need for whites to revert into the savagery of lynch law in order to preserve intact the evolutionary promise of the perfectible white nation. Dixon's archvillain in *The Clansman* was a mulatto demagogue whose name fairly called out for mob action, Silas Lynch. Lynch is the novel's Frankenstein monster, created by Senator Stoneman "as a cold-blooded scientific experiment" (183), an embodiment of the "Mulatto Republic" Stoneman hoped to found as his revenge on the South. It is Lynch who stirs the black Piedmont community into carrying the invasion of white space to its logical conclusion, when, in a clear instance of authorial ventriloquism, he announces the whites' deepest fear as the blacks' most pressing desire: "'The world is yours. Take it. Here and now I serve notice on every white man who breathes that I am as good as he is. I demand, and I am going to have, the privilege of going to see him in his house or his hotel, eating with him and sleeping with him, and when I see fit, to take his daughter in marriage'" (275). At Lynch's (and Lydia Brown's) instigation, the first act of the black-dominated Reconstruction legislature in Griffith's film version (visually designed after Pike's infamous description of the "mongrel legislature" in *The Prostrate State*) was to legalize racial intermarriage, putting the federal government behind even the ultimate "bad marriage," rape.[25]

The recollection of black Reconstruction outrages that surfaced reflexively in justifications of lynching implies that each violent seizure of authority by the white populace, whether in throngs of thousands or in small terrorist groups, ritually reenacted the mobilization of whites to overthrow Reconstruction itself. Any accusation of black "criminality," from theft to economic ascendancy, constituted an attempt to restage Reconstruction's "rape" of the "prostrate South," by this logic. Lynching's apologists, to be sure, did not overtly use the "one crime" in a metaphorical sense. They argued that only the terroristic violence against the black body that lynching provided served as a deterrent to more sexual assaults. But in explaining the southern mind-set that permitted such spontaneous recourse to torture and other forms of terroristic sadism, lynching's advocates habitually revisited Reconstruction as the lingering horror in the white southern imaginary that activated lynching. As the historical moment when the docile black population became infected with the dream of social equality, Reconstruction's legacy of black participation in the affairs of the nation had to be purged from southern life whenever it resurfaced in the transgressive behavior of the black masses.

At the same time that he declared that he could not "justify the practice of lynching on any ground whatever," Yale University's James Elbert Cutler observed in his 1905 investigation of lynch law that the practice made perfect sense from the southern point of view: "From the standpoint of the Southerners during the period of Reconstruction summary procedure [lynching] was wholly justifiable. To men living in a community where a particularly brutal and barbarous crime is committed on a white person by a negro, the prompt lynching of the negro, even with some torture and cruelty, seems entirely defensible" (226). For lynching's apologists, such as Methodist bishop Atticus Haygood, black criminality was a continuation of Reconstruction's imposition upon the forbearance of the southern people: "Southern white people have borne themselves, under trials *never known before in history*, as well as any people in the world could have borne themselves. . . . It is absolutely certain that, in their ordinary dealings with the negro, the Southern white people are kinder to him and more patient than any other people who come into relations with him. Cruelty of disposition does not explain the torture of the demon men burned to death for assaulting helpless women and tender little girls. The Southern people are not cruel and never were."[26]

Rather than defend lynchings of suspected thieves or perpetrators of other petty offenses, lynching's advocates chose the surer ground of representing rape as the "one crime." In "The Black Shadow in the South," Bishop Haygood, dean of southern "paternalists" and a self-proclaimed friend of what he was pleased to call "the brother in black," quoted a fellow clergyman's estimate that "three hundred white women had been raped by negroes within the preceding three months" (169). The bishop went on to speculate that his colleague had *underestimated* the true figures, recalling that he had never heard of more than a single case of "outrage" before the war. Haygood offered no proof of his or his colleague's assertions, but his alarming projections of the proliferation of black criminality and his previously quoted blanket defense of southern intentions toward blacks, coming from a self-styled advocate of black causes, were widely accepted as damaging "proof" that the black beast was more fact than fiction. Based on this single premise that lynching was irrevocably tied to the rape of white women, Haygood admonished "sane men" to consider the "provocation" as well as the barbarity of the lynching itself: "remember not only the brutish man who dies by the slow fire of torture; . . . also think of *the ruined woman, worse tortured than he*" (168; my emphasis).

Haygood's "ruined woman" served a dual role as archetypal female victim of black male sexual aggression and as the image of the white race incorporated, the "prostrate South" dominated by the postemancipation black brute. Haygood's injunction that nonsoutherners attend the sufferings of the "ruined woman" of the South rather than those of the black victim of lynching uses the analogy of "torture" to link their bodies as the twin foci of lynching's theater of cruelty. This symmetrical pairing of bodies through corporal punishment recalls Michel Foucault's discussion of torture as a "quantitative art of pain" executed to emphasize a correspondence between "the type of corporal effect, the quality, intensity, duration of pain, with the gravity of the crime, the person of the criminal, the rank of his victims" (34). Foucault's study of torture argues that, as a public "ceremonial by which a momentarily injured sovereignty is reconstituted," the aim of punishment was "not so much to re-establish a balance as to bring into play . . . the dissymmetry between the subject who has dared violate the law and the all-powerful sovereign who displays his strength" (48–49).

The frontispiece to Thomas Hobbes's *Leviathan* illustrates the collective citizenry whose assent in the king's personation of the state forms the immortal element in the secular metaphysics of sovereignty.[27] In lynching, where the "sovereign" was presumed to be the white racial mass itself, the terrorizing and displaying of the broken body of the condemned by the representatives of the white populace was key to the reconstitution of the violated socius. Unlike "a monarchy or a highly centralized form of government," according to Cutler, "[American] people consider themselves a law unto themselves. They make the laws; therefore they can unmake them. . . . To execute a criminal deserving of death is to act merely in their sovereign capacity" (269). As a counterritual to Reconstruction's "overthrow" of (white) majority rule, lynching presented itself as the righteous indignation of an aroused populace.[28] The rhetorical power inciting the community to lynch law, or at the very least, securing communal acquiescence in a lynching already performed by a small band, did not re-create as a rallying cry the image of an injured sovereign—the king's second body. Rather, it invoked the violated sanctity of the white population's idealized self-image, the injured, "prostrate South" under "Negro domination."

"In 1865 the South, prostrate and bleeding and helpless," intoned Ben Tillman in his 1907 "body of death" speech from the floor of the United States Senate, "a very Niobe of nations, had the dead carcass of slavery chained to it by the fourteenth and fifteenth amendments" (*Congressional Record*, January 21, 1907, 1443). Tillman's emotional wedge against lynching's critics was to frame the discussion entirely through images of female victimization, as when he painted a picture of "the white women of the South . . . in a state of siege" from the "African Minotaur" roaming freely through the South. Responding to the criticism of lynching from a northern senator, Tillman wove a hypothetical tale involving his critic's daughter caught alone at home or on the open road by the archetypal black brute: "she is choked or beaten into insensibility and ravished, her body prostituted, her chastity taken away from her and a memory branded on her brain as with a red-hot iron to haunt her day and night as long as she lives. . . . In other words, a death in life" (1441). Setting aside for the moment his evident enjoyment of the prospect of his opponent's daughter's victimization, Tillman revealed lynching's implicit equivalence between the "death in life" of the narrative's "ruined woman" and the "dead carcass of slavery" that pollutes her existence. The equivalence of the injured body politic and the condemned criminal was also a feature of the European tradition of torture and execution. To the body of the "injured sovereign" Foucault opposes the "symmetrical" image of "the body of the condemned man" (29). In Tillman's speech, "body of death" and "death in life" form a symmetrical, inverted rhetorical pair, linked, as will be shown, by the reproduction of the white victim's wounds on the body of the black condemned.

As many social historians have pointed out, the somatic differences of blacks from whites facilitated black embodiment of what Foucault has described as "the least body of the condemned" in the white imaginary (29). Lynching's condemned was an actor in a social role; his specific offense served to embellish the portrayal, but what really *fit* him (and the condemned was usually, though not always, male) for his role as cultural counterimage to the body politic was his typicality in difference. Lynch law ultimately obliterated identity because identity was not the key to this social role anyway, in spite of the theatrics of the ritual confession (produced, if at all, through the torture itself). In the South, genetic deviance within a community determined to preserve its homogeneity was crime enough and fit the actor to the role. Not even counting the frequent misidentifications, an entire category of lynchings was composed of "near misses," in which a relative or acquaintance of the person sought was lynched in the place of the intended target. According to Herbert Shapiro, "sometimes anyone who was black would do. The point was that for the supposed crime or insult the black community as a whole was accountable, and one black victim for the lynch mob would serves as well as another."[29]

Nothing could more clearly illustrate Eric Voegelin's contention that the racial other is, by definition, guilty of the capital offense of genetic deviance than the litany of "crimes" punished by communal torture and execution: bumping into whites, being "uppity," "talking disrespectfully," "writing an insulting note to a white girl," poisoning a mule.[30] These are classes of crimes that, with the single exception of the poisoning, did not exist for whites, crimes of which only a person at the debased social status occupied by blacks could be guilty. According to Voegelin, it is a small step from the proposition that favored "racial elements of the population are to be promoted by sociopolitical means" (Heilke, 134) to the criminalization of race difference itself: "Those who oppose the chosen race . . . do so not on voluntary grounds, but because they are not of the 'right' race. Their opposition is predetermined . . . genetically" (Heilke, 145). Any act in defiance of the superiority of whites becomes, in such a regime, a capital offense. "In the traditions of the region," said Gunnar Myrdal of the South after five decades of Jim Crow, "a break in caste rules against one white person is conceived of as an aggression against white society and, indeed, as a potential threat to every other white individual" (535). Thus crimes by blacks that might otherwise go entirely unpunished if committed against another black person or by a white against another white became the basis of the most severe punishment and torture imaginable if the accused had in some way, real or symbolic, "intruded upon white society" (Myrdal, 592).[31]

Southerners became, according to W. J. Cash, addicted to lynching "as an act of racial and patriotic expression, an act of chivalry, . . . having a definitely ritualistic value in respect to the entire Southern sentiment, and as an act which had had, in most concrete cases, the approbation and often the participation of the noblest and wisest" (118). "[A] broken head or even death was fair punishment for the sassy nigger (that is, *one guilty of any word or deed of assertion*)," as Cash put it, taking pains to point out that words or deeds contrary to authorized "white opinion" were all that would be needed to remind whites of the genetic deviant's danger to the social order (119; my emphasis). According to I. A. Newby, "lynching or the threat of lynching was the *sine qua non* of keeping the Negro in his place" (139), a sentiment expressed often by Mississippi race demagogue J. K. Vardaman: "How is the white man going to control the government? The way we do it is to pass laws to fit the white man and make the other people come to them. . . . If it is necessary every Negro in the state will be lynched; it will be done to maintain white supremacy" (Ray Stannard Baker, 246).

Lynching's strategy of stripping all individuality from the black body, violently producing the undifferentiated difference that typified the "black brute," makes intelligible why the black men who made the fatal white woman a staple of mythic black literature included many who could be cast in the "brute" role but also many others who simply went too far in aspiring to white male prerogatives. Chesnutt's Procrustean bed of racial undifferentiation prophetically identified both the socially progressive and the criminal elements as those most often singled out for punishment. The black male who "fell entirely out of society" (Williamson, *Crucible*, 58), the socially unhinged postemancipation black male pushed off the land by economic forces into a vagabond lifestyle, was ironically somewhat less a threat to the southern way of life than the industrious, upwardly mobile black male who merely attempted to secure the benefits of the "good life" advertised in the dominant culture. Enactments of the "brute" stereotype validated white nationalism, confirming the allochronistic distance between white and black. But black male desire for the prerogatives of whiteness was more threatening because it raised uncomfortable questions about the extent to which white Americans were willing to keep faith with their national ideals honoring freedom of speech, freedom of association, and social achievement based on individual merit.

Lynching's regulatory function of policing black intrusions into white time-space makes the astounding rationale given for one case—the lynching of a black for "trying to act like a white man"—paradigmatic, for who was more criminally deviant than someone who refused to remain within biologically determined behavioral parameters? Thus all black "criminality" was merely a degree of "uppitiness," of intrusion into the privileged space of whiteness, that permitted capital punishment as a deterrent. Charles P. Lane, editor of the *Huntsville (Ala.) Daily Tribune*, asserted,

> The menace to peace, the danger to society and white supremacy was not in the illiterate Negro, but in the upper branches of Negro society, the educated, the man who, after ascertaining his political rights, forced the way to assert them.
>
> . . . We regard each assertion as unfriendly encroachment upon our native superior rights, and a dare-devil menace to our control of the affairs of the state.
>
> . . . The way to dampen racial prejudice, avert the impending horrors, is to emasculate the Negro politically by repealing the XV Amendment. (Ray Stannard Baker, 241–42)

Fear of educated blacks stemmed also from an awareness that artificial constraints on advancement would make them increasingly alienated. In arguing that Negroes had "too much liberty," Charles Smith refuted Atticus Haygood's contention that education would prevent interracial rape, insisting that education for professions open only to whites made blacks discontented, unwilling to do menial work, improvident, and finally, criminally reckless (179–80).

Numerous instances of mobs taking political "emasculation" one step further into physical emasculation indicate the ease with which corporeal metaphors resulted in corporeal consequences. In arbitrarily selecting for torture and execution any exceptions to the rule that "the lowest white man must be higher than the highest black man," whites in the South had to imagine a social rupture by the upwardly mobile or self-assertive black that justified the prolonged torture of lynching. In the same way that no stock figure in literature was more absurd to bourgeois audiences than the obnoxious social climber, whites projected their own unease over competing American ideologies approving social mobility but disapproving rapid social change onto the intrusive black in popular culture, in literature, and on the minstrel stage, making him or her an object of ridicule and fear alike. The spatial determinism of black life in the Jim Crow South argued that a black citizen who rose above or fell below a range of permissible behavior might trigger white violence against the whole group. The vital connective between the promotion of rape as the "one crime" and the use of lynch law to police any acts of assertion by blacks contrary to white desires was the imagined victimization of the white national body, personified in the case of the rape victim but elsewhere abstracted as "white supremacy," "the southern way of life," or simply the South. The official preferment under law and custom for white bodies was what sustained the violence of black intrusion, be the criminal a rapist or a banker purchasing a first-class ticket on a rail car. The torture of lynching was justifiable in the first instance by the imagined suffering of the abused woman, and in the second, by the angst of the ethically compromised "superior race."[32]

World Upside Down

Because Reconstruction was a historical moment of collective black male assertiveness, re-creations of the era by southern sympathizers emphatically denounced even minimal black presence in governmental, business, or social elites as "Negro dominance." In the inverted world of Reconstruction, the black politician and the black rapist were indistinguishable: both were unlawful usurpers of power, and the violence of white Redemption often took on the atmosphere of popular revolt against an occupying force. "I want to say now that we have not shot any negroes in South Carolina on account of politics since 1876," explained Ben Tillman in his "body of death" speech. "We have not found it necessary. (Laughter.) . . . The action of the white men of South Carolina taking the State away from the negroes we regard as a second declaration of independence by the Caucasian from African barbarism" (1440). Celebration of the return of "lawful" white rule in the South had, therefore, a Fourth of July quality that became a signature aspect of post-Reconstruction lynchings. Arthur Raper described the carnival atmosphere following a 1930 lynching as a reaffirmation to lynching's multiple audiences of the lessons of the past: "the memories of the Reconstruction period have been revived, the protection of white womanhood has become something of an obsession, and the Negroes are more often reminded that they are Negroes and must 'stay in their place.'"[33]

That the mass lynchings often took on the aspect of carnival has a certain logic, given the era's characterization of Reconstruction. Though lynching's apologists explained its undeniable cruelty as a necessary remedy to the "one crime," they had a harder time justifying the festival atmosphere of the lynching itself. The brutality of the crowd, the lack of communal remorse, and the display of body parts taken as trophies and held as treasures long after the event raised doubts about explanations such as Haygood's of an "emotional insanity" that momentarily shook the mob free of civilized restraint. In another of its seemingly endless inversions, lynching's central agon found its ultimate articulation in the carnivalesque. In *The Politics and Poetics of Transgression* (1986), Peter Stallybrass and Allon White address what they call the "politics of carnival": "its nostalgia; its uncritical populism (carnival often violently abuses and demonizes *weaker*, not stronger, social groups—women, ethnic and religious minorities, those who don't belong—in a process of *displaced abjection*); its failure to do away with the official dominant culture, its licensed complicity" (19). Foucault read the carnival aspect of public torture in European history as a latent potential for the assembled crowd to identify with and to attempt to rescue the condemned who has suffered excessively at the hands of the king. Stallybrass and White, however, see the politics of carnival itself as socially conservative, not subversive, and merely using the pretense of hierarchical inversion to keep any actual revolt from materializing.[34]

Lynching's hybridization of popular revolt and social conservatism enables what may therefore be called a "carnivalization of politics" in order to enact its doubly parodic revolt—a phantom rebellion featuring the torture/murder of a mock despot. To make lynching's reactionary mock revolt seem appropriate, its apologists typically revived narratives of historical black transgressive behavior, invariably resorting to the carnivalesque as the proper register for conveying Reconstruction's "outrages." Ben Tillman equated the "Negro domination" of South Carolina with the British monarchy's tyranny over the American colonies in his "body of death" speech, but for him, one distinction was important: "Negro domination" was not merely despotic rule; it was despotic *mis*rule: "There was a condition bordering upon anarchy. Misrule, robbery and murder were holding high carnival. . . . There was riotous living in the statehouse" (1440). For Thomas Nelson Page, Reconstruction was a "riot of civic debauchery," a "mummery of government," and a "carnival of corruption and crime," and he noted that the barbarism of lynch law was a sign of white determination never to let "Negro domination" happen again (124, 264, 267).

Myrta Avary's greatest contempt fell upon whites whom she felt had deliberately imposed "Negro rule" on a helpless South in order to humiliate it. At one point, she described a speech by the "Carpet-Bagger-Philanthropist" Hayward, who told a packed audience of blacks at the Old African Church in Richmond, "*You may have a high carnival in whatever way you please. It is not for me to advise you what to do, for great masses do generally what they have a mind to*" (Avary, 233; my emphasis). In Avary's words, "[Emancipation] as it came, was inversion, revolution. Whenever I pass 'The House Upside Down' at a World's Fair, I am reminded of the South after freedom" (182). Avary's entire representation of the Reconstruction rested on this concept of biracial government as tragicomic inversion of social norms, figuratively making the South a "house upside down";[35] it adopts precisely the carnivalesque mode of discourse that Stallybrass and White describe as "world upside down (WUD) which encodes ways that carnival inverts the everyday hierarchies, structures, rules and customs of its social formation" (183).

The "world upside down" of Reconstruction had been invented and iconographed before the historical event itself, as blackface minstrelsy had permitted white audiences for decades to imagine an America without whites. For Avary, Reconstruction was a festival of incompetence comparable to the minstrel show, as whites treated the "mongrel Black and Tan" constitutional conventions presented with the task of dismantling the racist political culture of the South as a form of entertainment: "The funny sayings and doings of negroes, sitting for the first time in legislative halls, were rehearsed in conversation and reported in papers. Visitors went to the capitol as to a monkey or minstrel show."[36] Emblematic of this tragicomic spectacle of carnivalized politics was Avary's image of a "mongrel" legislature's inability to master even the basics of civilization: "Most of these darkeys, fresh from tobacco lots and corn and cotton fields, were as innocent as babes of any knowledge of reading and writing. . . . No sooner did darkeys observe that whites sent out and got newspapers that they did likewise; and sat there reading them upside down" (253–54). Avary's reference to minstrelsy's carnivalesque points up how blackface entertainment established an easily appropriable paradigm for Reconstruction's carnivalization of politics. To southern sympathizers, the figure of the black in high social circles was the realization of minstrelsy's pageant of social inversion, as racist propaganda, according to Cash, stirred southern indignation at the image of "their late slave, strutting about full of grotesque assertions" (114).[37]

"From the outset," notes Robert Toll, "minstrelsy unequivocally branded Negroes as inferiors. Although it offered its audiences no heroic white characters, it provided even more certain assurances of white common people's identity by emphasizing Negroes' 'peculiarities' and inferiorities" (67). Eric Lott's analysis of antebellum minstrelsy, *Love and Theft*, uncovers strong traces of desire for the somatic properties of black male bodies in minstrel performance, but this is a desire that found it necessary to "repress through ridicule" the object of its fascination (6). Because blackface minstrelsy "anticipated on stage what many Americans deeply feared: the blackening of America," according to Berndt Ostendorf, it created "a symbolic language and a comic iconography for 'intermingling' culturally with the African Caliban while at the same time 'isolating' him socially" (67). "After emancipation," Ostendorf contends, "blacks [were] increasingly depicted as uncontrollable animals with emotions that need to be disciplined. Accordingly the mode change[d] from humor (which includes) to satire and grotesque (which rejects)" (74).

To the tradition of politics as carnival during Reconstruction, lynching responded with its own festival atmosphere in keeping with what Foucault has called, after Vico, torture's "poetics of jurisprudence" (44–45). To ensure that the punishment "fit" the "crime," lynchings revisited the scene of the crime by mimicking the wounding of the victim on the body of the condemned, by replicating the victim's suffering at the criminal's hands, and by revisiting the ahistorical, "barbaric" time-space of black criminality through its own carnival atmosphere. The "politics of time" was crucial to the rhetoric of lynch law because widespread admissions by whites of "reversion to savagery" in the form of lynch mobs required an explanation. For Bishop Haygood, lynching's "anachronism" was regrettably an instance of "the Dark Ages surviving in modern and civilized life," yet justifiably so, given the unprecedented nature of southern suffering "under trials never known before in history" (171, 170). Lynching's retreat to prehistory to combat black "savagery" became a foundational element of the myth of the "one crime," the only crime, according to Walter Page, that *required* the rule of "law . . . [to be] permanently suspended" (307).[38] Lynching reactivated white barbarism, then, to root out the consequences of black atavism, a vital first step in reestablishing the spatiotemporal quarantine that Reconstruction's egalitarian idealism had disrupted. The reason that whites who defended lynching tolerated "white savagery" was ironically to reassure themselves that southern atrocities did not occur within or permanently preempt the time-space of the white civilization they thought they were saving.[39]

Not only did lynching's apologists refuse to avoid the issue of white savagery, but some of its practitioners approached it as an occasion for revelry. Ida B. Wells-Barnett's *A Red Record* (1895) published a photograph of a black man lynched in Clanton, Alabama, in August 1891 showing festive lynchers of all ages posing beneath the dangling corpse hanging in a tree. On the back of the photograph was written an explanation of how "this S-O-B," having been hung for murdering a young boy over thirty-five cents, represented "a good specimen of your Black Christians hung by White Heathens." Signed by "The Committee," the photo had been sent to Albion Tourgée (Wells-Barnett, *Lynchings: Red Record*, 55–56). As with the Boston Tea Party in the era of the Revolution, the heathen mask was an ironic reference to the populace's retreat to the ludic space of precivilization to shake off the yoke of a tyrannical ruler.

News accounts and commentaries on lynch mob behavior similarly noted (sometimes disapprovingly) that attention to formality and procedure at mass lynchings was conducted within a general atmosphere of levity and insobriety.[40] A Belleville, Illinois, lynching in 1903 inspired this news account: "The sentiment of the crowd was as remarkable as its composition. It was as if all had turned out for a frolic. They had gathered for a spectacle, and they made merry over the prospect. Loud laughter greeted jokes with violent death as their theme. Demands for blood were cheered. Women were in front of the jail with baby carriages" (Ralph Ginzburg, 51). At the lynching of Dan Davis in Tyler, Texas, in 1912, "the crowd jeered the dying man and uttered shocking comments suggestive of a cannibalistic spirit. Some danced and sang to testify to their enjoyment of the occasion" (Cassity, 244), while at the 1930 lynching of Oliver Moore in Edgecombe County, North Carolina, "whole families came together, mothers and fathers, bringing even their youngest children. It was the show of the countryside—a very popular show. Men joked loudly at the sight of the bleeding body. . . . Girls giggled as the flies fed on the blood that dripped from the Negro's nose" (Raper, 114). Because Reconstruction legislatures had sought to "privatize" capital punishment to avoid the possibility of mob action during a period of high emotions, lynching's festive celebration of ritual murder was in itself an act of defiance against the ghost of "Negro rule."

Lynching's narrators extended the language of the carnivalesque to cover practically every aspect of the ritual. The *Chicago Record-Herald* of September 2, 1902, reported that "in the most methodical and deliberate manner possible

Corinth [Mississippi] devoted Sunday afternoon to burning a negro to death. Even the victim, Tom Clark, seemed to enter into the spirit of the affair" (Ralph Ginzburg, 46). John Temple Graves, charging black rapists with inaugurating "such a carnival of crime as would infuriate the world and precipitate the anni-hilation of the negro race," likewise explained white festivity at lynchings on the mind-boggling grounds that blacks themselves "love[d] display" and "the spec-tacular element of a trial and execution," apparently willing to be victims of lynchings in order to get invited to them (quoted in Shufeldt, *Negro*, 168). As Bertram Wyatt-Brown has noted, "the invocation of the Lord of Misrule for the maintenance of order was usually directed toward . . . blacks" (12). Thus during the lynching of Henry Smith in Paris, Texas, in 1893, which helped to establish the ritual pattern of the mass lynching, the throng awaiting his return to the city from his point of capture placed him "upon a carnival float in mockery of a king upon his throne" and paraded him through the city "so that all might see the most inhuman monster known in current history" (Wells-Barnett, *Lynchings: Red Record*, 28). As martyr-king, Smith presided over the ritual reincarnation of southern honor, expiating his terroristic misrule through the spectacle of his pro-longed torture and immolation.

The carnivalization of lynching differed from the southern myth of Recon-struction as "world upside down" only in the fact that unlike the carnival of "Ne-gro domination," lynching's inversions included suspension of normal govern-mental processes in which only the whites participated, affecting normative race relations in degree but not in kind. Typically, lynching required the complicity of the constabulary, who either disappeared, allowed themselves to be overpow-ered, or turned the condemned directly over to the crowd to avoid destruction of property or loss of (white) lives. As one officer of the law explained, he "would not imperil the life of one man to save the lives of a hundred Negroes."[41] But even when the removal of prisoners from local authorities occasionally did prove excessive and a threat to public order, the spectacle of white citizens mobilized to punish black transgression reaffirmed racial hierarchy for a large segment of lynching's audience. The licensed anarchy of lynch law looked back nostalgi-cally to the tradition of postwar white extralegal violence against Reconstruction's unruly black bodies, and even further back to slavery's absolute bodily domina-tion of blacks. The romance of a people at war with a government unresponsive to the will of the white majority was a familiar and convenient narrative with which to energize particularly the disaffected white masses, who could, with the symbolic restitution of racial "order," be expected not to press their own com-plaints to the point of actual revolt. These mock revolts gave visual confirmation of a "white man's country," a concept easily lost in the heterogeneous routine. It was truly a herrenvolk festival, a celebration of carnival's egalitarian utopia as a privilege reserved "for whites only."[42]

Lynching's Three Bodies

Lynching departed from the minstrel carnivalesque in its staging of an aggressively sexual black grotesque. In Reconstruction's narrative of the "prostrate South," the implied sexual metaphor of "Negro domination" as rape required the direct confrontation of two racialized bodies that embodied the white nation and the allochronistic black "body of death." As Stallybrass and White indicate, the carnivalesque mode of representation typically balances two extreme body types in its politics of identity as well, and as in lynching's aesthetic politics, carnival's two bodies are a "high" classical body and a "low" grotesque body. Drawing on Bakhtin's discussion of carnival's polarities of bodily representation, Stallybrass and White conclude that this contrast of somatic forms figures into the ritual function of the carnivalesque in the cultural production of identity: "In Bakhtin the 'classical body' denotes the inherent *form* of the high official culture and suggests that the shape and plasticity of the human body is indissociable from the shape and plasticity of discursive material and social norm in a collectivity. . . . Clearly, as often as they are able, 'high' languages attempt to legitimate their authority by appealing to values inherent in the classical body" (21). For Bakhtin, the distinction between the austere, transcendent, pedestalized, classical body of high official culture and the grotesque body of the popular and festive occasion is the basis for carnival's inversive strategy of identity. Carnival suppresses the classical to allow full play of the "lower bodily stratum," which, in normative bourgeois culture, must be restrained. Where Stallybrass and White differ from Bakhtin is in their awareness that the grotesque body's exclusion from the normative is actually only a stage in its integration into the unconscious self of the cultural imaginary (Stallybrass and White, 191–201).

Similarly, I see lynching's fetishizing of the "ruined woman," whose body has been made alien and grotesque by violation of her lower bodily stratum, as a strategic element in the interpellation of a cherished white identity. Lynching's carnivalized "scene of the low Other" creates a new identity not through the substitution of the grotesque body of the black condemned in place of a classical white female body, as Bakhtin would have it, but by the juxtaposition of antithetical classical and grotesque bodies. The black body's transgressive presence was the centrifugal force that held the crowd in place, while the idealized white female body, always present rhetorically as an idealized figure of the white body politic whatever the actual offense to be punished, implicitly invoked the exculpatory rhetoric of "one crime." But even in cases where the transgression punished was clearly identified as nonsexual in nature, "one crime" rhetoric also facilitated lynching's primary function of identity formation. Stallybrass and White describe the carnivalesque mode as a "fundamental mechanism of identity formation [that] *produces* [a] second, hybrid grotesque at the level of the political unconscious *by the very struggle to exclude the first grotesque,* . . . an identity-in-difference which was nothing other than its fantasy relation, its negative symbiosis, with that which it had rejected in its social practices" (193). In lynching, the brutalization and utter obliteration of the body of the black grotesque could not be accomplished through the agency of the classical white female body politic. Only a second "hybrid grotesque," previously offstage, could reestablish the necessary "dissymmetry" of power to reconstitute the social norm. Lynching's tableau of white female and grotesque black male antipodes called forth as the new personation of the sovereign white populace the figure whose role was to reenact in a ritualized form upon the body of the black condemned the violence of southern "Redemption." That second, avenging white grotesque has been named—the "white heathen," the figure that Lawrence Friedman has called "the white savage"—and it was the interpellation of this cherished identity of southern manhood for which each lynching ritual aimed.

Thus lynching's rhetoric of two bodies staged a ritual designed, in fact, to elevate a third body, one that, as Stallybrass and White describe, mediated the classical and the grotesque through a hybridization of civilization's ideal of order with the "spectacle of excess" that the savage demands. The transformation of the southerner into savage was a prized cultural retention within the South's intensely felt code of "primal" honor, which Hiram Wyatt-Brown says in *Southern Honor* led to a "cultivation of ferocity" as a resource available in warfare, one that would signal to other white men one's trustworthiness as a warrior when under attack (39). The reason that accounts of lynchings could not suppress the apotheosis of white savagery was because this cherished identity was what the anticipatory rhetoric and its ritual enactment aimed to produce, and so news accounts that may seem at first glance uneasy about white savagery were in fact participating in the legitimizing and continuity of the ritual. The classic rendition of this culturally approved metamorphosis was given by Ben Tillman on the U.S. Senate floor in his 1907 speech: "[The black rapist] has sinned against the Holy Ghost. He has invaded the holy of holies. He has struck civilization a blow, the most deadly and cruel that the imagination can conceive. . . . Our brains reel under the staggering blow and hot blood surges to the heart. Civilization peels off us, *any and all of us who are men*, and we revert to the original savage type whose impulses under any and all such circumstances has always been to 'kill! kill! kill!'" (1441). Broadcasting white savagery from the Senate floor was no real contradiction for Tillman; it was simply of a piece with lynching's amplification of its ritual function.

Yet Tillman's and all other accounts of white female violation depended ironically on a ritualized absence of male protection as the origin of white female vulnerability, an absence that figures significantly in the forms that white savagery would take. This strategic absence creating the opportunity for black male aggression had, like lynching's carnivalesque, a historical origin in Reconstruction, in the wartime absence and the postwar political "emasculation" of white males in the South. Without this ritual white male absence, the violation could not have occurred. And yet in the paranoid post-Reconstruction South, the crime occurred over and over again, as news media and word of mouth magnified every conceivable boundary transgression by a black male as an attempt at or preliminary for a sexual assault. Because only white females not directly under white male supervision suffered this indignity, it does not surprise that such a narrative should become widely publicized in an era of agitation for women's political independence. A more critical reading of the motif of male absence and triumphant return after the fact suggests that the victimization of white females accomplished an act of white savagery *by black male proxy*, linking the brutalization of white women to the torture and political suppression of black males because both actions addressed specific threats to white manhood that required a ritual purgation.

To investigate lynching's primal scene of "rape" as an element in the ritual suppression of the two most conspicuous claimants to white male prerogative, I return here to a previously noted feature of lynch law apology, the figure of the "ruined woman." The "ruined woman" emerged in the justification of lynching veiled in mystery under the rhetorical sign of the *unspeakable*. According to Thomas Nelson Page, "the unnameable brutality with which the causing crime [that is, rape] was, in nearly every case, attended" made "death . . . generally the least of the . . . horrors. . . . They simply could not be put in print" (99). Myrta Avary similarly claimed to know of "no terms for dispassionate discussion" of the "one crime." Avary urged white men to "preserve [the rape victim] from memories that sear and craze," by endorsing "the prompt and informal removal from existence of the offender," whose continued physical presence on Earth would force the victim to relive the original violation. Avary's secondhand description of a rape victim, then, deliberately invoked the passion of a witness forced into a vicarious experience of the torture of black rape: "the most unspeakable pity of it all was her loathing for her own body; her prayers that she might die and her body be burned to ashes" (382). Note that the prescription of burning to purify the polluted body blatantly calls for the burning of the criminal through lynching's poetics of jurisprudence.

For lynch law apologists, the logic of summary execution was in large part based on the double jeopardy of the "one crime" for its victim, who might be further damaged by the publicity of a trial.[43] Thus accusations of assault rarely got to the point of investigation, since, protected by the crime's unspeakableness, the only witness was often not pressed to provide any proof of actual criminal behavior. Further, because the umbrella of "one crime" governed lynchings for all causes, crimes not involving accusations of rape could legitimize summary execution by appealing to this "tradition" of dispensing with the pretense of judicial procedure in the prosecution of "folk justice."

But if forcing the victim to relive the attack raised protests of the crime's unspeakableness, what made this unspeakableness ironic is that lynching's apologists seldom could resist teasing their audiences with sidelong glimpses into any crime that could be construed as having a sexual intent. In order to defend lynching, its apologists knew that they would have to make a case for the "fitness" of its savagery. According to Brundage, "accounts of alleged rapes of children dwelled upon the brutishness of the blacks and the innocence of their victims. With an eye toward lurid detail, whites speculated about the lifetime of unimaginable physical and psychological suffering that the victims would endure" (60). Bishop Haygood's determination not "to discuss for publication a subject both horrible and loathsome, or to offer to the public opinions about facts that make wise men mad" therefore easily yielded to his subsequent impulse to include a description of the crime leading to the 1893 lynching of Henry Smith in Paris, Texas: "think also of a white baby, four years old, first outraged with demoniacal cruelty and then taken by the heels and torn asunder in the mad wantonness of gorilla ferocity" (168). Haygood wanted his readers to know, then, that this "gorilla ferocity" established the standard against which the condemnations of white savagery must be gauged. In Charles Smith's account of the murder-rape of a twelve-year-old, whose assailant he pictures as whetting his knife while he lies in wait for her, the emphasis is on the tortured mind and the body of the victim:

"The thought of the awful misery of that child, as she agonized her innocent life away in the clutches of the fiend, is enough to freeze the heart of the Angel of Mercy" (182).

Smith's fascination with the abomination is a canonical moment in the rhetoric of lynch law. He tries to "see" the horror of the murdered twelve-year-old, to imagine her pain and the pain of her family as a basis for the "poetics of jurisprudence" governing the torture phase of lynching, and he concludes, "The lynching of such a monster, think many people in the South, is nothing—nothing compared with what he has done. If punishment, according to the old barbarous notion, should be proportioned to crime, . . . there is no torture that could suffice. Fire would be only too mild and instant death too speedy." Yet other accounts seem to dwell on the details of the crime with a barely concealed sadism. In his fabrication of the hypothetical rape of the northern senator's daughter, Ben Tillman seems to take delight in the idea that it would take the brutal violation of his opponent's daughter to stop his criticism of lynching. With "a memory branded on her brain as with a red-hot iron" to justify the torture of the condemned, the "ruined" girl "drags herself to her father and tells him what has happened" to spur him to manly revenge. "Is there a man here with red blood in his veins who doubts what impulses the father would feel?" Tillman asks gratuitously (1441).

The anguished but insistent contemplation of the "ravishing and tearing to pieces of white women and children" (Thomas Nelson Page, 114) does not seem inappropriate in many instances, given the emotions that fears of uncontrolled criminality tend to create. But by examining these visualizations of black brutality against the weak and unprotected in light of another body of rhetoric that envisioned savage assaults against white women by white *men*, we can detect a pattern of fantasy aggression against all white women who have become sexually intimate with black men, whether voluntarily or involuntarily. Like the dutiful father in Griffith's movie who will kill his womenfolk to spare them a fate worse than death, postwar fears of "miscegenation" produced a number of homicidal fantasies by white males who contemplated the spectacle of interracial sex between black men and white women: "I want to say that I would rather tear, screaming from her mother's arms, my little daughter and bury her alive than to see her arm in arm with the best nigger on earth," one Arkansas politician declared (Whitfield, 4). Ben Tillman was characteristically more histrionic: "I have three daughters, but, so help me God, I had rather find either one of them killed by a tiger or a bear and gather up her bones and bury them, conscious that she had died in the purity of her maidenhood, than have her crawl to me and tell me the horrid story that she had been robbed of the jewel of her womanhood by a black fiend" (1441). "Can you find a white preacher who would unite in holy wedlock a burly negro to a white lady?" asked Charles Carroll in *The Negro: A Beast* (1900). "Ah! parents, you would rather see your daughter burned, and her ashes scattered to the winds of heaven" (164). As these fantasies suggest, death alone could still the nagging doubts about the constancy of the white female, for death alone could halt speculation about the complicit desires of her own comparatively atavistic body.[44]

The permissible fantasy of white female brutalization by white males reveals an utter lack of regard for—perhaps even a perverse enjoyment of—white female suffering. The focus instead was on white male honor and the righteousness of a savage exercise of power in pursuit of it. Since it is clear that white fathers publicized these fantasies primarily to force female conformity to race chastity, it is possible to see a passive aggression likewise in the patriarchal absence that enabled the brutalization of women's bodies in lynching's "one crime" narrative. Moralizing about the "one crime" aimed at persuading two specific audiences—black men and white women—of the perils of defying white male authority, the common denominator being the physical and mental suffering of the woman, who, voluntarily or involuntarily, became a source of communal pollution and familial shame. Thus lynch law's erasure of the suspicion of white female depravity was incomplete, surviving, through meditation on the body of the "ruined woman," as an implicit warning to white women resistant to white male supervision. According to Hiram Wyatt-Brown, the term "ruined" meant physically, emotionally, and socially defiled (388), and to be so tagged publicly made women the objects of an intense, perverse fascination. As Jacquelyn Dowd Hall explains, "Rape and rumors of rape became a kind of acceptable folk pornography in the Bible Belt. As stories spread, the attacker became not just a black man but a ravenous brute, the victim a beautiful, frail, young virgin. The experience and condition of a woman (who could not be put on the witness stand to suffer the 'glare and stare of public curiosity') were described in minute and progressively embellished detail: a public fantasy that implies a kind of group participation in the rape of the woman almost as cathartic as the subsequent lynching of the alleged attacker" (150). Public fascination with the body of the victim of the alleged rape grew, in most cases, in proportion to the event's unspeakableness, with the additional irony that through this ritual evasion, the woman's own effective silencing within the community created more space for speculative embellishment.

Negro Passion

Philadelphia physician Robert Shufeldt provides an interesting study in the rhetoric of the "one crime" as displaced aggression against white women. Shufeldt justified, on the principle of unspeakableness, his refusal to divulge the details of black male crimes against white women, holding, "Scores of similar cases might easily have been retold in the pages of this book, *but for very obvious reasons I have refrained from doing so*" (Shufeldt, *Negro*, 13). But the very terms of his refusal to tell the details required that he document the savagery of the black brute. Thus Shufeldt, too, called attention to the 1893 Paris, Texas, case as the archetypal black crime, in terms that echo Haygood's.[45] After relating the newspaper account of the assault, Shufeldt pauses: "But enough; as I have said, nothing would be gained here by recounting in full such ghastly horrors. It takes a negro to assault a pretty and winsome little girl less than four years of age; then catch her by her feet and tear her body in twain; and afterwards to be so indifferent to the crime as to lie down and *sleep* by his mutilated victim all night" (13). Despite Shufeldt's insistence that this and other cases of assaults he has cited in his appendix "are by no means the most horrible known in the history of this country," he clearly chose the cases he highlights for their shock value, protesting all the while that there was nothing to be gained by dwelling on such details. But lynching's apologists knew that by raising the unspeakableness of the crimes that lynching punished, they must, given the great detail in which lynching brutalities were reported in the press, make the gravity of the crime as graphic as possible. The example of the 1893 Paris, Texas, crime became the type of the "one crime" that explained the unspeakableness of all others primarily through apologists like Bishop Haygood and Charles Smith, who produced a dubious quote by the lynched man, Henry Smith, that he had "split her open and throwed her off in the bushes" (181).

To enhance the portrayal of that event as the typical lynching, Shufeldt reprinted a series of seven photographs of the Paris lynching, including scenes of Henry Smith being tortured by the male family members of the deceased girl. The photos were taken from such a distance that it is difficult to ascertain any details, but Shufeldt captioned each photo as a running documentation of the event, emphasizing a terror that could both be spoken and shown, if only by means of the objectifying distance of the lens that his matter-of-fact descriptions mimic: "Fastening the negro, Henry Smith, to the stake on the scaffold, and burning his abdomen with a red hot iron"; "Lynching of Henry Smith. The Torture. Burning his feet with a red-hot iron." This picture, showing Smith on a scaffold on which the word "JUSTICE" was scrawled above his head, captures lynching's poetics of jurisprudence as a symbolic reenactment of the original crime upon the body of the condemned. Lynching's poetics not only required the male relatives to preside over the torture, but also that the torture reproducing the suffering of the child be publicly broadcast in direct proportion to the crime's unspeakableness.

But Shufeldt's inclusion of the pictures and his perfunctory descriptions of both the crimes and the punishment in detail are revealing in other ways. Consider Shufeldt's report of an atrocity that, like the hypothetical rape of a northern senator's daughter fantasized by Ben Tillman, *did not happen* but one that he allowed himself to imagine in far more graphic detail than he would have included about any actual event. The triggering incident of Shufeldt's fantasy was his personal involvement in the manhunt for the attempted rapist of a friend's daughter:

> The would-be raper was never discovered in this case. Fortunately, he did not have the necessary time to mutilate the child—a most lovely little girl and a great favorite—by which I mean he did not have the time to increase the size of her genital fissure by an ugly upward rip of his knife, a common practice among negroes when they assault little white girls. Such is the class of cases which for years past have terrified Southern mothers, which have filled fathers, husbands and brothers with apprehension throughout the great black belt of the South, and, owing to the peculiar nature of the knowledge, they cannot well communicate to their little growing daughters or even those of maturer years, without putting ideas in their minds. (134)

Shufeldt thus resolved the apparent dilemma of speaking the unspeakable: How can one describe a horror so thoroughly outside the realm of civilized behavior without creating the horror itself in a mind vulnerable to the very discussion? Yet how can one not speak of it, if speaking might prevent the actuality? The solution, then, was to make graphically evident the unspeakableness of the crime in the context of a hypothetical, rather than an actual, crime.

However, Shufeldt's explanation for breaking his own promise to forgo graphic description as a violation of propriety might sit better if not for a previous account of the author's own unambiguous sadism. Seven pages prior to his description of the averted mutilation of the family friend, he had bragged about how he had once bribed a black woman into letting him watch her as she went through childbirth without anesthesia or other medical assistance:

> With scarcely a word of persuasion, she was induced to remove every particle of clothing she had on. . . . She was instructed not to in any manner control her expressions of pain. . . . These instructions were cheerfully complied with, and the scene which followed was one of the most extraordinary in my entire medical experience. Her contortions were superb and utterly natural; her groans and screams were unconfined and were poured out without the least restraint. Not one bit of assistance did I render her . . . until everything was completely over. . . . It would have been a worthy subject for the modern biograph, and the lesson was by no means lost upon me. I have never forgotten so much as a single part of it, and it is only briefly described here with the sole view of throwing a single ray of light,—a sidelight—upon a certain phase of *negro passion*. (127–28; my emphases)

Missing from this explanation is why, for a man training to become a doctor, an event as routine as a childbirth should have been "one of the most extraordinary in [his] entire medical experience." But Shufeldt's penchant for dissecting black corpses suggests that the rupturing of black bodies may have had more of a recreational than professional appeal for him. Significantly, the end of this long paragraph finds Shufeldt wearily dismissing blacks as subjects of scientific observation: "Negroes are not responsible for the kind of men and women they are. It is in their nature, and they cannot possibly rid themselves of that, any more than skunks and polecats can cast away their abominable scent glands and the outrageous odors they emit." Never able to keep the mask of scientific objectivity in place for very long, except, of course, when graphically displaying scenes of torture, Shufeldt treated the woman's pain as an aspect of "negro passion" in order to shift attention from his own all too evident sexual excitement.

Nor is it insignificant that he framed the object of his fascination as a potentially cinematic event, one that, like the documenting of the Henry Smith lynching, he could relive over and over again. Turning the camera back toward Shufeldt as a lens into his own motivation, we can compare this achieved sadistic fantasy with the unaccomplished, unspeakable fantasy of child rape and mutilation that occurs pages later. His description of the woman—"a most voluptuous creature she was, to be sure"—places her on the surface in a quite different category from the "most lovely little girl" who survived the rape attempt. The first instance found him savoring the groans and contortions brought on by the actual pain of the black woman, for whom the surgical cutting of the vagina, which he withheld, would have brought relief. But in the second instance, the entirely imaginary cutting of the little white girl's vagina with a knife became the object of a second contemplation of "negro passion," with Shufeldt imagining the course of the crime from the point of view of a black male. By this time, it should be clear that "negro passion" is not really the subject of either episode, except that the delectation of a criminal fantasy through a black male body allowed Shufeldt a needed prophylactic, ocular distancing. The fantasy mutilation offers a vicarious experience of black maleness to conceal an unspeakable desire for the "favorite" girl, a violation that would presumably have resulted in an identical genital rupture of the child by any adult male.

"Lynchings . . . will continue to occur in the United States of America just so long as there is a negro left here alive, and there is a white woman living for him to assault," Shufeldt explained, by way of establishing the excessiveness of "negro passion" (*Negro*, 13). Responding to William Hannibal Thomas's suggestion that castration was a more appropriate punishment for rapists than lynching, Shufeldt (knowing full well that Thomas was a mulatto) countersuggested castration and subsequent extermination of *all* blacks: "What would Thomas think of this for a scheme?" he asked maliciously (145). Shufeldt declared that castration alone was insufficient, in any case, because "with the surgeon's knife actually pressing upon his scrotum; with the blazing fagots so near him that he could actually feel the heat of their flames, [the negro] would nevertheless seize his victim and outrage her . . . ninety-nine times out of a hundred" (150). There is no doubt as to the identity of the "surgeon" with the knife in this little drama, as his fantasies of genital wounding multiply to include black male castration to the vaginal mutilation of white and black women. To be a "negro" in Shufeldt's world was to be capable of a disinterested infliction of pain upon others. Recall his description of the quintessential "negro," Henry Smith, who was "so indifferent to the crime as to lie down and *sleep* by his mutilated victim all night." Descriptions of his dissecting experiences; his fascination with the details of the 1893 Paris crime to the extent of carefully—and pictorially—documenting the lynching; his intercutting of commentary on the deplorable state of the African "genus" with photographs of black male and female nudes "photographed from life by the Author": Shufeldt's contemplation of the human body in pain, being rent asunder, probed by knives, violated, exploited, rendered impotent, and opened to disinterested observation required the patina of scientific inquiry to cover for a sadism that elsewhere finds him detailing numerous accounts of African cannibalism. But the cannibal was not Shufeldt; it could not have been Shufeldt. It was the "negro." On this, we have no less an authority than Shufeldt himself, who exclaimed, "Thank Fortune, there were no black cannibals among my ancestors!" (154).

Lynching similarly brought ritual form to sadistic fantasies of dominance by ritually positioning white female and black male bodies as objects of reverence and contempt, linking them irrevocably through dual degradation. As a prelude to lynchings originating in alleged crimes against women, rumors of rape and the contemplation of the wounds of the victim became a standard public rite because in the South, public knowledge of genital "malformity" was a source of shame (Wyatt-Brown, 289–91), and thus sexual victimization by the black brute could not help but draw the prurient, degrading interest of the populace. Jacquelyn Dowd Hall notes that antilynching advocate Jesse Daniel Ames and her allies received letters from lynching advocates that "typify the way in which a lynching could become the occasion for the expression of aggressive fantasies ordinarily repressed. 'The crowds from here that went over to see [the victim] for themself,' wrote an anonymous Floridian, 'said he was so large he could not assault her until he took his knife and cut her, and also had either cut or bit one of her breast [sic] off'" (150–51). As in Shufeldt's fears for the unharmed child, the theme of genital mutilation to accommodate the monstrous black phallus appears here in a similar context—the fantasy of genital mutilation, not its actuality—that is suggestive of perhaps an unspeakable communal desire for the suffering of the woman who has, however blamelessly, brought defilement into the community. The white woman who was penetrated by the monstrous black penis *and did not* publicly suffer was the greatest threat imaginable to the whole structure of race/sex mythology because she offered living proof of the viability of transgression.

W. J. Cash's remark that a white woman in the South stood a greater chance of being struck by lightning than being raped by a black man only points up the magnitude of a paranoia so encompassing that no southern politician could be elected for nearly a century without paying homage to it (Cash, 115). In its elemental form, the fear of the black rapist was the fear of the monstrous black body itself—its unpredictable, transgressive, and destabilizing presence, always already at the very threshold of white space. The black male was literally a "brute," a shape-shifting "creature in human form" (Tillman, 1441) whose intermediate status between animal and human made him a contaminant—a corrupter of "cherished classifications" and hierarchies. Endless recitation of the lore of the black brute rapist kept southern women cowering in their homes and thus away from the types of political and social activism in which their northern sisters had begun to experiment.[46] Ironically, only by society's perpetual *speaking* of black rape's *unspeakableness* were white women made constantly to fear its horror.

If the horror of genital mutilation authored the unspeakableness of interracial rape in the white imaginary, that mutilation was a signifier with multiple referents. More than even the wounding blade, the black penis was the fearsome weapon wielded by the brute. William Lee Howard described the black male as a lycanthrope enslaved to the demands of a seemingly autonomous penis, a plaything of biological determinism powerful enough to pervert religious worship: "With their [that is, black men's] fathers and grandfathers phallic festivals were tribal institutions. In the days [when] . . . the camp meeting was instituted, . . . religion played no part. . . . These gatherings in the woods at midnight were merely to gratify sexual craving" (425). To Howard, the fact that "[sex] organs in the African [were] enormously developed" meant inevitably that "his whole life [was] devoted to the worship of Priapus." Apart from theories of an "instinctive" repulsion that made white women unwilling participants in interracial sex, Paul Broca speculated on a "unilateral hybridity" between the races based on a specific genital misalignment hindering productive intercourse between black males and white females.[47] Broca quoted Etienne Serres's observation that a double penalty thwarted the consenting white female, "who suffers in the act," since her uterine canal is not long enough to accommodate the "Ethiopian" penis: "the neck of the uterus is pressed against the sacrum, so that the act of reproduction is not merely painful, but frequently non-productive" (Broca, 28).[48] The proportional "gigantism" of the black female vagina, according to this medical folklore, makes black reproductive space easily available and exploitable by black and white males alike, but black male genital "gigantism" destroys the physical integrity and reproductive economy of the white vagina and womb.[49]

Howard, a Baltimore doctor who became friendly enough with Robert Shufeldt that the Philadelphia physician reprinted one of Howard's essays in its entirety in one of his books, speculated that black female genital "peculiarity" determined the perverse evolution of the black penis in size and shape. He then went on to even wilder fantasies. Howard described the biological determinism of black manhood as the result of the transmission of "sexual elements" from black father to black son "unchanged" from ages gone by. Thus, "whether he [was] a college professor or a laborer," the black male was a slave to his racial legacy of sexual madness originating in "the large but flexible sexual organ, which adapt[ed] itself to the peculiar sex organs of the female negro and their [*sic*] demands."[50] The excessive, allochronistic black penis, subject to a quantitative speculation rivaled only by the "very large brains" of white males, should not, by this "medical" evidence, have access to the white womb for which it was never intended. Nor could a white female "consent" to what her body had evolved specifically to prevent.

The horror attached to black male sexuality in this folklore, in fact, was undoubtedly an attempt to scare white women away from consensual interracial relationships as much as it tried to terrify them into remaining under strict male supervision. Yet if the intent of the folklore was also to discourage white women from interracial sex, it was only partially successful, for white males, prone themselves to curiosity about the hypersexuality of the "black Venus," could not entirely dismiss the possibility that the folklore of black male sexual gigantism would appeal to the sexual fantasies of some white women. Howard's friend Robert Shufeldt feared that there was "a large class of degraded, sensuous white women in this country who prefer[red] to copulate with black men, on account of the unusual length of time the act commonly last[ed] in them, but also on account of the immensity of their parts" (*Negro*, 103–4). Ironically, prolonged copulation by black males was, according to Howard, the physiological and psychic punishment exacted by nature for black males having too large a penis and too small a brain—they could never find relief.[51] Once again, black males and white females, unlike black females and white males, were doomed to physical suffering in interracial intercourse. The folklore of genital mutilation in part betrayed the fact that white female sexuality was still a socially destabilizing factor whose expression, in addition to the old religious and social proscriptions, was beginning to acquire new "scientific" barriers. In the South's system of socialization, honor reflected an exalted state of corporeal intactness: "In its most fundamental form, honor was a state of grace linking mind, body, blood, hand, voice, head, eyes, and even genitalia" (Wyatt-Brown, 49). Keeping in circulation an image of unsupervised white womanhood becoming degraded to the condition of African womanhood—that is, sexual "grotesqueness"—was a symbolic means of reestablishing the penalty of "social death" for racial unchastity. Deflowered, penetrated, open to public scrutiny, like the African woman's body in the cultural imaginary, the "ruined woman" of lynch lore served as a reminder of southern dishonor even if the lynching ritual reinstated the abstract ideal of white female purity.

Lynching's violations of black males and white females, like the institutionalized rape of black women during and after slavery, facilitated the performance of the transcendent rite of white maleness,[52] enabling the South to ward off meaningful social change for decades: "Thus the threat of rape cannot be seen, as reform rhetoric claimed, simply as a rationalization used to obscure the real function of lynching. Rather, the two phenomena were intricately connected, for the fear of rape, like the threat of lynching, served to keep a subordinate group in a state of anxiety and fear. It may be no accident that the vision of the Negro as threatening beast flourished during the first organizational phase of the women's rights movement in the South" (Hall, 153). By centering all discourse about lynching on the "one crime," lynching's advocates could amplify the threat to white womanhood in instances that did not involve accusations of rape.

By all accounts, the campaign to suppress white female activism and black male assertiveness was successful. Instinctively, many southern feminists and their northern allies tried to capitalize on the "one crime" hysteria to argue for political power sharing that otherwise risked heavy male censure, as white feminist critics of male privilege actually called for *more* white male protection in response to the black rape scare. Suffragettes complained that white males interested in neutralizing the black vote should have enlisted white women, who, on kinship grounds, had a stronger case for inclusion into full citizenship than did black men. Susan B. Anthony, commenting on the newly ratified Fifteenth Amendment, claimed that by "crowning" two million black men "with the honor and dignity of citizenship," the Republican Party had "dethroned FIFTEEN MILLION WHITE WOMEN—their own mothers and sisters, their own wives and daughters— and cast them under the heel of the lowest order of manhood" (Giddings, 66). Elizabeth Cady Stanton was even more graphic, equating black male suffrage with license to rape: "The Republican cry of 'Manhood Suffrage' creates an antagonism between black men and all women that will culminate in fearful outrages on womanhood, especially in the southern states" (Giddings, 66). Rebecca Latimer Felton, shortly after *Plessy*, attributed the occurrence of seven lynchings within a week, each resulting from the accusation of rape, to the fact that "white men equalized themselves at the polls with an inferior race." Thus "a crime nearly unknown before and during the war had become an almost daily occurrence" (Williamson, *Crucible*, 128). Felton demanded white male protection in the form of increased lynchings—"I say lynch a thousand a week if it becomes necessary"—setting off the spark that would later flare into the Wilmington riot.[53]

That lynching's body politics were primarily aimed at reaffirming white male prerogative comes through clearly in the language of southern "gyneolatry" (Cash, 86). For W. J. Cash, the social "remoteness" and inaccessibility of the white female to the black male was what fixed her value as a "mystic symbol of [the South] in the face of the foe." This symbolism stemmed from her principal function as "perpetuator of [their] superiority in legitimate line" (116), the guarantor of the right of white men's sons "in the legitimate line, through all the generations to come, to be born to the great heritage of white men." Outside of undeniable familial sentiment in the particular, white men rallied to the cause of race-exclusive white womanhood in the abstract because it was clearly a proprietary domain that ensured the stability of their entire way of life. As we have seen in the colonial slave statutes, the marking off of an exclusive phylogenetic space of whiteness became a property right with national implications, since the white woman's body was "a holy temple dedicated by God in which alone may continue the ever complicating warp and woof of evolution," as one race nationalist described it (Haller, 56). Such symbolism reinforced and drew authority from the southern tradition of husbands and fathers controlling a woman's property (Wyatt-Brown, 255). White womanhood was an irreplaceable resource in the transmission of white male social identity genetically, symbolically, and legally, but it could only perform this function as object, rather than as subject, of national desire.

Body/Sign

Looking at the causes of lynchings through this perspective clarifies their common purpose of asserting the unapproachableness of the persons, property, social prerogatives, and status of white men. Assaulting white men, taking their property (including their reputation as caste superiors), corrupting their women—these were, in order, the classes of events that typically erupted into lynchings. Arthur Raper's study *The Tragedy of Lynching* (1933) provides the following statistics: "Of the 3,693 mob victims between 1889 and 1929 in the United States, 1,394 or 37.7 per cent, were accused of murder; 214, or 5.8 per cent of felonious assault; 614, or 16.7 per cent, of rape; 247, or 6.7 per cent of attempted rape; 264, or 7.1 per cent, of theft; sixty-six, or 1.8 per cent, of insult to white person; and 894, or 24.2 per cent, of all other offenses" (36). To truly understand the workings of lynch law rhetoric, one must examine the list of "other offenses," which includes inciting racial troubles, suing whites, frightening children, acting like a white man, seeking employment in white business, approving of the murder of whites, strikebreaking, disrespect toward the president, using offensive language, keeping a gambling house, boasting, sympathizing with a lynch victim, and conjuring (Raper, 36–37). To Raper's list, we can add "other offenses"

from a list compiled by Ida B. Wells-Barnett in 1895, including unknown offenses, enticing a servant away, introducing smallpox, writing a letter to a white
woman, giving information, engaging in politics, and asking a white woman to
marry (*Lynchings: Red Record*, 93–94). In short, the second largest category of
alleged offense against lynch victims behind murder was miscellaneous crimes
against the sensibilities of the white race in general or particular. Even the idea
of white social norms and the race's reputation were race property and entitlements protected by mob violence.[54]

During the decades of greatest race violence, the largest statistical category of
lynchings was in retaliation for the murder, or attempted murder, of a white
male. Countless tales of whites contesting the rights of blacks to equality of treatment suggest that many of these murders erupted from confrontations over property and wages, as well as expressions of contempt for black aspirations to social
and political inclusion. White women were often part of the mob as active participants, mostly to add moral support but always to inspire the pursuit of racial
"manhood." Arthur Raper summarizes the role of women in the lynch mobs he
investigated in the year 1930: "Women figured prominently in a number of the
outbreaks. After a woman at Sherman had found the men unwilling to go into
the courtroom and get the accused, she got a group of boys to tear an American
flag from the wall of the courthouse corridor and parade . . . to incite the men to
do their 'manly duty.' . . . Other women held their babies high over their heads
and dared the soldiers to shoot. . . . It is reported that at Honey Grove[, Texas,]
the wife of one minister ran to the home of another minister and called to his
wife: 'Come, I never did see a nigger burned and I musn't miss this chance'" (12).
"One woman in a group of a dozen declared she wished they had burned every
nigger in Sherman. —— —— declared she wished she had been allowed to
fire the torch that burned him" (Raper, 338–39).

Stories abounded of women holding children up to see the events better. Ida
B. Wells-Barnett described the lynching of Lee Walker in Memphis, Tennessee,
to which "one man and woman brought a little girl, not over twelve years old, . . .
to view a scene which was calculated to drive sleep from the child's eyes for many
nights, if not to produce a permanent injury to her nervous system" (*Lynchings:
Red Record*, 52). Barnett's purpose was to use the very accounts by which lynchers exonerated themselves to point out the gross inconsistencies, as here, where
the idea of a frail white womanhood in need of lethal defense was contradicted
by the prominence of women and children among the curiosity seekers. The
black lore of the fatal white woman fed on such acts of racial malevolence, as
in the instance of the little old lady in Salisbury, North Carolina, who, taken to

see the still-hanging bodies at a multiple lynch site, proceeded to walk up to one of the bodies, cut off a finger as a souvenir, place it in her purse and depart (Williamson, *Crucible*, 188).

Not just this symbolic dowager but all of the South was compulsive about documenting lynching, whether to prolong its psychic benefits or to expand its potential base of influence beyond the participating community. Unlike forms of torture described by Foucault that used spectacle to enforce individual conformity, lynching had two important racial audiences for whom it accomplished different objectives. As it reassured whites of the availability of a terroristic tool to ensure black docility and deference, it warned blacks of the consequences of transgressing the boundaries of white space. Its message of conformity was differently nuanced for the parallel race worlds of the South because, despite numerous lynchings of whites in the early years of the epidemic, it quickly evolved into a race-specific ritual.[55] Further, its manipulation of the body of the condemned into a sign of both the crime and the state's overwhelming power over social caste inferiors was central to lynching's politics of identity. Lynching's black body of death itself became the chief documentation of unrestrained white savagery.

In the semiotics of lynching, the black body disintegrated under the weight of multiple significances. It was triply grotesque—first in its abjectness, second in its excessiveness, and finally in its plasticity. As parodic despot, it advertised black unworthiness for social equality, let alone "domination." The white audience was invited to laugh away its fears at the possibility of black competition for the world's resources, while the surviving blacks, powerless to prevent or respond to the message of their abjectness, were made to despair of any ambitions for inclusion into a community so committed to their humiliation. The ritual reliance on a grotesque black antithesis to white Christian womanhood ensured, in Alexander Manly's words, that "every negro lynched [was] called a Big Burly Black Brute" (quoted in Prather, 72–73). "Burliness" was as critical a factor as "blackness" in the semiotics of excess, which emphasized the imagery of boundary transgression and constitutional unrestraint by juxtaposing the physically imposing black body and the ethereal white female form. By ritual manipulation of the body through a repertoire of poetic tortures and mortal strokes, lynching literally carved and branded the condemned with the inscription that in the "white man's country," race is destiny.

One key element in the documentary impulse of lynching was the detailed nature of news accounts prepared for its different audiences. Driving the reportage was a phenomenon noted by Arthur Raper in his study of lynchings in 1930: "Whereas the Negro press in practically every case assumed that the person lynched was innocent, or that he was guilty of some crime less serious than that of which he was accused, the white press usually accepted as true all the rumored details of guilt" (24). Like the communities they served, white newspapers tended to denounce lynching in general but often justified it in the particular, especially when it occurred close at hand (Raper, 23). Both the white and the black press sought to exploit the fate of the condemned as evidence of the need for continued communal vigilance. The white press's more obvious function of articulating the white determination to lynch often appeared in the form of news items that announced lynchings in advance, including date, time, and site. In effect, these papers created the news they knew their readers wanted to see in print.

One very striking example was the role played by the white press in fomenting the 1906 Atlanta riot. Joel Williamson summarizes the effect of a shameful competition between Atlanta dailies to see who could sell the most papers by poisoning the racial atmosphere of the city on the eve of the riot:

> [*Atlanta News* editor Charles] Daniel proposed a law prohibiting white ladies from riding in the front seat of hacks with black drivers because a mere "touching of the garments" was enough to incite the beast to immediate and wanton sexuality. . . . Daniel offered a reward of $1,000 for the lynching of a rapist. [*Atlanta Constitution* editor John Temple] Graves shortly concluded that lynching was not deterrent enough, in part because satanic black ministers made martyrs of the lynched. He proposed that castration and branding an "R" on each cheek of the transgressor might be more effective. Later, he suggested that the rapist, in full view of the assembled black population, be required to ascend a tower and "pass over a slender bridge into a dark chamber where in utter darkness he perished by a terrible means never known to Negroes." Other people presented a host of suggestions in that racially fateful summer. Women should be armed and trained in shooting schools. Any white female of any age who shot and killed a would-be assailant should get a $10,000 reward. A long-term, but eventually perfect, cure was offered in the proposal to sterilize all black females. (Williamson, *Crucible*, 214)

The hatred and suspicion generated by the media campaign eventually exaggerated a series of unrelated occurrences into a "rape epidemic."

The 1934 lynching of Claude Neal for the murder of a white girl in Florida featured an itinerary that was broadcast by radio and newspapers. "All white folks are invited to the party," the announcement added, after listing a trip to the victim's farm where Neal was to be "mutilated by the girl's father," a trip to the site of the crime where Neal was to be killed, and finally a trip to the county seat so that his body could be "hung in the court house square for all to see" (Ralph Ginzburg, 221). "Bonfires have been started, piles of sharp sticks have been prepared, knives have been sharpened and one woman has displayed a curry-comb with which she promises to torture the negro," reported the *Macon Telegraph* on the day of the planned event. The paper's account reported the organizing committee's concern over the possible danger to "women with babes in arms," but no attempt was made to dissuade their attendance.[56]

While the black press seemed intent on magnifying the enormity of white terrorism in its explicit detailing of lynching's excesses, the white press often seemed, even when it condemned the lynching, to extend the cathartic benefits of the torture to a wider audience and, in emphasizing black criminality, to expand the destroyed black body's visibility as a sign of the white will to rule. Yet many papers in the South did report, though clearly lacking in expressions of moral indignation, the numerous cases of mistaken identity that resulted in the death of innocent people. Rather than use the occasion to speak out against lynching, papers often moved on to speculate about the fate of the next suspect. Because of the wide dispersal of lynchings in the various states, the news media performed a crucial function in maintaining a coherent ritual pattern across time and space. Seemingly unaware of the moral implications of their role in legitimizing lynching, the newspapers of the South provided a record sufficient in its specificity for subsequent studies to expose the myth of the "one crime" and to document the significance of the ritual to the whites who performed it.

The numerous photos that surfaced after lynchings, often showing whites posing alongside the remnants of the condemned, represented another attempt to document the white savage impulse. Pictures such as the one from 1908 showing five lynched blacks hanging from a dogwood tree in Sabine County, Texas (described in the epigraph to this chapter), indicate, through the poem printed below it and the acquisition of a copyright for it by the Harkrider Drug Company, that there was a market for such memorabilia that increased in commercial value in proportion to the publisher's ability to capitalize on its moralizing potential.[57] Framed as a warning to blacks to attend to "WHITE MAN'S RULE" and thereby avoid "the fate of the dogwood tree," the photo and poem, identified in the caption as "'U.S. Postcard,' 1908," reveal that far from unspeakable or removed from ordinary experience, the spectacle of lynching could be trivialized, mass-produced, made utterly casual by its commercialization as a form of intraracial greeting.[58] Defying the *Memphis Commercial-Appeal's* dictum that "it is not good business to kill [Negroes]" (Ralph Ginzburg, 82), the postcard proves that properly marketed, even dead black bodies were profitable, as the enterprising photographers at the Claude Neal lynching figured by hawking pictures of the corpse to latecomers who missed the "fun" (McGovern, 84–85). The Henry Smith lynching in Paris, Texas, not only spawned the photographic record of the event that Shufeldt ghoulishly reproduced, but someone marketed a gramophone recording of the condemned man's screams, documenting his suffering to extend that edification to those not present and to re-create it for those who were.

The process of social conditioning to appreciate lynching's brutalities began early, as in the cases of whites holding children aloft to see more clearly the torture of the condemned. What they saw that initiated them into the mysteries of whiteness was the black body itself, often stripped naked and subjected to sporadic acts of violence as well as the systematic program of torture. Wells-Barnett cited the New York Sun account of the poetic unspeakableness of the Henry Smith lynching in Paris as evidence of southern horrors: "Words to describe the awful torture inflicted upon Smith cannot be found. . . . His agony was awful. He pleaded and writhed in bodily and mental pain. . . . His clothes were torn off piecemeal and scattered in the crowd, people catching the shreds and putting them away as momentos [sic]" (Lynchings: Red Record, 29). More graphically than Shufeldt's account, the Sun documented how the father, brother, and two uncles of the slain child took turns administering hot irons to Smith, to the cheers of the crowd of ten thousand: "After burning the feet and legs, the hot irons— plenty of fresh ones being at hand—were rolled up and down Smith's stomach. Then the eyes were burned out and irons were thrust down his throat" (29).

An outraged black spectator, ridden out of town on a rail for overly protesting the sadistic torture, reported:

> One little tot scarcely older than Myrtle Vance [the murder victim] clapped her baby hands as her father held her on his shoulders above the heads of the people.
> "For God's sake," I shouted, "send the children home."
> "No, no," shouted a hundred maddened voices; "let them learn a lesson." (31)

The observer, a black preacher named Reverend King, noted "children of both sexes and colors," indicating that as of 1893, audiences for lynchings had not yet developed into race-exclusive gatherings. To King, "the little faces distorted with passion and the bloodshot eyes of the cruel parents who held them high in their arms" made him thankful he had no children of his own.[59]

Attention to the "poetics of jurisprudence" reveals, however, that a perhaps unconscious sense of fitness obtained in the presence of children at the execution of a man accused of murdering a child. But this justification did not explain other instances in which the entire spectrum of white society was represented at lynchings in retaliation for less spectacular offenses. Nor does it explain the tortures and mutilations in retaliation for alleged rapes that were performed before crowds that included many to whom parents could not describe the mechanics of rape for fear of poisoning their imaginations. But because mutilation, in particular, represented an unmediated reaction by whites to the intrusive presence of blacks, its performance could not be subtracted from the whole cultural context of lynching without a corresponding loss of coherence both in lynching's poetics and its interest in the grotesque. Lynching's ludic atmosphere permitted the strictly superficial contradiction of white savagery serving as a mode of education in the appropriate disciplining of unruly black bodies. Denied access to the inscriptions of white desire on the body of the condemned, the children would not learn the ultimate exhilaration of the asymmetrical power of whiteness, a power-knowledge that white adults acquired from the slaveholding generations before them. A key objective of the mutilation and torture was therefore faintly utopian—there was a presumption that as a sign of white will to rule, the lynching victim would exert a centrifugal pull sufficient to hold the momentarily visible empire of whiteness inviolate through posterity.

Indulging this sense of power, a mob in Vicksburg, Mississippi, in 1905 cut off the ears and fingers of a black man and woman, gouged out the man's eye with a stick, and used large corkscrews to tear out "big pieces of raw, quivering flesh" from the arms, legs, and torsos of the pair.[60] The lynching of Richard Coleman in Maysville, Kentucky, in 1899 involved children as attendants to the fire, which produced "teeth and bones and flesh" as relics for souvenir hunters (Harris, 9). Charles S. Johnson reported a story told to him of the castration of a three-year-old black boy who pulled at a four-year-old white girl's underpants (Shapiro, 220). A Kountze, Texas, mob removed the heart and genitals of a man accused of murdering a white woman, after dragging his body behind an automobile "for thirty-five minutes through the Negro section of Kountze to terrorize the negro population" (Ralph Ginzburg, 212). Though much of the mutilation involved the "lower bodily stratum" of the condemned, lynchers seemed to act on an impulse to render the faces of captives unrecognizable, and to attack other points of symbolic importance as well. In Newman, Georgia, in 1899, Sam Hose's heart and liver were removed and sold to the crowd: "Small pieces of bones went for 25 cents, and a bit of the liver crisply cooked sold for 10 cents" (Tolnay and Beck, 23). In Terre Haute, Indiana, in 1901, boys with knives auctioned toes and other body parts to trophy seekers, while in Leesburg, Texas, in 1921, "leaders of the mob drew lots for the part of the Negro's anatomy which they regarded as the choicest souvenir" (Ralph Ginzburg, 37, 155).

The lynching of Claude Neal in Florida in 1934, which, as previously reported, was announced in the press, did not go off precisely as planned. Rather than allow the scheduled mutilation by the father to start the events, because of crowd demands, "it was decided to do away with him first and then bring him to the Cannidy house dead." Therefore, the mob began the main event earlier than planned: "they cut off his penis. He was made to eat it. Then they cut off his testicles and made him eat them and say he liked it. . . . Then they sliced his sides and stomach with knives and every now and then somebody would cut off a finger or a toe" (McGovern, 80). After hours of mutilation and burning, Neal was killed, to the displeasure of the Cannidy family, who only got their chance at mutilation after Neal was beyond suffering. "They done me wrong," George Cannidy complained, bitter at not having gotten first crack at Neal (McGovern, 82). Nevertheless, a woman from the Cannidy household and neighborhood children did get their chance to plunge sharp objects into the corpse, after which it was kicked and run over by cars.

A similar incident in Moultrie, Georgia, in 1921, at which the suitably anonymous "negro Williams" was stripped, castrated, and made to swallow his penis (a portion of which "was sent by parcel post to Governor Dorsey, whom the people of this section hate[d] bitterly"), ended with "a hundred men and women, old and young, grandmothers among them," joining hands and dancing around while the Negro burned, followed by a gala community barn dance that same evening (Ralph Ginzburg, 153). For kissing a white girl, Charles Fisher had his lips and ears sheared off, and he was mutilated "in other ways below the belt" (Ralph Ginzburg, 90). In the 1922 triple lynching in Kirvin, Texas, three men, later discovered to be innocent bystanders in a feud between white Texas families that ended in the death of a white girl, were mutilated in a style that seems to sum up the entire significance of the practice: "Ears, toes, and fingers were snipped off. Eyes were gouged out, no organ of the negroes was allowed to remain protruding" (Graham, 197–98).

Lynching reveled in its power to destroy the materiality of the human form despite its avowed purpose of restoring purity, sanctity, and domestic pieties because the transgressive "burly black brute" that would not remain out of white space had to be physically prevented from committing further intrusion. This transformation coordinated two themes within the poetics of jurisprudence —

the divestment of the condemned's potential for intrusive, assertive behavior, on the one hand, and the violation of bodily integrity as revenge for the social injury allegedly perpetrated. Not only was any bodily part that blundered into white space, or which had the potential for doing so, ritually excised, but the black body itself was ruptured, invaded, probed, severed, dismembered, disintegrated. Genital wounding expiated genital wounding; crowds crying "too soon, too soon," reminded the masters of ceremonies to prolong the condemned's agony in reasonable imitation of the endless horror of the violated.

Conventions such as the use of burning, shooting, or hanging (or, in most cases, any combination of two or three) seemed to follow a certain logic that privileged the obliterating of the black body as a totality, while leaving traces that could be produced to document white race heroism. Burning purified the evil, even as it prolonged the death agony, a not inconsiderable detail, given the myth of black imperviousness to pain. According to Stephen Graham, southerners saw burning as appropriate to the nature of the black criminal: "'Like the animals, . . . he does not feel pain. When he is burned it is not the same as a white man burning'" (197–98). Further justification existed in the form of an attack on that which triggered black criminality: "for the negro is a thing of the senses, and with this race and with all similar races the desire of the senses must be restrained by the terror of the senses."[61] "God will burn . . . the Big African Brute in Hot Hell for molesting our God-like pure snowwhite angelic American Women," one apologist declared (Hall, 112), but why should God alone enjoy the spectacle? "Make 'em die slow" was the "watchword" in the South (Graham, 202).

Hanging, by using flagpoles, courthouses, Fourth of July trappings, and other sites of national and local power and prestige, debased the black body by making it a territorial marker of white exclusivity (Ralph Ginzburg, 139). Like burning, shooting obliterated the body to signal the power of the white nation, particularly in the numerous instances in which the entire assembled mob was able to effect the purification rite by emptying their guns into the body, guaranteeing its inability to return to life. The expression "shot to pieces" was a common description of the practice, in which thousands of rounds might be pumped into the body. On the occasions when whites did not trust the body signatures to convey their intentions adequately, they appended printed signs, many containing some variation of the sentiment "We Must Protect Our Southern Women."[62] Even the souvenirs were signed—"What is left of the niggers that shot a white man"—and displayed for public consumption (Ralph Ginzburg, 168). These trophies formed the ultimate class of lynch law documentation, as bits and pieces of

destroyed black bodies circulated in white communities across the nation, objects of ridicule and wonder, as though only by a specious homeopathy could the
threat of the black presence in America be rendered harmless. Englishman
Stephen Graham was stunned by the cruelty and the ferocity of the white citizenry, even after a lynching was over. But he was never so amazed as by the
southern obsession with documenting participation in the human sacrifice: "I
met Whites who boasted of having taken part in a lynching, and I have met those
who possessed gruesome mementoes in the shape of charred bones and grey dry
Negro skin. I said they were fools. Actually to have the signs upon them!" (Graham, 209). While Graham was concerned about his hosts having the signs of
criminal activity upon them, they were far more concerned that their signs effected the magic they required: "Beware all Darkies! You will be treated the
same way!" (Ralph Ginzburg, 15).

The black body, commodified, plundered, increased in exchange value in
proportion to its ensured docility—only the Nazis were able to improve on the
economics of lynching. Displayed upon shelves in parlors and shops; contained,
finally, in glass jars with preservatives to maintain its immobility and innocuousness; fetishized; exported as a keepsake for friends and as a warning to foes—the
black body was even more grotesque disassembled, the subject of wild imaginings stripped of any inherent power to harm. The final evidence of the autocracy
of race lies in the extent to which whites participated or acquiesced in such practices as proof of superiority. No "Negro domination" would ever leave them again
sleepless, gun in hand, waiting for the apocalypse. Jim Crowed or lynched—
docile or dead—each black body of death was a sign to blacks not to disturb the
dream of a white America.

Many blacks simply left, choosing to travel to all-black towns in the West and
to urban areas in the North to escape southern terrorism. But many others left
abruptly, going nowhere in particular, without choice and without prior notice,
as the logic of lynch law extended to the creation of white space counties all over
the South. In many cases, what began as lynchings turned into full-scale rioting—"pogroms against the whole black community" (Hall, 141)—as whites
sought to purify, by burning and looting, the "diseased" sections of their cities
where blacks, honky-tonks, and illicit interracial contact were to be found.[63] In
the prophetically named Whitesboro, Texas, all blacks were driven out after an
accusation of interracial rape led to an aborted lynching, after which whites
went on the rampage: "Guns were fired promiscuously in the negro section, and
the terror stricken negroes were ordered to leave at once. As a result outgoing

trains on all roads were filled with negroes" (Ralph Ginzburg, 61). According to Raper, "[Since Whitesboro, Negroes] have been forced out of Bells, Southmayd, Ruella, Hagermann, Pottsboro, and Saddler[, Texas]. In numerous communities in central southern Oklahoma immediately north of Grayson County and in Texas counties to the west, no Negroes are allowed. 'Nigger, don't let the sun go down on you here,' is a common phrase in these parts" (354–55). In Marion, Indiana, in 1930, a mob threatened to burn out the section of the city famed for interracial alliances after the double lynching of Abram Smith and Thomas Shipp, while in the previously all-white Shamrock, Texas, where blacks had not been able at one time to "stick their heads out of the train coaches," a determined sheriff had foiled a lynch attempt, leading to a mob bent on "burning out" the newly settled blacks (Raper, 451–52). But in Sherman, Texas, the mob nearly succeeded in burning out the entire black business district after a successful lynching, during which the county courthouse was razed to get to a protected prisoner: "Every Negro had disappeared from the Negro Section, even from districts which were not burning, . . . reported to be huddling in brush thickets on the outskirts of Sherman."[64] Deriding the town's self-image, the news account notes in closing that Sherman was "known as 'The Athens of Texas.'" Tazewell and Buchanan Counties in Virginia were early sites in a growing trend of violently establishing geopolitical white space, a route later followed by, among others, Forsyth County, Georgia (Brundage, 146, 122). Ray Stannard Baker reported the expulsion of all blacks from Evening Shade, Arkansas, for no apparent reason, forcing them to abandon all their property, while blacks in Waurika, Oklahoma, were ordered out in 1907: "Negroes, beware the cappers. We, the Sixty Sons of Waurika, demand the Negroes to leave here at once. We mean Go! Leave in twenty-four hours, or after that your life is uncertain" (71–72).

So powerful was lynching as a tool of race terrorism that it began to be used to cover up crimes actually committed by whites. White women, under social sanction to uphold the myth of white female purity, would sometimes invent a black rapist to protect a white lover.[65] According to Raper, "numerous cases [were] on record of white criminals who . . . blackened their faces to disguise themselves."[66] In one such instance, a young woman in Dade City, Florida, was attacked by a relative of hers by marriage who blackened his face to throw suspicion off himself (Ralph Ginzburg, 119). We are left, then, with the central paradox of lynching's politics of identity: the need for black bodies to define a range of activity forbidden to white bodies in relation to other white bodies, within a ritual context climaxing in the expulsion of black bodies as a sign of communal health.

No taboo existed for white males in relation to black bodies; they were largely free to rape, to murder, to loot, to torture and dismember blacks in the company of other whites, and with the acquiescence, if not outright approval, of their communities.

In their need to define crime as inherently a problem of black access to the white world, individuals could always costume themselves in black bodies to disguise criminality against other whites. But on another level, blackface crime merely extended the logic of blackface minstrelsy in creating a space of blackness within which the fantasy life of white America could unfold. As Ostendorf explains, "Those first white minstrels literally *incorporated* the role and circumscribed the symbolic space they wanted blacks to occupy. They assumed the face (mask, persona, role, identity), the bodies and the dresses of the unmanageable group and showed them who they 'really were'" (70). Having created that space, whites were free to occupy it themselves without stigma or personal consequence: "In minstrelsy Americans could be as uncivilized, barbaric and irrational as they pleased and then pass the buck to blacks" (Ostendorf, 80). Paradoxically, because of white determination that blacks should not "embody" with them, the mimicry of black bodies for comic and criminal purposes alike became foundational to the white imaginary, a conjunction of ideology, fantasy, and opportunity that, in inventing the dangerous and docile black bodies of popular culture, left an unmistakable imprint upon the black imaginary as well.

The system keeping black Americans in "their place" functioned both as physical and psychic violence, which ensured white male prerogative by establishing behavioral and identity parameters for white females and black people. "Moral regulation" of whites by whites decreased dramatically after the 1880s, focusing on sensational, capital crimes, allowing lynching as a first option of social control to become a largely race-specific form of punishment.[67] Lynching was a crucial component of a southern culture dedicated in the Progressive Era to the reinstatement of the legal, economic, and behavioral attributes of slavery's "social death" by forcing a state of nondifferentiation, nonassertion, and nonambition on the black population. Blacks and whites alike maintained this system, the motivation for black compliance being that assertive behavior by any would often result in white vigilantes singling out someone at random for punishment as an example to the rest. In this manner, whites turned the myth of black nondifferentiation into a powerful tool for terror, making clear that intrusions into the social space of privileged white activity was a form of "racial" assault for which they would punish the black "race" as a whole. As Ralph Ellison pointed out in

"Richard Wright's Blues," the system artificially induced in black Americans an irrational fear of performing any act that might call attention to themselves, since "to wander from the paths of behavior laid down for the group [was] to become the agent of communal disaster." Ellison, citing sociologist Edward Bland, identified this mass psychology as "pre-individualism,"[68] but its prevailing philosophy of social self-erasure was a prescription for a return to slavery's "social death" through the Brownlow tradition.

The Fatal Woman

The historical record indicates that black citizens contested the exclusivity of white space in the abstract and particular at almost every conceivable point of encroachment. Still, the fact of irregular enforcement against black assertiveness did not weaken the prevailing structure of relations, since any white could demand performance from any black and could claim communal support on the grounds of white "solidarity." The availability of myths of white female vulnerability especially invested their bodies with magical power in contests over public space. As a key component of Brownlow training, blacks defensively resorted to ritual behavior in approaching white females. Joel Williamson attributes white paranoia about "blacks 'bumping' whites, especially white women off the sidewalks," to a growing presumptuousness in the race that spelled rebelliousness (*Crucible*, 187). The importance of blacks "giving the wall" or yielding the sidewalk was an antebellum practice reinstated by the Brownlow tradition (Doyle, 55). Two black women in Statesboro, Georgia, in 1904 were dragged from a church, whipped violently, and expelled from the county after they were "said to have crowded two respectable white girls off the sidewalk" (Ray Stannard Baker, 182).

In the 1930s, Rollin Chambliss wrote in his master's thesis for the University of Georgia, "I have always understood that a Negro who touches a white woman must die. It is something that we learn in the South without knowing how or when or where. I have heard the statement made by men in the community who were models of right living. Somewhere out of the past this idea came, born of pride in our own culture and possibly of an unrecognized fear that it might not persist" (in Myrdal, 1194). Clearly Chambliss meant by "touching" some form of sexual overture, but the ambiguity is pertinent to the mythic unapproachableness of the white female. Profane, unauthorized advance toward this "holy of holies" would earn violent punishment for the transgressor, and eventually, "black men came generally to avoid being alone with white women, were careful not to meet feminine eyes with a level gaze, and guarded the tone of their voices in the presence of white females" (Williamson, *Crucible*, 117).

The mythic fatal white female ultimately played a crucial role in the reinstatement of slavery's lost spatial economies, providing the emotional lever that justified lynching, Jim Crow, and black male political "emasculation" in the Progressive Era. The boundary rituals involving the white female body had the additional effect of fetishizing the black male body, particularly the reproductive organs. According to Mary Douglas, in pollution behavior, there are no degrees of contamination: "the only material question is whether a forbidden contact has taken place or not" (130). The Jim Crow South took this principle one step further: the only material question was whether or not the forbidden contact had been conceivable.

There are court decisions on record that asserted the principle that any suspicion that a black man may have considered, planned, or been capable of sexual relations with a white woman was grounds for punishment. In *Jackson v. State of Georgia* (1893), the superior court ruled that because a black man, Major Jackson, had brought his genitals "within what may be termed 'striking distance' of the organs of the [white] female," by entering her room through a window, he should be considered guilty of attempted rape: "No actual touching of the woman's person is necessary to complete the assault. There need be nothing more than the intention to accomplish sexual intercourse presently by force" (Baughman, 117). Jackson's intrusion into the domestic space of the white female was sufficient violation, by communal standards, to warrant punishment for the "one crime," but to allay any doubts that it meant for the interracial nature of the encounter to be the main issue in the disposition of the case, the court affirmed the right of "social customs, founded on race differences, and the fact that the man was a negro and the girl a white person, might be taken into consideration" (Baughman, 118).

This legalistic code meant more often than not that the judge's own ideas on interracial relations were permissible and pertinent to the judicial process. William W. Callahan, an Alabama judge in one of the Scottsboro Boys rape trials in 1933, explained white female race chastity this way: "There is a very strong presumption under the law [that a white woman] would not . . . yield voluntarily to intercourse with . . . a Negro . . . whatever the station in life the prosecutrix may occupy, whether she be the most despised, ignorant and abandoned woman of the community, or the spotless virgin and daughter of a prominent home of luxury and learning" (Whitfield, 115). The sensational Scottsboro case showed that as the lynch craze waned in the thirties and forties, the institutional pattern of violently enforced race chastity still prevailed, with lynching supplemented and then supplanted by a system of "legal lynching." Of the 455 men executed by states for the crime of rape since 1930, 405 were black, with virtually all accused of assaulting white women (Whitfield, 116).

A 1911 case, *Kelly v. State of Alabama*, went even further than *Jackson v. Georgia*, arguing that the only possible outcome of an unsupervised encounter between a black male and a white female was attempted rape.[69] Such a legal history buttressed by the myth of autonomous black male sexuality made it seem "natural" that "political struggles over integration . . . take on the imagery of white rape" (O'Neill, 82). As with other ritual pollution behavior, interpellation of white male agency by the rhetoric of white female vulnerability occurred in response to otherwise negligible social infractions. Newspaper editorials, political rallies, and other semiofficial vehicles of race nationalism were constant sources of discourse about the inviolability of the white female body. In this way, the invocation of the idea of white female sanctity—the very words "white woman"—ultimately, in the discourse of race difference, acquired the magical power to render black bodies submissive.

In October 1913, a black man was lynched in Monroe, Louisiana, for making "an insulting remark" to a white woman, while a black man running for a train in Mississippi in 1916 accidentally bumped into the daughter of a white farmer and was lynched (Ralph Ginzburg, 89, 102). The NAACP's publication the *Crisis*, in its annual roundup of lynchings for 1914, reported a similar episode of "an impudent porter [who] pushed a white woman off the sidewalk and was lynched."[70] The article goes on to report the lynching of two men found in white women's rooms, while the previous year's roundup mentions the lynching of a man found *under* the house of a white woman. Ray Stannard Baker reported that a race riot in Danville, Illinois, in 1904 was caused by a starving black thief who knocked down a white woman as he fled her house, and the Brownsville incident of 1906 was sparked by white indignation after a woman was either grabbed or patted on the head by a passing black soldier as she stood inside her fence (Williamson, *Crucible*, 354). As we have seen, paranoia about black male intent made it unnecessary that there even be physical contact with white women for mob action to occur. Into this category of crime goes the "rape by leer" conviction of Matt Ingram in 1951, who spent two and a half years in prison for "assaulting" a white woman who was seventy-five feet away from him because of the "way he allegedly looked at her" (Berry and Blassingame, 124).

Visual appropriation of the white female form, a type of aggressive speculation, may have made whites nervous because it suggested the contemplation of
crime, but a black man who blundered into a white woman's field of vision without warning might also be suspected of harmful intent. In Atlanta, an elderly
white woman contributed to that city's riot by screaming when she saw a black
man on the sidewalk as she was closing her window blinds. Though the woman
recovered quickly and canceled her call for police assistance, the incident was
"chronicled in letters five inches high in a newspaper extra" as an "assault" and
became one of the triggering episodes of the bloody 1906 Atlanta race riot.[71] A
few months after the riot, one Atlanta newspaper, desperate to remain financially
viable, was still playing to white public opinion with incendiary editorials about
the menace to white women. Denying any "law of God or man" the authority to
forestall white male vengeance, one editorial promised to "double and treble
and quadruple the law of Moses" by hanging "off-hand" a black rapist or by proxy
lynching "two or three or four of the Negroes nearest to the crime" until blacks
understood that assaults on white women would not be tolerated (Ray Stannard
Baker, 25). Newspapers waged propaganda campaigns on behalf of white female
sanctity, even (or perhaps, especially) when no particular white woman was involved. The mere suggestion that every single white woman was not practicing
race chastity was cause for violent retaliation, according to these papers.

In other cases reported by the press, men were lynched for publicly kissing
their white women friends, for having love letters from white women, for specu-
lating about an uprising in which only white women were to be spared to become concubines of black men, and for dating white women while passing for
white (Ralph Ginzburg, 95, 159, 161, 172). In another case, a seventy-two-year-old
black man found walking with a white woman had his hands cut off and was
thrown in the Suwannee River to drown (Tolnay and Beck, 77). One Scooba,
Mississippi, official asserted that a 1930 lynching was incited by the alarming "increase of intimate relations between white women and Negro men" but then offered that the solution was the "establishment of a red light district, with white
and Negro women, in which only white men would be allowed" (Raper, 90).

Clearly, sexual contact between black men and white women never completely disappeared in the South, even during the era of lynching and rioting.
But just as clearly, the period ushered in an image of the fatal white woman who
could destroy black men with a single word or glance. Ray Stannard Baker related the story of a white woman who was amazed at the power she had to terrify
black men who came near her. She described her shoulder being brushed by "a

rather good-looking young Negro" hurrying along the sidewalk who had not noticed her: "'When he looked around and found it was a white woman he had touched, such a look of abject terror and fear came into his face as I hope never again to see on a human countenance. He knew what it meant if I was frightened, called for help, and accused him of insulting or attacking me. . . . It shows, does n't it, how little it might take to bring punishment upon an innocent man?'" (8). Baker also related an incident told to him by a bishop of the African Methodist Episcopal (AME) church, a "man of wide attainments," who, while serving at a rural post, once startled a white woman by appearing suddenly through a cluster of trees. The woman screamed and ran off. "'If I had been some Negroes,' said Bishop Gaines, 'I should have turned and fled in terror; the alarm would have been given, and . . . if I had been caught what would my life have been worth?'" (8). The bishop was able to save his life by following the woman and convincing her of his lack of harmful intent and apologizing for scaring her. Yet the incident shows the precariousness of life for even a committed community servant when the myths of the black beast and the fatal white woman collided.

If white women began to represent the possibility of instant death, they also possessed on rare occasions the magical power to bring the "dead" back to life. The story told by James Cameron of his miraculous escape from a lynch mob in Marion, Indiana, in 1930 illustrates the presumption that a black male's physical proximity to an unprotected white female could have no other intent than rape. An accomplice to a lover's lane murder of a white man, Cameron had run from the scene before his friends, Thomas Shipp and Abram Smith, pulled the trigger. But after the capture of Shipp and Smith, who named him as the ringleader, Cameron found himself faced with murder and rape charges. Alerted in jail by the sudden appearance of the city's mayor with a masked white man that his exact location in the jail was being charted to aid the lynchers in finding him, Cameron grew alarmed at the "carnival atmosphere" of the crowd outside the jailhouse: "The only thing that seemed to be missing was the vendors" (Cameron, 55). Law enforcement officials cooperated with and instructed the crowd on how to circumvent their pro forma efforts to prevent the lynching, and the front line of women and children participants provided a pretext for the jailers not to fire their weapons. Watching as first Shipp and then Smith were brutalized and lynched, Cameron found himself facing the menacing crowd.

With the rope around his neck, standing beneath the tree where his two friends were already hanging, Cameron heard a disembodied voice ring out: "Take this boy back. He had nothing to do with any raping or killing!" (Cameron, 74). Cameron's later investigation convinced him that no one else at the scene had heard this voice; yet for some reason, the mob transformed itself back into a sea of humanity and allowed him to walk back to the jail relatively unharmed. The inexplicable act of mercy by a bloodthirsty crowd, summoned unconsciously by the unheard woman's voice, made it possible for Cameron, after sweating out another planned lynching, to go to trial. The meaning of the disembodied voice that saved him later becomes clear when, during the trial, the female companion of the murder victim stunned the prosecution and the police by swearing in court that she had not been raped. For a second, miraculous time, a female voice had saved him from certain death. Cameron served time in prison and lived to write about his ordeal.

The Marion, Indiana, case highlights many of lynching's paradoxes, not the least of which includes the arbitrary enforcement of customs of race chastity. The racial antagonism in Marion, technically a northern city with only a small black population, stemmed from a core of working-class whites who avoided contact with blacks. According to Raper's extensive account of the lynching, though, the young woman in the case was widely reputed among whites (including skeptical newspaper reports) to be among those lower-class whites who were intimate with blacks. These whites asserted, in fact, that Mary Ball was actually a member of Cameron's gang whose function was to lure young white men to the lover's lane where the black gang members waited to rob them (Raper, 387–88).[72] The fact that the lynchers intended to send a message to those who strayed across the race line was clear from their attempted assault on the Johnston district, a poor section where interracial couples resided and informal interracial contacts were made (Raper, 406). One further aberration was the local NAACP's successful campaign to have some of the lynchers indicted and prosecuted (none were convicted) (Raper, 394).

To Raper, there was no question that the rape charge was a subterfuge, perhaps even a cover-up for transgressive white female behavior, and he used the fact that there were whites in jail at the time of the lynching who had committed more heinous crimes against other whites, including rape, dismemberment, and murder, to show that it was not the brutality of the alleged crimes or the social identity of the victims so much as the race of the criminals that made the lynchings possible (397). That a town that had tolerated interracial romances would lynch two men on a false charge of interracial rape reveals the shifting terms of white space boundaries that could make one day's permissible behavior another day's lynchable offense. Whatever sparked the lynching response, the event itself was a clear attempt to impose an ideology of separation on social practices disapproved of by the lynchers. The fabrication of a rape charge in an instance in which the real issue was white male rage over white female sexual nonconformity calls into doubt the many lynchings for sexual assault through the period of lynch law. Because of the high likelihood of a lynching in such cases, as well as the communal reluctance to have victims of assault take the witness stand, many cases reported as rapes were never subjected to close scrutiny. Over the years, the lore of the white woman who could bring death by bearing false witness against an innocent black man gained wide circulation among black Americans, owing in large part to the work of the first and most influential analyst of the rhetoric of lynching, Ida B. Wells-Barnett, who exposed the terroristic function of the "one crime" scare.

Southern Horrors

Based in economic, caste, and gender conventions of the time, the elaborate mythic apparatus of southern life conditioned black existence profoundly. Black writers implicitly recognized the power of racist discourse to constitute the subject position of white race identity. Their works were not simply protests but interventions in the discursive chain that naturalized white subjectivity and black objectification. To the reality of the South expressed by those whose entitlements arose from white race privilege, they offered an opposing subjectivity; to the mythology of race difference they offered countermyths. Writers such as Chesnutt and Hopkins produced no radical critique of American culture; when they questioned its color-consciousness, it was done in works that sometimes casually reflected prevailing theories of race difference. Perhaps the most penetrating analysis of race and capitalism outside of W. E. B. Du Bois came from a writer who did not specialize in literature but who was responsible for identifying a formula for tragedy in American life that influenced the literature that followed.

Ida B. Wells-Barnett introduced the mythic figure of the white witch in her exposés of the "one crime," *Southern Horrors* (1892) and *A Red Record* (1895). In her antilynching pamphlets, Wells-Barnett told of the incident that propelled her into national attention and a career as a spokesperson against lynching, when three black businessmen were lynched on March 9, 1892. Their crime was to open a grocery store that took business away from a white store owner, and they were arrested after a shootout with white officers whom the white store owner had called in on his behalf. These officers attempted to enter the back door of the black store in the dead of night, and the store's defenders opened fire. Three officers were wounded, but none died.

Thirty-one blacks were arrested on a charge of conspiracy, though they protested that the officers never identified themselves as lawmen. When the wounded men recovered, according to Wells-Barnett, "this hindered rather than helped the plans of the whites. There was no law in the statute books which would execute an Afro-American for wounding a white man, but the 'unwritten law.' Three of these men, the president, the manager and clerk of the grocery— 'the leaders of the conspiracy'—were secretly taken from jail and lynched in a shockingly brutal manner. 'The Negroes are getting too independent,' they say, 'we must teach them a lesson.' What lesson? The lesson of subordination" (*Lynching, Southern Horrors*, 19). Because the men were prominent in Memphis black business circles and known to Wells-Barnett, she was in a position to see at the outset of the lynching craze the complicity of white law enforcement, civic, business, and social interests in a campaign of terror aimed at curtailing black economic independence. Wells-Barnett's weekly newspaper, the *Memphis Free Speech*, counseled blacks to migrate rather than rebel.[73]

Her analysis needed no more than a cursory glimpse of the white press, however, which took the lead in narrating the race nationalist significance of the event:

> Aside from the violation of white women by Negroes, which is the outcropping of a bestial perversion of instinct, the chief cause of trouble between the races in the South is the Negro's lack of manners. . . . [The Negro] has taken up the idea that boorish insolence is independence, and the exercise of a decent degree of breeding toward white people is identical with servile submission.
>
>   We have had too many instances right here in Memphis to doubt this, and our experience is not exceptional. *The white people won't stand this sort of thing, and whether they be insulted as individuals are* [sic] *as a race, the response will be prompt and effectual.* (In Wells-Barnett, *Lynchings: Southern Horrors*, 17)

The article goes on to note that "the majority of [uppity blacks] are Negroes who have received educational advantages at the hands of white people," to drive home the fashionable criticism against educating Negroes "beyond their station in life" (17–18).

Wells-Barnett's twofold attack on lynch law was to dispute the emerging "one crime" justification by statistical analysis of the alleged causes of lynching and especially by contesting all crimes reported as rapes. By this method, she was able to demonstrate that factors other than the alleged epidemic of rapes lay behind the upsurge in lynchings. On the basis of the March lynchings, the threats against black assertiveness, and other incidents that she knew of in which lynchings had terminated consensual relations, using rape as an excuse, Wells-Barnett wrote an editorial in her paper on May 21, 1892, charging that the myth of the black rapist had been used to cover up eight lynchings in the South in one week and that "the same old racket—the new alarm about raping white women" had been prominent in five of the episodes (*Lynchings: Southern Horrors*, 4). The outrage in the white community over this "insult" to white womanhood resulted in the newspaper's business manager's expulsion from town, the destruction of Wells-Barnett's property, and her forced exile (she was out of town at the time of the mob attack) under threat of death. What so inflamed the whites was Well-Barnett's sarcastic suggestion that since "no one believes the old thread bare lie that Negro men rape white women," if whites were not careful, they would cause people to suspect "the moral reputation of their women" (4). The local white press was quick to demand violent retribution.[74]

Yet documented cases of interracial love affairs that ended in lynchings were being reported by the white press itself, and Wells-Barnett was resourceful enough to use such "unbiased" sources to buttress her claims (7–10). One of the May lynchings, for example, had reportedly resulted from a black man raping the "eight-year-old" daughter of a sheriff in Indianola, Mississippi. But according to Wells-Barnett, "the girl was more than eighteen years old, and was found by her father in the man's room, who was a servant on the place" (19). Wells-Barnett cited an 1887 incident in Montgomery, Alabama, in which J. C. Dukes of the *Montgomery Herald* was, "like the *Free Speech* proprietors, . . . forced to leave the city for reflecting on the 'honah' of white women," in suggesting that "white women attract negro men now more than in former days," because of the "growing appreciation of white Juliets for colored Romeos" (5–6). She then turned an entire chapter over to "The Black and White" of interracial romances involving white women, including some that ended in lynching, incarceration, and near execution when the woman cried rape under communal coercion.

Wells-Barnett's understanding of how the myth of the "one crime" silenced opposition to lynching was among her most lasting and significant contributions: "This cry has had its effect. . . . Men who stand high in the esteem of the public for Christian character, for moral and physical courage, for devotion to the principles of equal and exact justice to all, and for great sagacity, stand as cowards who fear to open their mouths before this great outrage" (14).[75] Even "the better

class of Afro-Americans," according to Wells-Barnett, were intimidated into acquiescence, "hoping and believing that education and financial strength would
solve the difficulty, and . . . devoting their energies to the accumulation of both."

While Wells-Barnett battled sensationalism in the press, she was more aggressively engaged in challenging the news medium's suppressions of consensual liaisons between white women and black men through lynch law, accomplished
by the manufacture of phony rape charges. Suppression of the existence of voluntary relations between white women and black men was important enough as
a social issue that noncombatants in the southern race war felt compelled to address it. Frances Willard of the Women's Christian Temperance Union spoke out
against Wells-Barnett's "statements . . . concerning white women having taken
the initiative in nameless acts between the races," insisting that she "had put an
imputation upon half the white race in this country that [was] unjust" (Wells-
Barnett, Lynchings: Red Record, 80). Willard warned Wells-Barnett "as a friend
and a well-wisher to banish from her vocabulary all such allusions" because they
hurt her antilynching crusade. In the WCTU publication, Union Signal, for December 6, 1894, the organization printed a resolution that denounced lynchings
but insisted that they were the result of "unspeakable outrages," demanding action so that "childhood, maidenhood and womanhood [would] no more be victims of atrocities worse than death."[76]

To Wells-Barnett, the "one crime" mythology boiled down to cases of actual
assaults augmented by white crimes committed in blackface, cases of scapegoating blacks for white crimes and misconduct, and instances of violent public reactions to the discovery of consensual relationships between white women and
black men that became classified as rapes because of communal pollution fears.
Her experience with press distortions in the triple lynching in Memphis led her
to investigations of the lynchings that had transpired in the interim: "I stumbled
on the amazing record that in every case of rape reported in that three months
became such only when it became public" (Crusade, 64–65). In A Red Record
she writes, "The question must be asked, what the white man means when he
charges the black man with rape. Does he mean the crime which the statutes of
the civilized states describe as such? Not by any means. With the Southern white
man, any mesalliance existing between a white woman and a colored man is a
sufficient foundation for the charge of rape. The Southern white man says that
it is impossible for a voluntary alliance to exist between a white woman and a
colored man, and therefore, the fact of an alliance is proof of force" (Lynchings,
11). Wells-Barnett was the first to recognize that white women, in effect, were

enjoined by custom, law, and national interest from giving nonwhite men access to their bodies, with the lynching of the boundary transgressor the new method of enforcement. As Hazel Carby notes, "Wells . . . was able to reveal how a patriarchal system which lost its total ownership over black male bodies used its control over women to completely circumscribe the actions of black male labor" (115).

The Wilmington, North Carolina, riot of 1898 was also set off in part by remarks regarding white female race chastity in the *Wilmington Record*, edited by Alexander Manly. Manly, who explained later that he was simply tired of the rape mythology used to defame black men, lashed out at Rebecca Felton's demand for more lynchings by laying the blame for the hysteria on white males' inability to force race chastity on white women: "Experience among poor white people of the country teaches us that women of that race are not any more particular in the matter of clandestine meetings with colored men than the white men with colored women. Meetings of this kind go on for some time until the woman's infatuation or the man's boldness brings attention to them, and the man is lynched for rape. Every negro lynched is called a Big Burly Black Brute, when, in fact, many . . . were not only not black and burly, but were sufficiently attractive for white girls of culture and refinement to fall in love with them, as is very well known to all" (Prather, 71–73).[77] Manly's remarks were exploited by radical political forces determined to end the final vestiges of Reconstruction biracialism in North Carolina (Williamson, *Crucible*, 197–98). Under threat of force, Wilmington's Republican city administration was ousted and Manly expelled from the city, but too late to stave off the bloodshed that followed (Williamson, *Crucible*, 195–201). The majority black city was sacrificed on the altar of white female sanctity.

Wells-Barnett's analysis of the role played by the myth of white female somatic inviolability became the foundation of the "white witch" as a type—the white seductress who, when faced with communal rebuke for her interracial dalliance, surrenders her lover to white communal punishment by charging rape. Wells-Barnett wrote in "defense of the Afro-American Sampsons [*sic*] who suffer themselves to be betrayed by white Delilahs." Among a gallery of "Delilahs," Wells introduced a Mrs. J. S. Underwood, wife of an Elyria, Ohio, minister, who had denounced her black lover William Offett as a rapist, only to recant after he had served four years of a fifteen-year sentence.[78] Wells-Barnett also cited a Memphis newspaper's account of a promiscuous and mysterious girl: "If Lillie Bailey, a rather pretty white girl seventeen years of age, who is now at the City Hospital, would be somewhat less reserved about her disgrace there would be some very nauseating details in the story of her life. She is the mother of a little coon" (*Lynchings: Southern Horrors*, 8). A stranger to Memphis, Bailey had been taken in at the Women's Refuge prior to giving birth, only to shock the attendants there with both the birth of the child and her refusal to divulge the story, whether one of "fearful depravity" or "rank outrage." As Wells-Barnett was quick to note, the story of Lillie Bailey was simply one of disappointed love, which, if the child had been white, would have allowed Bailey to remain in the refuge. "But a Negro[,] and to withhold its father's name and thus prevent the killing of another Negro 'rapist'[?] A case of 'fearful depravity'" (*Lynchings: Southern Horrors*, 9). No doubt the irony of the source—a Memphis newspaper like the ones that declared war on Wells-Barnett for libeling southern womanhood—added to her bitter awareness that the white press felt cheated out of a lynching by Lillie Bailey's refusal to play the offered role of "Delilah." Instead, she chose the social death of communal ostracism.

Those who would become the white witch of lynch lore likewise were women willing to risk, at least to a degree, the ostracism of the community, in order to test the boundaries of racialized gender constraints. Some were able to take lovers from men in their household employ, using the same economic leverage that white males had been able to exploit, in addition to the constant threat of public exposure. W. E. B. Du Bois told a story of a white woman who entered the office of a southern black lawyer located in the same public square where "men who [did] not like colored lawyers" worked, "and point[ed] to the white-filled square and sa[id], 'I want five hundred dollars now and if I do not get it I am going to scream.'"[79] Other women, by threatening to cry rape and by other uses of the precedence of race over gender, were able to coerce men into sexual relations that the men otherwise might not have dared. According to Arthur Raper, "In some cases, girls and women who had posed as victims acknowledged that they made these charges to cover their own derelictions, to divert suspicion from some white man, to reconcile their parents, to attract attention, or 'just to have a little excitement'" (37). That such women, who felt gender constraints as keenly as blacks felt racial ones, had always existed in the South (and always would) was Wells-Barnett's implicit contention. Lynching was simply a mechanism by which the South maintained the "lie that black men rape" by forcing complicit white women to denounce them and keep the foundational southern illusion of white female chastity alive.

But when southern white women like Lillie Bailey absolutely would not conform, there was still available as a form of coercion the social limbo into which their seventeenth-century sisters who married or had children by black bondsmen were cast. Historically, as Catherine Clinton reports, a white woman who consorted with a black man lost caste, throwing both of them into social marginality: "one of the marks of 'white trash' [as a social category] was that the women were said to 'associate'—sexually cohabit—with black men" (204). Philip A. Bruce noted that southern life had perpetuated the penalty of expulsion for white women who were deemed sexual transgressors: "The few white women who have given birth to mulattoes have always been regarded as monsters; and without exception, they have belonged to the most impoverished and degraded caste of whites, by whom they are scrupulously avoided as creatures who have sunk to the level of the beasts of the field" (55).

Often, other social misfits and malcontents who challenged white southern patriarchy were lumped into that category of "nonladyhood" as well. The southern woman's right to "protection" from white males "presupposed her obligation to obey" (Hall, 151), making her a resident in a glass prison. "When the southern white woman attempted to abandon her place on the pedestal," explains Jacquelyn Dowd Hall, "she was subject to attack by her protector." Jessie Daniel Ames and the members of the Association of Southern Women for the Prevention of Lynching (a group formed in 1930 to confront potential lynching situations before they could occur) challenged law enforcement officials to do their job and protect black citizens from lynch mobs. As a result, they often "found themselves in receipt of anonymous letters conveying threats in slimy words—threats against Southern white women by Southern white men" (Hall, 154).[80] The principled stand by this group of southern white women deprived the lynch mob of the cherished ideal of helpless, outraged, white Christian womanhood in need of defenders, at a time when the worsening economic conditions of the depression had already begun to produce an upswing in the number of lynchings (Hall, 160). If such church-oriented, middle-class white women could become the objects of vicious, obscene attacks for their extension of Christian charity to alleged black criminals,[81] it stands to reason that what W. J. Cash has referred to as southern "gyneolatry" was a rather thin phenomenon.

The ease with which the reverence for womanhood reverted to vilification based on adherence to race chastity explains one strand in the genealogy of the white witch. The definition of "witch" involved a specific sexual symbolism that could be applied to any white woman who took a black lover. But it was not for this reason that the Devil was traditionally described as the "black man." The Devil who arrived in America from Europe was already so designated, and the details of his mysteries illuminate the mythic inspiration for much of the severe proscription of black male freedom of movement in America. According to one "well-known exorcist," the Devil "would appear in the form of a small, black, shaggy man with a huge phallus. Then, coition with him was very painful, and his semen as icy as his embrace."[82] With an organ once described as "long and as thick as an arm" (Masters, 17–18) and a reputation for simultaneous sodomy and intercourse, the Devil was a phallic god whose worship centered on violent, prolonged, painful intercourse.[83] Thus the legends of genital mutilation as the price of sexual transgression with blacks predated the lynch craze as a social reinforcement of caste divisions.

The ability of white women to take protective cover behind the myth of race chastity in all of its forms allowed them to escape the stigma of violating the central prohibition of their caste. The power available to white women who gained both sexual mastery and life-and-death authority over a man, a power normally prohibited to them, did not come with the traditional liabilities of witchcraft then.[84] By giving in to communal pressure for a scapegoat more suitable than herself, she could escape ritual purification by fire, making possible an important deviation from the witch trial. The exorcism of the black "demon" allowed the woman identified as the site of his demonic intrusion to escape burning at the stake, even if her social life thereafter was marginal.[85]

Sexual relations between blacks and whites, with special attention to black men and white women, became in these counternarratives of race the functional equivalent of a pact with the Devil, though which partner was the Devil depended entirely on the social allegiance of the observer. In the fashion of the true mythologist, Wells-Barnett seized upon this pronounced cultural thread—suspicion of the female—as a basis for debunking the black rapist myth. Playing on white male fears of subterranean female passion, Wells-Barnett constructed a white femme fatale who was doubly duplicitous. To sustain her deception of the white community, the white "Delilah" must betray her black lover. The evolution of the white "Delilah" into the white witch required that suspicion of white females become a defensive racial reflex among black males, "the Afro-American Sampsons [sic] who suffer themselves to be betrayed by white Delilahs" (Lynchings: Southern Horrors, 5). Thus, the myth of the black rapist called forth its appropriate counternarrative of the white seductress who selfishly, perhaps even sadistically, lured black men to their death: "White men lynch the offending Afro-American, not because he is a despoiler of virtue, but because he succumbs to the smiles of white women" (*Lynchings: Southern Horrors*, 6).

Five years before Alexander Manly was run out of Wilmington, North Carolina, for a similar observation of white female sexual adventurism across the color line, Wells-Barnett was exiled from Memphis, Tennessee. Her charge that white female behavior toward black men had consequences for blacks as far reaching as the sexual exploitation of black women by white men was, despite qualification, designed to cast doubt on all allegations of rape against black men. Although Wells-Barnett invoked the imagery of female depravity in order to debunk white female race chastity, she was mostly concerned that "the Negro who was weak enough to take chances when accepting the invitations of these white women" could enable the "entire race [to] be branded as moral monsters" (*Crusade*, 71). Just as she had denounced the practice of black women gaining school appointments through illicit affairs with white school board members, her justification was couched in terms of the larger social consequences of individual behavior by blacks.[86]

Still, as her sympathetic discussion of the Lillie Bailey story proves, Wells-Barnett did not insist that black men practice race chastity, and she was not intent on demonizing white women so much as exposing the hypocritical society that forced on them false choices between the self and the "race": "there are many white women in the South who would marry colored men if such an act would not at once place them beyond the pale of society and within the clutches of the law. The miscegenation laws of the South only operate against the legitimate union of the races; they leave the white man free to seduce all the colored girls he can, but it is death to the colored man who yields to the force and advances of a similar attraction in white women" (*Lynchings: Southern Horrors*, 6). Wells-Barnett provided an illustration of how completely "beyond the pale" of society white women could go in her story of her visit to the home of Frederick Douglass shortly before she published *Southern Horrors* in 1892. At the time, Douglass was in his second marriage to his former secretary, a white woman named Helen Pitts, and when Wells-Barnett was preparing to leave his house, Douglass made a surprising expression of gratitude: "I want to tell you that you are the only colored woman save Mrs. Grimké who has come into my home as a guest and has treated Helen as a hostess has a right to be treated by her guest." Wells-Barnett reflects in her autobiography that she, too, wished Douglass had "chosen one of the beautiful, charming colored women of [her] race for his second wife," but she felt that "it was outrageous that [the Douglasses] should be crucified by both white and black people" for having fallen in love (*Crusade*, 72–73).

Even through her battles with Frances Willard and the WCTU, Wells-Barnett was able to indicate a sensitivity toward the systemic difficulties for white women who took a principled stand against their own communities (Ware, 190). The most dramatic example of her ability to avoid demonizing white women out of hand occurred on her first trip to England as an antilynching crusader. There she became associated with British antilynching activist Catherine Impey, who precipitated a controversy that nearly crippled the transatlantic campaign and cost Wells-Barnett the support of her major patroness, Isabella Fyvie Mayo (*Crusade*, 103–5). Impey's "indiscreet letter" declaring her love for a dental student from Ceylon who was a protégé of Mayo's caused the estrangement of the two white women, and Mayo cast Wells-Barnett "into outer darkness" along with Impey after demanding that the black woman choose sides. Impey's letter to George Ferdinands had explained that she was taking the initiative in expressing an affection "that she was sure [he] felt for her" because "she knew he hesitated to do so, being of a 'darker race'" (Ware, 190–91). Not only did Ferdinands not share Impey's feelings, but he immediately went to Mayo with the letter. Not content with accusing Impey of nymphomania, Mayo tried actively for years to discredit her through innuendo and outright accusation, culminating in her amazing editorial in the antilynching journal *Fraternity* in August 1894 in which she accused Impey of being none other than the fatal white woman who leads black men to their death: "There are women who will 'fancy' anything which will give them a sensation and a little passing notoriety. . . . Morbid egotists may only imagine that 'men fall in love with them.' Be it remembered that even this 'imagination,' if indulged in by a 'white woman,' regarding a 'nigger' in some of the States, would mean *the death of the man*, perhaps the more ignominious death, if he ventured to say in self-defence that the 'imagination' was wholly baseless" (Ware, 195). Mayo made her charge more explicit in her closing: "If the women in the South were all 'pure in heart and sound in head,' we should hear of fewer lynchings; and if British philanthropy . . . set aside the dubious help of these diseased imaginations . . . many good works which now flag and falter, would go on apace" (Ware, 196).

Mayo's withering attack did not stop Impey's work, though it made Wells-Barnett's public association with her more problematic. In *Beyond the Pale*, Vron Ware explains that "the ultimate significance of the episode is that it dramatized important aspects of Ida B. Wells' analysis of lynching" (197), an analysis that differed greatly from Mayo's:

> Isabella Mayo wrote as though it was the immoral and irresponsible behaviour of white women which contributed to the increase of lynching, taking a moralistic view of the activities of actual women. . . . Instead of blaming white women for immorality, [Wells-Barnett's] demand was that such voluntary relationships should be allowed to exist in the open. . . . In other words, Ida B. Wells was not interested in criticizing the behaviour of the white women who were implicated in lynchings; her argument was based on a perception of white womanhood as an ideological component of American racism. (Ware, 196–97)

Ware notes that Wells-Barnett's support of Impey over Mayo after spending one sleepless night "praying for guidance" demonstrates that her own research in the South had shown that white female interracial desire was not pathological but merely an object of cultural suppression: "Catherine, . . . she thought, had made a mistake but not committed a crime" (197). Ware is correct in her assessment of Wells-Barnett's evolving analysis, but she does not give detailed consideration to the imputations of white female duplicity that surfaced in Wells-Barnett's early pamphlets as the broad and, from the black point of view, necessary attack on the myth of white female race chastity that it was.

This episode, known at the time only within antilynching circles, had less immediate effect on the development of the white seductress as a type, though, than the case histories cited by Wells-Barnett to delineate the "white Delilah" archetype. In one instance, a Tennessee lynching took place after Richard Neal was accused of raping Mrs. Jack White in 1893. After Neal was caught, he was brought before Mrs. White, who gave an equivocal identification. The preparations to lynch Neal by hanging him from a tree limb "nearest the spot where the unpardonable sin was committed" (Wells-Barnett, *Lynchings: Red Record*, 64) set in motion the dramatic climax, as reported in the *Memphis Scimitar*, one of the very newspapers that had called for the lynching of Wells-Barnett eight months earlier, following her famous editorial: "Then Neal confessed. He said he was the right man, but denied that he used force or threats to accomplish his purpose. It was a matter of purchase, he claimed, and said the price paid was twenty-five cents. He warned the colored men present to beware of white women and resist temptation, for to yield to their blandishments or to the passions of men, meant death" (Wells-Barnett, *Lynchings: Red Record*, 64). Neal's revelation did not affect the outcome, however. Jack White, the husband of the alleged victim, performed the actual lynching as the party whose proprietary rights had been violated. But before the execution, another dramatic scene took place: "While [Neal] was speaking, Mrs. White came from her home and calling Constable Cash to one side, asked if he could not save the Negro's life. The reply was 'No,' and Mrs. White returned to the house." The fact that at the very moment Neal was accusing her of prostitution Mrs. White should request his release suggests some plausibility to Neal's tale, a detail that the news account does not discuss. More surprising is the fact that the paper printed as detailed an account as it did. Not only was Wells-Barnett an able propagandist in her analysis, but her skillful use of the very southern press that did so much to publicize the black rapist myth to debunk the myth was inspired journalism.[87]

An even more dramatic encounter had taken place almost exactly one year earlier in Texarkana, Arkansas, in the lynching of Edward Coy for rape. Wells-Barnett quotes a newspaper account written by Albion Tourgée describing the remarkable events. According to Tourgée, his investigation of the lynching and its cause revealed that both the alleged victim and her husband were known to be of "bad character"; that the woman "was publicly reported and generally known to have been *criminally intimate* with Coy for more than a year previous"; that "a large majority of the 'superior' white men" who led the mob were "the reputed fathers of mulatto children"; and that the woman was "compelled by threats, if not by violence, to make the charge against the victim" (*Lynchings: Red Record*, 62). Yet, when it came time for the lynching to take place, Coy's white lover was center stage: "When she came to apply the match Coy asked her if she would burn him after they had 'been sweethearting' so long." Her answer was unequivocal: after Coy had been treated to preliminary mutilation by men and boys, "[she] gladly set fire to him, and 15,000 persons saw him burn to death." Tourgée's acerbic conclusion was that "the woman was a willing partner in the victim's guilt, and being of the 'superior' race must naturally have been more guilty."

Wells-Barnett's anecdotes underscore that the demonization of white women in black literature and lore grew from white female complicity in the suppression of black male assertiveness. Whether she watched from a window as a helpless victim of circumstance or took the stage and set the "human torch" aflame herself, the moment of the white temptress in the black imagination was the moment of public exposure and humiliating execution for succumbing to the illusory American freedoms of life, liberty, and the pursuit of happiness. Not black criminality but thwarted black aspiration for unexceptional inclusion in the imagined American community anchors the social significance of lynch law. As whites intended, it became a sign of America's determination that blacks never gain a foothold in the time-space of the nation.

Wells-Barnett's formal appropriation of the Samson and Delilah tale emphasized the futility of the physical (that is, "natural") power of the black male in the face of the power of the repressive state, whose agent the white temptress becomes—a narrative whose subtextual moralizing on the danger of exogamic contamination reversed the dominant discourse of race purity. The black Nazarene who strayed from the sustaining embrace of his own nation brought about personal and communal calamity, and however careful Wells-Barnett was in avoiding a demand for black male sexual loyalty, his destructive lust for embodiment with the white other made inevitable such gallows philosophy as Richard Neal's admonition to his fellow black men to beware the fatal white woman. Out of such moments emerged the narrative of the black man who, in staying at home to guard the domestic circle, preserved his race "purity" and simultaneously avoided the extinction America wished upon him.

PART TWO

American Souls

CHAPTER FIVE

W. E. B. Du Bois and the Progress of the Black Soul

During the slave regime, the white man owned the Negro body and soul.
It was to his interest to dwarf the soul and preserve the body.
— Ida B. Wells-Barnett, *A Red Record*

Like the animals, [the Negro] has no soul either to lose or save.
— White folk saying

One of the unplanned outcomes of the campaign of violence against black bodies was the rapid development of a black national cultural consciousness. Because lynching presented a recurrent vision of a wished-for extinction of blacks, the idea of a black American renaissance had a meaning beyond its morale-building function in a time of political repression. It was strongly symbolic of black Americans' refusal to cooperate in their expulsion from history and thus from human kinship and national belonging. It was a refusal to accept quietly the black body of death rhetoric that encouraged the various piecemeal and wholesale solutions to the "Negro problem" in America.

W. E. B. Du Bois's *The Souls of Black Folk* would be his most celebrated attempt to contribute to the discussion of a black national renaissance, opening with an acknowledgment of that unspoken question echoing across the veil of race, "How does it feel to be a problem?" Du Bois's immediate answer to this question through the delineation of a pathology of racial self-awareness — "double-consciousness"—has tended to overshadow greatly the more sanguine conclud-ing image of a significant model for national belonging, black racial conscious-ness as a "gift . . . woven into the very warp and woof of this nation" that has al-ways "called out all that was best [in the nation] to throttle and subdue all that was worst" (*Souls*, 3, 187). In this chapter, I locate in Du Bois's trope of the black American's "two souls, two thoughts, . . . two warring ideals in one dark body" (a figure usually assumed to be simply a vivid rendition of "double-consciousness") the origin of the gift of the black Spirit to America that became the basis of his triumphal vision of African American world-historical status. In order to provide a counterimage to Washington's false choice between two body images of black America, the "separated fingers" or the "black body of death" chained to the white body politic, Du Bois offered his vision of a "two-souled" black American less as an admission of irrevocable black psychic self-division than as a sign of spiritual plenitude and eventual national reconciliation.

In introducing his trope of the two-souled black striver, Du Bois delved into autobiography to recount the anecdote of the haughty schoolgirl who was the first to raise the "veil of race" between him and his fellows.[1] In this section of his opening essay in *The Souls*, Du Bois claimed to be unaware as a boy growing up in Great Barrington, Massachusetts, that his presence in America was a "prob-lem," until the memorable day when a "tall newcomer" to the school brought the poison of racial caste consciousness with her. Du Bois says only that the girl refused his "visiting-card . . . peremptorily, with a glance." Yet if she stated no specific reason for her refusal, how did he conclude that the snub was racially motivated unless he was already conscious of himself as different in some im-portant way? Clearly, from other sources that describe his indoctrination into American racial prejudice as a more gradual process, Du Bois must already have suspected even before this encounter that he was being systematically isolated from his white companions (Lewis, *Biography*, 34).

Still, there is a sense from his strong response to the snub that this trivial episode carries too much allegorical weight in the essay. Du Bois cites no other incidents in *The Souls* that help explain either the desperate claustrophobia or the psychic turmoil of the life "within the veil" to which the girl consigned him, the social space of blackness where "the shades of the prison-house closed round about us all: walls strait [sic] and stubborn to the whitest, but relentlessly narrow, tall, and unscalable to sons of night who must plod darkly on in resignation, or beat unavailing palms against the stone" (2). As with the later anecdote of the black man and white woman arrested for talking together on Atlanta's Whitehall Street (128), the visiting card episode shows Du Bois's sensitivity to the way that American body politics sited the boundary between white and black social space on the white woman's body, and despite the seeming innocuousness of the encounter, it obviously stands for a whole range of experiences of social exclusion. As David Levering Lewis has noted, "interracial companionship has always been one of the first casualties of approaching puberty" (*Biography*, 33), but his statement requires amending to account for the fact that while white male puberty rites might actually involve seeking out black females for sexual initiation, the ritual initiation into white womanhood required strict observance of a physical distancing from those who might compromise her social status. Even the most profound racists were fond of pointing out that children in the South grew up together, regardless of race. The cutting off of unstructured interracial contact at the time of puberty created, as it was meant to, black males' consciousness of their exclusion from what Du Bois called "the dazzling opportunities" of life celebrated in the culture, but for black females, it developed a quite different consciousness of their official social exclusion complicated by clandestine white male sexual attentiveness.

Suddenly, or so it seemed to the black youth, their former playmates had to be addressed as "Mr." and "Miss," while if their childhood friends spoke to them at all, the familiar name was used to make their inferiority the unequivocal subtext of every conversation. This was an essential part of training for social "place," as Francis Broderick surmised when he explained that the visiting card exchange was a "juvenile (and therefore very serious) burlesque of a custom of their elders" (6). He might have gone further and pointed out that the exclusion of black boys from such social affairs was a more profoundly "serious . . . custom of their elders" aimed at demarcating the boundaries of reproductive access to ensure the perpetuation of color caste privilege. As a young adult, therefore, Du Bois could see clearly the gradual closing off to him of social opportunities and the encroaching "spiritual isolation in which [he] was living" in an America that was incapable of "conceiving" him in a capacity that rivaled the white professional class of his Massachusetts hometown (*Autobiography*, 106). "Unconsciously, I realized that as I grew older," Du Bois wrote in his autobiography, "the close cordial intermingling with my white fellows would grow more restricted. There would be meetings, parties, clubs, to which I would not be invited. Especially in the case of strangers, visitors, newcomers to the town would my presence and friendship become a matter of explanation or even embarrassment to my school-mates." On the verge of college, Du Bois understood by the means that such messages were typically communicated that there was no "place" for him there.

Du Bois's description in *The Souls* of the first moment "when the shadow swept across [him]" is largely symbolic, then, of the entire experience of reaching maturity in a town that followed its best instincts by supporting his educational ambitions but could not make a place for him socially and occupationally. Because of this, he presented the incident with the schoolgirl as if it were a universal of black experience, knowing that whatever the specifics, this necessary life discipline, this statement by the white world to the effect that "you cannot embody with us," inevitably found its way into the consciousness of the black American.

As an archetypal moment of white women's embodiment of exclusion from American belonging, the visiting card incident subsumes other episodes ranging from the unconscious insults of those like his childhood friend Mary Loop, who thought of him only when she could not find black servants,[2] to the open hostility of those like the white woman whom he slightly jostled on a Nashville Street, who reacted to his apology as if to an act of "barbarism": "The woman was furious; why I never knew; somehow, I cannot say how, I had transgressed the interracial mores of the South. Was it because I showed no submissiveness? Did I fail to debase myself utterly and eat spiritual dirt?" (*Autobiography*, 121). If Du Bois would not let white women make him "eat spiritual dirt," they did shape his consciousness by forcing a vigilant aloofness on him. Careful not to let the "veil of race" catch him unaware, Du Bois habitually raised it himself, not as in the Brownlow tradition, an acknowledgment of dwelling on a lower social plane, but with a mask of indifference that some interpreted as arrogance.

Yet the impression remains in Du Bois's work that because of their position at the gateway of American belonging, white women also inevitably represented all of the "dazzling opportunities" that racial caste privilege allowed. This is not to say that Du Bois felt in any way personally deprived by the ideology of white race chastity itself, but he did learn firsthand that there was more rhetorical wish fulfillment in the notion than fact. Du Bois's summer romance with Dora Marbach, the German daughter of his hostess in Eisenach during the summer before he entered the university at Berlin, gave him all the evidence he needed that racial barriers did not exist in "nature" but in the hearts and minds of people. Du Bois described the affair with Dora as a pastoral interlude: wanderings in forest glens, reciting poetry, and dancing, climaxing in their confession of love and Dora's insistence that she would marry him "'gleich!'" [at once] (*Autobiography*, 160–61). But Du Bois's refusal to marry her was based on his sense that he had a social mission to perform and that, like Douglass, he would be held in suspicion as a race spokesman if he had married Dora.[3] When an American white woman moved into the Marbach house for a month and proceeded to try to poison the family against him by explaining American racial etiquette, Du Bois again felt the veil of color caste division shaping his life from far across the ocean, but he was by then able to put it into context as less an indictment of his unworthiness than of American hypocrisy. Du Bois could not have included such an anecdote in *The Souls* for the same reason that he did not marry Dora. Having called for strategic endogamy in "The Conservation of Races" and especially considering that the lynching campaign grounded in the myth of "one crime" insisted that the object of all black male agitation for full inclusion had intermarriage as its ultimate goal, Du Bois could not surrender such a propaganda victory to his enemies. He would not subscribe to the logic that only in the arms of a white woman could he find a sense of personal fulfillment, regardless of their symbolic equation with "the good life," and he would not allow anyone to get the impression that he did.

But Du Bois's consciousness of white women's social significance informs a further substantive omission from *The Souls*, important to understanding the life "within the veil" because the incident had a direct bearing on his ascendance into visionary race leadership. The incident that, by his own estimation, halted his single-minded pursuit of science to take a more active role in race advocacy was the April 1899 lynching of Sam Hose, which cast "a red ray which could not be ignored" across his career path (*Dusk*, 67). Mary Church Terrell, in her 1904 article "Lynching from a Negro's Point of View,"[4] re-created the spectacle of the Sam Hose lynching, highlighting the *Atlanta Constitution*'s role in renarrating the details of Hose's attack on his landlord into the archetypal "one crime" to ensure a lynching: "A well-known, influential newspaper immediately offered a reward of $500 for the capture of Sam Hose. This same newspaper predicted a lynching, and stated that, though several modes of punishment had been suggested, it was the consensus of opinion that the negro should be burned at the stake and tortured before being burned" (859). Terrell went on to describe the lynching that ensued: "The Sunday on which Sam Hose was burned was converted into a holiday. Special trains were made up to take the Christian people of Atlanta to the scene of the burning, a short distance from the city. After the first train moved out with every inch of available space inside and out filled to overflowing, a second had to be made up, so as to accommodate those who had just come from church. After Sam Hose had been tortured and burned to death, the great concourse of Christians who had witnessed the tragedy scraped for hours among the ashes in the hope of finding a sufficient number of his bones to take to their friends as souvenirs." Though he did not mention the episode in detail in *The Souls*, Du Bois recounted in his autobiographical *Dusk of Dawn* (1940) his attempt to cull together the "evident facts" of the case in order to force the newspaper to retract its sensationalistic charges so as to prevent the lynching. Ironically, it was when he was walking from Atlanta University toward the office of the *Atlanta Constitution* to meet with "Uncle Remus" popularizer Joel Chandler Harris (who was working for the paper and whose racial paternalism Du Bois no doubt felt was more amenable to fair play than the race radicalism of editor John Temple Graves) that he got the news of the lynching: "Sam Hose had been lynched, and they said that his knuckles were on exhibition at a grocery store farther down on Mitchell Street, along which I was walking. I turned back to the University. I began to turn aside from my work" (67).

The grocer on Mitchell had been one of the "lucky" ones among the Christians described by Church Terrell, getting the knuckles that he proudly displayed to authenticate his participation in the lynching. Indeed, the "charm" clearly worked on Du Bois, casting a warning "red ray" that forced him to reverse his steps. Du Bois, though, described the incident as his annunciation into active leadership, the moment when he ceased being Saul and became Paul, by forcing him to shed his persona as a "calm, cool, detached scientist" for the role of race protagonist. One puzzling note emerges from Du Bois's retelling, however. What Du Bois characterized as the "evident facts" in the case were startlingly incorrect. Du Bois claimed in *Dusk of Dawn* that Hose had murdered "his landlord's wife." In fact, Hose was not even accused of murdering the wife but of murdering the landlord himself. This murder charge was very much later amended by the press with a false accusation that after the murder, the landlord's child was torn from its mother's breast and flung across the bloody floor, while "the wife was seized, choked, thrown upon the floor, where her clothing lay in the blood of her husband, and ravished." There was never, even in the rabid white press, a charge of murdering the wife herself.[5]

Du Bois's fuzzy recollection in *Dusk of Dawn* is curious for two reasons. First, he left this rendition of the events—the "murder" of the wife—unedited, repeating it verbatim in his autobiography, which he completed some twenty years after *Dusk of Dawn*. This is all the more surprising because Du Bois clearly knew the true events of the Hose affair. He gave a perfectly lucid and accurate account of it in an interview for the Oral History Project in 1960, after his work on both autobiographies: "What had happened was that . . . [Hose's] plantation owner hadn't settled with him, and Hose made a fuss about it, and they got into a fight, and the plantation owner was killed. They started then to find Sam Hose and they couldn't find him. And then, suddenly, there was the accusation that Sam Hose had raped the wife. . . . In order to arouse the neighborhood to find this man, they brought in the charge of rape. Even from the newspapers you could see there was no foundation to it."[6] Was Du Bois's assertion that Hose had killed the woman a Freudian slip, doubly significant because of its otherwise un-accountable repetition? Did Du Bois wish the woman dead, not even as an indi-vidual, perhaps, but as an abstraction whose ex post facto inscription into the narrative "veiled" the "evident facts," ultimately even from Du Bois himself?

To understand Du Bois's "red ray," then, means to understand that Du Bois was not reading the death of Sam Hose as an isolated tragic event. What stopped him on that Atlanta street was not even the generic sign of white supremacy ren-dered in the very body of the condemned as a demarcation of racialized space. What stopped him was the realization of how the specific nature of his own er-rand, to expunge charges of an assault against white womanhood from the offi-cial narrative of the crime, put him in a position similar to that for which Ida Wells-Barnett had been threatened and exiled and that one year earlier had caused Alexander Manly's exile, a coup d'état, and a riot in Wilmington, North Carolina. It must have come home to him in a flash that he was on his way to tell the very whites who had masterminded a lynching on faked rape charges that their communal fantasy of violated white womanhood, in fact, was a sham. With Sam Hose already dead, he was putting himself in harm's way to interrupt the whites-only celebration of his exclusion from American kinship.

The absence of this episode from *The Souls* is instructive. Despite its visceral pull, the lynching anecdote would have forced Du Bois out of his preferred tone of moderation. With the exception of the cold rage he displayed at the caste divi-sion in Atlanta that he blamed for the death of his son Burghardt (*Souls*, 146–51), Du Bois was generally successful in splitting the difference between the obse-quiousness of Washington and the militancy of those like William Monroe Trot-ter and Edward H. Morris, who had charged that Washington's acquiescence in American body politics was "largely responsible for the lynching in this country" (Lewis, *Biography*, 275).[7] Whether Du Bois's own career of race apostleship owed more to the psychic violence of racial etiquette or the corporeal violence of lynching mattered to him less than the fact that his vision of race "development" at the time of *The Souls* required changing the question from the Negro as a "problem" to the Negro as the solution to an imperfectly realized dream of egalitarian democracy in America. Thus, while Du Bois did not sidestep the issue of lynching or the myth of the "one crime," he did not wish to raise questions in *The Souls* that might compromise his presentation of the black contribution to America. More in keeping with his purpose was the expression of hope in the Sorrow Songs that "sometime, somewhere, men will judge men by their souls and not by their skins" (*Souls*, 186). After the 1906 Atlanta riots that threatened the safety of middle-class black neighborhoods, including the section where his wife and daughter were waiting alone for his return from a trip, Du Bois would give full vent to the rage that he had earlier suppressed after the lynching of Hose.[8] But in *The Souls*, Du Bois felt that to gain an audience, he would need to present a strong case for African American forbearance and generosity of spirit.

"The Conservation of Races"

While race baiters such as Dixon and Tillman fought to keep America's black and white bodies apart, Du Bois hoped to make black "soul" the basis of full national integration. Du Bois felt that he could change the course of the prolonged struggle over the inclusion of black Americans in the imagined community only if blackness lost its stigma of inferiority. "The real difference in Du Bois's conception," says Kwame Anthony Appiah, "is . . . that he assigns to race a different moral and metaphysical significance from the majority of his white contemporaries. The distinctive claim is that the Negro race has a positive message, a message that is not only different but valuable" (34).

Du Bois's adoption of the racial soul idea as a basis of national belonging was to have a lasting impact on future conceptualizations of black cultures worldwide. But as Stephen Graham discovered in his southern travels after World War I, there were still many who declared that African "soullessness" eternally divided black Americans from the rest of humanity. A Mississippi district attorney, asked about the social significance of lynching, told Graham, "'It doesn't make any difference to the Negro. . . . He hasn't got a soul. They don't go to heaven or hell. . . . They're just animals. . . . They were never in the Garden of Eden, for Adam and Eve were white. Consequently, as they had no part in original sin, they have no share in our salvation either. Christ did not come to save those who never fell from grace'" (Graham, 29). The district attorney was restating, with one important alteration, the thesis of Charles Carroll's *The Negro a Beast, or in the Image of God* (1900) and *The Tempter of Eve* (1902), both of which argued from the "whiteness" of Adam and Eve backward to the "whiteness" of God and forward to the need for perpetual racial exclusivity.[9] Unlike Graham's informant or James Anthony Froude, who also proclaimed that a bestial innocence protected blacks from penalty for their corrupt ways,[10] Carroll did give blacks a part in original sin. He asserted on philological evidence that mistranslations of the Hebrew word for "black" into "serpent" had completely distorted the Christian perception of what occurred in Eden: miscegenation *was* the original sin, and blacks were the agents of its becoming in the world.[11]

Throughout the history of ethnic relations in the Americas, defining African otherness as evidence of a divine curse foregrounded colonial justifications for policies of enslavement. To accomplish the legitimation of whiteness as a communal resource requiring special rules of preservation, more than just the color of skin or length of hair had to be involved; the psychic and physical violence that caste discrimination demanded acquired moral authority from the colonists' linkage of observable somatic features to an ineffable, transcendent "racial" essence for which only the racially "pure" body could serve as a container. In the early statutes, this authority clearly grew out of distinctions between the Christian "body politic" and the "ethnic" other.[12] The colonists extrapolated from the Christian idea of the "soul"—the transcendent essence of redeemed humanity—the notion of a "race soul" that authored the inherent mental and moral characteristics of whites.

The "condition of the mother" and the sales, as early as the 1650s, of black women and their offspring *for all time* facilitated the transition from a sacred to a secular race soul idea by invoking the concept of a transcendent, preformed, synchronic, encapsulated race womb. Eric Voegelin describes the "transcendentalist" idea this way: "All attempts to explain the unity of life [as in theories of 'race'] through divine creation and the encapsulation of all successive generations in the one originally created . . . are transcendent" (quoted in Heilke, 88). The preformatist brand of transcendentalist theorizing held that "God had originally organized inanimate matter into living entities at creation, and that He had encapsulated all future generations in the germ cells of the original parents" (Heilke, 89). Thus, to Voegelin, "what appeared as the formation of a new individual was simply the growth of an organized living thing which had been formed at the beginning of time" (Heilke, 89).

Racist tracts such as *The Negro: What Is His Ethnological Status?* (1876) by "Ariel" (Buckner H. Payne) and Carroll's *The Negro a Beast* restated the preformatist belief that "Eve . . . contain[ed] all future individuals of the human race in her original ova, which she then passed on to her descendants in a continual line of disencapsulation up to the present time" (Heilke, 90). Where Voegelin used "human race," race theorists substituted "white race" to extract biblical sanction for their condemnation of intermarriage as blasphemy.[13] The focus on the white female womb as an extension of Eve's womb positioned Eve as the source of both human corruption and, ironically, of "racial purity." Just as important, the womb as an analogue of "racial" history implies the equivalence of the woman's body and national time.[14] The state management of race-identified wombs, then, ultimately cited the urgency of keeping the pristine race body—the capsule of the racial essence—hermetically sealed against contamination by ethnic others. Those who policed the bodies of white women were not so much protecting the purity of the individual as the womb of their collective national imagining.

The practical problem of describing a race as a numerical average of somatic measurements that did not apply to any single *actual* body in the world was one that the science of race difference would never quite overcome, but as George Stocking explains, even if "pure" races and types could not be demonstrated, the idea of race could not be so easily discarded: "The fictive individual who embodied all the characteristics of the 'pure type' grew in the imagination, obliterating the individual variation of his fellows, until he stood forth for them all as the living expression of the lost, but now recaptured essence of racial purity" (59). If no one can say with finality where the lines between races are, how can anyone say for certain who does and does not share in the "soul" of the race? Finding no coherent, interdependent corporeal traits that are continuous over time through several generations, believers in a preformed, transcendental "racial essence" had to locate another vehicle of transmission.[15]

At best, according to Voegelin, "the individual members of a race are regarded more as constituents of a mass in motion that embodies the characteristics of the race than as individuals who live out a tradition of which . . . they are an integral part" (Heilke, 135). But the concept of a race soul gives each race member a stake in the behavior of all others, since the fate of the racial mass is directly tied to a unitary "race idea" that often cannot reach fulfillment in anything less than the formation of a state that governs its political interests (Heilke, 128). At the same time, envisioning race as "mass in motion" with no stable boundaries puts enormous pressure on individuals to "live" their race—to "prove" that they partake of the ineffable race soul by responding to any calls to arms made in the name of the race. They must "embody" the "race idea" in all they do.[16] Such a concept of performed race interrogates the individual body only to authenticate the performance.

The charges of black soullessness, both on the individual and group levels, had made it possible for blacks to be referred to as beasts and treated accordingly, as when public opinion exempted white violence against blacks from the rule of law. For black Americans to demonstrate a "racial genius" valuable to the march of world civilization would change public attitudes, making black national inclusion desirable, Du Bois felt. But rather than rely on an ideal of black racial "purity" to carry the ideological weight, Du Bois envisioned black America as a mass in motion living out the principles of an ennobling race idea. Du Bois had before him in Germany a recent example of the harnessing of race "genius" to transform the world's opinion of a people, and he had seen firsthand the power of the "race soul" at work in changing Germans' self-perception as well. Bismarck, he felt, had "made a nation out of a mass of bickering peoples," a nation whose Zeitgeist moved him deeply when, as a student in Berlin, he watched Wilhelm II prancing through the Brandenburg Gate. Du Bois felt moved enough despite his status as an outsider in Germany to shape his adult self-image in commemoration of this spectacle of the racial ideal. Thus he patterned his trademark Vandyke and moustache after the kaiser's, with whom he further identified because of the shared name William.[17]

Using the promise of a glorious racial destiny as a means of uniting the masses into collective action remained a potent ideal for Du Bois after Germany. The practical question for Du Bois was how a stateless black nation could come into being lacking anything like the Germans' historical claims to a specific national territory. Du Bois concluded that geopolitical boundaries were less important to national belonging than a shared concept of peoplehood, and perhaps, in the case of "bickering peoples," the question of geography was an unnecessary distraction. Thus Du Bois's imagined community of black America adapted the form of kinship that most typified American culture — "race." The value of having a black America as a political and cultural base far outweighed the likelihood of blacks, as individuals, effecting a change in America's distribution of privileges and encumbrances through a hierarchy of racial preferences. Black America would have to be a state of mind and of spirit only, an imagined community linked by the simultaneous resistance of its constituents to spaces of American confinement, until by collective effort it achieved full national inclusion.

Du Bois's foray into American body politics bore the stamp of his years at Harvard as well as his German experience. In effect, his education at Harvard can be described as a personal laboratory for the perfection of his idea of race advocacy. In his preamble to "The Conservation of Races" (1897), Du Bois begins with the premise "that any striving, no matter how intense and earnest, which is against the constitution of the world, is vain" (1), reaching the same conclusion as Chesnutt that the citadel of racism in America could not be taken by storm but could be changed over time from within its own value system.[18] Reconciled to working within American institutions for change, Du Bois honed a personal ethic of being "in" but not "of" the dominant order.[19] At the same time, Du Bois did not see his self-segregation as tantamount to an admission of inferiority, and he would make it plain that maintaining cultural distinction with no limit on access to institutional opportunities was both consistent with national idealism and imperative for the preservation of ethnic identity.

Du Bois contended that Harvard's faculty (better known, he said, but not better teachers than his Fisk instructors) challenged him to develop his ideas without shaking his resolve to help found a "Negro self-sufficient culture even in America" (*Autobiography*, 133, 135, 136). Absent from the list he provided of his most influential Harvard teachers was one—Nathaniel S. Shaler—whose writings outside his primary fields of natural history and geology were a direct challenge to Du Bois's self-ordained task.[20] Theirs was a complicated relationship. Du Bois had gotten good grades from the Kentuckian who had officered Union troops in the Civil War and who on one occasion had booted from class a prejudiced southerner who protested sitting near Du Bois (*Autobiography*, 143).[21] Shaler had written in support of Du Bois's Slater Fund applications, and perhaps out of gratitude, Du Bois did not single him out for rebuke.[22] Still, the tenor of Shaler's long series of articles in popular magazines on the American race situation could hardly have escaped Du Bois's eye.

Shaler's 1904 volume *The Neighbor*, on the surface a plea for tolerance and understanding (vii), was a compendium of the ideas about racial heterogeneity in America that he had proposed in numerous articles over the prior quarter century or more.[23] According to Shaler, black Americans' racially characteristic "arrest of development" left them indistinguishable in evolutionary terms from their ancestors, and they entered the new century hampered by an irremediable incapacity for developing or intellectually contributing to higher civilization (135, 136, 139). Lacking a "historic sense," blacks had created no transmittable "body of traditions," no art, no literature, no social polity—in short, no culture (151, 135). Because black individuation would require first the establishment of a "common mind," which their inability to engage in cooperative activity put beyond their reach, the best that could be expected of blacks in America was a slavish imitation of white culture, with black enterprise rising no higher than the low-average level of the white working class (252–53, 247, 135, 330, 334). Despite his personal experience with Du Bois and others at Harvard, Shaler expressed grave doubts that blacks could profit from a higher education or that any individual black achievements warranted a reevaluation of the group potential or social status (167, 136). Shaler was convinced that mulattoes, of whom he surely assumed Du Bois to be one, would die young and leave no heirs to trouble America with unwanted hybridity (160–62).

Most serious was Shaler's prognosis of black America as a veritable body of death attached to the American body politic. For Shaler, the "essential difference between the living and the dead" in societal terms was that the "living" are "able to gain by experience and transmit their acquisitions in a cumulative way to their successors" while the socially dead do not (236–37). Shaler felt that progress among such socially dead or "inorganic" individuals was strictly a zoological process of natural selection, while civilization required higher processes of cultural transmission for its advance. Having no ability to connect the past and present together to form meaningful and enduring lessons that would live in the "common mind," blacks could not build a real society, "a new kind of individual, which lives enduringly and stores in itself something of the profit won by its evanescent members" (272). Therefore, lack of innate capacity for transmittable culture meant that in social evolutionary terms blacks were "dead," and although they could become useful laborers for the state, they could not be expected to become what Du Bois would call in *The Souls* "co-workers in the kingdom of culture."

Shaler did not consider blacks to be on the level of "beasts of the field," but he did curiously think them "the most domesticable of all the lowly stocks" (324). Noting that "spiritual" diversification is the highest level of individuation (285), Shaler intoned that if the student of the human family "seeks for race characteristics of the spirit" among American blacks, he "is sure to be puzzled" (321), essentially charging that blacks lacked a racial spirit or "genius" like those peoples that had the ability to form cultures and create history. Based on these racial traits, Shaler had called the black presence a more serious obstacle to the nation's future than any other problem that any other nation had to bear.[24] Though Shaler denounced slavery, lynching, and prejudice as contributors to unnecessary social friction,[25] he might as well have asked Du Bois directly, "How does it feel to be a problem?"

The program of racial development that Du Bois outlined in his own series of essays at the turn of the century challenged, and therefore may rightly be said to have been negatively inspired by, Shaler's assumptions about black potential for collective action in the building of cultural institutions, and in a pointed act of defiance, Du Bois cited black spirituality as the race's most enduring "gift" to a dispiritualized, industrialized America. Clearly, Du Bois was already working out the details of his rebuttal during his time under Shaler's tutelage. Du Bois's claim that he was "in Harvard, but not of it" (*Autobiography*, 136) makes a certain sense as a defense mechanism against the casual circulation of attitudes that implicitly questioned the point of his being there at all.[26] Finding his "island within" to be a "fair country," Du Bois ultimately discovered that the imagined territory of caste isolation was very well populated by fellow seekers of opportunity. What discourses of racial alienation such as Shaler's had accomplished in league with the laws and customs assorting the population into racial castes was the creation of a "kinship" beyond the color line that became Du Bois's route to an epiphany of black spiritual empowerment.

Seeing black Americans as "one undifferentiated low-class mass" allowed whites to "entomb" all together in black social space, Du Bois felt.[27] In keeping with his determination to fight race privilege within its own structures, then, Du Bois would claim the "fair country" created by the social boundaries of undifferentiated difference:

> Thus this group of professional men, students, white collar workers and upper servants, whose common bond was color of skin in themselves or in their fathers, together with a common history and current experience of discrimination, formed a unit [around Harvard] which like many tens of thousands of like units across the nation had or were getting to have a common culture pattern which made them an interlocking mass; so that increasingly a colored person in Boston was more neighbor to a colored person in Chicago than to the white person across the street. (*Autobiography*, 137)

Du Bois's claim that black Americans shared a more intense sense of community with each other across wide geographical spaces than they shared with the whites among whom they lived fairly mocked the idea of the benevolent white "neighbor" so dear to Shaler. But more important to Du Bois was the fact that this potentially powerful "nation within a nation" might lose its coherence after winning increased access to the white world, which was the ultimate aim of his race advocacy. Thus Du Bois embarked upon the tricky task of using the existence of

a quarantined black America to expose America's violation of its creeds of freedom and equality, while at the same time seeking to hold together the imagined
community of black America as a political and cultural force in American society. Du Bois's dilemma was that in order to prove that biological "race" was irrelevant to one's capacity for national belonging, he had to assist in the formation
and maintenance of an exclusive "racial spirit" as an indispensable building
block for the cultural development of a people.

In a move that has raised questions about Du Bois's understanding of "race,"
he insisted in "The Conservation of Races," and continued to insist for some
time thereafter, that maintaining embodied "race" difference was crucial to the
evolution of a "racial spirit" or "message" that would ensure blacks their rightful
place among civilized peoples.[28] To meet this issue squarely, Du Bois identified
the philosophical crossroads that all serious black thinkers on the race issue
would have to negotiate — "What, after all, am I?": "If I strive as a Negro, am I not
perpetuating the very cleft that threatens and separates black and white America? Is not my only possible practical aim the subduction of all that is Negro in
me to the American? Does my black blood place upon me any more obligation
to assert my nationality than German, or Irish, or Italian blood would?" ("Conservation," 5). Implicit in these questions is the critical, centuries-old issue of
embodiment: Does "our sole hope of salvation [lie] in our being able to lose our
race identity in the commingled blood of the nation?" ("Conservation," 4). Du
Bois seemed to be referring to intermarriage into the American melting pot
as the way that African Americans might "lose" their race identity, given the tendency in human history toward the "integration of physical differences" among
peoples (3), the global trend toward hybridity that would help to define the first
of the existential paths described by Ryder in Chesnutt's "The Wife of His
Youth."[29]

But if the tendency of human history is toward a hybridized human population, what purpose would be served by blacks withdrawing from this process
while simultaneously attempting to integrate fully into American society? As Appiah has shown, Du Bois's definition of race in "The Conservation of Races" is at
best equivocal.[30] After calling attention to the unreliability of scientific definitions crudely based on "the grosser physical differences of color, hair and bone"
("Conservation," 2), Du Bois somewhat contradictorily declared, "It [is] the duty
of the Americans of Negro descent, *as a body*, to maintain their race identity until [the] mission of the Negro people is accomplished and the ideal of human
brotherhood has become a practical possibility" (7; my emphasis).

What concerned Du Bois more than the physical absorption of Negroes into white America was the greater potential for "spiritual" absorption—what he would later refer to as "spiritual and psychic amalgamation."[31] Du Bois felt that without a clear articulation of its ethos, no group would be accepted as a world-historical people, and that Negroes had not as yet "given to civilization the full spiritual message which they [were] capable of giving" ("Conservation," 4). The Du Boisian race soul would unite people of African descent in the struggle to articulate "the full, complete Negro message of the whole Negro race . . . to the world." It would be this concept of inspiriting race, not the embodied race idea, that Du Bois would urge the elite of the race to "develop" and "conserve," but the romantic tradition demanded a body image in whose features the racial essence could be scripted.

Thus in "Conservation," Du Bois quickly dismissed the idea that "self-obliteration [was] the highest end to which Negro blood dare[d] aspire" (5). Du Bois felt that wholesale somatic transformation through increased hybridity would undermine group integrity and cloud the racial "message." If his Shaleresque "new individual" of black culture did not unequivocally have an "African" identity—a black body image—then sophists like Shaler would simply attribute black progress to "white blood" or racial mimicry. The institution of a "body of traditions" would require a "living" body of black America to make sure that the world did not miss the point. Besides, the unilateral declaration of a raceless America was fraught with political risks. Du Bois defined a race as a group "voluntarily and involuntarily striving together" (2). Later, he would envision race advocacy as a struggle "not by choice but by inner and outer compulsion."[32] By acknowledging an "involuntary" affiliation maintained by "outer compulsion" in American body politics, Du Bois took note of the fact that "race" was not an entirely elective identity but a state-imposed classification crucial to the social, economic, political, and psychological constitution of America. Du Bois himself was not unaware of the epistemological difficulties of his overlapping, contradictory classificatory schema. It is clear to me that Du Bois understood that any discussion of race in America is by nature mythic and that one cannot battle myths of race difference in the political arena bolstered only by "scientific facts" that did not support "the constitution of the world."

As Du Bois would explain years later, "It is beside the point to ask whether we form a real race. Biologically we are mingled of all conceivable elements, but race is psychology, not biology; and psychologically we are a unified race with one history, one red memory, one revolt. It is not ours to argue whether we will be segregated or whether we ought to be a caste. We are segregated; we are a caste. . . . Our problem is how far and in what way can we consciously and scientifically guide our future so as to ensure our physical survival, our spiritual freedom and our social growth? Either we do this or we die."[33] For Du Bois, physical and spiritual survival of the "red memory" of the American experience had no practical alternative, and despite his obvious misgivings about the scientific evidence on "race," Du Bois clung to "the illusion of race" because discarding the idea of race in the hope that whites would acknowledge the illogic of race and voluntarily dismantle their own base of privilege was inexpedient to the leadership demanded by his age. If "race," constructed in language by the historical narratives of self-defining peoples, serves as a frame for historical consciousness in the world in which one lives, determining the distribution of rights and privileges of citizenship through a system of hierarchical social castes, then "races" exist regardless of the "final word of science." Du Bois would have been a fool to pretend otherwise. The illusion of biological race could not have been eradicated by the unilateral refusal of a politically marginal minority community to acknowledge its validity. In fighting a propaganda war against those gifted in the "science" of making "the world believe what is not true, provided the untruth is a widely wished-for thing like the probable extermination of Negroes" (*Dusk*, 151), Du Bois did not have the luxury of dismissing race as an illusion that would go away by virtue of his simple assertion.

Du Bois's attitude was that scientific race may be a fiction, but it represented a necessary fiction around which to organize political and cultural resistance. By framing the alternative as "self-obliteration," Du Bois declared blacks a de facto race that could either define itself or allow itself to be defined into oblivion by others. The collective tasking of the "advance guard of the Negro people" to realize a coherent expression of the race soul would work against the isolation and despair that made individual striving so hazardous. It would also change the terms of race belonging from a largely involuntary striving against racial barriers to a conscious, voluntary apostleship.

The distinction between voluntary and involuntary race is made implicit by Du Bois in "The Souls of White Folk" (1910). Here he differentiates between "the souls of them that are white" and "the souls of them that have become painfully conscious of their whiteness" by accepting the notion that "whiteness is the ownership of the earth, for ever and ever, Amen!" (25, 26). The "one-drop rule," relying on dubious genetics, had made race classification involuntary, and therefore much of the struggling against racial barriers was by those who found assignment to the lower racial caste an injustice. The foundational myth of Du Boisian race striving was that all world-historical races are self-created, if not self-chosen. In essence, Du Bois was banking on the persistence of white racism to deny blacks equal opportunity long enough for a "self-sufficient Negro culture" to develop. The focus of the would-be race leaders had to be on development "not as individuals, but as [a race]" (4), because to lose sight of the group ideal in pursuit of personal goals meant to jeopardize the collective historical mission: "For the development of Negro genius, of Negro literature and art, of Negro spirit, only Negroes bound and welded together, Negroes inspired by one vast ideal, can work out in its fullness the great message we have for humanity" (4). Because Du Bois had been trained at Harvard that "evolution" explained white mastery and black servitude, the story of black America would be an "evolutionary" struggle for "race development."[34] Thus the Du Boisian theme in black literature traces the saga of the racial "mass in motion" to maintain a group integrity while it generates its biographers who can, through collective self-imagining, bring its "race message" to fulfillment.[35] If the idea of a cultural renaissance was not original to Du Bois, he was destined to become the most celebrated early exponent of the politics of cultural rebirth.[36]

This group ethic would become important to the development of African American literature for several reasons. First, it assigned the artist a role in racial development, placing the creative writer at the center of race striving. Like most of his contemporaries, Du Bois considered the creative arts the epitome of cultural expression. He argued that a "stalwart originality which [would] unswervingly follow Negro ideals" would be necessary, if it was "to be proven for the first time in the modern world that not only [were] Negroes capable of evolving individual men like Toussaint the Saviour, but [were] a nation stored with wonderful possibilities of culture" (4). Race literature, then, of the variety that Chesnutt and Hopkins would shortly begin to write, would implicitly convey black modernity, individuation, and national status.

Further, because the Du Boisian "racial message" was a "work-in-progress," then literature would become a staging of the authors' interpretations of the African American ethos and of potential solutions to American racial strife. Despite his metaphysical bent, Du Bois knew that race development would be more a process of social construction than an "unveiling" of a transcendent racial ideal. Approaching transcendent race idealism as a riddle to be solved was one way of motivating a collective spirit of enterprise, but just as important, of forging the sort of habitual engagement with the historical past of which Shaler declared blacks incapable. Nor was Du Bois overly concerned that a contemplation of the meaning of the slavery experience would produce a stultifying despondency over prospects for black progress. His objective in "race development" was to reimagine slavery's inhibiting legacy as the very basis of black national belonging, by memorializing the slave past largely as evidence of the transformative power of the human will, a validation of the faith of the numberless enslaved Africans in their essential human worth. The function of writers would be to educate and inspire the strivers in their step-by-step progress, to "cheer the weary travelers" with tales of heroism and moral fortitude drawn from the tribulations of the past and hopes for the future.

In this vein, Du Bois's language of the racial soul also meant that losing "soul" as a result of frustration with the slow pace of black progress or as a result of trading on the racial genius for personal gain would become a staple narrative outline of his creative work. Because it would have to unite a highly differentiated black population with many hybrid members, thanks to the "one-drop rule," the racial idea demanded a performative, as opposed to a somatic, compliance. In practical and in literary terms, this meant that an individual need not conform to the Western prototype of "African" appearance to share in the racial soul, nor, conversely, need one be a physical hybrid to experience a "racial" identity crisis. The currency of "passing" narratives would remain strong among black writers as a way of dramatizing the centrality of the body in American culture, but Du Bois was already looking beyond the "tragic mulatto" as the central figure of African American letters. Instead, in narratives inspired by Du Boisian soul development, the protagonist might become "lost" to the racial mass by abandoning what Du Bois called "conscious striving together for certain ideals of life" (3). In this way, the danger of a dark-skinned protagonist "passing" out of the race by absorption into the Zeitgeist of white North America while in training for race leadership would ultimately supplant the "tragic mulatto" motif as the key identity crisis in literature steeped in Du Boisian racial idealism.

Finally, black literature would benefit specifically from Du Bois's heavy reliance on a mythic language of racial destiny. One thing Du Bois had learned from German romanticism was that the spirit of the race had a far greater chance of moving the masses when packaged as grand art and spectacle. Du Bois accordingly took seriously the role of racial seer and mythologist, appropriating folklore and biblical sources as needed. Indeed, the outlines of the great theme of the black soul quest would be one adapted by Du Bois from the work many Germans considered their most profound artistic statement of a Germanic "racial" spirit, Goethe's *Faust*.

Two Souls

Arnold Rampersad has noted that all discussions of Du Boisian duality must grapple with a fundamental ambivalence that existed in his youthful self-image: "Du Bois was facing a choice between [two] ways. One led to science and the other to art. The life of the scholar contested the life of the poet. This was the basic vocational dualism of Du Bois's life, out of which would come three careers: historian and social scientist, poet and novelist, and propagandist" (*Art and Imagination*, 40). S. P. Fullinwinder's less tempered statement of this dynamic is that Du Bois was "intellectually divided against himself" between the scientist and the "mystic." After "a brief struggle," the "mystic won and, in winning, made Du Bois a great protagonist for his race. In winning it also set the stage for the crisis in intellectual leadership" (48).[37] Hardly a man divided against himself by irreconcilable interests, however, Du Bois was instead consumed with a "world-historical"[38] mission that necessitated the role of the mythologist—one part scientist, one part artist, one part politician. Myth, as Du Bois used it, was not antithetical to "truth," though it was probably indifferent to sheer facticity. The self-conscious mythologist seeks merely to identify and enlarge upon the core values and issues by which a culture establishes its being in the world. Because the violence of lynch law and Jim Crow required active intervention, the mythologist of blackness in the Progressive Era had to be more than a reflective thinker; she or he had to become a propagandist of body politics.

At twenty-five, Du Bois wrote in his diary of his consuming passion to be simultaneously scientist, artist, and political leader: "is it egotism—is it assurance—or is [it] the silent call of the world spirit that makes me feel that I am royal and that beneath my sceptre a world of kings shall bow. . . . These are my plans: to make a name in science, to make a name in literature and thus to raise my race. Or perhaps to raise a visible empire in Africa thro' England, France or Germany" (*Against Racism*, 28–29). The eventual "divergence" of Du Bois from sociology to race propaganda stems from a duality, according to an orthodoxy that links Du Bois's famous description of the black American as "two-souled" to a struggle within Du Bois himself to follow two paths simultaneously.[39] Thus, his description of duality—"One ever feels his twoness,—an American, a Negro;

two souls, two thoughts, two unreconciled strivings; two warring ideals in one dark body, whose dogged strength alone keeps it from being torn asunder" (*Souls*, 3)—serves as a convenient starting point for scrutinizing Du Bois's career decisions as the archetypal African American crisis of cultural identity.

Yet Du Bois's diary does not set science against art. Rather, science and art as realms of intellectual endeavor are opposed to the idea of *literal* state building: creating a "visible empire." His choice of both literature and science in a project of "imagined community" building, then, represented no foundational dilemma for him. Du Bois always intended a political dimension to his race advocacy, the crucial distinction being between political organizing per se or leadership in crafting an imagined community. Just as the black American's mythic two souls were "unreconciled," not "unreconcilable," Du Bois seemed able to reconcile the scientist and the visionary artist in himself by becoming the mythologist of the imagined community.[40] In this sense, he never ceased being the scientist and never simply became the artist because the true quest of his life was not pursuit of either "Truth" or "Beauty" as mutually exclusive paths but, as he says in his diary, "multiply[ing] . . . Beauty by Truth and then Goodness, strength, shall bind them together into a solid whole" (*Against Racism*, 28). His long and incredibly productive public life suggests that the reconciliation did not arise from a career crisis but from his seizing of the challenges and opportunities that the era presented. Thus, not only did he reconcile science with art, but ultimately his roles as race visionary and political strategist as well.

David Levering Lewis has pointed out that Du Bois, as early as his Harvard days, toyed with the notion that epistemological dissociation of science and ethics from metaphysics had blinded Westerners to "the splendid goal of the unity of knowledge" (*Biography*, 94). His paper "The Renaissance of Ethics" assigned to "Duty" the task of reconciling matter ("what is," or Truth) and spirit ("what ought to be," or Beauty). Reconciliation of these into high principle—an "everlasting Ought"—would ultimately forge an "ethical science," Du Bois concluded (Lewis, *Biography*, 95). Du Bois's collegiate speculations on the power of the human will to do well as a force for unifying material and spiritual pursuits would evolve into his ethos of racial striving. Accommodating his multiple sensibilities and talents seems not to have been the source of pain for Du Bois so much as a liberating synthesis of complementary and pertinent angles of vision. As an artist, Du Bois would experience the unqualified imaginative freedom that those tasked with race development needed. His continued interest in science would give gravity and order to the performance of the mundane chores of racial uplift. If any significant crisis involving science seemed to trouble Du Bois, it was the deplorable state of scientific inquiry in an era that could not assess the "Truth" of race in its haste to legitimize the social policy trends toward violence, quarantine, and laissez-faire extermination.

Aspiring to the rigor of the physical sciences, the sociology of the day looked to data; it had a materialist bias that overvalued the quantitative and privileged the backward glance. It proclaimed, in the words of the young Du Bois himself: "Science is Mathematics. Mathematics is Identity. Science is Identity" (quoted in Broderick, 16). But those who sought to base Jim Crow advocacy in statistics adding up to black inferiority—what William B. Smith called rather pompously "the argument from numbers" (193)—were skilled in the manipulation of data to produce the desired results. Numbers were their god and could easily be marshaled in their cause. Their faith in race supremacy was marked by a tireless quest for the ultimate mathematics of difference, the quantification of somatic space as the determinant of racial destiny, and by a willingness to accept partial truths in the meantime.[41] Much of Du Bois's own early work involved a revisionary search for better, truer interpretations that would cast doubt upon the anthropometry and sociology that buttressed color caste difference.[42] Du Bois's original interest in subjecting the "Negro problem" to systematic scientific investigation produced in *The Philadelphia Negro* documentary proof that black America was "a striving, palpitating group, and *not an inert, sick body of crime*" (*Dusk of Dawn*, 59), but that would have been hard to tell from the uses to which hostile interpreters put his data.

Faced with a well-defined community of race propagandists, pseudoscientists, and unwitting popularizers of the statistical path, scholars who strike a pose of scientific objectivity can be dismayed to find their data wrenched out of context by their adversaries. Therefore when the advocates of racist social policy appropriated Du Bois's own sociological data to support the claim that blacks were unfit for survival in the modern metropolis, they made it impossible for him to maintain the pose of the objective statistician.[43] By 1897, when he wrote "The Strivings of Black Folk" (later revised as the opening chapter of *The Souls*, "Of Our Spiritual Strivings"), Du Bois was fully cognizant of this danger, dismayed that "while sociologists gleefully count[ed] his bastards and his prostitutes, the very soul of the toiling, sweating black man [was] darkened by the shadow of a vast despair" (*Souls*, 7). "Car-window sociology" would forever be the object of Du Bois's particular scorn—the epitome of unethical science (*Souls*, 107–8).[44] In a March 29, 1904, letter chastising Cornell economist Walter F. Willcox, predictor of black criminality and extinction, for trying to "spin a solution of the

Negro problem out of the inside of [his] office," Du Bois revealed that his own solution had been to defamiliarize statistical data through personal experience: "You simply have no adequate conception of the Negro problem in the south & of Negro character and capacity. When you have sat as I have ten years in intimate soul contact with all kinds & conditions of black men you will be less agnostic. . . . If you insist on writing about & pronouncing judgment on this problem why not study it? Not from a car window & associated press despatches . . . but get down here and really study it at first hand" (Aptheker, *Correspondence*, 75). Du Bois's reference to Willcox's total reliance on dubious interpretations of black evolutionary unfitness as "agnosticism" and his pride in his own prolonged "soul contact" as a superior source of wisdom point to the reforms Du Bois hoped to make in the practice of sociology. "Truth" and "Beauty" would necessarily form complementary reference points in Du Bois's ethical science, just as he would later argue that "the apostle of Beauty . . . becomes the apostle of Truth and Right not by choice but by inner and outer compulsion."[45]

Du Bois learned the hard way that uncontextualized assessments of the state of black America only aided and abetted enemies (Rampersad, 97). If he was going to be in a position to ask that Booker T. Washington, for example, cease to disparage all nonutilitarian black aspiration, he would himself have to couch his scientific work in terms that could not be interpreted detrimentally to the race. Understanding that the materialist bias of sociology could describe only a limited profile of a mythic black community brought into existence as a statistical mean, but that it could never render the emotional and philosophical history of real people or serve as an accurate index of their potential for the future, Du Bois complemented his Atlanta Studies project of developing a more reliable statistical black "identity" with poetic evocations of the vast and sociologically unquantifiable black soul. It is in the attempt to map the black "soul" that he employed the mythic quest motif, spatializing the nonspatial in his tropes of the "veil" and the "color line" and temporalizing the nontemporal with his myth of the "progress" of the black soul toward spiritual fulfillment.[46]

In keeping with his function as race mythologist, Du Bois appropriated the heroic language and archetypes from the Western classical and biblical traditions, combining these with his own rather bookish brand of Ethiopianism. His cosmos of race striving was replete with conventional figures of good and evil battling over the souls of black and white folk. Some of the more obscure references contribute to the "penumbra of vagueness and half-veiled allusion" that Du Bois felt served to cloud the meaning of his work for many readers.[47] The "half-veiled allusion" that most reveals the mythic context of the Du Boisian soul concept is, in all likelihood, the most often quoted phrase from *The Souls*: "two souls . . . in one dark body," for if Du Bois wanted to keep *The Souls* focused on the spiritual and psychic attributes of black Americans as opposed to their bodies, he paradoxically needed a body image to make that spiritual dimension manifest. One of Du Bois's models for the dual "soul" [48] is Goethe's *Faust*,[49] from the lines that translate,

> Two souls, alas, are dwelling in my breast,
> And one is striving to forsake its brother.
> Unto the world in grossly loving zest,
> With clinging tendrils, one adheres;
> The other rises forcibly in quest
> Of rarefied ancestral spheres. (Goethe, 145:1112–17)

Looking at Du Boisian soul in the context of Goethe's *Faust*, the West's great romantic myth of modernist angst and alienation, allows us to place Du Bois's concern for the two-souled black American's "two warring ideals in one dark body" into a specific mythic and historical frame.[50]

The Devil's Bargain

The crucial diary entry by Du Bois on the eve of his twenty-fifth birthday gives some indication of the romantic background to Du Bois's emerging definition of the race protagonist as the one entrusted with reconciling the debilitating split consciousness of racial division. Mimicking Faust in his tower conjuring the world spirit, Du Bois began his birthday celebration with a "'sacrifice to the Zeitgeist' of Mercy, God, and Work, and a curious ceremony with candles, Greek wine, oil, song, and prayer," followed by a dedication of his library to his deceased mother. The role of the lifelong seeker that Du Bois outlined for himself on the occasion has several points of interest: his sense of life as a "race" to be run, a metaphor on which he relies heavily in *The Souls*; his determination to defy God and the Devil in his quest; and his anxiety to be done with his Western apprenticeship so as to "enter the dark forest of the unknown world" as its discoverer/cartographer.[51]

For Du Bois, it would be a moment of reflection over the question faced ultimately by each talented race striver: "I am firmly convinced that my own best development is not one and the same with the best development of the world and here I am willing to sacrifice."[52] Convinced that an ethical "striving to make [his] life all that life may be" was a worthwhile aim, he claimed a willingness to limit "that strife only in so far as that strife [was] incompatible with others of [his] brothers and sisters making their lives similar." Du Bois's quest for the "fullest self" resolved itself into a desire for a "wholeness" that can best be visualized as a collective effort at producing the greatest good for the greatest number: "The general proposition of working for the world's good becomes too soon sickly sentimentality. I therefore take the work that the Unknown lays in my hands and work for the rise of the Negro people, taking for granted that their best development means the best development of the world." Rather than interpret Du Bois's commitment to work for the development of black people as strictly messianic, I would like to explore the Faustian aspect of his attempt to "make [his] life all that life may be" in concert with the brothers and sisters "making their lives similar."

Du Bois wished to differentiate his quest for self-development from that of the masses who seek lives of conformity, yet not in a way that would remove him from their elemental struggle for basic human necessities or disparage their mundane aspirations. Instead, Du Bois saw the development of the race as dependent on both the masses and a leadership class that would set national goals and direct progress. As he said in the opening line of "The Talented Tenth," an essay of the same year as *The Souls*, "The Negro race, like all races, is going to be saved by its exceptional men" (17).[53] It would be the job of this leadership cadre, not limited in their options by a Washingtonian materialist education in agriculture and the industrial arts, to serve as role models of ethical race striving, so that "the Best of this race . . . may guide the Mass away from the contamination and death of the Worst, in their own and other races" (17). Leaders of the race must paradoxically be both above and with the people in order to save them and be saved by them.

To dispel the notion of black preindividual nondifferentiation, the Du Boisian race protagonist would strive for personal excellence. But simultaneously, the race leader would have to resist unbridled individualism. Du Bois intended his "talented tenth" to be a social evolutionary advance over Spencerian competition, a postindividual collective agency that hinted of the utopian streak that later led Du Bois to socialism.[54] The dilemma of the Du Boisian race developer is akin to that of Faust in this fundamentally ambiguous relationship to the masses. In Goethe's tale of the soul bargainer, the lonely scholar in his tower escapes the temptation to despair and suicide only at the last moment by the chiming of church bells that proclaim the Easter Resurrection, and Faust, going among the people for the first time in years, comes "back into life" through the simple human contact that he is able to effect (12). In the springtime resurrection of his community, Faust discovers "the people's paradise": "Here I am human, may enjoy humanity" (13). However, when greeted by the villagers as an honored healer and the son of a healer, Faust demurs, knowing full well that his and his father's medicines had been "worse than the [disease]" itself (14). Faust's despair has arisen from the frustration at the limits of his study, which leave him, for all his learning, "The wretched fool [he] was before": "For all our science and art / We can know nothing. It burns my heart" (9).

Like Faust, the twenty-five-year-old Du Bois—alone in his room in Berlin, fighting off the "wild *sehnsucht* [yearning] for Eternity that makes [his] heart sick now and then," not knowing whether he is a "genius or a fool," because despite his long apprenticeship, he had little faith in the learning that the world had provided him—escaped from the temptation of death by the decision to plunge into the world. He declared that he would "seize the day" and press on toward his goal—development of "the greatest and fullest self—this end is the Good." He, like Faust, "yield[s] to magic"—to the "silent call of the world spirit," the call of the "dark forest of the unknown world"—delivering himself to the grand hopelessness of a life of endless seeking after that which Goethe called "what[ever] secret force / Hides in the world and rules its course." The completion of this ur-quest of scientific inquiry would make Faust both famous and powerful and be a boon to humanity as well through his massive project to raise, in Du Bois's words, "a visible empire" for the race.

According to Marshall Berman, the modern intellectual isolate/dramatic hero who would change the world must necessarily come to an understanding of the unity of the self and the world, even though it means that to better the world, "the self's destruction will be an integral part of its development" (39). The invocation of supernatural powers by both Faust and Du Bois served to fuse the seemingly antithetical yearnings that each scholar expressed: the desire for "a connection between the solidity and warmth of life with people—everyday life within the matrix of a concrete community—and the intellectual and cultural revolution that has taken place in his head" (Berman, 4). "This," says Berman, "is the point of [Faust's] famous lament, 'Two souls, alas, are living in my breast'": "He cannot go on living as a disembodied mind, bold and brilliant in a vacuum; he cannot go on living mindlessly in the world he left. He must participate in society in a way that will give his adventurous spirit room to soar and grow. But it will take 'the powers of the underworld' to pull these polarities together, to make such a synthesis work" (4). If Du Bois had struggled as a collegian to articulate the form that ethical science would take, he must have discovered in Faust an archetype of heroic striving able to fuse material and spiritual

questing. Du Bois would reconcile the polarities of race and nation with a categorical imperative of the greatest good for the greatest number, but by crediting
this commission to the "Unknown," Du Bois left open the possibility that "the
powers of the underworld" might be required to accomplish the task.

In the cases of the Faustian "developers"—individuals who can "bring material, technical and spiritual resources together, and transform them into new
structures of social life" (Berman, 7)—the mixture of the abstraction Progress
with the terms of existence of actual people sometimes produces tragedy. For
Faust, the destruction of the cottage of Baucis and Philemon along with the
chapel whose bell drives him to distraction clears the way for the construction of
a tower overlooking his land-reclamation project: "Goethe's hero is heroic by
virtue of liberating tremendous repressed human energies. . . . But the great developments he initiates . . . turn out to exact great human costs. This is the meaning of Faust's relationship with the devil: human powers can be developed only
through what Marx called 'the powers of the underworld,' dark and fearful energies that may erupt with a horrible force beyond all human control. Goethe's
Faust is the first, and still the best, *tragedy of development*" (Berman, 39, 40). For
Du Bois's development project, the "meaning of progress" was similarly to be
found in the forlorn schoolhouse on the hill in Tennessee that failed to alter the
tragic destiny of Josie and the other black children of the first school in which he
taught: "My log schoolhouse was gone. In its place stood Progress; and Progress,
I understand, is necessarily ugly. . . . As I sat by the spring and looked on the Old
and the New I felt glad, very glad, and yet—" (*Souls*, 50).

Having returned ten years after his last summer as teacher there, Du Bois
learned of the tragic fates of Josie and the others: "How shall man measure
Progress there where the dark-faced Josie lies? How many heartfuls of sorrow
shall balance a bushel of wheat? How hard a thing is life to the lowly, and yet
how human and real! And all this life and love and strife and failure,—is it the
twilight of nightfall or the flush of some faint-dawning day?" (52). Like the condition of many of the South's black colleges cited by Du Bois in "Of the Wings of
Atalanta," the schoolhouse serves as a symbol of a progress mentality that substitutes material progress for real human development.

Faust's intention to reveal the wonders behind the "veil"[55] of human experience makes him the prototype of Du Bois's "weary traveler" who steps within the
veil of race, a veil sustained, as we are told in "Of the Black Belt," by a spell.
Leading the reader by Jim Crow car into "the Black Belt,— that strange land of
shadows, at which even slaves paled in the past, and whence come now only·

faint and half-intelligible murmurs to the world beyond" (*Souls*, 79), Du Bois uncovers the soulless desolation of the "Land of the Unfenced," where "the Negro problem in its naked dirt and penury" lies revealed: "I could imagine the place under some weird spell, and was half-minded to search out the princess" (84). Du Bois hears the story of the spell on the Waters-Loring plantation as a parable of Reconstruction's failed promise, for though the "field-hands sang" at first, when "the Wizard of the North—the Capitalist" bought up the land, his abandonment of the land to rot and ruin sits like a "spell of dishonesty" on the Black Belt. Though men also "call the shadow prejudice," Du Bois's mythology focused attention on a devil that sympathetic northern audiences could potentially influence in a direct fashion: the power of capitalist America, the "Wizard of the North."

Du Bois's emphasis on "the training of men" differed from Faust's developmental ethic in some respects, for if Faust can afford to turn his back on the abstract realm of learning to embrace the immediacy of the sensual world, Du Bois knew full well that it would take the development of the latent resources of the race in an educational project so vast that the black intellectual could not discount any form of learning: "The would-be black *savant* was confronted by the paradox that the knowledge his people needed was a twice-told tale to his white neighbors, while the knowledge which would teach the white world was Greek to his own flesh and blood" (4). The savant manqué, on the other hand, despising the backbreaking, foundational work of race development, seeks after the "false god" of self-aggrandizement. Likewise, "by the poverty and ignorance of his people, the Negro minister or doctor was tempted toward quackery and demagogy, and by the criticism of the other world, toward ideals that made him ashamed of his lowly tasks."

Having described the failure of the apostles of Truth to see the Beauty of the race, Du Bois assessed the lapses of the disciples of Beauty who could not reconcile themselves to the Truth: "The innate love of harmony and beauty that set the ruder souls of his people a-dancing and a-singing raised but confusion and doubt in the soul of the black artist; for the beauty revealed to him was the soul-beauty of a race which his larger audience despised, and he could not articulate the message of another people." These too, then, would be liable to fall into despair because of the "waste of double aims, this seeking to satisfy two unreconciled ideals," leading them to "wooing false gods and invoking false means of salvation." Du Bois understood that unlike Faust's dual attraction to the life of the mind and of the flesh, the race protagonist would have to resolve the inescapable attraction of the American capitalist ideal of personal greed that would come with higher education and professional training. Otherwise the conflict between bettering the self and bettering the race would create a generation of self-doubters, who, in despair of ever effecting progress among the masses, would turn to cynical materialism.

To make sure that individuation would not verge into callow individualism, Du Bois insisted that the reconciling factor between knowledge and desire be morality—the everlasting "Ought"—as his February 23, 1893, diary entry makes clear:

> What is life but life, after all. Its end is its greatest and fullest self—this end is the Good. The Beautiful its attribute—its soul, and Truth is its being. Not three commensurable things are these, they are three dimensions of the cube—.... The greatest and fullest life is by definition beautiful, beautiful—beautiful as a dark, passionate woman, beautiful as a golden hearted school girl, beautiful as a grey haired hero. That is the dimension of *breadth*. Then comes Truth—what is, cold and indisputable: that is *height*. Now I will, so help my Soul, multiply breadth by height, Beauty by Truth and then Goodness, strength, shall bind them together into a solid whole. (*Against Racism*, 28)

Du Bois's geometry of self-development transcended duality to forge a meaningful synthesis, setting down the pattern for his race-development scheme as well, the expansion of the soul-beauty of the race as a base upon which the acquisition of race knowledge by accretions of "cold and indisputable" Truth would rest. For Du Bois, only those gifted with a sensitivity toward Truth and Beauty, reinforced by ethical striving, would achieve the "self-conscious manhood" of an integrated, three-dimensional self.

In Du Bois's scheme of race development, the necessary binding agent— Goodness, the "everlasting Ought"—would be what Du Bois was to call in *The Souls* by the term "The Gospel of Sacrifice." In his diary that February night, he was committing himself to a "limitation" of his own capacity for growth so as not to jeopardize his world-historical mission of race building: "I am firmly convinced that my own best development is not one and the same with the best development of the world and here I am willing to sacrifice. The sacrifice is the working for the multiplication of (Truth X Beauty)."[56]

It is in this "Gospel of Sacrifice" that Du Bois most clearly differentiated himself from the Faustian impulse to experience all that humanity may. Faust sets but two boundaries to his immersion in the world, one being that he never find a moment's satisfaction that will divert him from his self-willed ceaseless striving:

> If ever I recline, calmed, on a bed of sloth,
> You may destroy me then and there.
>
> . . . .
>
> If to the moment I should say:
> Abide, you are so fair—
> Put me in fetters on that day,
> I *wish* to perish then, I swear. (183–88)

As Marshall Berman explains, Faust's denial of unqualified sensual gratification makes his engagement in the physical world a powerful form of human development, a modern self-maximizing ethic of efficiency that allows no wasted effort, no squandered resource: "Universally modern . . . are the Faustian pressures to use every part of ourselves, and of everybody else, to push ourselves and others as far as we can go" (5).

But Faust's other condition, understated though it is, represents a qualification of the will to abjure satiation. For having cursed illusory "possessions that deceive" and "Mammon," whose treasures goad and whose "slothful pleasures" lure, Faust also disparages the antithetical impulse of self-restraint:

> You must renounce! You ought to yield!
>   [Entbehren sollst du! Sollst entbehren!]
> That is the never-ending drone
> Which we must, our life long, hear,
> Which, hoarsely, all our honors intone
> And grind into our weary ears. (175:1549–53)

Faust rebels against this ethic of self-restraint because in contrast to sensual experience it provides him with *no* satisfaction. His despair makes him rise with tears in his eyes in expectation of each day that will "scorn / [His] every wish—fulfill not one." Consequently, his "race" against time is driven by the promise of self-fulfillment minus the distraction of self-contentment: like Atalanta racing Hippomenes, he cannot linger over golden apples strewn by the roadside; but unlike Atalanta, he cannot leave any apple untasted.

It is in this second qualification, the refusal to renounce any experience, that Du Bois explicitly departed from the Faustian model, for reasons to which I will return shortly. Du Bois quoted Goethe's line "Entbehren sollst du! Sollst entbehren!" in several of his works, usually in the original German, though the occasions before and after he used the quotation in *The Souls* both included an English translation: "Thou shalt forego, shalt do without."[57] Schools such as

Atlanta University and Fisk were successful, Du Bois felt, in developing "that fine adjustment between real life and the growing knowledge of life, an adjustment which forms the secret of civilization" (*Souls*, 59). Du Bois's formula for development depends greatly on this "secret of civilization" to inspire the talented tenth to self-sacrifice: "Not at Oxford or at Leipsic [*sic*], not at Yale or Columbia, is there an air of higher resolve or more unfettered striving; the determination to realize for men, both black and white, the broadest possibilities of life, to seek the better and the best, to spread with their own hands the Gospel of Sacrifice,—all this is the burden of their talk and dream. . . . And here men may lie and listen, and learn of a future fuller than the past, and hear the voice of Time: 'Entbehren sollst du, sollst entbehren'" (58). In this image of the collegiate oasis, Du Bois turns *Faust* inside out, moving beyond Faustian egotism to find in sacrifice the key to a postindividualistic ideal of racial progress.

But in "The Problem of Amusement" (1897), the essay in which he first used the quotation from Goethe, Du Bois argued a position closer to Faust's. His subject for what was originally an address given at Booker T. Washington's alma mater, Hampton Institute, was the antagonism of black churches to secular public amusement, a social trend destined to produce the opposite effect than it intended:

> What the Negro church is trying to impress upon young people is that Work and Sacrifice is the true destiny of humanity. The Negro church is dimly groping for that divine word of Faust:
>
> 'Entbehren sollst du, sollst entbehren.'
> (Thou shalt forego, shalt do without.)
>
> But in this truth—properly conceived, properly enunciated—there is nothing incompatible with wholesale amusement, with true recreation. For what is true amusement, true diversion, but the re-creation of energy which we may sacrifice to noble ends, to higher ideals—while, without proper amusement, we waste or dissipate our mightiest powers? (36–37)

This qualification of the Gospel of Sacrifice, that amusement has its place as well, became the occasion for Du Bois to issue his sternest injunction, not against amusement, but against despair:

> For believe me, my hearers, the great danger of the best class of Negro youth to-day is not that they will hesitate to sacrifice their lives, their money and their energy on the altar of their race, but the danger is lest under continuous and persistent

proscription, under the thousand little annoyances and petty insults and disappoint-ments of caste system *they lose the divine faith of their fathers in the fruitfulness of sacrifice.* . . . There are creeping in among us low ideals of petty hatred, of sordid gain, of political theft, of place hunting and immodest self-praise that must be stifled lest they sting to death our loftier and nobler sentiments. (37) [58]

These corrosive forces threatening the group ideal of sacrifice would become personified by Booker T. Washington in Du Bois's works.

Du Bois had to modify Goethe's version of the Faust myth to fit the purposes of African American race striving because whereas Faust could complete his self-maximizing quest successfully *only* by forswearing both mindless indulgence and total abstinence, the myths of African unrestraint and incapacity for sus-tained gestures of self-sacrifice made it imperative that the black race protagonist adopt a posture of selfless striving. This ethical striving, as an alternative to Amer-ican capitalism as practiced in the Progressive Era, would serve as the racial "message" that would make black American world-historical status indisputable.

The Body of Death

In his Harvard commencement address, Du Bois first laid out the basis for this opposition of racial ideals in the American cultural landscape. In "Jefferson Davis as a Representative of Civilization" (1890), Du Bois depicted the southerner as the Strong Man: the Teutonic ideal of "Individualism coupled with the rule of might," the "advance of a part of the world at the expence [*sic*] of the whole" (in *W. E. B. Du Bois: A Reader*, 17–18). His opposite, the Submissive Man, the Ne-gro, enacted a different racial ideal. In contrast to the "Teutonic deification of Self," the Submissive Man benefited society by introducing the idea of "submis-sion of the strength of the Strong to the advance of all, not in mere aimless sacrifice, but recognizing the fact that 'To no one type of mind is it given to dis-cern the totality of Truth,' . . . that not only the assertion of the I, but also the sub-mission to the Thou is the highest Individualism (19).[59] Du Bois's explanation that the world needed an ideal of personal sacrifice to balance the "Personal As-sertion" of the Teuton helps to explain why Du Bois could not subscribe to Faust's overwhelming egotism, although he privileged the Germanic expression of per-sonal development (even his black Submissive Man in the allegory says "Ich Dein": "I serve"). Though Faust must resist self-abnegation to complete his quest, sacrifice became a "gospel" for Du Bois, though in his struggle with Booker T. Washington he would drop all references to "submission" as a model of pragmatic black leadership. In postulating "submission to the Thou" as a higher form of individualism than "assertion of the I," Du Bois revealed for the first time publicly a glimpse of his postindividual ethical striver who would transform America by resisting the Teutonic Zeitgeist through submission to the "everlasting Ought."

In his autobiographical reminiscence of the kaiser's entrance through the Brandenburg Gates during his student days in Germany, Du Bois revisited the black American soul dilemma: "I began to feel that dichotomy which all my life has characterized my thought: how far can love for my oppressed race accord with love for the oppressing country? And when these loyalties diverge, where shall my soul find refuge?" (*Autobiography*, 169).[60] In this excerpt Du Bois writes of a singular soul in personal, not racial, terms, but clearly the emphasis falls on the division of allegiance that fosters a psychic rupture. The trope of "double-consciousness," which typically focuses discussions of national belonging in Du Bois's works, is the precursor of this description of a "dichotomy" that plagued him. Yet Du Bois's abandonment of the term "double-consciousness" itself strongly supports Adolph Reed Jr.'s contention that the term has a historical context that should not be separated from its discussion.[61]

Because Du Bois used the "two souls" construct as a mechanism by which to reverse the debilitating split subjectivity of "double-consciousness," the confusion between the discourse of "souls" and of "consciousnesses" has accommodated divergent interpretations of the dual identity model of black America.[62] But just as he resolved the dichotomy between Teutonic assertion and black American submission with a "high[er] Individualism" of personal sacrifice, Du Bois saw black America's soul division as ultimately reconcilable. His opening discussion of "double-consciousness," however, leaves unclear the fact that there are three dualistic phases of black soul development that culminate also in a reconciliation. The first phase corresponds to what Du Bois called "double-consciousness," the pathological self-division based in intense self-loathing. The second phase was that of spiritual striving to develop black race idealism within and against a prevailing American ethic of materialistic striving, a phase most closely associated with the "two souls" figure. The third phase was one of spiritual reconciliation, a difficult equilibrium between black spiritual idealism and American materialism that would nudge the American success ethic away from its social Darwinist tendencies into a quest for the greatest good for the greatest number of people. The key to "Of Our Spiritual Strivings," the chapter in which Du Bois introduced the question of race and dualism, is its gradual replacement of the psychic dichotomy of "double-consciousness" with its concluding image of an America reconciled to the African American philosophical reflection on the American experience through its acceptance of black culture's already acknowledged imprint upon American idealism — its *spirituals* and folklore. Du Bois makes it clear at the end of this essay and at the end of the volume that black American dualism is a product of the way Americans think about race and not of race itself. The development of the black soul idea could not help but benefit America, then, because an America freed of its obsession with the meaning of race difference would be better able to fulfill its world-historical mission.

The difficulties implicit in "double-consciousness" (Du Bois's styling) as a meaningful characterization of black life reside in the ultimately pathological nature of "double consciousness," the disabling psychological condition that Du Bois posits as a preliminary stage of self-awareness. While the Faustian trope of dual souls captures the body politics of Henry Grady's image of the postwar South in his famous speech "The New South" (1886),[63] hysterical "double-consciousness" produced a body image roughly equivalent to that which surfaced in popular and scientific treatises on mulatto maladjustment. These emphasized physiological origins for the melancholy and discontent that supposedly afflicted racial hybrids, who were spatially divided into a white "side" and a black "side" compelled to disharmony by the laws of phylogenetic conflict.[64] Simple dual allegiance to race and to nation does not qualify, then, as "double-consciousness," the debilitating condition that entails self-doubt, self-hatred, and self-alienation.

Like the hysterical condition described by psychologist Alfred Binet, Du Bois's "double-consciousness" spawned a self-alienating, autonomous, preemptive identity.[65] In *On Double Consciousness* (1889, 1905), Binet described hysterical double consciousness, including cases of hemispherically self-divided individuals that strongly resemble images of mulatto bilateralism (12), as instances of "two distinct personalities, two egos united in the same person" (11). He particularly found that those with hysterical anesthesia in various limbs, organs, or spots on the body readily exhibited the doubling trait, strongly associating the condition with somatic insensibility akin to paralysis (12). Du Bois's appropriation of the trope captures something of this idea of self-division as producing a type of morbidity in the body itself.

The "double-conscious" black subject was therefore divided in a way that the romantic two-souled quester was not. Du Bois's Faustian equilibrium of race and nation gave way in "double-consciousness" to the false choice of self-objectification, of choosing nation over race. Binet had predicated his experiments on the practitioner's power to summon and manipulate the subject's second consciousness, whereas William James, Du Bois's Harvard teacher and mentor, whose *The Principles of Psychology* (1890) appeared in the year of Du Bois's matriculation, had pointed out that the mediumistic second consciousness seemed particularly susceptible to suggestion from the *"Zeitgeist."* [66] By consuming American culture unfiltered, the black subject necessarily absorbed the negative opinion of blackness so constitutive of American law and social practice. This produced a grotesque self-image that clashed with the subject's lived experience, a double's double, a being twice removed from reality, giving form to the myths of blackness circulating in the culture. Though Du Bois does not discuss this aspect in *The Souls*, the doubling process entails a mystification of embodied white America as the exalted and unattainable other that scoffs at black aspiration to escape its debased cultural status. Many years later Du Bois alluded to this secondary doubling, explaining that "the American Negro . . . is surrounded and conditioned by the concept which he has of white people and he is treated in accordance with the concept they have of him" (*Dusk*, 173). What Du Bois described as "double-consciousness" was the struggle between the internalized self-image and the "true" self for mastery of the black psyche, a struggle that the internalized critic could prolong or push to a negative conclusion. [67]

In "The Conservation of Races," Du Bois characterized a degree of self-doubt by black Americans as a predictable but ultimately damaging response to pervasive discourses of black inferiority and the seemingly endless struggle for dignity. The ur-statement of his cognitive dichotomy takes the form of a series of questions meant to register the black subject's existential dilemma: "What, after all, am I? Am I an American or am I a Negro? Can I be both? Or is it my duty to cease to be a Negro as soon as possible and be an American?" (5). In his discussion of a case study in dual consciousness, William James noted what Greisinger defined as a split between "an old familiar *me*" and a "strange, often astonishing and abhorrent *thou*," a "doubleness, [a] struggle of the old self against the new discordant forms of experience" that leads to a melancholic "cerebral malady" (1:376). James approximated the sensation of self-division, as Du Bois would seven years later, by a series of persistent questions that perplexed the victim of double consciousness: "Where is my old me? What is the new one? Are they the same? Or have I two?" (378). James concluded this passage with a somewhat dry observation, which seems equally applicable to the circumstances noted both by himself and by Du Bois: "Such questions, answered by whatever theory the patient is able to conjure up as plausible, *form the beginning of his insane life*" (378; my emphasis).

Du Bois, in "Conservation," reaches a similar conclusion, noting that "such incessant self-questioning and the hesitation that arises from it" result in the loss of psychic health, civic productivity, and effectual challenges to racism by the talented tenth, on the one hand, and in black demagoguery in the name of the race, on the other.[68] The patient whose case James cites described his delusions of bodily alienation in terms that also reflect a paralysis of will in hysterical double consciousness: "There was inside of me a new being, and another part of myself, the old being, which took no interest in the newcomer. . . . I was never really the dupe of these illusions, but my mind grew often tired of incessantly correcting the new impressions, and I let myself go and lived the unhappy life of this new entity. I had an ardent desire to . . . get back to my old self. . . . This desire kept me from killing myself." The patient who suffered from self-alienation ultimately surrendered to the invading new personality, but in Du Bois's *The Souls*, this is precisely what the soul quester *must not do*. Since Du Bois defined "double-consciousness" as a paralysis of will brought on by social exclusion and exacerbated by myths of black inferiority circulated in American culture, it was symptomatic of the paralyzing potential of the black body of death on individual striving.

The power of the body of black death to defeat the aspirations of Hopkins's and Chesnutt's characters is a prime instance of what Du Bois meant by "double-consciousness," particularly in its ability to produce characteristically vivid fantasy encounters with an "abhorrent thou": the original African mother as an invasive, revenant identity. To Binet, the "suggestibility" of the double conscious hysteric is on the order of the hypnotized subject, allowing the scientist to produce hallucinations spontaneously by implanting images in the subject's mind (69–73).[69] Laws and customs of exclusion created the psychic partitioning of "double-consciousness" for black subjects, as described by Du Bois, while the architects of white nationalism (and their apologists) exploited this division by battering the already weakened resistance of black America with constant suggestions of its inadequacy. The double's double was the black body of death psychically chained to the black consciousness in the era of Jim Crow and lynch law.

Despite the dogged will that permits striving toward incremental gains, the transitional "two-souled" figure is in danger always of regression into "double-consciousness" because of the nature of the two souls. Faust's two souls included one that clings "Unto the world in grossly loving zest" and another that "rises forcibly in quest / Of rarefied ancestral spheres." Du Bois's two-souled quester similarly desired mastery of the material world but simultaneously wanted to explore black "ancestral spheres" of wisdom. Because ancestral wisdom in the black American experience had much to do with avoiding the overreliance on material success with which white America was afflicted in the Progressive Era, the dual spiritual nature of the black American striver represented a dichotomy between materialism and idealism that, unreconciled, would leave the quester irreparably self-divided. It was a division that, pointedly, reflected an unreconciled split in American character generally, so that the resolution of the split in the black American would become the paradigm for American psychic wholeness as well.

In "The Development of a People," Du Bois explained that only leaders properly able to "discriminate between the good and the bad in the past" could divine what is beneficial in "that all-powerful spiritual world that surrounds and envelopes the souls of men" (212) and thereby avoid self-division. The reconciliation of "two warring ideals" of civilization required the development of a sui generis race idea that could never be "a servile imitation of Anglo-Saxon culture" because that culture was premised on white superiority. In addition, the Teutonic spirit encompassed a distracting American success ethic that inhibited incipient black idealism as it struggled to reify itself in a world that admired nothing so much as success. The potential for corruption of the fragile ideal of sacrifice, then, was as simple as a cessation of strife and resistance, a simple yes to the seductive lure of American acquisitiveness, which whispered, "What is the greatness of the country? Is it not money? Well then, the one end of our education and striving should be moneymaking. . . . What is personal humiliation and the denial of ordinary civil rights compared with a chance to earn a living?" (Du Bois, W. E. B. Du Bois: A Reader, 330). To Du Bois such loss of faith stemming from the "transformation of a fair far-off ideal of Freedom into the hard reality of bread-winning and the consequent deification of Bread" (57) brings the black soul striver to destruction. Against this event, Du Bois offered the time-tested "faith of the Fathers" that "some day the Awakening will come, when the pent-up vigor of ten million souls shall sweep irresistibly toward the Goal, out of the

Valley of the Shadow of Death, where all that makes life worth living—Liberty, Justice, and Right—is marked 'For White People Only'" (145).

To the degree that the ruling Zeitgeist of economic materialism was responsible for the oppression of black and brown people behind the color line, the greatest danger to the development of the leadership class needed for race striving would be, as Du Bois said in "The Problem of Amusement," that those trained in the "deification of self" by the American university system would quickly despair that the race could prevail over the long haul through sacrifice and submission to the greatest good. It was these would-be savants and artists, unable to reconcile the call of the Teutonic Zeitgeist with the faint promise of the African American *Volkgeist*, who would become the failed Du Boisian soul bargainers:

> What if the Negro people be wooed from a strife for righteousness, from a love of knowing, to regard dollars as the be-all and end-all of life? What if to the Mammonism of America be added the rising mammonism of the re-born South, and the Mammonism of this South be reinforced by the budding Mammonism of its half-wakened black millions? Whither, then, is the new-world quest of Goodness and Beauty and Truth gone glimmering? Must this, and that fair flower of Freedom which . . . sprung from our fathers' blood, must that too degenerate into a dusty quest of gold,—into lawless lust? (*Souls*, 57)

Before the fashionable modernist outcry against the materialism of the postwar era popularized the cultural wasteland motif, Du Bois had already proclaimed black America to be the "sole oasis of simple faith and reverence in a dusty desert of dollars and smartness" (*Souls*, 8).

No public figure better illustrated for Du Bois the temptation to exploit the debilitating potential of "double-consciousness" than the "Wizard of Tuskegee," Booker T. Washington, whose hostility to higher education as an immediate goal for African Americans inhibited progress toward articulation of a unique race ideal. Washington's decision to profit personally from a racially divided world with "a double life, with double thoughts, double duties, and double social classes" led to his casual indulgence in "double words and double ideals," a "Jesuitical casuistry . . . deterred by no ethical consideration in the endeavor" to profit from the relative powerlessness of the black masses (*Souls*, 142, 143).

In "Of Mr. Booker T. Washington and Others," the third chapter of *The Souls*, Du Bois had his finest moment in establishing the direction for his alternative to Washington's program of race development. Du Bois begins his assault on

Washington with masterful indirection, noting Washington's "singleness of vision and thorough oneness with his age" as the "mark of the successful man"
(32). From another, this might be high praise, but given Du Bois's criticism of
the materialistic bias of his age's Zeitgeist, it suggests that Washington's brand of
leadership masked a craftily concealed "deification of self." Du Bois thus goes on
to tie Washington's installation as black America's leader by hostile outside forces
to "that curious double movement where real progress may be negative and actual advance be relative retrogression" (33). This "double movement" is typified
for Du Bois by Washington's paradoxical acquiescence in "the alleged inferiority
of the Negro races" (36) as the key to his acceptability to white America. Thus,
in contrast to enlightened black leadership that knew "that relentless color-
prejudice is more often a cause than a result of the Negro's degradation" (38),
Washington agreed with his white benefactors that "the South is justified in its
present attitude toward the Negro" (41), and he assisted in "shift[ing] the burden
of the Negro problem to the Negro's shoulders" (42). Du Bois makes fairly plain
that the "double movement" of Washington has much to do with burdening the
masses with a paralyzing "double-consciousness," manipulating their latent self-
doubt to ensure his program's unchallenged authority.

To Du Bois, what Washington had accomplished from "the Atlanta Compromise" on was "aid[ing] and abet[ting] a national crime simply because it [was]
unpopular not to do so." The crime? Du Bois charged Washington with the entrapment of black America into the "double-conscious" double bind of "industrial slavery and civic death" (40). Du Bois's reaction to Washington's "body of
death" rhetoric was akin to charging that Washington had plotted the murder of
black America himself, for though he cites only the spiritual death of "industrial
slavery" and the "civic death" of disfranchisement at first, Du Bois subsequently
connects Washington's program and his rhetoric to complicity in genocide, "the
slow throttling and murder of nine millions of men" (42).[70]

The importance of this critique for both Du Bois's political agenda and his
evolving allegory of black national renaissance cannot be overstated. He seized
upon the implications of Washington's "body of death" rhetoric as a means of
rallying race leadership "by every consideration of patriotism and loyalty to oppose such a course by all civilized methods" (40). He would eventually challenge Washington's false choice between two body ideals for black America: the
black body of death—criminal, lust-driven, diseased, and ultimately doomed to
extinction; and the "industrial slave"—educated in "heart and hand" (but not in
head) to perform the manual labor for which whites did not wish to compete,

culturally extinct, intellectually stifled, dead to the life of the polis, economically dependent, and disciplined into a Brownlow black body by surrender of all legal recourse to the rights and entitlements of citizenship. To Du Bois, there was no meaningful distinction between acceptance of racial extinction and the social death of strategic withdrawal from national politics and culture in the hope of economic gains.

Alfred Binet had stumbled upon what he considered a "happy expression" for double consciousness as the "inhibition of a cause of inhibition" (88). Du Bois's "double-consciousness" countenanced the black subject's surrender of the inhibiting spiritual idealism that had staved off despair even in slavery, a surrender that might take the form of gross self-indulgence or an ethical collapse into tricksterism. In response, Du Bois offered his own postindividualist striver as an alternative to Washington's "double-conscious" opportunist, with one ear tuned in to the fears and doubts of the populace, the other alert to the main chance.

The Wizard and the Veil

In an essay published the year after *The Souls of Black Folk*, which he titled "The Development of a People," Du Bois used the same rhetorical ploy with which he began *The Souls*: an imaginary tour along and across the "color line." "I do not want you to see so much of the physical as the spiritual town," he explained. "Were you there in person I could not take you easily across the line into the world I want to study. But in spirit let me lead you across" ("Development," 206). As though he had to remind them, Du Bois warned his readers that this spiritual journey did not take place in the homogeneous, empty time of the nation, for the whole point of the "color line" was to produce a "mass of men isolated in space, [and] also isolated in time" (212). Du Bois then reveals that the remedy to this spiritual isolation is not the Washington ideal of industrial and agricultural training that Nathaniel Shaler favored but the development of race leaders trained in the progressive time of the [white] nation: "[The leader] must, in fine, stand to this group in the light of the interpreter of the civilization of the twentieth century to the minds and hearts of people who, from sheer necessity, can but dimly comprehend it. . . . This person is going to solve the Negro problem; for that problem is at bottom the clash of two different standards of culture." The essay appeared in the *International Journal of Ethics*, and as the invitation to cross the "color line" implies, Du Bois anticipated a white readership. Conceding black allochronism to this potentially sympathetic white audience, Du Bois seemed to support a saturation of black America with white American values and ideals of civilization.

But Du Bois's earlier "The Conservation of Races," his address before the American Negro Academy, had suggested to its black audience a different agenda for this leadership cadre. Du Bois envisioned the racial vanguard as the architects of a black America steeped in black ideals. The distinction shows that Du Bois was not above playing to his audiences and that despite his emphasis on ethical race striving, his insider/outsider posing reveals the maneuvering of a political pragmatist. More important, it emphasized Du Bois's role for the racial elite as interpreters and inhabitants of a socially partitioned "nation within the nation," whose territory was the black body itself.

The "veil" (or sometimes "Veil" or "shadow") became a vehicle for the expression of numerous features of the race question. In Du Bois's usage in *The Souls of Black Folk*, the veil signifies, first, the long history of black enslavement and degradation in the service of European capitalist expansion that deprived blacks of an understanding of their world-historical status (62). Second, it chiefly indicates the present fact of discrimination itself, based on that history, as interpreted through narratives of racial disaffiliation (63). Third, it demarcates the unstable boundary of the social space between the races (130), separating the allochronistic time-space of black America from the homogeneous, empty time of national simultaneity. Fourth, it signifies the consciousness of difference arising from that boundary, the cause of the self-loathing and despair that made black Americans, fifth, *self*-veiled—incapable of clear self-perception (3).[71]

Du Bois, as indicated in his 1897 paper at the Hampton Conference, saw nothing quite as threatening to the development of the black soul as the despair to which the black elite was subject when, self-veiled and self-doubting, they were oppressed by the "thousand and one little actions that go to make up" the "storm and stress" of black soul life. The "confused, half-conscious mutter of men who are black and whitened"—those whose soul division incapacitates them as race leaders—erodes the necessary spirit of sacrifice with unsettling second thoughts: "Suppose, after all, the World is right and we are less than men? Suppose this mad impulse within is all wrong, some mock mirage from the untrue?" (*Souls*, 63). This questioning inner voice, like the "inward voices" of the "demented" and the "possessed," reveals the onset of a crippling double consciousness (Binet, *On Double Consciousness*, 19).

Du Bois ends his ironically titled second chapter, "Of the Dawn of Freedom," the irony deriving from the final image of embodied black America at the crossroads of the new century: "And there in the King's Highways sat and sits a figure veiled and bowed, by which the traveller's footsteps hasten as they go. . . . Three centuries' thought has been the raising and unveiling of that bowed human heart, and now behold a century new for the duty and the deed" (29). Positioned just before Du Bois's third chapter, with its denunciation of Washington's leadership, this image of black America is the very emblem of the Washington idea in action. Like the crouching slave in the famous Tuskegee statue of Washington,[72] the figure's posture indicates an adjustment to the burden of the veil itself, as if the veil of race were imprinted into more than the consciousness—into the flesh itself. Du Bois's "bowed human heart," recalling the allegorical "Veiled Melancholy," embodies Du Bois's fear of "industrial slavery" and "civic death" as a psychophysiological state: a "soul" in the sense that Michel Foucault would later pronounce the "genealogy of the modern soul" to be "the present correlative of a certain technology of power over the body."[73] The veil of color, profoundly instituting a certain "reality-reference" by which the body's relation to the world came to be measured, affected "psyche, subjectivity, personality, [and] consciousness" (Foucault, 29).

In "The Negro Problems" (1915), after he had developed a stronger grasp of Marx, Du Bois listed as this "attempted solution" to the "Negro problem" that of white capitalism creating a "docile industrial class working for low wages" (W. E. B. Du Bois: A Reader, 51). Industrial America's hope was to inscribe itself, as with the Brownlow tradition, in the kinetic range of the worker, becoming a visible "prison of the body." Attracted himself to the self-conscious modernity of white America—he was, after all, hoping to emulate Bismarck—Du Bois was nonetheless frightened by what he saw as a descending veil of a spiritual numbness that would replace an older slavery with a newer one and replace an old quest for soul articulation with a modern spiritual anesthesia.

Du Bois held the Tuskegee leader accountable for contaminating the idealism of the black elite and the simple faith of the masses (Autobiography, 155). Washington's unabashed "Gospel of Money," in Du Bois's phrase, was thus the focal point, from the very inception of the Faustian framework of The Souls, for Du Bois's articulation of a "devil's bargain" that would compromise the project of black soul development. When Faust cursed Mammon for trying to entice him with treasures or seduce him into an irresistible "bed of sloth," he declared that it would take two devils to catch his soul. Du Bois's critique of Washington's "Atlanta Compromise" treated the speech as a bargaining of the black soul to two powerful, demonic forces of the North and South.

The grand wizards of the South who maintained the veil of color caste prejudice generally applauded the speech as acceptance of second-class status by a
prominent black American. At the same time, the financial wizards of the North
saw in the speech the possibility for a settlement of the racial unrest that had
made the South a dubious area for economic development. "Others less shrewd
and tactful," Du Bois noted, "had formerly essayed to sit on these two stools and
had fallen between them" (*Souls*, 31). But Washington's ability to "Brownlow" to
southerners and speak the language of "triumphant commercialism, and the
ideals of material prosperity to northerners" meant to Du Bois simply that Washington's willingness to serve both masters simultaneously spoke of a deep, ir-
reparable self-division. Washington's biographer, Louis R. Harlan, pointedly uses
the term "Faustian bargain" to describe Washington's manipulations of race and
power.[74] From Du Bois's perspective, the future enslavement of the race would
enlist wealthy whites and black soul brokers into a conspiracy to divide the spoils,
as the Washingtonian idea boasted of making available an exploitable, unenlightened black proletariat as a renewable material resource to be lapped up
by the bucketful by shrewd entrepreneurs.[75] Washington's "gospel of Work and
Money" in an age of "economic development" meant a complete overshadow-
ing of "the higher aims of life," then, because it necessarily had to ally itself with
the forces of racial disaffiliation and unabashed greed.

Taking note of white fears that higher education blurred certain distinctions
between blacks and whites, Washington presented to the American capitalist/
philanthropist class he courted the vision of a docile and upwardly immobile
black workforce and to the southerners with whom he wanted to coexist the vision of a regimented, "heart and hand" educated but mindless and voteless black
populace content to stay in its "place," justifying Du Bois's designation of his program as the "Tuskegee Machine" (*Dusk*, 7).[76] The machine was in this regard
more controlled by than it was controlling of the northern white capital disguised as philanthropy. Covetous of the cheap labor of the South but wary of the
potential for racial discord, northern capital saw Washington as a "godsend," according to Du Bois: "The control was to be drastic. The Negro intelligentsia was
to be suppressed and hammered into conformity. The process involved some
cruelty and disappointment, but that was inevitable. This was the real force back
of the Tuskegee Machine. It had money and it had opportunity, and it found in
Tuskegee tools to do its bidding" (*Dusk*, 7). Washington used his power as cajoler
and race disciplinarian to institute a docility shaped by the Brownlow tradition,
reinforcing the old etiquette with a new rationale of self-advancement through

nonassertiveness: "The young Negro of the South who would succeed cannot be frank and outspoken, honest and self-assertive, but rather he is daily tempted to be silent and wary, politic and sly; he must flatter and be pleasant, endure petty insults with a smile, shut his eyes to wrong; in too many cases he sees positive personal advantage in deception and lying. His real thoughts, his real aspirations, must be guarded in whispers; he must not criticise, he must not complain. Patience, humility, and adroitness must, in these growing youth, replace impulse, manliness and courage" (*Souls*, 144). Washington's threat to Du Bois's dream of soul development can be seen in its antagonism to the heroic struggle for a "self-conscious manhood."

Like Faust, Du Bois understood that the aim of striving was rending the "magic veils" that thwarted knowledge of any sort, but particularly self-knowledge: "In those sombre forests of his striving his own soul rose before him, and he saw himself, — darkly as though through a veil; and yet he saw in himself some faint revelation of his power, of his mission. He began to have a dim feeling that, to attain his place in the world, he must be himself, and not another" (*Souls*, 6).[77] This knowledge born of imposed self-alienation was a modification of the racial "fortunate fall," and it became the basis of Du Bois's "messianic" role for the black American.[78] Believing that knowledge of the corruption of founding American ideals entailed an obligation to strive for right, Du Bois envisioned the "best development" of the black race as the "best development" of America itself. And because Du Bois could see through the veil of race that "the striving [of blacks] toward self-realization [was] to the strife of the white world like a wheel within a wheel" (56), he knew that the Tuskegee idea was but a microcosm of the American technological soul that had to be resisted by some countervailing spiritual force. If that force was to be black American striving, then its civilizing message would produce an ethical modernity in America capable of elevating African Americans in the public esteem as the "tru[est] exponents of the spirit of the Declaration of Independence." The result of black American unqualified participation in national imagining can be represented by the term AMERICA — Houston Baker's figure for the perpetually anticipated fulfillment of America's "egalitarian promise" of freedom and opportunity (Baker, *Blues, Ideology*, 65). The end of all Du Boisian soul development was transforming America into AMERICA.

To accelerate the transformation, Du Bois pointed out in *The Souls* that the foundation for AMERICA had already been laid. For Du Bois, the first step away from soul cleavage lay in realization of the black American's veiled and therefore unacknowledged participation in American civilization from its inception. The myth of America as "white man's country" was *the* lie that Washington would have black Americans accept as a precondition for building a black world in the image of "white America."

> Your country? How came it yours? Before the Pilgrims landed we were here. . . . Out of the nation's heart we have called all that was best to throttle and subdue all that was worst. . . . Actively we have woven ourselves with the very warp and woof of this nation,—we fought their battles, shared their sorrow, [and] mingled our blood with theirs. . . . Our song, our toil, our cheer, and warning have been given to this nation in blood-brotherhood. Are not these gifts worth the giving? Is not this work and striving? Would America be America without her Negro people? (187)

By claiming "blood-brotherhood," in pointed contrast to Washington's appeal on the grounds of the servile devotion of blacks for their former masters, Du Bois thus denied a simplistic equation of the success ethic of "white America" with the essential American "soul" because black America's "gift of the Spirit" had been indelibly woven into the American character by active black participation in American life. This is why he takes pains to differentiate in "The Souls of White Folks" between white souls and white "consciousness" of being white. To counteract this false Strong Man ideal that had preempted American democratic idealism, Du Bois would offer the black "gift of the Spirit," a sensitivity to spiritual value he later identified as "the imprint of Africa on Europe in America" (*W. E. B. Du Bois: A Reader*, 54). The soul quester's discovery of an indispensable relation to American culture, evolved from an awareness of an indivisible American past, would make the task of the race protagonist as much the articulation of the black contribution to America as the realization of its full potential. The hero would be inspired by the guiding principle of Frederick Douglass, that black national belonging should be "*through* self-assertion, and not on other terms" (35). Du Bois carefully insisted, therefore, that for the black race protagonist to become a "co-worker in the kingdom of culture, to escape both death and isolation" planned by white America, she or he would first have to merge the "double self into a better and truer self" (3) without subordinating either the race or national idealism to the other.

Du Bois therefore defined what a reconciliation of the black American's "two souls" would be like, arguing in essence for a model of cultural pluralism. In "Conservation," he lists among his articles of faith that "unless modern civilization is a failure, it is entirely feasible and practicable for two races in such essential political, economic, and religious harmony as the white and colored people of America, to develop side by side in peace and mutual happiness, the peculiar contribution which each has to make to the culture of their common country" (7). Du Bois's model for the American future is a common national culture composed of stable but interactive ethnic components, along the lines of Faust's vision of the cosmos: "All weaves itself into the whole, / Each living in the other's soul" (99:457–58). Thus before the full emergence of the modern concept of cultural pluralism, Du Bois was already envisioning this paradigm as the best way to frame the indelible black contribution to America.[79]

Du Bois and Tuskegee

Washington solidified his grip on the emergent black middle class by playing the role of racial disciplinarian and dispenser of material boons. He emerged in Du Bois's analysis as a prototype of the neocolonialist, pseudo-Faustian dictators of the Third World, whom Martin Berman describes as benefiting their own fortunes and power through the manipulation of images of uplift and material progress (7). To Du Bois, Tuskegee became less a school than a vast intelligence-gathering agency—a network of rewards and punishments for the spiritual whitening of black Americans. Washington controlled thousands of political and teaching appointments through his powerful white benefactors and thereby was in a position to corrupt the ideals of the talented tenth. In this sense, Du Bois's whole program of developing Atlanta University as a knowledge base for the systematic development of black America was undermined by the Tuskegee power brokerage, which used its intellectual capital not to develop black America so much as to control it.

Ironically, the evolution of *The Souls of Black Folk* into its book form stands as perhaps the best illustration of the Faustian implications of black soul development. Du Bois was able to define the dilemma of the black American in Faustian terms because, like Faust, he too was tempted, almost coming under the spell of the "Wizard of Tuskegee" on several occasions. The first of these was the chance arrival of a job offer to the poor, newly married Du Bois a matter of days before he received an offer from Washington and Tuskegee (*Dusk*, 4). The second instance was a courtship of Du Bois after he had begun to experiment publicly with opposition to Washingtonian philosophy. In an era when the black press was being compromised by Washington's command of capital resources, the idea of white millionaires attempting to lure Du Bois to Tuskegee, inviting him to name his price, certainly suggested to Du Bois that what was being bargained for was not his services so much as a cessation of his attacks on the Tuskegee Machine (*Dusk*, 78–80). While Du Bois's plan to cure the world's wrong thinking about race through rigorous scientific documentation of black America seemed on the verge of foundering for lack of support, Washington was attracting unheard-of endowments, despite doubts about the quality of work being done at Tuskegee, such as the $600,000 grant from Carnegie in the year *The Souls* was published (*Dusk*, 58, 72, 78).

As he notes in *Dusk of Dawn*, the publication of his attack on Washington in *The Souls* "settled pretty definitely any further question of [his] going to Tuskegee as an employee" (8). The book was a rebuke to the bribes and veiled threats against Du Bois's home institution, Atlanta University, and the various development projects he attempted to institute, a bold stroke calculated to clear the air by asserting the right of the black intellectual to speak freely. Yet Du Bois did not see his gesture of independence, however much it implicated the wizard of the North as Washington's puppeteer, as a complete break with American capitalism. Capable of suggesting in *The Souls* that as a "partially undeveloped people [Negroes] should be ruled by the best of their stronger and better neighbors for their own good" (123), Du Bois was angling for some rapprochement with the white social elite that would buy time for a generation of black leaders to emerge. But the financial barons who had waved their checkbooks and brought forth the Tuskegee Miracle clearly lacked any incentive for bankrolling the scientific solution to America's race problem that Du Bois hoped to find.

In a 1904 high school commencement speech later published as "The Joy of Living," Du Bois set out to bring the students a word of hope to help them through the trials ahead. "This race calls for personal sacrifice—the sacrifice of position, of income, of social prestige, even of life itself for the sake of the larger welfare of a mighty people," he told them, enjoining the class from "blasphem[ing] against your mother race simply because the powers that be, love blasphemy" (221). He quoted "that heart wail of Faust"—"Selig der den er in Siegesglanze Findet" [Happy man whom Death shall find in victorious splendor]—prefatory to his explanation that in love and sacrifice for the race they would find the greatest joy they could know (220). But the race here, no longer an amorphous assembly of far-flung souls, has become in his handling a distinct personality, as Du Bois warms to the inspirational power of the myth:

Loose yourselves from that dark shadow that is creeping over these Negro public schools . . . seeking to degrade and cheapen them . . . to train black boys and girls forever to be the hewers of wood and drawers of water for the cowardly people who seek to shackle on minds as they shackled on hands yesterday.

Loose yourselves from that great temptation to curse and malign your own people and surrender their rights for the sake of applause and popularity and cash. . . . Work and sacrifice for the sake of the ancient Mother Race which has come up out of the house of bondage scarred and stricken but shining in Truth and Justice and Mercy. (222)

This appeal to striving in the name of the "ancient Mother Race" would become a staple of Du Bois's creative works, through which he sought simultaneously to encourage the foot soldiers in the struggle and to instruct the new leader-ship cadre in the meaning and terms of self-sacrifice for collective uplift. The "mother's return" in Du Boisian race development would be through a rehabili-tated black womanhood that would supplant the revenant black body of death in the public mind.

Because Washington had a critical advantage in disciplining the middle-class strivers through patronage and his veto power over job appointments, Du Bois knew that he would need to impact the lives of the people in some material way, to have any chance to stave off the onset of the spiritual death of black America. He felt that his opportunity lay in active organized struggle for civil rights coor-dinated with a literature of race striving that would influence the one thing Washington could not control—black Americans' ability to imagine themselves the equal to any in the nation by virtue of their newfound pride in racial identity.

In response to Washington's "body of death," Du Bois called, in "The Conser-vation of Races," for an artistic and political race renaissance, a renaissance that would be, as his earlier essay suggested, as much one of the spirit of ethical striv-ing as of tending those bodily needs that would prevent physical race extinction. The literary works of Chesnutt and Hopkins that responded to this and other calls for cultural rebirth were lacking in coherent political focus, however, and their privileging of the terminal angst of mulatto self-division as the voice of the embodied race provided little philosophical advance over Washingtonian laissez-faire individualism. Sutton Griggs, despite his more determined attention to poli-tics, could not provide an embodied image of black America any less ambivalent than the conflicting political solutions he dramatized.[80] Du Bois felt that if liter-ature and political commentary were to find consistent, coherent expression as vital elements in the articulation of the "race," he would have to become actively involved in promoting both, since so much of the black media had fallen under

Washington's control. To this end, his founding of the journals the *Moon*, the *Horizon*, and the *Crisis* in the first decade of the twentieth century helped to keep alive the principles of race development, to argue the need for continued struggle for civil rights, to establish an example of ethical striving for the "talented tenth" to emulate, and to nurture a literature of racial self-fashioning and national belonging.

CHAPTER SIX

The Quest of the Black Soul

W. E. B. Du Bois invoked the language of the black soul in his important essays of 1897 that evolved into *The Souls of Black Folk,* but the imaginative development of the theme of the progress of the racial soul toward self-realization would largely unfold as a collective enterprise among a number of writers around the turn of the century. Before Du Bois's creative writings in the short-lived periodicals the *Moon* and *Horizon,* his 1911 novel *The Quest of the Silver Fleece,* and his occasional pieces in the NAACP journal the *Crisis,* writers such as Pauline Hopkins and Sutton E. Griggs had begun to employ the discourse of the racial soul in their novels.

In its revision of the tragic mulatto motif, Frances E. Watkins Harper's *Iola Leroy, or Shadows Uplifted* (1892) probably did as much as any work to popularize the idea of black soul development, though largely in religious and moral terms. Iola Leroy, quadroon daughter of white Creole planter Eugene Leroy and his mulatto wife, Marie, refuses the marriage proposal of her white suitor Dr. Gresham for fear of his reaction, should "one of [their children] show unmistakable signs of color" (90). This fear of the revenant does not dominate her imagination the way it later would Chesnutt's and Hopkins's characters, though, and Harper stages numerous reunions between separated mothers and children after the Civil War, inaugurating a veneration of the slave mother in ritual emancipation from her fallen social condition. Iola is reunited with her own mother and grandmother, and later she becomes a teacher after hearing of the school mistress's mission to educate young black women to be "fit" mothers for their children. Her dedication to the education of mothers substitutes at first for her aborted dream of wifehood and a life of ease with Dr. Gresham.

Harper's theme of ethical race leadership, in fact, antedates Du Bois in its statement of the competing paths of self-fulfillment: "'To be,' continued Iola, 'the leader of a race to higher planes of thought and action, to teach men clearer views of life and duty, and to inspire their souls with loftier aims, is a far greater privilege than it is to open the gates of material prosperity and fill every home with sensuous enjoyment.'"[1] Iola later meets her ideal soul mate in mulatto Dr. Frank Latimer, a man of too much character to "forsake his mother's race for the richest advantages his [white] grandmother could bestow" (180). Harper's shaping of Latimer's racial allegiance as a choice between two female ancestors underscores her message of the need to reclaim slave mothers so as to redefine their "condition." United as they are in this mission, Iola experiences no obstacle to intimacy with Latimer, to whom "her soul went out," in contrast to Gresham, who "had never mingled" with the "aspirations in her soul" (204).

What differentiated Harper's "soul"-saving idealism from Du Bois's was his emphasis on a secular spiritualism of African origin. After Harper, works by women authors would focus strongly on the soul salvation of black women from the vestiges of slavery and residual paganism. But the relation of "paganism" to African spirituality was a key issue that Du Bois himself had to wrestle with at great length. Few, if any, of the black intelligentsia were willing to embrace what seemed on the surface a complete break from Western rationalism and Christian idealism. Thus even Du Bois, with his classicist and romantic sensibilities given full rein, conceived the path of black race development as a "pilgrim's progress" toward a transcendent Western idealism.

The writer who produced the most sustained early literary investigation of the progress of the black soul prior to the flowering of Du Bois's literary career was Baptist minister Sutton Elbert Griggs.[2] Griggs's first three works, *Imperium in Imperio* (1899), *Overshadowed* (1901), and *Unfettered* (1902), appeared before the publication of *The Souls*, but each bears a distinct connection to the Du Boisian racial soul idea. Wilson Jeremiah Moses claims that the didacticism of Griggs's work and the pasteboard quality of his characterizations tend to stage a Du Boisian "two-ness" through paired characters representing incompatible approaches to the question of continued black existence in a racist America (*Wings*, 226–27). This binary structuring lends itself to the lengthy debates that directly reflect on the lives of the characters through their emotional grapplings with the consequences of American racial division. Thus Du Bois's essays and Griggs's novels covered similar terrain, and while Griggs was in no sense the literary stylist that Du Bois was, his adaptations of Du Boisian explorations into the nature of the American race dilemma established several important dimensions of the emerging narrative of soul striving that would later be more fully developed or transcended in Du Bois's own works.

In Griggs's *Imperium in Imperio*, the question becomes not whether but how a race message will emerge. Berl Trout, the "traitor" to the secret black militant nation headquartered in Waco, Texas, interprets the oath of its mulatto leader, Bernard Belgrave, to have revenge on the murdering Anglo-Saxons as an indication that the Imperium has deteriorated from nationalism to terrorism under his leadership. Bernard's mixed racial background is crucial to this violent turn because it has led to his morbid fascination with Anglo-Saxonism, such that he sees history only in terms of conquest and racial violence.

The "pure" black Belton Piedmont, by contrast, counsels ceaseless agitation to "force an acknowledgment of equality from the . . . fierce, all-conquering Anglo-Saxon," but Bernard seems more concerned with settling a familial score against his white ancestry. He would engage Anglo-Saxon problem-solving methods in order to send whites a message they would understand, and his matching violence with violence proves that he has no interest in producing a uniquely "black" idea (247). In his speech urging the open political activity of the Imperium, Belton makes concessions confirming stereotypes of black inferiority that are clearly intended for a white readership.[3] Still, with the other options presented by members of the Imperium being voluntary self-obliteration through amalgamation, emigration to Africa, and race war, Belton's suggestion of inundating the state of Texas with blacks to take over the running of state politics is the only plan that fulfills Du Bois's vision of peaceful, but dignified, coexistence with whites: "Before we make a forward move, let us pull the veil from before the eyes of the Anglo-Saxon that he may see the New Negro standing before him humbly, but firmly demanding every right granted him by his maker and wrested from him by man" (244).

Wilson Jeremiah Moses oversimplifies Belton by calling him "the heroic Uncle Tom personality in the best sense" (*Wings*, 228). Belton is nonviolent, but only in the regard that he thinks Anglo-Saxon America needs time to adjust to the idea of a "New Negro." Struggling to produce a "transcendent thought" out of the gloom, Belton resolves that blacks take over the state of Texas, "working out our destiny as a separate and distinct race in the United States of America," but he also agrees to open warfare after a specified time if all else fails (247). Griggs's second novel, *Overshadowed*, raised the issue of black ideality with direct reference to Washingtonian submission as a possible expression of the black soul essence. In *Overshadowed*, Griggs shows Washingtonian appeasement as a bankrupt form of self-sacrifice under the conditions of the racist South. Erma Wysong, having been entrusted by her mother with her half brother John's "soul," comes under the spell of her former leader at Tuskegee, Booker T. Washington himself, who gives a speech urging submission: "May it not be that [the Negro's] anguish torn face and sorrow-laden prayer of faith are better weapons than the bomb of the Russian Nihilist and the tomahawk of the Indian?" (127).

Here is an appeal to total capitulation, unlike Belton's plan of forthright agitation and armed self-defense. Griggs shows the difference between the two in the fates of Belton and John. While Belton dies an honorable, principled death, John, after a remarkable Griggsian rescue from execution, dies ignominiously from illness incurred as a member of a chain gang. Allowed to choose, he has preferred to remain a prisoner in the American South rather than a free man in Africa. Erma berates herself for "having needlessly murdered her own brother, [for] having cast him into the midst of ravenous beasts, destitute of conscience and of feeling" (160). Even though one of these "beasts" does succeed in saving her brother's life, he is no less racialist for his belief that whites should hold themselves to a higher standard of behavior. The upshot is that Washingtonian acquiescence rests entirely on the good will of whites for the salvation of black souls and therefore leaves blacks as "overshadowed" by uncertain fate as they were in slavery. It is not a black idea at all, but a white idea in a new package.

The search for the black spiritual message is central to the whole subplot involving John, for the crime that condemns him to death is the murder of a northern unionist who calls himself, portentously, the Master Workman. The Master Workman "out-Heroded Herod in his denunciation of Negroes," making himself popular in the South on the basis of his plans to uplift white working men through exclusion of blacks from union jobs. Speaking the discourse of white hearth and home so important to southern suppression of black assertiveness, the Master Workman creates a social Darwinist scenario wherein the survival of white households depends on the destruction of black households. The higher "ideals and sentiments of homelife" among Anglo-Saxons require, says the Master Workman, a larger amount of money to operate than the less well developed home life of blacks. Paying blacks at the same rate as whites would thus give blacks an economic advantage in the racial struggle for survival: "Hence, we cannot afford to enter into competition with the Negro. For it would not be a question of dollars. It would be a question of home against home. So we of the Labor Unions have decided that either our homes must be crushed out or the Negro. And you know what the Anglo-Saxon does to a weaker foe that does not accept his standard. He simply destroys him" (100). By making Darwinist fabulation the core of the Anglo-Saxon idea, Griggs critiques Du Bois's claim in "The

Conservation of Races" that the "English nation stood for constitutional liberty and commercial freedom" ("Conservation," 4). Griggs instead offers his own more apt summary of Anglo-Saxonism: the "wedding between Thomas Jefferson and Charles Darwin, the truism of the household thus formed being 'All men are created equal, but the fittest survive'" (168).

When John Wysong murders the labor demagogue, he is submitting to the seductive logic of Anglo-Saxonism, that whites "will ignore all laws, defy all constituted authority, overthrow all government, defy all tradition" (101) that stands between them and mastery, and that since blacks do not understand that this white "spirit of oppression will yield only to force or the fear of it," they lack the spirit that will make them fit for entry into the progressive time of America (101–2). John keeps hearing the words of the Master Workman ringing in his ears, "If a foe stands in our way and nothing will dislodge him but death, then he must die" (102), and he gives in to the impulse to murder. The poetic justice of the Workman's death by means of his own preaching, though, does not serve the black spirit quest, since John here follows the Anglo-Saxon path entirely. This irony further informs John's blind submission to Erma's counsel of Washingtonian acquiescence, since John, of all people, should know what Anglo-Saxons do to their foes. Griggs doubly condemns John, then, for subscription to two false paths for the black soul quester—first for embracing white savagery, and then for succumbing to the idea that black spiritual difference can only be expressed as a passive martyrdom in the face of "the most aggressive and virile type of all time, the Anglo-Saxon" (5).

On the other hand, the punishment of Horace Christian, politician and man-about-town, forces on him the helpless fate of the human soul trapped in black flesh. In her efforts to create the kind of social atmosphere that will allow John to get a fair hearing when he goes to trial, Erma joins forces with a white social reformer named Mrs. Turner, who opens her salon to "young Negro women of the purest and highest type" so that their direct contact with members of the legislature will counterbalance public sentiment in favor of Jim Crow legislation (136). Christian's seduction of one of these young women, Margaret Marston, coupled with his admission that he had earlier instigated a lynching and then pretended to protect the condemned man from the mob so as to gain black votes, allows Lanier, the Speaker of the legislature, to execute a far-fetched scheme of poetic jurisprudence. Challenging Christian to go out on the town for a night of carousing in blackface, Lanier substitutes a drugged Christian for John Wysong on the eve of Wysong's impending execution, and Christian goes to his death protesting that he can't be executed because his only crime was that he once "killed a nigger."

While the notion that a white man chemically transformed to appear black lacks credibility, the fate of the significantly named Christian indicates that Griggs's preferred narrative mode is more allegorical than realistic. Having benefited directly from the exploitation of black bodies, Christian is appropriately punished by entrapment in a black body doomed to legal lynching, which, based on anthropometric measurements taken by Lanier, is so close in physical stature to Christian that only a few cosmetic touches in addition to the skin coloration serve to make him indistinguishable from John. Challenging the somatic basis of doctrines of race superiority, Griggs's answer to the semiotics of lynching is conveyed in a dream Christian experiences, in which he sees the corpse of the man whom he has caused to be lynched: "The face was ploughed up with bullets, his eyes were bulging out, his stomach was ripped open and his entrails were visible. On his breast there was a placard, and an inward voice seemed to say to me, 'Read!' . . . I crept up to the body, . . . and read these words: 'Whatsoever a man soweth, that shall he also reap.' I looked up at the bulging eyes, and they seemed to be trying to speak to me and say, 'Thou art the man'" (133–34). Falling forward, Christian, in his dream, tries to break his fall by grabbing the body, until they fall down together, Christian's head "getting caught under his mangled form." Prophetically entangled in the black body of death, Christian fulfills the prophecy through his sexual "entanglement" with Margaret Marston. Christian's appropriation of black features through blackface disguise, whose mythic sensual freedom he covets, ends ironically in his entrapment in the black body condemned to death. Griggs's clumsy dream symbolism is nonetheless a significant gesture that helps to inaugurate a tradition among black writers—the construction of racialized bodies as palimpsests of interracial desire.

The main plot likewise employs a black body inscribed with interracial desire, centering on the history of Erma's mixed racial ancestry. In Erma's story, several key elements of the black soul quest take shape within the tragic mulatto motif, extending beyond the simple design of racial ambivalence to raise issues like racial masking, race chastity, and the soul strivings of black women. Erma, whom the scion of a prominent white family has been attempting to seduce, represents the "natural," uncorrupted black woman who is forced to undergo numerous trials and afflictions because her ideal mate, Astral Herndon, decides to go away to school in order to gain a higher valuation in her eyes. While he is gone, James Lawson, white son of the state's former governor, uses a false name to secure the

services of Dolly Smith, a conjure woman and intrigant, to help Lawson bring
Erma under his control. Unknown to both Lawson and Erma, Dolly Smith is
really Erma's aunt, and her pose as Lawson's accomplice is part of an elaborate
revenge she has vowed upon the Lawson family.

Griggs employs Dolly to document what Du Bois would later call the "damnation of black women," a damnation that is expressed in terms of a classic soul
bargain. After being approached by the young Lawson, Dolly calls on Satan to
help her spring her trap. Dolly slips and reveals her awareness of Lawson's true
identity, causing Lawson to call her a "she devil." "'She devil, did you say? But
who made me a she devil? Who destroyed my soul? Who first started me on the
damnable mission of polluting the entire stream of the virtue of my race?'" (50).
Dolly does not continue her revelation here, but in a contrived courtroom scene
growing out of forgeries that Dolly has manipulated, she exposes the sordid history of Erma's parentage. Erma is really the young Lawson's half sister, daughter
of the former governor, who, as a young dry-goods merchant, had seduced
Erma's mother with Dolly's cooperation, using expensive gowns and other gifts
to entice them. Dolly's rage at the elder Lawson began after the girls were driven
in shame from their home and he refused them assistance. At the trial, her revelations are doubly effective as the young Lawson is convicted and jailed and the
elder Lawson goes mad and then dies.

When describing the means by which she will corrupt Erma on Lawson's behalf, Dolly really describes her own undoing, and, by inference, the path to damnation for young black women generally: "'Erma is to be driven to sin through
poverty. We must in the most merciless manner drive her to want; if need be,
drive her to the very door of starvation. Open but one door for her to walk out,
and let that be the door of sin. She will be less than human if she fails to come
out. Set riches before her, and there can be no failure. . . . Remember that Erma
is a woman, and that it is not impossible to get a woman to do as her mother and
grandmother did. She is no angel'" (89). Erma as Everywoman does prove in-
corruptible, though. But her friends among the newly educated class of black
women who slavishly follow every fashion and cultivate every mannerism associated with "ladyhood" are more susceptible to corruption than she is because of
their materialistic orientation.

In his considerations of the damnation of women, Griggs makes a powerful
argument against all forms of racial masking. When Erma places an ad in a
newspaper seeking work as a domestic, her school friends ostracize her for voluntarily squandering her education in an occupation they consider no better than

prostitution. They engineer her public dismissal from church, giving the Reverend Griggs an opportunity to sermonize on faithful service. These young women, says Griggs, are the perpetrators of a second enslavement of their emancipated mothers, "noble Negro women who, emerging from slavery, were at once enslaved again by their children and bore their heavy burdens uncomplainingly, in a vain attempt to build up upon their poor bruised shoulders an aristocracy such as they had left behind" (39). To the "heroic soul" named Aunt Mollie Marston, mother of Margaret Marston, Erma explains that the generation of former-slave black mothers are proof that domestic service need not be seen as shameful. Erma predicts that "this idea that work is disgraceful is destined to ruin thousands of young Negro girls who are going to try to play 'lady' and abstain from employment" (43), a prediction that comes true in the case of Margaret.

Erma's forthrightness, even to the point of urging John to confess his crime to whites, stands out as an instance of the "pure," undisguised, undiluted race soul struggling for expression. When Erma marries Astral Herndon, her pregnancy takes on the aura of an "annunciation": "When Erma knew that God would bless her with an offspring she besought Astral to allow her to leave Richmond and stay until her child was born. She asked to be separated from him and from the world until God had fully wrought upon the human being whom he was shortly going to introduce into the world through her" (198). Astral comprehends the symbolism and learns "to look upon his wife as being in an especial sense the handmaid of God."

After the birth of her son, a "crisis in two souls" frames the climactic death of Erma, when, in dedicating his life to his mother's will, Astral Jr. effects a soul bonding that allows Erma to feel that her life's work is done and she can die fulfilled. Left a widower, Astral challenges those gathered at the funeral to promise him that his son, a black Christ, will grow up in a land free of discrimination that will allow him to develop without interference from whites, "guided by the light of our own genius" (215). When he is counseled by Lanier to adopt Washingtonian acquiescence, humility, and material prosperity as a life path, Astral explains that one of the problems of living in America is having whites constantly give blacks unsolicited advice. Determined to live according to the dictates of his black soul, Astral refuses to let Erma be buried in America. When Lanier asks a black man for the second time in the novel if he will return to Africa, he gets a similar response: "It, too, is overshadowed. Aliens possess it" (216). Africa itself is compromised as a land for the nurturing of black genius by the intrusive presence of whites, and Astral, proclaiming himself "A CITIZEN OF THE OCEAN," buries his wife at sea.

Griggs's curious combination of stereotypical "plantation school" types and race militancy reveals a self-consciousness that vacillates between extremes of despair and elation—the sort of spirit that Du Bois describes as a result of blacks only being allowed to see themselves "through the revelation of the other world" (*Souls*, 3). Even so, his range of characterizations and attitudes toward blacks does not differ remarkably from the works of more celebrated contemporaries such as Chesnutt, Harper, Paul Laurence Dunbar, and Du Bois himself. Griggs's grappling with the philosophical issues surrounding American biracialism, however, at least approaches them with the idea that blacks have to work out their own destiny in their own way, as a racially distinct nation within a nation, while his contemporaries among black novelists typically portray their characters as helpless playthings in the hands of powerful social forces that severely limit their choices. One limitation that all black writers acknowledged was the unavailability of such conventions of melodrama as the marriage that serves to unite the warring parties in familial bonds. In Chesnutt's novels, interracial alliances are prescriptions for disaster, while Harper used mulatto and black alignments to signal a new spirit of intraracial cooperation. Griggs's black characters, with few exceptions, similarly confine their romantic yearnings within the race; only unscrupulous or foolish black women and opportunistic white males break the color line. As Mrs. Turner in *Overshadowed* explains, romance across the color line is more usually a source of tragedy than a practical resolution to racial strife: "Wherever and whenever, in other countries, race problems have arisen (and there have been many such to arise), the softening influences of the marriage tie and social intermingling have acted upon the icebergs of race prejudice like a southern sun. But . . . this factor must ever be missing [in America.] It is sad, sad, sad, but inevitable. The marriage tie we do not want" (150). Given white refusal of legal unions between the races and the determination of black thinkers to concentrate the genius of the race into the articulation of the black race message to the world, intermarriage, and therefore embodiment with white America, ceased to figure as a serious option among black intellectuals coming of age in the era of "one crime" and the Du Boisian soul quest.

While mass embodiment of blacks and whites within the American melting pot seemed less and less a practical solution to the race problem, the centering of black hopes on Africa as a territorial and spiritual "home" became increasingly popular, reaching its peak in the post–World War I period with Garveyism. Significantly, Griggs will not endorse back-to-Africa schemes, but in each novel, he presents a different rationale for dismissing this panacea. In *Imperium,* Belton regards African emigration as unpatriotic, while in *Overshadowed,* no clear, indisputably black race "message" can emerge from an Africa subdued by Europe either. In Griggs's third novel, *Unfettered,* the return to Africa is rendered irrelevant by having the newly rediscovered African prince, Dorlan Warthell, declare that his millions will go to the development of black Americans, since they are, by dint of their greater proximity to modern civilization, closer to the unleashing of the black soul than his still heathen African relatives are. Black Americans will thus serve as the vanguard of black race redemption by *not* returning to Africa. According to the messenger of Warthell's kingdom, who has been searching for him in America, the ideas of Herbert Spencer and Benjamin Kidd on why Africa has remained in "civilization's back yard" (165) have focused on the effect of heat and moisture in the tropics as an environmental barrier to the development of civilization. Until these barriers are overcome, he tells Warthell, there is no point in him returning to Africa, where his striving will be in vain.

Here Griggs seems to be deliberately evoking the third paragraph of Du Bois's "The Conservation of Races," which claims that "it is certain that all human striving must recognize the hard limits of natural law, and that any striving, no matter how intense and earnest, which is against the constitution of the world, is in vain" (1). This point resonates throughout *Unfettered,* for when Warthell at last gains a romantic understanding with his ideal "soul" mate, Morlene Dalton, she refuses to marry him until he can promise her that they will live in a world where soul striving is not pointless. Morlene proclaims her belief that a wife's mission is to be her mate's soul nurturer, and "in the South, the Negro wife is robbed of this holy task." Making clear the import of the book's title, Morlene describes the dragon Warthell must slay to win her hand:

> "I have firmly resolved, Mr. Warthell, to accept no place by a husband's side until I can say to his spirit, 'Go forth and fill the earth with goodness and glory.' . . . Mr. Warthell, in you may slumber the genius of a Pericles, but a wife in the South dare not urge upon you to become a town constable or a justice of the peace. Talk about slavery! Ah! the chains that fetter the body are but as ropes of down when compared to those that fetter the mind, the spirit of man. And think ye I would enter your home simply to inspire that great soul of yours to restlessness and fruitless tuggings at its chains!" (174)

Like Astral searching for a peaceable kingdom to nurture his black Christ child, Warthell is forced into grappling with a metaphysical and political dilemma before he can even attempt normal home life.

Warthell's task has an almost Faustian scope: "'I am to weld two hetero-geneous elements into a homogeneous entity. I am to make a successful blend of two races that differ so widely as do the whites and the Negroes. . . . Thomas Jefferson and Abraham Lincoln said the problem was incapable of solution, that the two races could not live together on terms of equality. They were great and wise, but not infallible'" (176–77). Eventually Warthell completes his task of outlining a resolution of the race problem, but its salient features involve a num-ber of contradictions and compromises. Acknowledging that "this adding to and taking from the national spirit is a most grave matter," Warthell makes a pitch for "giving the Negro the opportunity for untrammeled activity in the National Government" that will effect "an addition to and consequent alteration of our characteristic Americanism" (228). Cognizant of Du Bois's call in "The Striv-ings," Griggs uses Warthell to articulate a potential compromise that still gives black Americans a meritorious place in a reconstituted America. His plan calls for a concerted effort to develop black home life; a redirection of religious teach-ings to emphasize "ethical teachings, applicable to the world" (245) over other-worldly redemption; development of an educational system that encompasses in-dustrial education and university training; greater agricultural training; and land ownership.

Not only does Warthell call for the elimination of "Little Africas" in America's large cities, but Big Africa does not escape his reformism either. The most curi-ous part of his plan is the concession he makes to the "real world" of white Amer-ica. Aware, like Du Bois, that he has two demons to consider—one who wants to use the Negro as a tool, the other who thinks of contact with the Negro as conta-minating (200)—Warthell tries to accommodate both without surrendering the black soul to either. His plan calls for the redistribution of blacks across the United States so that they cannot concentrate in any one area, thereby raising fears of domination politically and "Africanization" culturally. Beyond calling on the civilizing "instincts" of the whites to "resist whatever Africanizing tenden-cies that anywhere show themselves" (267), Warthell reveals that he supports "the Americanization of the globe, and believe[s] that in due time the Negroes of America are to be the immediate agents of the Americanization of Africa." His solution to the Du Boisian dilemma does not therefore call for a whitening of Africa, since black Americans are to be the message bearers, but his plan for the dilution of the "Negro problem" of the South by spreading the "burden" more evenly seems a major concession to white fears, giving no assurances that black dispersion will not make blacks more vulnerable to white suppression. Warthell's simplistic solution is that by spreading blacks across the geographical map, they will cease to appear as an indigestible lump in the body politic.

At the very least, the plan marks a radical departure from proposals such as Belton's in *Imperium*, which argued that only the concentration of blacks within a defined territory—a nation within a nation—could provide protection from white political, psychological, and physical violence. Warthell's proposal to dismantle "Little Africas," distribute blacks across America into small, unthreatening groups, prevent block voting by blacks, and oblige whites all around them vigilantly to suppress "any Africanisms," leaves little on which to base black nationhood. The construction of a black nation, however, would be the special task of black artists and intellectuals, a realm of black creativity hermetically sealed against "Africanisms" yet fervently dedicated to struggle with the white world and the promulgation of its unique race message. The agents of this black imagined community would be, appropriately, an independent black press, whose function would be to establish a black American presence firmly in the time-space of the nation: "Daily newspapers and magazines favorable to the highest interests of the race, must be established so that the outpourings of the souls of Negro writers may have better opportunities of reaching the world. The poem, the novel, the drama must be pressed into service. The painter, the sculptor, the musical composer must plead our cause in the world of aesthetics" (274). Through Warthell, Griggs proposes a cultural nationalism that, denying interest in politics, would experience the widest latitude in expressing the black race idea. Griggs, in effect, called for a cultural renaissance as the literary imagining of an all-black nation.

The sticking point, however, is Africa, because key to Griggs's aesthetic sensibility is a reconstruction of Africa in the Western mind. The references to Warthell as a "Pericles," a nation builder in the classical mold, and elsewhere as an "ebony-like Apollo" (71) reflect the unabashed classicist impulse of many of the so-called Ethiopianists (including Du Bois) whose insistence on redeeming Africa into an "enlightened republic" (165) seemed to undermine their rhetoric of an emergent African idea.[4] To counteract the general low opinion of Africa, including his own, Warthell takes a stab at identifying the black race "message" with a reflection on ancient Egypt: "Some African genius of the long ago constructed a device, now unknown to earth, whereby the several strengths of individuals could be conjoined and the sum of their strengths thus obtained applied to the task of lifting the ponderous stones. . . . From these pyramids, eloquent in their silence, persistent reminders of the departed glory of Africa, let the scattered sons of that soil learn their first great need—Co-operation" (234). Griggs, through Warthell, offers racial cooperation as the alternative to a Darwinist struggle for racial survival, a black idea that would fulfill Du Bois's hope for a distinctive racial contribution to the world. But in tying his race idea to classical antiquity, Warthell offers no more than that cooperation become the basis for an Americanization of the world, including, and especially, Africa.

From an independent-minded idealist, Warthell seems to disintegrate under pressure from Morlene to reconstruct the racial world into an agent of American expansionism. On the one hand, he becomes prey to the Republican political machine he has abandoned. Congressman Bloodworth embodies the first of the demons besetting the black soul quester—the ambitious white who wants to exploit black talent to make his fortune and will stoop to anything, like tempting venal blacks to work against their own best racial interests. The second demon, more easily recognizable to black audiences who "regarded the Democratic party as the earthly abode of the devil" (127), is embodied by Lemuel Dalton, heir to the Dalton plantation from which Harry, Morlene, and the other black Daltons have been evicted. The imagination of Dalton's wife had been poisoned by press reports of black rapists roaming the countryside, and her paranoia was further inflamed by the deep antipathy toward blacks that makes Dalton evict all the black hands and replace them with white ones.

Expecting that any black man she encounters alone will unhesitatingly rape her, Eulalie Dalton refuses to stop to hear Tony Marshall's protestations of harmlessness. The encounter is a classic southern sight rape, a blundering of a black male into the visual field of a white woman without warning. Now certain that he will be lynched on the word of the fatal white woman if he lets her go, Marshall assesses his dilemma, giving her the name that will follow her through black literature: "'I'll swear I wish those "cops" had me safe in prison,'" says Tony. "'I have swapped the witch for the devil'" (191). Shooting Eulalie Dalton's horse to prevent her going for help, Tony causes her to be mortally wounded when the horse falls on her. He finds her still alive and puts his life in jeopardy by carrying her to her household, where she tells the story and secures her husband's promise that Tony will not be lynched and that he will work to dispel the "atmosphere of suspicion" that has caused her death. "'Circumstances killed my wife, sir,'" says Dalton. "'Circumstances—cold, cruel circumstances'" (195). The moment of the white witch, growing out of Wells-Barnett's discussion of the circumstantial victimization of black men by the socially pressured white women, in this instance leads to the potential for social cooperation with the white elite to make black coexistence in America less capricious. But, in the words of Warthell, she is merely "the prototype of hundreds," and so long as narratives of race difference continued to instill fear into the minds of whites, there would be many more instances of men unjustly lynched for accidental encounters with white women.

Griggs's 1905 novel *The Hindered Hand: Or, The Reign of the Repressionist*, which refers directly to Du Bois as "a seer linked to us by blood," makes an even more complicated analysis of the progress of the black race soul. The inclusion of a black militant insurrection, the lynching of Bud and Foresta Harper, the killing of Henry Crump, and numerous other subplots and digressions reveal a more distracted and a more bitter author than the one who endorsed Warthell's compromises, though Griggs clearly does not support the position of the militant insurrectionists. This novel, though, shows Griggs more committed to preserving black souls by preserving the integrity of black bodies and minds.

The story is set, appropriately, in "Almaville,"—that is, "Soulsville"—a place "so charged" by nature with "the spirit of the beautiful, that the men who later wrought in building the city found themselves the surprised and happy creatures of a lovely habitation" (9). The novel details how that naturally blessed environment came to ruin, telling the story of the Seabright family, whose collective soul is shattered by what Griggs calls "the cloven foot of American race prejudice" (307). We are presented with immediate evidence of racism's impact on families in the South by Griggs's opening scene aboard a train making its way to Almaville. The Jim Crow train in southern life is always, in Robert Stepto's words, a "nefarious design for the perpetuation of structure in instances where structure of site or place cannot hold sway" (75), and its separation of Eunice Seabright from her sister, whom the world will know as Tiara Merlow, only hints at the larger social forces that are sweeping down upon "Soulsville." Because Eunice travels as a white woman in the ladies car, and Tiara, her face covered by a veil, travels in the Jim Crow car, Eunice employs a dramatic subterfuge to gain access to the separate and unequal coach for a tender last farewell. She catches the eye of a passing porter and sends him a note—an innocent enough act whose implications are clear to Eunice, but she feels nevertheless that, as a white woman, she has put herself in no danger.

"'I don't want white girls passing me notes,' thought the Negro" (12). He sees before him a mental image of a lynching and is tempted to throw the note away, until after much tense self-consciousness about the ramifications of his even reading the note, he finds out that Eunice, who signs the note "The Girl That

Looked At You," wants him to give her fifteen minutes' notice before Almaville so that she can say goodbye to Tiara. Fear of an accusation of sight rape by the "looking" girl makes the porter refuse to go anywhere near Eunice afterward, but she succeeds in making her way to the Jim Crow car where Tiara sits, and she throws herself upon her sister, removing her veil in the process. When he first sees Tiara unveiled, Ensal Ellwood, seated opposite her, responds to her beauty in a way that makes clear that she will be the novel's chief soul striver, her beauty and physical form veiling a "soul of whom *they* are not even worthy" (18). If Tiara is the novel's soul protagonist, Eunice is its soul sufferer, and in a court-room confrontation that brings out all of the details of the women's pasts, their roles, and ultimately their social positions, will be reversed.

The two women are daughters of Arabelle Seabright, who has torn her family apart to execute a byzantine plot to use her children and other mixed-race persons who could pass for white to undermine the southern attitudes on race. She chooses Almaville as the site for her scheme to "shake the Southern system to its very foundation" (230) and thereby shake the nation. Arabelle's story is an enactment of a parable of the "condition of the mother." The wife of a mayor in Indiana, Arabelle saw her whole world destroyed with the birth of her third child, a dark-skinned daughter whom we know only by her adopted name, Tiara. To save her reputation from the charge of adultery, Arabelle reveals to her husband that she has black blood, only to find that he has been keeping a similar secret from her. Disturbed by the depth of color prejudice even in the North, Arabelle becomes unhinged by her family's ostracism after the birth of the throwback, and she fakes the deaths of her entire family in a fire so that no one will tie her to the plan for revenge against white America that she pursues.

She scatters her three children in different social planes in Almaville, forcing them to take on different names. Her son Percy Marshall[5] will become an influential white clergyman who can sway public ethics from the pulpit. Arabelle will use the child who remains with her, Eunice, as matrimonial bait for an up-and-coming politician, hoping that through Eunice's fortune, she can influence her son-in-law's politics. The third child, Tiara, can only foil the plot by revealing her kinship, and so Arabelle forbids the others to contact her.

The sign of domestic soul violation is Tiara herself. Cast off from her familial ties, forced to live in the shadows of the prosperous and socially prominent Seabrights, as well as the rising clergyman Percy Marshall, Tiara goes to Ensal Ellwood, a bachelor minister and moderate race leader in Almaville, as the proverbial "motherless child," nameless and alone in the world, and asks him to give her the name that she will be known by in Almaville, as a ceremonial break with her family. The name he chooses, Tiara, has two significances that will become clear, the first of which is a pun on the name "Seabright." When Arabelle finds Eunice in despair over never seeing her sister again after the move to Almaville, she tells Eunice, "You can't *see* how *bright* a future I have mapped out for you" (34; my emphases). Thus, when Ensal first looks at Tiara on the train without her veil, it enables him to come up with the name Tiara, because as a "man of faith," he can see how bright her soul is even behind the veil. Griggs's heavy-handed irony is that Eunice, however bright her outward appearance that allows her to pass for white, does not possess the concentrated soul force of Tiara, who, as her name implies, is black royalty in disguise.

Griggs reveals her symbolic importance in another play on words, when, at the conclusion of the trial that reveals her true relation to her siblings, she denounces the social circumstances in America that would not allow her family to remain together despite their color differences, with the same opportunity for development. Then turning to face Eunice, "Tiara stretched forth her hands, appealingly and said, "'Sister, come let us leave this country! Come'" (235). The gesture strikingly re-creates the supplicating slave of the abolitionist emblem who asks, "Am I Not A Woman And A Sister?" Even more strikingly, the wording calls attention to the biblical type of Ethiopia established in Ps. 68:31: "Princes shall come out of Egypt; Ethiopia shall soon stretch out her hands unto God." As Wilson Jeremiah Moses has shown, the verse's more typical rendering, "Ethiopia shall soon stretch *forth* her hands unto God," has been "a favorite with black preachers and other leaders, who, from the late eighteenth century to the present day, have never tired of explicating it": "Usually, it was seen as meaning that God had some mighty destiny planned for the black race. Thus 'Ethiopianism' involved a good deal more than mere allusions to Ethiopia in the songs, sermons and folklore of the African peoples. It was a historical mythology, presenting an exalted view of the black race and its cosmic messianic mission" (*Wings*, 113). Certainly Griggs, a preacher in the black messianic tradition, used the psalm in this sense, and by figuring Tiara, released now from the bondage of her mother's unholy scheme, as the embodiment of Ethiopia, he means to indicate the striving black soul returned to its rightful redemptive course.

But when Tiara stretches forth her hands to Eunice, Eunice rejects her contemptuously. Eunice's is the "hindered hand" of the title, hindered from reaching out to her sister's by the "reign of the repressionist." Standing before the court, Eunice proclaims herself to be, despite Tiara's story, "a white woman":

"My blood is the blood of the whites, my instincts, my feelings, my culture, my spirit, my all is cast in the same mold as yours. That woman who talked to you a few moments ago is a Negro. Don't honor her word above mine, the word of a white woman. I invoke your law of caste. Look at me!" (235–36). From the "Girl That Looked At You," Eunice has become the "Woman That Must Be Looked At" in order to regain the social place that she grew up enjoying.

Her invoking of caste privilege above Tiara, however, unleashes a recrimination against black womanhood that redounds upon her own head, for no sooner does the court pronounce her a Negro in accordance with the "one-drop rule" than she becomes subjected to her former community's humiliation. She rebukes Tiara a second time, spitting in her face to get rid of her, but before she can get clear of the courtroom, the "doom" she has been anticipating sets in. White men who had previously given her deference as a member of the white social elite now insult her by calling her Eunice, since race protocol forbids her being addressed as if she were a lady. She is openly propositioned by white males, once her black blood becomes public knowledge, and she is Jim Crowed out of her hotel, forced to leave through the back door, in fact. On the same train that brought her to Almaville in style, she is rudely ejected from first class into the Jim Crow coach. When she finally reaches her home, she asks her husband, also a light mulatto, whether there can ever be hope for Negroes in the South—the crucial question for all Griggsian domestic soul units. When he cannot offer her any more than a life of "sublime battling" for their son, he suddenly finds himself in the "presence of a soul about to make a final plunge into the dark, dark abyss of despair" (248).

Eunice's soul goes mad, following her mother's example, because, like her mother, she has succumbed to the corrupting spirit of white caste privilege. Having identified herself with white womanhood, she cannot withstand the pressure daily exerted upon black women's spirit, and by growing accustomed to the social deference her caste distinction afforded her, she repeats her mother's crime of destroying family ties in order to maintain social position. Her corruption by white Americanism becomes apparent on the second occasion of her riding the Almaville train, this time on her way out of the "city of soul." Once again she spots the same porter to whom she had given the note on her trip into Almaville, giving him a second note that reveals the transformation of the somewhat uncertain young girl into a manipulative white witch: "Mr. Porter: . . . you must see to it that this train stops after it has gone a few hundred feet into the long tunnel. Now you had better do as I tell you or else I will see that you have trouble. You know that any white woman can have a Negro's life taken at a word. Beware!" (82–83). The porter, reading the note, agrees to do her bidding after a recollection of cases that illustrated "the manner in which some white women used their unlimited power of life and death over Negro men, things that may in some age of the world's history come to light" (84).

A more humorous example of how a chance meeting contains the potential to develop into an encounter with the white witch occurs when the seldom seen Mr. Seabright becomes the victim of a nosy woman named Mrs. Marsh, who suspects that Seabright is hiding something. She bursts into his study and grills him for clues, but unable to get anything out of him, she decides to leave. Before she can go, however, Seabright asks her to sign a disclaimer: "This is to certify that I was in the presence of Mr. Seabright unaccompanied for a few moments and can testify that his treatment of me was in every way exemplary" (81). Mrs. Marsh, had she understood the purpose of the disclaimer, would have solved Seabright's "secret." For Seabright, conscious too of the "manner in which white women used their unlimited power of life and death over Negro men," was simply protecting himself against some future day when Mrs. Marsh, told of his black blood, might look upon their encounter alone as an opportunity to exert power over him.

Later, a racial moderate named Arthur Daleman Sr. tries to explain to his prospective son-in-law that if white women in the South were free to confess openly their involvement with black men, it might significantly reduce lynching in the South. No sooner is the word mentioned than a series of lynchings occur that exemplify Tiara's description of "the dehumanizing influence of caste": "You will be a great but a soulless race. This will come upon you when your heart is cankered with caste. You will devour the Negro to-day, the humbler white to-morrow, and you who remain will then turn upon yourselves" (233). The devouring begins with the white police murdering a black boy who escapes from a court after a racist judicial system orders him to the work farm for getting into a rock fight with white youths. Later, a black man is lynched for the murder of Arthur Daleman's daughter, and the brother and sister-in-law of the lynched man are brutally lynched in Mississippi in an episode that Griggs adapted directly from news reports of the double lynching of Luther Holbert and his wife in February 1904.[6] All die for committing what an anonymous white man explains is the "one crime," as far as the South is concerned—"being black" (136). To put emphasis on white soullessness, Griggs not only gives gruesome details of the prolonged torture and dismemberment of the husband and wife, but he also includes a chilling scene of a nine-year-old boy who sneaks out of his house to watch the lynching and returns with a souvenir: "Little Melville Brant found a piece of the charred flesh in the ashes and bore it home. 'Ben Stringer ain't got anything on me now,' said he as he trudged along in triumph. . . . The future ruler of the land!" (134–35).

Through it all, Griggs asserts the Du Boisian soul struggle against the "reign of the repressionist." His introduction of Arabelle, for instance, establishes the malady that will later strike her daughter Eunice in the form of madness and will drive others like Gus Martin to revolution—weariness of the soul strife brought on by race oppression. He contrasts the soul-weary and despairing with the soul strivers, represented in this work by Tiara and Ensal: "Others, fully conscious that they have been entrusted with a world message, confront a mountain with as much courage as they do a sand dune, and press onward, whether the stars are in a guiding or a hiding mood" (31). Later, Tiara offers another unattributed Du Boisian sentiment, when she exhorts those present at the trial, "Don't circumscribe the able, noble souls among the Negroes. Give them the world as a playground for their talents and let Negro men dream of stars as do your men" (235). Told that only the changing of social conditions in the South can restore his wife to sanity, Eunice's husband vows ceaseless strife until the "shadow" of race is removed from his soul. He pointedly dismisses the Tuskegee program of industrial education and obliquely suggests that Du Bois's fledgling Niagara Movement, which formed in the summer of 1905 and later merged into the NAACP, was at best only an initial step: "It is one thing to produce a Niagara and another thing to harness it" (254).[7]

More directly, Griggs cites Du Bois in Ensal Ellwood's letter of farewell upon going to Africa as a missionary, as "a seer linked to us by ties of blood" who predicts that the "paramount problem of our century will be the problem of the adjustment of the white to the darker races" (198). For Ensal, this adjustment places upon blacks the obligation to "maintain [their] ambition for race purity" to make sure that there is a "redeeming force specially equipped" for the uplift of Africa: "May it continue your ambition to abide Negroes, to force the American civilization to accord you your place in your own right, to the end that the world may have an example of *alien* races living side by side." Griggs's gloss of Du Bois concludes with the danger of seeking rights by the route of Arabelle Seabright and Eunice: "If through the process of being made white you attain your rights, the battle of the dark man will remain to be fought."

In this context, the incident of Tiara's naming and the cause of Ensal's abrupt departure come into focus. When Tiara asks Ensal to name her, he chooses "Douglass" as her last name, in honor of Frederick Douglass. Since Tiara traces her own unhappy family experience to racial intermixture, she refuses to take the name of Douglass, whose marriage to a white woman would make the name a constant reminder of a past she would like to forget. As if to explain the social significance of this, Griggs returns to the Douglass issue in his appendix, "A Hindering Hand," which is a prolonged harangue against Thomas Dixon Jr. that was excised from the first edition because it so completely halted the already crippled narrative flow. Griggs notes that Douglass became alienated from "his people" after his marriage to Helen Pitts and was never quite the same orator as he was before: "The delicate network of wires over which the inner soul conveys itself to the hearts of its hearers was totally disarranged by that marriage" (313). In a peculiar parallel to white social commentary on intermarriage, Griggs, whose novels are littered with characters born of illicit racial unions, was firmly against *legal* unions between blacks and whites.

Tiara, thus, is to be the soul striver within the race, the observer of race chastity who can, with a race-pure soul, "stretch forth her hands to God." But precisely this issue separates her from Ensal. After refusing the name of Douglass without explaining why, or telling Ensal anything of her history, she asks him his opinion on race mixing, without giving him a hint as to her personal beliefs, and he holds off his answer. Having been told of Tiara's private meeting with her disguised brother Percy Marshall, Ensal guesses wrong, assuming that Tiara approves of interracial romance, and to cut himself off from her completely, he delivers his stinging denunciation of blacks who seek "social absorption" into the white race.

Despite this seeming gradual movement toward a Pan-Africanist perspective, with Tiara as the embodiment of Ethiopia and Ensal actually going to Africa to stay, he thinks, forever, Griggs undermines any question of reconstructing popular opinions of Africa when, in his diatribe against Dixon, he cites a theory that Africans have been history's orphans because their physical ugliness has prevented the large-scale intermarriage that would uplift them into contact with the world: "The great races of the world, it is held, are the mixed races. When the Africans' environments robbed them of comeliness and attractive qualities, they were thrown off to their own one blood, no one courting alliance with them" (315). Griggs seems totally unaware of the contradiction of his preachment of race purity for blacks on the one hand and his endorsement of race mixture as the route to civilization on the other. Thus he adds to a list of already perplexing rationales for the separate consideration of Africa the fact that when it stretched forth its arms, its ugliness hindered other hands from reaching out in response.

This helps to explain, perhaps, why in works extolling race purity so many of Griggs's characters are mulatto. Perhaps he feared that audiences would not accept the love affairs of "ugly" Africans as a matter worthy of literature or that protestations of love and declarations of the arresting beauty of characters such as Erma Wysong, Morlene Dalton, and Tiara Merlow would not be taken as credible if they were anything but Caucasian in appearance. His one indisputably "pure" black character is the ebony Apollo Dorlan Warthell, but since physical beauty in a man bears less upon the sentiments of the audience, this is not so much a daring move as it might have been.

Sutton Griggs, in the end, could not get around his era's cramped biologism in charting a new direction for discussions of race. The African body was itself the source of racial deficiency, he concluded in *The Hindered Hand*. Griggs's continued bedevilment by the question of African bodies led him to an idealism that ran counter to his own practice. Despite her skin coloring, which, like the return of the repressed, forces the "condition of the mother" on Tiara's mother and Tiara's estrangement from her family, she remains a cultured mulatto, a very conventional type fitted only by her tanned skin and defense of the oppressed as the embodiment of a classicized, redeemed Africa.

One Blood, One Soul

Pauline E. Hopkins's novels were, like Griggs's, a conscientious response to Du Bois's call in "The Conservation of Races" for the development of a sui generis race idea. In her first work, *Contending Forces*, she paid homage to Du Bois himself by naming her Bostonian soul striver "Will" and by giving to him the task of mouthing the substance of Du Bois's American Negro Academy address.[8] Hopkins further delineated her tribute to Du Bois by having Will travel to Europe for education and return dedicated to the task of establishing a "school which should embrace every known department of science, where the Negro youth of ability and genius could enter without money and without price" (386). So far as Africa's spiritual gifts were concerned, though, Hopkins was rather dubious in *Contending Forces*: "Claiming kinship with the Egyptians and other black races of the Eastern continent, the Negro is thought to possess wonderful powers of necromancy. Races are like families. . . . But transplant them on a foreign shore and much of their supposed power vanishes. So with the Negro" (198). Hopkins consequently scoffed at conjure and other mystical practices as, at worst, the residue of pagan superstition and, at best, the vitiation of whatever spiritual power might have originated in Africa.

But in her later novel, *Of One Blood*, Hopkins revised this estimate of residual African spiritual power. In this novel, the remnants of the old kingdom of Meroe, ancient Ethiopia itself, hide in the underground city Telassar awaiting the return of a redeemer king descended from their long-lost ruling clan. The novel's hero, Reuel Briggs, has been passing for white in pursuit of a medical degree at Harvard, only to find himself compelled by financial circumstances to accept a position in an archaeological expedition that will lead him to this lost city and to knowledge of his past. The Telassarians certify Reuel's identity as the long-awaited Ergamenes by means of a distinctive birthmark, explaining to him that through defiance "of God's laws, worshiping Mammon, sensual, unbelieving," Meroe was turned from "the light of the world's civilization" into a "Necropolis" (556, 558).

Reuel reacts to this revelation with a reflection on the folklore of his past and the maternal origins of his extrasensory powers: "It was a tradition among those who knew him in childhood that he was descended from a race of African kings. He remembered his mother well. From her he had inherited his mysticism and his occult powers. The nature of the mystic within him was, then, but a dream-like devotion to the spirit that had swayed his ancestors; it was the shadow of Ethiopia's power" (558). "Perhaps the superstitious masses came nearer to solving the mysteries of creation than the favored elect will ever come," Reuel says, in summary of Hopkins's newfound respect for African spiritualism and the cultural resourcefulness of the folk community (469). By reconsidering her prior disdain, expressed in the theatrical occultism of Madame Frances in *Contending Forces* and the root working of Auntie Griffin in *Hagar's Daughter*, Hopkins achieved a partial resolution of her struggle with the literary value of somatic features. Though Anglo-Saxon in body, Reuel is linked to Africa through a spiritual force that redeems him from a life of racial alienation and petty careerism. By making Reuel spiritually African, Hopkins implies the irrelevance of his physical features to the task of soul development, an insight that she unfortunately could not carry forward to its logical conclusion.

More important than the mark that identifies him as Ergamenes is the spiritual mark of Africa that has sensitized Reuel to the supernatural. In his medical practice, Reuel has been fascinated by "what might be termed 'absurdities' of supernatural phenomena or *mysticism*" (442), knowing through his own powers the truth behind Alfred Binet's work on animal magnetism, hypnotism, and double consciousness.[9] This interest becomes focused on Dianthe Lusk, a featured soloist of the Fisk Jubilee Singers who appears to Reuel in a vision before he actually sees her in the flesh on stage. When Dianthe turns up in a hospital after a train derailment, stiffened to a catatonic condition, Reuel puts into practice a power that he has "stumbled upon" in his quest to understand the paranormal, "the reanimation of the body after seeming death" (464). Reuel's diagnosis that Dianthe had been "persistently subjected to mesmeric influences" leaving her in a state of suspended animation marks her as the genius of slumbering Ethiopia whom Reuel is destined to awaken. The "body of death" was an illusion: the problem of Dianthe, embodied black America, was the improper diagnosis of those lacking spiritual literacy. Like the biblical type Ethiopia, she reaches out to Reuel's hand through her long night of deliverance. More important, Reuel's reanimation of Dianthe obliquely responds to the era's "body of death" rhetoric continuing Hopkins's thesis from earlier works that the returning body of death was slavery itself.

In a trancelike state, Dianthe speaks of her own mystical powers: "I see much clearly, much dimly, of the powers and influences behind the Veil, and yet I cannot name them. Some time the full power will be mine; and mine shall be thine" (475). Indirectly identifying herself with Du Bois's "child of Emancipation" who, "darkly, as through a veil, . . . saw in [her]self some faint revelation of [her] power, of [her] mission" (*Souls*, 6), Dianthe speaks of herself in the third person. Such instances lead Reuel to describe her condition as a *"dual* mesmeric trance" (471). The dual sources of enchantment in Dianthe's life are clearly inspired by Du Bois's metaphorical construct "double-consciousness," which Binet's work on double consciousness associates with psychic splitting into autonomous personalities.

Dianthe suffers first from the residual spell of the slavemaster/scientist Aubrey Livingston, whose son Aubrey is Reuel's Harvard schoolmate, his confidant, his secret antagonist, and (even more secret) his brother. Impressed with his father's dabbling in mysticism, and desiring the spotlight for himself after Reuel's sensational reanimation of Dianthe, Aubrey relates at a social gathering how his father would place a young slave girl named Mira into a trance, making her perform tricks and render prophecies to entertain his party guests. Under hypnotic influence, Mira lost her repressed, enslaved personality, becoming a "gay, noisy, restless woman, full of irony and sharp jesting" (486). This personality change corresponds to Binet's "inhibition of a cause of inhibition," a sloughing off of slavery's enforced consciousness of social death to reveal the essential personality. Linking slavery to enchantment, Hopkins portrays Du Bois's trope of psychic dualism as the result of a cruel, unethical science of disaffiliation. The image of several generations of slavemasters whispering commands into the ears of helplessly compliant female slaves strikingly captures Hopkins's interpretation of Du Boisian "double-consciousness" through Binet's work on hysterical double consciousness.[10]

In "Plural States of Being," Binet had described a principle of personality division affecting those like Dianthe who exhibited somnambulistic and vigilambulistic traits.[11] "Two fundamental elements constitute personality—memory and character. . . . It frequently happens that the somnambulist does not relinquish the character that he had before he was put to sleep. . . . This does not, however, hold for the second element of personality—memory" (540). Unlike Mira's personality transformation under Livingston's spell, Dianthe's transformation chiefly involves the outpouring of a repressed memory. Dianthe's second source of enchantment, her "racial" heritage, came to her through her mother, Mira, along with the spell of the elder Aubrey Livingston, who is her father as well as Aubrey's and Reuel's. This "racial" soul manifests itself as an autonomous entity dwelling within Dianthe that returns her to self-awareness after lengthy amnesia. In effect, Mira personifies the "racial memory" that returns to guide Dianthe in her trancelike states as the second consciousness, commanding, as Binet prescribed, a stronger grasp of what has transpired than the amnesiac Dianthe. Like Binet's "somnambulistic ego," Mira "is not completely effaced when the waking state returns, but survives, coexists with normal thought, and gives rise to complex phenomena of division of consciousness." Her name contains a command (Mira: Look!) that draws Reuel's saving resuscitation but also draws Aubrey's lust and mesmeric power in the worst tradition of the slavemaster reborn as man of science. Her first message to Dianthe cryptically from the twelfth chapter of Luke singles out the veil of race as a temporary obstacle to a full disclosure of slavery's tangled "genealogies" and Jim Crow's myths of irremediable difference: "For there is nothing covered that shall not be revealed" (506).

One important instance of the "complex phenomena" of self-division in the novel (which include amnesia, catatonia, somnambulism, astral projection, and automatic writing) is Mira's emergence as a second "voice" that authoritatively reveals the racial memory of slavery. The mechanism of this living memory is the spiritual "Go Down Moses," which Dianthe spontaneously begins to sing one evening after Reuel has departed for Africa. The voice of Mira is detectable *within* Dianthe's as she sings: "A weird contralto, veiled as it were, rising and falling upon every wave of the great soprano, and reaching the ear as from some strange distance. The singer sang on, . . . the echo following it" (502). Anticipating Du Bois's description of the "master songs" in *The Souls*, which appeared in book form at precisely the moment that *Of One Blood* was serialized in *Colored American Magazine*, this veiled voice of the black mother calling Dianthe out of mental bondage simultaneously re-creates the past and relates Dianthe's present predicament to Reuel's in Africa.[12]

The tangled relations between the consanguineous trio, all of them Mira's children, once more affirm Hopkins's theme that "no man can draw the dividing line between the two races, for they are both of one blood!" (607). Having married Dianthe without knowing that she is his sister (but so close to his departure as to have left the marriage unconsummated), Reuel had been tricked into the two-year Ethiopian expedition by Aubrey, who felt that he could possess Dianthe himself in Reuel's absence. Through mesmerism and deceit, Aubrey attempts to murder Reuel, forces Dianthe to marry him after killing his own fiancée and then telling Dianthe that Reuel was dead, and later causes her to die by forcing her to drink poison. Aubrey's immersion in his slavemaster father's science of enchantment leads him to abuse his spiritual powers in part because the spiritual resources of his true mother, Mira, are "hidden" from him through a conventional "switched at birth" plot device.

The agent of Dianthe's recovery of her personal past is her grandmother, Aunt Hannah, a woman previously unknown to her. Aunt Hannah, "the most noted 'voodoo' doctor or witch in the country," reveals that the power by which Mira shadows Dianthe's voice and life is the legacy of their family's consecration to the god Osiris. Aunt Hannah's unaccountable silence and Mira's limited power to guide her children away from harm attest to the debased condition of the ancient worship. But her story's greatest interest is in the reconnection of spiritual links through mothers back to Africa. Like *Hagar's Daughter*, the novel tells of three generations of women physically evolving closer to the somatic features of the white slaveholders. In *Of One Blood*, however, the revelation that conjure stems from ancient African science leads away from an absolute translation of Western culture and appearance into "progress." The scenes in Telassar affirm that the immemorial African past was more spiritually progressive than the Anglo-Saxon present, that in the "heart of Africa was a knowledge of science that all the wealth and learning of modern times could not emulate" (576).

That knowledge of ethical science, the product of Meroe's own prolonged struggle with Mammonism, gives the Telassarians the ability to manipulate the spiritual realm as effectively as Westerners controlled the material world. In Telassar, the chief priest explains to Reuel the centrality of the concept of the oversoul, or "Ego": "'unless the Ego can wean the body from gross desires and raise it to the highest condition of human existence, it cannot be united to its Creator. The Ego preserves its individuality after the dissolution of the body. . . . The Ego can never be destroyed. For instance, when the body of a good man or woman dies, and the Ego is not sufficiently fitted for the higher condition of another world, it is reassociated with another body to complete the necessary fitness for heaven'" (562). The novel presents the interesting twist that unlike the revenant body of death that plagued Hopkins's earlier characters, the return of the slave mother spiritually protects and guides Dianthe. Mira's spiritual possession of Dianthe's body has been a refitting of her soul for heaven, while Dianthe's death scene is an overblown reunion with ancestral spirits whom she calls by name: "Candace, Semiramis, Dido, Solomon, David . . ." Hopkins imaginatively documents the transformation of slavery's double consciousness into a black American coming to awareness of an indwelling spiritual power of African provenance.

In the process of this multigenerational reincarnation, the physical features of the women's bodies undergo a transformation through the "accumulation of years of foulest wrongs heaped upon the innocent and defenseless women of the race" (594).[13] Hopkins undoubtedly sought to defuse criticism of her use of three quadroon characters as the protagonists of a novel about a reclamation of African heritage by concentrating on spiritual continuity. For two important reasons this strategy does not ultimately prove successful. First, Hopkins's body politics are defensible on technical grounds, but they curiously violate the very spirit of the work. Hopkins creates some of the confusion in an attempt to discuss knowledgeably the ancient Ethiopian body ideal as a point of differentiation between Ethiopia and Egypt: "Reuel noticed particularly the [picture] of a queen attired in long robe [sic], tight at neck and ankles, with closely fitted legs. . . . The figure was strongly marked by corpulency, a mark of beauty in Eastern women. This rotundity is the distinguishing feature of Ethiopian sculpture, more bulky and clumsy than Egypt, but pleasing to the eye" (537). Hopkins, however, shrinks from the implications of this aesthetic when the Telassarians take the stage. The chief priest Ai is described as passable for an "Arab, Turk, Malay, or Filipino" in America (584), while the description of Candace, an honorary title given each of the succession of virgin queens of the underground city, bears no resemblance to the ancient somatic ideal: "She reminded [Reuel] strongly of his beautiful Dianthe; in face, the resemblance was so striking that it was painful. . . . Yes, she was a Venus, a superb statue of bronze, molded by a great sculptor. . . . Long, jet-black hair and totally free, covered her shoulders like a silken mantle; a broad, square forehead, a warm bronze complexion, . . . a delicate nose with quivering nostrils. . . . She seemed the embodiment of all chastity" (569). Given the opportunity to develop a somatic ideal in keeping with her theme, Hopkins stubbornly fell back on "classical" aesthetics to elevate Candace into "the embodiment of all chastity." Neither Candace, an "unmixed" Ethiopian, nor her near twin Dianthe, who "was not in any way the preconceived idea of a Negro" (453), shows any sign of "rotundity" as a distinguishing feature. And neither bears any resemblance to the family matriarch Aunt Hannah, the only one of the family who is unequivocally dark skinned, "crisp-haired," and "flat featured" (603, 606). If Hannah is the "original" African body, why does her quadroon granddaughter bear a stronger "family" resemblance to the Telassarians than she does?

Candace's evocation of the "bronze Venus," in fact, dramatizes the point Hopkins makes in her companion magazine article to the serialized novel, "Venus and Apollo Modeled from Ethiopians." In this article, Hopkins challenged the "scientific" use of anthropometrical dimensions based on measurements from classical sculpture to establish African somatic inferiority. She cites unnamed "authorities in the art world" as the basis of her claim that "the Venus de Milo and the Apollo Belvedere" were sculpted from "Ethiopian slave models." Incredibly, she explains that the length of the arms of the Apollo Belvedere is an important clue to the statue's Ethiopian somatic foundation: "A curious fact about the Negro race is that their arms are, as a rule, longer than those of people of the white race. This may be because they *are more recently evolved from the ape ancestors*" (465; my emphasis). Hopkins clearly did not think through the implications of simultaneously granting Ethiopians greater cultural antiquity, despite "more recent" evolution than whites. Taken together, these reflections on racial bodies suggest Hopkins's lingering ambivalence about the biological legacy of Africa.

A second flaw in the novel's body politics is actually tangential to the novel itself but speaks to the contradictions of the era. The ads that ran in *Colored American Magazine* during the novel's serialization included several for skin whiteners, hair dekinkers, and other "beauty" aids. The ads typically featured "before and after" illustrations that promised emancipation from the artists' conception of African features. These ads reiterated the power of the literature to transform consumers into a fantasized ideal, subtly provoking the very double consciousness that the novel overtly condemns. If, as the novel's subtitle hints, the veiled, hidden, African self is the subject of a complex spiritual revelation that will eventually restore Africans to a position of esteem in the world, the magazine's advertising and editorial policy suggest that demonstrably African bodies were inadequate and perhaps even inappropriate vehicles for the expression of this racial renaissance.

Thus, when Dianthe, on her deathbed, addresses Aunt Hannah as "Mother" and relates a vision to her, we must wonder what Hopkins had in mind. "A very golden cloud is printed with the fleecy words of glory. 'I will return.'. . . O, will our spirits come, like setting suns, on each tomorrow of eternity?" (613). The mother's return is simultaneously the spirit's triumph, a dramatic refiguration of the revenant body of death that characterized the narratives of racial escape into national belonging. Mira, whom Reuel sees with "spiritual eyes," points the way to this new image of African motherhood as the mystical body of the race spirit itself. But though the revenant African body as a trope of racial essence gives way in Hopkins's work to the spiritual renaissance of Africa, it does so without challenging the cultural erasure of the African body itself. It would remain for W. E. B. Du Bois to connect the African spiritual ideal in literature to a distinctively African aesthetic of embodiment that can, for the first time, move unapologetically center stage.

CHAPTER SEVEN

The Darkness of the Mother

In the service of his great theme—how can African Americans gain full access to America without losing their cultural integrity, their black soul?—Du Bois necessarily had to address the question of religious leadership among the masses. As he explained in *The Souls of Black Folk* in "Of the Faith of the Fathers," "The Negro church of to-day is the social centre of Negro life in the United States, and the most characteristic expression of African character" (136), and any attempt to define and conserve African character had to find a secular equivalent to the type of religious uplift popularized by Harper's *Iola Leroy*. Du Bois, particularly in his early poetry and essays, used mythic forms from a variety of cultural sources as a means of familiarizing his audiences with his brand of "secular" spiritual development. In describing these cultural sources, Wilson Jeremiah Moses has identified a dualistic base of mythic formalism in Du Bois's work: the European tradition of interpretive mythology and the literary-religious tradition of "Ethiopianism" (Andrews, *Critical Essays*, 92–93). The Ethiopianist strain, according to Moses—ranging from a neutral belief in the deliverance of black people worldwide from bondage to whites, to the more aggressive belief that blacks would not stop with freedom but someday would actually come to rule whites (93)—has two components: "Rising Africa" and "The Decline of the West" (94–95). An early indication of this type of binarism in the work of Du Bois emerges in his opposition of the Teutonic Strong Man and the black Submissive Man in his Harvard graduation address. The "feminized" Submissive Man sheds his gender ambiguity entirely in the ringing conclusion, where Du Bois admonishes the audience, "You owe a debt of humanity for this Ethiopia of the

Out-stretched Arm, who has made her beauty, patience, and her grandeur, law"
(*W. E. B. Du Bois: A Reader*, 19).[1]

In a moment that would become typical of the many pageants, poems, and
race allegories he produced as morale boosters and homiletic inquiries into the
nature of caste prejudice, Du Bois apotheosized the race spirit as "Rising Africa."
In a parallel movement, he replaced the supermasculine Strong Man with a
conventionally feminized America who embodied the "Decline of the West."
These dramatis personae had counterparts in his more realistic creative writing,
giving an overt allegorical cast to all of his work. His core narrative would be a
modified version of Wells-Barnett's tale of the white Delilah and black Samson,
with the important qualification that a fierce racial dignity would not allow Du
Bois to depict a white female as an object of black male desire. Still, the black
male quester's choice between the feminized "Rising Africa" or the feminized
"Decline of the West" enacted the crucial transition from a naïf plagued by double
consciousness to a spiritually focused race striver, a mythicized variant of the
marriage plot as initiation into national belonging.

S. P. Fullinwinder, in an attempt to portray Du Bois as an irresponsible mystic
who turned his back on science to become a race propagandist, has argued that
Du Bois indulged in myth in order to identify with the masses from whom he
had become alienated (72). Fullinwinder's premise, that "true" intellectuals deal
in facts and not myths, would be hard to prove from the writings of many intellectuals, especially those of Du Bois's era. Du Bois's use of myth is simply characteristic of his thinking, with or without regard to his relation to the black
masses. By addressing black and white audiences through cosmologies that provided a common sign system, Du Bois did no more or less than any other self-
conscious user of language — he adapted extant forms to his own purposes. When,
for example, he sought to describe how the oppressive demand for public expressions of religiosity at his first teaching job at Wilberforce clashed with his
own sense of mission, he did so in a fashion both characteristic and ironic: "To
remain at Wilberforce without doing my ideals meant spiritual death" (*Darkwater* 20). Describing public profession of the "faith of the fathers" as "spiritual
death" is not the way to connect with the black masses.

What Du Bois did was to find an inspirational language of uplift that could introduce his brand of secular activism to both the masses and the "talented tenth"
who were to lead them. He never abandoned "science," which provided much
of the content of his race appeals. But ironically, his language of black spiritualism had an inescapable materialist bent. Du Bois knew that spiritual practice by

blacks historically had had deleterious effects for which the Sorrow Songs only partially compensated, since the indefinite deferral of rewards into the "next world" led to an endemic fatalism about "this-worldly" striving.[2] Du Bois's appropriation of religious rhetoric and biblical forms can be described, then, as a reorientation of black Christianity's otherworldly fatalism into this-worldly optimism.

But to the degree that the black church itself was one of the inhibiting factors on the development of the home, the site of sociological tinkering and experimentation, not to mention nationalist race development, Du Bois had to wrest religio-mythic discourse from both its white origins and its "misuse" in black dogma.[3] And to the extent that he saw the development of the race as resting on a base of material security, Du Bois had to take care to differentiate that gainful striving of the soul he advocated from the "cynical practical religion of success": the belief that "the sole and sufficient object of work is wealth" ("Joy of Living," 218). In the Du Boisian cosmos, the Decline of the West not only signifies the irrational power of race hatred, but as embodied female she also serves as a catalyst for the protagonist's double-conscious crisis of faith in the future of the race. She dominates those who fall into a self-serving exploitation of talent—the abandonment of race striving by his heroes for "aims [no] higher than their bellies, and no God greater than Gold" ("Talented Tenth," 20). She lures him, whispering the "sound of the Zeitgeist": "Earn a living: get rich, and all these things shall be added unto you. . . . Conciliate your neighbors, because they are more powerful and wealthier, and the price you must pay to earn a living in America is that of humiliation and inferiority" (*W. E. B. Du Bois: A Reader*, 330). Rising Africa, on the other hand, enacts the spirit of sacrifice that undergirds the slow, frustrating task of collective striving. She is the guardian of the soul quest and the will to world-historical status for the race.

Of the Coming of the Black Patriarchs

Du Bois's interest in contributing to an ethical literature, an important phase of his project of racial soul development, accounts for his inclusion of a fictional piece, "Of the Coming of John," in *The Souls of Black Folk*. In this short fable of black aspiration and despair, Du Bois gives us two Johns—one black, one white—inhabitants of opposite ends of the social order of the southeastern Georgia town of Altamaha who are both done to death by the blindness of race ideology. At the moment that black John accidentally touches the arm of white John's date at the

New York performance of *Lohengrin*, he has been transported by the music into a dream of transcending his social limitations in pursuit of some mighty life purpose. With the music of the violins, "there came to him the vision of a far-off home, the great eyes of his sister, and the dark drawn face of his mother. And his heart sank below the waters" (167).

The possibility of spiritual transcendence for black John becomes complicated by two factors: the physical presence of the white woman as the very symbol of his imperfect access to white world culture, and the intruding awareness that the dream of rising above the veil brings with it the responsibility to uplift the race, personified by the dark mother and sister. This incident is the metaphorical complement to the autobiographical episode of the scornful schoolgirl in "Of Our Spiritual Strivings," which seemed to suggest at the outset of *The Souls* that transcendence of the veil was a matter of reining in personal ambition. But here, nearly at the end of the journey "beyond the Veil," Du Bois reinforces his ethic of sacrifice with an image of the women who have devoted themselves to the "coming of John" into household and race leadership.

The bloody conclusion, in which the whites of Altamaha gallop in pursuit of black John to lynch him for the murder of the white John, fills out the picture of the race/sex tangle of the South. The judge, white John's father, has agreed to let black John teach at the Negro school on the condition that he forswear any attempt to "reverse nature, and rule white men, and marry white women, and sit in my parlor" (172). Yet John also suffers alienation from the black folk to whom he has dedicated himself when he speaks at his welcoming reception about the material tasks of building schools and banks and of establishing unity and charity. The assembly takes his offhand remark that differences of religious belief are inconsequential to the task of nation building as a sign of religious skepticism. John's this-worldly crusade thus gets off to a slow start, but after a month, he can see glimmers of progress in his school. However, after the return of the white John from the North, bringing word that black John had, in New York, tried to force himself into a seat next to a white woman in a theater, the judge summarily dismisses John from his teaching position. Coming upon white John tussling with his sister Jennie, black John, already ripe for despair, delivers a death blow and then awaits the mob.

Du Bois's parable serves several purposes. Coming before his discussion of the Sorrow Songs, the story contrasts John's despair with the determination of the singers of the spirituals to persevere. At the same time, Du Bois's critique of religious fundamentalism in "Of the Coming of John" undercuts any sense that the songs of that fatalistic folk religion represent anything like a final statement of the black race message. The songs may "cheer the weary traveller," but they cannot bring his travels to a successful conclusion. Du Bois presents black folk religion as bedeviled by superstition and manipulated by self-serving preachers. The strained relationship between the ethical race developer and the older class of religious leadership shows in John's rationalist appeal to unity and common striving for uplift. It will take, Du Bois was saying, the coming of many "Johns" to move the race the next logical step beyond the anticipation of sorrow into hope that worldly striving can effect real social change.

John Jones is the type Du Bois referred to in "The Development of a People" as the new priesthood of cultural interpreters (212). Coming to an awareness of the color line, this priestly class must be gifted with the ability to see the "spiritual" time-space of black America, which included a consciousness of how, for "nearly half a millennium, the Christian world fattened on the stealing of human souls" (210), and how for nearly half a century after, on the shackling of human spirits. This historical knowledge, however, must be tempered by a vision of the future. Based on Nathaniel Shaler's assertion that the establishment of patriarchy was the origin of complex social organization and of all ethnic distinction, we might call this moment the coming of the black patriarchs, those who would establish the "authority of the fathers, the customs of the past in a nation without grandfathers."[4] Du Bois's leadership role in this black patriarchal project would use the sign of the black mother in much the same way, as we will see, that whites had manipulated white females as territorial markers.

Balancing tradition with modernity, this priestly class would establish the direction of group striving, taking care not to circumscribe any legitimate aspirations. John Jones is learning this delicate balance, when suddenly the veil entraps him. I do not agree with the interpretation offered by Rampersad and endorsed by Nellie McKay that John Jones's possible suicide at the story's conclusion gives the work a mood of unrelieved pessimism.[5] To see John Jones's death in isolation misses an important point. Du Bois paints a grim picture of the South, but to an interracial audience that he feels is just as likely to see itself reflected in white John as black John. Thus, he refrains from identifying white John with unmitigated evil: "He was not a bad fellow,—just spoiled and self-indulgent, and as headstrong as his proud father" (174). In other words, both Johns are products of their environment—not inherently evil or saintly people, but the sum of their life experiences, opportunities, and choices. The "Coming of John" refers to both men, who together represent the future of the South. Educated away, both men have more in common culturally with New York (and, ironically, with each other) than they do with their families and friends, and both are reluctant to take on the burden of leading their respective communities in Altamaha as their families have planned. If black John stumbles in finding a proper accommodation to his newfound knowledge of the veil, white John blunders equally in his insistence on planter class sexual license, as though emancipation had never happened. Du Bois's point, then, is that their deaths at each other's hands are twin catastrophes that the South cannot afford. The story is a warning to those whom Du Bois escorts behind the veil that only a change in the racial environment of the South will save both races by making the "Coming of the Johns" of the New South an event that saves the region, instead of perpetuating the ages-old antagonism.

John Jones's act of murder and (possibly) suicide are preventable calamities, drawing attention to two southern customs—the fatal white woman and the exploitable black female—that would have to change if black development and southern progress were ever to occur. The fact that black John has tripped one of the invisible wires of race difference in the South, the vast network of hindrances and restrictions erected against black aspiration in the name of protecting white female purity, does not mean that Du Bois sees John's experience as prescriptive of all black race agency. John is clearly a pioneer in the most difficult phase of the new racial accommodation in the South. According to Du Bois, the incipient black patriarchy will necessarily face resistance from white males, whose hegemony it threatens: "the race question is at bottom simply a matter of the ownership of women; white men want the right to own and use all women, colored and white, and they resent any intrusion of colored men into this domain."[6] In raising the question of whether blacks could become a "peculiar people" in "The Conservation of Races," Du Bois acknowledged that the key element of this race ideal is a movement toward racial integrity. Black America could not unite on principles of corruption, immorality, and exploitation, Du Bois held, but must come together to stop black disease and black criminality and "to guard the purity of black women and to reduce the vast army of black prostitutes that is marching to hell" (6).

Thus Du Bois, however reluctantly, agreed with William Archer's malicious observation that blacks could become a "peculiar people" only through the institution of female race chastity, a prospect at which Archer openly scoffed.[7] Black John and white John are victims of this new phase of race adjustment, the coming of the black patriarch. If white John takes it into his mind idly to pursue the habit of black female concubinage, nothing will stop such a habit but a black patriarchy united for the protection of black females. Whether sexual exploitation was in fact white John's intention is not clear, but southern custom was solidly on his side if it was, and it was this legacy that black John was striking out against. Thus, the price may inevitably be the martyrdom of some transitional black males like John Jones, but until the principle of defending black females from sexual exploitation became accepted by both sides, a few dead white Johns might be the only thing that would convey black communal resolve for racial exclusivity. Du Bois therefore saw this conflict over the ownership of women as a necessary first stage in the development of the black nation, not an indication of an endless cycle of hopelessness and despair awaiting the black missionary elite.

On this same point, we cannot overlook black John's own race/sex dilemma. Before the encounter in the theater and the accidental touch across the color line, John had been rather taken in by the Zeitgeist of cosmopolitan New York. Directionless, he blindly surrenders himself to the crowd, following a couple—a "tall, light-haired young man and a little talkative lady"—until he finds himself swept into the theater line. If his very presence in the theater stems from an impulse to lose consciousness of his caste difference in the crowd, then his loss of self-consciousness in the sweep of the Teutonic music represents a looming crisis of "double-consciousness." Inevitably, a white woman sits next to him, making her body the boundary between the new black patriarch and the new white one, and whether his touching of her hand is entirely accidental or suggests an unconscious attempt by a second self at physically manifesting its spiritual contact with the white world, black John responds to her snub with "a deep longing [that] swelled in all his heart to rise with that clear music out of the dirt and dust of that low life that held him prisoned and befouled" (167). If he had not before been beset by the prospect of eating "spiritual dirt," the onset of "double-consciousness" after seeing himself through the woman's eyes certainly makes that inevitable.

Heretofore, John has been rather too absorbed in a "half-daze minding the scene around him" to settle into his characteristic fretting about race prejudice. But suddenly, he is back in the depths, back in the foul "prison-house" of caste. What has put him there, if not the rejection of his humanity by the woman? If we cannot strictly call John's touch an "invitation" across the line of race, as in Du Bois's visiting card episode earlier recounted in The Souls,[8] it still is clear that John's reaction expresses a regret that "a world like this lay open to [white] men" but not to him. Later, Du Bois reverses their positions in a way that recalls the function of puberty as a dividing line in race/gender role socialization. Having denied black John the white-world initiation of incidental physical contact with the white female, white John seemingly attempts to pursue his own initiation into manhood by physically handling his other childhood playmate, black John's sister. Despite black John's sense of rejection, the pattern of white male control of women is not complete until Du Bois juxtaposes black female vulnerability to white female unapproachableness.

John Jones's dismissal from the theater at white John's request reaffirms the association of the white woman with spaces in America prohibited to him. The white woman who stands for that closed world causes his heart to sink, but significantly, though it sinks immediately also when he thinks of his obligation to his mother and sister back home, by the end his heart has lifted. The rather inert icons of defenseless black womanhood, who have sacrificed to give him his education, become for him in this double-conscious phase first a burden and then the very embodiment of "some master-work, some life service, . . . without the cruel hurt that hardened his heart and soul" (167), saving him from the "listless[ness]" and "idle[ness]" of the whites in the audience. Scorned by a white woman but sworn to self-realization through service to black ones, John resigns himself to the Gospel of Sacrifice that marks him as the new black patriarch. Determined now to end his escapist adventure in New York, he sends a letter saying, "Dear Mother and Sister—I am coming—John" (168). "'I will go in to the King, which is not according to the law,'" he tells himself, "'and if I perish, I perish.'"

Although Du Bois gives us only one clue, John Jones's murder of white John is not simply an act of protection of his sister but also a revenge for the double insult at the New York theater. What black John sees as he rushes angrily forward to help his sister is not white John, his childhood friend, but "a tall and fair-haired man" (175). The white couple that black John had unthinkingly followed to the theater in New York was the identically described white John and his date, and the repetition of the generic description of white John at these two critical moments ensures that the episodes of psychological and physical violence between the two Johns cancel each other out. The closing of this circle reveals this insight: black John had followed the couple to the theater and had touched the woman's arm because of his unconscious desire to be in the place of the "tall, light-haired young man," his doppelgänger, white John. That he unconsciously strikes out in hatred at that figure in direct proportion to his earlier unconscious attraction suggests that beyond the allegorical import, Du Bois was investigating the complex transracial psychology of fear and desire that complicated the rise of a black patriarchy.

The Burden of Black Women

In his role of "seer," in this, the only fictional effort in *The Souls*, Du Bois does not dwell in unrelieved pessimism, but neither does he paint an overly optimistic picture of race relations in the South, as he often accused Washington of doing. He wanted race strivers to know what they were in for and what the stakes were, but he did not want to scare them away from the struggle ahead. It is as seer, then, that he described the shouldering of the "Burden of Black Women" as a phase in the solution of the Negro problem, as well as his utopian vision of Rising Africa as the installation of the black mother in the shrine of the "little yellow house" with the "flower-bed struggling sturdily with the clay" ("Development," 212). The early Du Bois, swept up in his zeal for a moral revolution in the black South at the instigation of an ethical, priestly cadre of race builders, became a stern critic of those social trends that clashed with his patriarchal impulse, particularly the issue of black female unchastity. Patricia Morton summarizes his depiction of black womanhood in his early sociological work: "Du Bois's early sociological research focused heavily upon the contemporary black woman's sexual behavior. He pointed, for example, to the high rate of illegitimate births as what 'represents the unchastity of large numbers of women,' arguing that their historically 'lax morality' had been compounded by the dislocation associated with recent black migration to the city. Thus, while articulating an environmentalist interpretation of racial behavior, Du Bois also reiterated denigrating images of black womanhood" (58). Asserting that Du Bois's "apparent objective presentation of fact often masked the moralistic perspective underpinning these images," Morton cites *The Philadelphia Negro* as a particular example of his "judgmental, sexual puritanism": "In this, Du Bois advised, for example, that the 'colored girl' had too much freedom, and what she needed was a strict home life. It was 'the duty of Negroes' to 'solve' the problem of female 'unchastity' by 'keeping little girls off the street at night, stopping the escorting of unchaperoned young ladies to church and elsewhere'" (58–59). Small wonder that his enemies quoted him as a source on the moral unfitness of the race.

The first step toward race development, the domestication of the black female, was the focus of Du Bois's 1902 essay "The Work of Negro Women in Society," which appeared in the *Spelman Messenger*, a publication of the black women's college in Atlanta. Du Bois's essay reads the history of "civilization" in terms of women's roles, their primary one being homemaking: "[Motherhood] demands strength, courage, and infinite sacrifice. It is neither a pastime, a joke, nor a dissipation, but a solemn human occupation to be assumed with forethought and reverence. At the same time it is a duty. *The perpetuation of the race, the transmission of culture, the ultimate triumph of right depend primarily upon the physical motherhood of the nation. There is no use trying to rear a race or nation on the physical foundation of mothers too weak or wanton to bring forth healthy children*" ("Negro Women in Society," 139–40; my emphasis). Du Bois then charged "the better class" of black women (that is, the Spelman students) with shirking their duty—the "everlasting Ought" that particularly pertained to women—to help blacks "keep progress with the *virile races* of the world," by deferring marriage and families, although he favored decreasing the number of children they should have relative to their parents' generation as a matter of racial "efficiency" (140). The most unfortunate aspect of this shirking of motherhood was their "leaving the making of the next generation to the worst elements of our population." This argument, very popular among eugenicists as well, was the inevitable culmination of a "progress" narrative. With each new generation coming from the poorest social elements, Du Bois said, the race started further and further back, rather than building upon its leading, materially secure edge.

Second, Du Bois laid a charge for black women to be "spiritual" builders as well, for, "to make a real home—there is need of mind and soul to guide the hands." Taking up his cudgel against Washington and organized religion again, Du Bois contended that "no amount of material prosperity, political expansion, or religious formalism [could] arrest ruin, if the homes of the people [were] deteriorating in vice, excess and ignorance."[9] Here Du Bois defined the establishment of the black home out of the "wilderness" of slavery's despoliation of black familial integrity as the central task of race striving: "Our homes are *new* things, *experiments* little more than a generation old—sudden efforts reared on a foundation of polygamy, communism, and concubinage. If we succeed in founding and strengthening real home life among us, then there is no power on earth to hinder these nine millions of men from establishing and maintaining a place in the civilized world beside the other races of men and perhaps above them." Du Bois challenged the women of his audience not to regard homemaking as "soul-wasting drudgery" but as "a way of thinking, a habit of doing; a system of human education, an insight into the beauty of things; an ideal of goodness and a reverence for God's truth." Though he has dropped the Germanic capitals, Du Bois manages to insert Beauty, Goodness, and Truth into the mission of home crafting as an indispensable part of his race-building formula. In sum, the "spiritual" function of motherhood was to "interpret life and the world to the little group about you, until they in turn can give back to the world a soul and a purpose." Thus the black homemaker was nothing less than the high priestess of the new class of cultural missionaries/interpreters, who in her third, "civilizing" function knitted individual households into a nation (142).

Gradually, Du Bois would downplay both his strident denunciation of the failings of black womanhood and his demands on the "best" women to outprocreate their poorer sisters. More and more he focused on the historico-mythic contributions of black women to civilization and to the race. It is important to note, however, that even though his enemies convinced him that it was counterproductive to carry on a moral campaign against the black Venus, his more celebratory evocations of black female essence still betray unmistakable traces of a patriarchal desire for silent, acquiescent, race-chaste womanhood. For Du Bois, the "ownership of women" had to be accomplished rhetorically before it could be achieved practically. Thus the literature most directly influenced by his vision of soul development illustrates his own struggle toward an emancipatory project that challenged racial hierarchies without disturbing gender hierarchies.

One of his earliest investigations into the relation of the black female experience to the development of a sui generis race idea, The Quest of the Silver Fleece, was begun in late 1905 or early 1906 (perhaps as Du Bois's response to Griggs's The Hindered Hand or Dixon's The Clansman, or both),[10] but it was not completed until 1911. During that time, Du Bois edited two journals, the Moon (1905–6) and the Horizon (1907–10), in which a number of creative efforts of his appeared, as would later be the case with the Crisis (1911-).[11] His "Credo," first published in 1904 and later used as an introductory statement in Darkwater (1920), set the tone for his creative efforts in its establishment of the themes that would prevail in his works for years to come. He begins with an affirmation of his belief in the brotherhood of the races, "made of one blood" by God and "alike in soul and in the possibility of infinite development" (229).

Du Bois's third paragraph is one of the more important ones, affirming his belief in the possibility of coexistence between races that do not embody with each other: "I believe in pride of race so chivalrous as neither to offer bastardy to the weak nor beg wedlock of the strong, knowing that men may be brothers in Christ, even they be not brothers-in-law." In his fifth paragraph, Du Bois outlines his cosmology: "I believe in the Devil and his angels, who wantonly work to narrow the opportunities of struggling human beings, especially if they be black." These demonic forces are they who deprive blacks of the "space to stretch their arms and their souls," while working tirelessly to imprison blacks in the time-space of the veil.

In his penultimate paragraph of "Credo," Du Bois touches on his conflict with Washington that leaves no doubt as to the Faustian basis of his philosophy of soul striving: "I believe in the training of children, black even as white; the leading out of little souls into the green pastures . . . not for self or peace, but for Life lit by some large vision of beauty and goodness and truth; lest we forget, and the sons of the fathers, like Esau, for more meat barter their birthright in a mighty nation" (229–30; my emphasis). Those most susceptible to bartering their black birthright of beauty and goodness and truth for immediate satisfaction were those who lacked "Patience," the final quality in which Du Bois pledges belief, the quality typified by the long-suffering black mother.

The Blackness of the Mother

Du Bois's deification of black womanhood as the embodiment of Rising Africa presents a surprising analogue to two key discussions in Charles Darwin's *The Descent of Man* (1871). In outlining the evolution of human social organization, Darwin paused to note a distinction between humans and other animals that centers on the role of the mother. Darwin thought human society was founded in the resolution of opposed instincts through the institution of a moral code.[12] Through a constant reflection possible only for the human mind, the "social instinct" of sympathy and compassion became stronger than the intermittent and immediately assuagable biological instincts. Darwin's parable of the swallow, who abandons her young by succumbing to the stronger instinct to migrate, was an image of biological motherhood devoid of the moral capacity to place the greater social good over immediate desire (1:87).

This model of motherhood, as we have seen, fit the prevailing image of black women in the Progressive Era. Nathaniel Shaler's summary of Darwin's thinking on social evolution in *The Neighbor* moves from the communal lifestyles of animals to the development of human sympathy, citing also the role of the mother in establishing an example of selfless devotion to others that underlies the moral order (262–65). Yet Shaler may not have meant this evolutionary train to include blacks, having previously noted black maternal indifference in terms reminiscent of Page and Thomas. Reiterating Joseph Tillinghast's slander that blacks were incapable of "lasting sacrificial friendship,"[13] Shaler characterized black biological motherhood as a uterine filiation too weak in associative claims to prevent maternal neglect but that surprisingly, with proper white supervision, did not prevent black women from becoming excellent mammies. Du Bois himself would lash out at the hypocrisy of mammy worship in his 1912 essay "The Black Mother," charging that whites' excessive demands on black domestics left them indifferent to their own households and that whites only disparaged black women's maternal qualities to ensure themselves of a cheap source of domestic help.[14]

For Darwin, the crucial term that established the leap from animal communities to human sacrificial relationships was "*ought.*" Even morality had a physiological source: "The imperious word *ought* seems merely to employ the consciousness of the existence of a persistent instinct, either innate or partly acquired" (1:88). The fact of consciousness in no way implied the moral superiority of the persistent instinct. Its greater strength and frequency alone explain its success, although Darwin does say that communal disapprobation would likely be the force compelling the "moral" choice. As we have seen, Du Bois from the very beginning placed the "everlasting *Ought*" at the center of all race development. In the Du Boisian scheme, the mother *ought* to stay home with her young: "Let the present-day mammies suckle their own children. . . . Let the colored mother of today build her own statues, and let it be the four walls of her own unsullied home" (*W. E. B. Du Bois: A Reader*, 294). Following this prescription, the S/ness of the mother would come to stand for Self-Sacrifice.

In return the would-be black patriarch *ought* to declare allegiance to the sacrificial path of black motherhood over the various instincts urging him to self-gratification. Though Du Bois did not indicate a specific awareness of Darwin's *Descent*, a second critical move in his program of "race conservation" echoed Darwin. Despite the prevailing wisdom that races had developed through natural selection in response to specific environmental conditions, Darwin felt that a lack of evidence that specific "racial" characteristics were necessary to survival in a particular environment required an alternative explanation to natural selection. In *The Descent of Man, and Selection in Relation to Sex*, the second part of which often disappears from the title, Darwin developed the theory of sexual selection to explain evolutionary traits that had no obvious environmental survival functions, but also to explain the presence of extreme variation among all animal populations.

For Darwin, only if *all* members of the race had to have a trait or risk extinction could there be any proof that "race" was an adaptation to a specific geographical or social environment. The polygenist idea of race-specific zones was only an illusion created by grandfathering populations into their locations during the period of European expansion and historical documentation. The wide variety in somatic traits *within* the "races," including hair texture, skin color, body form, and the like, certified the absence of a nondifferentiated difference that would set each population apart (1:217). For whites to be a "race" in the sense that they used the term, they would have to be a nondifferentiated population whose eye color, hair color and texture, and skin color were uniform and directly responsible for their survival. If survival in tropical climates required dark skin, why were there people lacking this trait who inhabited tropical zones outside Africa? Darwin did not rule out climatic factors entirely. Instead, he argued that ample evidence of protean polymorphism meant that individuation within a general somatic range arose as a tool for enhancing reproductive opportunities, not as an aid to natural selection. Human variety arose, according to Darwin, not as the efflorescence of transcendent spiritual characteristics but out of the competition for mates. Races were the result of the systematic sexual selection of specific aesthetic traits among certain populations.[15]

According to Darwin, this process critically involved the female because in human communities, it was typical that men selected mates for beauty, whereas women exerted their degree of choice toward the better provider and protector, with less attention to appearance. Thus, the aesthetic choices that resulted in "racial" characteristics were largely a reflection of masculine ideals of beauty systematized over the centuries.[16] Darwin gives examples from numerous non-Western cultures that preferred their own standards of beauty even after exposure to Europeans, noting that the distinct Hottentot female anatomy and physical enhancements represent a type of beauty greatly encouraged by the males (2:329). He further cites the Somali practice of judging the beauty of females by first examining their posteriors (2:330). The black Venus, however parodic a principle to other Westerners, was very real to Darwin.

Du Bois argued a Darwinian position in his race advocacy, perhaps unknowingly. In his 1920 essay "The Damnation of Women," Du Bois reflected on the world's demand that white women be beautiful and ornamental, while defining black women as ugly: "when the white world objects to black women because it does not consider them beautiful, the black world of right asks two questions: 'What is beauty?' and, 'Suppose you think them ugly, what then? If ugliness and unconventionality and eccentricity of face and deed do not hinder men from doing the world's work and reaping the world's reward, why should it hinder women?'" (*W. E. B. Du Bois: A Reader*, 310). Du Bois's approach grew more sophisticated in his piece "Social Equality and Marriage" (1922), where he argued against intermarriage on the grounds that each population had its own standard of somatic beauty, and therefore "the preservation and development of this interesting and stimulating variety in mankind is a great human duty" (*W. E. B. Du Bois: A Reader*, 374). In short, blacks *ought* to practice race chastity to conserve variety and avoid the "dead level sameness" of hybridity (373). Du Bois's appeal to "differences of taste as to human types of . . . beauty" shows an increased assuredness in the cultural pluralist argument but a simplistic understanding of genetics, if he truly believed that intermarriage would decrease variety. But if William B. Smith could declare that blacks merited extinction on the grounds that "*Selection*" produced "the preservation of favoured individuals and favoured races" (13), Du Bois would counter that black survival had always rested and would continue to rest with the *selection* of black womanhood as a ritual confirmation of the wisdom of the ages.

In his poetry, short sketches, and other creative efforts, Du Bois moved steadily toward an enunciation of an aesthetic revaluation of black womanhood, to the extent of overloading female bodies with allegorical significance. He honed the mythic images of the white female as embodiment of the temptation to participate in Western spiritual decline, and of the black female as the presiding race genius. In conjunction with a radical shift in color symbolism attached to these figures, he made the whiteness of the witch synonymous with death, disease, and destruction and switched the onus of black race corruption away from the black female. The black mother's reverential presentation accords with her embodiment of self-sacrifice, while the Devil's white angel, offering personal success at the expense of the race, embodies spiritual death. Although he did not dispense with the madonna/whore classification system as such, despite his revaluation of the color symbolism, Du Bois's sociologically driven schema gradually replaced the language of women's natures with a language of role socialization.

His 1906 poem "A Litany of Atlanta" was written in response to the Atlanta riots of that year as Du Bois traveled back to the city from his research project in Alabama. Describing Atlanta itself as a female demon, "from [whose] loins sprang twin Murder and / Black Hate," Du Bois calls upon a "Silent" and perhaps even "sleeping" or "dead" God to curse the black "devils" whom the news accounts had blamed for the "epidemic" of rapes that touched off the rioting: "When our devils do deviltry, curse Thou the doer and the deed / . . . do to them all and more that [sic] ever they have done to / innocence and weakness, to womanhood and home" (*Creative Writings*, 7).[17] But pursuing a line of argumentation he had begun in *The Souls*, Du Bois refused to let denunciations of black rapists go without referring to the "hereditary weight of a mass of corruption from white adulterers, threatening almost the obliteration of the Negro home" (*Souls*, 6). Du Bois expresses near despair in wondering, "Surely Thou too are not white, O Lord, a pale, bloodless, heartless / thing?"—as if by asking a negative question, he wills into being a concept of black divinity.

This poem, "Done at Atlanta, in the Day of Death, 1906," reflects an important turn in Du Bois's mythic representations. The ironic questioning of God's "race" both stimulated experimentation with the concept of a black God and inaugurated in African American literature a black aesthetic that reverses the typical elevation of whiteness as the highest attainment of goodness, beauty, and truth. Ethiopianists had long established the basis for a black God, but Du Bois was the first important literary artist to "read" racial features of skin color through a reversed valuation. Du Bois depicted arrogant pride in whiteness as an absence of humanity, a lack of "soul," while blackness signified vitality. Thus, in "The Song of the Smoke" (1907), he not only gave voice to an emphatically black protagonist ("I am the Smoke King / I am black!"), but his black king is a mythologist who, like Du Bois, "whiten[s]" black men and "blacken[s]" whites: "I am daubing God in night, / I am swabbing Hell in white" (*Creative Writings*, 10–11). This mythological process involves the rewriting of history from a black viewpoint, "For blackness was ancient ere whiteness began." "The Song of the Smoke King" is Ethiopianism with a vengeance, bringing to bear a more fully developed historical perspective to supplant Du Bois's naive references to "race childhood" in *The Souls*.

In a 1905 prose piece, Du Bois had approached the figure of embodied blackness with a restrained self-consciousness. Mother Earth questions her daughter "Ethiopia" about her comparative lack of achievement: "Ethiopia, my little daughter, why hast thou lingered and loitered in the Sun? See thy tall sisters, pale and blue of eye—see thy strong brothers, shrewd and slippery haired—see what they have done! Behold their gardens and their magic, their halls and wonder wheels! Behold their Gold, Gold, Gold!"[18] Ethiopia can, at this stage, offer only flowers, "the echo of a Song's song," humility, and finally, a promise of

"Stories and Songs" in the future to tell of her experiences. But two years later, Du Bois's "The Burden of Black Women" would, applying the confidence gained from his new aesthetic proclaimed in "The Smoke King," reconsider the relation between "Ethiopia" and her siblings. Du Bois, by this time, had moved beyond the scolding of black women for holding the race back, to an image of black womanhood more in keeping with its spiritual mission. Although sociology could serve the quantitative aims of black motherhood's first function, physical motherhood, Du Bois was clear on the failure of sociology even to address spiritual motherhood. Du Bois the visionary, then, sought to define this function appropriately in the language of the "soul," of "wisdom clothed in beauty" (that is, "Truth X Beauty"): poetry (*Creative Writings*, x). "The Burden of Black Women" represents the transformation of Rising Africa from obedient "daughter" to "Mother of God," an awakening to a life calling that redeems the self and the world. The poem opens with an invocation to the "Dark daughter of the lotus leaves" who is the "Wan spirit of a prisoned soul a-panting to be / free" to rise up and claim her heritage: "Crying: Awake, O ancient race! Wailing: O woman arise!" (*Creative Writings*, 12).

This dreamer's awakening, though, is stifled by the white world, specifically, "the Burden of white men." At the moment that the world spirit calls out to the race to give its message, then, the corruption of black womanhood by white men hinders that awakening. Here we are in familiar territory, as Du Bois details the corruptions and its attendant consequences for race development:

> The White World's vermin and filth:
>   All the dirt of London,
>   All the scum of New York;
>   Valiant spoilers of women
>   And conquerors of unarmed men;
>   Shameless breeders of bastards
>   Drunk with the greed of gold.
>   Baiting their blood-stained hooks
>   With cant for the souls of the simple,
>   Bearing the White Man's Burden
>   Of Liquor and Lust and Lies! (12–13)

The rigorous denunciation of the West raises the question of why Du Bois, seeing the "modern" worlds in these terms, should want blacks to join it. The very enumeration of the white world's corruptions convulses the speaker with anger: "I hate them, Oh! / I hate them well, / I hate them, Christ! / As I hate Hell" (13).

Here Du Bois elaborates on his claim that blackness was "ancient ere whiteness began." It was a point that Du Bois was to make with greater conviction in the coming years, that whites had benefited from earlier civilizations of dark peoples and then, while at the pinnacle of their world power, began to rewrite history to support the claim that civilization was synonymous with white skin, and savagery with dark. "Who raised the fools to their glory / But black men of Egypt and Ind?" he asks. This reading of history makes "Ethiopia," as personification of Africa, the "mother" of civilization. Du Bois adds the warning that all the despised peoples of the dark world—blacks, Chinese, the Hebrews, and the "mongrels of Rome and Greece"—had "raised the boasters" and, when they got tired of the boasting, would "drag them down again." This "shearing" of the "Devil's strength" would culminate in the "married maiden, Mother of God, / Bid[ding] the Black Christ be born!" Du Bois's anger over the social and political developments in America had moved him, only four years after The Souls, to a much more pessimistic vision of the possibility for racial coexistence, given the speaker's declaration that "If I were God / I'd sound their knell / This day!" In that same month's issue of the Horizon, Du Bois included a poem for blacks to use as a substitute when singing "My Country 'Tis of Thee," which begins "My country 'tis of thee, / Late land of slavery / Of thee I sing." [19]

But the very next month, December 1907, almost as if in atonement for this outburst, Du Bois published a poem that reads almost like a warning to himself not to let anger drive him to the three temptations he enumerated in The Souls—Hate, Despair, and Doubt (Souls, 152). The poem "Death" is a parable— a wedding of a dark warrior to Death in female form: "the maid / Stands motionless—her pallid form / Swathed in the cold and clinging night" (Creative Writings, 16). This poem is the prototype of James Weldon Johnson's "The White Witch," published seven years later in Du Bois's own Crisis magazine. [20] The "bold black face" of the warrior strikingly announces Du Bois's new aesthetic. "World and Warrior, Maid and Mist, / Met each other—met and kissed." In the confrontation between white witch and black warrior, the maid acts out the classic role of the "White Goddess," the muse of all "true" poetry in Robert Graves's formulation. [21] The kiss, like the witch's withering touch or evil eye, proves deadly to the warrior just as the hate, despair, and doubt that bedevil the poet of black national striving might push him, Du Bois felt, toward a fatal embrace of the very spiritual deadness he wished to destroy. More than the "burden of white men," the white witch would become the allegory of a tempting but corrupt white civilization that must be resisted in order to be transcended.

In the months of November and December 1907, Du Bois had mapped out his spiritual alternatives through imaginative encounters with these two female forms, the black mother of the dark world epiphany and the pale white maiden of death. In April 1907, Du Bois had made a preliminary sketch of the figures as the old black hag and the white lady of "Wittekind." These women conduct a mock battle for the racial destiny of South Carolina. In this contest, the witchlike black hag gets the better of the white lady, who thinks that the arrival of six hundred white servants and laborers aboard the ship "Wittekind" will tilt the balance in favor of white numerical superiority, until the hag informs her that eighteen thousand black babies had been born in Carolina in the last six months (*Creative Writings*, 63). Important to the allegorical intent is the name of the ship, suggesting the historical figure Hermann Witekind, who wrote a treatise on witchcraft in sixteenth-century Germany (Carlo Ginzburg, 156–58). In pitting the black woman's generative powers against the transatlantic transport of Europeans, Du Bois for the first time, perhaps, articulated a vision of black national emergence as a battle between the organic magic of black motherhood and the technological witchcraft of white civilization.

In poems published in February and March 1908, Du Bois began to elaborate on and codify these feminized forces. In "The Song of America," he personified America as the "Great I Will," leaving no doubt that the pallid maid "Death" in the earlier work was the soul image of white America, and explains why she signifies death for the black warrior:

> I doom, I live, I will,
> I take, I lie, I kill!
> I rend and rear
> In deserts drear—
> I build and burrow well.
> With wrack and rue
> I hound and hew
> On founding stones in Hell:
> My Temples rise
> And split the Skies,
> My winged wheels do tell

The woven wonders of my hand,
The witch-work of my skill!
I writhe, I rave,
I chain the Slave
I do the deed, I kill!
Now what care I
For God or Lie?
I am the great
I WILL. (*Creative Writings*, 18)

Du Bois discovered in the image of the "witch-working" American spirit, living and building in "deserts drear," the perfect vehicle for his Faustian theme.

But Du Bois particularizes the image by making the American spirit of manifest destiny the engine of its mythic machinery, for if there were an inherent temptation in American culture for the race builder, it would be the "can-do" spirit of American pragmatism, which, isolated from any sustaining purpose but self-aggrandizement, Du Bois saw as spiritually corrupting. America's apotheosis as the "Great I Will" in Du Bois's poetry revived and extended the old iconic tradition figuring America as a cannibal female, an "American Amazon" often depicted as carrying the severed head or limbs of her human victims in many of the earliest artistic renderings of the new continent. Hugh Honour's *The New Golden Land* (1975) documents European perspectives on America, tracing the earliest imaginings of America as a naked female headhunter in the age of discovery to later allegorical renditions of the nation as a young female social climber "cannibalizing" the European aristocracy in the late Victorian period (84–89, 248–53), a figure called *"die Dollarprinzessin"* — "the Bitch Goddess Success worshiped in the Gilded Age and beyond," in the words of Martha Banta (487).

Against the "dazzling opportunities" laid out before the individual of talent by this culture, Du Bois offered the counterimage of sacrifice and patient striving, the black madonna. In "Ave! Maria!," published one month after "The Song of America," Du Bois returned to this image as his inspirational messenger of race commitment and collective agency. Anchored by the black woman's experience of sorrow in America, this icon achieves redemption through good works and faith in the human potential for change. Thus, the "Mother-maid" is a "Mother of Miracles" — an alternative developmental path to the witch's philosophy of more, better, sooner. In "Ave! Maria!" Du Bois calls upon this race mother to "gather" in the "Daughter [*sic*] of Sin": "Gather them in!" (*Creative Writings*, 19).

His use of "Maria" rather than the more usual honorifics suggests the dual possibility of Mary as virgin mother and as Mary Magdalen, to say nothing of the
connections to his own mother, Mary Burghardt. In "The Prayer of the Bantu,"
she is called "Spirit of Wonder, / Daughter of Thunder" and "Adorable One"
(*Creative Writings*, 20). In the brief sketch "The Woman," she is the black woman
pleading before the "Great White Throne" of the king that she is not worthy to
be "Bride of God," until God "swept the veiling of his face aside and lifted up
the light of his countenance upon her and lo! it was black." (*Creative Writings*,
78). In a 1913 pageant, "The People of People and Their Gifts to Men," she appears first as the "Veiled Woman," who, holding Fire in her right hand and Iron
in her left, inaugurates humanity's slow climb into civilization. (*Creative Writings*, 1). At the end of the pageant, she reappears with the other black givers of
gifts as "the All-Mother, formerly the Veiled Woman, now unveiled in her char-
iot with her dancing brood, and the bust of Lincoln at her side" (4).

In these allegories of the white witch and black madonna, Du Bois hinted at
the dramatic potential inherent in the critical functions of the white female,
black female, and black male bodies in the social maintenance of race difference
and all that it entailed, organizing his own and others' creative works around a
narrative core articulating the desires, resistance, and embedded ambivalence of
the American race dilemma. Counterpointing the alienating spirit of American
materialism to the soul-preserving agency of black motherhood, Du Bois designed a narrative frame wherein the black nation builder would be forced to
choose allegiance with white American cultural values or with an evolving racial
epic of African redemption in America. Du Bois overdetermined his preferred
choice for the race protagonist by opposing a fickle, sometimes fatal white bride
to a nurturing black mother, and conveyed moral urgency through the free adaptation of Christian symbolism to a secular variety of spiritual agency. Adapting
the marriage plot to his brand of ethical race striving, Du Bois revised the type of
the fatal white woman to encompass a whiteness of "spirit" as well as of body.
This required the reinvention of the mulatta as a spiritually "white" though
legally "black" woman who tempts the quester to "spiritual amalgamation" without raising the thorny question of intermarriage.

The Quest of the Silver Fleece

W. E. B. Du Bois's first novel is a tale of race development in the South that takes
a black soul quester through a series of trying experiences in order to test his

commitment and worthiness. Carrying a name like Blessed Alwyn, he cannot be seen as anything other than a figure in a passion play. His name ironically echoes that of the novel's "black" white witch, Caroline Wynn, who refuses to leave the likelihood of "winning" to chance. She tests Blessed (Bles, for short) in his conviction that "all" should "win," rather than just the ambitious few, and in the process, he learns important spiritual lessons on black womanhood, the temptations of leadership, and the paralyzing power of the veil.

The novel's chief black mother—Elspeth—is not, ironically, the story's black madonna; instead, she is the novel's black Venus as witch—the image of sexually depraved black womanhood still under the thrall of slave immorality. Her daughter Zora, whom she has raised in a house in the swamp, becomes the novel's Madonna-without-child. The child of a prostitute, driven into prostitution herself by Elspeth to service the white planter class of Tooms County, Alabama, Zora bodies forth "The Burden of Black Women," which presented a dilemma for the aspiring black patriarchy (52). Bles, who wants to answer the spiritual call of Zora by marrying her, has been taught morality by the teachers at Mrs. Smith's school but little of the history of black womanhood or of the primacy of spirit in making decisions. Zora sees the white world as devoid of spirituality and therefore looks askance at its profession of morality because she, unlike Bles, has seen white depravity up close in the swamp. When Bles tries to coax the wild swamp girl who has befriended him to go to school, she replies that whites don't have all the answers: "They don't really rule; they just thinks they rule. They just got things,—heavy dead things. We black folks is got the *spirit*. . . . Black folks is wonderful" (46).

Such a thematically freighted observation by a twelve-year-old is symptomatic of her rigidly symbolic function, limiting the extent of her development through the novel and helping to center all narrative tension on the experiences of the male quester, Bles. Zora's only real changes are superficial ones, in keeping with Du Bois's emphasis on black womanhood's latent, unconscious spiritual gift. Paradoxically, only her later transformation into a "lady" permits Bles to look past appearances deeply enough to recover his initial belief in her essential goodness. But through characters such as Mary Taylor, Caroline Wynn, and Mrs. Vanderpool, Du Bois portrays white ladyhood as merely a refinement that either embellishes a stout soul or disguises a weak one. Each of these women is potentially a nurturer of Bles's soul striving, but only Zora becomes that soul-sustaining force in his life. The others become white witches whose selfish greed, ideological blindness, or ambition causes them to exploit Bles's trusting nature to further their own ends.

Bles's first instinct is to be the agent of Zora's salvation, until he succumbs to double consciousness, "seeing" her through the eyes of whites as a sexually corrupt figure of social scorn. Bles has brought Zora to Mrs. Smith's school and instructed her in Christian ethics in the spirit of mutual uplift. He constructs a canopy of branches and leaves to cover her "throne" in a black oak tree, turning it into a shrine where Zora could sit "hidden and alone in silent ecstasy." Bles completes the shrine by placing "on the rough main trunk, a little picture in blue and gold of Bougereau's Madonna" (97). In her contemplation of the meaning of the Madonna's whiteness and her virgin motherhood, Zora asks, "What's purity—just whiteness?" (98). Zora interprets Bles's response, that purity means "being good—just as good as a woman knows how," as an endorsement of her own reformed behavior since coming under Bles's tutelage. Later, Du Bois sums up the significance of Zora's force as a "latent" motherhood: "She would, unhindered, develop to a brilliant, sumptuous womanhood; proud, conquering, full-blooded, and deep-bosomed—a passionate mother of men. Herein lay all her early wildness and strangeness. Herein lay, as yet half hidden, dimly sensed and all unspoken, the power of a mighty all-compelling love for one human soul, and, through it, for all the souls of men" (125). Bles's dim awareness of the possibility of a "mightier mingling of souls" (126) with Zora becomes an unconscious refuge from his growing sensitivity to the veil of race, which his education has more clearly defined for him. When Mary Taylor, a teacher at Miss Smith's school for black children, and Harry Cresswell, heir to the largest cotton plantation in the county, chance upon Bles and Zora alone in the woods, locked in an innocent embrace, Cresswell's remark that Zora is "notorious" falls "like a blow" on the pair (166).

Bles soon discovers that the contempt for Zora expressed by Cresswell is mysteriously connected to the veil of race that has taken so much of his youthful innocence from him, and "he dared not question the awful shape that sat somewhere, cold and still, behind his soul" (167). That shape emerges, however, as one of the Du Boisian three mortal temptations—"shivering doubt" (167)—when Mary Taylor joins in Cresswell's denunciation of Zora: "'It's a damned lie!' he shouted to the trees. '*Is it?—is it?*' chirped the birds. . . . '*Is it?—is it?*' whispered the devils within" (168). "'I thought you knew,'" Zora vainly argues, "'and I thought that—that purity was just *wanting* to be pure.'" With this resolution of his doubt and the dissipation of his "livid anger" at Zora, Bles is left to grapple with the third deadly sin of the soul striver, "despair" (171).

The separation of Zora and Bles by the revelation of her sexual history and his inability to withstand the scorn of the white world on her behalf marks a divergence in their paths but not a disconnection. The narrative focuses thereafter on the compact of the demons and the gathering force of the white witches over the fates of the pair. In John Taylor and Harry Cresswell, Du Bois has created the would-be "Wizard of the North" and the demon of the South, who, together, attempt to control the economics of the black belt. They seal their alliance by conventionally swapping sisters as wives, after Mary Taylor, John's sister, allows her earlier idealism on behalf of Miss Smith's colored school to erode in the face of a life of leisure as Mrs. Harry Cresswell. She aligns herself from this point on with forces who seem intent on monopolizing black education in the South to move it toward the Booker T. Washington model of industrial training—a prospect that pleases the bigot Cresswell and the industrialist Taylor, who both require a docile black labor pool for their plans to succeed. Taylor has no real fear of a black elite, since by all indications, they will become pawns in his power game, too: "A few of them with brains will help us rule the rest with money" (390). The task for Zora, who has fallen from her status as Bles's Madonna to become Mrs. Vanderpool's black "Venus of the Roadside," is to help Miss Smith protect her program of unrestricted black education against the united interests of the capitalists and the philanthropists who want to turn the school into a Tuskegee-style "hearts and hands" institution, an "intelligence office for furnishing servants to the nation" (177).

Bles, meanwhile, goes off to Washington, D.C., to pursue a civil service position, where he meets Caroline Wynn, a woman "so cold and formal and precise, without heart or marrow" (235), that Bles at first thinks she is a white woman. A schoolteacher in Washington, Wynn must play politics to keep her position. She is one of the class of alienated blacks whose "curious coldness and aloofness" make them seem "like black white people—strangers in way and thought" (240) to Bles. Wynn's coldness comes of a despair brought on by discrimination, but characteristic of her class, all of her allusions to the color line are veiled in a language that Bles cannot decipher. She therefore represents the type whose "double-consciousness" "give[s] rise to double words and double ideals," tempting her to "pretence" and "hypocrisy" (Souls, 142). She surprises Bles with her cynicism, letting him see gradually that she "had little faith in Truth and Goodness and Love" (263). She leaves him aghast with her story of how she finessed a school board appointment from a judge who had demanded sexual favors in return for the job, and when Bles protests at her continued association with him, she replies: "What would you have? I use the world; I did not make it; I did not choose it. He is the world. Through him I earn my bread and butter" (265). Unwilling to strive to reform the world, she is the novel's best example of a tenor in black social life that caused Du Bois to remark in *The Souls* that "the price of culture is a lie" (144).

Wynn's spiritual concubinage with the white patriarchy raises the question of "purity" in a fashion that ennobles Zora, who has simply lacked moral training growing up under Elspeth in the swamp. Caroline Wynn's literal virginity serves merely to emphasize her lack of passion and her commodification of chastity to secure for herself the most politically advantageous marriage. Her refusal to strive against injustice, but merely to turn it to her advantage, eventually turns her, in the city of "Washington," to thoughts of power politics: "Why not take this young man in hand and make a Negro leader of him—a protagonist of ten millions? . . . Would he be amenable to her training and become worldly wise?" (269). The temptation that Wynn will offer to Bles is the "dazzling opportunity" of political race leadership—the course for which he has prepared all his early adulthood— but even she is uncertain of how he will respond to the price.

Zora, meantime, has been taken in hand by another cynic, the world-weary Mrs. Vanderpool. "Had she been compelled to earn a living she would have made a successful teacher or manipulator of men." But Mrs. Vanderpool, who was "essentially . . . unmoral, . . . stooped to no intrigue, because none interested her" (247). Only in the prospect of "making something out of" Zora does she show any interest in life. In their first meeting, Zora strikes a chord in Mrs. Vanderpool's imagination, sending her a vision of Zora that confirms her image of the girl as the "Venus of the Roadside": "her mind seemed to leap backward a thousand years; back to a simpler, primal day when she herself, white, frail, and fettered, stood before the dusky magnificence of some bejewelled barbarian queen and sought to justify herself" (223). Mrs. Vanderpool's intimation that, in some important sense, Zora had been sent to judge her forces her to take note of Zora as a person, and not merely a black girl who needs to be trained for a career of serving whites. Ultimately this recognition of common humanity across the color line allows this "tired woman of fashion" to make Zora her personal companion, and within a week she finds herself sinking back "contentedly into Zora's strong arms" (225). Du Bois's hint that Mrs. Vanderpool's interest in Zora is erotic creates a distinct contrast to Bles's passionless relationship with Caroline Wynn. Because the physical contact between the women is in the tradition of black female nurturance, he is freer to explore the witch's sexual attraction to a dark body than he would have been with a heterosexual pair.

The story lines intersect when Bles, after stumping for the Republican Party to get out the black vote in a close presidential election, comes up for an unsought political reward. Caroline Wynn, seeking to maneuver Bles into a high government position that she can control through him, suggests to the influential Senator Smith, brother of the school founder Miss Smith, that Bles receive a position as register of the Treasury. But unknown to her, Zora has also been at work, using her influence with Mrs. Vanderpool to try to get Bles considered for an unprecedented cabinet appointment as the first black secretary of the Treasury.[22] Zora's plan has much in common with Caroline's, but with the very different motivation of redeeming his faith in black womanhood. With redemption as her only reward for helping Bles to the top, Zora still dreams a greater dream for him than does the worldly wise and personally ambitious Caroline Wynn.

Du Bois's division of women into forces for good and evil stems from a Victorian mind-set that limited women's freedom of movement and broadly classified women according to their degree of adherence to prescribed social roles. Not encouraged to be agents of their own destinies, they were trained to pursue their life objectives through men. Whatever social prominence they achieved was generally a reflection of their ability to turn appearance, reputation, or wealth into power over influential men. This is, of course, a static view of society and certainly not reflective of universal female experience. But it was a view of society that Du Bois largely shared for much of his life, and, because black women would be judged by it whether or not they accepted its assumptions about gender roles, Du Bois felt that concessions had to be made to it. One concession, as he made clear in "The Work of Negro Women in Society," was that black patriarchal interests would have to be secured before an expanded social role for women could be entertained.

Still, Du Bois showed some impatience with this division of labor in *The Quest*. In contrast to his unfavorable treatment of schemers like Caroline Wynn and Mrs. Vanderpool, who are obsessed with power, he admits the necessity of Zora and Miss Smith engaging in politics in selfless causes. Later, he would denounce social limitations on women to domestic roles in "The Damnation of Women," proclaiming that the "horror of free womanhood must pass if we are ever to be rid of the bestiality of free manhood; not by guarding the weak in weakness do we gain strength, but by making weakness free and strong" (*Darkwater*, 165). Pointing to the important work done by women in the war years after publication of *The Quest*, Du Bois explained his new conviction that the world was better off with husbandless black working mothers than with childless white wives languishing in high fashion (*Darkwater*, 184–85).[23]

Prior to this awakening, though, Du Bois's moralistic dyad of women's roles, depending on whether they influenced men to do uplifting or selfish deeds, served as a reliable frame for his witch/madonna dichotomy. Women who wished social redemption would have to restrain their activity to the reproduction, education, and spiritual encouragement of males. In a forecast of his criticism of the childless white odalisques of the North in *Darkwater*, Du Bois in *The Quest* distinguished Caroline Wynn from Zora by their attitudes toward the Du Boisian prime directive, "motherhood." "It is a deep ethical query, is it not, how far one has the right to bear black children to the world in the Land of the Free and the home of the brave," says Caroline (278). She laughs when Bles offers that having children means more fighters for the cause, but Bles is willing to overlook this attitude. As opposed to the swampland of black female unchastity from which Zora arose, Bles's aspirations in Washington become focused on considering how the stylish Caroline "would complete a house" (279). "He kept thinking what a mistress of a mansion she would make" (280), and seeing his eyes "surveying her," as he would a set of furniture, she smiles encouragement. Childless idealists like Zora and Miss Smith, on the other hand, were investing their energies in the education of black youth, rather than schemes of occupying the "big house."

When the moment of crisis comes for Bles, the women indirectly compete for his soul. After it becomes clear that the price of his appointment to the cabinet will be abandonment of his principled defense of black civil rights, Bles turns to Caroline, whose speech makes clear that it is within his power to become what Booker T. Washington was—the political boss of black America: "Mr. Alwyn, the line between virtue and foolishness is dim and wavering, and I should hate to see you lost in that marshy borderland. By a streak of extraordinary luck you have gained the political leadership of Negroes in America. Here's your chance to lead your people, and you stand here blinking and hesitating. Be a man!" (277). To make this veiled reference to Washington more pointed, Du Bois has Tom Teerswell, a longtime suitor of Caroline's, plant the lie that Bles has been bribed to betray black civil rights for a six-thousand-dollar-a-year job with the *Colored American*, once the magazine had become secretly bought out and controlled by Washington's Tuskegee Machine.[24] When Teerswell, Cresswell, and assorted other self-servers conspire to isolate Bles from his political base, he turns again to Caroline, wondering, "I want to do the best thing, but I'm puzzled. I wonder if

I'm selling my birthright for six thousand dollars?" (316). Caroline's answer says all we need to know about her allegiances: "In case of doubt, do it."

Zora, though, has been watching from the shadows, and she seizes the moment of Bles's uncertainty to send him an anonymous message of hope, a quotation from Henley's "Invictus," that he is "the captain of [his] soul" (318). Though her "better self" really wants Bles to stand on principle and become a man whom she can respect but not marry with into a life of poverty, Caroline decides that she, in fact, does not want Bles to "be a man." She goes to Mrs. Vanderpool to persuade her to use her influence to make Bles sell out his ideals, putting the white woman in the curious position of being asked by Zora to help Bles get his position without cost to his manhood, and then by Caroline to force him to "bow to the yoke" (319). When Bles loses the appointment by refusing to compromise himself, it means that he has ignored the entreaties of Caroline Wynn and Mrs. Vanderpool, obeying instead the "Voice from nowhere calling to him," telling him that "Right always triumphs" (328).

On hearing that Bles was engaged to Caroline, Zora had wandered into a church and heard there a message—in effect, Du Bois's favorite sermon—that gives her the focus to continue her efforts on Bles's behalf, the lesson of "Supreme Sacrifice": "Only in a world of selves, infinite, endless, eternal world on world of selves—only in their vast good is true salvation. The good of others is our true good; work for others; not for *your* salvation, but the salvation of the world. . . . Go down to the South where we writhe. Strive—work—build—hew—lead—inspire!" (295). In answering this call to sacrifice, Zora understands that she must guide Bles past the temptation she has inadvertently caused to be thrown in his path. The only way for "all" blacks to "win" is for Bles to lose the appointment as the "chosen" black who will control the others. She understands too that Mrs. Vanderpool has also been willing to sacrifice—to sacrifice Zora, that is—in the hope of salvaging a political appointment for her husband. Zora's "Voice from nowhere" represents a "call" to Bles's soul to stand against the witch whom he wants to marry and the witch whom Zora serves. After Mrs. Vanderpool's double cross, Zora leaves her, wondering, "Where was the poor spoiled woman? Who was putting her to bed and smoothing the pillow? Who was caring for her, and what was she doing?" (335). It happens that Mrs. Vanderpool was in the process of acting on her vow that her husband would be confirmed ambassador to France "'if I have to mortgage my immortal soul'" (336). She wins the battle but loses the war when her husband, upon commission to the post, dies of apoplexy.

The novel's final movement takes place in Toomsville, again, as Bles returns to take a position with Miss Smith's school, and Zora, using Mrs. Vanderpool's conscience money to make good her commitment to protect all black girls from the poverty and corruption to which she was subjected, devises an intricate plan for a communalistic cooperative that would ensure the future of black economic striving, the safety of black girls, and the educational autonomy of the Smith school. At the center of her design is the "Home [for girls] and the School" (404), capitalized, no doubt, to give emphasis to Du Bois's bedrock institutions of race development. But before Zora commits this vision to Bles's direction, she rescues him from yet another of the witches, Mary Taylor Cresswell, who has returned from Washington.

Mary has lost a child after being infected with her husband's syphilis, and she has lost her youth and beauty in the process. After her husband emotionally abandons her, she revives her fantasy that Bles is secretly in love with her, and, unwilling to face her emotions, she exposes him to danger by inviting him into the home she shares with her father-in-law, Colonel Cresswell. But Zora saves Bles from the vindictiveness of Mary, who, after he disappoints her romantic expectations by telling her that he still loves Zora, makes it possible for Colonel Cresswell to kill Bles in the name of protecting white womanhood. Zora trades on her own bad reputation with the Cresswells and the general low esteem in which black women were held to save Bles from Cresswell, who has been look-ing for an excuse to put Bles "in his place." Her subjection of herself to humili-ation to save his life reverses the last vestiges of Bles's double consciousness, opening his eyes to the true worth of black womanhood, which, in addition to the burden of sexual exploitation by whites, has had to endure the contempt of black men.

When Zora brings Bles to her "den" to secure his commitment to her devel-opment plan, he sees there a representation of her soul: "A thick green rag-carpet covered the floor; a few pictures were on the walls—a Madonna, a scene of mad careering horses, and some sad baby faces. The room was a unity; things fitted together" (399). Bles does not quite understand the significance of the shrine, despite its clear connection to the bower he had built for Zora in the swamp years before. He does not read the shrine's thwarted domesticity—its Madonna flanked by the faces of unborn children—as a plea for redemption in matri-mony; in fact, Bles decides that he has to sacrifice his dream of winning Zora back to him in order to make her dream of communal development a reality. In the end, their love prevails, in spite of the continued meddling of Mary and the

Colonel Cresswell's bargain with the "evil spirit" of race prejudice reminiscent of Carteret's role in Chesnutt's *The Marrow of Tradition*. Colonel Cresswell unleashes the oppressed poor whites to destroy the black development project as a dangerous experiment in social equality (418). Sparked by the news of white women and children mixing with blacks at Zora's home for girls, the poor whites, afraid of competing with blacks economically, burn, loot, riot, and lynch.

In kneeling before the injured embodiment of black womanhood and proclaiming his unworthiness of Zora, Bles redeems her from the part he has played in maintaining her social stigma, and fulfills the latent Madonna in her. Du Bois ends on a note of realistic uncertainty of whether the climate of race hatred in the South would permit black development to go unchallenged by white violence, but with hope that strivers like Zora and Bles would continue the fight.

Some scholars have applauded Du Bois's creation of a hero and heroine who are dark skinned, and especially, a dark-skinned woman who is beautiful because of her non-Caucasian facial features.[25] Indeed, Du Bois's scene in which Bles "blazes" Zora in near-Shakespearean stychomythia, trailing iambs throughout, contains elements that, if placed unaltered in a minstrel routine, would have been perceived by white audiences as drolly comic:

> "You are tall and bend like grasses on the swamp," he said.
> "And yet look up to you," she murmured.
> "Your eyes are darkness dressed in night."
> "To see you brighter, dear," she said.
> "Your little hands are much too frail for work."
> "They must grow larger, then, and soon."
> "Your feet are far too small to travel on."
> "They'll travel on to you—that's far enough."
> Your lips—your full and purple lips—were made alone for kissing, not for words."
> "They'll do for both." (165–66)

When Bles touches her hair, Zora becomes self-conscious, saying, "It does not fly with sunlight," which gives Bles the opportunity to respond, "No. . . . It sits and listens to the night."

Du Bois's adoration of the black body is not idle, for to praise Zora's height and her smallness of feet and hands is deliberately to contradict the catalog of somatic deformities that passed for objective fact in the literature of race difference. And to single out for attention her "midnight" eyes, "full and purple lips," and her mass of hair, sitting on her forehead "like some shadowed halo" (124), was to claim as beautiful features that were the specific objects of white sarcasm as far back as Shakespeare's antiblazon, Sonnet 130: "My Mistress' Eyes Are Nothing Like the Sun." Ironically, Bles would go on to take away Zora's beauty by the end of this very scene, when, rather than trust his own reading, he allows Harry Cresswell and Mary Taylor to veil Zora's beauty from him behind their hypocritical morality. Du Bois was adamant in "The Damnation of Women" that white standards of beauty held black women in a particularly difficult position, since women who are not "pink and white and straight-haired" will not have their message heard in a world that asks "that a woman primarily be pretty" (*Darkwater*, 183, 184). Bles's contemplation of Zora's physical perfection qualifies, then, as what Du Bois referred to as "the cultural and spiritual desire to be one's self without interference from others." The interference of whites in Bles and Zora's idyll distorts Bles's ability to receive Zora's "message," destroying "that anarchy of the spirit which is inevitably the goal of all consciousness" (*Dusk*, 134). Bles's "anarchy of spirit" represents a race idealism that, once surrendered, will take him much subsequent striving to regain.

CHAPTER EIGHT

The Whiteness of the Witch

Is this the life you grudge us, O knightly America? . . . Are you afraid lest
peering from this high Pisgah, between Philistine and Amalekite, we sight
the Promised Land?
 —W. E. B. Du Bois, *The Souls of Black Folk*

New York City is the most fatally fascinating thing in America. She sits like
a great witch at the gate of the country.
 —James Weldon Johnson, *The Autobiography of an Ex-Colored Man*

James Weldon Johnson's contribution to the fatal white female and sacrificial
black mother motifs in African American literature would rely more heavily on
Western tradition than Du Bois did, and though less explicitly messianic, his allegorical treatments of the coming of the black patriarch would retain and expand on the aesthetic and philosophical choices required of a black striver faced
with the changed circumstance of a rapidly urbanizing twentieth-century America. Contributing to these representations was, as Robert Graves explains in *The
White Goddess* (1948), an entire Western tradition depicting feminine archetypes as the coincidence of opposites, objects of fear and desire. In a description
that identifies the Western antecedents of the dual archetypes, Graves portrays
the figure he calls the "Triple Goddess" as both Muse and demon: "The Goddess is a lovely, slender woman with a hooked nose, deathly pale face, lips red as
rowan-berries, startlingly blue eyes and long fair hair; she will suddenly transform herself into sow, mare, bitch, vixen, she-ass, weasel, serpent, owl, she-wolf,
tigress, mermaid or loathsome hag" (24).

Graves's description of the goddess's Aryan features obscures her origins, which he vaguely traces to Mesopotamia. He is by his own admission more interested in the Celtic representations of the goddess, but he does quote Apuleus, who traces her ultimately to Egypt. When the goddess speaks to Apuleus, she praises the Egyptians as "excellent in all kind of ancient doctrine and by their proper ceremonies accustom to worship me, do call me by my true name, Queen Isis" (Graves, 73). Isis, though, is for Graves but one of the incarnations of the goddess. His etymology of Isis connects her to the "onomatopoeic Asianic word, *Ish-ish*, meaning 'She who weeps,'" making her the "pre-Christian original of the *Mater Dolorosa.*" As Isis triumphs by bringing forth life from the body of death (her brother/husband Osiris), she also weeps for that death (337). Her incarnation as Io reveals the basis of Graves's designation of her as "Triple Goddess": "the New Moon is the white goddess of birth and growth; the Full Moon, the red goddess of love and battle; the Old Moon, the black goddess of death and divination" (70). In this tradition of the lunar goddess's mutability lies the secret of the multiple faces of the goddess. Graves suggests that her colors, white, red, and black, through time evolved into white, red, and dark blue (70).

Still, Graves's insistence that white is the goddess's "principal colour" because of her association with the new moon of birth and growth does not square with her nightmarish figure. Admitting the ambivalence of the associations, he arrives again at a union of opposites: "In one sense it is the pleasant whiteness of pearl-barley, or a woman's body, or milk, or unsmutched snow; in another it is the horrifying whiteness of a corpse, or a spectre, or leprosy." Thus he quotes approvingly the lines from Coleridge's *Rime of the Ancient Mariner* that describe the image of the phantom woman dicing with Death:

> Her lips were red, her looks were free,
>> Her locks were yellow as gold,
> Her skin was white as leprosy.
> The Nightmare Life-in-Death was she,
>> Who thicks men's blood with cold. (433–34)

Graves's description aims to explain the color attributes, then, as vestiges of the white goddess's multiple functions from virgin to mother to hag. Her white skin and red lips show her in her vampiric aspect. But in her migration northward, she gained blue Aryan eyes and lost, Graves would have us believe, her Nilotic features. Yet numerous other scholars recognize in Isis not only the original of the Mater Dolorosa but, in her maternal pose suckling the baby Horus, also the original virgin mother. Dark of skin, Isis was the model for the black madonnas of Europe.[1]

If both the white goddess—the white witch—and the black madonna derive from the Egyptian Isis, their representation in black American literature as antithetical paths toward national inclusion likewise conceals ideological correspondences between them. The black madonna's apotheosis as All-Mother subsumes two key ideological transformations: her evolution from black Venus to black mammy, the disloyal black mother; and her emancipation from black mammy to domestic black goddess, the sign of black patriarchal enterprise. The white witch's duality as Life-in-Death mirrors the black madonna's duality as joy bringer and Mater Dolorosa of the slavery experience. The separation of the dark goddess from the light signifies the specifically Western appropriation of color symbolism in accordance with what Abdul JanMohammed has termed its "Manichean aesthetic" (JanMohammed, 3). Graves thus describes the quest for the white goddess as an undertaking that only the "true poet" can comprehend, let alone achieve: "Constant illiterate use of the phrase 'to woo the Muse' has obscured its poetic sense: the poet's inner communion with the White Goddess, regarded as the source of Truth. . . . The poet is in love with the White Goddess, with Truth: his heart breaks with longing and love for her" (448).

In black American literature, writers would associate the witch figure with white America rather than with Truth, though the element of unrequited love would become a more pronounced link to Graves's goddess. According to R. H. Robbins, the "white witch" of European tradition was a healer whose magic benefited society, by using an "exact knowledge of the secrets of nature" to cure illness or prevent natural disasters (Robbins, 540). The dogmatic church fathers found something threatening about the power to heal in the hands of women, though, and eventually the opinion prevailed that "white magic" was "more horrible and detestable" than black magic because by promoting faith in human skill without divine assistance she would lead people away from God (Robbins, 540–41). Thus, the "white and the black [witch] are both guilty alike in compounding with the Devil." They ought to be persecuted too, felt Cotton Mather, since there was "none that doeth good, no, not one" (541).

Mary Douglas's more succinct definition of white magic, though, spells out the significance of the "white witch" as one whose powers "are exerted on behalf of the social structure; they protect society from malefactors against whom their danger is directed" (99). The "whiteness" of the witch refers in this usage to her defense of the status quo, a role that requires that she be socially marginal as well so that she can police the boundaries that come under assault. In this way, the witch becomes a key figure in a tradition that examines the ambivalent attachment of the black male striver to the "dazzling opportunities" of the white world that might potentially result in the spiritual death of black America. The materiality of the white witch in the black literary tradition is therefore an important register of her symbolism of immediate gratification as an alternative path to American inclusion to that of patient striving, the sacrificial path reified in the maternal black spirit.

James Weldon Johnson's application of the witch lore would give a racial accent to the sadomasochistic worship of the deified white muse of poetry. The narrator of his 1915 poem "The White Witch"[2] warns his "brothers" that the only safety from the "white witch" is to flee, "For in her glance there is a snare, / And in her smile there is a blight" (*Saint Peter*, 34). In subsequent stanzas, Johnson reveals the following important characteristics of the "witch": she does not look like the "ancient hag" she really is but appears deceptively "in all the glowing charms of youth"; behind her smile lurks the "shadow of the panther" and the "spirit of the vampire"; it is the "Antaean strength" of her victims that attracts her — "the great dynamic beat / Of primal passions," "the echo of a far-off day, / When man was closer to the earth." The speaker identifies himself as a victim of the witch who has been "bound" by her yellow hair, his strength drained from his soul as he lay helplessly entranced in the arms of the vampire woman. In all particulars, Johnson's white witch is Graves's white goddess. Yet for the black poet, the sociohistorical connections of the white witch to the white Delilah of Wells-Barnett removes this nightmare vision from the realm of the purely aesthetic.

The poem, written during the early stage of the massive migration of blacks northward during and after World War I, superimposes the significance of the Du Boisian white witch upon an evolving discourse of the failed promises of the northern black experience, with the important exception that Johnson's women will not be cold, "spiritually white" mulattoes but women who socially classify themselves as white. Johnson's enumeration of the witch's "properties" becomes one of the signatory aspects of the motif, especially the great importance he attaches to color symbolism:

Her lips are like carnations red,
Her face like new-born lilies fair,
Her eyes like ocean waters blue,
She moves with subtle grace and air,

And all about her head there floats
The golden glory of her hair. (34)

His chromatic scheme suggests overlapping symbolic economies—the Aryan so-matic ideal, revealed as the red, white, and blue of the American flag, with the "golden glory" of the national wealth thrown in for good measure. As Michel Fabre's semiotic reading of Ralph Ellison's Circean white witch in the "Battle Royal" scene of *Invisible Man* reveals, such codes of race/nationalist desire in-scribing her feminine form with the myths of freedom and opportunity make her vampiric seduction of the "brothers" a striking critique of American democ-racy and capitalism, even in their most benign manifestations (Fabre, 127).

Johnson's "companion" poem, "The Black Mammy," envisions the alternate interracial fantasy, white male/black female, and comparison of the two helps to explain the social context of the urban migration that ultimately transformed black Americans from rural southerners to prisoners of the inner cities. Pub-lished in the *Crisis* five months after "The White Witch" appeared, "The Black Mammy," according to Johnson's biographer Eugene Levy, was actually com-posed in 1900, although Levy's description of that version of the poem seems dif-ferent from the version of 1915 (Levy, 70). As "foster-mother" to the white race, the mammy is economically locked into a position of dubious allegiance to her race:

So often hast thou to thy bosom pressed
The golden head, the face and brow of snow;
So often has it 'gainst thy broad, dark breast
Lain, set off like a quickened cameo. (*Saint Peter*, 40)

Here the female form is more explicitly objectified as a site of competing male desires, using the mammy's age to mask the implicitly sexual tug-of-war. Unlike the white witch, the black mammy is a truly nurturing female, but the "bosom pressed [to] / The golden head" gives strength to the "sons of the masters of the land," to the detriment of her own black child. Implicitly, Johnson invokes the "bad mother" lore of black womanhood's abandonment of her own household and neglect of her own children to tend to the children of her white employer.

As with Johnson's witch and her victim, the exploitation of the black body by a parasitical white figure defines interracial contact. Though the image of child-hood innocence that includes her own body in the delightful "cameo" seduces the old mammy, the phrase "golden head" creatively conveys capitalist exploita-tion of black labor as the subtext of the tableau. While Johnson's earlier poem warned the black male nation builder to beware becoming ensnared in the witch's golden hair, here he explicitly questions the ability of the mammy even to understand the nature of the trap into which the white [male] child draws her. More than her lack of political astuteness, the poem raises doubts about the loyalty of the black female to her own domestic responsibilities: "Came ne'er the thought to thee, swift like a stab, / That [the golden head] some day might crush thy own black child?"

The framing of the question reveals an identification between the adult observer and the deposed infant whom the "golden head" supplants. At the same time, no black female perspective emerges from either poem: the mammy here is silent, not allowed to answer the rhetorical question that concludes the poem, while the witch poem unfolds as a conversation among "brothers." The mammy's absorption into American culture as a marker of white prestige thus masks her treachery against incipient black domesticity,[3] and, by extension, against black patriarchal interests as yet unfounded. The white male colonization of her physical form, from a black male perspective, appears as a rejection with sexual overtones. Noting how often she has pressed her bosom to the golden head, the speaker insinuates that far from grudgingly submitting to the demands of her employment, she envisions the golden head as the key to a fantasy of transcending her sociogenetic history through the mothering of a white child with the white patriarch. The golden head displaces the absent black child not just out of economic necessity, then, but out of the mammy's self-negation as a mere backdrop to the "face and brow of snow." On the other hand, no similar appeal to domestic responsibility interrogates the "brothers'" aesthetic preference for the white witch.

Taken together, the poems reveal that these oppositional female archetypes coincide with respect to a pervasive distrust of the feminine—a black male deracination so profound that neither in the compromised domesticity of the South nor in the impermanent sexual commerce of the North is there any hope of sanctuary. The white witch, siren of false hopes, projection of internalized self-doubt, blocks the advance of the black male into American national subjecthood, while the treacherous black mother mortgages his refuge in the black world of the Jim Crow South. In the end, both betray the black male to secure their own marginal positions in the white world. Johnson's cosmos of black male striving is a bleaker one than Du Bois's, absent a committed, sacrificial black madonna, which leaves the black male subject paralyzed between emasculating feminine ideations. After Johnson, the presentation of the feminine in black male texts (especially in prose and drama) will typically employ this misogynistic interracial construct.

Prospects of AMERICA

Juxtaposing the white witch and the black mother, as in Chesnutt's "Uncle Wellington's Wives," formalizes a North-South dialectic in black twentieth-century thought.[4] Johnson's two poems hold out no hope of assistance from either North or South in the black soul's progress and use the opposed female images to investigate the conflicting emotions of the black deraciné. The question of embodiment during the northern migration takes a definitive turn from earlier formulations that assumed that white women would betray black lovers to lynch mobs rather than suffer social death. The literature of the early twentieth century recognizes the changed circumstances of interracial relations brought on by the northern urban experience. The white woman's body, a symbolic enticement into the promised good life of America, betrays the black quester by creating a psychic barrier to the inclusion he seeks.

The blazon of the white witch in Johnson's poem, in her red, white, and blue, is only one element in Johnson's rich symbolism, extending his critique of the American "spirit of the vampire" to cultural and economic exploitation. Johnson, in effect, sounds one of the earliest literary warnings against cultural appropriation—the exploitation of black cultural productivity as native American exotica. Though Johnson often expressed a naive faith in the liberating potential of the coming vogue of primitivism, which because of his experiences on the New York and European theatrical scenes he predicted would become an important social force, in "The White Witch" he reveals a structural ambivalence that would resonate through the decades of fluctuating African American access to the American cultural capital of New York. His white witch is the American consumer par excellence—the slummer, the bored habitué of Negro nightlife, the avant-garde stalker of novelty who would turn black Harlem within a decade into a peep show. The striver's "strong young limbs" and "laughter loud and gay," remind the witch of "a far-off day, / When man was closer to the earth":

She feels the old Antaean strength
In you, the great dynamic beat

> Of primal passions, and she sees
> In you the last besieged retreat
> Of love relentless, lusty, fierce,
> Love pain-ecstatic, cruel sweet. (35–36)

The witch parodies "Liberty" by sneering at the greatest of white-world social taboos, interracial sex. In a sense, the homogenizing effect of American culture is a by-product of her assault on the racial margin, for as she goes from victim to victim, she consumes the "primal passions" of each black Antaeus, leaving each soul drained and pacified—forms empty of content. Her victims, therefore, do not speak from the grave but remain trapped in a death-in-life paralysis of will: "twined [in] her arms, / And bound . . . with her yellow hair" (36). The reference to Antaeus "grounds" Johnson's core narrative of black deracination. Like Antaeus, the black quester as primitive draws his strength directly from nature, in which, unlike the men of the industrialized North, the southern black has been firmly rooted. But as we learn from Johnson's companion poem, the Earth Mother of the South whose nurturance he needs is similarly enthralled and colonized by the white patriarchy. Deprived of a nurturing southern soil to stand upon as his own, the black Antaeus dies a slow painful death in the North.

The blazon of the white witch in Johnson's poem becomes a staple of the motif for this reason, that the "display" of the witch's "parts" is an element in the attempted territorial conquest of racially restricted American space, involving "simultaneously an act of unfolding, offering to the eye, and the more static sense of something to be gazed upon and seen":

> The economic motive of itemizing—the detailing of a woman's parts as an inventory of goods—makes explicit an aspect of the rhetorical tradition's [that is, "blazing"] own relation to natural plenitude, copia, wealth, or increase. . . .
>
> The "matter" of discourse, then, is to be made plentiful, by a shaper outside it who "opens" it to the gaze, but also to be kept firmly under control. The inventory or itemizing impulse of the blazon . . . would seem to be part of the motif of taking control of a woman's body by making it, precisely, the engaging "matter" of male discourse, a passive commodity in a homosocial discourse or male exchange in which the woman herself, traditionally absent, does not speak. (Parker, 127, 131)

In both the witch and mammy poems, the underlying theme of black male victimization thwarts the proprietary impulse, arguing by negation the unfairness of a universe in which no woman can, finally, be owned by black men.

The blazon of the witch reflects a specific response to the topos of AMERICA. The tradition of the white witch demonstrates the paradox of living in an America determined to make AMERICA impossible as specifically an assault on black manhood. It adopts the mode of the "prospect"—the gaze across the horizon at "gendered sign[s] of the territory to be conquered and occupied" (Parker, 131, 140–41), yet it simultaneously announces America's resistance to such occupation. The racial seer who, like some new Columbus, canonizes his entry into New York Harbor as a communion with America's myth of immigrant origins rends the veil of duplicity to reveal the disparity between the promise and the actuality. Calvin Hernton's observation that "any oppressed group, when obtaining power, tends to acquire the females of the group that has been the oppressor" assumes that black nation builders as "prospectors" of AMERICA read the white female form as allegory of "Liberty" (Hernton, 79). But in a society that racializes genders and genders races, the gaze that colonizes is the witch's, not the black male watcher's. It is in this sense that James Weldon Johnson's witch casts a "blight" on her prey through an evil eye that complements the sexual nature of her vampirism—like her southern sister, she punishes the black male who wanders into her visual field with a ligature that, if not unto death, certainly invests black male spatial adventurism with imminent peril.

The tradition of the white witch consequently focuses on the boundedness of America through images of a spatially "closed" female white America that, once "penetrated" by the black male nation builder, becomes a space of confinement. Peter Stallybrass identifies three positions in the discourse of the "enclosed" female body, the third of which is that of the "class aspirant":

> Like members of the male elite, the class aspirant has an interest in preserving social closure, since without it there would be nothing to aspire *to*. But, at the same time, that closure must be sufficiently flexible to incorporate *him*. His conceptualization of woman will as a result be radically unstable: she will be perceived as oscillating between the enclosed body (the purity of the elite to which he aspires) and the open body (or else how could he attain her?), between being "too coy" and "too common." (Stallybrass, 134)

Johnson's witch subverts the appropriating male gaze by beguiling her victims into the illusion that they have chosen her, even as she assails their "last besieged retreat" of "primal passions." Johnson's "feminizing" rhetoric of black primitivism thus shifts subjectivity from the gaze of the male to that of the witch herself,

making the black quester the commodified object of the discourse. His acknowledgment of the situational masculinity of the white woman in an interracial relationship makes her the phallic woman, reducing the black male to an impotence
and exploitation escapable only through flight. It is he who ends "enclosed":
"Around me she has twined her arms, / And bound me with her yellow hair."
The black male's quest for freedom ends with the image of an enslavement more
profound for its implicit emasculation.

American Babylon

Both Du Bois and Johnson contributed to the tradition of representing black
Americans as deluded by the dream of American freedom in the North, a tradition that resonates from the slave era to the era of Jim Crow and beyond as a profound critique of American ceremonial and iconographic idealism and the myth
of northern liberal egalitarianism. In 1833, Maria W. Stewart had portrayed black
Americans as subjects of a captivity narrative of biblical dimensions: "America
has become like the great city of Babylon. . . . She is indeed a seller of slaves and
the souls of men; she has made the Africans drunk with the wine of her fornication; she has put them completely beneath her feet, and she means to keep them
there" (Porter, 134). Stewart's condemnation of a feminized America denies misleading sectional distinctions between the slave South and free North, anticipating Du Bois's figure of Progressive Era America as the "Great I Will."

If Du Bois continued Stewart's characterization of America as corrupter of the
"chosen" people, he also drew on other classical representations of demonic
women. In *The Souls of Black Folk*, Du Bois appropriated the national symbolism of the American eagle to portray the black predicament: "if . . . we debauch
the race thus caught in our talons, selfishly sucking their blood and brains in the
future as in the past, what shall save us from national decadence?" (63). Du Bois
used a self-inclusive "we" in referring to America, largely, I think, to stress the necessity of black American political agency as a force in American cultural perfection. Still, his characteristic referent for America in *The Souls* is "she." It
might, under the circumstances, be provocative to envision Du Bois's "America"
as more harpy than eagle, a suggestive figure that would look backward to Stewart's American Babylon. Key to this interpretation is Du Bois's use of "debauchery" and "decadence" to describe the nature of interracial relations, as Stewart
had previously figured such relations as "fornication."

In his 1902 novel *The Sport of the Gods*, Paul Laurence Dunbar, better known for his dialect poetry, depicted a black family's disastrous migration north to New York:

> To the provincial coming to New York for the first time, ignorant and unknown, the city presents a notable mingling of the qualities of cheeriness and gloom. If he have an eye at all for the beautiful, he cannot help experiencing a thrill as he crosses the ferry over the river . . . and catches the first sight of the spires and buildings of New York. If he have the right stuff in him, a something will take possession of him that will grip him again every time he returns to the scene and will make him long and hunger for the place when he is away from it. Later, the lights in the busy streets will bewilder and entice him. . . . The subtle, insidious wine of New York will begin to intoxicate him. Then, if he be wise, he will go away, any place. . . . But if he be a fool, he will stay and stay on until the town becomes all in all to him. . . . Then he is hopeless, and to live elsewhere would be death. (507–8)

As Houston Baker has pointed out, the assumption that Dunbar, in the words of Robert Bone, "was urging Negroes to stay in the South, where they could provide a disciplined labor force for the new plantation economy" fails to take into account the fact that the originary act in the family's disintegration occurs in the South—in fact, was peculiar to the South—and was compounded by the southern black community's self-protective, "pre-individualistic" hostility to the family's thrifty, upwardly mobile ethic (Baker, *Blues, Ideology*, 119, 125–38). Thus Dunbar's portrayal of the provincial's initial encounter with New York is laden with conditionals, evidencing a functional ambivalence toward the city that is not transferable to the North generally, nor should it be misconstrued to read that other places in the South are correspondingly less fatal to black aspirations. Rather, Dunbar posed the seeming contradiction that those who "have the right stuff" are *more*, not less, vulnerable to the city's enticements.

Dunbar's portrait of New York as "bewildering," "enticing," "subtle," "insidious," and "intoxicating" presents the (conventionally) masculine newcomer's journey to New York as a one-sided love affair with a cold, cruel temptress: "A new emotion will take his heart as the people hasten by him,—a feeling of loneliness, almost of grief, that with all of these souls about him he knows not one and not one of them cares for him. . . . After he has got beyond the stranger's enthusiasm for the metropolis, the real fever of love for the place will begin to take hold upon him" (507). Dunbar's watchful newcomer is artistically inspired by this unrequited love, associating the city's points of interest with his creativity:

"The Bowery will be his romance, Broadway his lyric, and the Park his pastoral, the river and the glory of it all his epic, and he will look down pityingly on all the rest of humanity" (508).

Notably absent from his list of romantic places is the Tenderloin—ironic, in that what the Tenderloin will inspire is "his novel." The Banner Club—"an institution for the lower education of negro youth" (523)—serves as the Tenderloin in microcosm, a backdrop for the corruption of young Joe Hamilton, just up from the South with his mother and sister after the false imprisonment of his father for theft. One of the revelations of the Banner Club for the newcomer, which "drew its pupils from every class of people and from every part of the country," was, in the words of Du Bois in *The Souls*, that while the color line keeps the "best" of both races apart, "at the bottom of the social group, in the saloon, the gambling-hell, and the brothel, that same line wavers and disappears" (130). Dunbar presents the Banner as a dark world visited by white curiosity-seekers—"those who were young enough to be fascinated by the bizarre, and those who were old enough to know that it was all in the game" (523–24). Of this latter group, Dunbar introduces us to Skaggs, a reporter for the yellow journal the *New York Universe*, and his girlfriend, Maudie. Perhaps this was a daring move by turn-of-the-century novelistic standards, the voluntary presence of a white woman in a black Manhattan saloon—more daring, that is, for Dunbar than it would have been for Rider Haggard or Rudyard Kipling—but Maudie is merely one more element in the decadence of the club life. She comes closest to enacting the Decline of the West while doing a ragtime two-step with a black woman named Mamie Lacey.

The putative case against black immigration into New York rests largely on the passages in which the denizens of the Banner inveigh against wide-eyed southerners coming north: "They wanted to preach to these people that good agriculture is better than bad art,—that it was better and nobler for them to sing to God across the Southern fields than to dance for rowdies in the Northern halls. They wanted to dare to say . . . that even what they suffered [in the South] was better than what awaited them in the great alleys of New York. Down there, the bodies were restrained, and they chafed; but here the soul would fester" (567). The narrator imagines blacks coming from the South in a "stream . . . dashing itself against the hard necessities of the city and breaking like waves against a rock," becoming human "sacrifices to false ideals and unreal ambitions," attributing to New York the role of siren, and thus paving the way for James Weldon Johnson's later depiction of the city as cruel enchantress.

Whether one feels that Dunbar was agitating against black immigration or that he was simply preparing the inevitable "untrained negroes" for the disillusionment they would surely find, his writing here is striking for its pointed rejection of the myth of New York that had achieved worldwide currency. In the tradition of the naturalists and the muckrakers, Dunbar's environmental determinism looked critically at black immigration in an era when foreign-born immigrants (and, obviously, blacks too) were writing home about the wonders of New York. The divergent experiences of foreign-born immigrants and native-born blacks were always a sore point with black Americans, who watched as every stage of European immigration brought over groups who were given latitude to develop individually and collectively, such that, within generations, they would begin to "melt" into the genetic pot—to "embody" with America. Dunbar, like Chesnutt before him, could not unconditionally endorse black immigration into the realm of the great "I Will," for fear of what blacks would do when they were told "You Can't."

In his 1912 novel *The Autobiography of an Ex-Colored Man*, James Weldon Johnson connected Dunbar's theme of black immigrant spiritual decay in New York to Du Bois's discourse of soul development to produce the most artistically successful black work of the first two decades of the century. Johnson revisits Dunbar's entry into New York as a canonical moment of cultural significance and racial awakening:

> The buildings of the town shone out in a reflected light which gave the city an air of enchantment; and, truly, it is an enchanted spot. New York City is the most fatally fascinating thing in America. She sits like a great witch at the gate of the country, showing her alluring white face and hiding her crooked hands and feet under the folds of her wide garments—constantly enticing thousands from far within, and tempting those who come from across the seas to go no farther. And all these become the victim of her caprice. Some she at once crushes beneath her cruel feet; others she condemns to a fate like that of galley slaves; a few she favors and fondles, riding them high on the bubbles of fortune; then with a sudden breath she blows the bubbles out and laughs mockingly as she watches them fall. (65–66)

Johnson's depiction of the city as a white-faced witch disguising her haglike deformity beneath the "folds of her wide garments" would evolve into the "white witch" of his 1915 poem—the "ancient hag" of "unnumbered centuries" who "appears / In form of youth and mood of mirth." Given Johnson's connection to the musical comedy theater of New York's "Great White Way," the pun on New

York as "Great White Witch" in the 1915 poem would be an apt expression of the city's deceptive promise of wealth and fame to talented black Americans.[5]

Johnson fulfills Stewart's vision of America as Babylon, Dunbar's immigrant wasteland, and Du Bois's American harpy by condensing the gendered national space, America, into a gendered urban space, New York City, and then into the gendered icon universally associated with the myth of America's nurturance of the immigrant dispossessed—the Statue of Liberty. Johnson cleverly renders "Liberty" as the symbol of the cruel irony of northern black migration, whose outcome he foreshadows in the image of the white witch city "hiding her crooked hands and feet under the folds of her wide garment . . . crush[ing black immigrants] beneath her cruel feet." Here he echoes Maria Stewart's allegorization of America as Whore of Babylon crushing Africans "completely beneath her feet. . . . Her right hand supports the reins of government, and her left hand the wheel of power, and she is determined not to let go her grasp" (Porter, 134). By making this cruel violation of black Americans the apotheosis of American "Liberty," Johnson sets in motion a new series of metaphorical possibilities keyed to the more fluid interpersonal relations of the northern experience.

However, unlike the classicized icon "Liberty" (as, for example, the one sculpted by Hiram Powers in the mid-nineteenth century),[6] these "cruel feet" reflect a significant revision. Powers was working within an iconic tradition in which Liberty was depicted as "trampl[ing] on the symbols of monarchy or oppression: the key to the Bastille, a crown, shackles, and the like" (Joshua C. Taylor, 11). Taylor describes a 1789 statue, "with her foot on the head of the conquered British lion, . . . called 'America,'" as definitive of "now what America meant to optimistic Europeans and proud inhabitants of the United States." Thus Powers attempted to locate his "America," precursor to the Statue of Liberty, within the "Liberty" iconography by designing first a diadem, then a set of broken chains with a scepter, and finally, just the broken chains beneath the left heel of "America."[7]

Johnson's caricature of Liberty crushing the immigrants beneath her feet is in the spirit of those mid-nineteenth-century critics who challenged the idealistic depiction of America as liberator (including, at one point, Powers himself) at a time when the country was being torn apart by the slavery question (Yellin, 115–19). His revisionist iconography is in keeping with the function of the black mythologist to deconstruct hypocritical images of achieved idealism in order to defend the very ideals misrepresented. Du Bois similarly critiques American liberty in an anecdote about his return through New York Harbor after his

European studies: "A new land loomed there beyond the horizon and we began searching the skies. I who was born there was also approaching something new and untried after 24 years of preparation. At last it loomed on the morning when we saw the Statue of Liberty. I know not what multitude of emotions surged in the others, but I had to recall that mischievous little French girl whose eyes twinkled when she said: 'Oh yes the Statue of Liberty! With its back toward America, and its face toward France!'" (*Autobiography*, 182). In the hands of Du Bois and Johnson, Wells-Barnett's white Delilah had evolved into a complex cultural sign, a transfiguration of the second, white female revenant in the black American imagination, announcing the eternal return of American "race" distinctions as a determining factor in human destiny: the white goddess Liberty—the Dollar Princess—as the revenant white body of death. The turn that Johnson takes with the evolving myth, however, proves crucial in shaping black literary modernism, which would subsequently fail to envision an American future uncomplicated by body politics.

The Witch and the City

The white women who frequented the black Bohemia of the Tenderloin were at first socially marginal figures, but the increasing trendiness of the Bohemian lifestyle of the early twentieth century attracted more and more women of high social status—women with enough power and wealth to feel themselves immune from public opinion. James Weldon Johnson's novel documents one such woman, known only as the "widow," who frequents the "Club" on the arm of a well-tailored and pampered black youth. However schematic his poem's depiction of the witch as a predator, the white women in his novel resist easy classification as witches, and the fatal meeting with the widow is one of a series of interracial encounters by the book's unnamed narrator—whose erasure of any racial or personal identity makes him the prototypical anonymous burgher, an "eX"-man in color and courage—that invest the work with a realism often lacking in the novels of Griggs and Du Bois. Based on the events of *The Autobiography of an Ex-Colored Man* and his own later autobiography, *Along This Way* (1933), Johnson's statement in "The White Witch" cannot be reduced to a mere protest against individual white women who cruise the black world for adventure, but must be discussed in terms of the larger systemic features of American body politics.

No doubt, part of the widow's attractiveness for the "ex-colored" protagonist (I will call him "X") is her whiteness. Capable himself of passing for white, X is the child of a quadroon mother and a prominent white man, whose last visit to their Connecticut home X remembers as the occasion of his father's breaking off with the family in order to marry a white woman. His father's farewell gift of a piano becomes the means both by which X earns a living and by which the bicultural aspect of the racial question enters the text most persuasively. Though he is at first a regular performer (elevated to the level of "professor") at the "Club," X's more lucrative employment by a mysterious private white benefactor gradually transforms him from an employee into a regular customer. Warned by friends that the widow's flirtations would lead to trouble with her black lover, X still cannot resist her: "I resolved to stop the affair before it should go any further; but the woman was so beautiful that my native gallantry and delicacy would not allow me to repulse her; my finer feelings entirely overcame my judgment" (89). But he is not fooled by the attention from this woman, knowing that she is using him to make her boyfriend jealous. In the tradition of Du Bois, X euphemizes his emotional investment into "finer feelings." When her lover shoots her through the neck with his gun, X runs out of the Club and keeps going until he gets to Paris with his wealthy white patron.

Johnson later wrote his own autobiography, *Along This Way*, in part to make clear that he was not X (*Along*, 239). Though he gives X some of his talents and opinions, along with more than a few of his experiences, from all indications X is based largely on Johnson's friend Judson Douglass Wetmore, whom Johnson calls "D——" in his autobiography (Levy, 16–17, 62–63). Wetmore had been a boyhood friend of Johnson's, a classmate at Atlanta University, a law partner in Jacksonville, and later, he had followed Johnson to New York. Through the years, he had been a person of white appearance in the black world, until in New York he began to pass for white, like X, for business and romantic reasons (*Along*, 241). When he married a Jewish woman, D—— did not cut off his ties to his black friends but in the huge anonymity of New York was able to live, in effect, a double racial life (256). When D—— divorced and later remarried, it was to a white Louisianian, whom he also told of his racial past and who, like his first wife, accepted his racial duality as a part of what made him interesting. D——'s surrender to double consciousness became the paradigm for X's race betrayal.

Johnson seizes upon this second marriage of D—— to make an observation about the mythic semipermeability of the color line:

> It is possible that Dame Nature never kicks up her heels in such ecstatic abandon as when she has succeeded in bringing a fair woman and a dark man together; and vice

versa. . . . It would [not] be more difficult for a colored man to win the love of a white woman . . . than for a white man to win the love of a colored woman, . . . a thought well nigh impossible for the average white man to think. . . . The primitive spirit of possessive and egotistical maleness is broad enough to embrace the women of other men, but its egotistic quality brooks no encroachment on the women of the clan. (390–91)

Johnson does not accuse whites of being peculiar in this regard but says that the Negro in the South, having the same impulse, merely lacks "power to give it authority."

Johnson's application of the idea that interracial romance works against the territorialist male sentiment for race chastity suggests one element in the evolution of "The White Witch." Wetmore's fascination with white women undoubtedly had something to do with his gradual disappearance from the black world, creating the impression that he had pursued women across the color line. But even those who could not have changed their racial allegiance if they wanted to were given to such pursuits. Though Johnson was not one of these, he knew well the temptation. Although he had visited New York as a boy and considered himself born to be a New Yorker, Johnson as a young man with aspirations in the world of musical theater experienced the city as "an alluring world, a tempting world, a world of greatly lessened restraints, a world of fascinating perils" (*Along*, 47, 152). He later gives this "alluring," postadolescent view of New York more definition in his description of the clubs of the black Bohemia of the Tenderloin, with their gambling, drinking, and "white sightseers and slummers," including "a considerable clientele of white women who had or sought to have colored lovers" (156).

Johnson somewhat deflects the impression that he himself was a candidate for such attention in his praise of the "handsome, deep-bosomed, fertile women" of the South whom he had seen in a brief experience as a rural schoolteacher:

Here, without question, was the basic material for race-building. I use the word "handsome" without reservations. To Negroes themselves, before whom "white" ideals have so long been held up, the recognition of the beauty of the Negro women is often a remote idea. Being shut up in the backwoods of Georgia forced a comparison upon me, and a realization that there, at least, the Negro woman, with her rich coloring, her gayety, her laughter and song, her alluring, undulating movements—a heritage from the African jungle—was a more beautiful creature than her sallow, songless, lipless, hipless, tired-looking, tired-moving white sister. (121)

Even though he expresses a proprietary interest in the black women of Georgia as the "raw" material for "race-building," Johnson's own concept of the finished product was a racially fused ideal of womanhood: "perhaps, the perfection of the human female is reached in the golden-hued and ivory-toned colored women of the United States, in whom there is a fusion of the fierceness in love of blond women with the responsiveness of black" (75).[8]

A fair-skinned woman of this type nearly cost Johnson his life in his hometown of Jacksonville, Florida, when, after a great fire had brought many rural militiamen into the city to police the martial law in force, he was almost lynched for "Being with a white woman" (167–68). The woman, whom Johnson had gone to meet in a public park, was not white but was apparently not interested in publicizing her ancestry. After soldiers with dogs tracked the pair down and proceeded to brutalize Johnson, he was able to save himself by establishing intellectual contact with the lieutenant in charge of the patrol and thereafter was able to plead his case before a major whom he knew as a fellow member of the Jacksonville bar. Johnson remarks that this May 1901 encounter disturbed his sleep with a horror complex not completely exorcised until, as field secretary for the NAACP, he was able to work toward passage of federal antilynching legislation.[9] The incident left Johnson with the conviction that "in the core of the heart of the American race problem the sex factor [was] rooted; rooted so deeply that it [was] not always recognized when it show[ed] at the surface." For Johnson, all the rationalizations for white superiority complexes stemmed from this sexual conflict, whose "strength and bitterness [were] magnified by and intensified by the white man's perception, more or less, of the Negro's complex of sexual superiority" (Along, 312–13).

A case in point, someone he had reason to see perhaps as something of an alter ego because of their similar names, was the boxer Jack Johnson. James Weldon knew John Arthur "Jack" Johnson three years before he became the first black heavyweight champion in 1908 (Along, 208). Though James Weldon Johnson would say in his autobiography that Jack Johnson had contributed to the race struggle, despite "his big and little failings," it is almost certain that what he euphemized as "failings" prominently included the fighter's sensational experiences with white women. It is also certain that the boxer was at least one of the models for his "black Antaeus" in "The White Witch." When the poem was published in March 1915, Johnson had just recently signed to fight Jess Willard, another in the series of "white hopes" who were attempting to redeem the honor of Anglo-Saxons by taking the crown from Johnson. It would prove to be the fighter's swan song as race protagonist, as, on April 5, 1915, he lost to Willard in twenty-six rounds in a fight that he said later was fixed.[10] James Weldon Johnson would write a boxing eulogy for his friend in April 1915 in the *New York Age* under the title "The Passing of Jack Johnson," in which he described the former champion as "one lone black man against the world" (Gilmore, 140).

It is not clear if Johnson anticipated the boxer's defeat and was, in "The White Witch," attempting to draw the same type of general racial significance that nearly all commentators on Jack Johnson's career ultimately considered, relative to the influence that his flamboyant lifestyle would have on white perceptions of blacks and black perceptions of the North as the "promised land" of black social mobility. He was simply the most popular and best-known black figure of his day, with the exception of Booker T. Washington, who, growing uncomfortable with Johnson's climb to success by physically beating white men and openly conducting flamboyant interracial affairs, urged Johnson to drop the sporting life and to adopt a Washingtonian "simplicity and humility of bearing" (Gilmore, 53).

What made the Texas-born boxer almost irresistible as a subject of racial sermonizing was his simultaneous smashing and legitimizing of racial stereotypes, particularly in regard to his public flaunting of his preference for white women. When, in 1912, his first white wife, Etta Duryea, committed suicide, Johnson became almost immediately embroiled in controversy after a Minnesota mother accused him of kidnapping her daughter. The girl in question, Lucille Cameron, put the accusation to rest, but within weeks a second allegation involving violation of the Mann "White Slavery" Act with another white woman, Belle Schrieber, was entered in federal court.[11] Three weeks after his acquittal on the abduction charge for lack of evidence, Johnson married Cameron. Within a two-month period, Jack Johnson had become a scandal-ridden and disgraced figure whose black defenders were hard pressed to account for his seeming fatal attraction to a class of women in whose name southern blacks were still being lynched by the score.[12]

According to Al-Tony Gilmore, Jack Johnson's significance as a national figure stems from his embodiment of two distinct black stereotypes at once, the "bad nigger" and the "uppity nigger" (16). As the brute "bad nigger," Johnson scoffed at convention and "undoubtedly took pleasure in aggravating and annoying whites":

> For example, upon entering his integrated nightclub in Chicago—his city of residence—the Cafe de Champion, one was first met by a larger than life portrait of the

champion embracing his white wife. As if that were not enough for openers, the champion would grace the bandstand with his bass violin and sing his favorite song, "I Love My Wife." But, perhaps, his most daring and potentially explosive act came during his sparring sessions when he played on the innermost fears of white men and the fantasies of white women by wrapping his penis in gauze bandages, enhancing its size for all onlookers, and strolled around the ring affecting the awe and admiration of all. (14)

A "bad nigger" who scoffed at racial prohibitions, Johnson also enacted the "uppity nigger's" economic independence with his fast cars, his extravagant entourage, and his indulgence of himself and his consorts in high fashion.

The image of this bald-shaven, muscular epitome of the "black brute" almost always accompanied by a "darling pink lady dangling on his bulging biceps" (17) raised the propaganda stakes of a sport in decline in the public interest because the myth of white evolutionary "fitness" in direct combat against a competitive "species" was so thoroughly undermined by the sight of Johnson mercilessly beating white men and publicly flouting his sexual conquest of white women. On the occasion of his important fight with Jim Jeffries on July 4, 1910, antifight campaigners warned the state of Nevada against "serv[ing] the devil" by staging the fight, even while others, including ardent Anglo-Saxonist writer Jack London, had been building up the fight as the ultimate showdown between the "small-brained" African's "soul shallowness and lack of imagination" and the white man's "intellectual advantage"—a testament, once and for all, to white supremacy.[13]

Johnson's marriage to his second white wife prompted a call for his lynching by at least one southern governor, numerous newspapers, and at least two southern ministers; calls for special lynching trains from the South to show the northerners how to handle blacks who forgot their place; and regrets from governors that the "sacred rite" of matrimony had been "desecrated" by a "blot on our civilization" (Gilmore, 106–9). Even blacks who had risen to Johnson's defense when it appeared that white reporters were playing off Cameron's youth and naïveté against Johnson's physical impressiveness were less charitable toward Johnson after he supposedly bragged to Cameron's mother, "I can get any white woman in Chicago I want," and after many black males began to lose their jobs in a backlash against black male assertiveness.[14] "Jack Johnson, Dangerously Ill," proclaimed one headline in a black newspaper: "Victim of White Fever" (Gilmore, 99). Johnson did not help matters by letting it be known that he was not sexually interested in black women, prompting many to characterize him as "a man who strove to get away from his race" (Gilmore, 153, 141). Eventually, one black publication applied the racist rhetoric of the black brute stereotype as the measure of its disgust at the whole affair, implicitly identifying Johnson with the "body of death": "To carry Jack Johnson," it said, "the race had a dead corpse attached to it" (Gilmore, 141).

Worse in some ways than if he had been literally "lynched," Johnson's "social death" through dishonor and exile was for many image-conscious blacks exactly what anyone who tampered with forbidden fruit should expect, a message whites were anxious that blacks receive. When Lucille Cameron emphatically refused to accept the role of "white witch," government prosecutors simply went on to locate in the jilted Belle Schrieber a woman who was willing to take the part. The lesson seemed clear to blacks who followed the events: "white women of a mercenary order have come in and brought about [the] undoing . . . [of] another one of the race's idols" (Gilmore, 122). Thus James Weldon Johnson's "The White Witch," in the context of Jack Johnson's exile from America after his conviction under the Mann Act and his Havana match against another in a series of white hopes, seems to describe poignantly the "death-in-life" of a man whose "Antaean strength" could not overcome the witch's wiles. By boldly accepting and turning against whites the image of phallic warrior, Jack Johnson had made it inevitable that his disastrous "entanglements" with white women would be seen by his public as a symbolic castration.

If James Weldon Johnson's own near lynching, Douglass Wetmore's defection, and Jack Johnson's spectacular downfall had not given him enough on which to base his poetic treatment of interracial involvement, the strange circumstances of Booker T. Washington's March 1911 trip to New York City alone should have convinced Johnson that the city was a great white witch. After giving talks to segregated audiences at a black and a white church on Sunday, March 19, the uncharacteristically unaccompanied Washington went to an address just north of the unofficial boundaries of the Tenderloin district, which had been moving steadily up the West Side since its heyday in the mid-nineties (Jervis Anderson, 13–15). In a building occupied entirely by whites, Washington had paced for about an hour, seeming to be searching for an address. First, he was passed by a "slim attractive brunette about thirty years old," later identified as a "Mrs. Ulrich," who claimed afterward that on her second encounter with Washington, he had called out to her, "Hello, sweetheart" (Harlan, *Booker T. Washington*, 2:379–80). Shortly thereafter, two young women passed him on the way to their apartment. Then, suddenly, a man identified later as Henry Albert Ulrich rushed at

Washington, accused him of peeping into the keyhole of his apartment, and began savagely beating Washington with a stick. Only the good fortune of running into a plainclothes policeman saved Washington from more serious injury (2: 380–81). The Tuskegee Machine immediately launched a damage control operation that tried to give some plausibility to Washington's incoherent statement that he was looking for an address at which he had been told he could find friends of a university lawyer who lived in New Jersey. In the end, Ulrich was acquitted of assault charges, despite the fact that the woman in question was not his wife and that both had shady reputations. Newspaper accounts of the trial could not agree whether a subtle race bias against Washington or Washington's vague responses under questioning were the cause of the verdict (2:391).

The event, which many Washington loyalists had originally responded to as an outrage, especially in that it occurred in New York, gradually shook the faith of many of his followers and gave ammunition to those whom Washington had alienated with his covert political heavy-handedness. Louis Harlan is inclined to think that Washington's habit of dissembling figured heavily into the cloud of uncertainty still lingering over the incident: "It may have been that Washington's lifelong habit of duplicity, secretiveness, and mendacity in his public affairs caused him, in the shock of the beating and the panic of being arrested, to make up what seemed in his confused state a credible untruth instead of a less creditable truth. Deception had become for Washington almost a reflex action, much as a squid inks the waters" (2:402). Harlan notes that after the incident, Washington became a more forceful critic of injustice, omitting "his usual weasel words," but Harlan finds irony in the fact that Washington, running "bleeding through the New York streets," must have reached the conclusion at some point that "in the atmosphere of American racism even Booker T. Washington was lynchable."

A further irony found Washington criticizing Jack Johnson's conduct after the Cameron and Schrieber stories broke, less than a year after the Ulrich trial, breaking Washington's own pledge not to prejudge the case. Washington took the occasion of the boxer's legal quandary to make sure that this rival for the public's adoration never would challenge him again, declaring Johnson to be an obstacle to race uplift, whose actions did not "meet with the approval of the colored race" (Gilmore, 101–2). Washington deplored Johnson's "grave injustice to his race," continuing with the hypocritical, self-serving observation, "It only goes to prove my contention that all men should be educated along mental and spiritual lines in connection with their physical education. A man with muscle minus brains is a useless creature." Jack Johnson counterpunched, blues style, reminding Booker T. Washington about the Ulrich affair: "I never got caught in the wrong flat. I never got beat up because I looked in the wrong keyhole" (Gilmore, 104). Gilmore explains that after black publications and leaders across the country responded angrily, bringing up Washington's fiasco in New York, "he never again made the mistake of publicly denouncing Johnson" (102).

A Mess of Pottage

The murder of the widow in a New York cabaret in Johnson's novel does not convince X of the fatality of color-line transgressions, although in France he would receive another lesson in the tragedy of American race relations. The highlight of this trip to Paris is an encounter reminiscent of the theater scene in Du Bois's "Of the Coming of John." With a wink in Du Bois's direction, Johnson makes the musical occasion of this encounter not *Lohengrin* but Berlioz's *The Damnation of Faust*: "At the end of the act I noticed that my neighbor on the left was a young girl. I cannot describe her either as to feature, or color of her hair, or of her eyes; she was so young, so fair, so ethereal, that I felt to stare at her would be a violation; yet I was distinctly conscious of her beauty" (98). Every so often stealing a glance at the girl, X will not allow himself to violate her innocence with his proprietary gaze; thus, while he can describe her general effect, he cannot enumerate her "parts." Yet when he extends his glance toward the male sitting next to her, he receives a shock that elevates his personal tragedy above that of Faust: "My glance immediately turned into a stare. Yes, there he was, unmistakably, my father! looking hardly a day older than when I had seen him some ten years before. . . . Before I had recovered from my first surprise, there came another shock in the realization that the beautiful, tender girl at my side was my sister." The pathos of the encounter overwhelms X, making him want to fall "at her feet and worship her": "Slowly the desolate loneliness of my position became clear to me. I knew that I could not speak, but I would have given a part of my life to touch her hand with mine and call her 'sister.' I sat through the opera until I could stand it no longer. . . . I felt an almost uncontrollable impulse to rise up and scream to the audience: 'Here, here in your very midst, is a tragedy, a real tragedy!'" Where black John had touched a white woman's hand without conscious volition, X's consciousness of the social barriers that will not allow him to touch his own sister's hand foreshadows his emotional odyssey into white America. His Faustian quest will, in fact, end in damnation, caused as much by his own lapse into double consciousness as by an American structural denial of his humanity sufficiently potent to haunt him across the ocean.

Like black John in Du Bois's parable, whose despair at belonging is mitigated by the vision of sacrificial black womanhood, X's first inclination is to affirm his black heritage, perhaps because the newfound sister who embodies his exclusion from American belonging is *not* a black woman. He decides to leave his employer to become a race builder through his interest in universalizing (that is, "classicizing") black folk and popular music. But a lynching that he witnesses in the South shakes X's confidence in his ability to live as a "voluntary Negro"— one whose "place" in the black race cannot be fixed by somatic evidence. As he falls into "double-consciousness," his shame in blackness overrides his shame in a country that could allow white savagery, and so rather than repudiate the white nation, he allows himself to be absorbed into it. Pointing to the national import of his defection, he decides that "to forsake one's race to better one's condition [is] no less worthy an action than to forsake one's country for the same purpose" (139), determining that he would make "a white man's success: . . . money" (141). His renunciation of the Du Boisian demand that the talented race striver resist despair and remain dedicated to the slow process of race development leads inevitably to his abandonment of his project of classicizing and conserving the spirituals. He becomes a real estate speculator and a slum landlord, thus joining not only the white race but perhaps even the oppressor class of that race that made full black participation in the American dream in New York impossible. His soul bargain is no abstraction, either, since he directly profits from the exploitation of blacks by real estate agents who were carving up the northern metropolises into residential facsimiles of the imagined color line in society.[15]

X eventually meets a woman who agrees to marry him and to whom he feels obliged to explain his family tree. His description of her looks forward to the blazon of the white witch in the poem: "She was almost tall and quite slender, with lustrous yellow hair and eyes so blue as to appear almost black. She was as white as a lily, and she was dressed in white. Indeed, she seemed to me the most dazzlingly white thing I had ever seen. But it was not her delicate beauty which attracted me most; it was her voice, a voice which made one wonder how tones of such passionate color could come from so fragile a body" (144). The dissonance between the whiteness of her body and the "color" in her voice makes her a siren of a particular sort. X is responding to the "color" in her "soul" that will manifest itself later when he tells her of his ancestry.

Johnson gives a prime example of what he calls in *Along This Way* the "Man-Negro dualism" in American society (209), when X's beloved looks at him for the first time in the knowledge of his racial history: "I felt her hand grow cold, and when I looked up, she was gazing at me with a wild, fixed stare as though I was some object she had never seen. Under the strange light in her eyes I felt that I was growing black and thick-featured and crimp-haired" (149). X's fantasy metamorphosis into the revenant black brute of the white imaginary "under . . . her eyes" attests to a witchlike power—an evil eye—that ties her to his poetic white witch. The moment recapitulates X's moment of discovery of the veil of race in a childhood episode reminiscent of Du Bois's visiting card fiasco. Unmasked by an insensitive teacher who publicly rebukes him when she calls for the white students in the class to stand and tells him, portentously, that he must sit down and "*rise* with the *others*," he goes home and examines himself in a mirror and then runs to his mother demanding, "'Mother, mother, tell me, am I a nigger?'" (11–12). His awareness of himself for the first time as a racially constructed individual immediately forces a reevaluation of his mother too in light of this new knowledge: "I looked at her critically for the first time. I had thought of her in a childish way only as the most beautiful woman in the world; now I looked at her searching for defects." Finding his mother still beautiful but different "from the other ladies" he knew in skin and hair, X rediscovers in his beloved's eyes a self transformed by the "condition" of this revered but deficient mother, which sets him to curse "the drops of African blood in [his] veins and [wish he] were really white" (149).

Seeing his "intended" again at the theater in the company of another man, X "feel[s] weak and powerless, like a man trying with his bare hands to break the iron bars of his prison cell" (151). But his love proves to be true; she marries him despite his social handicap, and they have two children, a dark-haired girl and then a boy—"fair like his mother, a little golden-headed god"—whom his wife bears only to die soon after of complications. Significantly, the "golden-haired" boy who three years later would measure racial allegiance for the speaker in "The Mammy" appears in this novel as the being who "occupies an inner sanctuary" of X's heart. Notwithstanding his ability to evoke the sacrificial motherhood of X's wife, his golden hair here, as later, represents the materiality of a "white man's success" that has replaced X's nobler dream of striving for black race development.

The novel's understated ending finds X materially secure but regretful of having sacrificed his "racial" talent in favor of personal gain: "Beside [the gallant band of colored men who are publicly fighting the cause of their race,] I feel small and selfish. I am an ordinarily successful white man who has made a little money. They are men who are making history and a race. I too might have taken part in a work so glorious. . . . I cannot repress the thought that, after all, I have chosen the lesser part, that I have sold my birthright for a mess of pottage" (154). X's "birthright" refers to the "souls of black folk," captured in the spirituals, to which he no longer has any claim after his defection from black America. His dream of revealing the world-historical stature of black America by musical reinterpretation of traditional black folk melodies has, in the end, withered into a sheaf of "yellowing manuscripts, the only tangible remnants of a vanished dream, a dead ambition, a sacrificed talent." By burying his "talent," X gains comfortable mediocrity but squanders his race soul.

Johnson was not in New York at the time of the Ulrich affair, though he was just arriving there with the manuscript of *The Autobiography of an Ex-Colored Man* when the case went to trial in November 1911.[16] The case would certainly have reinforced his characterization of New York as a great witch of a city, but behind the novel's adaptation of Du Bois's Faustian theme lies a crisis in Johnson's own philosophical leanings that sheds additional light on the novel's "soul bargain." Johnson had come under the influence of Washington in 1905 at the peak of his career as a member of the songwriting team of Cole and Johnson Brothers, whose successes on Broadway were responsible for black performers being gradually emancipated from the coon song tradition in musical theater (Woll, 15). Around this time, Johnson also made the acquaintance of W. E. B. Du Bois, then a professor at Atlanta University, Johnson's alma mater. In 1905, Johnson was one of the men to whom Du Bois extended an invitation to join in the formation of the Niagara Movement. Johnson, according to Eugene Levy, declined, because he did not want to antagonize Washington, whom he understood to be the target of Du Bois's group. Johnson had been tabbed by Washington ally Charles Anderson during the 1904 presidential race to work for the Republican ticket, and in 1905 Anderson offered Johnson a position in the consular service, part of the decreasing political largesse still available to loyal black Republicans (Levy, 105–6). In effect, Johnson was being offered choices very much like those that had been tendered to Du Bois in 1902 to bring him into the Washington camp. Johnson, despite the immediate financial hardship of the low-paying consular post and the likelihood of drawing an unglamorous assignment, accepted the offer, hoping that eventually it would lead to an appointment later as "American Minister to somewhere" (Levy, 107–8). Rather than continue his more lucrative career in musical theater or join Du Bois's band of race strivers, Johnson cast his lot with the Washington political machine.

Johnson's theatrical success and his college background caused Charles Anderson to celebrate that the coup of securing Johnson's loyalty to Washington would be a propaganda victory against the talented tenth types who felt that Washington did not speak for the black professional class.[17] "Thus, you see," Anderson crowed in a letter to Washington, "it will serve two purposes: to take care of Johnson, and, at the same time give the enemy a black eye" (Harlan, *Booker T. Washington*, 2:19). Unlike Douglass Wetmore, who left behind his thriving business and political career in Florida and settled in New York that year against Johnson's advice, moving in with him at the studio apartment in the Marshall Hotel on West Fifty-third, Johnson at least had not deliberately set out to sell his services to the political faction that promised the most.[18] But five years later, after continuous consular service in low-paying, thankless posts in Venezuela and Nicaragua, Johnson, now married to Grace Nail, was relentless in going through every official and unofficial political channel to get a better, if not better-paying, assignment (*Along*, 116–17). Thus, in the year that his protagonist lamented having sold "his birthright for a mess of pottage," there could be no doubt that Johnson saw the diminishing career returns of his own political affiliation with Washington as a Faustian bargain.

In the years of his writing and publishing *The Autobiography of an Ex-Colored Man*, then, Johnson was still politically connected to Washington, and this relationship shows in the novel as Johnson balances his Du Boisian sensibilities against his indebtedness to Washington. Despite its Du Boisian themes and explicit reference to *The Souls* as a model for black intellectual and artistic striving (123), Johnson politically gives his highest praise for race development to Washington, whom he describes as the epitome of "that small but gallant band of colored men who are publicly fighting the cause of their race" (154). Ironically, this praise for those who were "making history and a race" while X settled for making money is clearly in Du Boisian terms of culture building and political agitation. However, Johnson's setting of a key scene of his novel at a Paris opera, like Du Bois's "Of the Coming of John," might well be an implicit critique of Washington's directive to Tuskegee students that "the opportunity to earn a dollar in a factory just now is worth infinitely more than the opportunity to spend a dollar in an opera-house" (Farr, 45), especially if the opera is *The Damnation of Faust*.

Eugene Levy notes Johnson's skill in keeping to a middle course in the Washington–Du Bois controversy, sitting on "two stools," as it were, and Johnson, even after refusing Du Bois's offer to be one of the founders of the Niagara Movement, was able to keep the channels of communication open sufficiently that Du Bois published several of his poems in the *Crisis* and was publicly and privately commendatory toward him.[19] Not until after the death of Washington would Johnson feel able to declare forthrightly his allegiance to the Du Boisian path by joining the NAACP staff, and thereafter he downplayed his important early identification with Washington to the point of near erasure.[20]

Within the metaphorical tradition of the witch established by Du Bois and Johnson, the white female body became in black literature a flexible trope of insubstantial desires for social inclusion, a longed-for path to "embodiment" with the nation that eventually proves fatally delusive by reinstating the rupture it seeks to repair. That this fatal entrapment seemed a greater danger to men of some success and men living on the edge of legality—famous athletes, cultured men of the black republic, race visionaries, and desperadoes: "uppity niggers" and "bad" ones too—was a point not stressed by Johnson or Du Bois but implicit in their handling of the subject. It was a tradition that some were bound to misunderstand, taking its ambivalence as merely a sign of deception. Thomas Dixon Jr., for example, outraged by the NAACP campaign against the showing of *Birth of a Nation* in northern cities, targeted Du Bois and Johnson particularly, among what he termed the "Negro Junta" for retaliation. In 1939, his novel *The Flaming Sword* depicted a vicious rape in the South carried out by a black brute whose northern black friend had sent him the version of Johnson's poem "The White Witch" published in Du Bois's the *Crisis* for use as a rapist training manual![21]

The White City

The work of Du Bois and Johnson undoubtedly set the tone for the imagery of entrapment and despair in the northern metropolis that permeates the poetry of Jamaican-born Claude McKay, an immigrant like Du Bois and Johnson in the American city famed for its "openness" to outsiders. McKay reached New York in spring 1914, already embittered by two years in the South and midwestern plains of Kansas over the cruel race prejudice for which his Jamaican upbringing had not prepared him.[22] In "The White House," the poem that occasioned McKay's vilification of Alain Locke, McKay's Marxist critique envisions Du Bois's "Great I Will" as a national space enclosed against black male aspiration.

In this poem, the "door" shut against the "tightened face" of the "chafing savage" forces him to "keep [his] heart inviolate / Against the potent poison of your hate" (*Poems*, 78). McKay complained that Locke had changed the title of the poem to "White Houses" without consulting him, in fear that the original title "The White House" would be misconstrued as a criticism of the president, thereby jeopardizing McKay's ability as a resident alien to return to the country from Europe. In his autobiographical *A Long Way from Home*, McKay gives some insight into the whiteness of the enclosed spaces of his poetic landscape: "My title was symbolic," he says, "not meaning specifically the private homes of white people, but more the vast modern edifice of American Industry from which Negroes were effectively barred as a group." Locke, said McKay, distorted the meaning of the poem, "making it appear as if the burning desire of the black malcontent was to enter white houses in general" (*Long Way*, 313–14). When McKay looked to Africa as a possible refuge, he found a still colonized African body politic the plaything of the modern white nations. "The sciences were sucklings at thy breast," McKay exclaims in "Africa." Yet despite Africa's history as the mother of all civilization, it had since been "swallowed" by "darkness" and now has become "the harlot, . . . / Of all the mighty nations of the sun" (*Poems*, 40). Like Johnson before him, McKay's despair emerges as disbelief in the millenarian triumph of Du Bois's Mother Africa, a view that not even his later visit to Africa would materially alter (*Long Way*, 295–305).

Looking no further than the possibility of a perpetual torture in America that perversely bestows a measure of redemption through conscientious resistance, McKay renders New York as a stark labyrinth where exclusion becomes a form of entrapment in the cruel talons of Liberty. In "The City's Love" the city comes alive for him in a form clearly influenced by Johnson's white witch city:

> For one brief golden moment rare like wine,
> The gracious city swept across the line;
> Oblivious of the color of my skin,
> Forgetting that I was an alien guest,
> She bent to me, my hostile heart to win,
> Caught me in passion to her pillowy breast. (*Poems*, 66)

The city as feminized space shows the poet her tempting face, testing his "inviolate" heart by "[sweeping] across the line." Denied "masculine" prerogative in the maintenance and transgression of boundaries, however, the speaker is the one whose spatial integrity is at issue here, a circumstance magnified by his inability to hold the city's attention beyond "one flame hour." The passage might refer to one of those moments when McKay, among a group of radical artists and writers associated with the journals the *Masses* and the *Liberator*, found some respite from the raging color consciousness of the era, although he was to find sufficient prejudice within socialism to make him an outcast among outcasts.[23]

However, such idylls are eventually disturbed by vampiric figures that link McKay to Du Bois and Johnson before him, as in the moments of "loveliness" described in "The City's Love":

> Oh cold as death is all the loveliness,
> That breathes out of the strangeness of the scene,
> And sickening like a skeleton's caress,
> Of clammy clinging fingers long and lean. (53)

McKay's adaptation of Johnson's witch, who twines her arms about her victim and binds him with her hair, is more fully realized in his sonnet "America":

> Although she feeds me bread of bitterness,
> And sinks into my throat her tiger's tooth,
> Stealing my breath of life, I will confess
> I love this cultured hell that tests my youth!
> Her vigor flows like tides into my blood,
> Giving me strength erect against her hate.
> Her bigness sweeps me like a flood. (59)

McKay's earlier "Tiger" had similarly explored the sexual suggestiveness and sado-masochism of black/white contact, imagining the "white man [as] a tiger at" his throat, "muttering that his terrible striped coat / Is Freedom's" (47). "America" employs the tiger image in a heterosexual encounter, in the tradition of Johnson's witch. She is a phallic mother, simultaneously exploiting and nourishing the en-trapped immigrant "stand[ing] within her walls with not a shred / Of terror, mal-ice, not a word of jeer" (59). The cruel paradox of life in a racist America is that the race hero stands "erect" only through *resistance* to America's resistance.

Similarly, McKay's "The White City" finds his victimization strangely invigo-rating:

> My being would be a skeleton, a shell,
> If this dark Passion that fills my every mood,
> And makes my heaven in the white world's hell,
> Did not forever feed me vital blood. (*Poems*, 74)

Only the hate engendered in the poet by the city's callous disregard keeps him alive, keeps him from being drained, and because that hatred is an ever renewing source of energy, his death-in-life is eternal. McKay captures that simultaneous exclusion and enclosure in the image of the city veiled by a "mist." Thus his failed "inventory" leads to a perversely gratifying hatred of that which he can see dimly through the veil of whiteness but never seemingly possess.

With McKay, exclusion from the myth of "Liberty" in New York necessitates a paradoxical protective self-enclosure. The act of self-restraint becomes itself the imprisonment against which the poet's spirit rebels. McKay envisions the black American, then, as having internalized his own oppression sufficiently to love the possibility of AMERICA, while hating the self that both disallows participation in that freedom and protectively numbs the spirit against such desire. As Houston Baker has suggested, it has been this eternally deferred possibility of an egalitarian social order that has alienated black Americans, and McKay's poetry reveals clearly how entrapment in this myth of AMERICA is the form that social exclusion often takes. McKay thus became the forerunner of poet Langston Hughes and novelists Richard Wright, Ann Petry, Ralph Ellison, and James Baldwin, who would explore the contradictions of the urban ghetto's proximity but incomplete access to the wealth and power of America.

Taken as a whole, McKay's works reiterate the earlier immigrant experience of Du Bois and Johnson in giving voice to two distinct narratives of New York: the mythic New York as the gateway to America, and the cruel, indifferent New York as the destroyer of dreams. In the context of the black northward migration, this body of work collectively reveals the anti-"prospect" as a characteristic stance of black literary production—a gaze upon the seductive myth of American spatial freedom that yields only visions of further enslavement and misery. This vision is acutely modern in that its consciousness of alienation does not quite extinguish the quest for cherished ideals. It betrays the would-be race hero as always potentially a masochistic product of a slave mentality, in love with that which hates him. The gaze from without fails to penetrate; the gaze from within is mesmerized by its spell.

More important, McKay's symbolism returns the focus to what, in Du Boisian terms, might be called the "whiteness" of the witch. Du Bois's white witches, as we have seen, did not have to be racially identified as "white" to serve as agents of American materialism: for Du Bois, the "white soul" was more threatening than the white body. As the center of the American capitalist myth machinery, New York symbolized the social "space" of "whiteness" in American culture, dwarfing the literally white sites of governmental authority in Washington, D.C., in the public imagination. The "whiteness" of America was a myth that had to be resisted because it had but one implication that all blacks could agree on—the death of blackness. McKay is Graves's "true poet," in love with the pitiless goddess Liberty, who would as soon crush him as embrace him. It is the colossal ambivalence of his posture that inaugurates the Harlem Renaissance as the public fantasy of America's two social bodies living inside each other's soul.

CHAPTER NINE

Conclusion

In a book review of William B. Smith's *The Color Line*, W. E. B. Du Bois accused Smith of stating "flatly and with unnecessary barbarism a thesis that is the active belief of millions of our fellow countrymen."[1] Later, in "The Souls of White Folk," he speculated on the grip with which racial disaffiliation held white Americans:

> I . . . know that today to the millions of my people no misfortune could happen, of death and pestilence, failure and defeat, that would not make the hearts of millions of their fellows beat with fierce, vindictive joy. Do you doubt it? Ask your own soul—what would it say if the next census told it that half Black America was dead and the rest dying?
>
> . . . Am I in my blackness the sole sufferer? I suffer. And yet, somehow, above the suffering, . . . surges in me a vast pity—pity for a people prisoned and enthralled, hampered and made miserable for such a cause, for such a fantasy.
>
> I sit and see the souls of White Folk daily shriveling and dying in the fierce flame of this new fanaticism. ("Souls," 27)[2]

In response to this pervasive fantasy of black biological extinction and its inevitable corollary of historical erasure, Du Bois had joined others his generation in calling for and becoming a force in a racial "renaissance."

In the early days of the literary reimagining of black America, many writers contributed to a developing ethos. The "color line" narratives of Harper, Hopkins, and Chesnutt had made the "marriage plot" central to the literature of ethnic preservation, while Griggs had imaginatively responded to Du Bois's call for conservation of the body and "soul" of black America. Du Bois, building on the archetypal "white Delilah" introduced by Wells-Barnett, had allegorized the self-centered, materialistic white America that Johnson would call "The White Witch," a figure whose function within the marriage plot was to serve as a test for the race protagonist. Only by choosing the rehabilitated ideal of black woman-hood, the domestic madonna, would that hero overcome a crippling "double-consciousness" undermining black collective striving for inclusion in America and thereby go on to articulate the indispensable African contribution to world civilization. Dunbar's *The Sport of the Gods*, Johnson's *The Autobiography of an Ex-Colored Man*, and McKay's poetry, though, would lead the way into the diffi-cult modernist phase of this evolving epic of race survival, a phase marked by an imperfect inclusion that would end as entrapment in new spaces of American confinement.

With the emergence of Harlem as the "Culture Capital" of black America, the renaissance gained a galvanizing spatial identity.[3] The ensuing ethnic revival within the larger boom of the "Jazz Age" drew its artistic inspiration increasingly from the modernist revolt and not from the Du Boisian ethic, already a quarter century old. The fact that his own NAACP was like a club for literary race strivers tended to dilute rather than to concentrate Du Bois's influence with the postwar generation. In addition to Du Bois and James Weldon Johnson (whose *The Autobiography of an Ex-Colored Man* was reprinted in 1927 under his own name, the same year as *God's Trombones*), the organization could boast the work of Johnson's assistant, Walter White, and of Du Bois's literary editor at the *Crisis*, Jessie Fauset.[4] Yet the still younger generation of writers coming of age in the twenties had other sources of support and inspiration, and the friendships White and Johnson maintained with those on the modern scene whom Du Bois thought most responsible for leading the young artists astray left him in an increasingly isolated position on the necessity to pursue "racial" rather than individual goals in art. Despite his attempt to regenerate a sense of mission among the emerging artists with his 1926 symposium on racial representation in literature and his manifesto, "Criteria of Negro Art," Du Bois would never become more than a symbolic influence for the postwar artists, refusing to put the full weight of the *Crisis* and the NAACP behind arts patronage.[5]

Du Bois's charge was that the "New Negro" generation had gone "wooing false gods" who urged, as Carl Van Vechten did in the March 1926 the *Crisis*, that black artists supply America with a steady stream of urban exotica.[6] By his reck-oning, the precocious self-centeredness of the Harlem literati seemed a fulfillment of Du Bois's fear of the seduction of the "talented tenth" by the materialist Zeitgeist. In his "Talented Tenth: Memorial Address" (1948), Du Bois reconsidered his ideal of a dedicated "racial aristocracy": "I realized that it was quite possible that my plan of training a talented tenth might put in control and power, a group of selfish, self-indulgent, well-to-do men, whose basic interest in solving the Negro problem was personal; personal freedom and unhampered enjoyment and use of the world, without any real care . . . as to what became of the mass of any people. My Talented Tenth, I could see, might result in a sort of interracial free-for-all, with the devil taking the hindmost and the foremost taking anything they could lay hands on" (*W. E. B. Du Bois: A Reader*, 348–49). As a summation of the "spiritual truancy" of the period, Du Bois's retrospective helps to explain why "the new-world quest of Goodness and Beauty and Truth [went] glimmering." The voice of the Zeitgeist offering success as a substitute for striving had made a specific appeal to the young artists: "Here is a way out. Here is the real solution of the color problem. . . . Keep quiet! Don't complain! Work! All will be well! . . . What is the use of your complaining; do the great thing and the reward is there."[7] Du Bois offered once more an aesthetic of striving, a sublime combination of Beauty, Truth, and Goodness that would resonate far more with future generations of writers than with the Harlem literati: "all Art is propaganda and ever must be" ("Criteria," 296). Instead, the New Negroes seemed more inclined to go about in what Du Bois called the "second-hand soul clothes of white patrons" ("Criteria," 297).

When Is a Renaissance Not a Renaissance?

When is a renaissance not a renaissance? Literally, when there are no births. One striking feature of the New Negro renaissance was the way that Caroline Wynn's observation in *The Quest of the Silver Fleece* — "how far [does] one [have] the right to bear black children to the world" — reverberated through the twenties and thirties literature. The decades that saw a huge population explosion in the northern metropolises, dispelling the twin myths of black unfitness for modernity and eventual extinction, witnessed a remarkable inhospitality to black children in their literature. Despite Alain Locke's inclusion of an illustration titled "The Brown Madonna" as the frontispiece to his *The New Negro* (1925), most literary works by black writers shared Caroline Wynn's pessimism. Jean Toomer's *Cane* (1923) had begun promisingly with glimpses of the black madonna as evidence of an incipient spiritual reawakening among the black folk. But since Toomer saw the folk spirit as doomed to extinction by the forces of industrialization and by rapid black out-migration from the South, these intimations of spiritual rebirth gave way to images of infanticide.[8]

The various infelicitous alliances of the sexes in *Cane* were prelude to Toomer's own spiritual emancipation from American racial definitions, as he imitated his ambivalent narrator John in "Theater" by opting to preserve the "soul-beauty" of the women of the South but to abandon their bodies.[9] Karintha has a child in the woods, whose body she destroys in a "pyramidal sawdust pile," while her soul, "a growing thing ripened too soon," atrophies. Becky, the white woman liminally positioned as the threshold guardian between the black and white sides of the "veil," becomes after her exclusion from the white world an ironic "black" madonna. She gives birth to two black sons who bear allegiance to neither side and who eventually leave her behind to die. Fern becomes a "virgin" when deprived of the spiritual fulfillment of dependable male companionship. Louisa goes mad, Avey becomes an "orphan-woman," and Esther's dream annunciation represents only a psychic compensation for her spiritual and economic dissociation from the black folk. All these possibilities of black motherhood fail to come to fruition because of the residual effects of the plantation sexual economy in stifling black patriarchy. In spite of Barlo's momentary epiphany and the numerous prophetic drawings of black madonnas on courthouse walls and barns, the lasting image of motherhood in *Cane* is that of the lynched mother Mame Lamkins in "Kabnis" whose Caesarian fetus the lynchers crucify. "It was living; but a nigger baby aint supposed t live," says Layman (90). This was a curious tone to take in the midst of a renaissance, and it got worse before it got better.

As Claudia Tate has shown, before even the seizure of masculine prerogative as a form of social protest by the new women of the twenties, Angelina Weld Grimké had explored the meaning of lynching's violence as a "curse" on black motherhood in her works. In her 1916 play *Rachel*, Rachel Loving's fantasy of motherhood falls victim to a fear of lynching that psychically unbalances her: "[Rachel] slips into madness imagining that she hears her unborn children appealing to her not to give them life in a racist society" (Tate, 215). In Nella Larsen's *Quicksand*, Helga Crane similarly ponders, "Why add any more unwanted, tortured Negroes to America? Why *do* Negroes have children?" (103). At the other extreme, the "quicksand" of Larsen's novel is the mind-numbing vortex of black motherhood, while her second novel includes a character who, in a statement that extends far beyond the hazards of "passing," explains, "But, of course, nobody wants a dark child."[10] Whether in the fear of producing new victims of racial violence in Grimké's *Rachel*, of atavistic birth in *Passing*, or of multiple births in *Quicksand*, the issues of social obligation, personal freedom, and self-actualization complicated an unequivocal black modernist embrace of sacrificial motherhood.

Fear of the revenant turned comic in George Schuyler's *Black No More* (1931). The one flaw of Dr. Crookman's skin-whitening process is that it cannot be genetically transmitted, meaning that women who appear to be white begin to have black babies as a result of pandemic color line crossings. Schuyler's antirenaissance themes that blacks were culturally indistinguishable from other Americans and that the driving mechanism of race striving was not a "conservation" of blackness but a displaced desire for "self-obliteration" in whiteness reach their farcical climax in the revelation of the disguised hybridity of even America's white social elite. And though some intrepid mothers in the North allow their mulatto babies to "keep" their color, the erasure of blackness is so complete that "even in Mississippi, Negroes were quite rare."[11] From the self-defeating ambivalence of his poetic reflections on America, Claude McKay would go on to document the sterile carousing of "spiritual truants" Jake and Banjo.[12] In the meantime, Langston Hughes and Zora Neale Hurston, signaled their independence from Du Bois by choosing Van Vechten and Charlotte Osgood Mason as their spiritual godparents.[13] Wallace Thurman was on to something when he made the "infants" of his second novel, *Infants of the Spring*, a group of spoiled New Negro artists. The spiritual blight of the renaissance's failed promise had, in Thurman's mind, stifled the budding artists, offering them only a moment's celebrity as reward.

Du Bois's own judgment of the Harlem literary period was by any standard even harsher. He was unwilling to dispense with the Victorian baggage of his early training and characterized the period's experimentations with newfound freedom in American social life as a wild debauch, like most of the other moralists of the day. In "The Negro College" (1933), Du Bois assessed the Harlem Renaissance as a failed experiment, calling its creative production a "literature written for the benefit of white people and at the behest of white readers and starting out privately from the white point of view. . . . On such an artificial basis no real literature can grow" (*W. E. B. Du Bois: A Reader*, 71–72).

The depression that sealed the doom of the Jazz Age helped to return black writers to a more politicized literature through a Marxist analysis of the black American experience and again later, when the cultural revolutions of the civil rights and black power movements would usher in the politicized art of the "black aesthetic." But Du Bois had made a final attempt to lead the New Negro Renaissance by example before the depression years with his 1928 novel *Dark Princess*, a work that the New Negroes justifiably thought artistically heavy-handed and out of step with the times.[14] It reflected Du Bois's continuing attempt to elaborate a definitive racial contribution by Africans to world civilization, fleshing out his thesis that human "racial" division was an unfolding "family" drama: "The father and his worship is Asia; Europe is the precocious, self-centered, forward striving child; but the land of the mother is and was Africa" (*Darkwater*, 166). Because it brings full circle the question of race as an American institution defined through women's bodies, *Dark Princess* will serve as a useful coda for my discussion of the first, pre-Harlem phase of modern black literature.

Dark Princess

If the issue of bearing black children is, as Caroline Wynn suggests, a moral one, separating those who doubt the future of the black body in America from those who refuse to conceive of an America without blacks, then faith in the future of blackness separates Caroline from Du Bois's incipient madonna, Zora, and also from the heroine of *Dark Princess*, Kautilya, Maharanee of Bwodpur, who bears Matthew Towns a child out of wedlock. A high-caste Indian, Kautilya uses her maternity to establish her faith in American blacks to develop a world-historical civilization. Since the novel's underlying question is whether or not the black race has the capacity to join the dark Asiatics in a global color line revolt against the white West, Kautilya's pregnancy is literally the most dramatic response that she can make.[15] The out-of-wedlock pregnancy was also Du Bois's way of indicating to the New Negroes that his complaint with the young artists was not subject matter so much as treatment. Du Bois commented in "Criteria of Negro Art": "We can afford the Truth. White folk today cannot" (297).

Before *The Quest of the Silver Fleece* was published, Du Bois had already embarked on a series of important changes and new experiences that would make *Dark Princess* possible some seventeen years later. In August 1910, Du Bois began his first tenure with the NAACP as director of research and publications. Two months later, in October 1910, he published an essay in the *Independent* called "Marrying of Black Folk," in which he set down specific terms by which he could accept the possibility of racial intermarriage. Acknowledging that "wholesale intermarriage of races during the present generation would be a social calamity by reason of the wide cultural, ethical and traditional differences," Du Bois concluded, though, that "a desire to impose on future generations one's own judgment . . . by physical force, [was] *prima facie* evidence of the logical weakness" of prohibitions to intermarriage ("Marrying," 34).[16]

In 1911, the year of *The Quest*, Du Bois attended the First Universal Races Congress in London, where he was hosted by Her Highness the Ranee of Sarawak, whom Mary White Ovington identified as the prototype of Kautilya.[17] In 1919 Du Bois helped to convene the First Pan-African Congress in Paris, devoted to formulating a plan for African development based on disposition of the former German colonies (*Autobiography*, 271–72).[18] Thereafter, in 1921, 1923, and 1927, Du Bois helped to organize subsequent Pan-African congresses. Collectively, these developments helped to expand Du Bois's concern beyond the American race question to the global color line, such that his 1928 novel's adaptation of the marriage plot forces the black male quest hero to choose between a Chicago New Woman and an Indian princess.

More than even Caroline Wynn, Sara Andrews, the "black" white witch of *Dark Princess*, embodies the force she represents. Physically, she "gave an impression of cleanliness, order, cold, clean hardness, and unusual efficiency" (109). Predictably, Sara "could pass for white" (111), largely because her manner, like Caroline's, is so cold and formal. "Neither a prude nor a flirt," Sara "simply had a good intellect without moral scruples," and this ethical vacuum extends to her "clear idea of the communal and social value of virginity, respectability, and good clothes" (114). She is the real force behind the neo-Washington ward politician, the Honorable Sammy Scott, whose personal ambition masquerades as political progress for the race. After Matthew thwarts a terrorist attack on the Klan train that lynched the porter Jimmie, he goes to jail, only to be released into the protective custody of Sara and Sammy. They proceed to turn the zombified Matthew into a political operative, trading on his talented tenth panache. Sara, like Caroline Wynn in the earlier work, uses Matthew to seize power that she cannot hope to gain directly as a woman, and when she decides to marry him, she and Matthew seal their engagement with a handshake because she so loathes human contact. Sara's attitude toward motherhood is easily captured in her reaction to Matthew's offhand mention of "a baby": "Certainly not!" (153). Small wonder that after the wedding ceremony, when Matthew tries to place his arm around her shoulder, she snaps at him, "'Be careful of the veil'" (144).

The key term in Sara's description is "efficiency," for as Du Bois revealed in *Dusk of Dawn*, his first visit to Africa in 1923, after years of idealizing the continent in his work, taught him a fundamental "truth" that helped to define the distinction that he was searching for as a "race message." "And the Great Truth was this: efficiency and happiness do not go together in modern culture. Going south from London, as the world darkens it gets happier" (*Dusk*, 125). For Du Bois, Africa's isolation was both a blessing and a curse, the latter because, lying outside the communications network of the West, commonplaces in America that would prevent much suffering were unheard of in Africa. On the other hand, "African life with its isolation has deeper knowledge of human souls. The village life, the forest ways, the teeming markets, bring in intimate human knowl-edge that the West misses, sinking the individual in the social. Africans know fewer folk, but know them infinitely better. Their intertwined communal souls, therefore, brook no poverty nor prostitution—these things to them are un-understandable" (*Dusk*, 128–29). Despite this bit of firsthand idealization of Africa, Du Bois admitted his personal preference for New York with all its faults (128).

Du Bois was more emphatically literal in his articulation of the soul bargain as plot device in *Dark Princess* than he had been in *The Quest*, perhaps not trusting the younger generation to understand the motivation of someone who turns down wealth and power for a life of poverty and manual labor. When Kautilya returns into Matthew's life, her purpose in becoming an external conscience that will reawaken his dormant idealism is to "save [his] soul from hell" (209). "'Too late,' he murmured. 'I have sold it to the Devil.'" Gently, though, Kautilya re-stores his faith in himself so that he is no longer torn asunder by "double aims." His return to Truth and Beauty and Goodness is embodied in the dark princess's dreams of global self-determination: "The world was one woman and one cause" (210). Their passionate liaison in his apartment, which he has maintained as a soul retreat from his sterile marriage to Sara, almost immediately results in a pregnancy. The impression that Matthew has abandoned his race for this exotic woman becomes the basis of a further irony. The public, unaware of Sara's cor-rupting influence on him, sees his running away with Kautilya after all Sara has done for him as "the Sunday School example of one who has sold his soul to the devil, . . . punished . . . for following lust and desecrating the home" (263). Du Bois rescues Matthew from this contradiction of appearances by investing Kautilya's pregnancy and childbirth with the significance of a "race-message," saturating Kautilya's "Asian" body with the "mother-idea" of the black world.

In his essay "The Damnation of Women" (1920), Du Bois had made his most definitive statement on the world's indebtedness to black womanhood, which he associated with the figure of "Veiled Melancholy."[19] But as in the development of his own concept of the black madonna, "Veiled Melancholy" reveals her true features as the "All-Mother" of Du Bois's pageant "The People of Peoples and Their Gifts to Men": [20]

> The world must heed these daughters of sorrow, from the primal black All-Mother of men down through the ghostly throng of mighty womanhood, who walked in the mysterious dawn of Asia and Africa; from Neith, the primal mother of all, whose feet rest on hell, and whose almighty hands uphold the heavens; all religion, from beauty to beast, lies on her eager breasts; her body bears the stars, while her shoulders are necklaced by the dragon; from black Neith down to

> "That starred Ethiop queen who strove
> To set her beauty's praise above
> The sea-nymphs," [21]

> through dusky Cleopatras, dark Candaces, and darker, fiercer Zinghas, to our own day and our own land. (*Darkwater*, 165–66)

Du Bois traces a line of descent from mythological mother images to the "Veiled Melancholy" of African American experience to make the point that black American women are, in fact, the local manifestation of a universally recognized generative/nurturing principle who "walked in the mysterious dawn of Asia and Africa." Drawing on several sources, Du Bois mythologizes the derivation of the "mother-idea" from African cultural practice: "In subtle and mysterious way, despite her curious history, her slavery, polygamy, and toil, the spell of the African mother pervades her land. Isis, the mother, is still titular goddess, in thought if not in name, of the dark continent" (*Darkwater*, 166). A few years after writing this paean, Du Bois's first visit to African soil confirmed this anticipation of African maternal provenance: "Different, Immense, Menacing, Alluring. It is a great black bosom where the spirit longs to die." [22]

For Du Bois, the fact that in his personal experience it was "mothers and mothers of mothers who seem[ed] to count, while fathers [were] shadowy memories" (*Darkwater*, 168) explained why black women survived slavery with their souls intact. "To no modern race does its women mean so much as to the Negro nor come so near to the fulfilment of its meaning" (*Darkwater*, 173). Du Bois concluded with a tribute to black womanhood: "For this, their promise, and for their hard past, I honor the women of my race. Their beauty,—their dark and mysterious beauty of midnight eyes, crumpled hair, and soft, full-featured faces—is perhaps more to me than you, because I was born to its warm and subtle spell; but their worth is yours as well as mine" (186). Du Bois's extension of that spiritual message to the Indian princess and through her to the world is consistent with his idea of making the black contribution to world civilization plain, but it seems in conflict with his notion that "transmitting human culture" is an argument for "group solidarity" and against intermarriage (W. E. B. Du Bois: A Reader, 373). As with the "race soul" concept generally, this leap reflects more than a little inconsistency.

Black elevation to world-historical status serves, in Dark Princess, as a rationale for Kautilya's embodiment of the soul force that saves Matthew. In effect, it is the black woman's "soul" that Kautilya bears, since her message to Matthew to survive through faith is his mother's message passed on through her. In contrast, the soul of white America resides in the woman who is technically a black American. The move extends Du Bois's established use of black women as embodiments of the white American "spiritual ideal" to its logical conclusion, but in so doing, it demonstrates the utter emancipation of "race" from the body. If Kautilya is not herself a black woman, her worthiness to bear this message comes through in her spiritual apprenticeship to the black woman whom she perceives . as the epitome of motherhood: "Oh, Matthew, you have a wonderful mother. Have you seen her hands? Have you seen the gnarled and knotted glory of her hands? . . . Your mother is Kali, the Black One; wife of Siva, Mother of the World!" (220).

Du Bois's characterization of Mrs. Towns is another of the signal reversals of this novel from the earlier The Quest of the Silver Fleece. If Mrs. Towns has any counterpart in The Quest, it is Elspeth, the swamp witch and symbol of black female degradation. Elspeth is a conjure woman who, despite her power to drag Zora down into corruption with her, nonetheless is the bearer of the seeds from Africa that become the first cotton crop that establishes black economic independence, the "silver fleece." Elspeth plants the seed, but only the next generation can reap it—the generation of Zora and Bles. In short, Elspeth embodies the slave mothers' unworthiness to found the black nation; only their daughters, trained by American cultural missionaries, could prevent the corruption of race nationalism at its domestic base. Du Bois's black madonna in The Quest is not an actual mother at all but a projection of a reformed black motherhood that would take what was valuable from the past in order to build for the future—an interpreter/priestess/cultural missionary whose firsthand knowledge of the "damnation of black women" would forge in her the commitment to make hers the last generation of black women to bear the stigma of the black Venus.

In *Dark Princess*, Du Bois, having come to terms with the history of black womanhood, creates in Mrs. Towns an utterly transformed icon of black womanhood. Though she, like Elspeth, has personally endured the slave experience, she serves as a triumphant reminder of black female heroism, not a community scandal. Since Du Bois holds her offstage until the very end of the work, we see her only through the eyes of Kautilya, who recognizes her universality and mythic stature as a corn goddess: "And when I saw that old mother of yours standing in the blue shadows of twilight with flowers, cotton and corn about her, I knew that I was looking upon one of the ancient prophets of India and that she was to lead me out of the depths in which I found myself and up to the atonement for which I yearned" (221). Kautilya starts, after this first meeting, a planned seven-year apprenticeship under Mrs. Towns, timed to end with Matthew's release from prison: "We prayed to God, hers and mine, and out of her ancient lore she did the sacrifice of flame and blood which was the ceremony of my own great fathers and which came down to her from Shango of Western Africa."

Testimony to Du Bois's changed perspective is his attitude toward African cultural retentions. In *The Souls*, Du Bois is vague about precisely what undiluted Africanisms he would have black Americans hold on to. His discussion of the one area in which African practices had enjoyed acknowledged longevity in African American culture—folk religion—was at best ambivalent about the African legacy. Describing the black folk preacher as the successor to the "Priest or Medicine-man" (138), Du Bois had earlier pictured the spiritual world of the slave plantation as a world beset by supernatural forces: "Endowed with a rich tropical imagination and a keen, delicate appreciation of Nature, the transplanted African lived in a world animate with gods and devils, elves and witches; full of strange influences,—of Good to be implored, of Evil to be propitiated. Slavery, then, was to him the dark triumph of Evil over him. All the hateful powers of the Under-world were striving against him, and a spirit of revolt and revenge filled his heart" (139). Du Bois's rationale for the importation of the Faustian theme into his description of the African American worldview was that a cosmic battle against witches and devils had been integral to black folk culture all along. But in the telling, black religion became a dubious vehicle for cultural transmission, and its function would be ceded to the priesthood of cultural interpreters if Du Bois had his way.

Du Bois's disapproval of "superstition" in *The Quest* seems at first focused on Elspeth's powers. Through a later bizarre encounter in the swamp with the figure that Zora thought of as a demon, Du Bois reveals that not conjure but traffic with the unhallowed lusts of whites is the source of Elspeth's corruption. Nevertheless, there remains a residue of the sensational and luridness attached to the "supernatural" events in the swamp. The rationalist who had looked askance in *The Souls* at the "resources of heathenism"—"exorcism and witchcraft, the mysterious Obi worship with its barbarous rites, spells, and blood-sacrifice even, now and then, of human victims" (139)—was, in *The Quest*, still not convinced that African retentions did not represent more of a hindrance than a blessing.

But in *Dark Princess*, Mrs. Towns unabashedly presides over a Shangoist "blood" sacrifice and draws Kautilya's praise for keeping this tradition alive. The ceremony is not Kautilya's true spiritual initiation, however, which comes about by walking in the everyday life "path" of her new mother. She becomes initiated into the rites of black womanhood by reenacting the tribulations of Mrs. Towns, first as a domestic worker in Richmond (where she is sexually attacked by her white employer, just as "Mother" warned she would be). Later, she becomes a to-bacco factory worker, a waitress in Philadelphia, and then a box factory worker and labor union organizer in New York's Lower East Side. The novel's ending, with Matthew's atonement through physical labor among the masses, his divorce from Sara, and his marriage to Kautilya (now a mother herself of the new maharajah of Bwodpur) suggests Du Bois's shift in interest on the question of race development toward an international project of uniting dark people around the globe with similar experiences of color-line discrimination and toward Marxism as a basis of social struggle.

Later, in *Dusk of Dawn* (1940), Du Bois would go far beyond even this revision of his original concept of race striving, admitting that race is something that he "can feel better than [he] can explain" (*Dusk*, 116). What "race" is, Du Bois says in *Dusk of Dawn*, he does not know, "nor does science know today" (117). The only constant, then, is a common history of oppression, which can be shared by those not physically identical: "The physical bond is least and the badge of color relatively unimportant save as a badge; the real essence of this kinship is its social heritage of slavery; the discrimination and insult; and this heritage binds together not simply the children of Africa, but extends through yellow Asia and into the South Seas" (117). This older, less equivocally socialist Du Bois acknowledged his part in the mythic construction of race difference as an expedient against oppression, noting that the "race concept" was in fact "a group of contradictory forces, facts, and tendencies" that he ultimately found "illogical" and "irreconcilable" (133). There are no race "souls" because there are no "races," only the illusion of "integrating souls" produced by analogizing the social group to a body: "The soul is still individual if it is free."[23]

In changing the question of race difference from a matter of somatic difference to one of spiritual difference, Du Bois had exposed the paradox identified by Kwame Anthony Appiah—that of making the body ultimately irrelevant in the formulation of race, despite his reliance on somatic features as a basis for collective striving. His final word on race, though, again warned that a cultural, rather than biological, concept of race entailed a palpable risk in the form of a predominantly political definition: "the black man is a person who must ride 'Jim Crow' in Georgia" (*Dusk*, 153). Kautilya's exploration of a common heritage of "discrimination and insult" that she has personally experienced in Bwodpur at the hands of the white West because of the "badge" of color suggests that the triumph of the African "mother-idea" is the universalization of reverence for a new productive, nondecorative ideal of womanhood: woman as "co-worker in the kingdom of culture."

Ironically, Du Bois's move in *Dark Princess* (which he subtitled *A Romance*) away from realism freed him to pursue a concept of "race" more compatible with the ongoing "scientific" dismantling of embodied race. Du Bois's creation of a nonbiological "black" madonna underscored his belief that the mother idea was a gift to the world and dictated a new direction for the priestly class of cultural interpreters to pursue, the global dissemination of this rehabilitated ideal of womanhood. Black motherhood as a performative, rather than biological, phenomenon would become the basis of a secular "spiritual" reformation of historic dimensions. Thus, in *Dark Princess*, though he agrees that race has more to do with culture and history than with the body, he reminds the New Negro generation that certain bodies have developed a common culture because of their shared history—a history they would be doomed to repeat without a collective commitment to preserve and broadcast the best of that culture to the world.

Notes

Preface

1. William B. Smith, *The Color Line: A Brief in Behalf of the Unborn* (New York: McClure, Phillips and Co., 1905). In *Outcasts from Evolution: Scientific Attitudes of Racial Inferiority, 1859–1900* (Urbana: University of Illinois Press, 1971), John S. Haller Jr. summarizes the arguments supporting the theory of the "natural extinction" of blacks (203–10).

2. See *The National Cyclopedia of American Biography*, 223–24, for biographical details on Smith's career. See also "People in the Foreground," *Current Literature* 38 (June 1905): 509.

3. See William B. Smith, 165–74. Smith's stance against higher education for blacks put him at odds also with his own College of Arts and Sciences dean, James Hardy Dillard, for whom Dillard University was named. See John P. Dyer, *Tulane: The Biography of a University, 1834–1965* (New York: Harper and Row, 1966), 83 n. 14.

4. See George W. Stocking Jr., *Race, Culture, and Evolution: Essays in the History of Anthropology* (1968; Chicago: University of Chicago Press, 1982), 209–10.

5. W. E. B. Du Bois, *The Souls of Black Folk* (1903; New York: Bantam, 1989).

6. See Frederick L. Hoffman, "Race Traits and Tendencies of the American Negro," American Economics Association, *Publications* 11 (August 1896).

7. See Willcox's lecture in Southern Society for the Promotion of the Study of Race Conditions and Problems in the South, *Race Problems of the South: Report of the Proceedings of the First Annual Conference* (Richmond: B. F. Johnson Publishing Co., 1900), 155–56 (hereafter cited as "Southern Society").

8. See Joel Williamson, *New People: Miscegenation and Mulattoes in the United States* (New York: Free Press, 1980), 62–75, for a discussion of the evolution of the "one-drop rule."

9. See William B. Smith, 8–10 and 15, for the rationale behind the racial "double-standard." As I make clear in chapter 1, the restrictions on this specific form of interracial reproductive alliance are based in gender ideas and patriarchal privileges that go back to the beginnings of racial classification in American slavery.

Ironically, Smith may have showed more interest in the "unborn" of the race than in his own fascinating children. His oldest child, Merrill Neville Smith, died young. Yeremya Kenly (Y.K.), Kathryn (Katy), and William Benjamin Smith Jr. (Bill Smith) were the adolescent playmates of Ernest Hemingway at Horton's Bay in Michigan, and they figured in many of his important early experiences and literary creations. One anecdote related by Hemingway biographer James R. Mellow highlights an irreligious streak in Smith and a seeming lack of concern about his children: "A family story had it that, once, when Y.K. and his friends were out sailing on the lake and a severe storm came up, [Professor Smith's sister-in-law], frantic about the children, ran to Professor Smith's study to rouse him. The professor walked down to the lakeshore and shouted over the waters, 'Oh, Lord, give up Thy dead,' then turned and went back to his work" (*Hemingway: A Life without Consequences* [Boston: Houghton Mifflin, 1992], 37). On the other hand, compare Warren Browne's recollection of Smith as very spiritual and personally attentive to his son Y.K. during a bout of typhoid fever. Browne cites Smith's sister-in-law's vicious defamation of him during and after his life as a source of much misinformation. See *Titan vs. Taboo: The Life of William Benjamin Smith* (Tucson: Diogenes Press, 1961) x, 88–89. For the controversy over Smith's religious views in *Ecce Deus* (1911) that resulted in public outrage and an investigation by the university, see Dyer, 173–74. For more about the Smith children and Hemingway, see Mellow; Gioia Diliberto, *Hadley* (New York: Ticknor and Fields, 1992); and Donald St. John, "Interview with Hemingway's 'Bill Gorton,'" in Bertram D. Sarason, *Hemingway and "The Sun" Set* (Washington, D.C.: National Cash Register Co., 1972), 151–88.

10. Quoted in I. A. Newby, *Jim Crow's Defense: Anti-Negro Thought in America, 1900–1930* (Baton Rouge: Louisiana State University Press, 1965), 4. See Smith's adoption of this principle in William B. Smith, 17.

11. See Nancy Leys Stepan's discussion of this theory in "Race and Gender: The Role of Analogy in Science," in *Anatomy of Racism*, ed. David Theo Goldberg (Minneapolis: University of Minnesota Press, 1990), 44–52.

12. See Tamar Lewin, "The Balkans Rapes: A Legal Test for the Outraged," *New York Times*, January 16, 1993, B16.

13. See Werner Sollors's discussion of this illustration in *Beyond Ethnicity: Consent and Descent in American Culture* (New York: Oxford University Press, 1986), 75–78.

14. See Houston A. Baker Jr., *Modernism and the Harlem Renaissance* (Chicago: University of Chicago Press, 1987), 91.

15. See Houston A. Baker Jr., "The Promised Body: Reflections on Canon in an Afro-American Context," *Poetics Today* 9, no. 2, 353.

16. See Roland Barthes, *Mythologies*, selected and trans. Annette Lavers (1957; New York: Farrar, Straus, and Giroux, 1972), 131 ff.

17. See Arnold Rampersad, "W. E. B. Du Bois as a Man of Literature," in *Critical Essays on W. E. B. Du Bois*, ed. William L. Andrews (Boston: G. K. Hall, 1985), 59. I am using a different conception of myth than, for instance, that proposed by Robert Stepto in his 1979 study of early modern African American literature, *From Behind the Veil: A Study of Afro-American Narrative* (Urbana: University of Illinois Press, 1979). Stepto also calls attention to the crucial way that the spatial limitations of black life have defined African American experience, by highlighting W. E. B. Du Bois's metaphor for color discrimination—the "veil"—as a boundary between white and black social space. In his discussion of the beginnings of a distinctive black literary tradition, he attempts to establish a least common denominator for the tradition's "major" texts—literally, a myth of origins. He adapts Northrop Frye's concept of preliterary "shared stories or myths" that help to "shape the forms that comprise a given culture's literary canon" into what he calls "pregeneric myths" of a culture (Stepto, xv). According to Stepto, the "primary pregeneric myth for Afro-America is the quest for freedom and literacy," a quest narrative that takes the black hero on journeys between spaces of relative social confinement and relative social freedom. My own discussion of what is mythic in black life and literature includes the ritual performances of race difference required of blacks at different times and places, the theories of race difference on which such performances rested, and the counterritual appropriations of such formal traditions as gestures of defiance toward and demystification of theories of black inferiority. I make no distinction between shared cultural tales, ritual behavior enacting race difference, and the scientific folklore of race difference because all discourse that invents or maintains the idea of race in America—that different "origins" require different destinies among the citizenry—is functionally mythic behavior.

Chapter One: American Body Politics

1. Ralph Ellison, "What America Would Be Like without Blacks," in *Going to the Territory* (1986; New York: Vintage, 1995), 104, 110, 107.

2. See Orlando Patterson, *Slavery and Social Death: A Comparative Study* (Cambridge: Harvard University Press, 1982), 13. Patterson explains that "natal alienation" suggests "what is critical in the slave's forced alienation, the loss of ties of birth in both ascending and descending generations. It has the important nuance of a loss of native status, of deracination . . . from any attachment to groups or localities other than those chosen for him by the master" (7).

3. See Ellison's "Twentieth-Century Fiction and the Black Mask of Humanity," in *Shadow and Act* (New York: Random House, 1964), 24–44.

4. See also Thomas F. Gossett's chapter "Literary Naturalism and Race" in *Race: The History of an Idea in America* (New York: Schocken Books, 1965), 198–227.

5. Joseph A. Tillinghast, *The Negro in Africa and America* (1902; New York: Negro Universities Press, 1968), 1.

6. See Nathaniel S. Shaler, *The Neighbor: The Natural History of Human Contacts* (Boston: Houghton Mifflin, 1904), 327–28.

7. See Nathaniel S. Shaler, "The Negro Problem," *Atlantic Monthly* 54 (November 1884): 699.

8. See Joel Williamson, *The Crucible of Race: Black-White Relations in the American South since Emancipation* (New York: Oxford University Press, 1984), 140–79, on Dixon and Page.

9. See pt. 3 of John H. Bracy, August Meier, and Eliot Rudwick, eds., *Black Nationalism in America* (Indianapolis: Bobbs-Merrill, 1970).

10. Quoted in Hortense J. Spillers, "Mamma's Baby, Papa's Maybe: An American Grammar Book," *Diacritics* 17 (Summer 1987): 72.

11. Williamson, *New People*, 7. My assumption here, of course, is that "Negro" refers to a female, since said infraction with a male might have warranted further vituperation with biblical overtones. See A. Leon Higginbotham Jr., *In the Matter of Color: Race and the American Legal Process*, The Colonial Period (New York: Oxford University Press, 1978), 23.

12. George Washington Cable uses the example of Pocahontas to distinguish white sentiments toward a nonblack racial other, in "The Freedman's Case in Equity," in *The Silent South* (New York: Charles Scribner's Sons, 1885), 35. See Sollors, 75–81, for the significance of Pocahontas in the tradition of the American "melting pot."

13. See Higginbotham, 42, for the uncertainties about the Davis case.

14. See ibid., 52, for the 1705 law declaring slaves to be "real estate."

15. See, for example, ibid., 128, 159, 194, 252.

16. Jordan also cites a Maryland transaction of 1649 that shows that colony's projection of slave status onto black bodies indefinitely into the future—the deeding of "two Negro men and a woman 'and all their issue both male and Female.'" See Winthrop Jordan, *White over Black: American Attitudes Toward the Negro, 1550–1812* (Chapel Hill: University of North Carolina Press, 1968), 75.

17. See Higginbotham, 55–57, for the colonial laws that allowed owners to kill disobedient slaves; for laws allowing dismemberment by nonowners against unruly slaves; and for laws that compensated owners for slaves killed as a disciplinary or terroristic act to ensure the docility of other slaves.

18. See Michael J. Cassity, *Legacy of Fear: American Race Relations to 1900* (Westport, Conn.: Greenwood Press, 1985), 20, 32, for the regulations regarding white male interracial sex. Cassity points out that this act "may also be one of the last instances in which the impulse toward interracial sex is attributed to the 'Lascivious & Lustful desires' of white women." The dominant myth of white "ladyhood" would extend the assumptions of race chastity, if not strict sexual innocence, to white women who denied voluntary

participation in interracial sex, as a rule. But as Martha Hodes has demonstrated, the tradition of condemning white female depravity in interracial unions continued, especially in court cases involving divorces and those involving white vigilantes acting as "moral regulators." See Hodes, "The Sexualization of Reconstruction Politics: White Women and Black Men in the South after the Civil War," in *American Sexual Politics: Sex, Gender, and Race since the Civil War* (Chicago: University of Chicago Press, 1992), 59–60, 67–69. See also James Hugo Johnston, *Race Relations in Virginia and Miscegenation in the South, 1776–1860* (Amherst: University of Massachusetts Press, 1970), 258–68.

19. See Higginbotham, 44, and Jordan, 138.

20. Exceptions, of course, did exist. See the case recounted by Jordan of the mulatto, Gideon Gibson, accused of "whitewashing" his progeny through his white wife's womb (172–73).

21. See Lincoln's thoughts below. See Hinton Rowan Helper's extended discussion of Jefferson in *Nojoque: A Question for a Continent* (New York: George F. Carleton and Co., 1867), 26–29.

22. See Jordan, 465–69.

23. See ibid., 475.

24. By contrast, Jefferson encouraged intermixture between whites and American Indians, whose savage condition he attributed not to the distinctive Indian body but to environmental factors. See ibid., 477–80.

25. I do not intend to rehash the circumstances of the Hemings case. Winthrop Jordan's suspicion falls upon Jefferson's father-in-law, John Wayles, though he states that "Jefferson's paternity can be neither refuted nor proved from the known circumstances" (466–67). See also Bertram Wyatt-Brown's promotion of Jefferson's nephews Peter and Samuel Carr as the most likely suspects in *Southern Honor: Ethics and Behavior in the Old South* (New York: Oxford University Press, 1982), 310.

26. In fairness, I should point out that the entire text of the *Notes* unfolds along this narrative pattern. This does not mitigate the fact, however, that Jefferson's reputation as a philosopher, statesman, and egalitarian lent incalculable weight to his speculations on race difference, which accounts for his frequently being cited as an "objective" observer who came to the same conclusions as the unabashed racists.

27. Translated and quoted in Thomas W. Heilke, *Voegelin on the Idea of Race: An Analysis of Modern European Racism* (Baton Rouge: Louisiana State University Press, 1990), 59.

28. Samuel Sewall, *The Selling of Joseph* (1700; New York: Arno Press and the New York Times, 1969), no page numbers in the original.

29. In the words of Winthrop Jordan, "A darkened nation would present incontrovertible evidence that sheer animal sex was governing the American destiny and that the great experiment in the wilderness had failed to maintain the social and personal restraints which were the hallmarks and the very stuff of civilization. A blackened posterity would

mean that the basest energies had guided the direction of the American experiment and that civilized man had turned to beast in the forest. Retention of whiteness would be evidence of purity and of diligent nurture of the original body of the folk. Could a blackened people look back to Europe and say that they had faithfully performed their errand?" (543).

30. See Martha Banta, *Imaging American Women: Ideas and Ideals in Cultural History* (New York: Columbia University Press, 1987), 490, fig. 11.14.

31. Theodore Galle's 1600 representation of the "meeting" of Amerigo Vespucci and his namesake, America, considerably softens the savage temperament of the Indian Queen by placing her in a hammock, passively awaiting the approaching, towering European. See Joshua C. Taylor, *America as Art* (New York: Harper and Row, 1976), 4. Vespucci carries a banner on a pole surmounted by a cross, signifying his gift of Christianity to the heathen clime, but his dominant relation to the recumbent Queen is as heavily invested in his symbols of modernity as his phallic posture. Carrying a compass, dressed in European fashion (in contrast to the Queen's nudity), and flanked by his ships in the harbor, Vespucci is clearly the emissary of a "masculine" civilization awakening a dormant tropical giantess.

32. Taylor, though asserting that "America was chiefly seen as an extension of the European mind," does not explain why people who identified themselves with "the insignias that stood for their national origin and political patronage" (5) did not transfer such images to their local enterprises.

33. See Hugh Honour, *The New Golden Land: European Images of America from the Discoveries to the Present Time* (New York: Random House, 1975), 84–117.

34. This point is made very well by Taylor himself (11–20).

35. E. McClung Fleming considers it no accident that the "Sons of Liberty" chose to dress as Indians during the 1773 Boston Tea Party, without giving an explanation. See "The American Image as Indian Princess, 1765–1783," *Winterthur Portfolio* 2 (1965): 69. Perhaps he felt that the association of the Indian with warlikeness and independence of spirit was conventional enough as a cultural concept to obviate further discussion.

36. See E. McClung Fleming's "From Indian Princess to Greek Goddess: The American Image, 1783–1815," *Winterthur Portfolio* 3 (1967): 46.

37. See, for example, illustrations of this figure in Taylor, 14, and in Fleming, "Indian Princess to Greek Goddess," 52, 53.

38. See Jean Fagan Yellin, *Women and Sisters: Antislavery Feminists in American Culture* (New Haven: Yale University Press, 1989), 4, 6, 11, 16, 18, 20, for a series of representations of enslavement, with and without the accompanying figure of nation or personified virtue.

39. See Cassity, 26–28, and Jordan, 79.

40. See Jordan, 110.

41. See Hugh Honour, *The Image of the Black in Western Art*, vol. 4, *From the American Revolution to World War I* (Houston: Menil Foundation, 1989), pt. 1, p. 34.

42. U.S. Army Corps of Engineers captain Edward B. Hunt's analysis of the physical geography of North America, *Union Foundations: A Study of American Nationality as a Fact of Science* (New York: Van Nostrand, 1863), employed the vision of America as a living organism to describe the southern revolt as "unnatural," on the grounds that it attempted to "dismember" the body politic (16).

43. See George M. Fredrickson, *The Black Image in the White Mind: The Debate on Afro-American Character and Destiny, 1817–1914* (New York: Harper and Row, 1971), 150.

44. See chapter 2.

45. According to Lillian Smith, each individual body in the Jim Crow South served as a microcosm of the social order: "when we as small children crept over the race line and ate and played with Negroes . . . we felt the same dread fear of consequences, the same overwhelming guilt we felt when we crept over the sex line and played with our bodies." Smith was well aware that the emphasis southern culture placed on alienating children from their own bodies was directly related to efforts to alienate white bodies from black ones, and her analogy of racial equality to masturbation convincingly illustrates the somatic context of the sex/race equation that permeated southern mythology. Lillian Smith, *Killers of the Dream* (1949; New York: W. W. Norton, 1978), 84.

46. Joel Williamson describes the postwar South as "an organic society" that imagined a "social body" in which "every part would have its place and function." But "since some parts of the body are more vital than others," there must be an absolute hierarchy: "A hand is expendable, a head is not" (*Crucible*, 24, 28).

47. See Graves's comments in "Southern Society," 53.

48. I have paraphrased liberally from Barthes's "Myth Today," in *Mythologies*, esp. 118, 120, 124, 127, 129, 130, 131, 132, 142, 144.

49. See Barthes, 119: "the fundamental character of the mythical concept is to be *appropriated*."

50. See Goldberg's critique of Cornel West's assertion that racist thought is unified at the discursive level ("Social Formation of Racist Discourse," in Goldberg, *Anatomy of Racism*, 299). Goldberg acknowledges only two levels of racist discourse, the preconceptual and the discursive (or formal) level. Like Barthes, he insists that analysis of racist discourse must involve both the grammatical (discursive, formal) level and the preformal level (298).

51. "*Differential exclusion* is the most basic primitive term of the deep structure definitive of racist discourse. As the basic propositional content of racist desires, dispositions, beliefs, hypotheses, and expressions (including acts, laws, and institutions) racial exclusion motivates the entire superstructure of racist discourse" (Goldberg, "Social Formation of Racist Discourse," 304).

52. W. E. B. Du Bois provides graphic depictions of the "colored world within" the white world in his autobiographical *Dusk of Dawn* (Millwood, N.Y.: Kraus-Thomson, 1975). Du Bois explains the impression of black Americans' "double environment" of black space surrounded by white space as being entombed behind a "thick sheet of invisible but horribly tangible plate glass" that leaves them increasingly "hysterical" about getting the attention of the white world beyond. See *Dusk*, 173, 131.

53. See Stocking, 21–28.

54. Benedict Anderson describes the effect as one produced "by temporal coincidence, and measured by clock and calendar" (24).

55. Anderson claims that "one could argue that every essential modern conception is based on a conception of 'meanwhile'" (24).

56. If, according to Darwin, evolutionary change was "natural" to the human species, then the "failure" of African people to evolve was evidence of their "natural" separation from white Europeans. See Robert F. Shufeldt, *America's Greatest Problem: The Negro* (Philadelphia: F. A. Davis Co., 1915), 84.

57. See address of Hillary Herbert in Southern Society, 25.

58. See Shaler, *Neighbor*, 135–36, on the futility of educating blacks into full citizenship. See also Haller's summation of white attitudes toward black education in the social Darwinist era (141–47).

59. See Du Bois, *Dusk*, 99. Thomas Dixon Jr. asserts a three-thousand-year evolutionary gap in *The Leopard's Spots: A Romance of the White Man's Burden, 1865–1900* (New York: Doubleday, Page and Co., 1902), 394, while Shufeldt arbitrarily pegs the time differential at one million years (*America's Greatest Problem*, 51), increasing Du Bois's "one thousand years" one thousandfold.

60. See Stephen Jay Gould, *The Mismeasure of Man* (New York: W. W. Norton, 1981), 73, and Gossett, 44–51.

61. See Georg W. F. Hegel, *The Philosophy of History* (New York: Willey Book Co., 1900), 99. See also Hunt, 48–49, and Gossett, 91.

62. See Haller for a thorough discussion of Nathaniel Shaler's "cradle-land theory," a revision of Aggassiz's "zoological provinces" (166–87).

63. See also Stocking, 41–68, for a comprehensive discussion of the relationship between polygenism and late-nineteenth-century racism.

64. Quoted in Haller, 89.

65. See Gossett, 353–58, for the eugenics campaign of Madison Grant; 387–89, for the moral campaign against non-Aryan culture by Henry Fairfield Osborn; and 390–94, for the secular vision of Lothrop Stoddard. Though these writers gave their primary attention to the threat to white America from foreign immigrants, they were largely extending established racialist concepts into finer and finer areas of distinction.

66. See Haller, 3–39. See Shaler, *Neighbor*, 135–36, for his views on the "arrested de-

velopment" of Africans. See Tillinghast, 91–95, for his summary of the physical and psychic limitations of African bodies.

67. Tillinghast, 21–27.

68. Heilke, 108. As I will show later, this reading of the external form as an index of character is an indispensable element of the witch and madonna figures.

69. See Gould, 113–22, on recapitulation and neoteny.

70. See Haller, 187–202, for a discussion of Edward Drinker Cope's terms "accelerated" and "retarded" as temporal classifications of racial difference.

71. The advent of more rigorous social science methodology did not disturb the popularity and usefulness of race gendering. As late as the 1950s, the sociologist Robert Park offered that "*he* [i.e., "the Negro"] is, so to speak, the *lady* among the races" (quoted in Fredrickson, 327; my emphases). That Park could simultaneously envision the black race as a masculine entity— "he"—while attributing feminine qualities to it speaks volumes about the arbitrariness of race gendering.

72. See Charles Darwin, *The Descent of Man, and Selection in Relation to Sex* (New York: D. Appleton and Co., 1871), 2:302, 306, 310–12.

73. See Gould's discussion of recapitulationist analogies of gender and race (115–18).

74. Justice Henry Brown's majority decision in *Plessy* cites as precedence the ruling by Chief Justice Shaw of the Supreme Judicial Court of Massachusetts, who held in favor of Boston's segregated school system: "When this great principle [i.e., equality of citizens before the law] comes to be applied to the actual and various conditions of persons in society, it will not warrant the assertion, that men and women are legally clothed with the same civil and political powers, and that children and adults are legally to have the same functions and be subject to the same treatment; but only that the rights of all, as they are settled and regulated by law, are equally entitled to the paternal consideration and protection of the law for their maintenance and security" (quoted in Otto H. Olsen, *The Thin Disguise: Turning Point in Negro History. Plessy v. Ferguson: A Documentary Presentation (1864–1896)* [New York: Humanities Press, 1967], 109). Brown does not have to announce the implied connective here, for his audience would have immediately recognized its conceptual basis. Female and Negro inequality to the adult white male norm is sanctioned by, and in turn gives further validity to, "a central feature of the analogical science of inferiority"—"that adult women and lower races were more childlike in their bodies and minds than white males" and therefore are entitled to the same treatment as children (Stepan, "Race and Gender," 51). They form a class of second-order citizens who must alike depend on the "paternal consideration and protection of the law" but may not presume to paternal authority themselves. Thus the language of Jim Crow serves a second function in the maintenance of the status quo: by defining the relations between the races in terms of immutable gender roles, it simultaneously reinscribes woman's social space as fixed by "natural" physical limitations, even as it decrees blacks to be spatially confined

owing to their "physical difference" from the norm. The associative ring closes further with popular references to the amorality and savagery of children, and, as Stepan points out, references to women as the "primitive" gender (40). The gendering of race makes possible the racialization of gender.

75. Although, as Gould points out, the paradigmatic shift in this century to a belief in the relative benefits of neoteny led some scientists to use exactly the opposite argument to prove black inferiority: blacks were not as neotenous as whites, and therefore their rapid acceleration into maturity was a sign of biological inferiority. In the new paradigm, retardation is good, so it is whites who are the most neotenous. See Gould, 119–22.

76. See Tillinghast, 21–27, 30, 68–69, 95.

77. John Temple Graves told the 1900 Montgomery Race Conference that an instinctive aversion operated to keep the races separated: "the evil is in the blood of races, the disease is in the bones and the marrow and the skin of antagonistic peoples" (Southern Society, 55). Even the supposed racial moderate Methodist bishop Atticus Haygood excused white belligerence and incivility to blacks as evidence of an "inbred race instinct for racial purity" that would "never be satisfied . . . whether . . . the white race approve[d] or disapprove[d]" until "it realize[d] itself in complete separation" (quoted in Fredrickson, 218).

78. See Willcox and Barringer in Southern Society, 154, 186–87. See also Tillinghast, 91, 96.

79. See Haller's chapter "The Politics of 'Natural' Extinction" (203–10) for instances of open advocacy of black extinction.

80. Robert W. Shufeldt, *The Negro: A Menace to American Civilization* (Boston: Gorham Press, 1907), 115.

81. See Fredrickson, 251–52. See also Haller, 51–58.

82. See Shaler, *Neighbor*, 285, for individuation as a distinction between animal and human varieties. Compare, however, Shaler's discrediting of a "uniformity" of physical appearance among blacks in "Science and the African Problem," *Atlantic Monthly* 66 (July 1890): 39. In "Our Negro Types" (*Current Literature* 29 [July 1900]: 44–45), Shaler describes the variety he perceives in the southern black population, the most common type of which is the "real or Guinea negro," in whose expression "the human look is blended with a remnant of the ancient animal who had not yet come to the careful stage of life" (44). Shaler explains in *The Neighbor* that the stage of individuation for humans was typically puberty, meaning that despite his overt rejection of nondifferentiation as a "race trait," Shaler described the overwhelming majority of blacks in America as cases of arrested development. His only positive comments were in regard to the "6 percent" of blacks who showed a capacity to rise to the level of "ordinary" whites. Despite his experience with Du Bois, Shaler was thoroughly unimpressed with mulattoes as a group.

83. Quoted in Hazel Carby, *Reconstructing Womanhood: The Emergence of the Afro-American Woman Novelist* (New York: Oxford University Press, 1987), 86.

84. Shaler's particular brand of Lamarckianism in higher social process leaves open the

question of whether such an "instinct" is culturally acquired or biological, however. At least one of his contemporaries, Myrta Lockett Avary, was willing to admit bluntly to cultural training in discrimination, cutting through the pseudoscientific explanations to lament that "foreigners without the saving American race prejudice" were actually socially unaware enough to marry blacks. See Avary, *Dixie after the War: An Exposition of Social Conditions Existing in the South, during the Twelve Years Succeeding the Fall of Richmond* (Freeport, N.Y.: Books for Libraries Press, 1906), 394. Ralph Ellison half-jokingly notes that learning to use the word *nigger* served European immigrants as an initiation ritual into American society ("What America Would Be Like without Blacks," in *Going to the Territory* [1986; New York: Vintage, 1995], 111).

85. See Nathaniel S. Shaler, "Race Prejudices," *Atlantic Monthly* 58 (October 1886): 511, 514.

86. See Tourgée's "Assignment of Errors" and "Brief for Homer A. Plessy" in Olsen, 75, 81.

87. See James F. Davis, *Who Is Black?: One Nation's Definition* (University Park: Pennsylvania State University Press, 1991), 15–16, for the "one-drop rule." See also Williamson, *New People*, 1, 2.

88. Harlan's opinion borrows from Albion Tourgée's brief and is worth citing in detail: "Personal liberty," it has been well said, "consists in the power of locomotion, of changing situations, or of removing one's person to whatsoever places one's inclination may direct, without imprisonment or restraint, unless by due course of law." . . .

If a State can prescribe, as a rule of civil conduct, that whites and blacks shall not travel as passengers in the same railroad coach, why may it not so regulate the use of the streets of its cities and towns as to compel white citizens to keep on one side of the street and black citizens to keep on the other? Why may it not, upon like grounds, punish whites and blacks who ride together in street cars or in open vehicles on a public road or street? (Olsen, 115–16)

89. See Fredrickson, 180, for his discussion of political versus social equality in race relations in the postwar South. Fredrickson concludes that "'equality before the law' could readily be translated as de facto inequality in a 'naturally' stratified social system."

90. Robert B. Stepto, *From Behind the Veil: A Study of Afro-American Narrative*, 2d ed. (Urbana: University of Illinois Press, 1991), 75.

91. See *The Negro*, 92–93.

92. As a paternalist like Shaler, Thomas Nelson Page asserted that there were clear differences between blacks, which roughly amounted to a distinction between docile "good" Negroes and unmanageable "bad" Negroes. Page, though, like Smith, believed that the numerical preponderance of "bad" Negroes meant that policy decisions should be based on containing the "bad" Negroes rather than rewarding the "good" Negroes. See Page, *The Negro: The Southerner's Problem* (New York: Charles Scribner's Sons, 1904), 61–64.

93. See Stocking, 192–94. Boas demonstrated that even if somatometric data showed a

higher average among whites, that anthropometry had to suppress the importance of evidence that individual blacks had always surpassed individual whites in order to conclude that "race" accounted for differences in capacity and achievement. Thus, some factor other than "racial" markings must have been responsible for the difference in averages, otherwise all whites (the beneficiaries, by Smith's reasoning, of natural selection) would have scored above all blacks. Boas would go on to pioneer the idea that "culture" explained differences that biology did not (Stocking, 227–33). See William B. Smith's response to evidence of the overlapping distribution of ability: "It may very well be that some dogs are superior to some men" (15).

Chapter Two: Meanwhile, in Black America

1. Hazel Carby, introduction to *The Magazine Novels of Pauline Hopkins* (New York: Oxford University Press, 1988), xxxv.

2. The popularity of this verse in the antislavery and antiracist campaigns throughout the nineteenth and into the twentieth century is the subject of an extensive discussion by Sollors (60–65). Sollors does not cite Hopkins or Dixon, but he does mention contemporaries of theirs such as William Dean Howells, Paul Laurence Dunbar, Charles W. Chesnutt, W. E. B. Du Bois, and Mary Antin.

3. See also *The Neighbor*, 157, in which Shaler declares that Africans are not a "state-building race."

4. Richard H. Brodhead, ed., *The Journals of Charles W. Chesnutt* (Durham, N.C.: Duke University Press, 1993), 140.

5. Quoted in Darwin Turner, introduction to *The House behind the Cedars*, by Charles W. Chesnutt (New York: Collier, 1969), xiv.

6. See chapters 1 and 3 for Tourgée's important role in *Plessy v. Ferguson*.

7. See, for example, Ann duCille, *The Coupling Convention: Sex, Text, and Tradition in Black Women's Fiction* (New York: Oxford University Press, 1993), which traces the "subversive" uses of the marriage plot "as a trope through which to explore not only the so-called more compelling questions of race, racism, and racial identity but complex questions of sexuality and female subjectivity as well" (3–4). Claudia Tate has argued recently that civil marriages among the emancipated slaves certified an official civic participation and that among the Victorian black bourgeoisie fictionalized by turn-of-the-century black women authors, stories about marriage were allegories reflecting the desire to build the sort of equitable society that would promote such a marriage. See Tate, *Domestic Allegories of Political Desire: The Black Heroine's Text at the Turn of the Century* (New York: Oxford University Press, 1992), 91, 101.

8. See chap. 2 in Sollors, esp. 56–65.

9. See, for example, Shaler in *The Neighbor*: "the fact that groups are separated by that rather obscure interval which we term specific is safely to be taken as indicating that they should not be bred together" (160).

10. Louis Harlan, ed., *The Booker T. Washington Papers* (Urbana: University of Illinois Press, 1972-), 3:585 (hereafter cited as "*BTW Papers*").

I am greatly indebted to my colleague Patricia Boyer, without whose fascinating discussion of textuality as a "body of death" I would have entirely missed the import of this rhetorical tradition. In her unpublished manuscript entitled "Medusan," Boyer asserts that all artistic efforts are figurative encounters with death and that textual traces of this elemental struggle with mortality and immortality constitute a "body of death." My discussion relates to a historically situated rhetoric accusing black Americans of corrupting the American body politic, but as I will argue, the very pervasiveness of this discourse of the "black body of death" gave urgency to the concept of a black American cultural renaissance.

11. See Baker, *Modernism and the Harlem Renaissance*, 32–33, on the minstrel performance of Washington. See Louis Harlan, *Booker T. Washington* (New York: Oxford University Press, 1972–83), 1:124, and *BTW Papers*, 4:191, for other examples of Washington's "large fund of henhouse stories," and David Levering Lewis, *W. E. B. Du Bois: Biography of a Race, 1868–1919* (New York: Henry Holt and Co., 1993), 239, for public reaction to Washington's "darky" humor.

12. See Harlan for Du Bois's firsthand observation of Washington's skill in manipulating whites: "he was most popular among [whites], because if he was talking with a white man he sat there and found out what the white man wanted him to say, and then as soon as possible he said it" (*Booker T. Washington*, 2:134). See also vol. 1 for Washington's own admission of playing up to his white audience at the exposition: "I was determined from the first not to say anything that would give undue offense to the South and thus prevent it from thus honoring another Negro in the future" (211–12).

13. Associating black Americans with evolutionary extinction was widespread long before Hoffman's full study appeared in 1896, however. According to Haller, "Hoffman's conclusions mirrored the cumulative tendencies of a century of American and European medical and somatometric studies on race" (60). Hoffman himself had already come to his prediction of racial extinction by 1892, when he announced in "Vital Statistics of the Negro": "No one can foretell the probable future of the colored population . . . with any *absolute accuracy*, but . . . tendencies . . . warrant us to believe that . . . the negro, like the Indian, will be a vanishing race" (*Arena* 29 [April 1892]: 542).

14. Quoted in Harlan, *BTW Papers*, 7:119.

15. "Why is it that the South to-day is bound to a body of death? Five cent cotton is like the man hugging the bear, and can't turn him loose, simply because the farmers of the South are not intelligent enough to raise a diversified crop." Quoted in Victoria Earle Matthews, ed., *Black Belt Diamonds: Gems from the Speeches, Addresses, and Talks to Students of Booker T. Washington* (Miami: Mnemosyne Publishing Co., 1969), 112.

16. "That which for three centuries had bound master and slave, yea, North and South, to a body of death, could not be blotted out by four years of war." See Harlan, *BTW Papers*, 4:286. Colonel Robert Gould Shaw was the white commander of the Massachusetts Fifty-fourth Regiment who died at Fort Wagner, South Carolina, along with his black

troops. See also Shufeldt, *America's Greatest Problem*, 65, for his designation of slavery as a "cadaver."

17. See Harlan, *BTW Papers*, 4:71.

18. *Congressional Record*, January 21, 1907: 1443.

19. Harlan, *Booker T. Washington*, 2:452. See Hoffman's estimate that "at least three fourths of the colored population are cursed with one kind or another of the many diseases classified as venereal" ("Vital Statistics," 534). See Haller, 51–57, for a summary of nineteenth-century linkage of blacks and venereal disease.

20. Hoffman backed off his extravagant 1892 claim of 75 percent black venereal disease infection in "Race Traits and Tendencies" (1896). However, he insinuated on anecdotal evidence provided by S. E. Bishop that like the Hawaiian islanders, blacks would "fall victims to other maladies" owing to "a general impairment of constitutional vigor . . . by venereal disease" (quoted on 322). Thus susceptibility to illness or physical exhaustion in blacks might be, in fact, due to venereal disease, though not specifically attributed to it in medical reports. Hoffman undoubtedly did not find the expected mortality rates for syphilis in black Americans and therefore hoped to build an indirect case that "the root of all evil [lay] in the fact of an immense amount of immorality, which [was] a race trait, and of which scrofula, syphilis, and even consumption [were] the inevitable consequences" (95).

21. See Harlan, *Booker T. Washington*, 2:452.

22. See Daniel J. Boorstin, ed., *An American Primer* (Chicago: University of Chicago Press, 1966), 470.

23. See Williamson, *Crucible*, 178–79, on the fabrication of the myth of Reconstruction as a period that spawned an epidemic of black rapes of white women in the defeated South.

24. This important event is the subject of H. Leon Prather's *We Have Taken a City: Wilmington Racial Massacre and Coup of 1898* (Rutherford, N.J.: Fairleigh Dickinson Univeristy Press, 1984).

25. See Williamson, *Crucible*, 196–97.

26. See Southern Society, 43.

27. This may be an oblique reference to J. Kinnard Jr.'s thesis in "Who Are Our National Poets?" (1845) that since poor blacks originated the songs that America listened to, they were de facto rulers of the nation. See Bruce Jackson, ed., *The Negro and His Folklore in Nineteenth-Century Periodicals* (Austin: University of Texas Press, 1967), 23–35.

28. See Prather, 68 ff., for an account of how local presses kept up a nonstop campaign of white supremacy and solidarity.

29. See Stocking, 29–31.

30. Kate Chopin's short story "Desiree's Baby" turns as well on the birth of an atavistic child, although the plot twist makes the father the "guilty" party after the initial suspicion falls upon the mother, driving her away from the home in self-imposed exile.

31. Shufeldt replays the entire episode almost verbatim in his later work, *America's Greatest Problem* (1915).

32. See Southern Society, 189.

33. See Tate, 62–64, for a discussion of skin color politics in black women's "domestic" literature.

34. See Sollors, 155–60.

35. See Newbell Niles Puckett, ed., *Popular Beliefs and Superstitions: A Compendium of American Folklore from the Ohio Collection of Newbell Niles Puckett* (Boston: G. K. Hall, 1981), 1:403 (#10189), for lore on the poisonous bite of the "blue gum." See also Versh's tale to frighten Benjamin in William Faulkner's *The Sound and the Fury* (New York: Random House), 84–85, about "blue gums" who devour people.

36. See W. E. B. Du Bois, *W. E. B. Du Bois: A Reader*, ed. David Levering Lewis (New York: Henry Holt and Co., 1995), 25. The importance of this essay to Du Bois's literary contribution is discussed fully in chapter 5 below.

37. See Sollors, 166–68.

Chapter Three: The S/ness of the Mother

1. According to Jordan, this libel had a larger cultural import because the ape was not simply beast but "the Demon" himself, since "associations of apes . . . with devils was common in England." Jordan notes that "James I linked them in his *Daemonology*" (30). Fragments of this ape libel surfaced in the nineteenth-century craniometric comparisons of African and primate skulls; in the discourse of the "apelikeness" of black bodily and facial features; and in discourse emphasizing the "grotesque and simian" imitativeness of blacks, and particularly black women (Haller, 9–18; William Archer, *Through Afro-America: An English Reading of the Race Problem* [London: Chapman and Hall, 1910], 8).

2. A 1795 lithograph by J. Pafs reproduced in Jan Nederveen Pieterse, *White on Black: Images of Africa and Blacks in Western Popular Culture* (New Haven: Yale University Press, 1992), 180, indicates the extent to which even the possibility of African female beauty was held up to ridicule. The crowned figure of the African woman, naked but for her leopard skin robe, poses as a European monarch, with bow and arrows as emblems of "state" (that is, her "primitive" state). Gilman notes that it was this fascination with black female genitalia that fed polygenetic arguments throughout the nineteenth century: "If their sexual parts could be shown to be inherently different, this would be a sufficient sign that the blacks were a separate (and, needless to say, lower) race, as different from the European as the proverbial orangutan"; see Sander L. Gilman, "Black Bodies, White Bodies: Toward an Iconography of Female Sexuality in Late Nineteenth-Century Art, Medicine, and Literature," in *"Race," Writing, and Difference*, ed. Henry Louis Gates Jr. (New York: Routledge, 1991), 235.

3. According to Helper, "women . . . , or rather a species of sexless creatures in petticoats—human hermaphrodites in female garb—have . . . begun to . . . [hold] public meetings for the purpose of propping up and sustaining the nature-blasted representatives

of Black" (84). Helper goes on to say how "infinitely better [it would] be for these brazen-faced and babyless personators of women" to be forced into motherhood to prevent their attempts at gaining political equality for blacks and for themselves: "White women, or rather the white hermaphrodites who personate women, like all the Indians, negroes, mu-lattoes, and other swarthy numskulls [sic], are utterly unfit to be allowed to participate, in any manner, in the more important political affairs of our country" (85). Although Helper stops short of prescribing therapeutic rape for feminists, he does suggest enforced mother-hood as a way of simultaneously forcing them to submit to masculine authority and to the will of the "race," whose proprietary claim to their wombs supersedes their "unnatural" social ambitions.

4. See William Hogarth, *The Analysis of Beauty* (Oxford: Clarendon Press, 1955), chap. 7, "Of Lines."

5. See poster art and photos of Baker in Bryan Hammond, comp., and Patrick O'Connor, biographer, *Josephine Baker* (Boston: Little, Brown, 1988). In "Selling Hot Pussy: Repre-sentations of Black Female Sexuality in the Cultural Marketplace," in *Black Looks: Race and Representation* (Boston: South End Press, 1992), bell hooks places Baker's use of her posterior in the iconic tradition of the Hottentot Venus (63).

6. See Shaler, *Neighbor*, 263–65.

7. The slave marriage legalization is an issue not only in Chesnutt's "Uncle Welling-ton's Wives" (see below) but also in his story "The Wife of His Youth." See Herbert G. Gutman, *The Black Family in Slavery and Freedom, 1750–1925* (New York: Pantheon, 1976), 414–25.

8. See ibid., 458–59.

9. See Patricia Morton, *Disfigured Images: The Historical Assault on Afro-American Women* (New York: Praeger, 1991), 27–53, 67–85.

10. See ibid., 45–47 and esp. 73.

11. See Morton's summary of the Victorian "bad" woman as "by definition the woman without male protectors" (11–12).

12. Like Theodore Parker, who quipped that "the Negro girls of Boston [were] only chaste in the sense of being run after" (quoted in Fredrickson, 120 n. 47), Thomas felt that race chastity was not a legitimate issue until sexual continence could be instilled in black girls. Having been informed by "a trustworthy physician" who had examined more than nine hundred black females between the ages of ten and twenty-five that only two had been virgins, Thomas concluded that blacks have no future as a race without a radical constraint on black female sexuality; see William Hannibal Thomas, *The American Ne-gro: What He Was, What He Is, and What He May Become: A Critical and Practical Dis-cussion* (New York: Macmillan, 1901), 197. By way of contrast, Ray Stannard Baker's gloss on black female sexuality is generous, if only in its suggestion that moral instruction and relocation in the North might have lasting benefits: "I have heard a great deal South and North about the immorality of Negro women. Much immorality no doubt exists, but no

honest observer can go into any of the crowded coloured communities of Northern cities and study the life without coming away with a new respect for the Negro women"; see Baker, *Following the Color Line: An Account of Negro Citizenship in the American Democracy* (1908; Williamstown, Mass.: Corner House Publishers, 1973), 141.

13. Dollard, for example, reports that as late as the thirties, black women working as domestic servants earned only $1.50 to $2.00 per week. See John Dollard, *Caste and Class in a Southern Town* (New Haven: Yale University Press, 1937), 107–8.

14. See Morton's observation that "Mammy and Jezebel were also two sides of the same coin of Southern mythology" (10). See also Deborah White's discussion of the political value of the archetypes in *Ar'n't I a Woman?: Female Slaves in the Plantation South* (New York: W. W. Norton, 1985), 60–61.

15. See Gossett, 282; Fredrickson, 250; Jordan, 518–21; Lawrence J. Friedman, *The White Savage: Racial Fantasies in the Postbellum South* (Englewood Cliffs, N.J.: Prentice-Hall, 1970), 122–25.

16. See also Shufeldt's lengthy quotes of articles detailing the dangers of infectious black bodies in *America's Greatest Problem*, 239, 248–50.

17. Archer, 214–15. Fascinating in Archer's description of the corruption of white manhood is his acknowledgment that "animal nature takes little account" of social restrictions. This same author's initial response to the sight of "alien" blacks taking up "half the elbow-room of life" in America was the abhorrence at the thought of spatial coexistence with people who excited such "natural" antipathy because of their pronounced physical differences, "all the most striking of these differences [being] in the direction of what our deepest instincts, inherited through a thousand generations, compel us to regard as ugliness" (8). Archer is at least consistent in his evaluation of black women's "ugliness"; he attributes their seductiveness to their being "physically well-developed," not to their aesthetic appeal. Otherwise, his illogic that, on the one hand, sexual appetite is "instinctive" and, on the other hand, revulsion toward black women is likewise "instinctive" reveals yet again that the radical inconsistencies of race mythology are rarely obstacles to its persistence.

18. Herbert Gutman cites one incident in which a black man named Daniel Wood was taken from his home at night by whites and shot because his wife's white employer believed that Wood had given his own wife and another black girl who worked in the employer's household a venereal disease (396). Though the black man was the immediate target of violence here, his "crime" was possible only because of the access that the black females had to the white household and the access that the white male had to the black females.

19. Dixon, of course, uses "leopard" as the defining animal of Lydia Brown's nature because of its resonance with the biblical quotation from which he adapted the title of his earlier novel, *The Leopard's Spots.* Lydia cannot change her "spots," although there is some question as to whether, as an "Ethiopian," she has successfully changed her skin. A

second likely referent for Dixon is the 1900 novel by J. Cameron Grant, *The Ethiopian: A Narrative of the Society of Human Leopards* (1900; New York: Black Hawk Press, 1935), a fictionalized account of the Leopard Society "cannibal" cults in Africa.

20. See Williamson, *Crucible*, 380, which cites Mississippi race demagogue Senator James K. Vardaman's speech on unsegregated streetcars and the incidence of assaults on white women.

21. See also William B. Smith's defense of dining prohibitions (10–11).

22. See *The Neighbor*, 177–79.

23. See Arnold van Gennep's categorization of magical practice in *The Rites of Passage*, trans. Monika B. Vizedom and Gabrielle L. Caffee (Chicago: University of Chicago Press, 1960), 4–10. The complete categorization by van Gennep's scheme would be sympathetic, contagious, direct negative magic.

24. See van Gennep, 15–25. Of particular importance is van Gennep's discussion of threshold rituals, 20 ff., 57–61. Given the heavy emphasis in the South on which doors could and could not be entered by blacks, this aspect of southern magical practice helps to fill in the mythic landscape of black life.

25. Striking here is the transformation in gender that the black rider undergoes. A "nurse" in charge of children is logically female, but Tourgée frames his protest in such a way that aspiration to equality transforms the hypothetical rider into a "man." Tourgée fails to note the ubiquitous presence of subservient black men as cooks, waiters, and porters.

26. See Brodhead, 112, for a journal account of a similar experience and reaction by Chesnutt himself, though he was riding in the car with the workers because he paid for a second-class accommodation, not because he was compelled to do so by Jim Crow laws. Chesnutt was offended enough to refer to the laborers as "darkies," and he "empathise[d]" with a white fellow traveler who stuck his head out of the window to escape the smell of the group. But he grudgingly approved of the "merriment" they brought to the trip and their camaraderie.

27. See Charles A. Lofgren, *The Plessy Case: A Legal-Historical Interpretation* (New York: Oxford University Press, 1987), 118–21, for the details of the Miles case. Lofgren also makes the point that gender distinction became one of the enabling conditions of Jim Crow (117).

28. Although, see Lofgren, 24, for a disavowal of the nurse exclusion in Arkansas. Lofgren concludes that populist sentiment against women wealthy enough to have nurses was the basis for denying the exemption, and not the principle itself.

29. For example, consider this excerpt from his final chapter, "The Negro Gets By": "It seems that there are no racial antagonisms that cannot be overcome by scrupulous adherence to etiquette. When a new situation arises that produces racial conflict, it may generally be changed to bring about harmony if only the groups will revert to the etiquette of race relations. . . . A Negro will occasionally be called upon to use the traditional forms. If

he does use the forms, he plays at the practice, as at an amusing game. He feels no inferiority or superiority. And this, in the broadest sense, is the true emancipation of the Negro" ([Chicago: University of Chicago Press, 1937], 168).

30. Quoted in Peter Stallybrass and Allon White, *The Politics and Poetics of Transgression* (Ithaca, N.Y.: Cornell University Press, 1986), 20.

31. According to Doyle, "To the present situation [the Negro] brings the assets of personal and racial adaptability gained under the harsh regime of slavery. He has learned to smile, to be pleasant, and . . . moreover, he has learned that the surest method of retreating from a difficult position is to express himself in ways that show he meant no offense" (170).

32. Friedman, 32; my emphases. It is unclear whether Friedman himself was aware of his phrasing here — "docile Negroes" but "insolent, disrespectful blacks."

33. See Wright's fullest elaboration of the "etiquette of living Jim Crow" in *Black Boy: A Record of Childhood and Youth* (New York: Harper and Brothers, 1945).

34. Bailey, quoted in Bertram W. Doyle, 141. Defining this phenomenon in ideological terms, C. Vann Woodward explains that "the Jim Crow laws, unlike feudal laws, did not assign the subordinate group a fixed status in society. They were constantly pushing the Negro farther down" such that "no negro in the world [would be] the equal of the 'poorest, lowest-down white man'"; see Woodward, *The Strange Career of Jim Crow*, 3d rev. ed. (New York: Oxford University Press, 1974), 108, 107.

35. "What the white southern people see who 'know their Negroes' is the role that they have forced the Negro to accept, his caste role. . . . It is perhaps this fact which often makes Negroes seem so deceptive to white people; apparently our white caste wishes the Negro to have only one social personality, his caste role, and to *be* this with utter completeness" (Dollard, 257).

36. See Sollors, 77–78.

37. Paul Laurence Dunbar's *Sport of the Gods* (1902), for example, plays on this theme, not to glorify the South as "the only place for the black man," but to dispel the mythology of the North as an unproblematic haven for blacks. See chapter 8 below.

38. See Gutman, 301n., for Irish jokes among blacks. See also Daryl Dance, *Shuckin' and Jivin': Folklore from Contemporary Black Americans* (Bloomington: Indiana University Press, 1978), chap. 10, for a collection of Irish jokes.

39. See Houston A. Baker Jr., *Workings of the Spirit: The Poetics of Afro-American Women's Writing* (Chicago: University of Chicago Press, 1991), 19–37.

40. See Shaler, *Neighbor*, 141, and Tillinghast, 65, 160. Both Shaler and Tillinghast leap from this supposed phenomenon to a larger claim that Africans lack even the most elemental trait of other-directedness and sympathy upon which to found meaningful kinship patterns, for reasons that I take up in chapter 5.

41. Chesnutt works within received racial stereotypes: the greedy, lecherous preacher, the domineering black woman, the shiftless black man, and troublesome pickaninnies.

Even the Irish woman, given to strong drink and unparticular about matrimonial relations, shows how the local color conventions of magazine fiction influenced Chesnutt's characterization. See Dance, chap. 5 (41–76), for black folklore and humor directed at preachers.

42. Chesnutt, himself a resident of Ohio, was by no means criticizing black migration to the North. The mythology of the North that leads to Wellington's disillusionment makes him unfitted to prosper there, and Chesnutt's story must be seen as countermythological in the sense of adjusting black expectations to fit with probable experience.

43. Griggs may have based this episode on the accounts of a lynching that took place in Arcadia, Louisiana, in March 1892. The victim, Dennis Cobb, was a black man who had been targeted for violence because of his prosperity. After hanging him from a tree and shooting him numerous times, the mob left. Cobb was still alive, and he was strong enough to crawl back home before dying of his wounds. See Stewart E. Tolnay and E. M. Beck, A Festival of Violence: An Analysis of Southern Lynchings, 1882–1930 (Urbana: University of Illinois Press, 1995), 71–72.

44. See Goldberg's discussion of discursive interpellation in "Social Formation of Racist Discourse," 309.

45. Thomas Dixon belatedly disputed this characterization of an "ancient African chastity" claimed by Du Bois, in The Flaming Sword (Atlanta: Monarch Publishing Co., 1939), 20.

46. See Frederick Douglass, Narrative of the Life of Frederick Douglass, an American Slave (New York: Penguin, 1982), chaps. 6, 7. Harriet Jacobs tells of the "The Jealous Mistress" in chap. 6 of Incidents in the Life of a Slave Girl: Written by Herself (Cambridge: Harvard University Press, 1987).

Chapter Four: The "White Delilah"

1. See Lawrence W. Levine's use of blues lyrics in Black Culture and Black Consciousness: Afro-American Folk Thought from Slavery to Freedom (Oxford: Oxford University Press, 1977) to illustrate the folk belief that "in general dark skin could be trusted more than light complexions":

Yaller gal's yourn
An de black gal's mine,
You can never tell
When de yaller gal's lyin'. (288)

2. According to Ronald Takaki,

in 1821 white citizens of Pennsylvania petitioned the legislature to declare mixed marriages void and to make it a penal action for a black to marry a "white man's daughter." . . . In a petition to the legislature of the Indiana territory, whites sought to prevent the settlement of blacks because they believed white wives and daughters would be insulted and abused by "those Africans." At the Illinois constitutional convention of 1847, a delegate warned that the lack of a restriction on black migration was tantamount to allowing blacks "to make proposals to marry our daughters." . . . A delegate to the New York constitutional convention of 1821 favored [black] disfranchisement because he wanted to avoid the time "when the colors shall intermarry."

In Wisconsin, Takaki notes, Democrats feared that "the extension of political rights to blacks would encourage them to marry 'our sisters and daughters.'" See Takaki, *Iron Cages: Race and Culture in Nineteenth-Century America* (New York: Oxford University Press, 1990), 114–15.

3. See Mary Douglas, *Purity and Danger: An Analysis of Concepts of Pollution and Taboo* (New York: Frederick A. Praeger, 1966), 53, on holiness as a function of social order. Perhaps the flaming sword that guards Dixon's "holy of holies" cuts both ways, as Michael Rogin explains: "The sword guards the female genitalia not only to protect the white woman from the black phallus but also to keep her from acquiring a phallus of her own"; see Michael Paul Rogin, *Ronald Reagan, the Movie, and Other Episodes in Political Demonology* (Berkeley and Los Angeles: University of California Pres, 1987), 220.

4. See Forrest G. Wood, *Black Scare: The Racist Response to Emancipation and Reconstruction* (Berkeley and Los Angeles: University of California Press, 1968), 53–79, for a full discussion of the *Miscegenation* controversy.

5. See the cover illustration reproduced in Wood, plate 5.

6. See George L Mosse, *Toward the Final Solution: A History of European Racism* (New York: Howard Fertig, 1978), fig. 7.

7. See Sander Gilman, "The Jewish Nose," in *The Jew's Body* (New York: Routledge, 1991), 169–93.

8. Ransom Dexter's 1874 article "The Facial Angle" included a striking illustration of this generic teleology reprinted by Haller (Haller, 13). A drawing from Robert Knox's *The Races of Men* (1850) used the facial angle in a way that anticipated the Seaman pamphlet illustration. Using straight lines traced according to Camper's specifications over profiles of an Apollonian white male and an orangutan, the drawing shows the angular disparity between the species (Haller, 10). But the disparity between species served only as a referent for the distinction between races, as the illustration gives not the full profile but only the prognathous lower jaw of a Negro male jutting out in near silhouette behind the white male, symmetrical to the snout of the primate. Thus, as Camper claimed, the "African profile" falls right at the dividing line between man and ape, at an angle of 70 degrees, while the "Caucasian profile" conforms to the 100-degree ideal established by the "*Grecian antique.*"

9. See Fredrickson, 78.

10. See Gould, 33, fig. 2.1. See also Banta's reproduction of illustrations from Lavater and Guyot that use hierarchies of human and animal types that feature the Apollonian ideal at the top of the scale.

11. See Newby, 93–100, for the pre-Adamite position.

12. See Honour, *Image of the Black*, 12–21, esp. 16–17. Stephen Graham in *Children of the Slaves* (London: Macmillan, 1920) quotes Fanny Kemble's travel diary (an obvious source and model for an Englishman traveling through America) as recording John Quincy Adams's observation that "it served Desdemona right for marrying a 'nigger.'" Kemble "imagines the fine effect which some American actor in the role of Iago might obtain by substituting for "I hate the Moor" "I hate the Nigger," pronounced in proper Charleston or Savannah fashion. "Only think what a very new order of interest the whole tragedy might receive acted from this standpoint and called 'Amalgamation, or the Black Bridal'!" (80).

13. See, for example, Ida B. Wells-Barnett, *On Lynchings: Southern Horrors, A Red Record, Mob Rule in New Orleans* (Salem N.H.: Ayer, 1991), 12, and Mary Church Terrell, "Lynching from a Negro's Point of View," *North American Review* (June 1904): 862.

14. Bertram Wyatt-Brown, however, says that divorces for poor white males, even and especially for a wife's adultery, were extremely difficult to get under any circumstances (301).

15. See Walter T. Howard, *Lynchings: Extralegal Violence in Florida during the 1930s* (Cranbury, N.J.: Associated University Presses, 1995), and Tolnay and Beck. W. Fitzhugh Brundage in *Lynching in the New South: Georgia and Virginia, 1880–1930* (Urbana: University of Illinois Press, 1993), for instance, has argued that reading lynching as "an endlessly repetitive ritual, performed again and again, year after year" that "celebrated and renewed fixed white social values and traditions" makes sweeping assumptions that "threaten to obscure the complexities of southern mob violence" (17–18). Brundage takes note of variations in lynchings that make them hard to typify, including differences in "size, organization, motivation, and extent of ritual" (18–19). Because of these variables and differing notions among whites on the meaning of white supremacy, a simplistic reading of lynchings as ceremonial expressions of white supremacy risks seeing communal consensus in events that were the actions of only a few interested parties.

16. As early as the pioneering work of Wells-Barnett, the attack on lynching's apologists has given priority to statistical and anecdotal refutation of rape as a motivating factor for all lynchings. See *Southern Horrors* (1892) and *A Red Record* (1894) in *On Lynchings*. Yearly statistics on lynching were also published in W. E. B. Du Bois's *Crisis*.

17. This drawing was reproduced in Wood, plate 12.

18. See Joe Gray Taylor, *Louisiana Reconstructed, 1863–1877* (Baton Rouge: Louisiana State University Press, 1974), 245–48.

19. In a compelling image, Gunnar Myrdal envisioned white female interracial sex as an inundation of white space: "Sex relations between Negro men and white women . . . would be like an *attempt* to pour Negro blood into the white race. It cannot succeed, of

course, as the child would be considered a Negro. But the white woman would be absolutely degraded—which the white man in the parallel situation is not." See Myrdal, *An American Dilemma: The Negro Problem and Modern Democracy* (New York: Harper and Row, 1944), 589.

20. Griffith here changes the rape scene from *The Clansman*, in which the Lenoirs, a widow and her daughter Marion, are raped by the soldier Gus in their home, having no white male to protect them. But the change keeps intact the symbolism of the white household as a sanctuary under siege during Reconstruction.

21. See a reproduction of the ad for the original New York showing of the film in Thomas Cripps, *Slow Fade to Black: The Negro in American Film, 1900–1942* (1977; New York: Oxford University Press, 1993), 54.

22. One apparent change was the inclusion in the film of a pair of "faithful souls" in the Cameron household. These characters are drawn more from the paternalistic "plantation school" types popularized by Page than from Dixon.

23. See Haller, 49, for Van Evrie's theories of black retentions of anthropoidal characteristics.

24. See Helper, 57–58, on the deformity of black feet. See also William B. Smith's catalog of African anatomical abnormalities, 46–49, including flat feet and "lark heel."

25. Dixon and Griffith charged that the passage of laws allowing intermarriage during Reconstruction was part of a Radical Republican revenge against the South, allowing black men to take the daughters of the slavemasters as their wives. As Gutman explains, the prominence of intermarriage provisions early in Reconstruction was part of an effort to eliminate black female concubinage by depriving white men who exploited and abandoned black women of a legal escape clause (400–402).

26. Atticus G. Haygood, "The Black Shadow in the South," *Forum* 16 (October 1893): 170; my emphasis.

27. See Michel Foucault, *Discipline and Punish: The Birth of the Prison*, trans. Alan Sheridan (New York: Pantheon, 1977), on the "King's Body," 28–29. See also John O'Neill, *Five Bodies: The Human Shape of Modern Society* (Ithaca, N.Y.: Cornell University Press, 1985), 67–77.

28. Newby took note of the prevalence of the rhetoric of the "sovereign" mob: "According to Charles E. Woodruff, an Army surgeon, lynch law was merely an expression of democracy, for it was 'the highest prerogative of the sovereign democracy to make and execute their own laws.' Since Southern lynch mobs sometimes 'constitute all the sovereigns' in a community, there could be no objection to them as undemocratic. . . . Lynch law, [Tom Watson] felt, was a good sign . . . that the sense of justice yet lived among the people" (139).

29. See Herbert Shapiro, *White Violence and Black Response: From Reconstruction to Montgomery* (Amherst: University of Massachusetts Press, 1988), 30. See also specific instances of proxy lynchings in Ralph Ginzburg, 39, 44, 77 and 166.

30. See Williamson, *Crucible*, 282.

31. See Ray Stannard Baker's investigation into crime and punishment in the South within and without the hermetic categories of "race." Baker shows, for example, that whites who committed capital crimes were sometimes sentenced to little or no imprisonment. At the same time, blacks typically received longer sentences, regardless of the race of the victim, but the severity of punishment sharply escalated when they were accused of criminal violations of the "color line" (183–84, 193–94, 204–5).

32. See Williamson, *Crucible*, 301–35, for a discussion of lynching as scapegoating and the psychic cost of white solidarity.

33. Arthur F. Raper, *The Tragedy of Lynching* (Chapel Hill: University of North Carolina Press, 1933), 119. For Raper, the coincidence of depressed cotton prices and increased lynchings suggests an economic causality (30–31). Yet, given lynching's festive atmosphere, a case could also be made from this data for a survival of fertility ritual themes and practices. See also Tolnay and Beck, 142–49, on the seasonal connection between cotton planting (but not harvesting) and lynching.

34. See also Hiram Wyatt-Brown's discussion of ritual scapegoating in southern culture as a socially conservative tradition (437).

35. Having previously described the typical antebellum southern plantation as "in effect, a great social settlement for the uplift of Africans" (179), and having described slavery itself as the bondage of white mistresses, "body and soul," to their Negroes (181), Avary overplayed her rhetorical hand in describing Reconstruction as social "inversion." Nevertheless, she satirized countless displacements of social order as the norm. Blacks "keep parlour" while their employers tend the kitchen; a gentleman discovers that his illiterate stable boy has become a lawyer; blacks ride in coaches and demand deference from their former owners, and on streetcars, they sit while whites stand. It was an unreal world where the publicly haughty and obnoxious former servants privately visited their old masters and mistresses to grovel before them in order to be "'jes myse'f den,'" as Avary, characteristically resorting to invented dialogue in dialect, was pleased to report (255).

36. Avary, 253. Compare Bowers's discourse of black Reconstruction as "pollution" in his description of Louisiana: "Visitors from the North organize 'slumming expedition' to the Legislature or go as to a zoo"; see Claude Bowers, *The Tragic Era: The Revolution after Lincoln* (Cambridge, Mass.: Literary Guild of America, 1929), 364.

37. To Thomas, "the grotesqueness of Reconstruction was further accentuated for the reason that the ignorant and credulous freedmen ha[d] no conception of their shortcomings. Devoid of discernment and sober judgment, they pose[d] as the peers of their immediate white fellow-citizens, such [was] their colossal conceit, and [were] imbued with the belief that the people of the North [stood] ready to support and defend them in these pretensions" (227).

38. As Avary explained, "No other crime offers such problems; . . . it is so outside of civilisation that there seem no terms for dispassionate discussion, no fine adjustment of civil trial and legal penalty" (382).

39. See Friedman's study of white radicalism (169): "White skin entitled Caucasians to behave barbarically toward blacks as they overthrew 'Negro rule.' Yet because whiteness represented civilization, the conduct of the whites was not characterized as actual barbarism. Only blacks could behave like savages." In fact, many whites like Haygood did acknowledge white savagery as a phylogenetic reservoir of instinctive racial will to survival.

40. See Cassity, 239.

41. Quoted in National Association for the Advancement of Colored People, *Thirty Years of Lynching in the United States: 1889–1918* (New York: NAACP National Office, 1919), 19. Yet even the instinct of self-preservation does not explain Raper's discovery that of the one hundred lynchings he surveyed, at least half involved law enforcement participation, while nine-tenths elicited law enforcement approval (Jacquelyn Dowd Hall, *Revolt against Chivalry: Jessie Daniel Ames and the Women's Campaign against Lynching* [New York: Columbia University Press, 1979], 139).

42. See Fredrickson, 51, for a discussion of van den Berghe's concept of herrenvolk democracy.

43. Avary's source goes on to quote a doctor who refused to have the victim relive the event by identifying suspects brought before her: "'I would be signing that girl's death warrant if I let you in there to make her tell that horrible story over again" (382).

44. See Stepan's "Race and Gender" for myths of female atavism, 39–40.

45. I am forced to include the date here on each occasion in order to distinguish this instance from the other Paris lynchings.

46. See Brundage's account of a white woman in the 1930s who was afraid to be home alone but who nevertheless realized that the threat of the "Big Black Nig" did not have a similar effect on her granddaughter (71).

47. See Paul Broca, *On the Phenomena of Hybridity in the Genus Homo*, trans. and ed. C. C. Blake (London: Longman, Green, Longman and Roberts, 1864), 27–29.

48. Haller summarized the complicity of anthropology in the mythologizing of sex and race: "By determining the direction of the vagina, the position of the hymen, and the general structure of the sexual organs, white doctors could set the African apart as a distinct and inferior species of man. The conclusion generally drawn from sexual differentiation was that while sexual intercourse between Caucasian male and Negro female was possible and fertile, it was 'unnatural' and unproductive between the Negro male and the Caucasian female" (55).

49. See also Myrdal: "The belief that Negro males have extraordinarily large genitalia is to be taken as an expression of . . . sexual envy and, at the same time, as part of the social control devices to aid in preventing intercourse between Negro males and white females" (108).

50. Quoted in Shufeldt, *America's Greatest Problem*, 99.

51. See William Lee Howard, "The Negro as a Distinct Ethnic Factor in Civilization," *Medicine* 15 (May 1903): 424. Howard's thesis is that insufficient evolution leaves blacks with less-developed nervous systems and therefore less "sensitiveness of the terminal

fibers which exist in the Caucasian." Thus, the inability of the African ever to satisfy the inordinate lust that controls his life leads to "sexual madness and excess." The severity of punishment meted out to blacks in and out of slavery also derives from the myth that they do not feel pain like whites do. See William B. Smith, 47.

52. See Brundage, 72.

53. For the full story on Felton's connection to the Wilmington riot, see Prather, 171–73. See also Williamson, *Crucible*, 124–30, 197.

54. Tolnay and Beck's recent study arrived at different figures, using slightly different dates and using data only on lynchings in the South. They found that between 1882 and 1930, 33.6 percent of lynchings were for sexual assaults, 47.1 percent were for murders and assaults, and 17.5 percent were for miscellaneous causes (48). Among the miscellaneous causes were throwing stones, vagrancy, voodooism, voting for wrong party, being obnoxious, and demanding respect (47). Even by Tolnay and Beck's figures, almost 65 percent of lynchings were not for sexual crimes and reflected the same trend that shows up in Raper's statistics: lynchings stemmed from affronts to the persons, property, and/or status demands of whites in the preponderance of incidents.

55. Hall notes that while the proportion of lynchings moved to 95 percent southern by the 1920s, "over the same period the proportion of lynch victims who were white decreased from 32 percent to 9 percent. Lynching had become virtually a southern phenomenon and a racial one" (133).

56. For a full account of the Claude Neal lynching, see James R. McGovern, *Anatomy of a Lynching: The Killing of Claude Neal* (Baton Rouge: Louisiana State University Press, 1982). On the press involvement, see 74–75.

57. See Henry Louis Gates Jr., "The Face and Voice of Blackness," in *Facing History: The Black Image in American Art, 1710–1940*, ed. Guy C. McElroy (San Francisco: Bedford Arts, 1990), fig. 6.

58. See also the postcard photo of the lynching of Claude Neal in McGovern, 83. Ralph Ginzburg reports the existence of a postcard of a severed head of a black man lynched in Memphis in 1917, which the *Chicago Defender* of September 8, 1917, reprinted (112–13).

59. Wells-Barnett's autobiography recounts a story passed on to her in the wake of the lynching: "Miss Laura Dainty-Pelham was traveling through Texas a year later and she often told how the wife of the hotel keeper kept talking about [the lynching] as if it were something to be proud of. While she talked, her eight-year-old daughter, who was playing about the room, came up to her mother and shaking her by the arm said, 'I saw them burn the nigger, didn't I Mamma?' 'Yes, darling, you saw them burn the nigger,' said the complacent mother, as matter-of-factly as if she had said she saw them burn a pile of trash"; see Ida B. Wells-Barnett, *Crusade for Justice: The Autobiography of Ida B. Wells*, ed. Alfreda M. Duster (Chicago: University of Chicago Press, 1970), 85. Wells-Barnett's dismay at the socialization of white children to see lynching as normative white behavior explains the fascination of reporters with the presence and even participation of children.

60. See Trudier Harris, *Exorcising Blackness: Historical and Literary Lynching and Burning Rituals* (Bloomington: Indiana University Press, 1984), 2. Also reported in Ralph Ginzburg, 62–63.

61. John Temple Graves, quoted in Shufeldt, *The Negro*, 168.

62. Ralph Ginzburg, 11. See also 15, 58, and 130. See Brundage, 42–43, for more on body signs.

63. See Stallybrass and White's chapter on the social construction of "filth" in Victorian culture (125–48).

64. See Ralph Ginzburg, 184–85. See also Raper, 319–55.

65. See Raper, 37, for an incident that ended with the discovery in time to save a black man from execution, and Ralph Ginzburg, 120–21, for an instance in which the lynching did occur, almost certainly to protect a woman's reputation.

66. Raper, 37. See also Laurence Alan Baughman, *Southern Rape Complex: Hundred Year Psychosis* (Atlanta: Pendulum Books, 1966), 164.

67. See Tolnay and Beck, 93–96, and Brundage, 86–102.

68. See *Shadow and Act*, 83–84. Ellison's use of Bland's term "pre-individual," however, shows the influence of social science's allochronistic distancing of white and black communities, since it announces a perceived failure of black Americans to progress toward the "higher" evolutionary state of whites, and since it describes black nonindividuation as normative in the South. See 89–91. Elsewhere, Ellison is more circumspect about such generalizations about black life.

69. When the defendant, Red Kelly, accosted a thirteen-year-old white girl as he drove a buggy past her, asking her if she wanted a ride and later chasing her a short distance after she refused, he was committing an act of de facto rape, presumably, by the logic of *Jackson v. Georgia*, for bringing his sexual organs into "striking distance" of the girl. The Alabama court ruled that "the fact that the defendant was a Negro boy, and Miss Guin was a white girl, proved an indication of an attempt to rape" (Baughman, 120). A "Negro boy" could have no other possible reason for pursuing a white girl, according to the prevailing concepts of "Negro boyhood," than rape. To be a Negro boy, in race mythology, meant that "sexual desire [was] an imperative need, raw and crude and strong": "It is to be satisfied when and wherever it arises. It does not proceed tortuously through devious detours of flirtation, but flies straight to its mark with the blind compulsion and devouring intensity of a speeding bullet" (David L. Cohn, *God Shakes Creation* [New York: Harper and Brothers, 1935], 110).

70. *Crisis*, vol. 9, no. 4 (February 1915): 198.

71. Ray Stannard Baker, 211, 9. Baker's entire first chapter looks at the causes and consequences of the shocking riot that featured the assault on middle-class property owners for possession of firearms and attacks on unwary blacks leaving the business district. See Williamson, *Crucible*, 209–23, for another account of the affair.

72. Cameron does not refer to Raper's findings, nor does he give any hint that Mary Ball was a part of the robbery plot. In his memoir, though, he seemed very certain that the

girl would corroborate his innocence, an assurance that Wells-Barnett considered a fool-ish assumption by black males in interracial relationships (see below). As for interracial sexual relations, Cameron does recount sex parties in prison involving white prostitutes to which he was invited (but understandably did not attend). He also notes the almost unan-imous support for him from white fellow prisoners, despite the nature of the accusation against him; see James Cameron, *A Time of Terror: A Survivor's Story* (Baltimore: Black Classic Press, 1994), 160, 163.

73. See Tolnay and Beck, chap. 7, "The Great Migration and the Demise of Lynching" (202–33), in which the authors suggest that the disappearance of the cheap black labor force into northern cities gave economic impetus to propertied whites to exert pressure to halt lynchings.

74. One white paper, the *Daily Commercial*, warned that "the fact that a black scoundrel [was] allowed to live and utter such loathsome and repulsive calumnies" at-tested to the patience of whites, although there were "some things that the Southern white man [would] not tolerate" (4–5). The threat urged by the *Memphis Evening Scimi-tar* was more explicit: "it is the duty of those whom he has attacked to tie the wretch who utters these calumnies to a stake at the intersection of Main and Madison Sts., brand him in the forehead with a hot iron and perform upon him a surgical operation with a pair of tailor's shears" (5). The presumption that the "wretch" must be a male gives clear indica-tion of the imputation of "rape" by innuendo against white womanhood.

75. In *A Red Record*, she took exception to the rhetoric of Atticus Haygood in regard to his remarks on the Paris, Texas, lynching of Henry Smith and to the general representa-tion of every physical assault attributed to a black person as sexually motivated: "The truth was bad enough, but the white people of the community made it a point to exaggerate every detail of the awful affair, and to inflame the public mind so that nothing less than immediate and violent death would satisfy the populace. As a matter of fact, the child was not brutally assaulted as the world has been told in excuse for the awful barbarism of that day. Persons who saw the child after its death, have stated, . . . only a slight abrasion and discoloration was noticeable and that mostly about the neck" (in *On Lynchings*, 25). Wells-Barnett accused Haygood of "maliciously falsifying" his report of the child "torn asunder," charging him with a "cold blooded, deliberate, brutal falsehood" to bolster his plea that the white community had gone justifiably insane (26). See Haygood's remarks in "The Black Shadow in the South," 167–73.

76. Wells-Barnett, *Red Record*, in *On Lynchings*, 88. The highlight of the ensuing war of words between the women activists was Wells-Barnett's challenge of the Willard-backed resolution, to which Willard responded that Wells-Barnett should not "blame [Willard] for [her] rhetorical expressions" (89).

77. The editorial was widely enough known that Chesnutt referred to it in *The Marrow of Tradition*, in *The African-American Novel in the Age of Reaction: Three Classics*, ed. William L. Andrews (New York: Penguin, 1992), 399–402, as did Thomas Dixon in *The Leopard's Spots* (411).

78. Mrs. Underwood expressed fear that at the time of the false charge, neighbors had seen Offett on the premises, that she was afraid she had "contracted a loathsome disease," and that she feared giving birth to a Negro baby.

79. See "Criteria of Negro Art," *Crisis* 32 (October 1926): 292.

80. "'You may have yourself a nigger if you want one, but do not force them on others,' wrote one expatriated southerner. 'If you want a Negro man, OK. Otherwise lay off white supremacy,' read a telegram to an ASWPL leader in Mississippi" (Hall, 154). The process could also work in reverse, as happened with attempts to downplay the questionable past of Victoria Price, star witness for the prosecution in the Scottsboro Boys case. She "'might be a fallen woman,' commented a spectator, 'but by God she is a white woman'" (Hall, 204). Significantly, it was Price's complicity in the state's prosecution that reestablished her racial affiliation.

81. Hall cautions that the ASWPL program should not be confused with political liberalism or "social equality": "[They] were primarily moralists, not social theorists." Although the political activism in which they engaged led increasingly to awareness of the fundamental inequities of southern life, the membership, covering a wide spectrum of political positions, by and large gave no mandate for radical social change: "The lowest common denominator of their crusade was an impulse toward social order, and many of the women whose names appear on ASWPL membership lists probably shared the white supremacist views of their contemporaries" (209).

82. R. E. L. Masters, *Eros and Evil: The Sexual Psychopathology of Witchcraft* (New York: Matrix House, 1966), 13. Other references to the Devil as "black man" in specific case histories occur at 12, 14, 15–17, 21, 22, and 61. See also Carlo Ginzburg, *Ecstasies: Deciphering the Witches Sabbath*, trans. Raymond Rosenthal (New York: Random House, 1991), 108, for the black man as leader of a diabolic cult.

83. "The penes of demons were most often described as being made of horn, or of half flesh and half iron. Some said that they were covered with scales and that these, once penetration had been effected, might open out like barbs, so that each withdrawal movement was excruciatingly painful. It was reported in this connection that witches often screamed and groaned during intercourse with incubi, and that they bled copiously during the act or after it was completed" (Masters, 17). "Claudia Fellet said she herself had often experienced something forced into her, swollen to such a size, that no matter how capacious a vagina a woman might have, she would not be able to hold it without extreme pain" (Rossell Hope Robbins, *The Encyclopedia of Witchcraft and Demonology* [New York: Crown Publishers, 1959], 466).

84. According to Masters, "the sexual act between the demon and the witch also bound the witch to his service in a magical way, while she gained from it *an increase in the potency of her supernormal powers*. The coition was an essential part of the pact between the two, and some held that in essence it *was* the pact, with the additional ceremonies, oath-taking, etc., no more than mere trappings and folderol" (56; my emphasis).

85. On lynching as "exorcism," see Harris.

86. See *Crusade*, 36–37. See also the episode in which Wells-Barnett's own reputation was slandered by a black preacher, and her determination to confront him directly because she "had no brother or father to protect it" for her (42–45).

87. See *Southern Horrors*: "Most of these cases were reported by the daily papers of the South" (in *On Lynchings*, 8).

Chapter Five: W. E. B. Du Bois and the Progress of the Black Soul

1. Lewis speculates on the source and significance of the anecdote in *Biography*, 33–34.

2. Du Bois once recalled with withering sarcasm his correspondence with former neighbor and playmate May Loop, "an orphaned hoyden of an old but poor family," who wrote to him after he had gone to school in the South to ask if he could find her a colored servant. He "couldn't" (*Autobiography*, 86). May Loop's instincts were correct by prevailing social customs. The adult Du Bois, however educated, would have been closer socially to the servant class in Great Barrington than to her own life station. Du Bois reported a similar incident of a wealthy benefactress of Tuskegee and Hampton Institute who complained to him that in spite of her philanthropy she still could not find "decent servants" (W. E. B. Du Bois, *Darkwater: Voices from within the Veil* [New York: Harcourt, Brace, 1921], 109).

3. "I knew that this would be unfair to her and fatal to my work at home, where I had neither property nor social standing for this blue-eyed stranger" (*Autobiography*, 161).

4. *North American Review* 178 (June 1904): 853–68.

5. Quoted in Ralph Ginzburg, 18. See Ginzburg's reprints of the news coverage of the sensational Hose lynching (12–21), marred by the fact that Ginzburg unaccountably refers to Hose as "Holt" throughout. See also Frank Shay, *Judge Lynch: His First Hundred Years* (New York: Ives Washburn, 1938), 108–9. See Shapiro, 63, 88–99, 123, and Wells-Barnett, *Mob Rule in New Orleans*, 45, in *On Lynchings*, for other perspectives of the Hose affair. See William Ivy Hair, *Carnival of Fury: Robert Charles and the New Orleans Race Riot of 1900* (Baton Rouge: Louisiana State University Press, 1976), 107, 108, and Williamson, *Crucible*, 204–5, for connection between the Hose lynching and the Robert Charles incident in New Orleans. On Charles, see also Wells-Barnett, *Mob Rule in New Orleans*, in *On Lynchings*.

6. Quoted in Shapiro, 481 n. 42.

7. In a passage in *Dusk of Dawn*, Du Bois apotheosized Washington, William Monroe Trotter, and himself as the embodiments of the three responses to strategies of disaffiliation that he describes in "Of Mr. Booker T. Washington and Others": "My thoughts, the thoughts of Washington, Trotter and others, were the expression of social forces more than of our own minds. These forces or ideologies embraced more than our reasoned acts. They included physical, biological and psychological forces; habits, conventions and

enactments" (96). Trotter, the publisher of the *Boston Guardian*, was the emblem for Du Bois of the first approach, "revolt and revenge" (34). See Lewis, *Biography*, 275, 298–304. The second approach of adjustment and "submission" to the dominant group was represented by Washington, while Du Bois was the standard-bearer for those who wanted only the middle course of "self-realization and self-development despite environing opinion." By depicting Washington as the embodiment of "the old attitude of adjustment and submission" (36), Du Bois simultaneously shed his own "Submissive Man" academic exercise and charged the Tuskegee leader with looking back to slavery for a solution to a twentieth-century problem.

8. See Du Bois's poem "A Litany of Atlanta" in the *Independent*, October 11, 1906, 856–58.

9. See Newby's discussion of Carroll, 93–99.

10. A few years before Carroll's *The Negro, a Beast*, James Anthony Froude produced the following polygenist fantasy about black West Indians: "they sin but they sin only as animals sin, without shame because there is no sense of wrong doing; they eat the forbidden fruit, but it brings with it no knowledge of the difference between good and evil—in fact these poor children of darkness have escaped the consequences of the fall, and *must come of another stock after all.*" Quoted in Hoffman, 239.

11. Carroll was rehashing arguments made in various antebellum essays by a Louisiana doctor named Samuel A. Cartwright. See Fredrickson, 87–89, 277. Graham seems to confirm the sources cited by Newby that Carroll had maintained an immense, even "scriptural," popularity among poor whites, though Newby himself discounts this, holding that "the suggestion that Negroes are beasts of the field was so totally at variance with popular interpretations of the Bible that it probably had little influence among any group, even in the deep South" (96). But for Graham, the widespread expressions of black soullessness were among the foundational tenets of the southern racial "creed." See Graham, 197–200. See Williamson, *Crucible*, 119, for another intriguing aspect to the Carroll story, the mistaken impression that Carroll was "himself a black man."

12. See Sollors, 25, for the origins of "ethnic" as a term of oppositional identification and its use in distinguishing Christian from non-Christian.

13. According to "Ariel," "You cannot elevate a beast to the level of a son of God—a son of Adam and Eve—but you may depress the sons of Adam and Eve, with their *impress* of the Almighty, *down to the level of a beast.* . . . A man cannot commit so great an offense against his race, against his country, against his God, in any other way, as to give his daughter in marriage to a negro—a beast—or to take one of their females for his wife" ([Buckner H. Payne, pseudonym "Ariel"], *The Negro: What Is His Ethnological Status? Is He a Progeny of Ham? Is He a Descendant of Adam and Eve? Has He a Soul? Or Is He a Beast in God's Nomenclature? What Is His Relation to the White Race?* [Cincinnati: N.p., 1867], 48).

14. Ariel's version of the unpardonable transgression is voluntary surrender of salvation history by moving *downward* along the divine chain of being ([Payne], 48).

15. This line of inquiry culminated in what Stocking has called "the passing of a romantic conception of race—of the ideas of racial 'essence,' of racial 'genius,' of racial 'soul,' of race as a supraindividual organic identity" (194).

16. In "The Souls of White Folk," in *Literature and the Body: Essays on Populations and Persons*, ed. Elaine Scarry (Baltimore: Johns Hopkins University Press, 1988), Walter Benn Michaels has explained the use of sheets as a masking device by the Ku Klux Klan showing how race identity supersedes individual identity: "The purpose of the sheets is not to conceal the identities of individual clansmen for, far from making their visible identities invisible, the sheets make their invisible identities visible. The Klan wear sheets because their bodies aren't as white as their souls, because *no* body can be as white as the soul embodied in the white sheet" (190). The possession of a white body as a precondition for inclusion into rights and privileges reserved for the individual expressions of the white race soul necessarily marks that idealized soul *as* white and serves to strengthen the sense of identity and interdependency between all whites.

17. See *Autobiography*, 126, 169. In his recollections, Du Bois, who certainly would have referred to the kaiser as "Wilhelm" when in Germany, insists on referring to him as "William II."

18. See chapter 2.

19. See *Autobiography*, 132–39, on Du Bois's acceptance of caste separation at Harvard as a trade-off for educational opportunity.

20. I think this is a potentially significant omission because Du Bois did include Shaler among the list of outstanding faculty members in *Dusk of Dawn*, from which he liberally borrowed passages for his later autobiography. See *Dusk*, 37.

21. In *The Neighbor*, Shaler explains, "Where a [black] youth fit for professional work appears, he should be trained in colleges with the whites," this despite the fact that he thought there was "nothing to be gained by pushing them towards the professions," since after training, blacks could not be expected to "find their way to satisfactory employment" (167).

22. In retrospect, given Shaler's generally low opinion of black potential, his letter praising Du Bois as "decidedly the best specimen of his race that we have had in our classes" (Lewis, *Biography*, 125) seems a bit ambiguous.

23. See Haller, 166–87, for a thorough summary of Shaler's thinking on race and specific listings.

24. See Shaler, "Negro Problem," 699.

25. On the other hand, Haller points out Shaler's explanation of lynch law as an attempt to protect defenseless women and children, for which he refused to apologize (185).

26. See *Dusk*, 98, for Du Bois's encounter with the sophisticated racism of evolutionary science at Harvard.

27. See ibid., 183, 185, 130.

28. According to Lewis, the questioning began as soon as Du Bois had given the address at the American Negro Academy. See *Biography*, 173.

29. See chapter 2.

30. See Kwame Anthony Appiah, "Illusions of Race," in *In My Father's House: Africa in the Philosophy of Culture* (New York: Oxford University Press, 1992), 28–46.

31. "On Being Ashamed of Oneself: An Essay on Race Pride," Lewis, *Reader*, 76.

32. See "Criteria of Negro Art," 296.

33. "The Negro College" (1933), in Lewis, *Reader*, 74–75.

34. See *Dusk*, 98, for Harvard's emphasis on the evolutionist argument for racial caste.

35. This likely is what Du Bois had in mind by calling *Dusk of Dawn* "An Essay toward an Autobiography of a Race Concept." See Lewis, *Biography*, 19.

36. See Hazel Carby's discussions of Frances E. Watkins Harper, Anna Julia Cooper, Victoria Earle Matthews, and Pauline E. Hopkins, precursors and contemporaries of Du Bois who articulated various appeals for a racial renaissance in *Reconstructing Womanhood: The Emergence of the Afro-American Woman Novelist* (New York: Oxford University Press, 1987).

37. I will return to Fullinwider's charge of a "crisis in intellectual leadership," a phrase that attempts to turn Du Bois's own sense of the racial "crisis" (the term he chose for the title of the official NAACP journal) against him.

38. See Williamson, *Crucible*, 408–9, for a discussion of Du Bois in this role.

39. See Arnold Rampersad, *The Art and Imagination of W. E. B. Du Bois* (Cambridge: Harvard University Press, 1976), 9.

40. Rampersad notes that "Du Bois took unto himself the primary responsibility of the would-be mythmaker. . . . It is only slight exaggeration to say that wherever the Afro-American subsequently went as a writer, Du Bois had been there before him, anticipating both the most vital ideas of later currency and the very tropes of their expression." See "W. E. B. Du Bois as a Man of Literature," 59.

41. Gould critiques the "allure of numbers" as the self-delusion of "apostles of objectivity": "Science is rooted in creative interpretation. Numbers suggest, constrain, refute; they do not, by themselves, specify the content of scientific theories. Theories are built upon the interpretation of numbers, and interpreters are often trapped by their own rhetoric. They believe in their own objectivity, and fail to discern the prejudice that leads them to one interpretation among many consistent with their numbers" (74).

42. Rampersad laments, for example, the misguidedness of some volumes in Du Bois's Atlanta University Publications because their usefulness is limited by the language and methodology of an untenable anthropometric view of human identity (*Art and Imagination*, 55).

43. See ibid., 97–98. To name a few already cited, Ray Stannard Baker quotes Du Bois in an unfavorable description of the rural black family (100), while William B. Smith,

who singles out Du Bois and anthropologist Franz Boas for attack, uses *The Philadelphia Negro* for statistics showing the depravity of the black urban family (243–46; 258). See also Tillinghast's frequent quoting of Du Bois to assert black inferiority (182, 183, 190, 200, 203–4).

44. Biographer David Levering Lewis points out the sharp turn in Du Bois's language and temperament from *The Philadelphia Negro* to "The Strivings of the Negro People" in 1897. See *Biography*, 199.

45. See "Criteria of Negro Art," 296.

46. Heilke summarizes Voegelin's soul concept in this way: "The soul, a nonspatial, non-temporal entity, organizes inorganic matter into a body that concretely expresses the character of the soul" (48). For a discussion of the "Veil" as a spatial concept enabling the quest motif, see Stepto, 52–91.

47. See Du Bois's own review essay on *The Souls* in the *Independent*, November 17, 1904, 1152.

48. See Rampersad, *Art and Imagination*, 74, for his discussion of "double consciousness."

49. Lewis's biography takes note also of Du Bois's interest in Goethe's *Faust*. See *Biography*, 165, 281, 282.

50. Lewis concludes that Du Bois's "two souls" trope "echo[ed] almost surely his beloved Goethe's words in *Faust*" (ibid., 281), and he later notes that the construct of the divided self was important to Goethe's work as a whole (282).

51. The passage reads,

I am glad I am living, I rejoice as a strong man to run a race, and I am strong—. . . . I know that I am either a genius or a fool. . . . This I do know: be the Truth what it may I will seek it, on the pure assumption that it is worth seeking and Heaven nor Hell, God nor Devil shall turn me from my purpose till I die.

I will in this second quarter of my life, enter the dark forest of the unknown world for which I have so many years served my apprenticeship—the chart and compass the world furnishes me I have little faith in—yet, I have none better—I will seek till I find—and die. (Du Bois, *Against Racism*, 27–28)

See also Du Bois's slightly altered version in his *Autobiography*, 170–71.

52. The wording here is from the *Autobiography*, since Aptheker's transcription from the diary substitutes "now" for "not," which substantially changes the sentence's meaning. See also Francis L. Broderick, *W. E. B. Du Bois: Negro Leader in a Time of Crisis* (Stanford: Stanford University Press, 1959), 29.

53. As Carby has noted, the idea of a missionary elite of racial strivers predated Du Bois by at least Frances E. W. Harper's *Iola Leroy*. See Carby, *Reconstructing Womanhood*, 84.

54. See Lewis, *Biography*, 144, 313, 338, for Du Bois's evolving interest in socialism.

55. I loathe the knowledge I once sought.

In sensuality's abysmal land

Let our passions drink their fill!
In magic veils, not pierced by skill,
Let every wonder be at hand! (Johann Wolfgang von Goethe, *Faust*, trans. Walter
  Kaufman [New York: Anchor, 1963], 187; my emphasis)

56. I have chosen Broderick's transcription here over Aptheker's, since Aptheker quotes "Youth x Beauty," which does not make sense in this context. See Broderick, 28.

57. Two of the occasions stemmed from Du Bois's reflections on the meaning of the black university in the South, published first in "Of the Wings of Atalanta" in *The Souls* and later incorporated into *Autobiography*, 212. A second use of the phrase in *The Souls* finds the line "Thou shalt forego!" at the end of "Of the Passing of the First Born," in which Du Bois expressed preparedness for any sacrifice *but* the death of his son Burghart, which the essay commemorates (151). Another occasion was an essay "The Problem of Amusement" (discussed below) in the *Southern Workman* 26 (September 1897): 36, which antedates *The Souls* by six years, published one month after the essay that first used the "two-souls" figure, "The Strivings of the Negro People," *Atlantic Monthly* 80 (August 1897).

58. Rampersad explains that while Du Bois did not openly break with Washington until 1903, he had begun to attack the Washington philosophy in his writings as early as the 1900 essay "The Religion of the American Negro." The essay on black amusement and sacrifice shows, however, that Du Bois had, in fact, begun to attack Washington's "Gospel of Wealth" as early as 1897, for the essay was originally given at the General Conference of Negroes at Washington's alma mater of Hampton Institute, and if Washington himself was not present, his functionaries certainly were. See *Autobiography*, 212–13, for Du Bois's recollection of the Hampton and Tuskegee Conferences, on which he based the later series of Atlanta University Conferences.

59. See Shaler, *Neighbor*, 321 for Shaler's version of Du Bois's contrast between strength and submissiveness. In the process of explaining that "the Negro is not an Aryan in a black skin," Shaler undertakes to explain "how very good this primitive may be." The "primary" beneficial race trait to Shaler "is that of devotion to the strong man who is recognized as the overlord." Given Shaler's insistence that blacks are useful to civilization under proper white supervision, it is not clear whether he influenced Du Bois's allegory or Du Bois influenced him.

60. It may be significant that this observation comes in the 1958 *Autobiography* rather than in the 1940 *Dusk of Dawn*, Du Bois's "Autobiography of a Race Concept," in which he admits to the illogic of the racial attitudes he grew up with and helped to perpetuate. See chapter 9 below.

61. See Adolph Reed Jr., "Du Bois's 'Double Consciousness': Race and Gender in Progressive Era American Thought," *Studies in American Political Development* 6 (Spring 1992): 93–139.

62. Literary critics have closely attended Du Bois's metaphor of "double-consciousness" as his most intriguing contribution to the discourse of race difference, a tendency

that Adolph Reed says has more to do with "presentist" politics of each generation of interpreters than with the salience of "double-consciousness" as an enduring description of African American life. See ibid., 102–5.

63. "But the future holds a problem, in solving which the South must stand alone. . . . This problem is to carry within her body politic two separate races. . . . She must carry these races in peace—for discord means ruin. She must carry them separately—for assimilation means debasement. . . . She must carry them even to the end, for in human probability, she will never be quit of either." See John Temple Graves, Clark Howell, and Walter Williams, eds., *Eloquent Sons of the South* (Boston: Chapple Publishing Co., 1909), 254.

64. Williamson reports that "neurologists decided that the electrical signals that control the body run in one direction in white people and in the opposite direction in black people. Mulattoes, obviously, were bound to be highly confused people" (*New People*, 95–96).

65. See Alfred Binet, *On Double Consciousness: Experimental Psychological Studies* (1889: Chicago: Open Court Publishing Co., 1905), 10–11.

66. See William James, *Principles of Psychology* (New York: Henry Holt and Co., 1890), 1:394.

67. Du Bois "stages" such a conflict between personifications of his "white and colored environment" in *Dusk of Dawn*, giving his representative of white America the name Roger Van Dieman, perhaps both an allegory and an allusion to the "racial spirit" of death that had authorized the extermination of the Tasmanian people of Van Diemen's Land.

68. "It is such incessant self-questioning and the hesitation that arises from it, that is making the present period a time of vacillation and contradiction for the American Negro; combined race action is stifled, race responsibility is shirked, race enterprises languish, and the best blood, the best talent, the best energy of the Negro people cannot be marshaled to do the bidding of the race. They stand back to make room for every rascal and demagogue who chooses to cloak his selfish deviltry under the veil of race pride" (5).

69. "Suggestion, when successful, consists of an idea impressed upon a person and reigning dominant in the consciousness of that person; reason, critical powers, and will are impotent to restrain it. . . . For suggestion to develop itself, accordingly, it is necessary that the subject's field of consciousness do [sic] not contain too many antagonistic ideas. Now, it is exactly this psychological situation that is found realized in the duplication of consciousness" (72–73). Binet found that suggestion did not create double consciousness so much as it exploited a prior condition and that "as a consequence of such a phenomenon of bipartition, each of the consciousnesses occupies a more narrow and more limited field than if there existed one single consciousness" (72, 73).

70. The reference seems to echo Du Bois's earlier essay "The Meaning of All This"

(1899), in which he had lamented that "if, in a land of freemen, eight millions of human beings were found to be dying of disease," the calls of "Heal them!" would immediately be "broken by counter-cries and echoes, 'Let them die!'" (Lewis, *Reader*, 163–64).

71. In this sense of self-veiling, Du Bois's trope has an analogue in Binet's studies on double consciousness. In order to test his theory of double consciousness, Binet used a screen to block his subjects from seeing what their hands or other anesthetic body parts were doing (*Double Consciousness*, 13). Behind his screen, Binet would induce activity in the affected body parts, explaining that "the sensations and movements of the anaesthetic limb, by grouping themselves together, formed a second consciousness," (57) an aggregate of neuromuscular motor activity. This "second consciousness" centered in the body itself was the subject of a further experiment by Binet involving patients again screened from visual contact with their own body parts. Using the "transitory anaesthesia" of "distraction" (*Double Consciousness*, 78), Binet found that he could induce a functioning second consciousness in nonhysterics, an "automatic" personality residing in the motor operations of the body itself, creating "intelligences of a parasitic kind." See Alfred Binet, "Plural States of Being," *Popular Science Monthly* 50 (February 1897): 541. I have developed Binet's ideas in some detail here because, as I show in chapter 6, he served as Pauline Hopkins's source for a literary exploration of the phenomenon following Du Bois's racial appropriation of the term.

72. In Ralph Ellison's *Invisible Man* (New York: Random House, 1972), 36, the narrator questions whether Washington is unveiling the slave or lowering the veil "more firmly in place."

73. See Foucault, 29.

74. For example, in vol. 2 of *Booker T. Washington*, Harlan notes that "Washington was always hungry for evidence that the Faustian bargain he had made for black leadership and regional influence was worth the cost" (256). In vol. 1, Harlan had similarly made use of this figure to describe Washington's only serious competition for southern white patronage, William Hooper Councill: "At the end of Reconstruction, Councill had sold his black soul for white Conservative favor. . . . This faustian bargain gave him great power, for he fulfilled the Alabama white man's conception of a Negro leader more completely than Washington. . . . He could out-Booker Booker, and he frequently did" (169).

75. "The tendency is here, born of slavery and quickened to renewed life by the crazy imperialism of the day, to regard human beings as among the material resources of a land to be trained with an eye single to future dividends. Race-prejudices, which keep brown and black men in their 'places,' we are coming to regard as useful allies with such a theory, no matter how much they may dull the ambition and sicken the hearts of struggling human beings" (*Souls*, 67).

76. Claude McKay remembered Tuskegee as dominated by a "semi-military, machine-like existence," and despite his continuing reverence for Washington, he left the school within weeks of his arrival. See Wayne F. Cooper, *Claude McKay: Rebel Sojourner in the*

Harlem Renaissance: A Biography (Baton Rouge: Louisiana State University Press, 1987), 65–66.

77. See Goethe, 191, where in answer to Faust's fear for the success of his self-development scheme, Mephistopheles comforts him:

You're in the end—just what you are!

Put wigs on with a million locks

And put your foot on ell-high socks,

You still remain just what you are.

78. "Apparently one consideration alone saved me from the conformity with the thoughts and confusion of then current social trends; and that was the problem of racial and cultural contacts. Otherwise I might easily have been simply the current product of my day" (*Autobiography*, 15). It is illuminating to compare Du Bois's revision of the "fortunate fall" with Washington's entirely characteristic resuscitation of the old racist logic that slavery had been beneficial "as an early version of citizenship training" (Lewis, *Biography*, 169).

79. See Stocking, 195–233, for the early tentative steps of Franz Boas toward the modern anthropological concept of culture. In *Dusk of Dawn*, Du Bois would finally acknowledge that his concept all along had been based on "culture" rather than biological "race," first as a result of his late introduction to "African feeling" (115) and later through his university training and other experiences in Europe (102).

80. See chapter 6.

Chapter Six: The Quest of the Black Soul

1. See William L. Andrews, ed., *The African-American Novel in the Age of Reaction: Three Classics* (New York: Penguin, 1992), 164.

2. See Sutton E. Griggs, *Imperium in Imperio: A Study of the Negro Race Problem: A Novel* (1899; New York: Arno Press, 1969), v, for details on Griggs's background. As I show in chapter 8, Paul Laurence Dunbar's *The Sport of the Gods* (1902) was a more profound study of black American spiritual crisis than any single one of Griggs's efforts, but for sheer volume and variety of treatment, Griggs was far and away the most prolific.

3. Among these are the approval of the "fortunate fall" of blacks into American slavery, and therefore civilization, and the curious nonresistance to white mob violence when, "by violence, a member of a despised race assails a defenseless woman" (232, 238). Simply put, Bernard endorses lynch law for the "one crime."

4. See the discussion of Hopkins's article on the black models for classical statuary, "Venus and Apollo Modelled from Ethiopians," below.

5. Griggs does not give two names for these characters because there are so many characters to follow and so little characterization that any summary of events would be

impossible. Thus, we are not told Perry's name before the split up, nor are we ever told Tiara's.

6. See Ralph Ginzburg, 62–63.

7. See Du Bois, *Autobiography*, 138, 248–51.

8. "I believe that the same rules which govern all races will be applicable to mine. . . . If men are rude and foolish, down they must go. When at last in any race a new principle appears, an idea, *that* conserves it. Ideas only save races. If the black man is feeble and impotent, unimportant to the existing races—not on a parity with the best races, the black man must serve and be exterminated. *But*, if he carries within his bosom the element of a new and coming civilization, he will survive and play his part" (295).

9. Reuel cites Binet's "The Unclassified Residuum," and his knowledge of research on hysterical anesthesia, double consciousness, and mesmerism suggests that he would have been familiar with Binet's works such as *Alterations of Personality* (1896), *Animal Magnetism* (1892), and *On Double Consciousness* (1889, 1896).

10. The whispering voices have a curious analogue in the studies of Binet, which may cast a certain light on the connection between Du Bois's concepts of "double-consciousness" and the veil of race. By whispering in the subject's ear, Binet used direct or indirect suggestion in the form of "an image conjured up in the mind of the patient" ("Plural States," 542) to activate the second consciousness. The artificially induced second consciousness was highly suggestible to the experimenter's whisperings when he approached the subject from behind, where the subject could not see him. These suggestions were "screened," in effect, from the primary consciousness, which could not hear and did not respond to them. Such suggestion was a "partial hypnotisation" of the body's second, neuromuscular-centered consciousness to Binet, which might share either a complementary or antagonistic relationship with the primary "ego." The Du Boisian equivalent was the mesmeric power of the man called the "Wizard of Tuskegee," the ally of the powerful "Wizard of the North" and chief apologist of the wizards of the South, who distracted the soul quester from ethical striving by whispering of personal gain through acceptance of industrial slavery and civic death.

11. See "Plural States of Being," 539, for Binet's distinction between somnambulism at night (noctambulism) and in the day (vigilambulism).

12. See Du Bois's description of the Sorrow Songs as artifacts of cultural identity: "Ever since I was a child these songs have stirred me strangely. They came out of the South unknown to me, one by one, and yet at once I knew them as of me and mine" (177). *Of One Blood* was serialized between November 1902 and November 1903. *The Souls* appeared almost midway during this serial run, in April 1903.

13. Compare with Du Bois in *The Souls*: "two centuries of systematic legal defilement of Negro women . . . meant not only the loss of ancient African chastity, but also the hereditary weight of a mass of corruption from white adulterers" (6).

Chapter Seven: The Darkness of the Mother

1. As Broderick reports, Du Bois had recorded in his 1888–90 diary prior to the Jefferson Davis speech the more qualified opinion that "Ethiopia shall in these days stretch forth her hands to God," but "the spectacle of the colored dame in this rather unbalanced position in regard to the Anglo-Saxon God has become somewhat nauseating to the average young Negro of today" (23). The passage may reveal that Du Bois's use of the figure to end the speech was a calculated attempt to curry the favor of powerful whites, given his own strong reservations.

2. According to Du Bois, "this deep religious fatalism . . . came soon to breed, as all fatalistic faiths will, the sensualist side by side with the martyr. Under the lax moral life of the plantation, where marriage was a farce, laziness a virtue, and property a theft, a religion of resignation and submission degenerated easily, in less strenuous minds, into a philosophy of indulgence and crime. Many of the worst characteristics of the Negro masses of to-day had their seed in this period of the slave's ethical growth. Here it was that the Home was ruined under the very shadow of the Church, white and black; here habits of shiftlessness took root, and sullen hopelessness replaced hopeful strife" (*Souls*, 140).

3. On Du Bois's attempts to isolate the black home from the influence of the church, see "The Work of Negro Women in Society," in *Writings by W. E. B. Du Bois in Periodicals Edited by Others*, ed. Herbert Aptheker (Millwood, N.Y.: Kraus-Thomson, 1982), 1:143; "The Problem of Amusement," 33–39; and "The Talented Tenth," in *Writings by W. E. B. Du Bois in Non-Periodical Literature Edited by Others*, ed. Herbert Aptheker (Millwood, N.Y.: Kraus-Thomson, 1982), 22. On his attempt to distinguish secular from religious striving, see "The Joy of Living," in *Writings by W. E. B. Du Bois in Periodicals Edited by Others*, 216–21.

4. See Shaler, *Neighbor*, 263–65.

5. See Andrews, *Critical Essays*, 68. See also Rampersad, *Art and Imagination*, 75–76.

6. Quoted in Morton, 55.

7. See Archer, 215n.

8. See *Souls*, 2.

9. "Negro Women in Society," 141. See also on that same page Du Bois's gratuitous swipe at Tuskegee: "But unless we do this, no amount of education, wealth, or, if I may dare say it—industrial training—can save us from wavering, falling, and disappearing before more strongly organized men."

10. See undated letter to Walter Page in Herbert Aptheker, ed., *The Correspondence of W. E. B. Du Bois* (Amherst: University of Massachusetts Press, 1973), 1:113, and also n. 1.

11. See Rampersad, *Art and Imagination*, 100–104.

12. See 1:84–86.

13. See *Neighbor*, 141. See Tillinghast, 65–66.

14. See Lewis, *Reader*, 294.

15. See Darwin, chap. 7, "Of the Races of Man" (209–41).

16. 2:352–58. Darwin, though, cites evidence of greater male differentiation within human populations and speculates that with respect to certain traits, "it is the male which has been chiefly modified" (2:306). Thus greater female modification through sexual selection may be balanced by greater male variability through natural selection, an interesting way of justifying his observation that white females were closer to the "lower races" (311).

17. Du Bois did not know at the time the extent of the exaggeration of the "epidemic" but seemed convinced that at least some of the claims were true. See Williamson, *Crucible*, 215, for Ray Stannard Baker's estimate that nearly half of the reported assaults were clearly unfounded.

18. Quoted in Wilson J. Moses, "The Politics of Ethiopianism: W. E. B. Du Bois and Literary Black Nationalism," in Andrews, *Critical Essays*, 95.

19. *Creative Writings by W. E. B. Du Bois: A Pageant, Poems, Short Stories, and Playlets* (White Plains, N.Y.: Kraus-Thomson, 1985), 15. Both poems were published in November 1907.

20. See chapter 8.

21. Ibid.

22. Du Bois uses these offices knowing that black readers will not find the prospect utterly unbelievable, since patronage in Treasury had been a traditional political reward for black votes in key states. See Williamson, *Crucible*, 366, 380–81, where Williamson discusses the assault on the position of register of the Treasury, a patronage position that had been designated as a political plum for black Republicans from 1896 until Wilson's presidency.

23. "We cannot imprison women again in a home or require them all on pain of death to be nurses and housekeepers. . . . The uplift of women is, next to the problem of the color line and the peace movement, our greatest modern cause" (181).

24. See Carby, introduction to *Magazine Novels of Pauline Hopkins*, xxx. Hopkins's affiliation with the magazine was in the pre-Washington days when it was published in Boston. See Harlan, *Booker T. Washington*, 2:41. See also Lewis, *Biography*, 314–15, for Du Bois's revelation of Washington's corruption of the black press.

25. See Arthur P. Davis, *From the Dark Tower: Afro-American Writers, 1900 to 1960* (Washington, D.C.: Howard University Press, 1974), 22. See also Rampersad, *Art and Imagination*, 131–32, and Nellie McKay, "W. E. B. Du Bois: The Black Women in His Writings: Selected Fictional and Autobiographical Portraits," in Andrews, *Critical Essays*, 230–32.

Chapter Eight: The Whiteness of the Witch

1. See Ean Begg, *The Cult of the Black Virgin* (London: Penguin, 1985), 13.

2. See the *Crisis* 9 (March 1915): 239. See also James Weldon Johnson, *Saint Peter Relates an Incident: Selected Poems by James Weldon Johnson* (New York: Viking Press, 1935), 34–36.

3. On the sexual content of southern mammyolatry, see Lillian Smith, 132–34; Catherine Clinton, *The Plantation Mistress: Woman's World in the Old South* (New York: Pantheon, 1982), 202; and Graham, 160.

4. See Stepto, 86–91, for the Washington–Du Bois debate. See Houston A. Baker Jr., *Blues, Ideology, and Afro-American Literature: A Vernacular Theory* (Chicago: University of Chicago Press, 1984), 119–22, for the debate with particular reference to Dunbar's *Sport of the Gods*.

5. See Johnson's discussion of personal success amidst a continuing climate of racial discrimination in the New York theater in James Weldon Johnson, *Along This Way: The Autobiography of James Weldon Johnson* (1933; New York: Penguin, 1990), 194–201.

6. See Yellin, 114, fig. 20.

7. See Yellin's extensive discussion of the evolution of the final design (113–19).

8. This physical type generally corresponds to his descriptions of the first serious sweetheart of his youth, to whom he coyly refers as "Heart's Desire," and also to Grace Nail, his New York–born wife who, at least on one occasion, was mistaken for a white woman (63, 379). See Eugene Levy, *James Weldon Johnson: Black Leader, Black Voice* (Chicago: University of Chicago Press, 1973), 114, for a physical description of Grace Nail, and *Along*, facing 212, for photo of Grace Nail.

9. *Along*, 170. See 314–26; 361–74.

10. See Al-Tony Gilmore, *Bad Nigger!: The National Impact of Jack Johnson* (Port Washington, N.Y.: Kennikat Press, 1975), 135. See also Finis Farr's critique of the story that the fight was fixed, in *Black Champion: The Life and Times of Jack Johnson* (New York: Charles Scribner's Sons, 1964), 204–7.

11. See Farr, 72 ff., 170, for Belle Schreiber's role.

12. See Gilmore's account of the legal tangles of Johnson (95–125).

13. Quoted in Gilmore, 35–37. See also Farr, 83, for a description of a *Chicago Defender* cartoon in which the black newspaper showed Johnson in the ring with Jeffries, the Devil as referee, and "Race Hatred," "Prejudice," and "Negro Persecution" crowding around Jeffries, with a caption, "HE WILL HAVE THEM ALL TO BEAT."

14. Gilmore, 105, 103, 100. In a further irony, Farr notes that the "beauty and the beast" motif had earlier been the hook for a vaudeville act featuring Johnson and Etta Duryea early in their marriage (79).

15. See *Along*, 191, for Johnson's regret that he had not invested more of his money in

Florida real estate. By contrast, his in-laws, the Nails, became wealthy from real estate deals. See Jervis Anderson, *This Was Harlem: A Critical Portrait, 1900–1950* (New York: Farrar, Straus, and Giroux, 1982), 53. There is no direct evidence that X was involved in tenement houses for blacks, but according to Anderson, the real estate market in New York covering the time of the novel's events was engaged in a conspiracy to restrict the black population to certain areas. Rogue agents created a white stampede out of Harlem by settling blacks into one house on the block at a steep increase in rental. See James Weldon Johnson, *Black Manhattan* (1930; New York: Da Capo, 1991), 145–51, for the black "invasion" of Harlem during this period. Thus, whether he was one of those colluding to restrict blacks or one profiting from renting to blacks in segregated neighborhoods at well over the prevailing rent, X's wealth depended in some way on the white space real estate wars in New York. See Jervis Anderson, 11–12, 49–56.

16. See Levy, 116–17, 126.

17. Johnson owed his consular position to Washington's political clout, though he later declined to describe himself as a part of Washington's political machine, and political operatives who were important players in the disposition of the Ulrich affair were Johnson's contacts with the Tuskegee group. See Levy, 99–109. See *Along*, 219–21, for Johnson's description of his relationship to Washington operative Charles Anderson.

18. Levy, 133. See also *Along*, 222.

19. See Levy, 153, 179.

20. The ease with which Johnson moved into the Du Bois orbit in the declining years of Washington as a power broker can partially be explained in light of the references to Washington in his autobiography, *Along This Way*. In this book, written nearly two decades after Washington's death and after the NAACP had been long established as the major black organization, Johnson reveals that, apart from a certain reticence of character and a southerner's ability to find common ground with southern whites, he really had no strong personal or philosophical attachment to the conservative Tuskegee idea. Though he describes himself as an informal member of the "Black Cabinet" during the days of his consular service, Johnson cleverly leaves out the fact that Washington controlled the group, giving the impression that the cabinet somehow functioned as a presidential advisory group on race issues independent of Washington, just as he leaves out any mention of Washington's role in securing his consular position. See *Along This Way*, 239. See also Levy, 104 n. 14. Then, in reference to the issue of "social equality," he attacks Washington's "Atlanta Compromise" in terms that Du Bois had first used in *The Souls* but that his long affiliation with Washington had made impossible for Johnson to endorse at the time. Calling the speech a "stroke of consummate diplomacy," Johnson decries its illogic and "ineptitude": "There ought not be any intellectual dilemma in this question for a self-respecting Negro. He can, without apology to himself or to anyone else, stand for social equality on any definition of the term not laid down by a madman or an idiot" (312).

Johnson then launches into a history of the NAACP's origins and antagonism to the Tuskegee Machine without a single indication that his own political apprenticeship had been in the Washington camp (313).

21. See Dixon, *Sword*, 164–79, esp. 173, 179. See also Johnson's discussion of the use of the poem at the *Birth of a Nation* trial in Boston in 1915 (*Along*, 306).

22. See Cooper, 63–65.

23. See ibid., 146–48.

Chapter Nine: Conclusion

1. See "The Southerner's Problem" in the *Dial*, May 1, 1905, 317. "The Souls of White Folk" is therefore a continuation of the line of discussion Du Bois engages in his review of Smith and Thomas Nelson Page's *The Negro: The Southerner's Problem*.

2. See *Dusk*, 99, where Du Bois observes with satisfaction, "I lived to see every assumption of Hoffman's 'Race Traits and Tendencies' contradicted."

3. See James Weldon Johnson, "Harlem: The Culture Capital," in *The New Negro*, ed. Alain Locke (New York: Boni and Liveright, 1925), 302.

4. White's novels, *Fire in the Flint* (1924) and *Flight* (1926), were firmly in the Du Boisian tradition of a propagandistic literature of race striving, though *Flight*, like Fauset's *Plum Bun* (1928), framed the narrative within the "passing" genre. Fauset's earlier *There Is Confusion* (1924) featured the lives of upper-middle-class blacks in their attempt to find personal fulfillment while battling the confining American racial caste system.

5. See David Levering Lewis, *When Harlem Was in Vogue* (New York: Oxford University Press, 1981), 176–78.

6. See p. 219: "The squalor of Negro life, the vice of Negro life, offer a wealth of novel, exotic, picturesque material for the artist. . . . Are Negro writers going to write about this exotic material while it is still fresh?"

7. See "Criteria of Negro Art," 294.

8. See Darwin Turner, introduction to *The House behind the Cedars*, by Charles W. Chesnutt (1900; New York: Collier Books, 1969), xxii.

9. See Felipe Smith, "Alice Walker's Redemptive Art," *African American Review* 26 (1992): 437–51.

10. See Nella Larsen, *Quicksand* and *Passing* (New Brunswick, N.J.: Rutgers University Press, 1986), 134–55 and 168 respectively.

11. See George Schuyler, *Black No More* (1931; Boston: Northeastern University Press, 1989), 132.

12. See Claude McKay's *Home to Harlem* (1928; Boston: Northeastern University Press, 1987) and *Banjo* (New York: Harper, 1929). See Alain Locke's review of Claude McKay's *A Long Way from Home*, "Spiritual Truancy," in *Voices of the Harlem Renaissance*, ed. Nathan Irvin Huggins (New York: Oxford University Press, 1976), 404–6.

13. See Lewis, *Harlem*, 151–53.

14. See ibid., 229.

15. Lewis thinks the positive vote for black America by the other "colored" victims of Western imperialism was condescending, given Du Bois's vocal advocacy of race pride. See ibid., 201.

16. See further clarification of Du Bois's ideas on intermarriage in "Social Equality and Racial Intermarriage," in Lewis, *Reader*, 372–74. See also Du Bois's response to a letter in the *Crisis* 32 (March 1926): 218.

17. Herbert Aptheker, introduction to *Dark Princess: A Romance*, by W. E. B. Du Bois (Millwood, N.Y.: Kraus-Thomson, 1974), 7–8. See also Du Bois, *Autobiography*, 262–63.

18. The conference was not, in fact, the first of its kind, despite the title. The first conference had been held in London in 1900, and Du Bois attended but did not preside. See Lewis, *Biography*, 248–51.

19. For a discussion of the iconic representation of Melancholy as a swarthy female with connections to ancient Egyptian art, see Erwin Panofsky, *The Life and Art of Albrecht Dürer* (Princeton: Princeton University Press, 1955), 161, 162. Cited in Yellin, 84–85.

20. See *Creative Writings*, 1.

21. A quote from Apollodorous, "Perseus," describing Cassiopeia, queen of Ethiopia, mother of Andromeda. See Edith Hamilton, *Mythology: Timeless Tales of Gods and Heroes* (New York: New American Library, 1969), 146.

22. Quoted in Rampersad, *Art and Imagination*, 154.

23. *Dusk*, 153. See Appiah's observations on the practical significance of this evolution in Du Bois's concept of race (40–42).

Works Cited

Anderson, Benedict. *Imagined Communities: Reflections on the Origin and Spread of Nationalism*. 1983. Rev. and expanded. London: Verso, 1991.

Anderson, Jervis. *This Was Harlem: A Cultural Portrait, 1900–1950*. New York: Farrar, Straus, and Giroux, 1982.

Andrews, William L., ed. *The African-American Novel in the Age of Reaction: Three Classics*. New York: Penguin, 1992.

——, ed. *Critical Essays on W. E. B. Du Bois*. Boston: G. K. Hall, 1985.

Appiah, Kwame Anthony. *In My Father's House: Africa in the Philosophy of Culture*. New York: Oxford University Press, 1992.

Aptheker, Herbert, ed. *The Correspondence of W. E. B. Du Bois*. 2 vols. Amherst: University of Massachusetts Press, 1973.

——, ed. *Pamphlets and Leaflets by W. E. B. Du Bois*. Millwood, N.Y.: Kraus-Thomson, 1986.

——, ed. *Writings by W. E. B. Du Bois in Non-Periodical Literature Edited by Others*. Millwood, N.Y.: Kraus-Thomson, 1982.

——, ed. *Writings by W. E. B. Du Bois in Periodicals Edited by Others*. 4 vols. Millwood, N.Y.: Kraus-Thomson, 1982.

Archer, William. *Through Afro-America: An English Reading of the Race Problem*. London: Chapman and Hall, 1910.

Avary, Myrta Lockett. *Dixie after the War: An Exposition of Social Conditions Existing in the South, during the Twelve Years Succeeding the Fall of Richmond*. Freeport, N.Y.: Books for Libraries Press, 1906.

Ayers, Edward L. *Vengeance and Justice: Crime and Punishment in the Nineteenth-Century American South*. New York: Oxford University Press, 1984.

Baker, Houston A., Jr. *Blues, Ideology, and Afro-American Literature: A Vernacular Theory*. Chicago: University of Chicago Press, 1984.

——. *Modernism and the Harlem Renaissance*. Chicago: University of Chicago Press, 1987.

——. "The Promised Body: Reflections on Canon in an Afro-American Context." *Poetics Today* 9, no. 2 (1988): 339–54.

——. *Workings of the Spirit: The Poetics of Afro-American Women's Writing*. Chicago: University of Chicago Press, 1991.

Baker, Ray Stannard. *Following the Color Line: An Account of Negro Citizenship in the American Democracy*. 1908. Williamstown, Mass.: Corner House Publishers, 1973.

Banta, Martha. *Imaging American Women: Ideas and Ideals in Cultural History*. New York: Columbia University Press, 1987.

Barringer, Paul B. *The American Negro, His Past and Future*. Raleigh, N.C.: Edwards and Broughton Printers, 1900.

——. "The Sacrifice of a Race." In *Race Problems of the South: Report of the Proceedings of the First Annual Conference*, 178–94. Richmond: B. F. Johnson Publishing Co., 1900.

Barthes, Roland. *Mythologies*. Selected and translated by Annette Lavers. 1957. New York: Farrar, Straus, and Giroux, 1972.

Baughman, Laurence Alan. *Southern Rape Complex: Hundred Year Psychosis*. Atlanta: Pendulum Books, 1966.

Begg, Ean. *The Cult of the Black Virgin*. London: Penguin, 1985.

Berman, Marshall. *All That Is Solid Melts into Air: The Experience of Modernity*. New York: Simon and Schuster, 1982.

Berry, Mary Frances, and John W. Blassingame. *Long Memory: The Black Experience in America*. New York: Oxford University Press, 1982.

Binet, Alfred. *On Double Consciousness: Experimental Psychological Studies*. 1889. Chicago: Open Court Publishing Co., 1905.

——. "Plural States of Being." *Popular Science Monthly* 50 (February 1897): 539–43.

Blassingame, John W. *Black New Orleans: 1860–1880*. Chicago: University of Chicago Press, 1973.

Bleckley, L. E. "Negro Outrage No Excuse for Lynching." *Forum* 16 (October 1893): 300–302.

Boorstin, Daniel J., ed. *An American Primer*. Chicago: University of Chicago Press, 1966.

Bowers, Claude. *The Tragic Era: The Revolution after Lincoln*. Cambridge, Mass.: Literary Guild of America, 1929.

Bracy, John H., August Meier, and Eliot Rudwick, eds. *Black Nationalism in America*. Indianapolis: Bobbs-Merrill, 1970.

Broca, Paul. *On the Phenomena of Hybridity in the Genus Homo*. Translated and edited by C. C. Blake. London: Longman, Green, Longman and Roberts, 1864.

Broderick, Francis L. *W. E. B. Du Bois: Negro Leader in a Time of Crisis*. Stanford: Stanford University Press, 1959.

Brodhead, Richard H., ed. *The Journals of Charles W. Chesnutt*. Durham, N.C.: Duke University Press, 1993.

Browne, Warren. *Titan vs. Taboo: The Life of William Benjamin Smith*. Tucson, Ariz.: Diogenes Press, 1961.

Bruce, Philip A. *The Plantation Negro as a Freeman: Observations on His Character, Condition, and Prospects in Virginia*. New York: G. P. Putnam's Sons, 1889.

Brundage, W. Fitzhugh. *Lynching in the New South: Georgia and Virginia, 1880–1930*. Urbana: University of Illinois Press, 1993.

Cable, George Washington. *The Silent South*. New York: Charles Scribner's Sons, 1885.

Cameron, James. *A Time of Terror: A Survivor's Story*. Baltimore: Black Classic Press, 1994.

Carby, Hazel. Introduction to *The Magazine Novels of Pauline Hopkins*. New York: Oxford University Press, 1988.

———. "'On the Threshold of Woman's Era': Lynching, Empire, and Sexuality in Black Feminist Theory." In *"Race," Writing, and Difference*, edited by Henry Louis Gates Jr., 301–16. Chicago: University of Chicago Press, 1985.

———. *Reconstructing Womanhood: The Emergence of the Afro-American Woman Novelist*. New York: Oxford University Press, 1987.

Carroll, Charles. *The Negro, a Beast, or in the Image of God*. St. Louis: American Book and Bible House, 1900.

Cash, W. J. *The Mind of the South*. New York: Knopf, 1941.

Cassity, Michael J. *Legacy of Fear: American Race Relations to 1900*. Westport, Conn.: Greenwood Press, 1985.

Chambers, Bradford, ed. *Chronicles of Black Protest*. New York: New American Library, 1968.

Chesnutt, Charles W. *Collected Stories of Charles W. Chesnutt*. Edited by William L. Andrews. New York: Penguin, 1992.

———. *The House behind the Cedars*. 1900. New York: Collier Books, 1969.

———. *The Marrow of Tradition. The African-American Novel in the Age of Reaction: Three Classics*. Edited by William L. Andrews. New York: Penguin, 1992.

Christian, Barbara. *Black Women Novelists: The Development of a Tradition, 1892–1976*. Westport, Conn.: Greenwood Press, 1980.

Clinton, Catherine. *The Plantation Mistress: Woman's World in the Old South*. New York: Pantheon, 1982.

Cohn, David L. *God Shakes Creation*. New York: Harper and Brothers, 1935.

Congressional Record—Senate. Washington, D.C. January 21, 1907.

Conrad, Joseph. *Heart of Darkness*. Edited by Ross C. Murfin. 1899. New York: St. Martin's, 1996.

Cooper, Wayne F. *Claude McKay: Rebel Sojourner in the Harlem Renaissance: A Biography*. Baton Rouge: Louisiana State University Press, 1987.

Cox, Earnest Sevier. *White America*. Richmond: White America Society, 1923.

Cripps, Thomas. *Slow Fade to Black: The Negro in American Film, 1900–1942.* 1977. New York: Oxford University Press, 1993.

[Croly, David Goodman, and George Wakeman.] *Miscegenation: The Theory of the Blending of the Races, Applied to the American White Man and Negro.* New York: H. Dexter, Hamilton and Co., 1864.

Cutler, James E. *Lynch-Law: An Investigation into the History of Lynching in the United States.* New York: Longmans, Green, and Co., 1905.

Dance, Daryl. *Shuckin' and Jivin': Folklore from Contemporary Black Americans.* Bloomington: Indiana University Press, 1978.

Darwin, Charles. *The Descent of Man, and Selection in Relation to Sex.* 2 vols. New York: D. Appleton and Co., 1871.

Davis, Arthur P. *From the Dark Tower: Afro-American Writers, 1900 to 1960.* Washington, D.C.: Howard University Press, 1974.

Davis, James F. *Who Is Black?: One Nation's Definition.* University Park: Pennsylvania State University Press, 1991.

Dijkstra, Bram. *Idols of Perversity: Fantasies of Feminine Evil in Fin-de-Siècle Culture.* New York: Oxford University Press, 1986.

Diliberto, Gioia. *Hadley.* New York: Ticknor and Fields, 1992.

Dixon, Thomas, Jr. *The Clansman: An Historical Romance of the Ku Klux Klan.* Lexington: University Press of Kentucky, 1970.

———. *The Flaming Sword.* Atlanta: Monarch Publishing Co., 1939.

———. *The Leopard's Spots: A Romance of the White Man's Burden, 1865–1900.* New York: Doubleday, Page and Co., 1902.

Dollard, John. *Caste and Class in a Southern Town.* New Haven: Yale University Press, 1937.

Douglas, Mary. *Purity and Danger: An Analysis of Concepts of Pollution and Taboo.* New York: Frederick A. Praeger, 1966.

Douglass, Frederick. *Narrative of the Life of Frederick Douglass, an American Slave.* New York: Penguin, 1982.

Doyle, Bertram W. *The Etiquette of Race Relations in the South: A Study in Social Control.* Chicago: University of Chicago Press, 1937.

Doyle, Laura. *Bordering on the Body: The Racial Matrix of Modern Fiction and Culture.* New York: Oxford University Press, 1994.

Du Bois, W. E. B. *Against Racism: Unpublished Essays, Papers, Addresses, 1887–1961.* Edited by Herbert Aptheker. Amherst: University of Massachusetts Press, 1985.

———. "An Attack." In *Writings by W. E. B. Du Bois in Non-Periodical Literature Edited by Others,* edited by Herbert Aptheker, 66. Millwood, N.Y.: Kraus-Thomson, 1982.

———. *The Autobiography of W. E. B. Du Bois: A Soliloquy on Viewing My Life from the Last Decade of Its First Century.* N.p.: International Publishers, 1968.

———. "The Conservation of Races." In *Pamphlets and Leaflets by W. E. B. Du Bois,* edited by Herbert Aptheker, 1–8. Millwood, N.Y.: Kraus-Thomson, 1986.

——. *Creative Writings by W. E. B. Du Bois: A Pageant, Poems, Short Stories, and Play-lets: The Complete Published Works of W. E. B. Du Bois*. Edited by Herbert Aptheker. White Plains, N.Y.: Kraus-Thomson, 1985.

——. "Credo." In *Writings by W. E. B. Du Bois in Periodicals Edited by Others*, edited by Herbert Aptheker, 1:229–30. Millwood, N.Y.: Kraus-Thomson, 1982.

——. "Criteria of Negro Art." *Crisis* 32, no. 6 (October 1926): 290–97.

——. *Dark Princess: A Romance*. Millwood, N.Y.: Kraus-Thomson, 1974.

——. *Darkwater: Voices from within the Veil*. New York: Harcourt, Brace and Co., 1921.

——. "The Development of a People." In *Writings by W. E. B. Du Bois in Periodicals Edited by Others*, edited by Herbert Aptheker, 1:203–15. Millwood, N.Y.: Kraus-Thomson, 1982.

——. *Dusk of Dawn*. Millwood, N.Y.: Kraus-Thomson, 1975.

——. "The Joy of Living." In *Writings by W. E. B. Du Bois in Periodicals Edited by Others*, edited by Herbert Aptheker, 1:216–22. Millwood, N.Y.: Kraus-Thomson, 1982.

——. "Marrying of Black Folk." In *Writings by W. E. B. Du Bois in Periodicals Edited by Others*, edited by Herbert Aptheker, 2:32–34. Millwood, N.Y.: Kraus-Thomson, 1982.

——. "The Problem of Amusement." In *Writings by W. E. B. Du Bois in Periodicals Edited by Others*, edited by Herbert Aptheker, 1:32–39. Millwood, N.Y.: Kraus-Thomson, 1982.

——. *The Quest of the Silver Fleece: A Novel*. New York: Arno Press, 1969.

——. Review. *The Souls of Black Folk. Independent* 57 (1904): 1152.

——. *The Souls of Black Folk*. 1903. New York: Bantam, 1989.

——. "The Souls of White Folk." In *Writings by W. E. B. Du Bois in Periodicals Edited by Others*, edited by Herbert Aptheker, 2:25–29. Millwood, N.Y.: Kraus-Thomson, 1982.

——. "The Southerner's Problem." *Dial*, May 1, 1905, 315–18.

——. "Strivings of the Negro People." *Atlantic Monthly* 80 (August 1897): 194–98.

——. "The Talented Tenth." *Writings by W. E. B. Du Bois in Non-Periodical Literature Edited by Others*, edited by Herbert Aptheker, 17–29. Millwood, N.Y.: Kraus-Thomson, 1982.

——. *W. E. B. Du Bois: A Reader*. Edited by David Levering Lewis. New York: Henry Holt and Co., 1995.

——. "The Work of Negro Women in Society." In *Writings by W. E. B. Du Bois in Periodicals Edited by Others*, edited by Herbert Aptheker, 1:139–44. Millwood, N.Y.: Kraus-Thomson, 1982.

duCille, Ann. *The Coupling Convention: Sex, Text, and Tradition in Black Women's Fiction*. New York: Oxford University Press, 1993.

Dunbar, Paul Laurence. *The Sport of the Gods. The African-American Novel in the Age of Reaction: Three Classics*. Edited by William L. Andrews. New York: Penguin, 1992.

Dyer, John P. *Tulane: The Biography of a University, 1834–1965*. New York: Harper and Row, 1966.

Ellison, Ralph. *Invisible Man*. New York: Random House, 1972.

——. *Shadow and Act*. New York: Random House, 1964.

——. "What America Would Be Like without Blacks." In *Going to the Territory*, 104–12. 1986. New York: Vintage, 1995.

Fabian, Johannes. *Time and the Other: How Anthropology Makes Its Object*. New York: Columbia University Press, 1983.

Fabre, Michel. "Looking at the Naked Blonde—Closely (or, Scrutinizing Ellison's Writing)." *Delta* 18 (April 1984): 119–31.

Farr, Finis. *Black Champion: The Life and Times of Jack Johnson*. New York: Charles Scribner's Sons, 1964.

Faulkner, William. *The Sound and the Fury*. New York: Random House, 1956.

Fitzgerald, F. Scott. *The Crack-Up*. Edited by Edmund Wilson. 1945. New York: New Directions, 1964.

Fleming, E. McClung. "The American Image as Indian Princess, 1765–1783." *Winterthur Portfolio* 2 (1965): 65–81.

——. "From Indian Princess to Greek Goddess: The American Image, 1783–1815." *Winterthur Portfolio* 3 (1967): 37–66.

Foucault, Michel. *Discipline and Punish: The Birth of the Prison*. Translated by Alan Sheridan. New York: Pantheon, 1977.

Fox-Genovese, Elizabeth. *Within the Plantation Household: Black and White Women of the Old South*. Chapel Hill: University of North Carolina Press, 1988.

Fredrickson, George M. *The Black Image in the White Mind: The Debate on Afro-American Character and Destiny, 1817–1914*. New York: Harper and Row, 1971.

Friedman, Lawrence J. *The White Savage: Racial Fantasies in the Postbellum South*. Englewood Cliffs, N.J.: Prentice-Hall, 1970.

Fullinwinder, S. P. *The Mind and Mood of Black America: Twentieth-Century Thought*. Homewood, Ill.: Dorsey Press, 1969.

Gates, Henry Louis, Jr. "The Face and Voice of Blackness." In *Facing History: The Black Image in American Art, 1710–1940*, edited by Guy C. McElroy, xxix–xlvi. San Francisco: Bedford Arts, 1990.

——, ed. *"Race," Writing, and Difference*. Chicago: University of Chicago Press, 1986.

——. *The Signifying Monkey: A Theory of African-American Literary Criticism*. New York: Oxford University Press, 1988.

Giddings, Paula. *When and Where I Enter: The Impact of Black Women on Race and Sex in America*. New York: Bantam, 1984.

Giles, James R. *Claude McKay*. Boston: G. K. Hall, 1976.

Gilman, Sander L. "Black Bodies, White Bodies: Toward an Iconography of Female Sexuality in Late Nineteenth-Century Art, Medicine, and Literature." In *"Race," Writing, and Difference*, edited by Henry Louis Gates, 223–61. Chicago: University of Chicago Press, 1986.

——. *The Jew's Body*. New York: Routledge, 1991.

Gilmore, Al-Tony. *Bad Nigger!: The National Impact of Jack Johnson*. Port Washington, N.Y.: Kennikat Press, 1975.

Ginzburg, Carlo. *Ecstasies: Deciphering the Witches' Sabbath*. Translated by Raymond Rosenthal. New York: Random House, 1991.

Ginzburg, Ralph. *One Hundred Years of Lynchings*. 1962. Baltimore: Black Classic Press, 1988.

Goethe, Johann Wolfgang von. *Faust*, pt. 1 and sections of pt. 2. Translated by Walter Kaufman. New York: Anchor, 1963.

Goldberg, David Theo, ed. *Anatomy of Racism*. Minneapolis: University of Minnesota Press, 1990.

——. "The Social Formation of Racist Discourse." In *Anatomy of Racism*, 295–318. Minneapolis: University of Minnesota Press, 1990.

Gossett, Thomas F. *Race: The History of an Idea in America*. New York: Schocken Books, 1965.

Gould, Stephen Jay. *The Mismeasure of Man*. New York: W. W. Norton, 1981.

Graham, Stephen. *Children of the Slaves*. London: Macmillan, 1920.

Grant, J. Cameron. *The Ethiopian: A Narrative of the Society of Human Leopards*. 1900. New York: Black Hawk Press, 1935.

Graves, John Temple, Clark Howell, and Walter Williams, eds. *Eloquent Sons of the South*. Boston: Chapple Publishing Co., 1909.

Graves, Robert. *The White Goddess: A Historical Investigation*. 1948. New York: Farrar, Straus, and Giroux, 1966.

Griggs, Sutton E. *The Hindered Hand: Or, The Reign of the Repressionist*. 3d ed., rev. 1905. New York: AMS Press, 1969.

——. *Imperium in Imperio: A Study of the Negro Race Problem: A Novel*. 1899. New York: Arno Press, 1969.

——. *Overshadowed*. 1901. Freeport, N.Y.: Books for Libraries Press, 1971.

——. *Unfettered*. Nashville: Orion Publishing Co., 1902.

Gutman, Herbert G. *The Black Family in Slavery and Freedom, 1750–1925*. New York: Pantheon, 1976.

Hair, William Ivy. *Carnival of Fury: Robert Charles and the New Orleans Race Riot of 1900*. Baton Rouge: Louisiana State University Press, 1976.

Hall, Jacquelyn Dowd. *Revolt against Chivalry: Jessie Daniel Ames and the Women's Campaign against Lynching*. New York: Columbia University Press, 1979.

Haller, John S., Jr. *Outcasts from Evolution: Scientific Attitudes of Racial Inferiority, 1859–1900*. Urbana: University of Illinois Press, 1971.

Hamilton, Edith. *Mythology: Timeless Tales of Gods and Heroes*. New York: New American Library, 1969.

Hammond, Bryan, comp., and Patrick O'Connor, biographer. *Josephine Baker*. Boston: Little, Brown, 1988.

Harlan, Louis. *Booker T. Washington*. 2 vols. New York: Oxford University Press, 1972–83.

——, ed. *The Booker T. Washington Papers*. 14 vols. Urbana: University of Illinois Press, 1972-.

Harper, Frances E. W. *Iola Leroy, or Shadows Uplifted. The African-American Novel in the Age of Reaction: Three Classics*. Edited by William L. Andrews. New York: Penguin, 1992.

Harris, Trudier. *Exorcising Blackness: Historical and Literary Lynching and Burning Rituals*. Bloomington: Indiana University Press, 1984.

Haygood, Atticus G. "The Black Shadow in the South." *Forum* 16 (October 1893): 167–75.

Hegel, Georg W. F. *The Philosophy of History*. Rev. ed. Translated by J. Sibree. New York: Willey Book Co., 1920.

Heilke, Thomas W. *Voegelin on the Idea of Race: An Analysis of Modern European Racism*. Baton Rouge: Louisiana State University Press, 1990.

Helper, Hinton Rowan. *Nojoque: A Question for a Continent*. New York: George F. Carleton and Co., 1867.

Hernton, Calvin. *Sex and Racism in America*. New York: Grove Weidenfeld, 1965.

Higginbotham, A. Leon, Jr. *In the Matter of Color: The Colonial Period*. New York: Oxford University Press, 1978.

Hodes, Martha. "The Sexualization of Reconstruction Politics: White Women and Black Men in the South after the Civil War." In *American Sexual Politics: Sex, Gender, and Race since the Civil War*, 59–74. Chicago: University of Chicago Press, 1992.

Hoetink, Harmanus. *The Two Variants in Caribbean Race Relations*. London: Oxford University Press, 1967.

Hoffman, Frederick L. "Race Traits and Tendencies of the American Negro." American Economics Association, *Publications* 11 (August 1896).

——. "Vital Statistics of the Negro." *Arena* 29 (April 1892): 529–42.

Hogarth, William. *The Analysis of Beauty*. Oxford: Clarendon Press, 1955.

Honour, Hugh. *The Image of the Black in Western Art, IV: From the American Revolution to World War I*. Nos. 1 and 2. Houston: Menil Foundation, 1989.

——. *The New Golden Land: European Images of America from the Discoveries to the Present Time*. New York: Random House, 1975.

hooks, bell. "Selling Hot Pussy: Representations of Black Female Sexuality in the Cultural Marketplace." In *Black Looks: Race and Representation*, 61–77. Boston: South End Press, 1992.

Hopkins, Pauline. *Contending Forces: A Romance Illustrative of Negro Life North and South*. 1900. Carbondale: Southern Illinois University Press, 1978.

——. *The Magazine Novels of Pauline Hopkins. (Hagar's Daughter, Winona, and Of One Blood.)* Edited by Henry Louis Gates Jr., with an introduction by Hazel Carby. New York: Oxford University Press, 1988.

——. "The Test of Manhood." *Colored American Magazine* 6 (December 1902): 113–19.

——. "Venus and Apollo Modelled from Ethiopians." *Colored American Magazine* 6 (May-June 1903): 465.

Horsman, Reginald. *Race and Manifest Destiny: The Origins of American Racial Anglo-Saxonism*. Cambridge: Harvard University Press, 1981.

Howard, Walter T. *Lynchings: Extralegal Violence in Florida during the 1930s*. Cranbury, N.J.: Associated University Presses, 1995.

Howard, William Lee. "The Negro as a Distinct Ethnic Factor in Civilization." *Medicine* 15 (May 1903): 423–26.

Hunt, Edward B. *Union Foundations: A Study of American Nationality as a Fact of Science*. New York: Van Nostrand, 1863.

Hurston, Zora Neale. *Tell My Horse: Voodoo and Life in Haiti and Jamaica*. 1938. New York: Harper and Row, 1990.

Jackson, Bruce, ed. *The Negro and His Folklore in Nineteenth-Century Periodicals*. Austin: University of Texas Press, 1967.

Jacobs, Harriet. *Incidents in the Life of a Slave Girl: Written by Herself*. Cambridge: Harvard University Press, 1987.

James, William. *The Principles of Psychology*. 2 vols. New York: Henry Holt and Co., 1890.

JanMohammed, Abdul R. *Manichean Aesthetics: The Politics of Literature in Colonial Africa*. Amherst: University of Massachusetts Press, 1983.

Jefferson, Thomas. *Notes on the State of Virginia*. 1785. New York: Harper and Row, 1964.

Johnson, James Weldon. *Along This Way: The Autobiography of James Weldon Johnson*. 1933. New York: Penguin, 1990.

——. *The Autobiography of an Ex-Colored Man*. 1912. New York: Penguin, 1990.

——. *Black Manhattan*. 1930. New York: Da Capo, 1991.

——. "Harlem: The Culture Capital." In *The New Negro*, edited by Alain Locke, 301–11. New York: Boni and Liveright, 1925.

——. *Saint Peter Relates an Incident: Selected Poems by James Weldon Johnson*. New York: Viking Press, 1935.

——. "The White Witch." *Crisis* 9 (March 1915): 239.

Johnston, James Hugo. *Race Relations in Virginia and Miscegenation in the South, 1776–1860*. Amherst: University of Massachusetts Press, 1970.

Jordan, Winthrop. *White over Black: American Attitudes toward the Negro, 1550–1812*. Chapel Hill: University of North Carolina Press, 1968.

Kinney, James. *Amalgamation!: Race, Sex, and Rhetoric in the Nineteenth-Century American Novel*. Westport, Conn.: Greenwood Press, 1985.

Larsen, Nella. *Quicksand* and *Passing*. New Brunswick, N.J.: Rutgers University Press, 1986.

Levine, Lawrence W. *Black Culture and Black Consciousness: Afro-American Folk Thought from Slavery to Freedom*. Oxford: Oxford University Press, 1977.

Levy, Eugene. *James Weldon Johnson: Black Leader, Black Voice*. Chicago: University of Chicago Press, 1973.

Lewin, Tamar. "The Balkans Rapes: A Legal Test for the Outraged." *New York Times*, January 16, 1993, B16.

Lewis, David Levering. *W. E. B. Du Bois: Biography of a Race, 1868–1919*. New York: Henry Holt and Co., 1993.

——. *When Harlem Was in Vogue*. New York: Oxford University Press, 1981.

Locke, Alain, ed. *The New Negro*. New York: Boni and Liveright, 1925.

——. "Spiritual Truancy." In *Voices of the Harlem Renaissance*, edited by Nathan Irvin Huggins, 404–6. 1976. New York: Oxford University Press, 1995.

Lofgren, Charles A. *The Plessy Case: A Legal-Historical Interpretation*. New York: Oxford University Press, 1987.

Lott, Eric. *Love and Theft: Blackface Minstrelsy and the American Working Class*. New York: Oxford University Press, 1995.

Masters, R. E. L. *Eros and Evil: The Sexual Psychopathology of Witchcraft*. New York: Matrix House, 1966.

Matthews, Victoria Earle, ed. *Black Belt Diamonds: Gems from the Speeches, Addresses, and Talks to Students of Booker T. Washington*. Miami: Mnemosyne Publishing Co., 1969.

McGovern, James R. *Anatomy of a Lynching: The Killing of Claude Neal*. Baton Rouge: Louisiana State University Press, 1982.

McKay, Claude. *Banjo*. New York: Harper, 1929.

——. *Home to Harlem*. 1928. Boston: Northeastern University Press, 1987.

——. *A Long Way from Home: An Autobiography*. London: Pluto Press, 1970.

——. *Selected Poems of Claude McKay*. New York: Bookman, 1953.

McKay, Nellie. "W. E. B. Du Bois: The Black Women in His Writings: Selected Fictional and Autobiographical Portraits." In *Critical Essays on W. E. B. Du Bois*, edited by William L. Andrews, 230–52. Boston: G. K. Hall, 1985.

Mellow, James R. *Hemingway: A Life without Consequences*. Boston: Houghton Mifflin, 1992.

Michaels, Walter Benn. "The Souls of White Folk." In *Literature and the Body: Essays on Populations and Persons*, edited by Elaine Scarry, 185–209. Baltimore: Johns Hopkins University Press, 1988.

Miller, Kelly. *Race Adjustment* and *The Everlasting Stain*. 1908. New York: Arno Press, 1968.

Morrison, William S. "The History of South Carolina, 1865–1909." In *The South in the Building of the Nation*, 92–121. Richmond: Southern Historical Publication Society, 1906.

Morton, Patricia. *Disfigured Images: The Historical Assault on Afro-American Women*. New York: Praeger, 1991.

Moses, Wilson Jeremiah. *Black Messiahs and Uncle Toms: Social and Literary Manipulations of a Religious Myth*. University Park: Pennsylvania State University Press, 1982.

——. "The Politics of Ethiopianism: W. E. B. Du Bois and Literary Black Nationalism."
In *Critical Essays on W. E. B. Du Bois*, edited by William L. Andrews, 92–105. Boston:
G. K. Hall, 1985.

——. *The Wings of Ethiopia: Studies in African-American Life and Letters*. Ames: Iowa
State University Press, 1990.

Mosse, George L. *Toward the Final Solution: A History of European Racism*. New York:
Howard Fertig, 1978.

Myrdal, Gunnar. *An American Dilemma: The Negro Problem and Modern Democracy*.
New York: Harper and Row, 1944.

National Association for the Advancement of Colored People. *Thirty Years of Lynching in
the United States: 1889–1918*. New York: NAACP National Office, 1919.

Newby, I. A. *Jim Crow's Defense: Anti-Negro Thought in America, 1900–1930*. Baton
Rouge: Louisiana State University Press, 1965.

Olsen, Otto H. *The Thin Disguise: Turning Point in Negro History. Plessy v. Ferguson: A
Documentary Presentation (1864–1896)*. New York: Humanities Press, 1967.

O'Neill, John. *Five Bodies: The Human Shape of Modern Society*. Ithaca, N.Y.: Cornell
University Press, 1985.

Osofsky, Gilbert, ed. *The Burden of Race: A Documentary History of Negro-White Relations in America*. New York: Harper and Row, 1967.

Ostendorf, Berndt. *Black Literature in White America*. Brighton, Sussex: Harrenton Press,
1982.

Page, Thomas Nelson. *The Negro: The Southerner's Problem*. New York: Charles Scribner's Sons, 1904.

Page, Walter H. "Last Stronghold of the Southern Bully." *Forum* 16 (October 1893): 303–14.

Panofsky, Erwin. *The Life and Art of Albrecht Dürer*. Princeton: Princeton University
Press, 1955.

Parker, Patricia. *Literary Fat Ladies: Rhetoric, Gender, Property*. London: Methuen, 1987.

Patterson, Orlando. *Slavery and Social Death: A Comparative Study*. Cambridge: Harvard University Press, 1982.

[Payne, Buckner H., pseudonym "Ariel"]. *The Negro: What Is His Ethnological Status? Is
He a Progeny of Ham? Is He a Descendant of Adam and Eve? Has He a Soul? Or Is He
a Beast in God's Nomenclature? What Is His Relation to the White Race?* Cincinnati:
N.p., 1867.

"People in the Foreground (William Benjamin Smith)." *Current Literature* 38 (June
1905): 509.

Petesch, Donald A. *A Spy in the Enemy's Country: The Emergence of Modern Black Literature*. Iowa City: University of Iowa Press, 1989.

Pieterse, Jan Nederveen. *White on Black: Images of Africa and Blacks in Western Popular
Culture*. New Haven: Yale University Press, 1992.

Pike, James S. *The Prostrate State: South Carolina under Negro Government*. New York: Loring and Mussey, 1873.

Porter, Dorothy, ed. *Early Negro Writing, 1760–1837*. Boston: Beacon Press, 1971.

Prather, H. Leon. *We Have Taken a City: Wilmington Racial Massacre and Coup of 1898*. Rutherford, N.J.: Fairleigh Dickinson University Press, 1984.

Puckett, Newbell Niles, ed. *Popular Beliefs and Superstitions: A Compendium of American Folklore from the Ohio Collection of Newbell Niles Puckett*. 3 vols. Boston: G. K. Hall, 1981.

Rampersad, Arnold. *The Art and Imagination of W. E. B. Du Bois*. Cambridge: Harvard University Press, 1976.

———. "W. E. B. Du Bois as a Man of Literature." Andrews, ed. In *Critical Essays on W. E. B. Du Bois*, edited by William L. Andrews, 57–72. Boston: G. K. Hall, 1985.

Raper, Arthur F. *The Tragedy of Lynching*. Chapel Hill: University of North Carolina Press, 1933.

Reed, Adolph, Jr. "Du Bois's 'Double Consciousness': Race and Gender in Progressive Era American Thought." *Studies in American Political Development* 6 (Spring 1992): 93–139.

Robbins, Rossell Hope. *The Encyclopedia of Witchcraft and Demonology*. New York: Crown Publishers, 1959.

Rogin, Michael Paul. *Ronald Reagan, the Movie, and Other Episodes in Political Demonology*. Berkeley and Los Angeles: University of California Press, 1987.

St. John, Donald. "Interview with Hemingway's 'Bill Gorton.'" In Bertram D. Sarason, *Hemingway and "The Sun" Set*, 151–88. Washington, D.C.: National Cash Register Co., 1972.

Sarason, Bertram D. *Hemingway and "The Sun" Set*. Washington, D.C.: National Cash Register Co., 1972.

Schuyler, George. *Black No More*. 1931. Boston: Northeastern University Press, 1989.

Seaman, L. *What Miscegenation Is!: What We Are to Expect, Now That Mr. Lincoln Is Re-elected*. New York: Waller and Willetts, 1864.

Sewall, Samuel. *The Selling of Joseph*. 1700. New York: Arno Press and the New York Times, 1969.

Shaler, Nathaniel S. "African Element in America." *Arena* 2 (November 1890): 660–73.

———. "The Future of the Negro in the South." *Popular Science Monthly* 57 (June 1900): 147–56.

———. "The Negro Problem." *Atlantic Monthly* 54 (November 1884): 696–708.

———. "The Negro since the Civil War." *Popular Science Monthly* 57 (May 1900): 29–39.

———. *The Neighbor: The Natural History of Human Contacts*. Boston: Houghton Mifflin, 1904.

———. "Our Negro Types." *Current Literature* 29 (July 1900): 44–45.

———. "Race Prejudices." *Atlantic Monthly* 58 (October 1886): 510–18.

———. "Science and the African Problem." *Atlantic Monthly* 66 (July 1890): 36–45.

Shapiro, Herbert. *White Violence and Black Response: From Reconstruction to Montgomery.* Amherst: University of Massachusetts Press, 1988.

Shay, Frank. *Judge Lynch: His First Hundred Years.* New York: Ives Washburn, 1938.

Shufeldt, Robert W. *America's Greatest Problem: The Negro.* Philadelphia: F. A. Davis Co., 1915.

———. *The Negro: A Menace to American Civilization.* Boston: Gorham Press, 1907.

Smith, Charles H. "Have American Negroes Too Much Liberty?" *Forum* 16 (October 1893): 176–83.

Smith, Felipe. "Alice Walker's Redemptive Art." *African American Review* 26 (1992): 437–51.

Smith, James McCune. "A Word for the Smith Family." *Anglo-African Magazine* 2 (March 1860): 77–83.

Smith, Lillian. *Killers of the Dream.* 1949. New York: W. W. Norton, 1978.

Smith, William B. *The Color Line: A Brief in Behalf of the Unborn.* New York: McClure, Phillips and Co., 1905.

Sollors, Werner. *Beyond Ethnicity: Consent and Descent in American Culture.* New York: Oxford University Press, 1986.

Sommer, Doris. *Foundational Fictions: The National Romances of Latin America.* Berkeley and Los Angeles: University of California Press, 1991.

Southern Society for the Promotion of the Study of Race Conditions and Problems in the South. *Race Problems of the South: Report of the Proceedings of the First Annual Conference.* Richmond: B. F. Johnson Publishing Co., 1900.

Spillers, Hortense J. "Mamma's Baby, Papa's Maybe: An American Grammar Book." *Diacritics* 17 (Summer 1987): 65–81.

Stallybrass, Peter. "Patriarchal Territories: The Body Enclosed." In *Rewriting the Renaissance: The Discourse of Sexual Difference in Early Modern Europe,* edited by Margaret Ferguson, Maureen Quilligan, and Nancy J. Vickers, 123–42. Chicago: University of Chicago Press, 1986.

Stallybrass, Peter, and Allon White. *The Politics and Poetics of Transgression.* Ithaca, N.Y.: Cornell University Press, 1986.

Stepan, Nancy Leys. *The Idea of Race in Science: Great Britain, 1800–1960.* London: Macmillan, 1982.

———. "Race and Gender: The Role of Analogy in Science." In *Anatomy of Racism,* edited by David Theo Goldberg, 38–57. Minneapolis: University of Minnesota Press, 1990.

Stepan, Nancy Leys, and Sander L. Gilman. "Appropriating the Idioms of Science: The Rejection of Scientific Racism." In *The Bounds of Race: Perspectives on Hegemony and Resistance,* edited by Dominick La Capra, 72–103. Ithaca, N.Y.: Cornell University Press, 1991.

Stepto, Robert B. *From behind the Veil: A Study of Afro-American Narrative*. 1979. 2d ed. Urbana: University of Illinois Press, 1991.

Sterling, Dorothy, ed. *The Trouble They Seen: Black People Tell the Story of Reconstruction*. New York: Doubleday, 1976.

Stewart, Maria W. "An Address, Delivered at the African Masonic Hall, Boston, February 27, 1833." In *Early Negro Writing, 1760–1837*, edited by Dorothy Porter, 129–35. Boston: Beacon Press, 1971.

Stocking, George W., Jr. *Race, Culture, and Evolution: Essays in the History of Anthropology*. 1968. Chicago: University of Chicago Press, 1982.

Takaki, Ronald. *Iron Cages: Race and Culture in Nineteenth-Century America*. New York: Oxford University Press, 1990.

Tate, Claudia. *Domestic Allegories of Political Desire: The Black Heroine's Text at the Turn of the Century*. New York: Oxford University Press, 1992.

Taylor, Joe Gray. *Louisiana Reconstructed, 1863–1877*. Baton Rouge: Louisiana State University Press, 1974.

Taylor, Joshua C. *America as Art*. New York: Harper and Row, 1976.

Terrell, Mary Church. "Lynching from a Negro's Point of View." *North American Review* (June 1904): 853–68.

Thomas, William Hannibal. *The American Negro: What He Was, What He Is, and What He May Become: A Critical and Practical Discussion*. New York: Macmillan, 1901.

Thurman, Wallace. *Infants of the Spring*. 1932. Boston: Northeastern University Press, 1992.

Tillinghast, Joseph A. *The Negro in Africa and America*. 1902. New York: Negro Universities Press, 1968.

Tocqueville, Alexis de. *Democracy in America*. Translated by Henry Reeve. New York: Colonial Press, 1894.

Toll, Robert C. *Blacking Up: The Minstrel Show in Nineteenth-Century America*. New York: Oxford University Press, 1974.

Tolnay, Stewart E., and E. M. Beck. *A Festival of Violence: An Analysis of Southern Lynchings, 1882–1930*. Urbana: University of Illinois Press, 1995.

Toomer, Jean. *Cane*. New York: Boni and Liveright, 1923.

Turner, Darwin. Introduction to *The House behind the Cedars*, by Charles W. Chesnutt. 1900. New York: Collier Books, 1969.

van Gennep, Arnold. *The Rites of Passage*. Translated by Monika B. Vizedom and Gabrielle L. Caffee. Chicago: University of Chicago Press, 1960.

Wallace, Michele. *Black Macho and the Myth of the Superwoman*. New York: Dial Press, 1978.

Ware, Vron. *Beyond the Pale: White Women, Racism, and History*. London: Verso, 1992.

Wells-Barnett, Ida B. *Crusade for Justice: The Autobiography of Ida B. Wells*, edited by Alfreda M. Duster. Chicago: University of Chicago Press, 1970.

———. *On Lynchings: Southern Horrors, a Red Record, Mob Rule in New Orleans*. 1892, 1895, 1900. Salem, N.H.: Ayer, 1991.

White, Deborah. *Ar'n't I a Woman?: Female Slaves in the Plantation South*. New York: W. W. Norton, 1985.

White, Walter. *Rope and Faggot: A Biography of Judge Lynch*. New York: Knopf, 1929.

Whitfield, Stephen J. *A Death in the Delta: The Story of Emmett Till*. New York: Free Press, 1988.

"William Benjamin Smith." In *The National Cyclopedia of American Biography*, 23:223–24. New York: J. T. White, 1898.

Williamson, Joel. *The Crucible of Race: Black-White Relations in the American South since Emancipation*. New York: Oxford University Press, 1984.

———. *New People: Miscegenation and Mulattoes in the United States*. New York: Free Press, 1980.

Wintz, Cary D. *Black Culture and the Harlem Renaissance*. Houston: Rice University Press, 1988.

Woll, Allen. *Black Musical Theatre: From Coontown to Dreamgirls*. Baton Rouge: Louisiana State University Press, 1989.

Wood, Forrest G. *Black Scare: The Racist Response to Emancipation and Reconstruction*. Berkeley and Los Angeles: University of California Press, 1968.

Woodward, C. Vann. *The Strange Career of Jim Crow*. 3d rev. ed. New York: Oxford University Press, 1974.

Wright, Richard. *Black Boy: A Record of Childhood and Youth*. New York: Harper and Brothers, 1945.

Wyatt-Brown, Bertram. *Southern Honor: Ethics and Behavior in the Old South*. New York: Oxford University Press, 1982.

Yellin, Jean Fagan. *Women and Sisters: Antislavery Feminists in American Culture*. New Haven: Yale University Press, 1989.

Index

Africa: represented as female, 86; spirituality of, 249, 256, 269–75

African American literature: "passing" narratives in, 53, 65, 217, 321; marriage plot in, 56–58, 76–77, 277, 296, 364 (n. 7); revenant in, 65, 71–72, 74–77, 79, 246, 262, 275, 331, 343; African mother's return in, 70, 71, 77–80, 83, 118–19, 246, 271–75; "daughter's departure" in, 73, 80, 108; debate over having black babies in, 302, 342, 345; and white patronage, 341, 343

African Americans: extinction of, vii, x, xi, xiii, 3, 7, 43–44, 58, 63–65, 67, 88, 93, 237, 238, 290, 339; as "Negro problem," viii, 3, 6, 56, 137, 199, 211, 240, 258; "race traits and tendencies" of, ix; racial renaissance of, xiii, 85, 199, 216, 237, 259, 275, 339, 341; disaffiliated from national kinship, 3, 4, 36, 72; as unfit for modern civilization, 4, 36, 39–41, 64, 66, 104, 136–37, 138, 147, 221, 288; expulsion of, from America, 5, 7, 21, 22, 31, 37, 42, 46, 99, 175; family life of, 6, 89–92, 112, 114, 120, 258, 285–86; white efforts to accelerate extinction of, 8, 43–44; black nationalism among, 8, 199, 209, 259, 282; Pan-Africanism among, 8, 267, 345; as repulsive to whites, 20–21, 23, 29, 43, 48, 49, 56, 67, 86, 267–68, 289, 369 (n. 17); somatic and mental inferiority of, 20–23, 39–41, 87, 88, 234, 237; ape libel against, 24, 85, 137, 367 (n. 1); neoteny of, 40–41; atavistic regression by, 41, 45, 58, 65, 66, 67, 68, 69, 70, 72, 76–78, 81, 88, 89, 112–13, 128, 131, 137, 148, 274; diseases of, requiring quarantine, 42–44, 46–47, 61, 93–94; immorality of, 42, 74, 88, 91–94, 284; undifferentiated difference of, 45–46, 48–51, 66, 68, 78, 86, 88, 123, 142, 143, 176, 212, 223, 289; as "body of death," 58–62, 65, 82, 84, 132, 167, 246, 253, 270, 327, 365 (nn. 10, 15, 16); criminality of, 62, 123, 138; and self-obliteration, 75, 78–79, 214–15, 343; matriarchal family structure of, 89–90; households of, as wilderness, 116–18, 285; immortal soul of, 206, 209, 326; capacity for cultural development of, 210–11; spiritual giftedness of, 212, 243, 249, 252, 268, 279, 280, 349, 351; development of race message or soul of, 214, 215, 216, 217, 221, 226, 230, 236, 248, 249–53, 255, 257, 259–60, 271, 278, 282, 346–49; extermination of, 215; somatic traits of, 291, 293; "spiritual amalgamation" or "truancy" of, 296, 341;

African Americans (*continued*)
  migration to North of, 316–20, 337; as New
  Negro, 341; retention of Africanisms by, 349
African-Indian Boy, 26–27
Africans: and cannibalism, 7, 68, 88; and
  uterine filiation, 88–89, 119, 120, 288
Allochronism, 34–36, 45, 68, 104, 105, 106, 116,
  137
America, representations of: as "melting pot,"
  xii, 57, 107; as female, 24; as Columbia, 24,
  27, 29; as Indian Princess, 24–26; as Indian
  Queen, 24–26, 29, 358 (n. 31); as allegory of
  racial identity, 24–29; as Liberty, 25–27,
  320–21; as Plumed Greek Goddess, 26–27;
  as AMERICA, 242, 315, 337; as "Great I Will,"
  294–95, 316; as Amazon headhunter, 295;
  as Dollar Princess, 295; as Babylon, 316;
  as eagle, 316
Ames, Jesse Daniel, 161
Anglo-Saxonism, 230–31, 251–52

Binet, Alfred, 232–33, 234, 270, 271
Blackface: as caricature, 126, 147–48; as
  disguise, 176, 253
Black social space, 9, 41, 49, 102–3; and
  Jim Crow segregation, 94, 101, 102
Boas, Franz, viii, 50
Body, human: as metaphor for society, xii, 3, 9,
  22, 31–32

Cameron, James: attempted lynching of, 181–83
Carnivalesque, 147, 148, 152
Chesnutt, Charles W., 52, 54–55; *The Marrow
  of Tradition*, 62–67, 75–76, 101–2; "The
  Sheriff's Children," 75; "The Wife of His
  Youth," 76–78; *The House behind the Cedars*,
  78, 80–83; "Her Virginia Mammy," 79–80;
  "Uncle Wellington's Wives," 107–10, 313
Classicism, 25–26, 27, 126–28, 133; and
  personified virtue, 24–25, 133
Colored American Magazine, 53, 272, 274–75, 302
"Color line," xii, 33, 103, 106, 238, 330, 343;

ritual observance of, 98, 103, 104, 106, 107, 111;
  violations of, 139, 144, 161, 318
Conrad, Joseph: *Heart of Darkness*, 45

Darwin, Charles, xi, 252; *The Descent of Man*,
  287–89
Devil, 190, 241
Dixon, Thomas, Jr.: *The Clansman*, 53, 56,
  95; *The Leopard's Spots*, 59, 98; *Birth of a
  Nation*, 136, 334; *The Flaming Sword*, 334
Double consciousness, 232–34, 270, 271.
  See also Du Bois, W. E. B.: "double-
  consciousness" theory of
Douglass, Frederick, 116, 191, 267
Du Bois, W. E. B., viii, x, xiii, 238, 332, 333,
  334, 339–41; on "Veil" of race, 31, 239; *Dark
  Princess: A Romance*, 122–24, 344, 345–51;
  The Souls of Black Folk, 199, 245, 276, 316;
  "double-consciousness" theory of, 199–200,
  231–36, 270–71, 282, 298, 330; "two-souled"
  theory of, 200, 218–19, 231, 233, 235, 243;
  and Dora Marbach, 202–3; as ethical
  scientist, 204, 224, 284; "The Conservation
  of Races," 210, 213–14, 234; and race
  message development, 217, 239, 242, 266;
  as mythologist, 218–19, 277–78, 349; and
  "everlasting Ought," 219, 227, 231, 285, 288,
  290; on "The Talented Tenth," 223, 234–39,
  244, 341; and "The Gospel of Sacrifice," 227,
  229–30, 235, 245, 246, 283, 285, 303; "Jefferson
  Davis as a Representative of Civilization,"
  230–31; as visionary race leader, 242, 244, 245,
  246, 249; idea of mother as race message of,
  246, 290, 346–51; "Of the Coming of John,"
  278–84, 333; secularization of folk religion
  by, 279, 280; *The Quest of the Silver Fleece*,
  286, 296–306, 341, 345, 346, 348, 349–50
Dunbar, Paul Laurence: *The Sport of the Gods*,
  317–18

Ethiopianism, 8, 221, 263, 269–75, 276, 291–93
Ethnicity, 46

Faustian bargain, 287, 290, 303, 326, 329, 332, 333, 346. *See also* Goethe, Johann Wolfgang von: *Faust*

Felton, Rebecca Latimer, 164, 187

Goethe, Johann Wolfgang von: *Faust*, 222–30, 245

Graves, Robert: *The White Goddess*, 293, 307–9

Griffith, D. W.: *Birth of a Nation*, 135–39

Griggs, Sutton E., 248, 249; *Imperium in Imperio*, 111–15, 250; *Overshadowed*, 250–57; *Unfettered*, 257–61; *The Hindered Hand: Or, The Reign of the Repressionist*, 261–68

Grimké, Angelina Weld: *Rachel*, 342

Harper, Frances E. Watkins: *Iola Leroy, or Shadows Uplifed*, 248–49

Haygood, Atticus, 139–40, 146, 380 (n. 75)

Hemings, Sally, 20–21, 357 (n. 25)

Hoffman, Frederick L., viii–ix, 59, 61, 365 (n. 13)

Holbert, Luther: lynching of, with wife, 265

Hopkins, Pauline, 52; *Hagar's Daughter*, 53, 69–75; *Of One Blood*, 53–54, 269–75; *Contending Forces*, 117–20, 268–69; "Venus and Apollo Modeled from Ethiopians," 274

Hose, Sam: lynching of, 203–5

Hybridity, 47, 66, 114, 213, 290, 324

Hybridophobia, 47, 67–69, 78, 81

Impey, Catherine, 192

Interracial marriage, 10, 14–15, 98, 107–8, 139, 203, 267, 344; prohibition against, 14, 15, 30, 56, 58, 71, 125, 191, 208, 213, 256, 345

Interracial sex: as blood pollution, viii–ix, 22, 44–45, 55, 65, 74; involving white women, ix, 11–12, 14, 15–19, 313, 321–23, 326; defilement of white bodies via, 10, 11, 28, 44; prohibition of, 12, 14, 15, 185–86, 326; assault of white women in, 17, 88, 96, 129, 132, 138, 145, 148, 153, 154, 156, 164, 169, 184, 185, 188, 291; exploitation of black women in, 28–30, 58, 73, 82–83, 95–96, 102, 116, 118, 125, 191, 254, 273, 281–83, 292, 304, 311; victimization of white men in, 94–96, 129. *See also* Men, black: as brute rapists; Women, white: as "White Delilah"; Women, white: as "white witch"

James, William, 233–34

Jefferson, Thomas, 19–21, 23, 252

Jim Crow segregation, 43–44, 46–49; on railway cars, 49, 261, 262. See also *Plessy v. Ferguson* decision

Johnson, James Weldon, 332–34; "The White Witch," 293, 310–11, 312–16, 320, 324–27, 334; "The Black Mammy," 311–14; *The Autobiography of an Ex-Colored Man*, 319–22, 329–32, 333, 340; *Along This Way*, 321, 322–24; attempted lynching of, 324

Johnson, John Arthur "Jack," 324–27, 329

Larsen, Nella: *Quicksand*, 102, 342–43; *Passing*, 343

Lawrence, Richard, 28

Lincoln, Abraham, 31, 54

Locke, Alain, 334–35; *The New Negro*, 341

Lynching: psychohistorical analysis of, 130; defense of, 132; and genital mutilation, 133, 160–62, 171, 172, 173, 190; offenses punished by, 142, 165, 179–80; as carnival, 145, 146, 149, 151, 153, 171, 181; complicity of lawmen in, 150; as ritual reaffirmation of white manhood, 150–53, 154, 164–65, 169; of Henry Smith, 150, 154, 157–60, 170, 380 (n. 75); representation in media of, 158, 167, 168; role of white women in, 166; socialization of whites by means of, 167, 170–71, 173–74; role of press in, 168, 203, 326; body parts as souvenirs of, 172–74, 204; of Abram Smith, 175, 181–82; of Thomas Shipp, 175, 181–82; "legal," 179; attempted, of James Cameron, 181–83; of Sam Hose, 203–5;

Lynching (*continued*)
of Luther Holbert and his wife, 265;
attempted, of James Weldon Johnson, 324

Manly, Alexander, 187
Mayo, Isabella Fyvie, 192
McKay, Claude, 334; "The White House,"
334–35; "Africa," 335; *A Long Way From
Home*, 335; "The City's Love," 335–36;
"America," 336; "Tiger," 336; "The White
City," 336
Men, black: as brute rapists, 61–62, 124, 128–29,
131, 135, 137–38, 140–41, 143–44, 152, 162, 167,
172, 175, 194; social assertiveness of, 63, 137,
139, 143, 144, 145, 325–26; patriarchy of,
92–93, 110, 114–15, 118, 281–82, 284, 286, 301,
307, 309, 314, 315; genital "gigantism" of,
162–63; as "black Samsons," 187
Men, white: sexual access to women of, ix, 15,
16, 17, 18–19, 20, 28–30; honor and shame
among, 10–11, 150, 155–57; property rights of,
12, 28, 165, 173; patriarchal interests of, 16, 28,
164; and restriction on spatial adventurism,
40, 101–2, 176; status requirements of, 131,
166; and political control of South, 135, 151,
176; moral regulation of white women by,
175, 185, 187, 189
Miscegenation controversy, 125–26
Murphy, Edgar Gardner, 60

Nation: and race, 3–5, 10–11, 15, 54; as
imagined community, 3–4, 34–37, 63;
descent and consent as means of identity
with, 56–58, 71, 78–79
"Negro domination," 62, 135, 145, 146, 151

Pike, James S.: *The Prostrate State: South
Carolina under Negro Government*, 132–33,
134
Plessy v. Ferguson decision, viii, 47, 97, 100
Poetics of jurisprudence, 148, 154, 155, 158, 170
"Prostrate South," 61, 132–34, 140, 141

Race: concept of gender in discourse about,
xi–xii, 9–10, 13, 40, 61, 97, 101, 102, 132, 316,
361 (n. 74); and kinship, 3–4, 6–8, 17, 34–
36, 52, 53, 54, 67, 79, 89, 209, 329–30, 344;
and social death, 10, 14, 46, 99, 104–7, 163,
211, 238, 327; difference as distance in, 32–
33, 34, 50; "pure type" idea of, 50, 208; as
performance of social death, 104, 112, 176,
177, 238; pre-Adamite theories of, 127, 207;
as performance, 209, 217; liberation of
concept of, from the body, 350–51
Race characteristics: state preference for white,
22–23, 29, 48–49, 208; African Americans'
preference for white, 23–24, 64, 66, 72–74,
75–76, 273–75; of "white goddess," 308
Race chastity, 15, 92, 114, 125, 129, 134, 163, 165,
178–79, 182, 187, 193, 281, 290, 323
Race soul: 207, 208, 348. *See also* African
Americans: development of race message
or soul of
Racial classification: "one-drop rule" of, ix,
44–45, 54, 55, 65, 66, 68, 76, 77, 215, 217;
and slavery, 10, 12–13; and "condition of the
mother," 10–12, 13, 17, 27–28, 68–70, 71, 74,
77, 80, 83, 88; involuntary, 214, 215; voluntary,
215, 290, 330
Reconstruction: and race, 3; as rape of white
body politic, 133, 139
Roosevelt, Theodore, 98

Science, vii–viii, 5, 12, 16–17, 48, 81, 90, 138,
208, 213, 215, 216, 220, 271, 350–51
Sewall, Samuel, 22
Shaler, Nathaniel S., 6; *The Neighbor*, 210–11,
287–88
Shufeldt, Robert, 157–61
Slavery, 12
Smith, Abram: lynching of, with Thomas Shipp,
175, 181–82
Smith, Henry: lynching of, 150, 154, 157–60,
170, 380 (n. 75)
Smith, James McCune, vii, xi

Smith, Lillian, xii, 31, 359 (n. 45)

Smith, William Benjamin: *The Color Line*, vii–viii, xv, 37, 38–39, 44, 135, 339; on Du Bois, x; children of, 354 (n. 9)

Social sciences: anthropology, viii, 43, 126–27; social Darwinism, x, 37–38, 39–43, 251, 290; and race, 292

Stothard, Thomas: *The Voyage of the Sable Venus*, 29

Tillman, Ben, 60, 141

Tocqueville, Alexis de, 30

Toomer, Jean: *Cane*, 341–42

Tourgée, Albion, 47, 55, 100, 194

Van Vechten, Carl, 340–41

Washington, Booker T., viii, 98, 101, 332, 333; "Atlanta Exposition Address," 58–59, 237, 240; and "body of death," 58–61, 200, 237; accomodationist policies of, 236–46, 250–51; "Gospel of Work and Money," 240–41; Faustian bargain of, 241; "Tuskegee Machine," 241, 302, 332; on Jack Johnson, 325; and Ulrich affair, 327–29

Wells-Barnett, Ida B., 183–95

"Whitecapping," 130

"White savagery," 148–49, 152–53, 167, 169, 171

White solidarity, 130, 131, 177

White space: geographical, vii, ix–x, 38, 46, 49–51, 103, 174–75, 337; social, ix–x, xii, 5, 10, 30–37, 100, 103, 105, 123, 337; somatic, 98, 122, 135; domestic, 99, 103, 136

White superiority, 20, 22, 31, 33, 174

White supremacy, ix, 33, 50, 63, 130, 143, 326

Willard, Frances, 186, 192

Willcox, Walter, viii, 220–21

"Wilmington Massacre," 62, 63, 164

Wilson, Woodrow, 136

Women, black: as race womb, 13, 17, 68, 85; and social death, 16; as threat to white race purity, 17, 94–95; as black Venus, 24, 28–29, 85, 88, 95, 120, 163, 286, 289, 297, 309, 348; sexual depravity of, 24, 82, 84–94, 115, 116, 281, 284, 297, 302, 348; physical beauty of, 75, 227, 273–75, 289–90, 305–6, 323, 347; as mammy, 79, 80, 85, 86–88, 108–9, 119, 120, 288, 311–12; genital "abnormality" of, 85–88, 162; as "Hottentot Venus," 85–86; bodies in shape of S of, 87, 95, 101; as bad or indifferent mother, 93, 102, 287, 312; and "black lady" ideal, 96, 115, 254–55; as matriarchs, 109; virtuousness of, 110, 112–14, 115, 117, 118, 281; as domestic black madonna, 113, 114, 119, 309, 341; as "Rising Africa," 277, 293; as embodiment of self-sacrifice, 283, 285, 286, 290, 296, 307, 330, 331, 343; preferred by black men, 290–91, 305–6, 323, 325–27, 347; disloyalty of, 312–13. *See also* Africa; African American literature; Du Bois, W. E. B.: idea of mother as race message of; Interracial sex: exploitation of black women in; Racial classification: and "condition of the mother"

Women, mulatta: as "black" white witch, 297, 345

Women, white: as race property, 11, 14, 16–18, 28, 165; enslavement of, 11–12, 14–16; as race womb, 14, 17, 18, 29, 207–8; sexual depravity of, 14, 128–29, 156, 163, 188, 191; and "color line," 16, 29–30, 45, 101, 102, 116, 124, 201, 282–83, 322–23; as symbol of social acceptance, 83, 200–203, 279, 311–12; as "ruined woman," 140, 151, 153, 156, 163; as fatal woman, 166, 178, 181, 190, 260, 264–65, 293, 296, 307–9; as "White Delilah," 187–89, 193, 277; as "white witch," 189, 294, 309–16, 319; as "Decline of the West," 277–78, 318; as embodiment of spiritual death, 277–78, 290, 292–95. *See also* America: representations of, as "melting pot"; Interracial sex; Johnson, James Weldon: "The White Witch"

Zenneck, A.: "Murder of Louisiana," 133